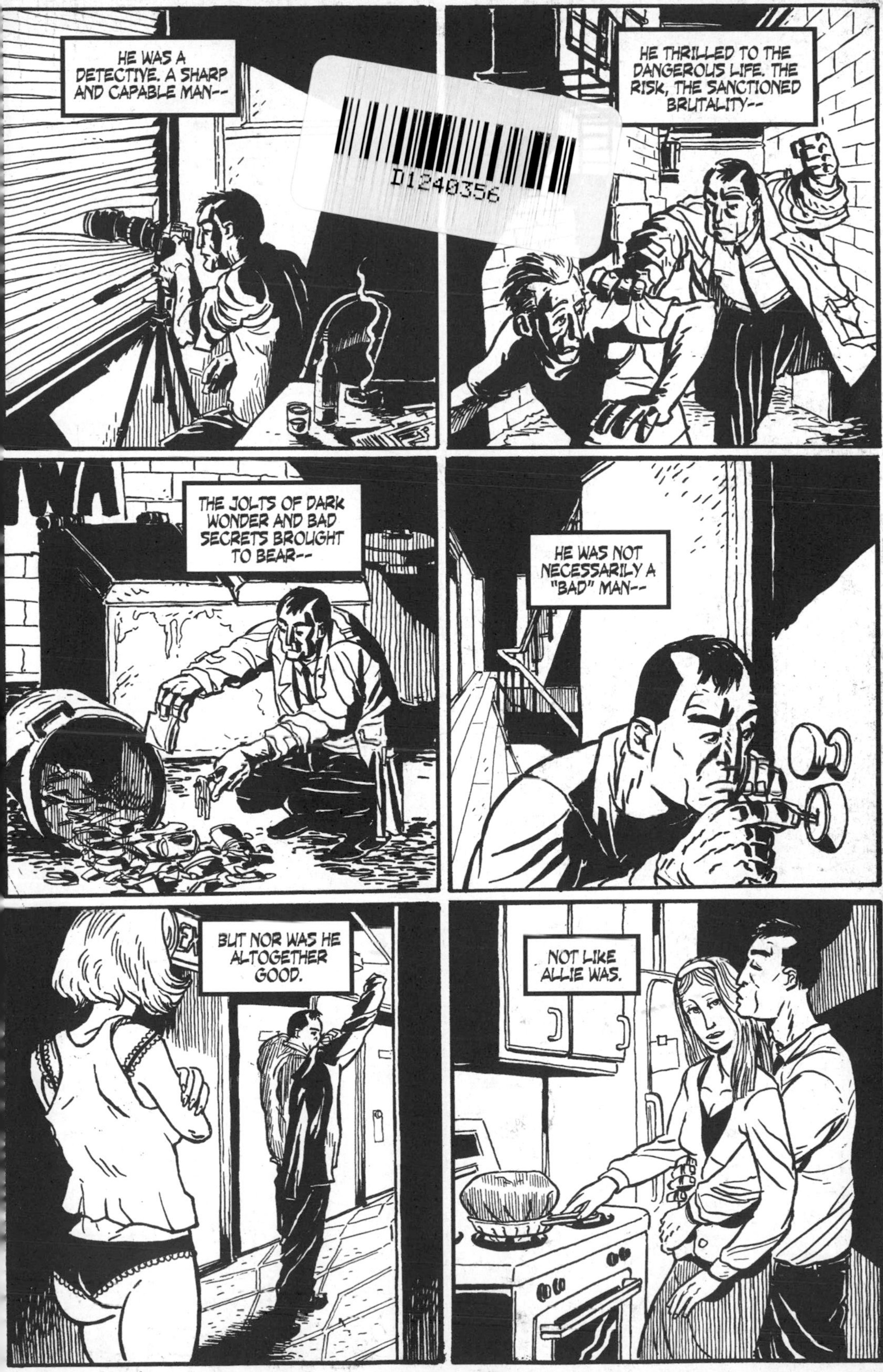
HE WAS A DETECTIVE. A SHARP AND CAPABLE MAN--
HE THRILLED TO THE DANGEROUS LIFE. THE RISK, THE SANCTIONED BRUTALITY--
THE JOLTS OF DARK WONDER AND BAD SECRETS BROUGHT TO BEAR--
HE WAS NOT NECESSARILY A "BAD" MAN--
BUT NOR WAS HE ALTOGETHER GOOD.
NOT LIKE ALLIE WAS.

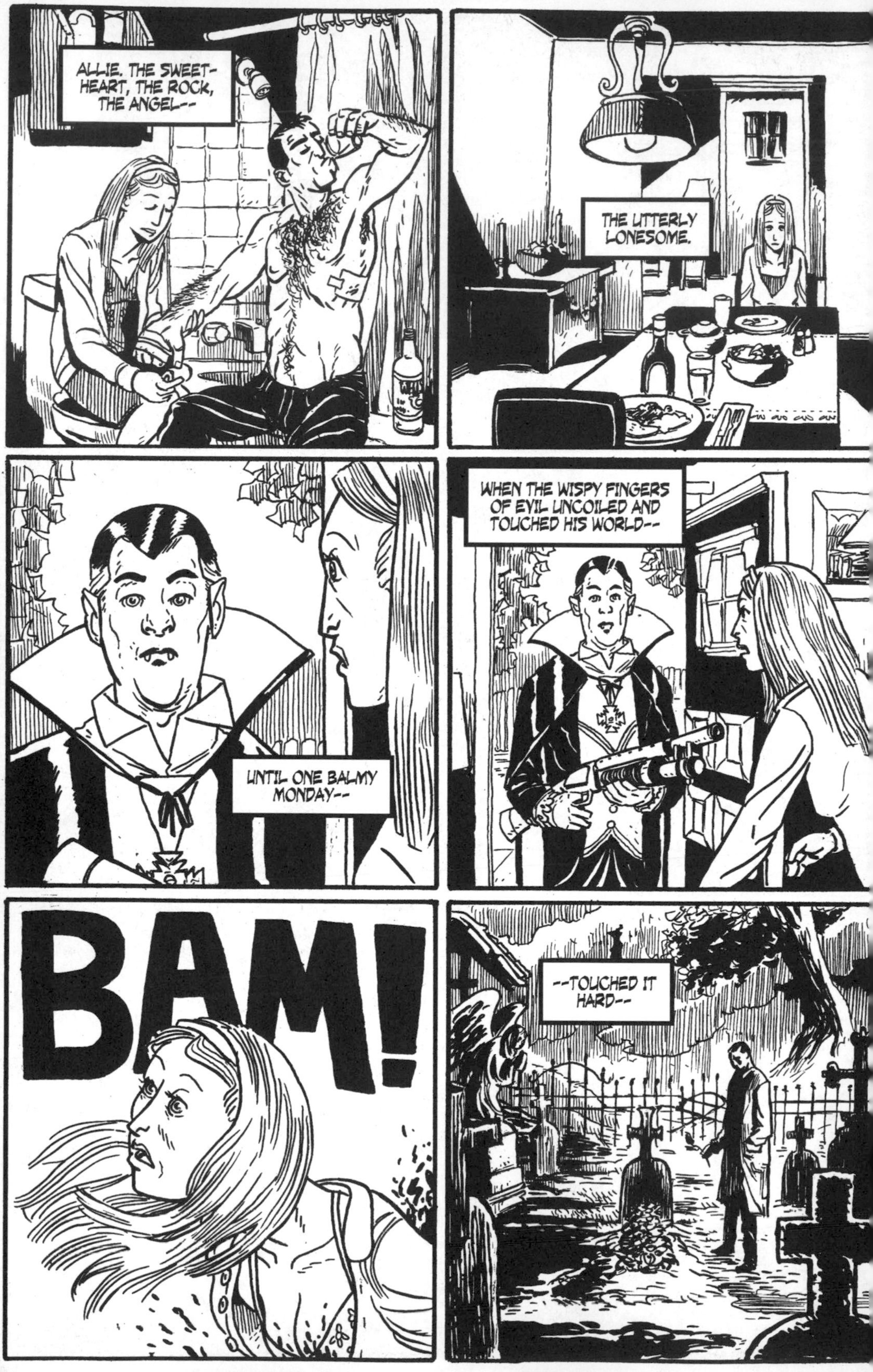
ALLIE. THE SWEET-HEART, THE ROCK, THE ANGEL--
THE UTTERLY LONESOME.
UNTIL ONE BALMY MONDAY--
WHEN THE WISPY FINGERS OF EVIL UNCOILED AND TOUCHED HIS WORLD--
BAM!
--TOUCHED IT HARD--

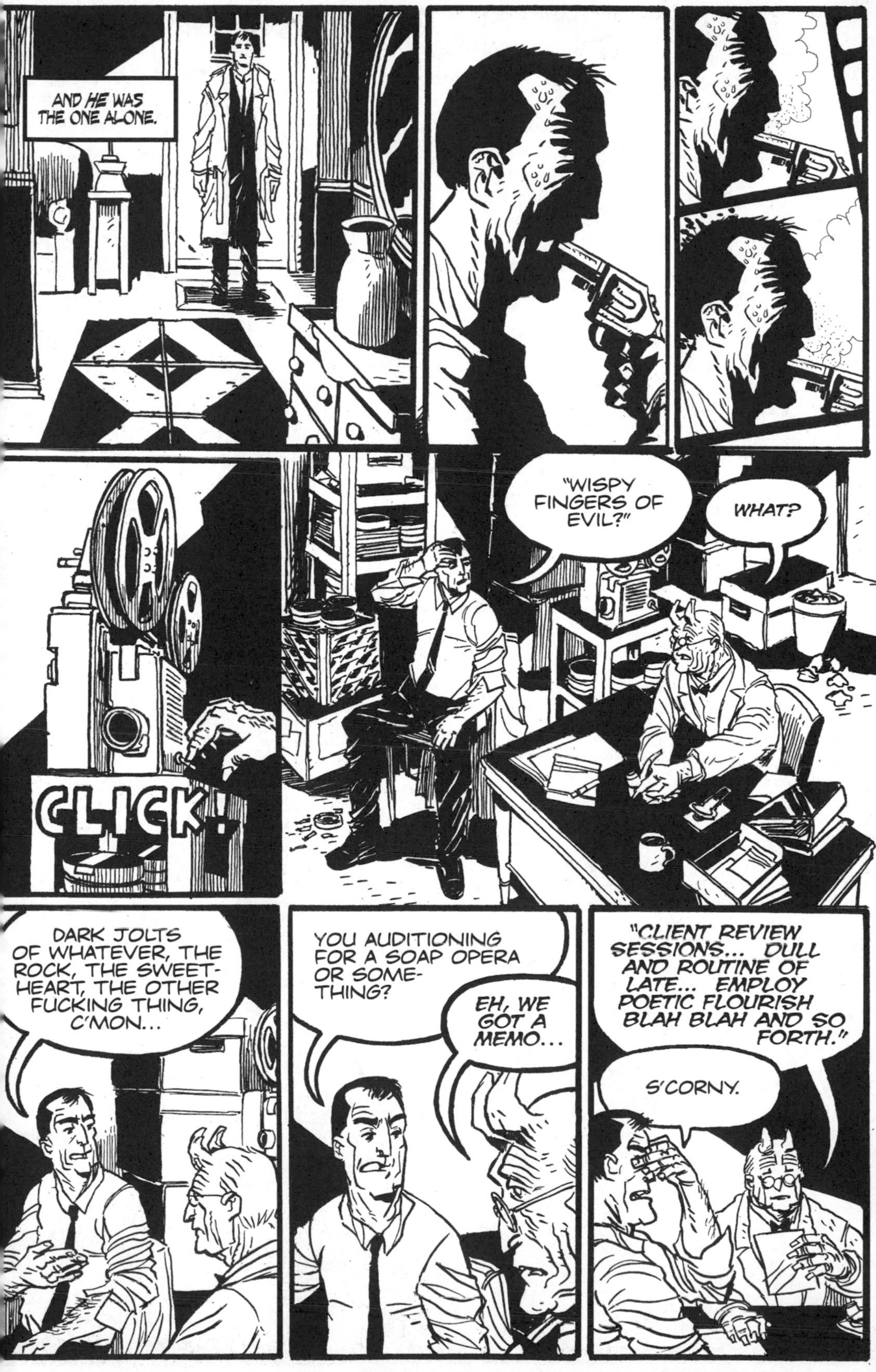
AND HE WAS THE ONE ALONE.
"WISPY FINGERS OF EVIL?"
WHAT?
CLICK!
DARK JOLTS OF WHATEVER, THE ROCK, THE SWEET-HEART, THE OTHER FUCKING THING, C'MON...
YOU AUDITIONING FOR A SOAP OPERA OR SOME-THING?
EH, WE GOT A MEMO...
"CLIENT REVIEW SESSIONS... DULL AND ROUTINE OF LATE... EMPLOY POETIC FLOURISH BLAH BLAH AND SO FORTH."
S'CORNY.

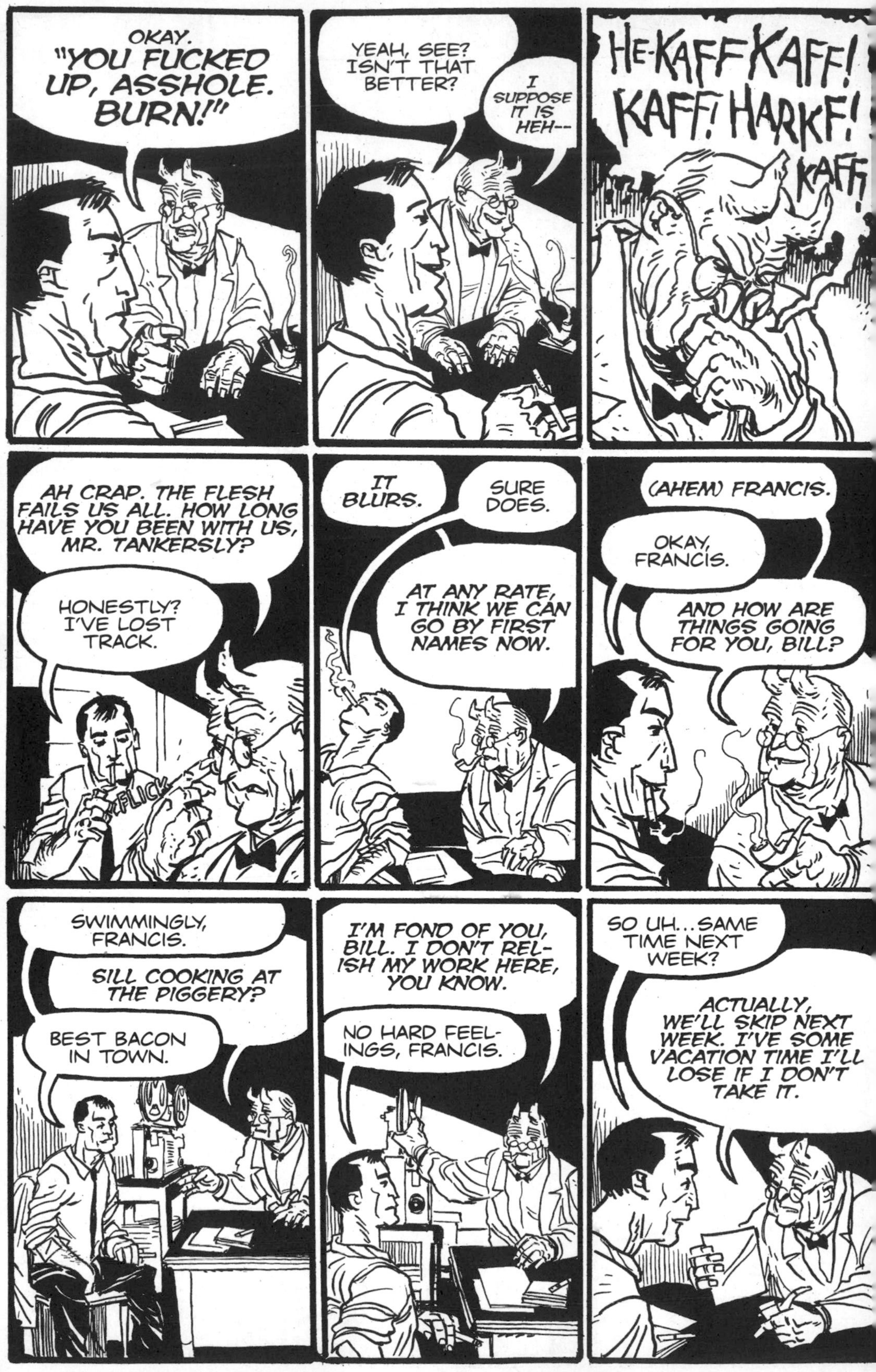
OKAY. "YOU FUCKED UP, ASSHOLE. BURN!"
YEAH, SEE? ISN'T THAT BETTER?
I SUPPOSE IT IS HEH--
HE-KAFF KAFF! KAFF! HARKF! KAFF!
AH CRAP. THE FLESH FAILS US ALL. HOW LONG HAVE YOU BEEN WITH US, MR. TANKERSLY?
HONESTLY? I'VE LOST TRACK.
FLICK
IT BLURS.
SURE DOES.
AT ANY RATE, I THINK WE CAN GO BY FIRST NAMES NOW.
(AHEM) FRANCIS.
OKAY, FRANCIS.
AND HOW ARE THINGS GOING FOR YOU, BILL?
SWIMMINGLY, FRANCIS.
SILL COOKING AT THE PIGGERY?
BEST BACON IN TOWN.
I'M FOND OF YOU, BILL. I DON'T REL-ISH MY WORK HERE, YOU KNOW.
NO HARD FEEL-INGS, FRANCIS.
SO UH...SAME TIME NEXT WEEK?
ACTUALLY, WE'LL SKIP NEXT WEEK. I'VE SOME VACATION TIME I'LL LOSE IF I DON'T TAKE IT.

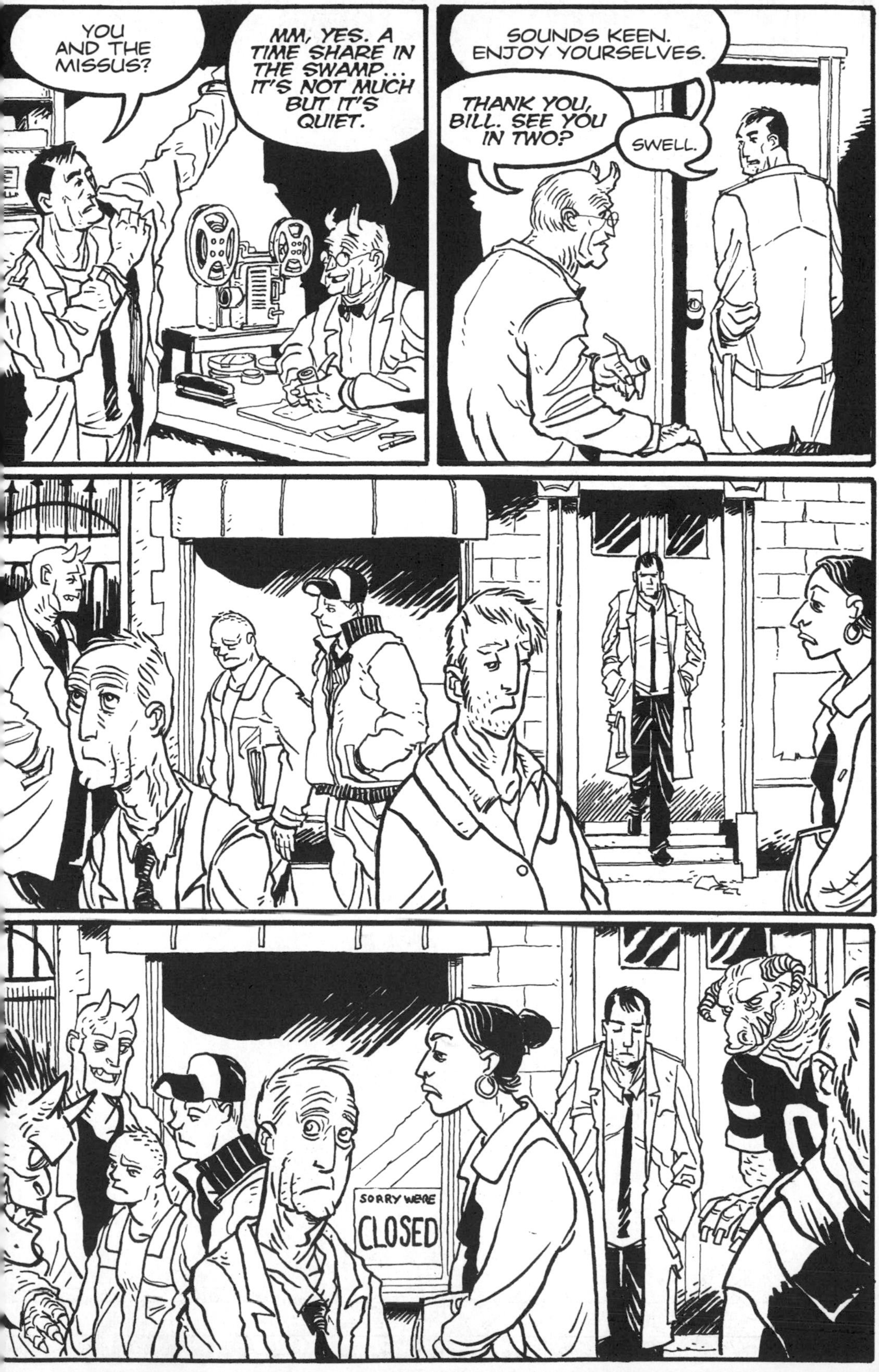
YOU AND THE MISSUS?
MM, YES. A TIME SHARE IN THE SWAMP... IT'S NOT MUCH BUT IT'S QUIET.
SOUNDS KEEN. ENJOY YOURSELVES.
THANK YOU, BILL. SEE YOU IN TWO?
SWELL.
SORRY WE'RE
CLOSED

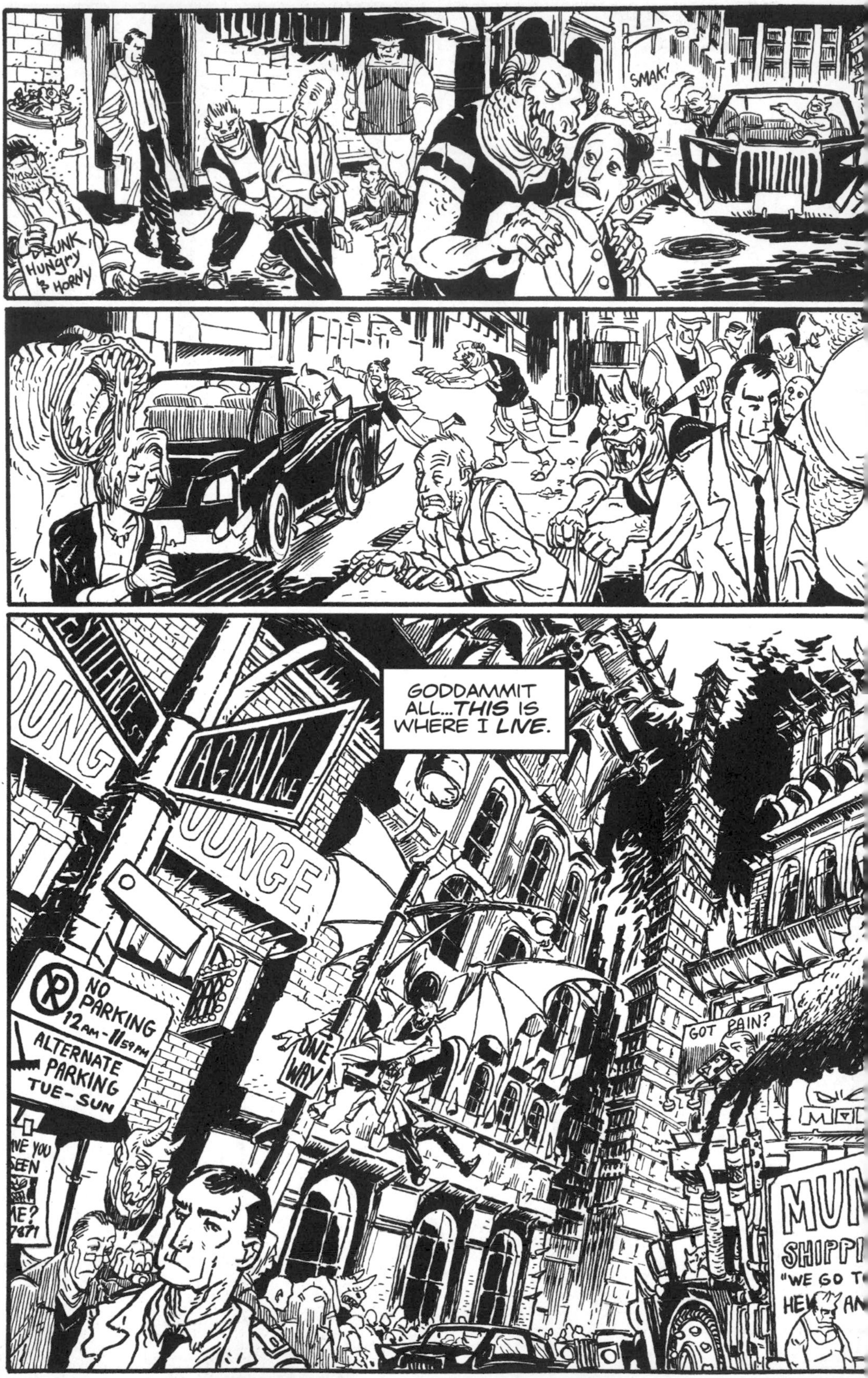
DRUNK, Hungry & HORNY
SMAK!
GODDAMMIT ALL...THIS IS WHERE I LIVE.
PESTILENCE ST
AGONY AVE
LOUNGE
NO PARKING 12AM-11:59PM ALTERNATE PARKING TUE-SUN
ONE WAY
GOT PAIN?

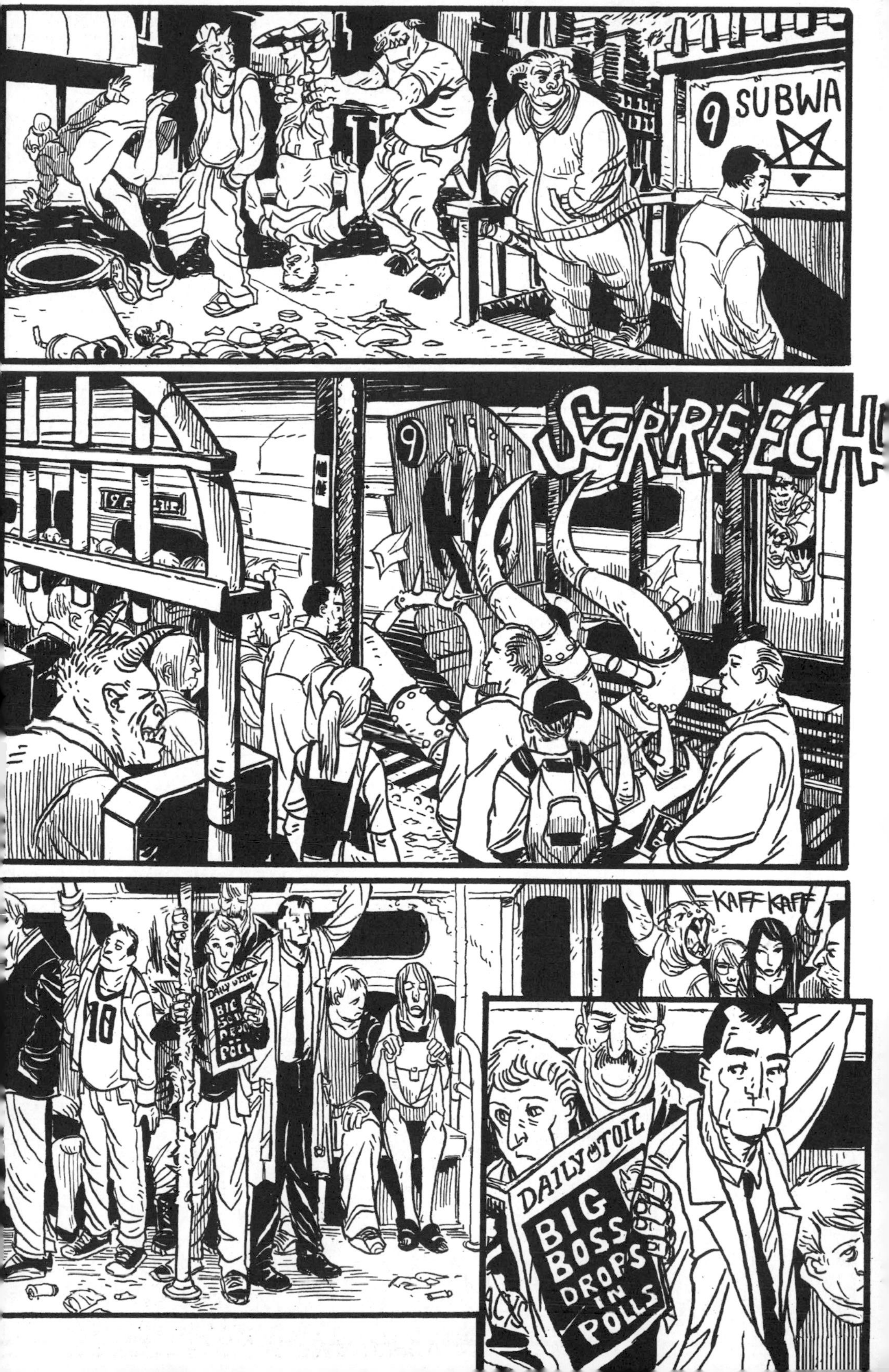
9 SUBWA
SCRREECH
KAFF KAFF
DAILY TOIL
BIG BOSS DROPS IN POLLS

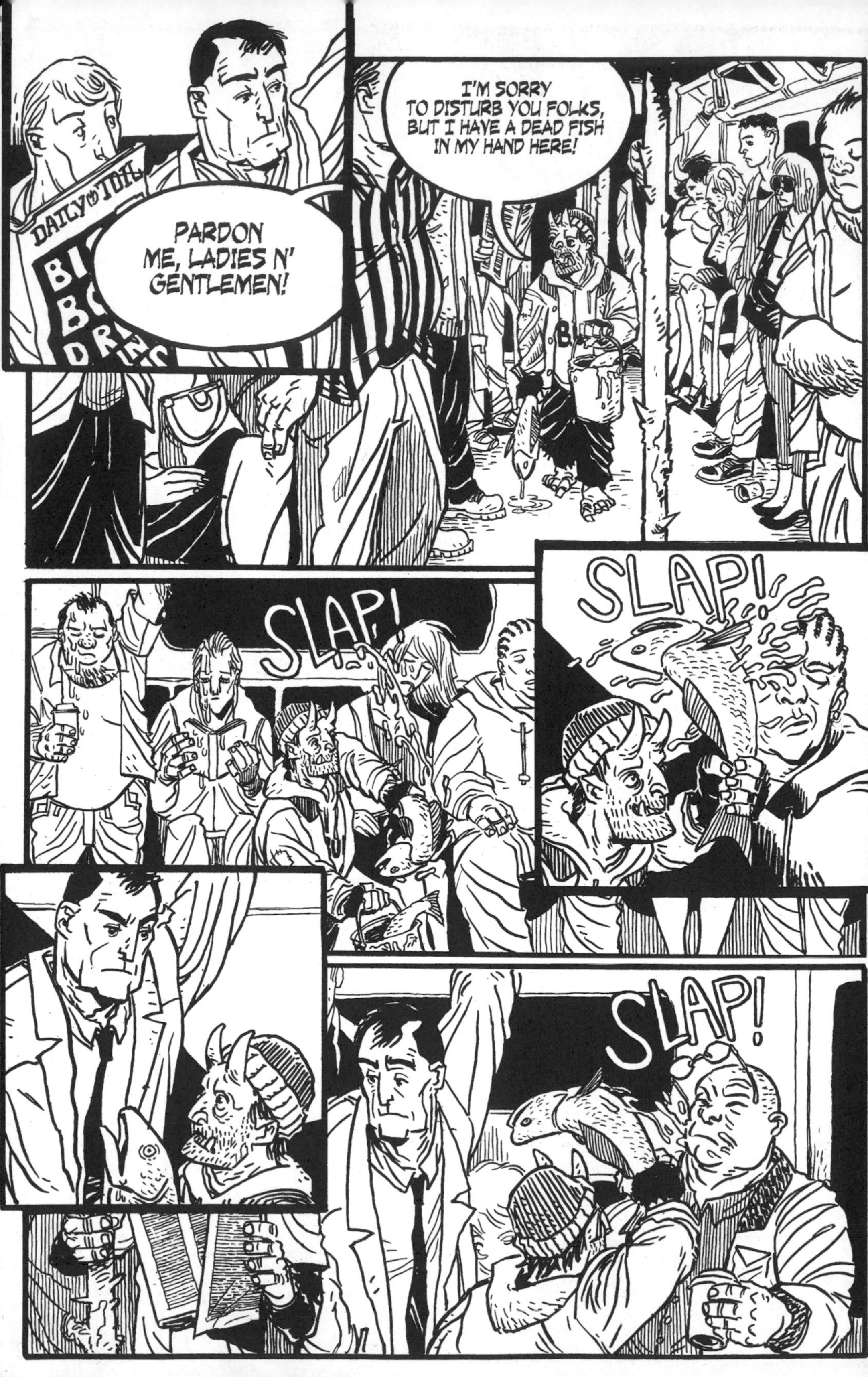

DAILY TOIL
PARDON ME, LADIES N' GENTLEMEN!
I'M SORRY TO DISTURB YOU FOLKS, BUT I HAVE A DEAD FISH IN MY HAND HERE!
SLAP!
SLAP!
SLAP!

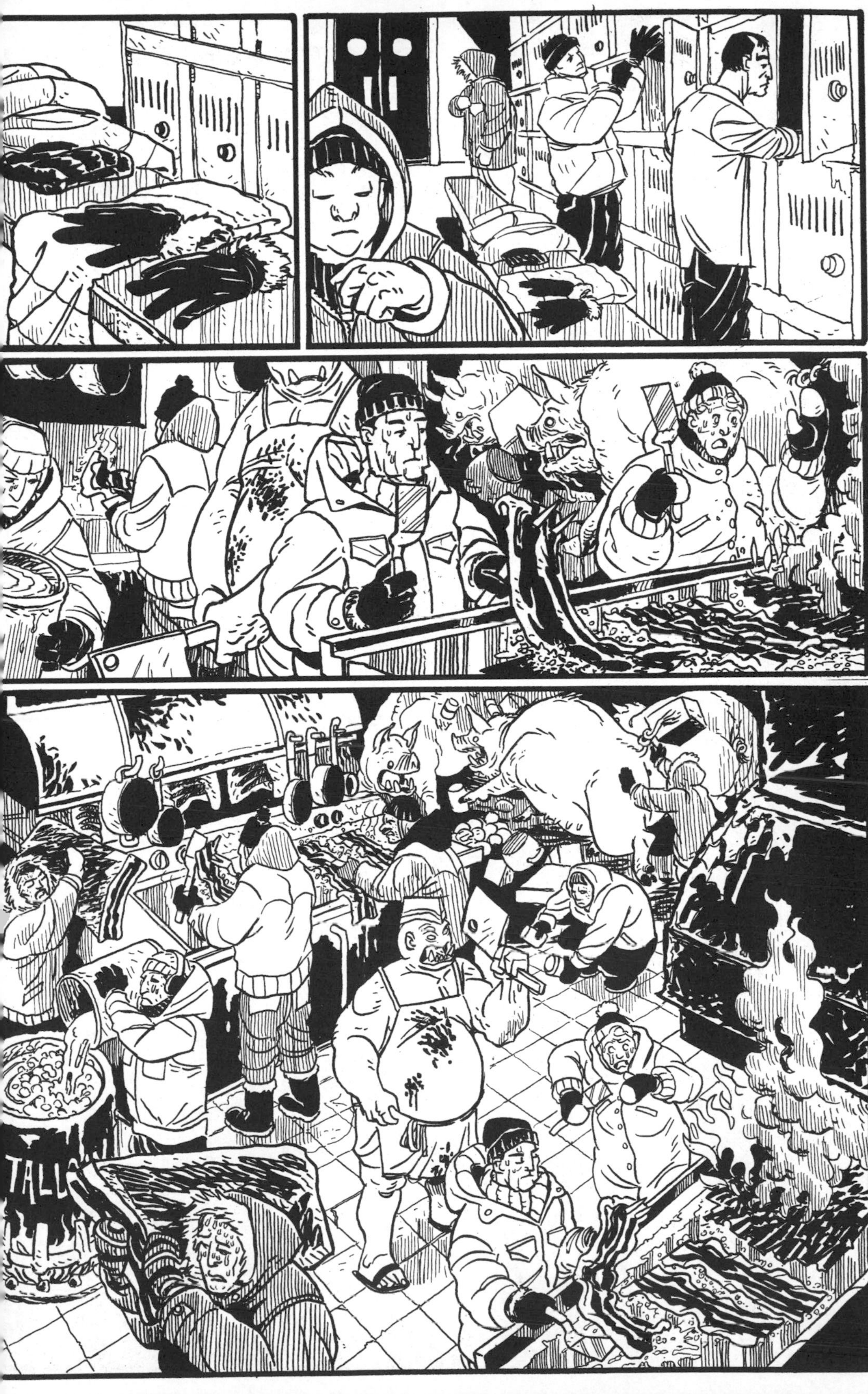
TALL

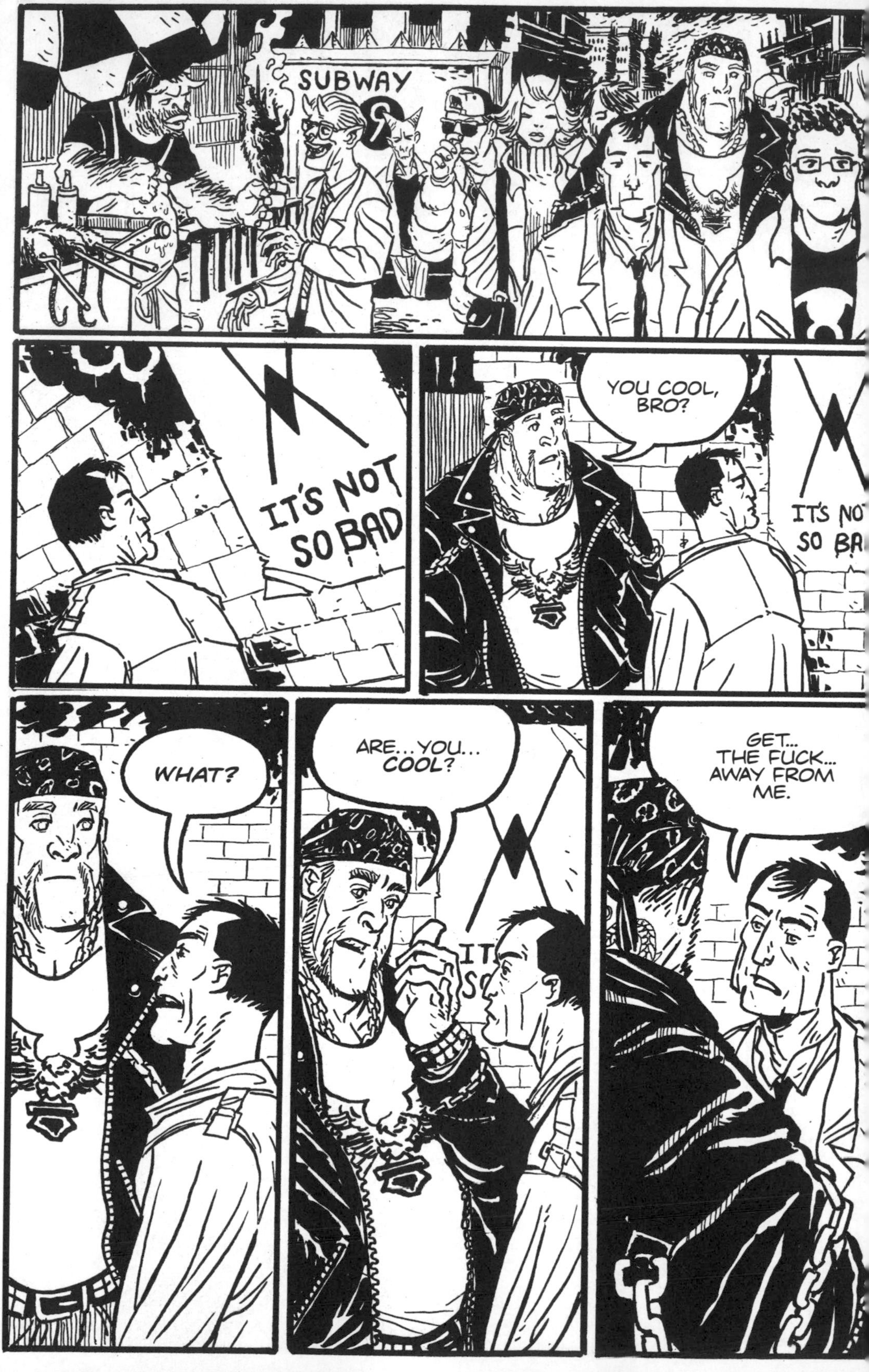
SUBWAY
IT'S NOT SO BAD
YOU COOL, BRO?
IT'S NOT SO BA
WHAT?
ARE... YOU... COOL?
GET... THE FUCK... AWAY FROM ME.

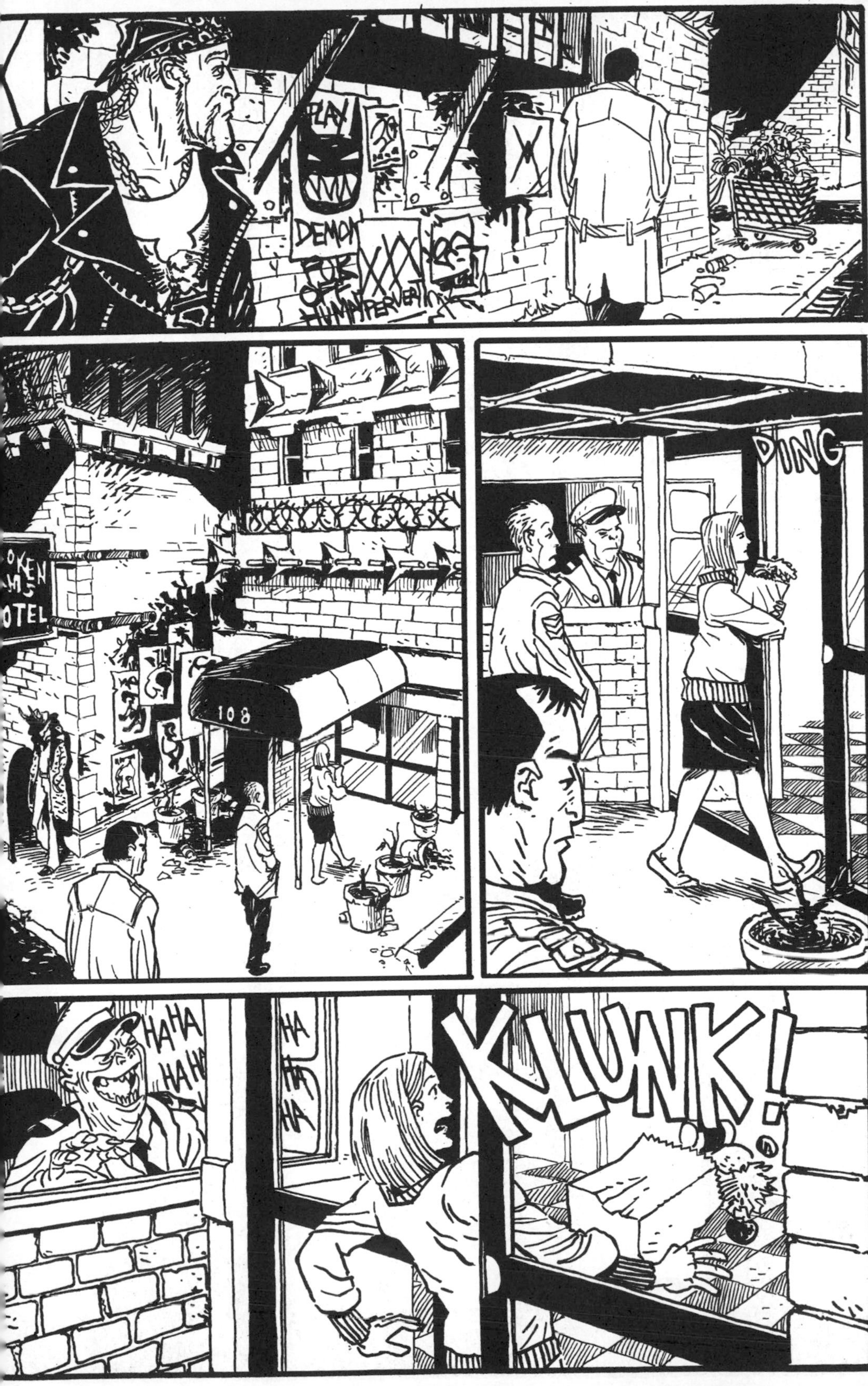
PLAY
DEMON
FUK OFF
HUMAN PERVERT
OKEN
OTEL
108
DING
HA HA
HA HA
HA
HA
HA
KLUNK!

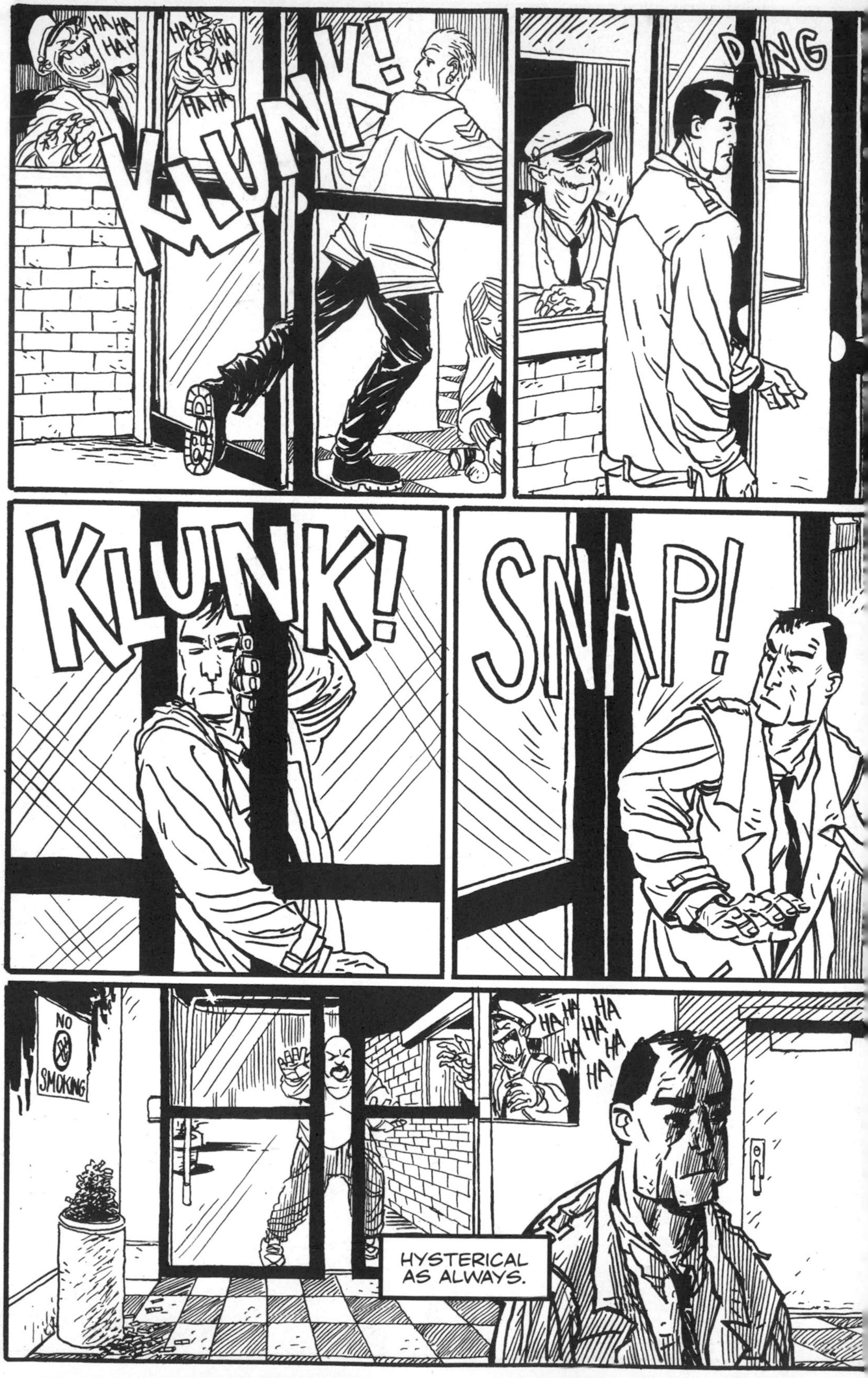
HA HA HA HA
HA HA HA HA
HA HA
KLUNK!
DING
KLUNK!
SNAP!
NO SMOKING
HA HA HA HA HA HA HA HA
HYSTERICAL AS ALWAYS.

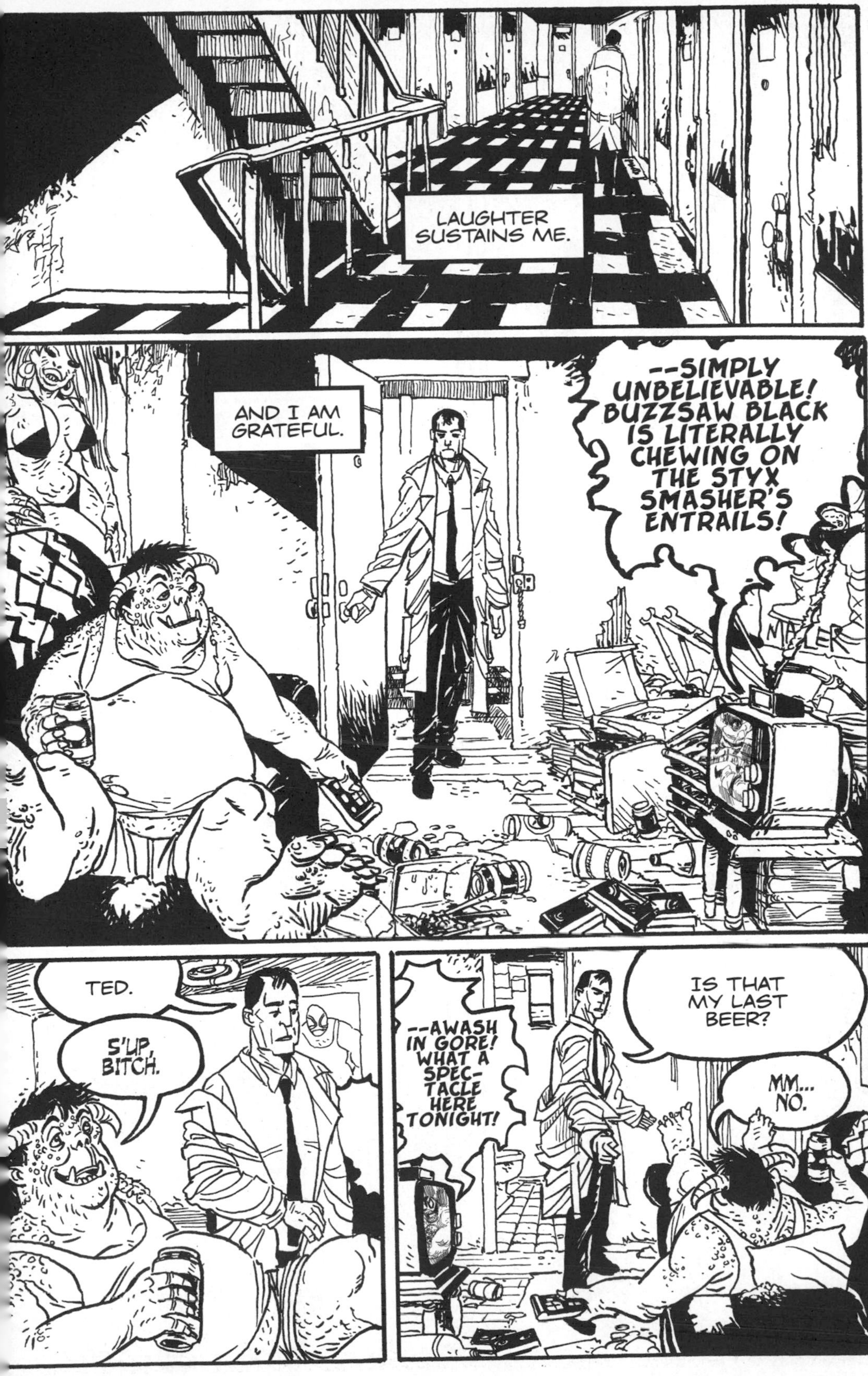
LAUGHTER SUSTAINS ME.
AND I AM GRATEFUL.
--SIMPLY UNBELIEVABLE! BUZZSAW BLACK IS LITERALLY CHEWING ON THE STYX SMASHER'S ENTRAILS!
TED.
S'UP, BITCH.
--AWASH IN GORE! WHAT A SPEC-TACLE HERE TONIGHT!
IS THAT MY LAST BEER?
MM... NO.

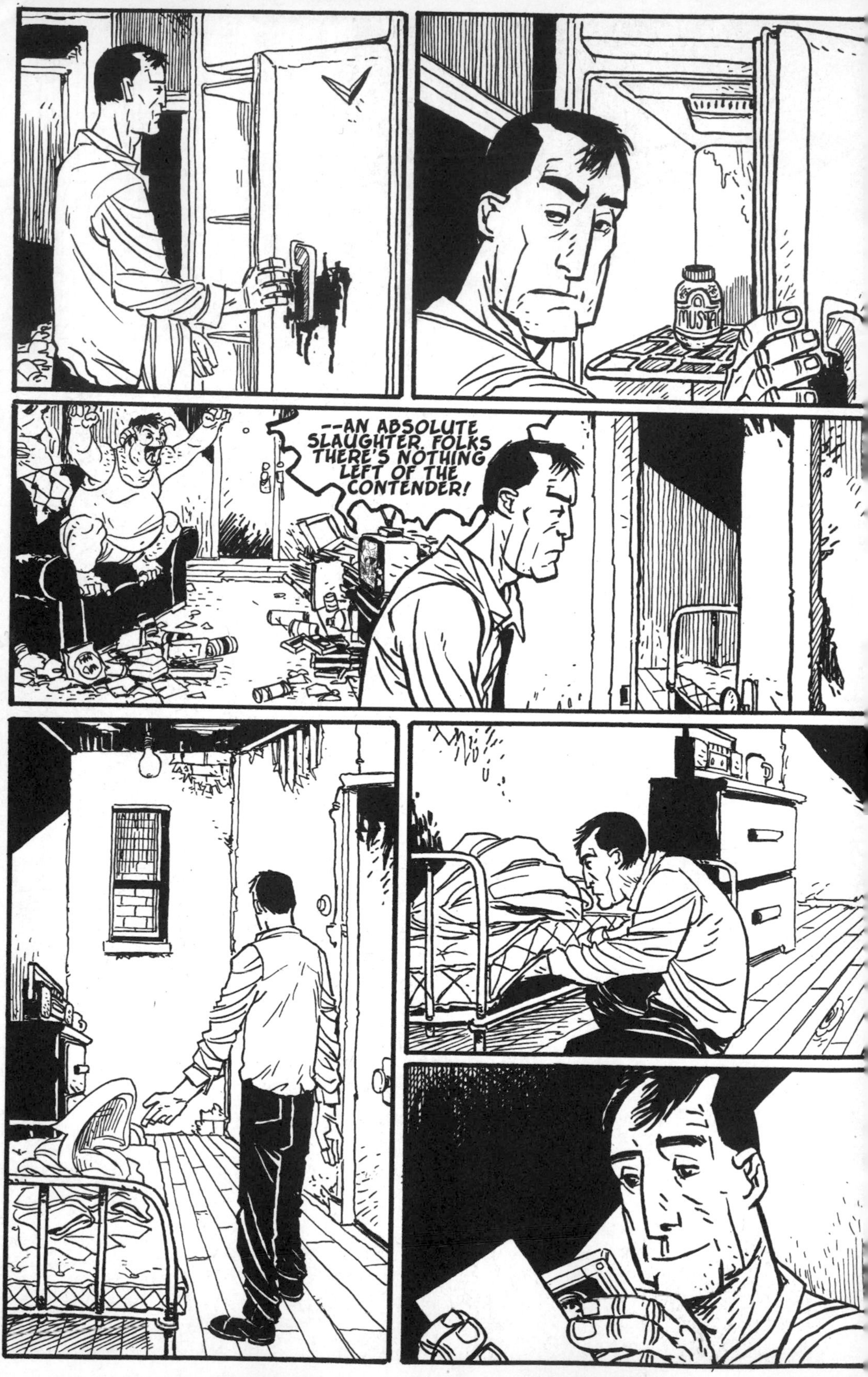
--AN ABSOLUTE SLAUGHTER, FOLKS THERE'S NOTHING LEFT OF THE CONTENDER!

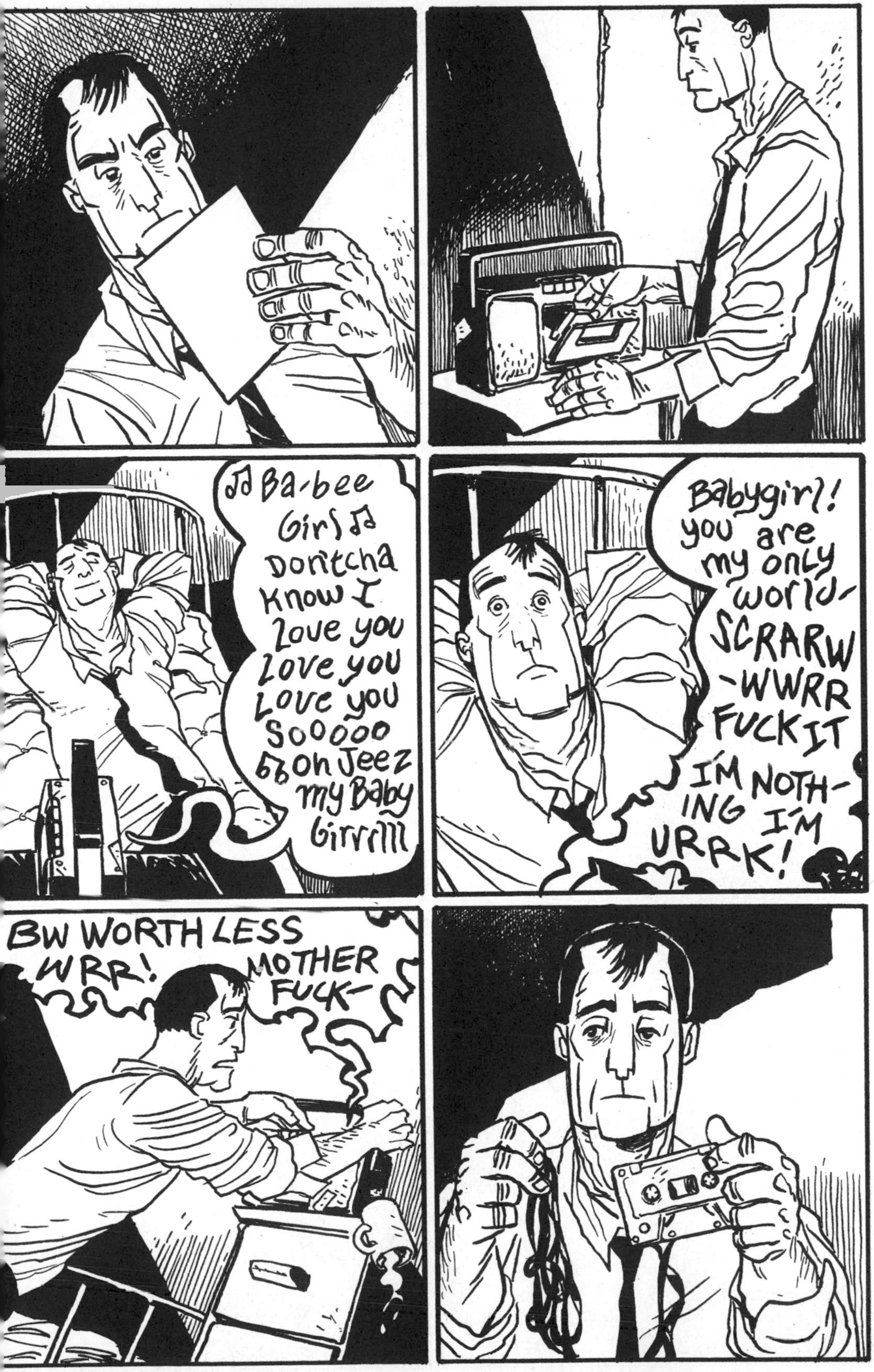
♫ Ba-bee Girl ♫ Don'tcha Know I Love you Love you Love you Sooooo ♫ oh Jeez my Baby Girrrlll
Babygirl! you are my only world- SCRARW -WWRR FUCK IT
I'M NOTH-ING I'M URRK!
BW WORTH LESS WRR!
MOTHER FUCK-

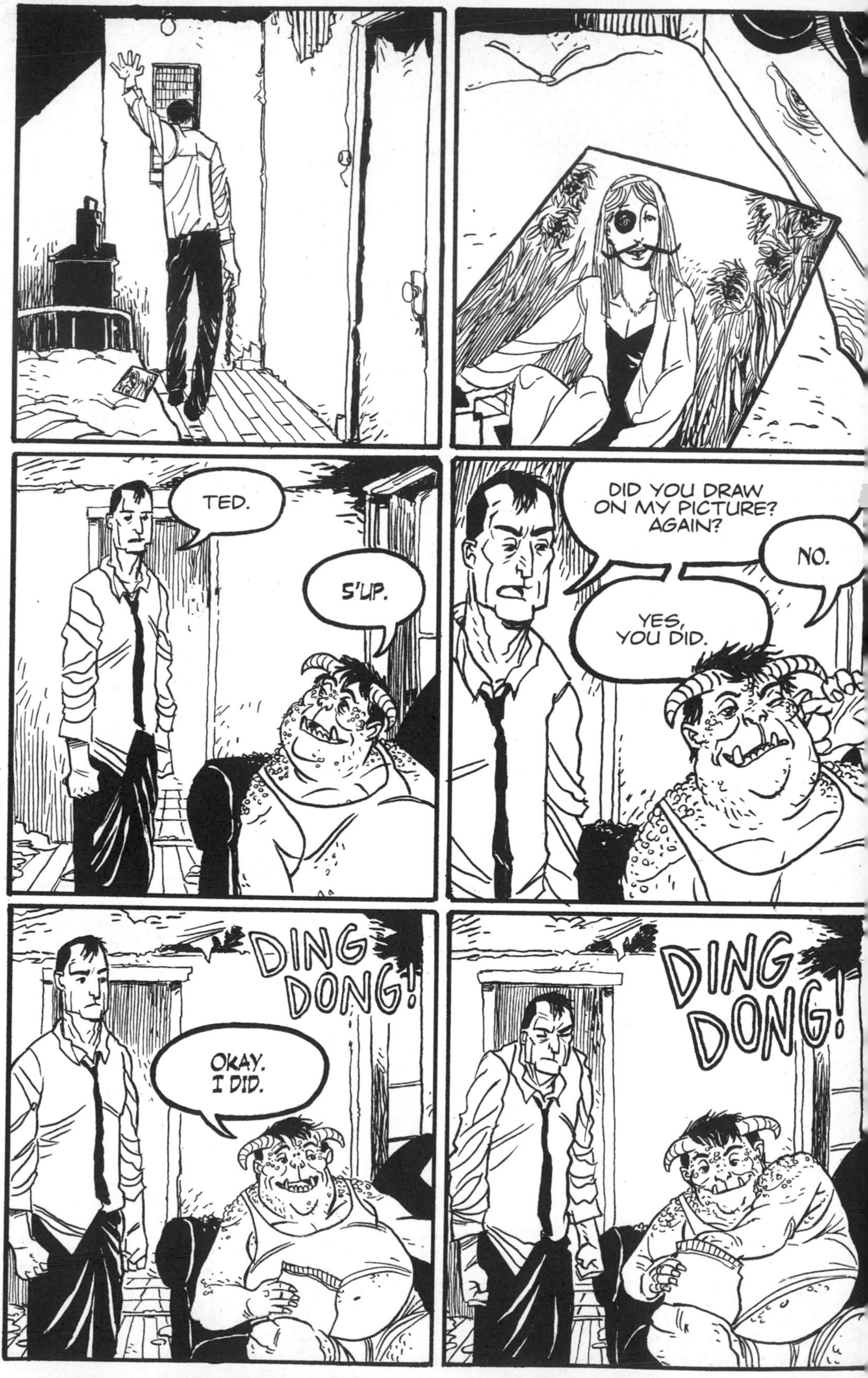
TED.
S'UP.
DID YOU DRAW ON MY PICTURE? AGAIN?
NO.
YES, YOU DID.
DING DONG!
OKAY. I DID.
DING DONG!

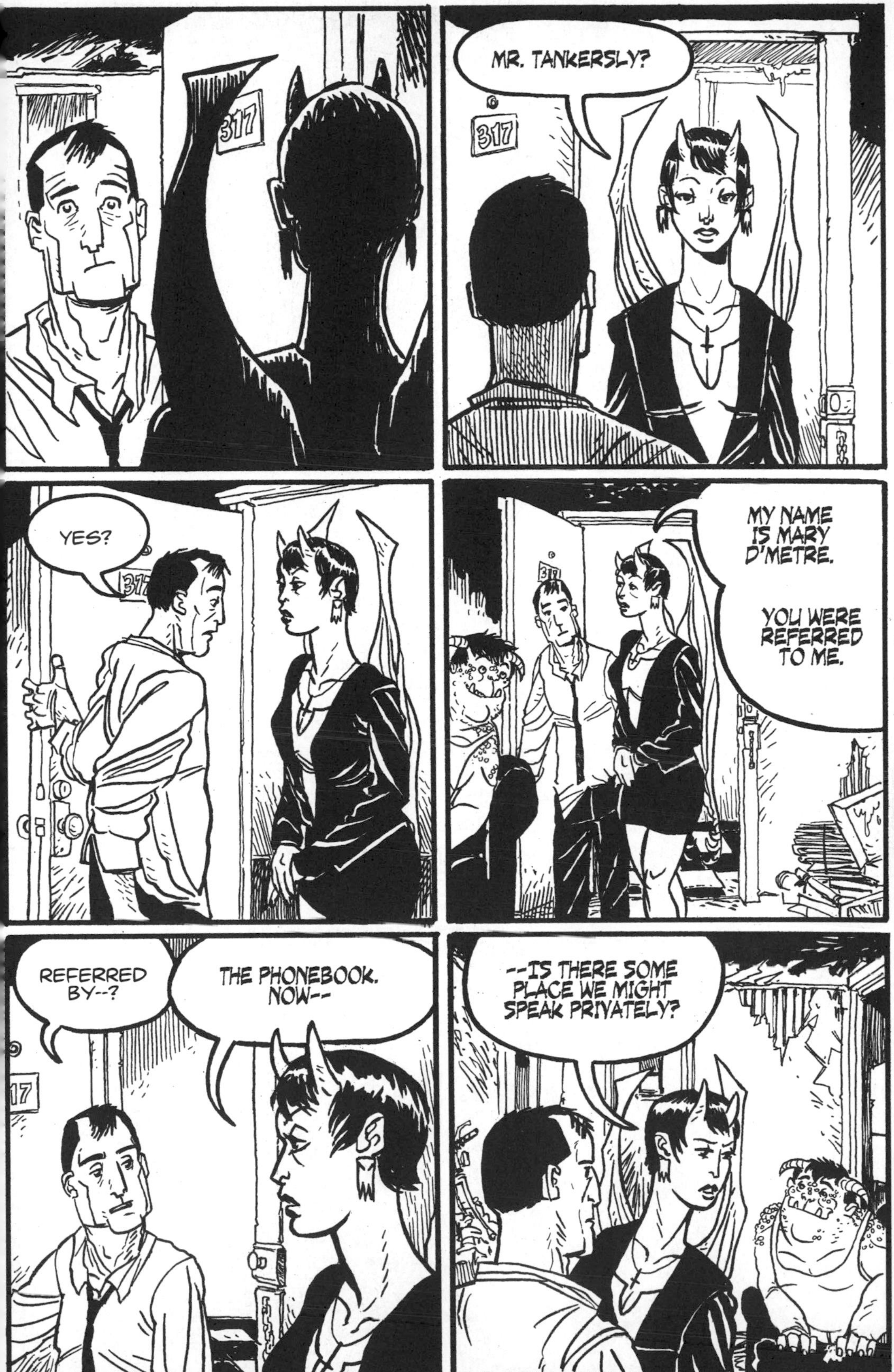
MR. TANKERSLY?
YES?
MY NAME IS MARY D'METRE.
YOU WERE REFERRED TO ME.
REFERRED BY--?
THE PHONEBOOK. NOW--
--IS THERE SOME PLACE WE MIGHT SPEAK PRIVATELY?

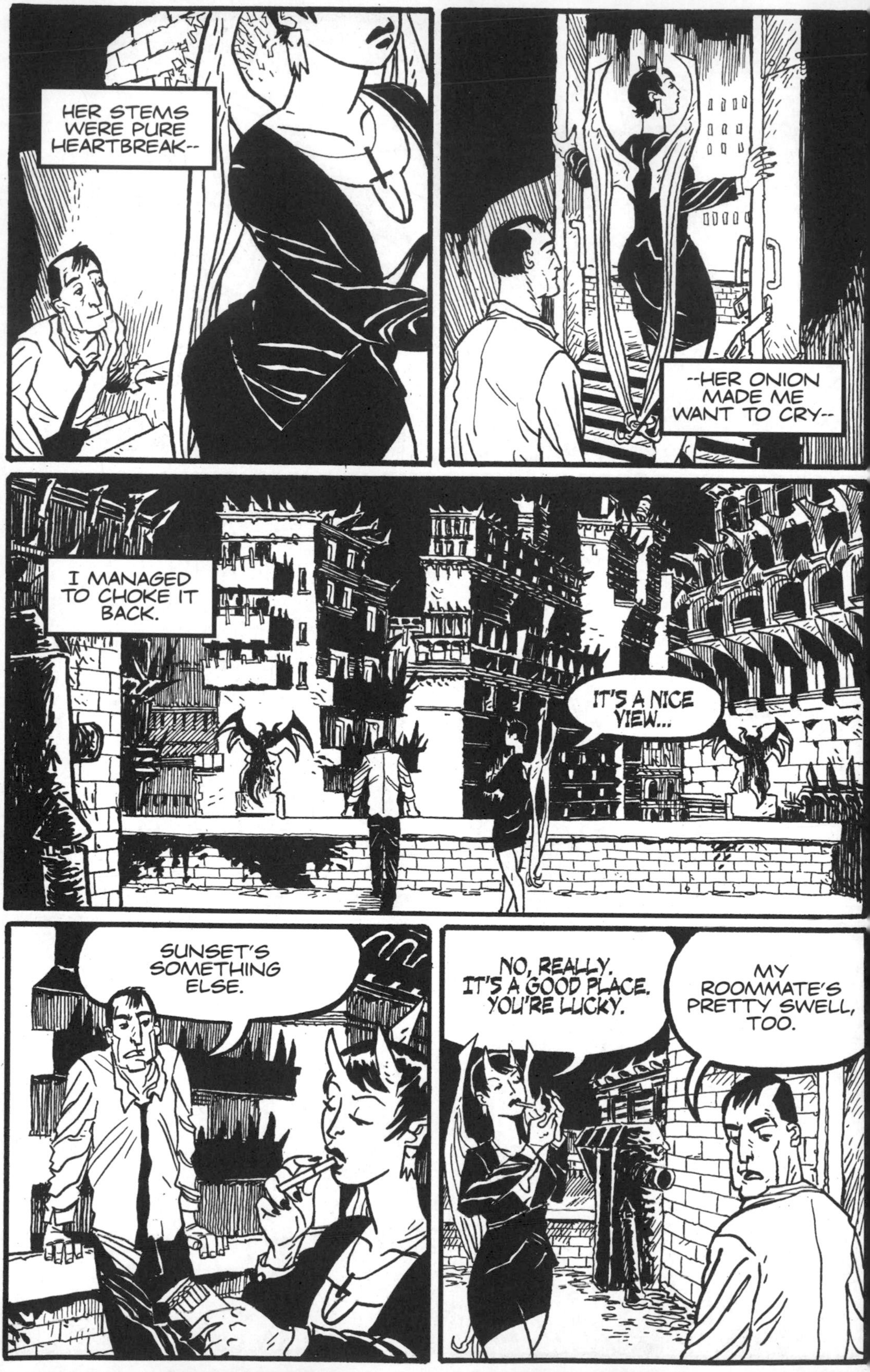
HER STEMS WERE PURE HEARTBREAK--
--HER ONION MADE ME WANT TO CRY--
I MANAGED TO CHOKE IT BACK.
IT'S A NICE VIEW...
SUNSET'S SOMETHING ELSE.
NO, REALLY. IT'S A GOOD PLACE. YOU'RE LUCKY.
MY ROOMMATE'S PRETTY SWELL, TOO.

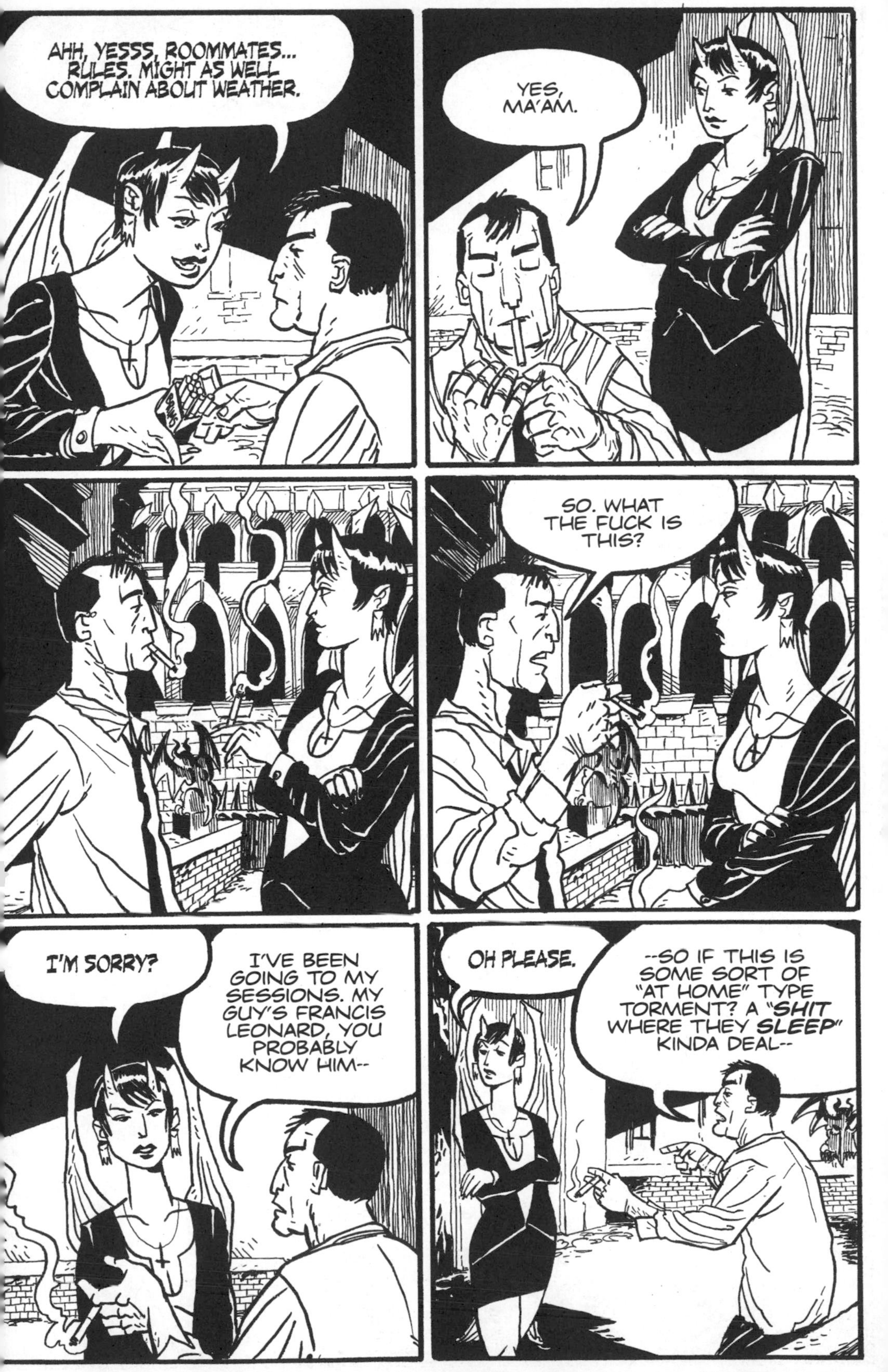
AHH, YESSS, ROOMMATES... RULES. MIGHT AS WELL COMPLAIN ABOUT WEATHER.
YES, MA'AM.
SO. WHAT THE FUCK IS THIS?
I'M SORRY?
I'VE BEEN GOING TO MY SESSIONS. MY GUY'S FRANCIS LEONARD, YOU PROBABLY KNOW HIM--
OH PLEASE.
--SO IF THIS IS SOME SORT OF "AT HOME" TYPE TORMENT? A "SHIT WHERE THEY SLEEP" KINDA DEAL--

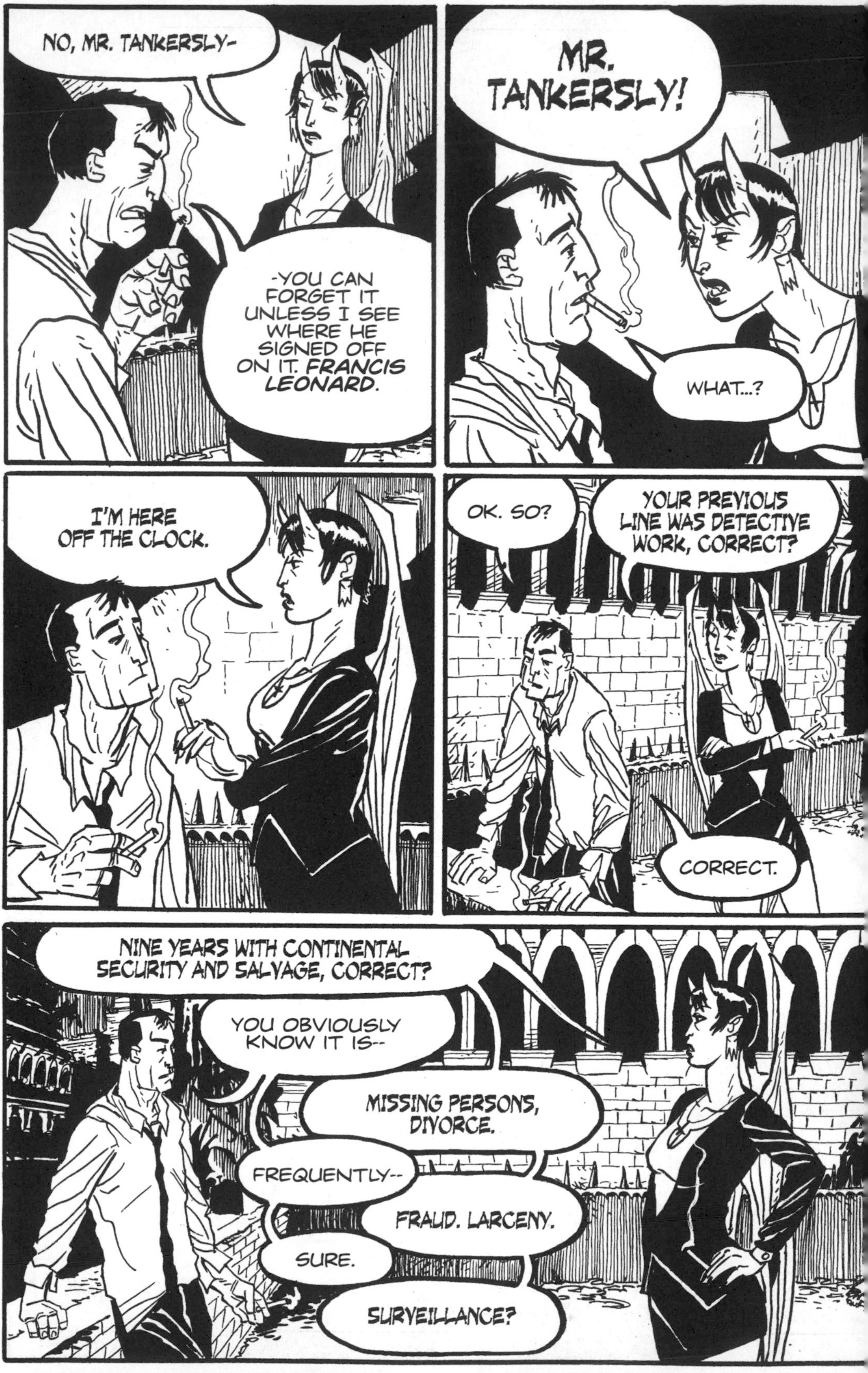
NO, MR. TANKERSLY-
-YOU CAN FORGET IT UNLESS I SEE WHERE HE SIGNED OFF ON IT. *FRANCIS LEONARD*.
MR. TANKERSLY!
WHAT...?
I'M HERE OFF THE CLOCK.
OK. SO?
YOUR PREVIOUS LINE WAS DETECTIVE WORK, CORRECT?
CORRECT.
NINE YEARS WITH CONTINENTAL SECURITY AND SALVAGE, CORRECT?
YOU OBVIOUSLY KNOW IT IS--
MISSING PERSONS, DIVORCE.
FREQUENTLY--
FRAUD. LARCENY.
SURE.
SURVEILLANCE?

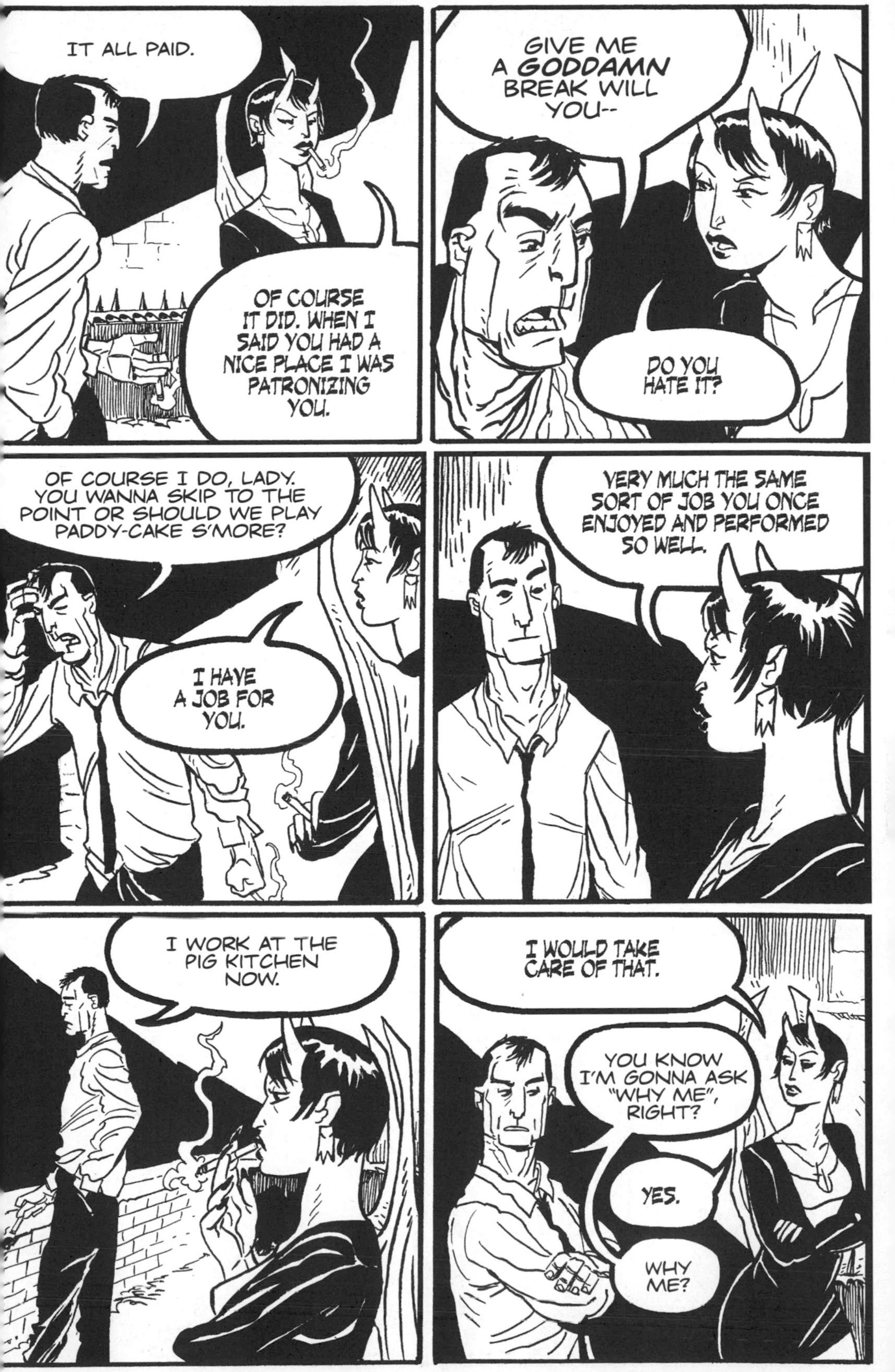
IT ALL PAID.
OF COURSE IT DID. WHEN I SAID YOU HAD A NICE PLACE I WAS PATRONIZING YOU.
GIVE ME A GODDAMN BREAK WILL YOU--
DO YOU HATE IT?
OF COURSE I DO, LADY. YOU WANNA SKIP TO THE POINT OR SHOULD WE PLAY PADDY-CAKE S'MORE?
I HAVE A JOB FOR YOU.
VERY MUCH THE SAME SORT OF JOB YOU ONCE ENJOYED AND PERFORMED SO WELL.
I WORK AT THE PIG KITCHEN NOW.
I WOULD TAKE CARE OF THAT.
YOU KNOW I'M GONNA ASK "WHY ME", RIGHT?
YES.
WHY ME?

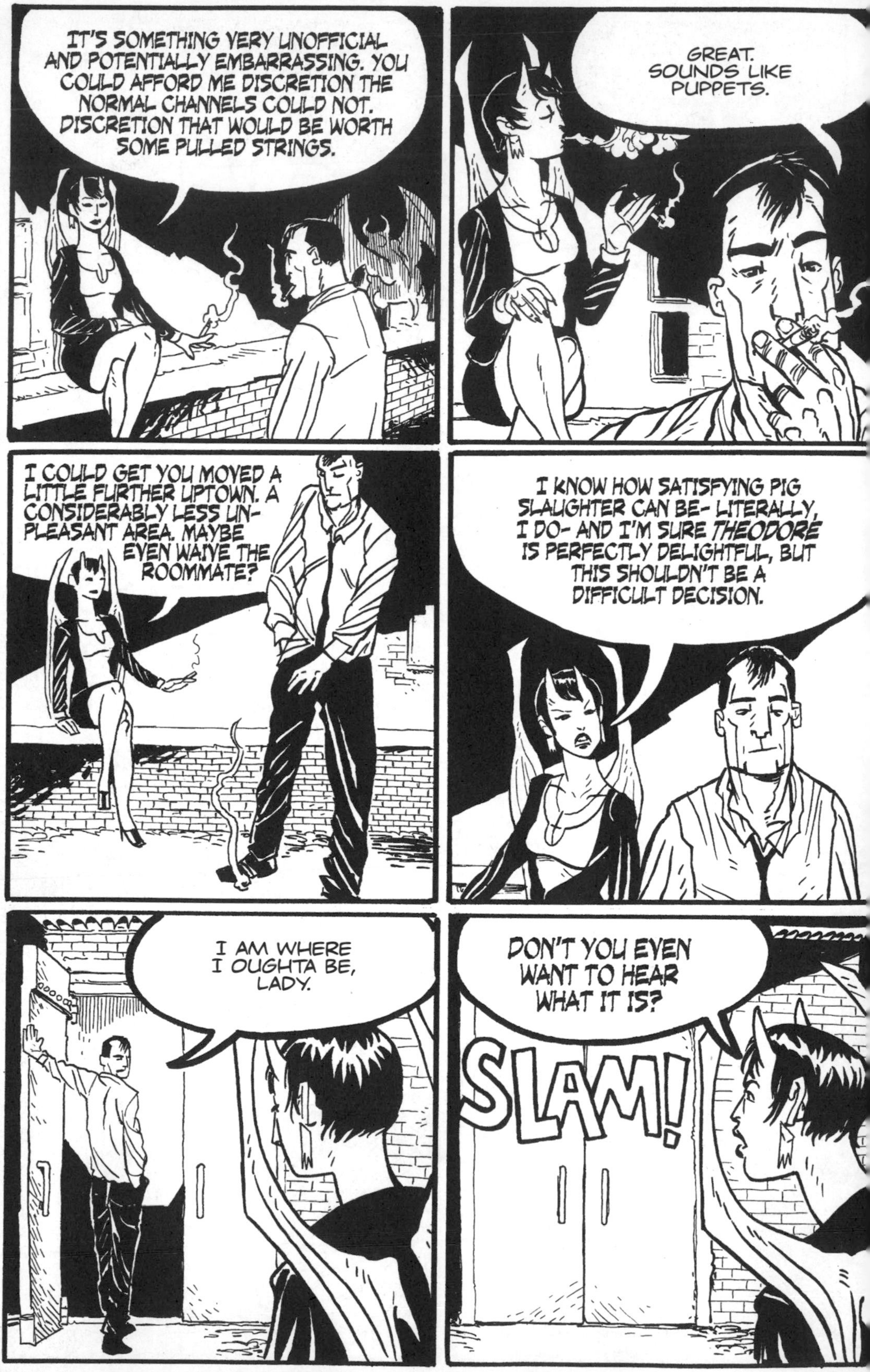
IT'S SOMETHING VERY UNOFFICIAL AND POTENTIALLY EMBARRASSING. YOU COULD AFFORD ME DISCRETION THE NORMAL CHANNELS COULD NOT. DISCRETION THAT WOULD BE WORTH SOME PULLED STRINGS.
GREAT. SOUNDS LIKE PUPPETS.
I COULD GET YOU MOVED A LITTLE FURTHER UPTOWN. A CONSIDERABLY LESS UN-PLEASANT AREA. MAYBE EVEN WAIVE THE ROOMMATE?
I KNOW HOW SATISFYING PIG SLAUGHTER CAN BE- LITERALLY, I DO- AND I'M SURE THEODORE IS PERFECTLY DELIGHTFUL, BUT THIS SHOULDN'T BE A DIFFICULT DECISION.
I AM WHERE I OUGHTA BE, LADY.
DON'T YOU EVEN WANT TO HEAR WHAT IT IS?
SLAM!

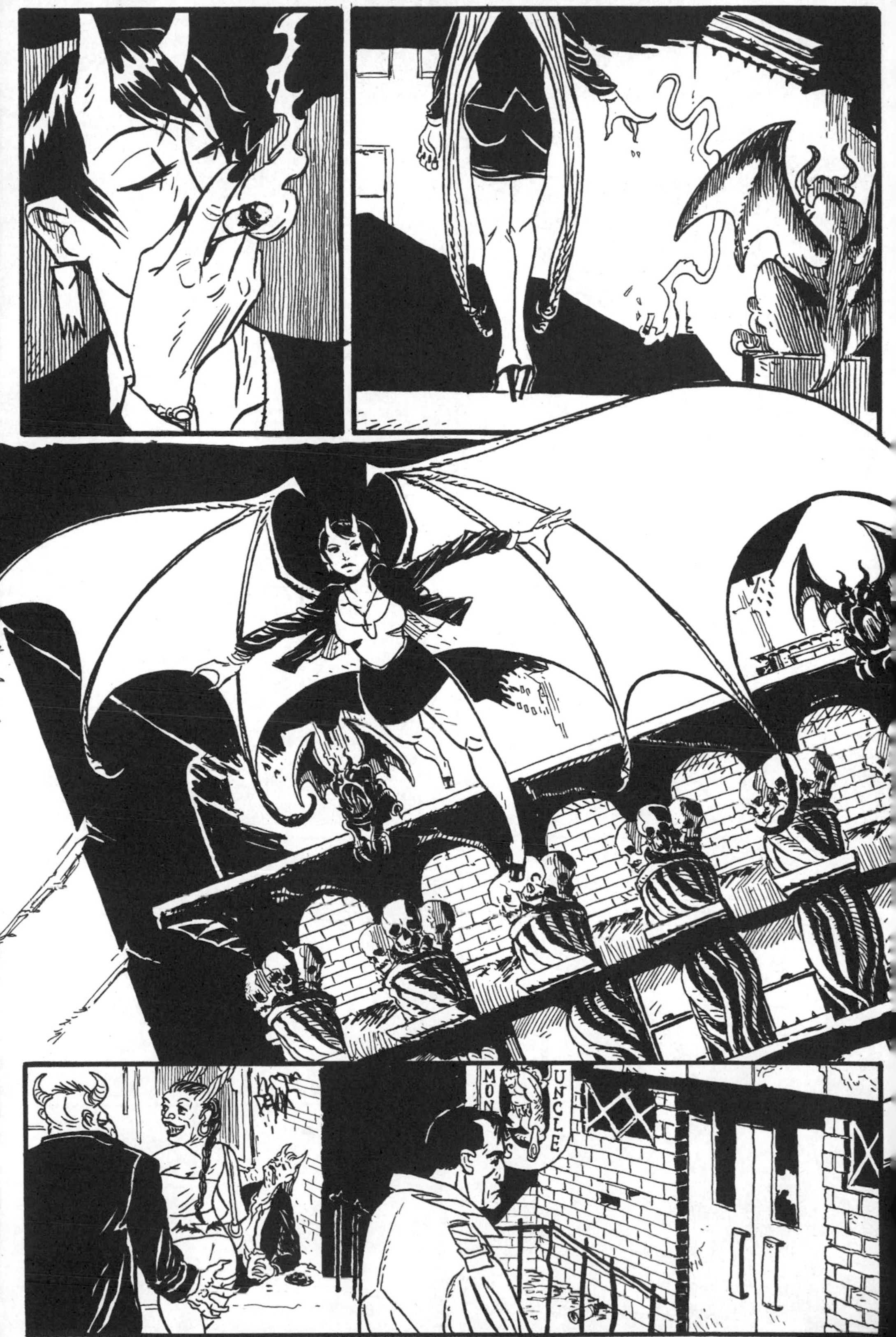
MON
S
UNCLE

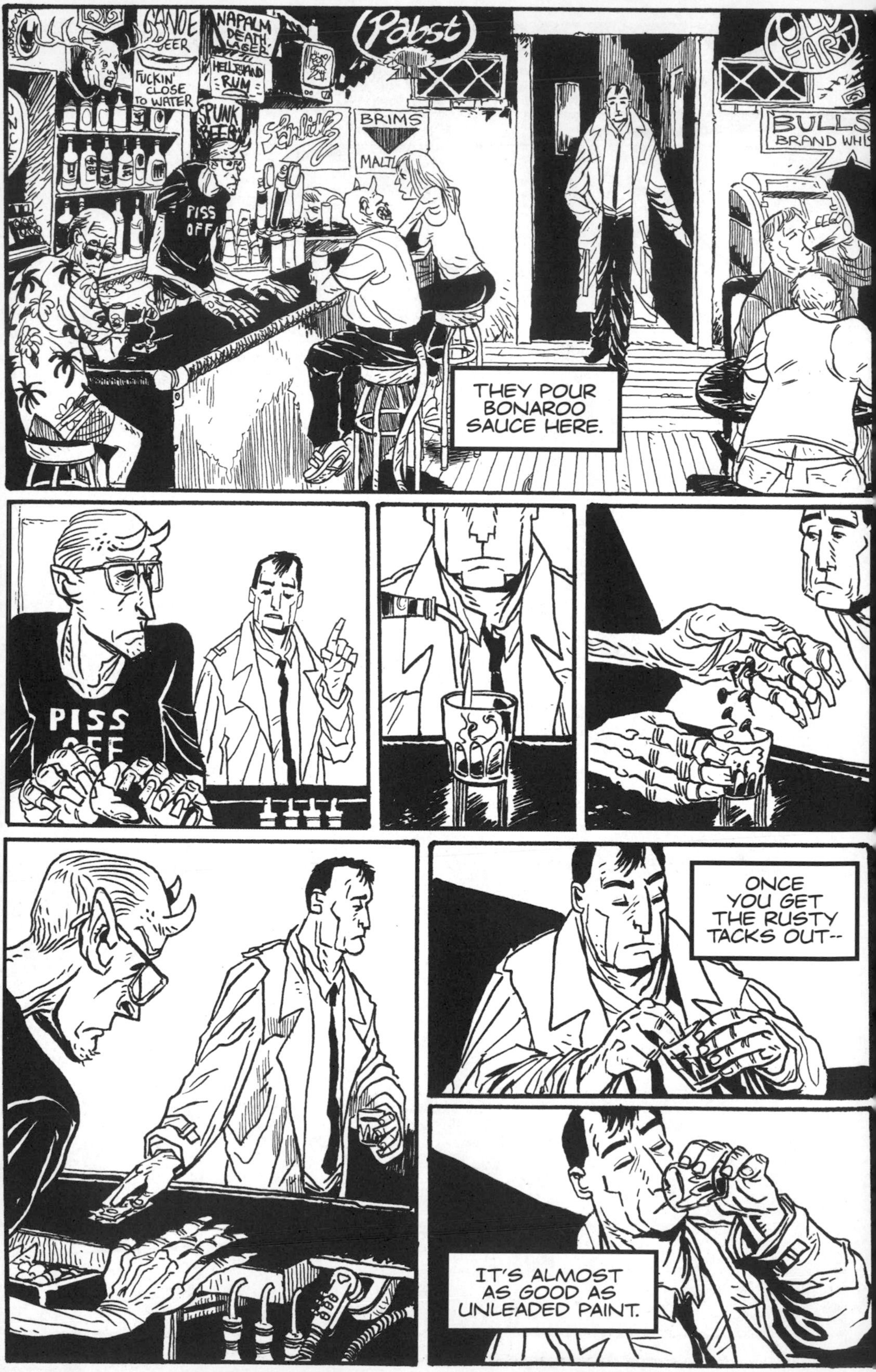
NAPALM DEATH LAGER
FUCKIN' CLOSE TO WATER
SPUNK BEER
Pabst
BRIMS
MALT
PISS OFF
THEY POUR BONAROO SAUCE HERE.
PISS OFF
ONCE YOU GET THE RUSTY TACKS OUT--
IT'S ALMOST AS GOOD AS UNLEADED PAINT.

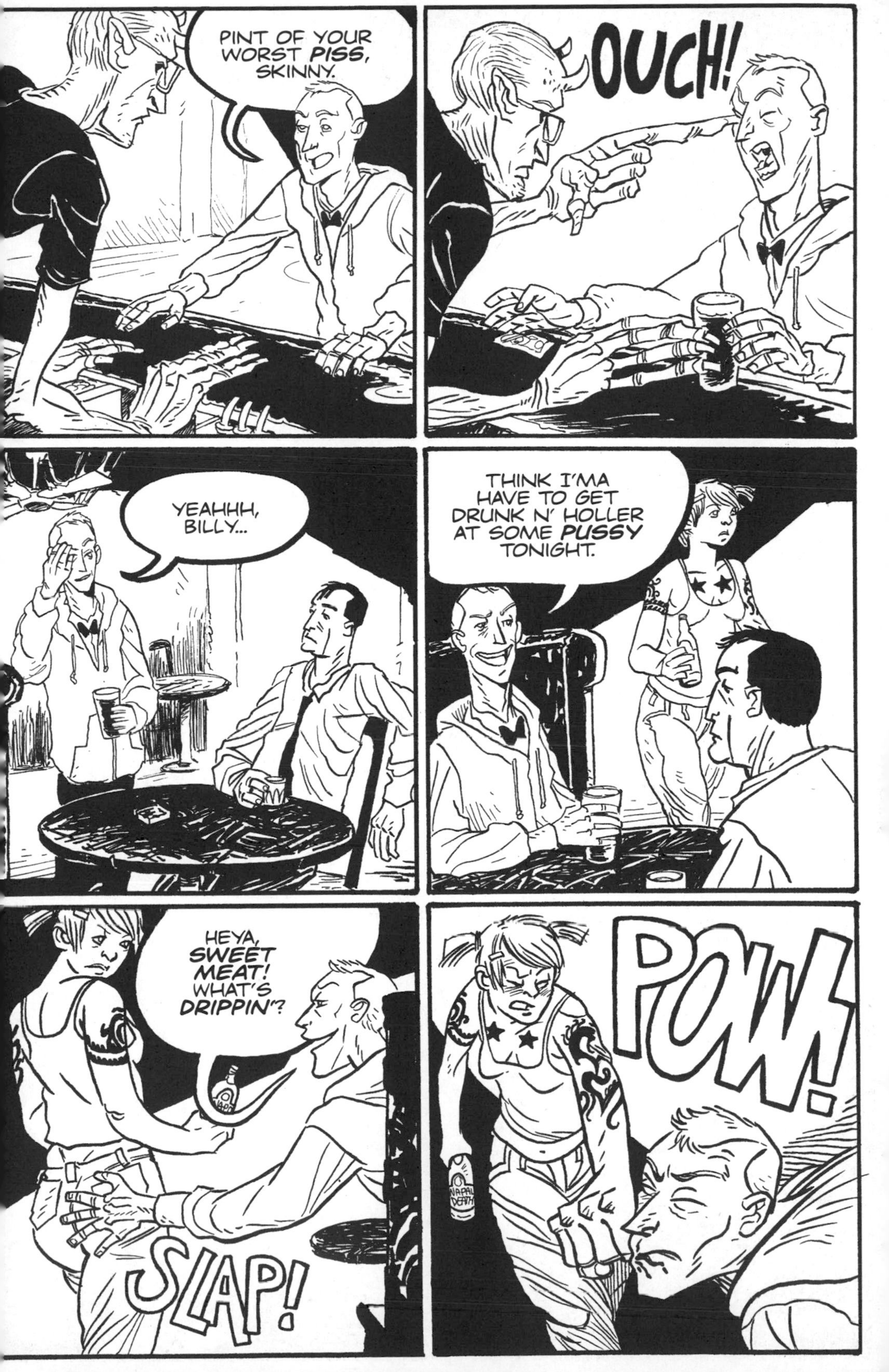

PINT OF YOUR WORST PISS, SKINNY.
OUCH!
YEAHHH, BILLY...
THINK I'MA HAVE TO GET DRUNK N' HOLLER AT SOME PUSSY TONIGHT.
HEYA, SWEET MEAT! WHAT'S DRIPPIN'?
SLAP!
NAPALM DEATH
POW!

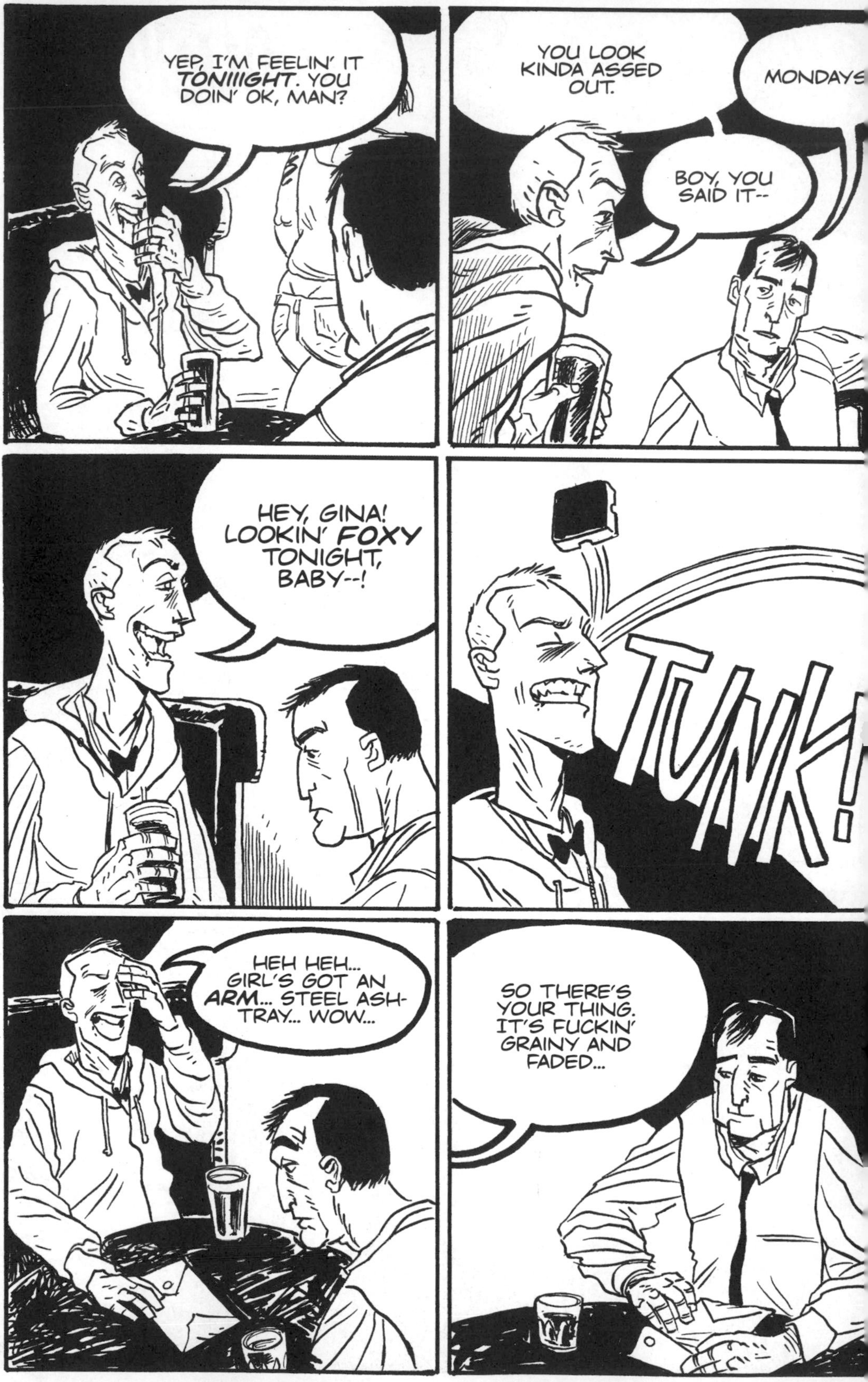
YEP, I'M FEELIN' IT TONIIIGHT. YOU DOIN' OK, MAN?
YOU LOOK KINDA ASSED OUT.
MONDAYS
BOY, YOU SAID IT--
HEY, GINA! LOOKIN' FOXY TONIGHT, BABY--!
TUNK!
HEH HEH... GIRL'S GOT AN ARM... STEEL ASH-TRAY... WOW...
SO THERE'S YOUR THING. IT'S FUCKIN' GRAINY AND FADED...

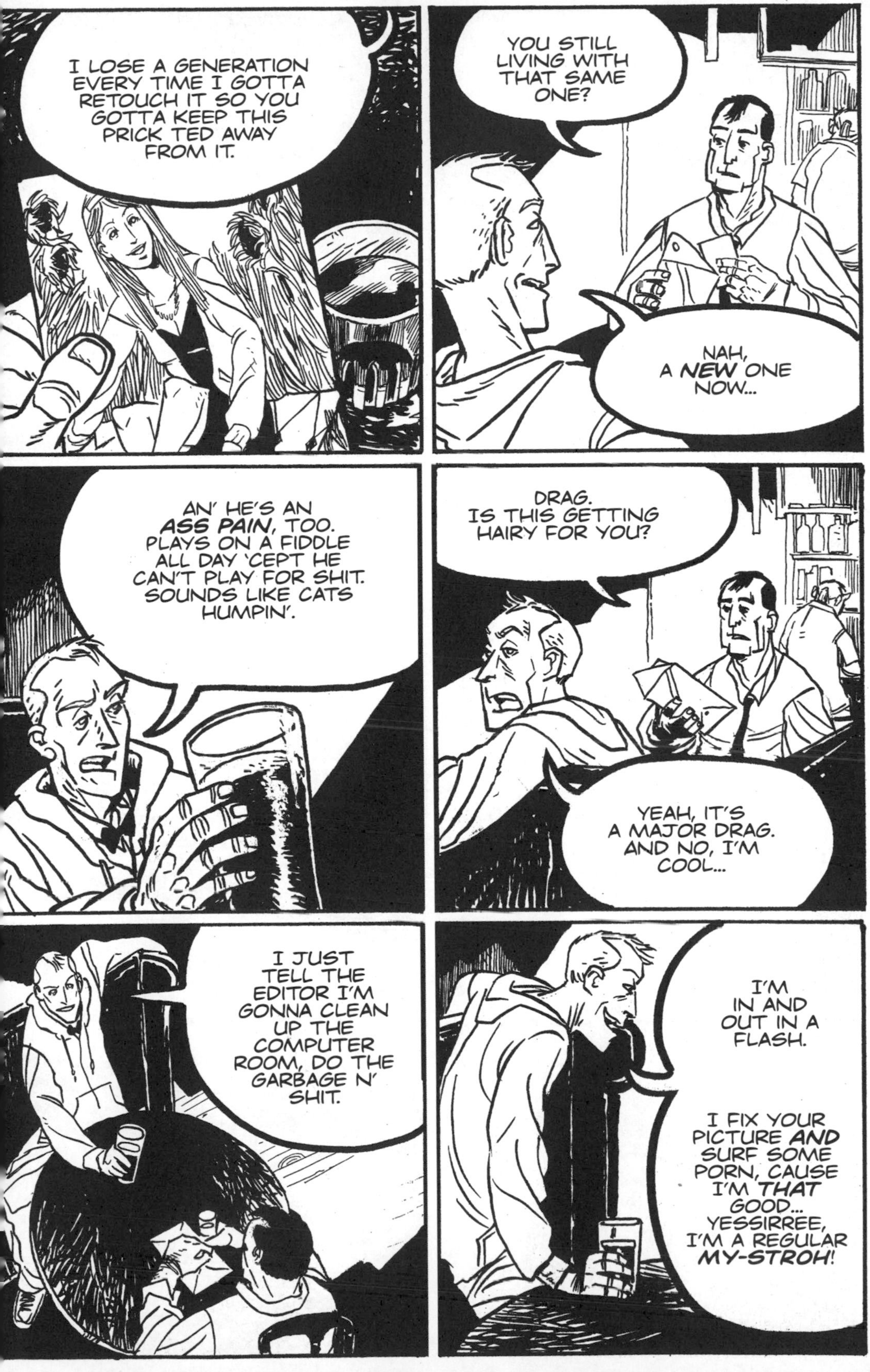
I LOSE A GENERATION EVERY TIME I GOTTA RETOUCH IT SO YOU GOTTA KEEP THIS PRICK TED AWAY FROM IT.
YOU STILL LIVING WITH THAT SAME ONE?
NAH, A NEW ONE NOW...
AN' HE'S AN ASS PAIN, TOO. PLAYS ON A FIDDLE ALL DAY 'CEPT HE CAN'T PLAY FOR SHIT. SOUNDS LIKE CATS HUMPIN'.
DRAG. IS THIS GETTING HAIRY FOR YOU?
YEAH, IT'S A MAJOR DRAG. AND NO, I'M COOL...
I JUST TELL THE EDITOR I'M GONNA CLEAN UP THE COMPUTER ROOM, DO THE GARBAGE N' SHIT.
I'M IN AND OUT IN A FLASH.
I FIX YOUR PICTURE AND SURF SOME PORN, CAUSE I'M THAT GOOD... YESSIRREE, I'M A REGULAR MY-STROH!

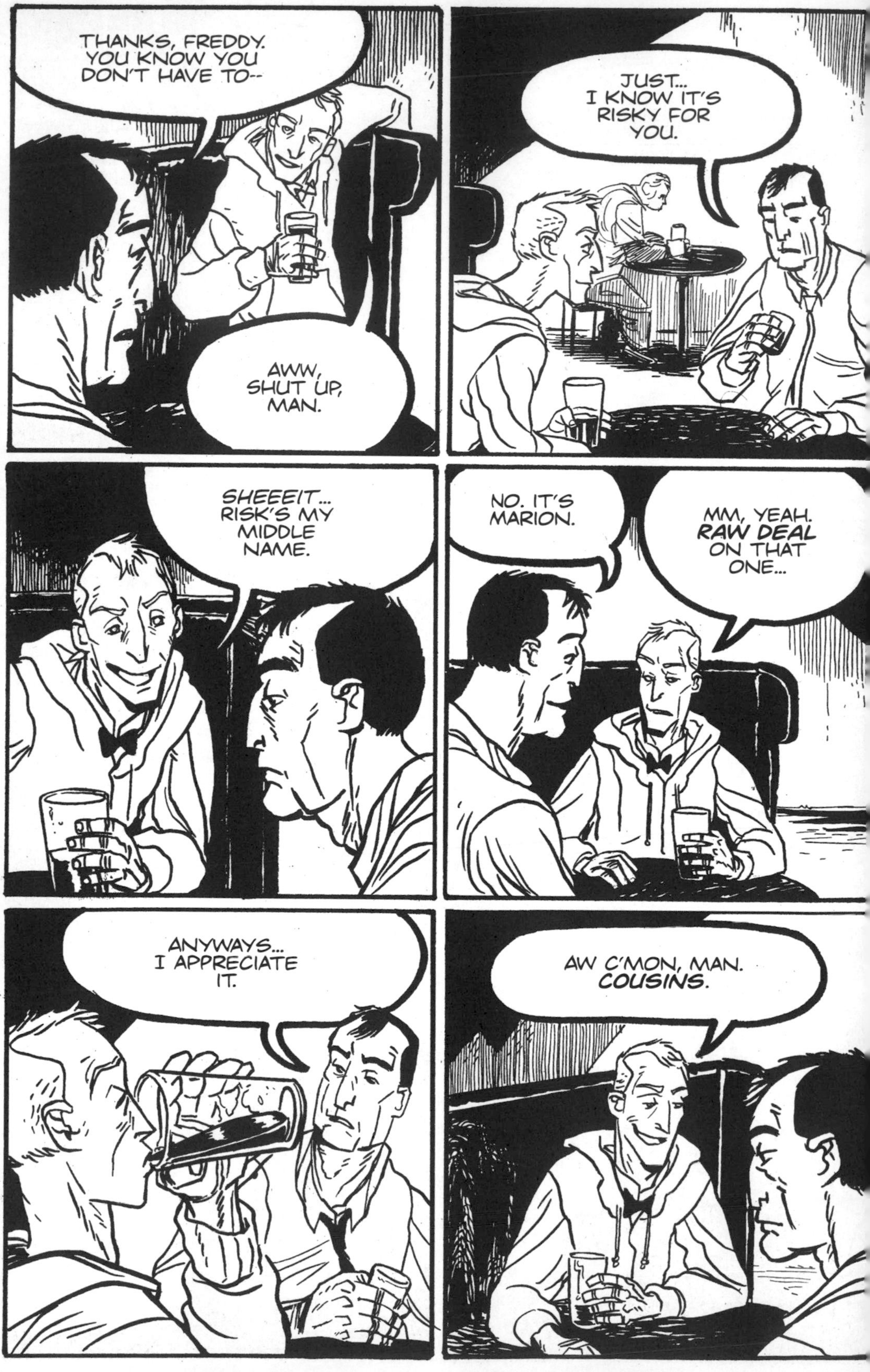
THANKS, FREDDY. YOU KNOW YOU DON'T HAVE TO--
AWW, SHUT UP, MAN.
JUST... I KNOW IT'S RISKY FOR YOU.
SHEEEIT... RISK'S MY MIDDLE NAME.
NO. IT'S MARION.
MM, YEAH. RAW DEAL ON THAT ONE...
ANYWAYS... I APPRECIATE IT.
AW C'MON, MAN. COUSINS.

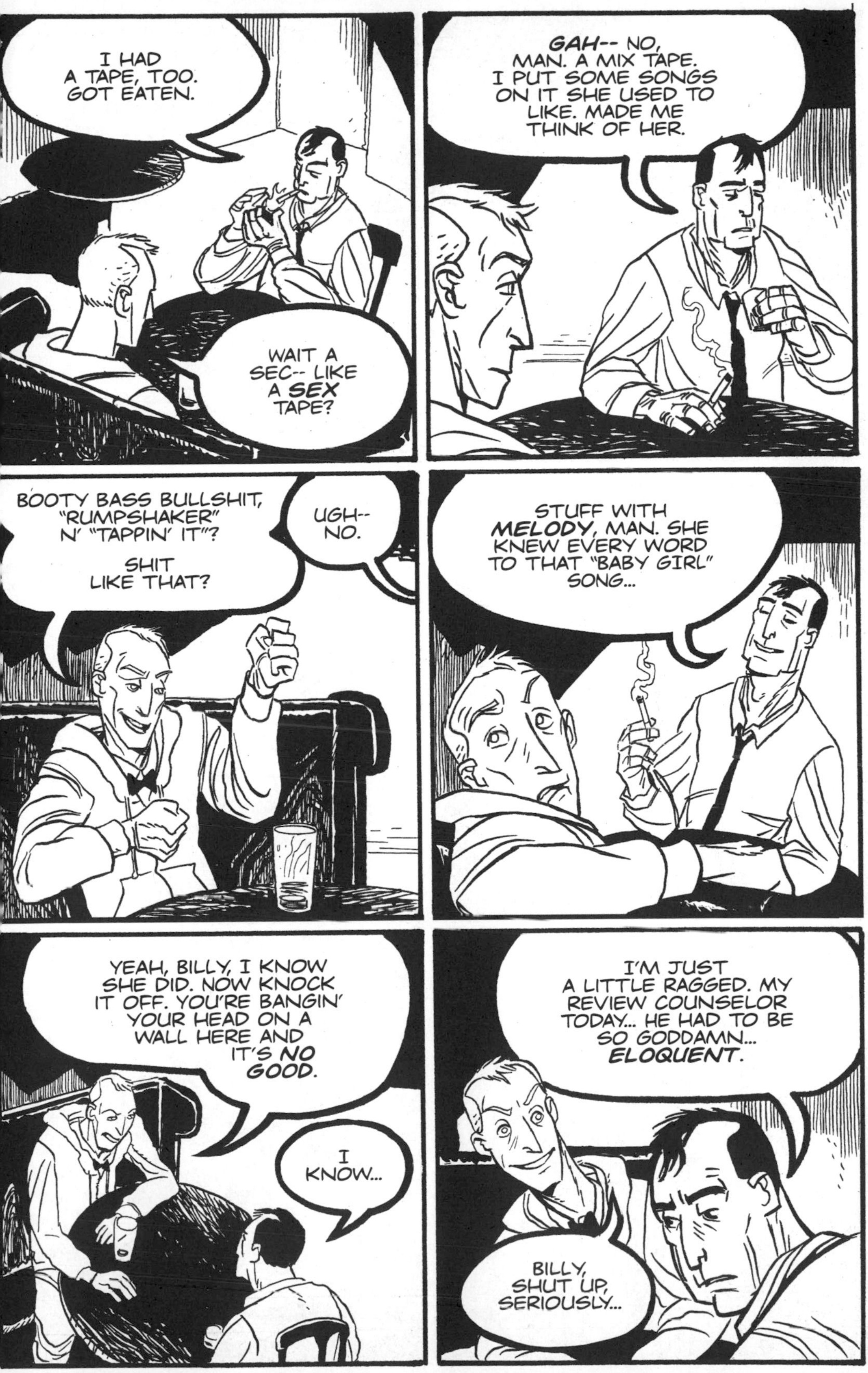
I HAD A TAPE, TOO. GOT EATEN.
WAIT A SEC-- LIKE A SEX TAPE?
GAH-- NO, MAN. A MIX TAPE. I PUT SOME SONGS ON IT SHE USED TO LIKE. MADE ME THINK OF HER.
BOOTY BASS BULLSHIT, "RUMPSHAKER" N' "TAPPIN' IT"?
SHIT LIKE THAT?
UGH-- NO.
STUFF WITH MELODY, MAN. SHE KNEW EVERY WORD TO THAT "BABY GIRL" SONG...
YEAH, BILLY, I KNOW SHE DID. NOW KNOCK IT OFF. YOU'RE BANGIN' YOUR HEAD ON A WALL HERE AND IT'S NO GOOD.
I KNOW...
I'M JUST A LITTLE RAGGED. MY REVIEW COUNSELOR TODAY... HE HAD TO BE SO GODDAMN... ELOQUENT.
BILLY, SHUT UP, SERIOUSLY...

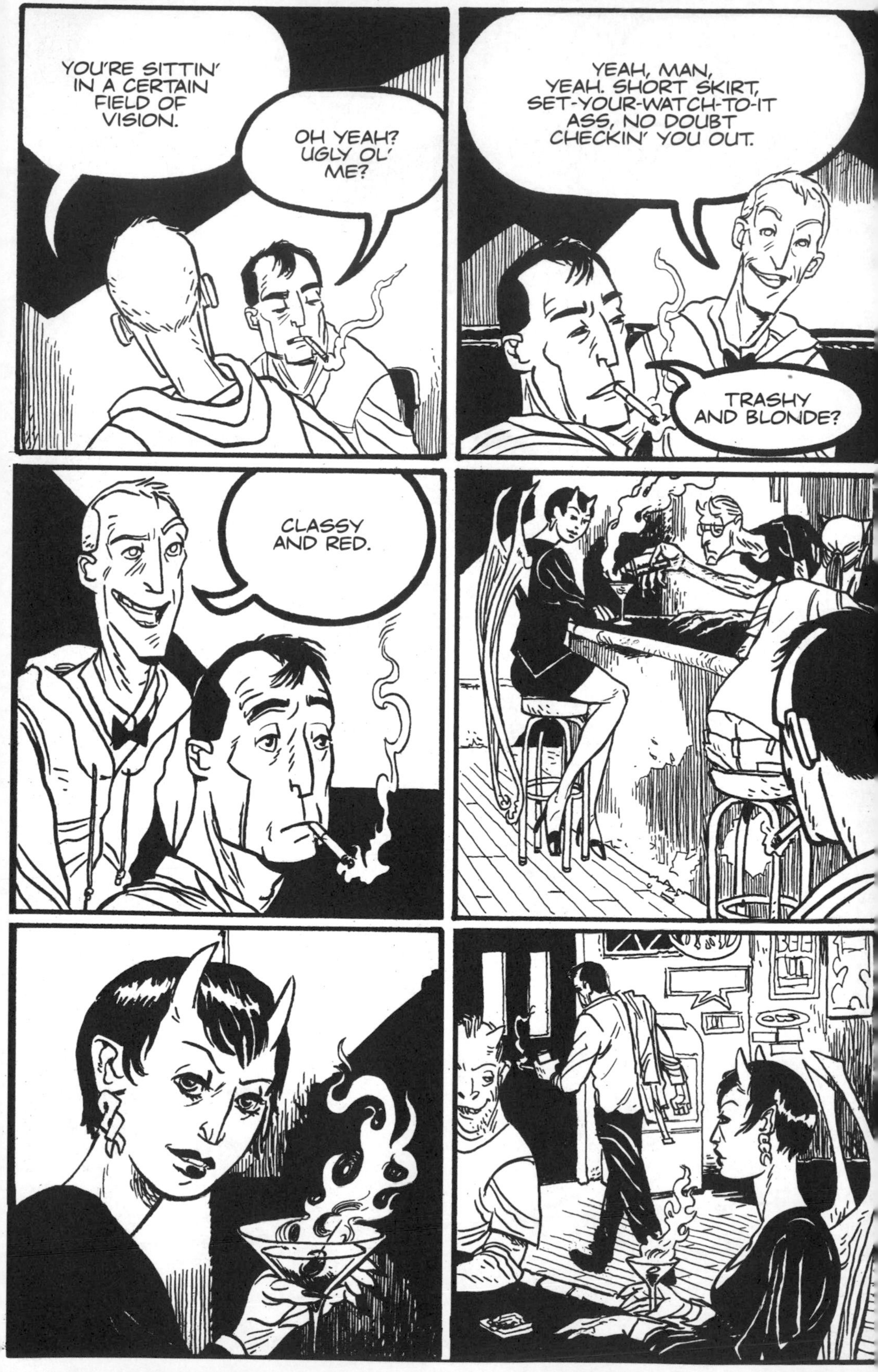
YOU'RE SITTIN' IN A CERTAIN FIELD OF VISION.
OH YEAH? UGLY OL' ME?
YEAH, MAN, YEAH. SHORT SKIRT, SET-YOUR-WATCH-TO-IT ASS, NO DOUBT CHECKIN' YOU OUT.
TRASHY AND BLONDE?
CLASSY AND RED.

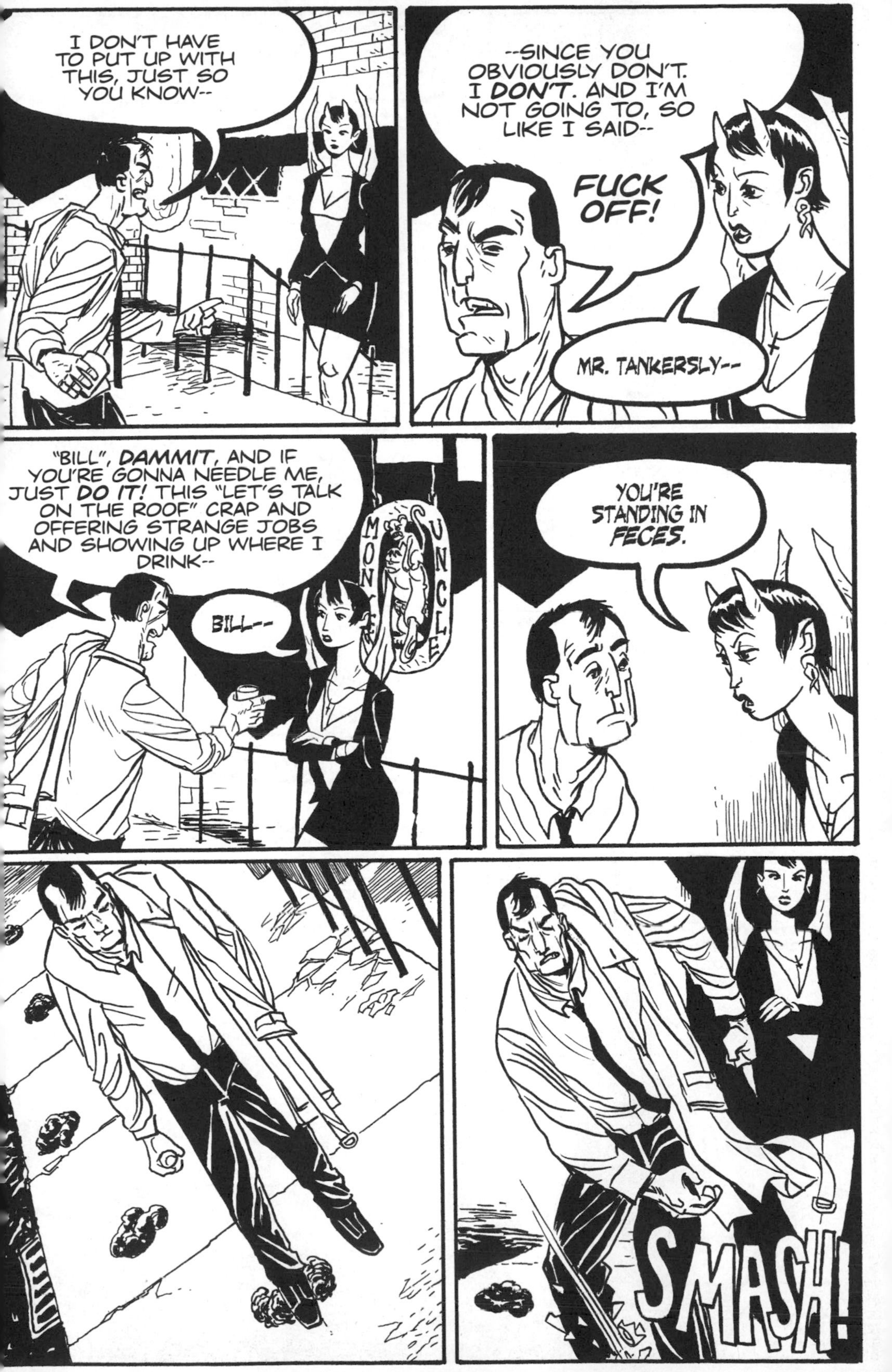
I DON'T HAVE TO PUT UP WITH THIS, JUST SO YOU KNOW--
--SINCE YOU OBVIOUSLY DON'T. I DON'T. AND I'M NOT GOING TO, SO LIKE I SAID--
FUCK OFF!
MR. TANKERSLY--
"BILL", DAMMIT, AND IF YOU'RE GONNA NEEDLE ME, JUST DO IT! THIS "LET'S TALK ON THE ROOF" CRAP AND OFFERING STRANGE JOBS AND SHOWING UP WHERE I DRINK--
BILL--
UNCLE
YOU'RE STANDING IN FECES.
SMASH!

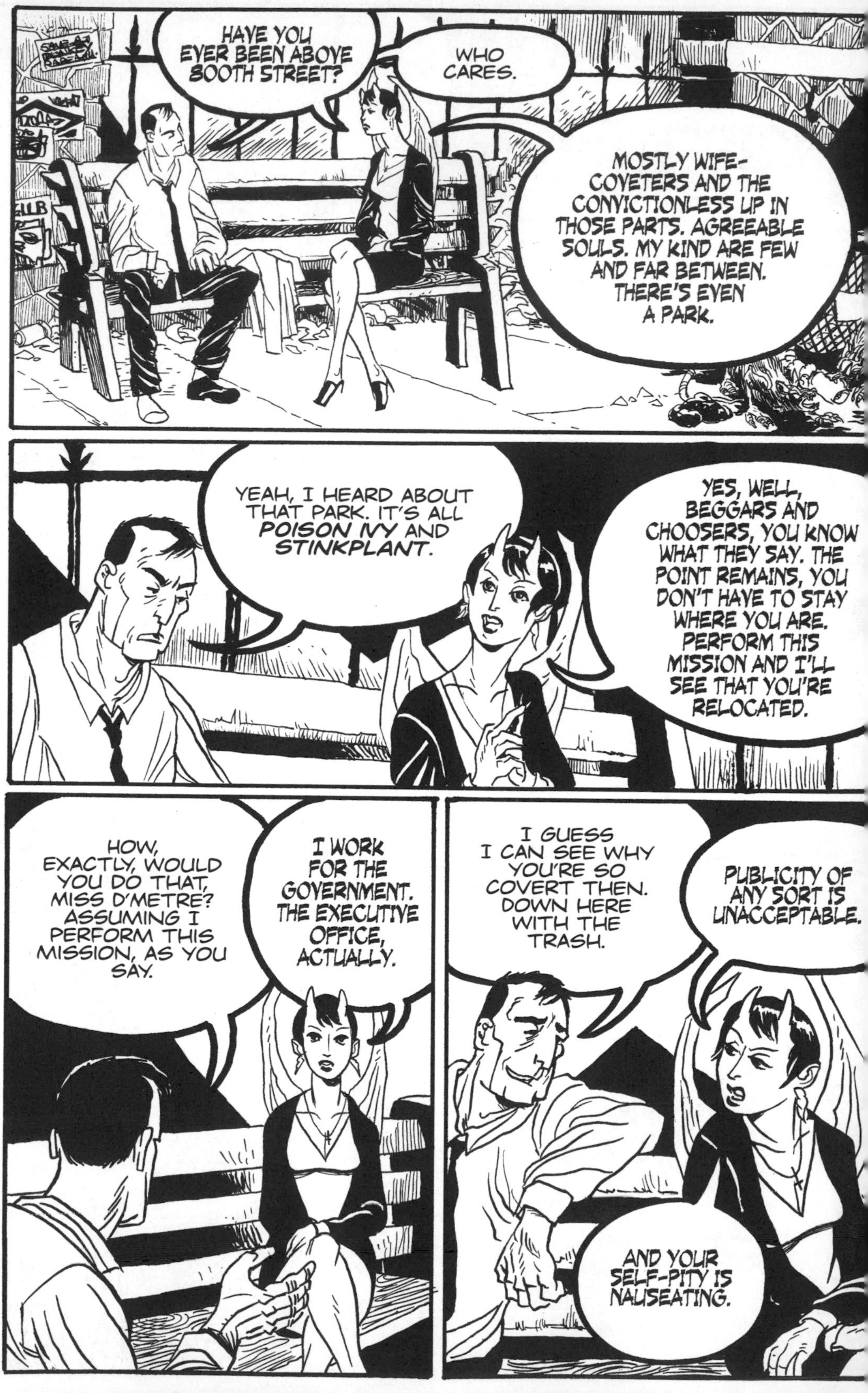
HAVE YOU EVER BEEN ABOVE 800TH STREET?
WHO CARES.
MOSTLY WIFE-COVETERS AND THE CONVICTIONLESS UP IN THOSE PARTS. AGREEABLE SOULS. MY KIND ARE FEW AND FAR BETWEEN. THERE'S EVEN A PARK.
YEAH, I HEARD ABOUT THAT PARK. IT'S ALL POISON IVY AND STINKPLANT.
YES, WELL, BEGGARS AND CHOOSERS, YOU KNOW WHAT THEY SAY. THE POINT REMAINS, YOU DON'T HAVE TO STAY WHERE YOU ARE. PERFORM THIS MISSION AND I'LL SEE THAT YOU'RE RELOCATED.
HOW, EXACTLY, WOULD YOU DO THAT, MISS D'METRE? ASSUMING I PERFORM THIS MISSION, AS YOU SAY.
I WORK FOR THE GOVERNMENT. THE EXECUTIVE OFFICE, ACTUALLY.
I GUESS I CAN SEE WHY YOU'RE SO COVERT THEN. DOWN HERE WITH THE TRASH.
PUBLICITY OF ANY SORT IS UNACCEPTABLE.
AND YOUR SELF-PITY IS NAUSEATING.

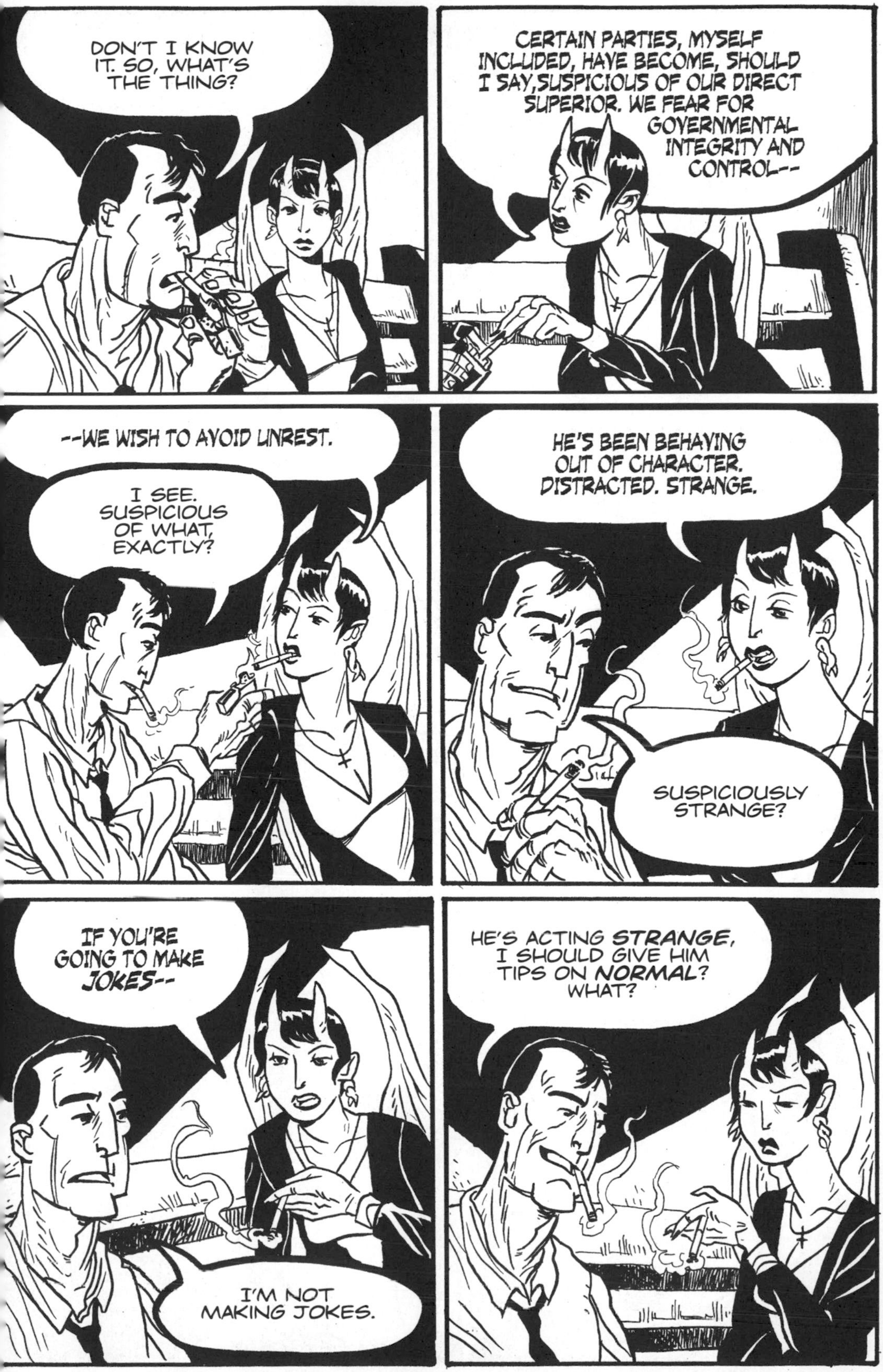
DON'T I KNOW IT. SO, WHAT'S THE THING?
CERTAIN PARTIES, MYSELF INCLUDED, HAVE BECOME, SHOULD I SAY, SUSPICIOUS OF OUR DIRECT SUPERIOR. WE FEAR FOR GOVERNMENTAL INTEGRITY AND CONTROL--
--WE WISH TO AVOID UNREST.
I SEE. SUSPICIOUS OF WHAT, EXACTLY?
HE'S BEEN BEHAVING OUT OF CHARACTER. DISTRACTED. STRANGE.
SUSPICIOUSLY STRANGE?
IF YOU'RE GOING TO MAKE JOKES--
I'M NOT MAKING JOKES.
HE'S ACTING STRANGE, I SHOULD GIVE HIM TIPS ON NORMAL? WHAT?

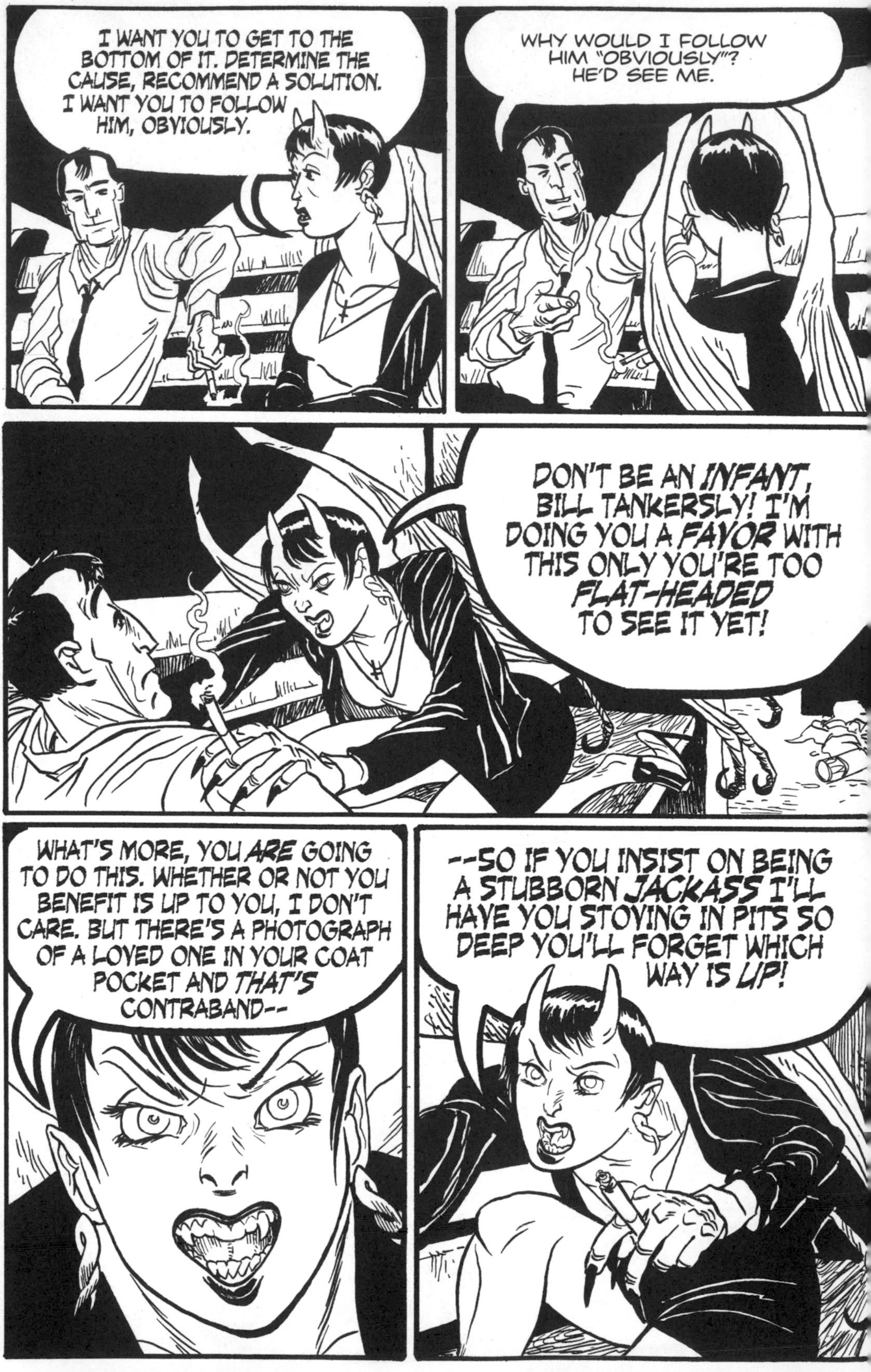
I WANT YOU TO GET TO THE BOTTOM OF IT. DETERMINE THE CAUSE, RECOMMEND A SOLUTION. I WANT YOU TO FOLLOW HIM, OBVIOUSLY.
WHY WOULD I FOLLOW HIM "OBVIOUSLY"? HE'D SEE ME.
DON'T BE AN INFANT, BILL TANKERSLY! I'M DOING YOU A FAVOR WITH THIS ONLY YOU'RE TOO FLAT-HEADED TO SEE IT YET!
WHAT'S MORE, YOU ARE GOING TO DO THIS. WHETHER OR NOT YOU BENEFIT IS UP TO YOU, I DON'T CARE. BUT THERE'S A PHOTOGRAPH OF A LOVED ONE IN YOUR COAT POCKET AND THAT'S CONTRABAND--
--SO IF YOU INSIST ON BEING A STUBBORN JACKASS I'LL HAVE YOU STOVING IN PITS SO DEEP YOU'LL FORGET WHICH WAY IS UP!

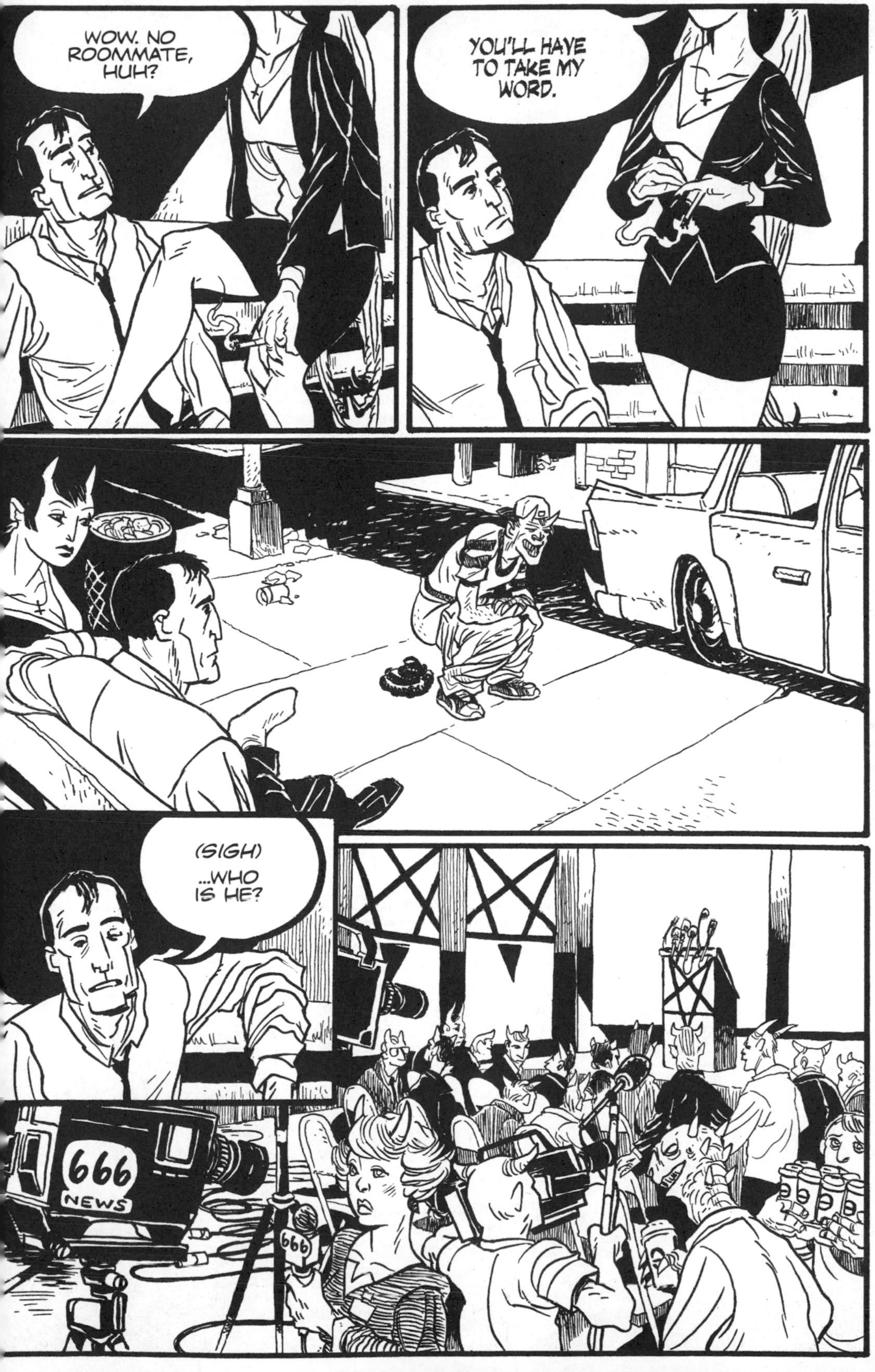
WOW. NO ROOMMATE, HUH?
YOU'LL HAVE TO TAKE MY WORD.
(SIGH) ...WHO IS HE?
666 NEWS
666

THANK YOU, SIR. *BOB FLINT* FROM THE *DAILY TOIL*. IF THE TWO OFFICERS WHO WERE SO BRUTALLY ATTACKED LAST WEEK WERE VICTIMS OF A SO-CALLED ANARCHIST CULT, THEN WHAT DOES THAT SAY ABOUT THE STATE OF *AUTHORITY* IN HELLCITY, THAT SUCH AN ORGANIZATION COULD EXIST AND OPERATE, AND ALSO WHAT DO YOU INTEND *TO DO* ABOUT IT?

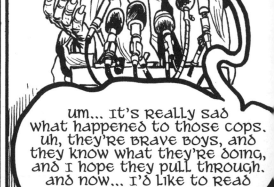

UM... IT'S REALLY SAD WHAT HAPPENED TO THOSE COPS. UH, THEY'RE BRAVE BOYS, AND THEY KNOW WHAT THEY'RE DOING, AND I HOPE THEY PULL THROUGH. AND NOW... I'D LIKE TO READ YOU A POEM I WROTE.

IT'S CALLED "WHAT I LOOK FOR". **(AHEM)** I SMASH THE TELEVISION BECAUSE YOU'RE NOT ON TONIGHT. I BURN THE MOVIE THEATER BECAUSE YOUR DOUBLE FEATURE HASN'T OPENED. I READ THE PAPER AND CHOKE THE LITTLE PAPERBOY, BECAUSE YOUR STORY WAS SECOND PAGE. **YOU** ARE THE ONLY THING I LOOK FOR.

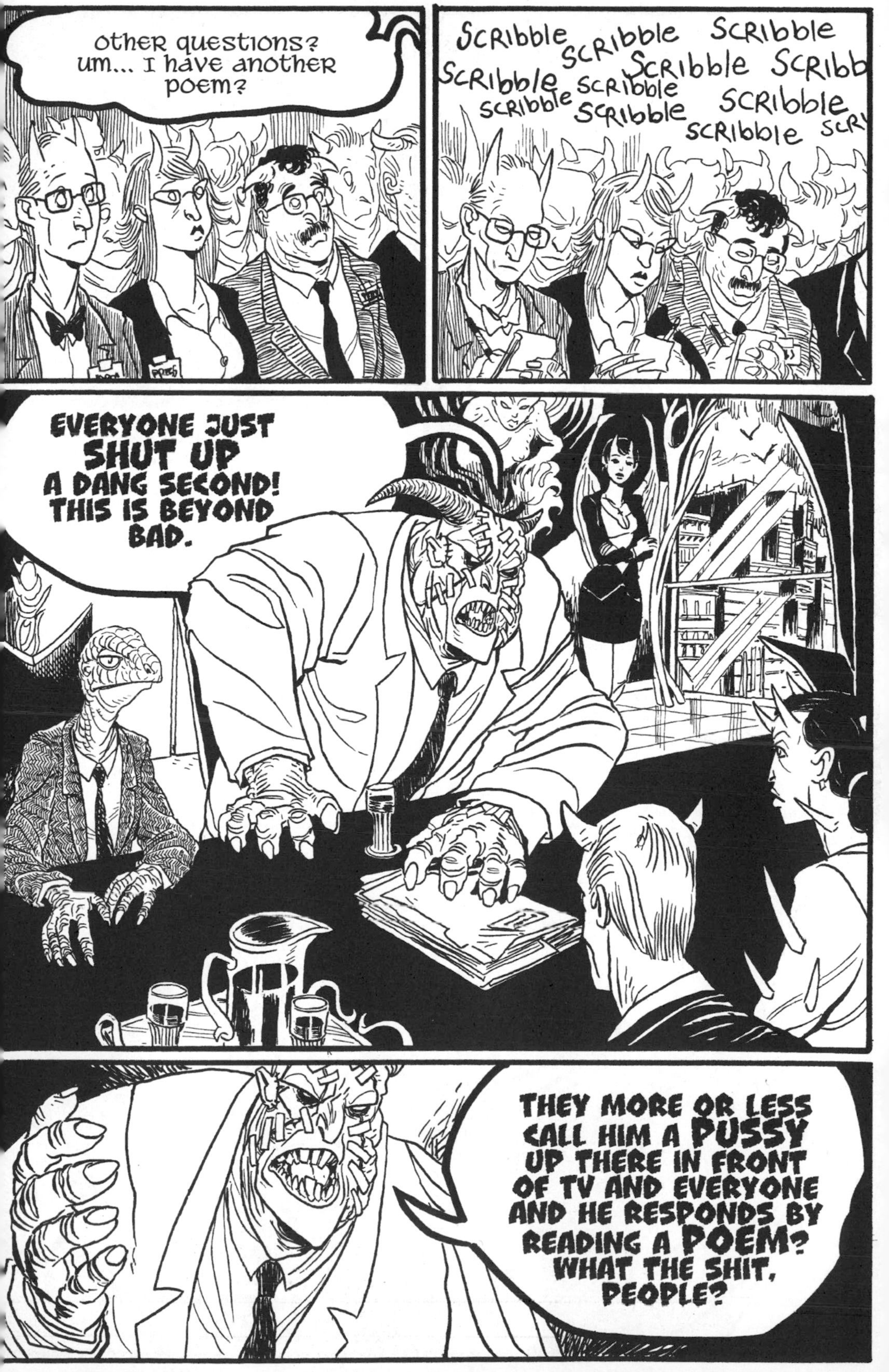
other questions? um... I have another poem?
SCRIBBLE SCRIBBLE SCRIBBLE SCRIBBLE SCRIBBLE SCRIBBLE SCRIBBLE SCRIBBLE SCRIBBLE SCRIBBLE SCRIBBLE
EVERYONE JUST SHUT UP A DANG SECOND! THIS IS BEYOND BAD.
THEY MORE OR LESS CALL HIM A PUSSY UP THERE IN FRONT OF TV AND EVERYONE AND HE RESPONDS BY READING A POEM? WHAT THE SHIT, PEOPLE?

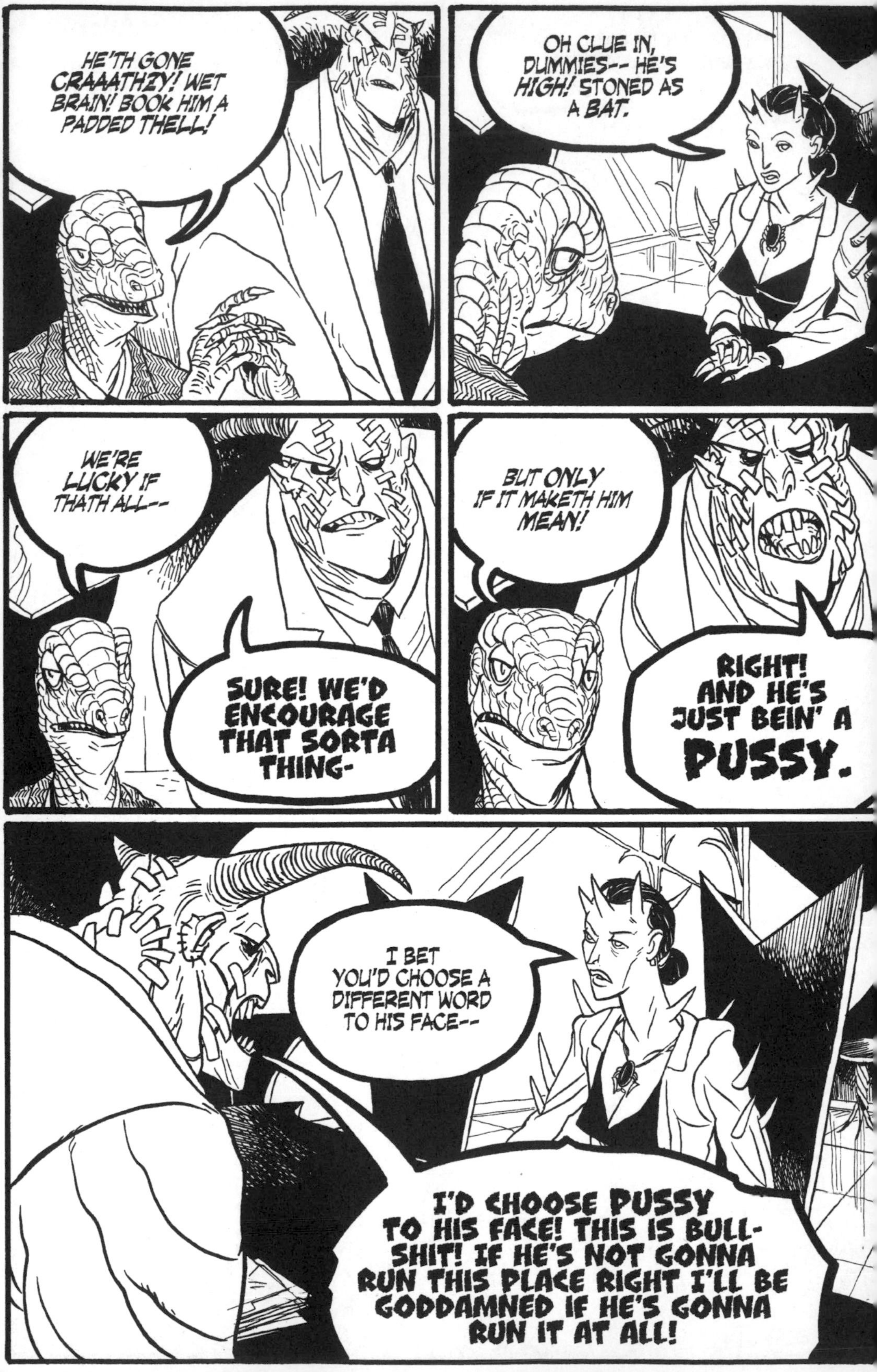
HE'TH GONE CRAAATHZY! WET BRAIN! BOOK HIM A PADDED THELL!
OH CLUE IN, DUMMIES-- HE'S HIGH! STONED AS A BAT.
WE'RE LUCKY IF THATH ALL--
SURE! WE'D ENCOURAGE THAT SORTA THING-
BUT ONLY IF IT MAKETH HIM MEAN!
RIGHT! AND HE'S JUST BEIN' A PUSSY.
I BET YOU'D CHOOSE A DIFFERENT WORD TO HIS FACE--
I'D CHOOSE PUSSY TO HIS FACE! THIS IS BULL-SHIT! IF HE'S NOT GONNA RUN THIS PLACE RIGHT I'LL BE GODDAMNED IF HE'S GONNA RUN IT AT ALL!

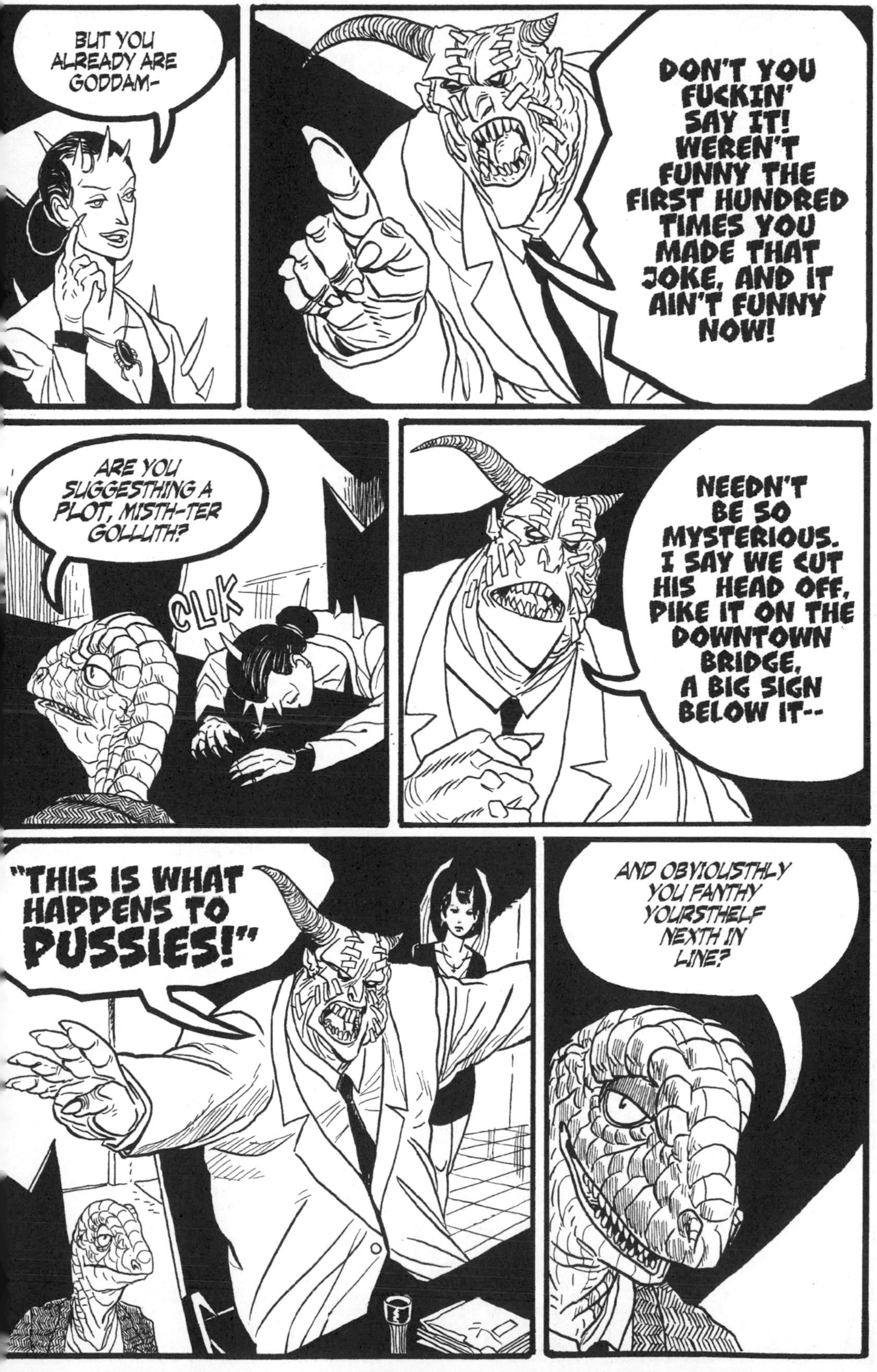
BUT YOU ALREADY ARE GODDAM-
DON'T YOU FUCKIN' SAY IT! WEREN'T FUNNY THE FIRST HUNDRED TIMES YOU MADE THAT JOKE, AND IT AIN'T FUNNY NOW!
ARE YOU SUGGESTHING A PLOT, MISTH-TER GOLLUTH?
CLIK
NEEDN'T BE SO MYSTERIOUS. I SAY WE CUT HIS HEAD OFF, PIKE IT ON THE DOWNTOWN BRIDGE, A BIG SIGN BELOW IT--
"THIS IS WHAT HAPPENS TO PUSSIES!"
AND OBVIOUSTHLY YOU FANTHY YOURSTHELF NEXTH IN LINE?

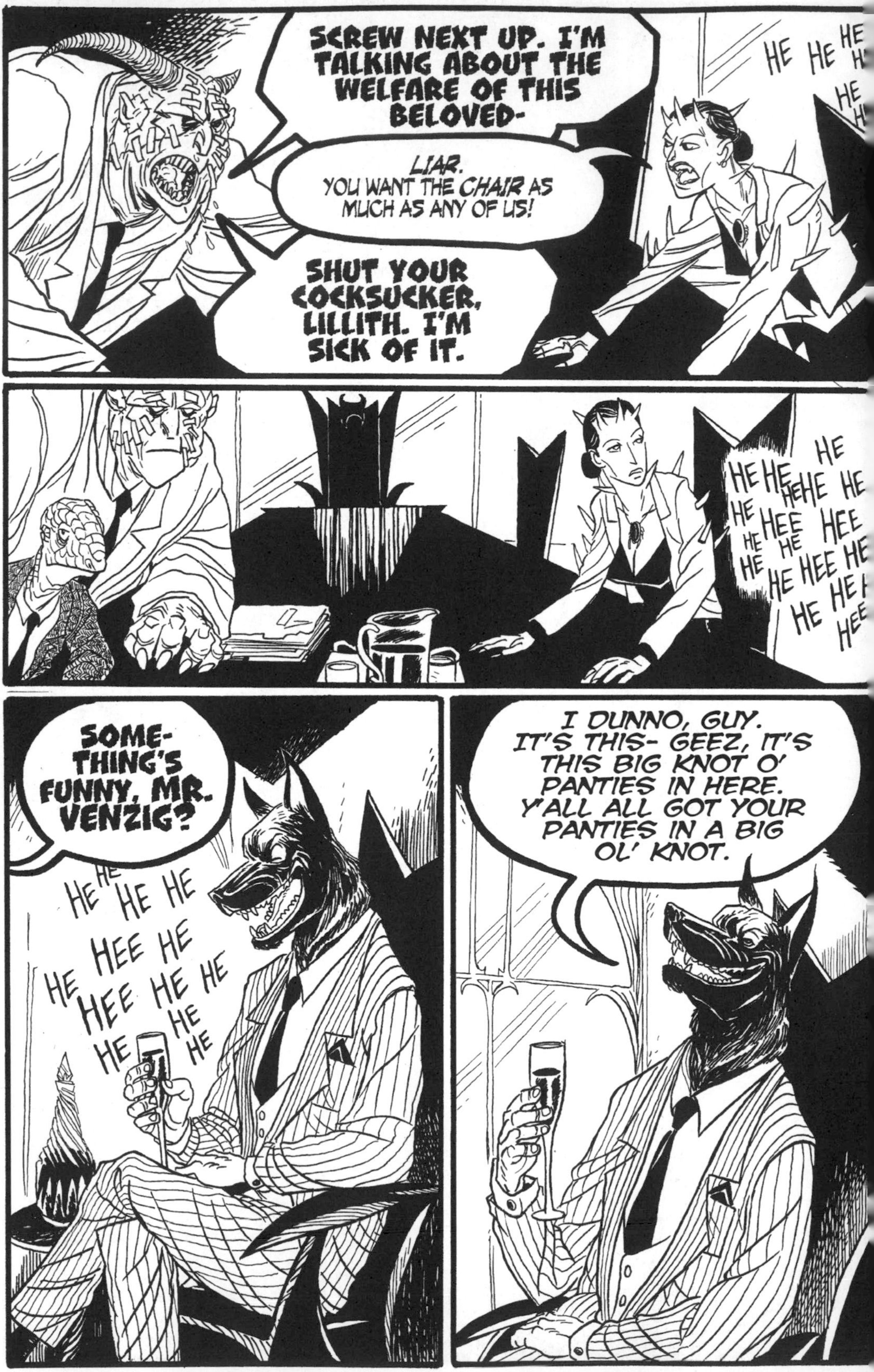
SCREW NEXT UP. I'M TALKING ABOUT THE WELFARE OF THIS BELOVED-
HE HE HE
LIAR. YOU WANT THE CHAIR AS MUCH AS ANY OF US!
SHUT YOUR COCKSUCKER, LILLITH. I'M SICK OF IT.
HE HE HE HE HE HE HE HE HEE HEE HE HE HE HEE HE HE HE HE
SOME-THING'S FUNNY, MR. VENZIG?
HE HE HE HE HE HEE HE HEE HE HE HE HE HE
I DUNNO, GUY. IT'S THIS- GEEZ, IT'S THIS BIG KNOT O' PANTIES IN HERE. Y'ALL ALL GOT YOUR PANTIES IN A BIG OL' KNOT.

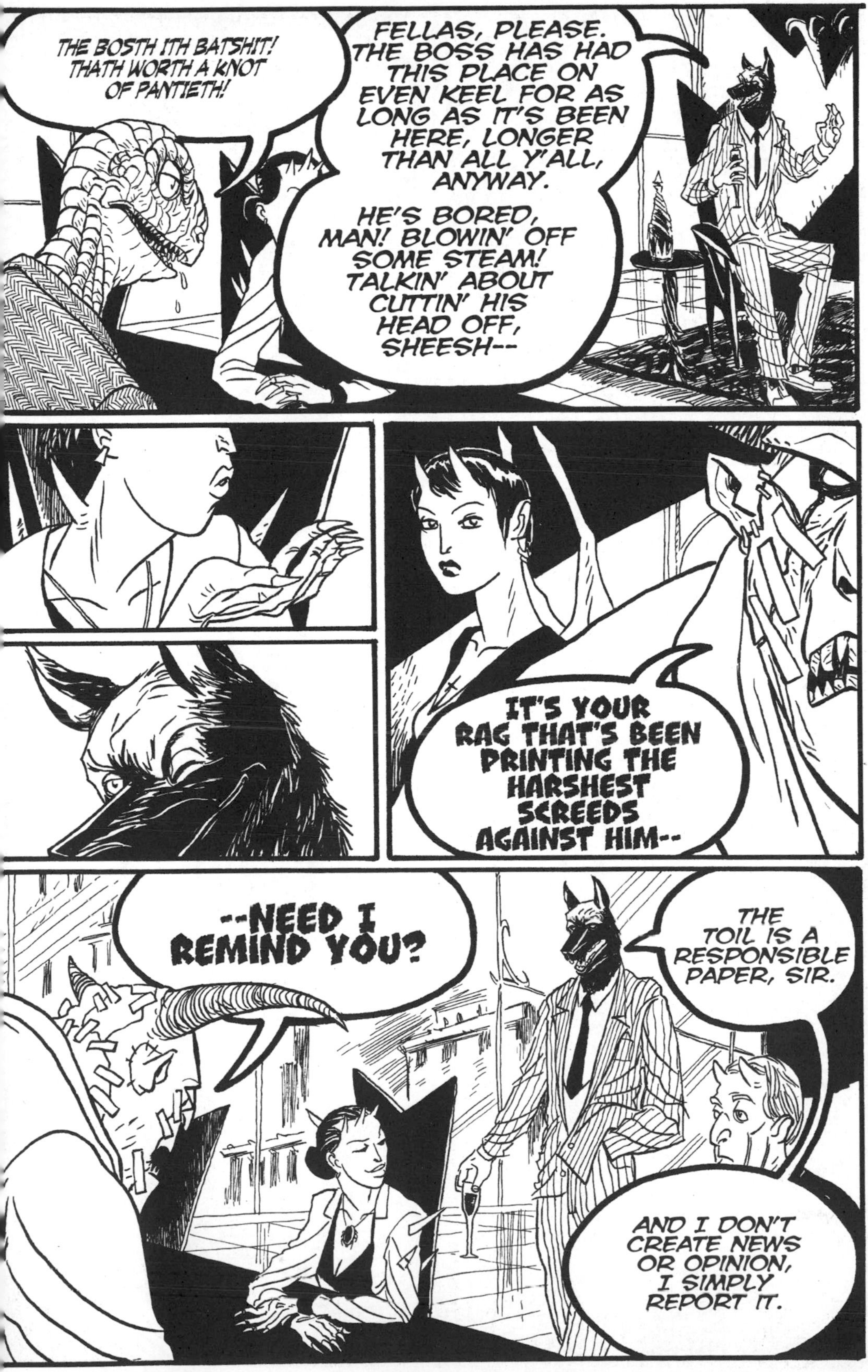
THE BOSTH ITH BATSHIT! THATH WORTH A KNOT OF PANTIETH!
FELLAS, PLEASE. THE BOSS HAS HAD THIS PLACE ON EVEN KEEL FOR AS LONG AS IT'S BEEN HERE, LONGER THAN ALL Y'ALL, ANYWAY.
HE'S BORED, MAN! BLOWIN' OFF SOME STEAM! TALKIN' ABOUT CUTTIN' HIS HEAD OFF, SHEESH--
IT'S YOUR RAG THAT'S BEEN PRINTING THE HARSHEST SCREEDS AGAINST HIM--
--NEED I REMIND YOU?
THE TOIL IS A RESPONSIBLE PAPER, SIR.
AND I DON'T CREATE NEWS OR OPINION, I SIMPLY REPORT IT.

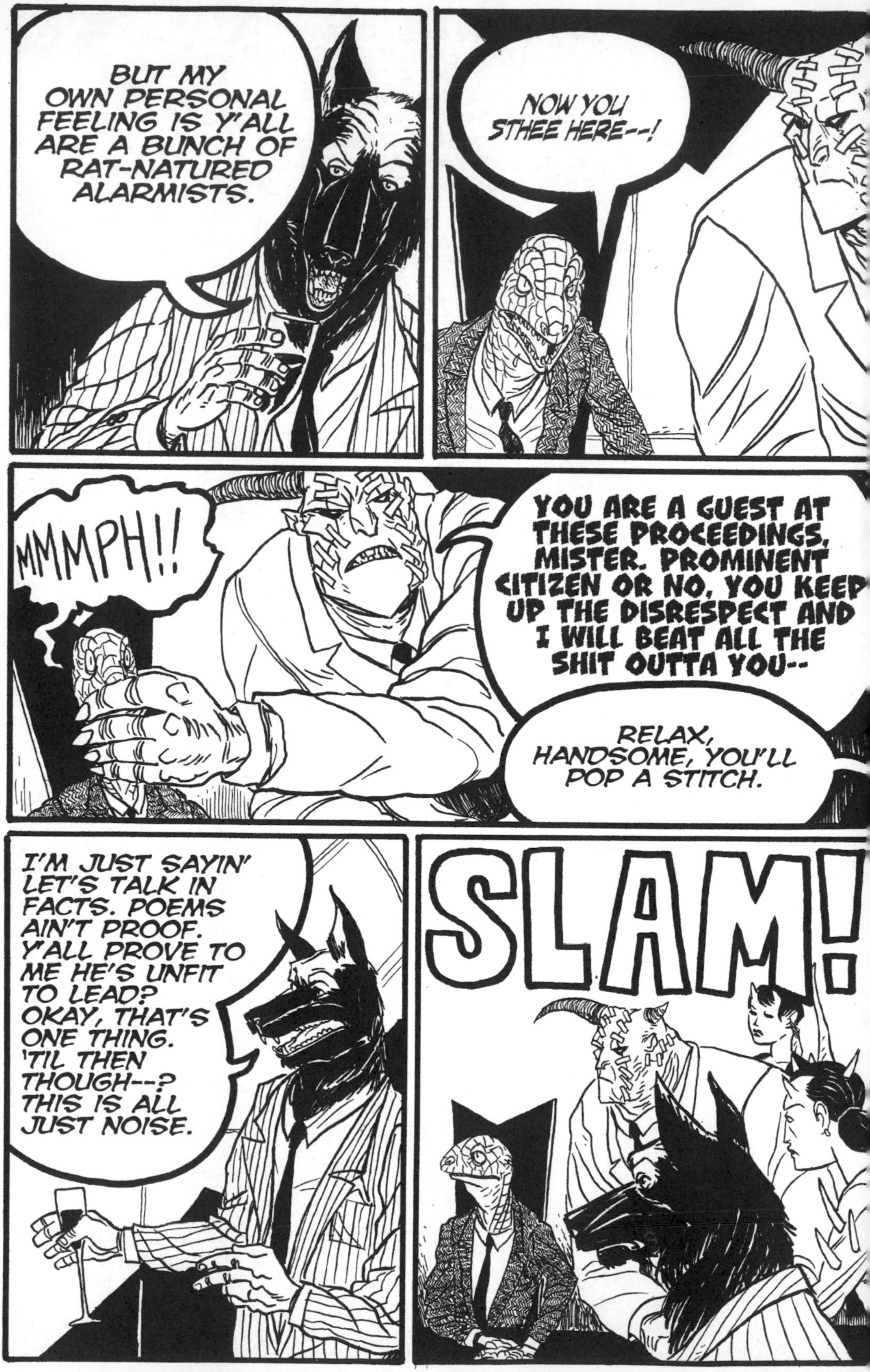
BUT MY OWN PERSONAL FEELING IS Y'ALL ARE A BUNCH OF RAT-NATURED ALARMISTS.
NOW YOU STHEE HERE--!
MMMPH!!
YOU ARE A GUEST AT THESE PROCEEDINGS, MISTER. PROMINENT CITIZEN OR NO, YOU KEEP UP THE DISRESPECT AND I WILL BEAT ALL THE SHIT OUTTA YOU--
RELAX, HANDSOME, YOU'LL POP A STITCH.
I'M JUST SAYIN' LET'S TALK IN FACTS. POEMS AIN'T PROOF. Y'ALL PROVE TO ME HE'S UNFIT TO LEAD? OKAY, THAT'S ONE THING. 'TIL THEN THOUGH--? THIS IS ALL JUST NOISE.
SLAM!

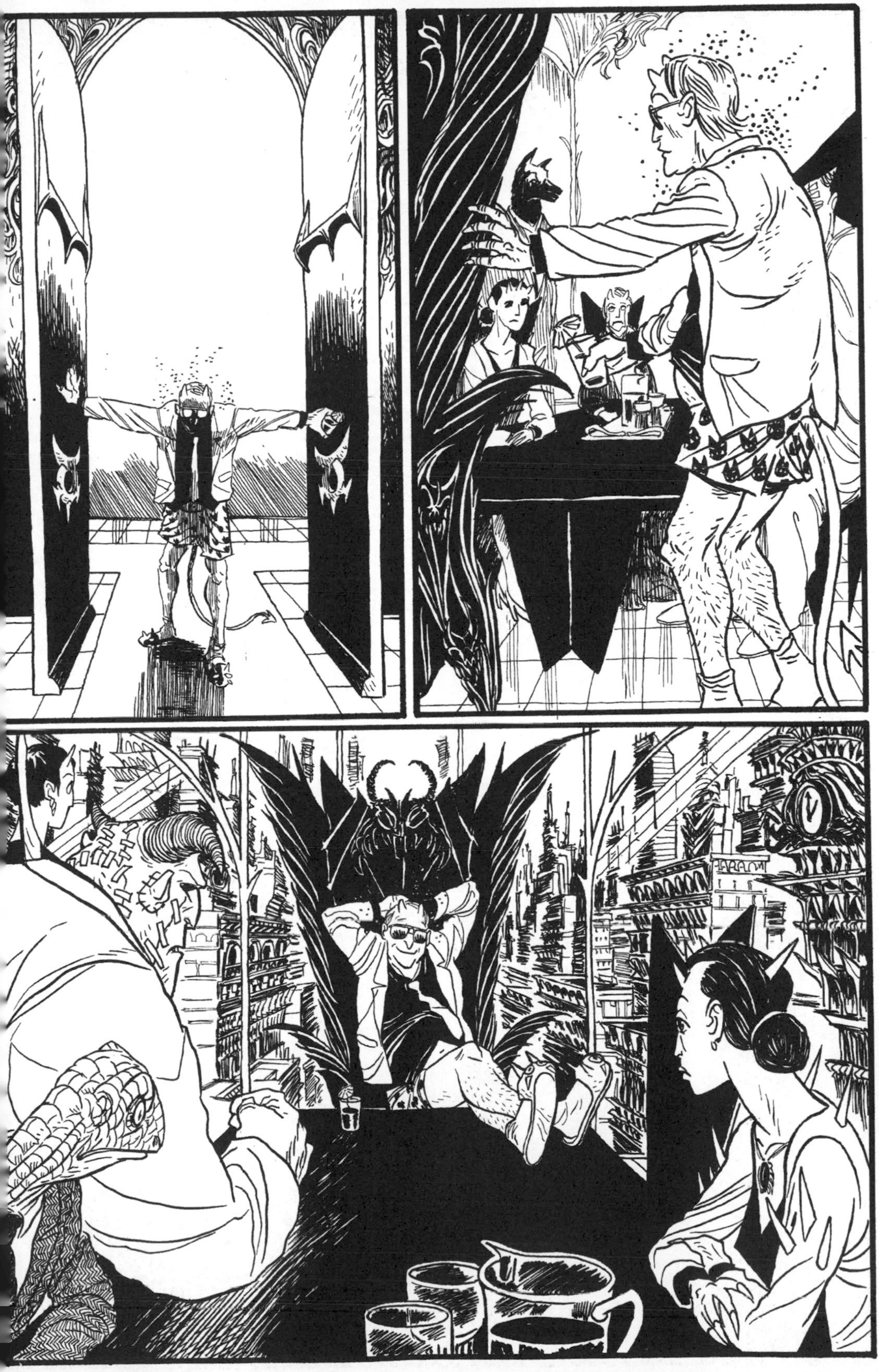

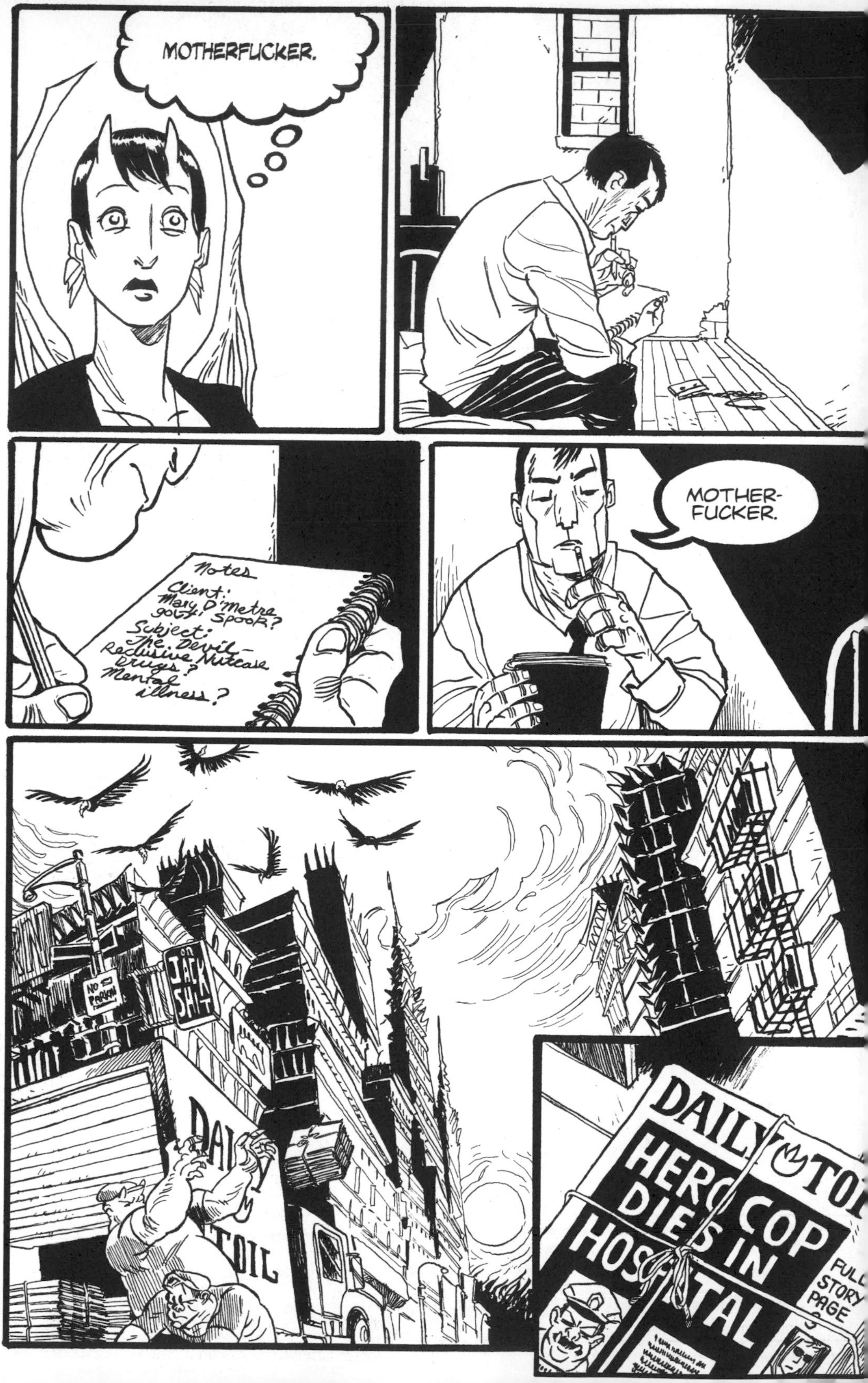
MOTHERFUCKER.
Notes
Client: Mary D'metra govt. spook?
Subject: The Devil- Reclusive Nutcase drugs? Mental illness?
MOTHER-FUCKER.
NO PARKING
JACK SHIT
DAILY TOIL
DAILY TOIL
HERO COP DIES IN HOSPITAL
FULL STORY PAGE

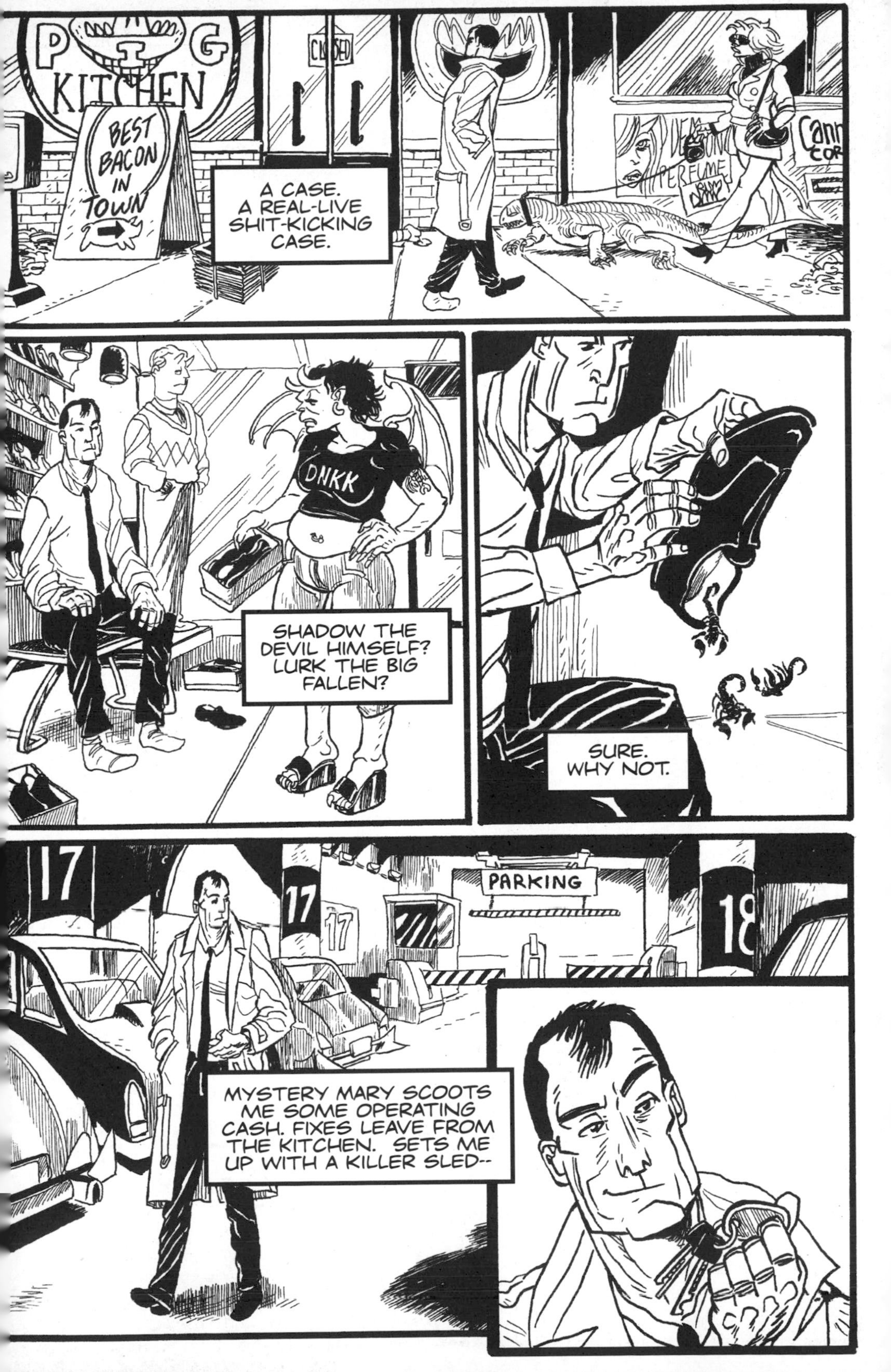
KITCHEN
BEST BACON IN TOWN
CLOSED
A CASE. A REAL-LIVE SHIT-KICKING CASE.
PERFUME
DNKK
SHADOW THE DEVIL HIMSELF? LURK THE BIG FALLEN?
SURE. WHY NOT.
17
17
17
PARKING
18
MYSTERY MARY SCOOTS ME SOME OPERATING CASH. FIXES LEAVE FROM THE KITCHEN. SETS ME UP WITH A KILLER SLED--

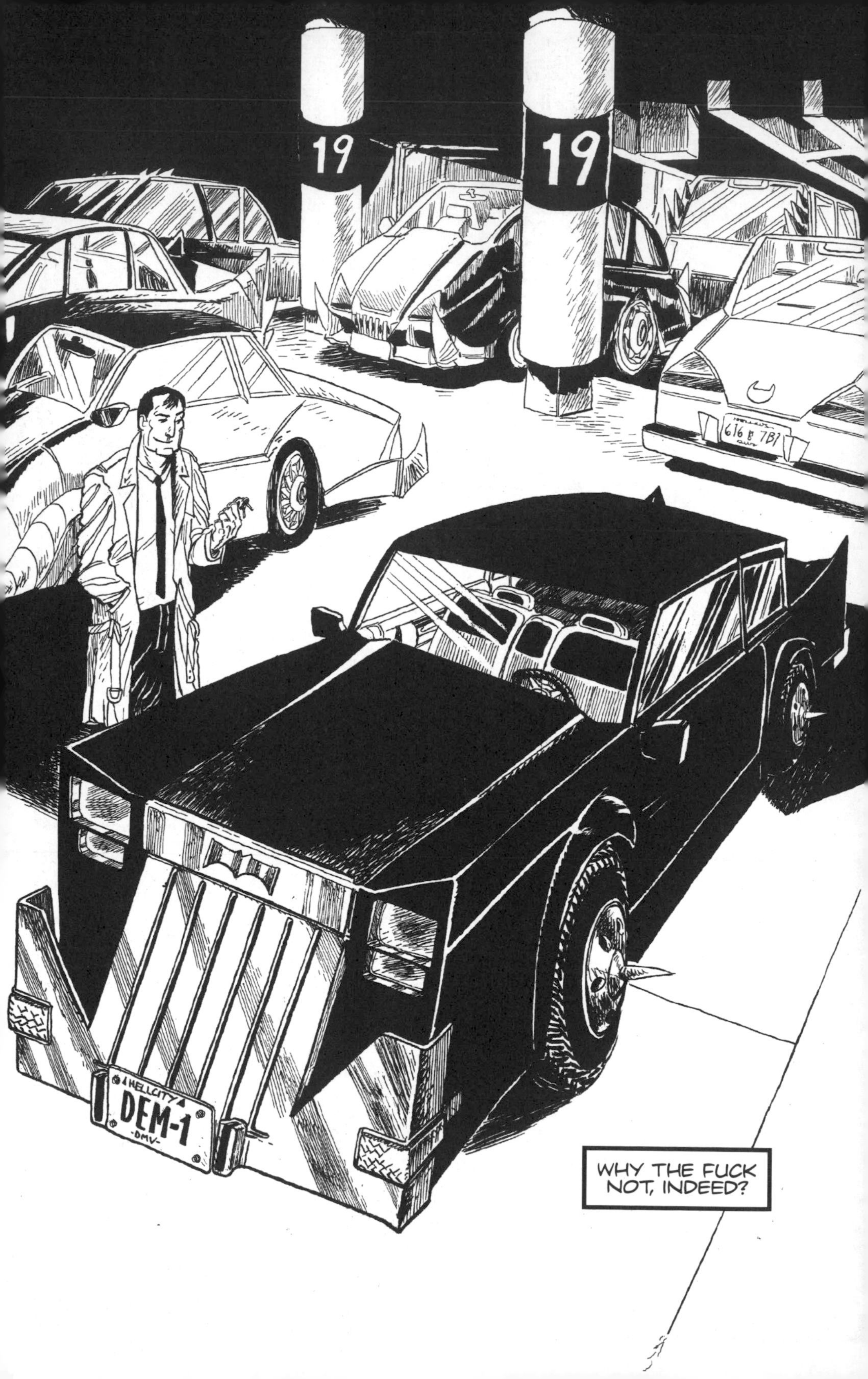
19
19
HELLCITY
DEM-1
DMV
WHY THE FUCK NOT, INDEED?

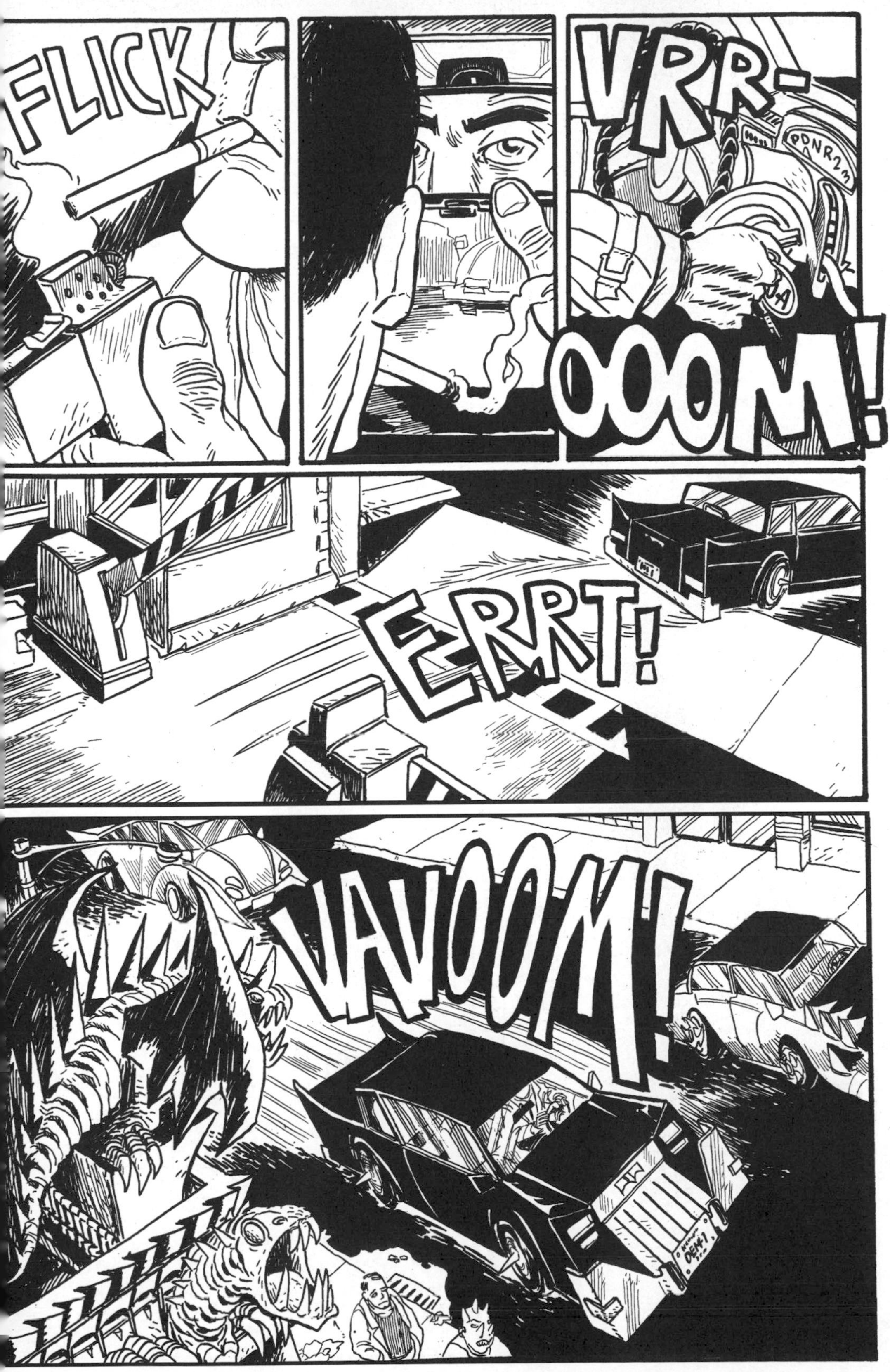
FLICK
VRR-
OOOM!
ERRT!
VAVOOM!

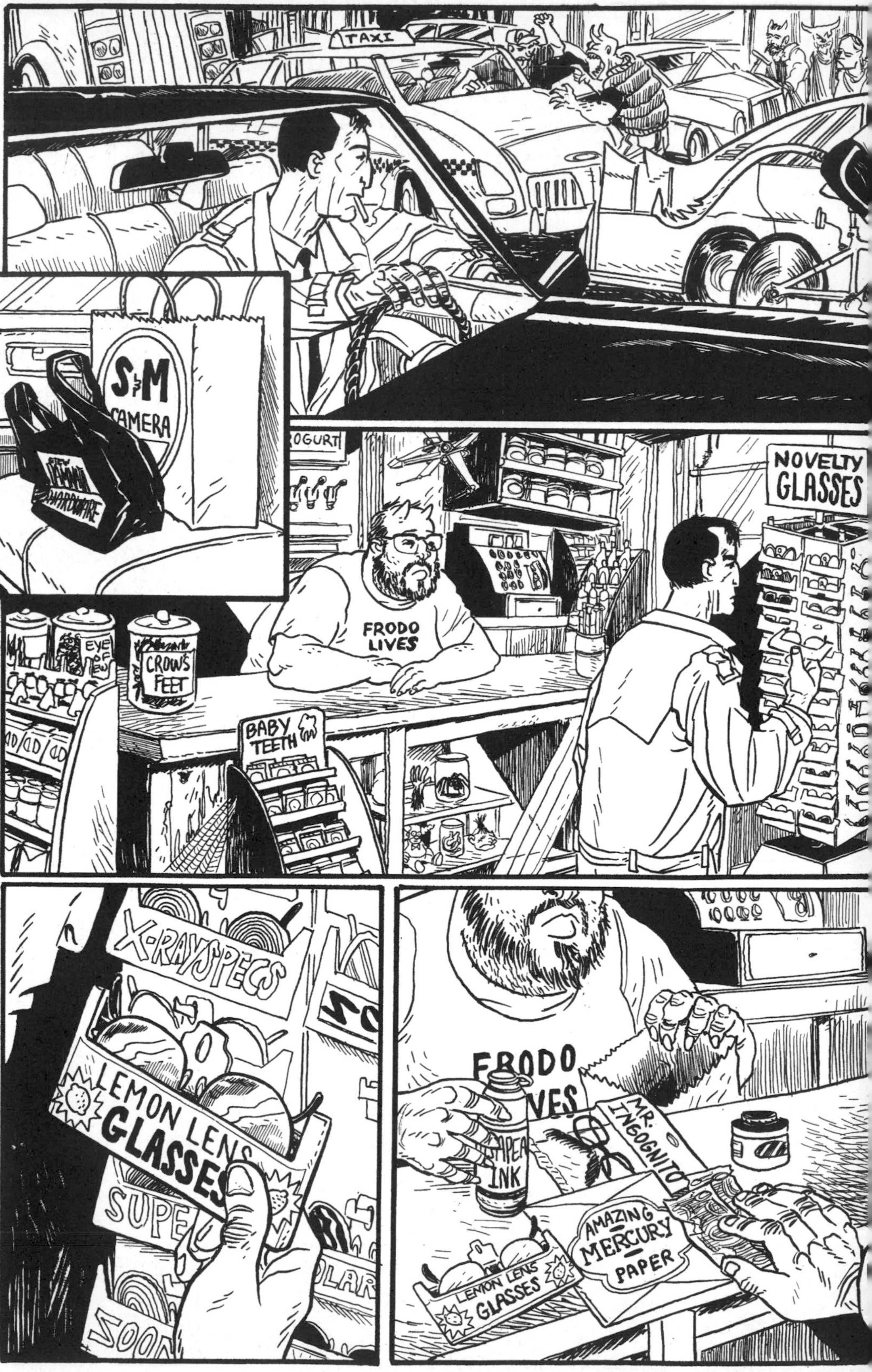
TAXI
S&M
CAMERA
HARDWARE
ROGURT
NOVELTY
GLASSES
FRODO
LIVES
CROW'S
FEET
BABY
TEETH
X-RAYSPECS
LEMON LENS
GLASSES
SUPE
FRODO
VES
MR.
INCOGNITO
INK
AMAZING
MERCURY
PAPER
LEMON LENS
GLASSES

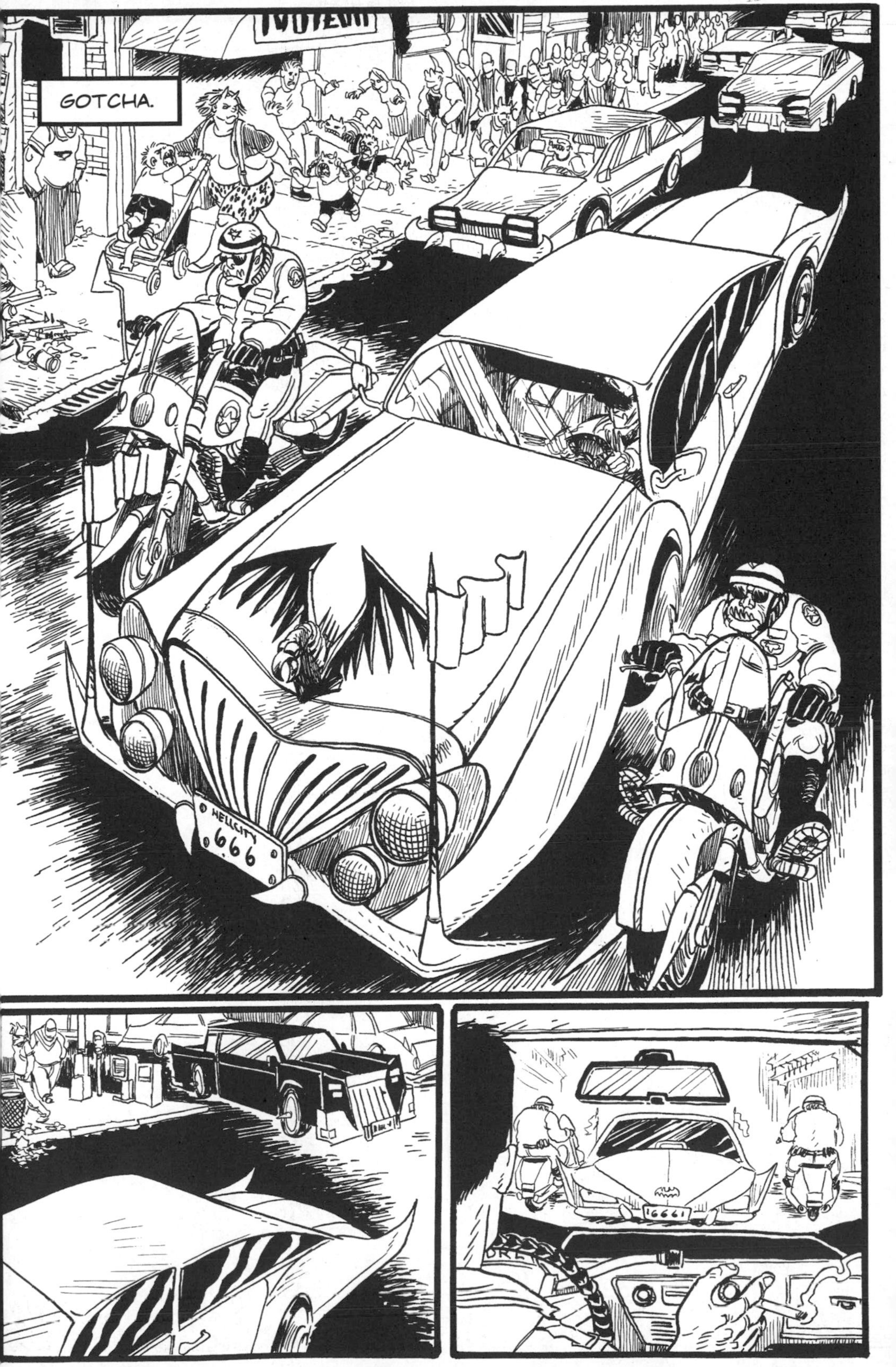
GOTCHA.
HELLCITY
666

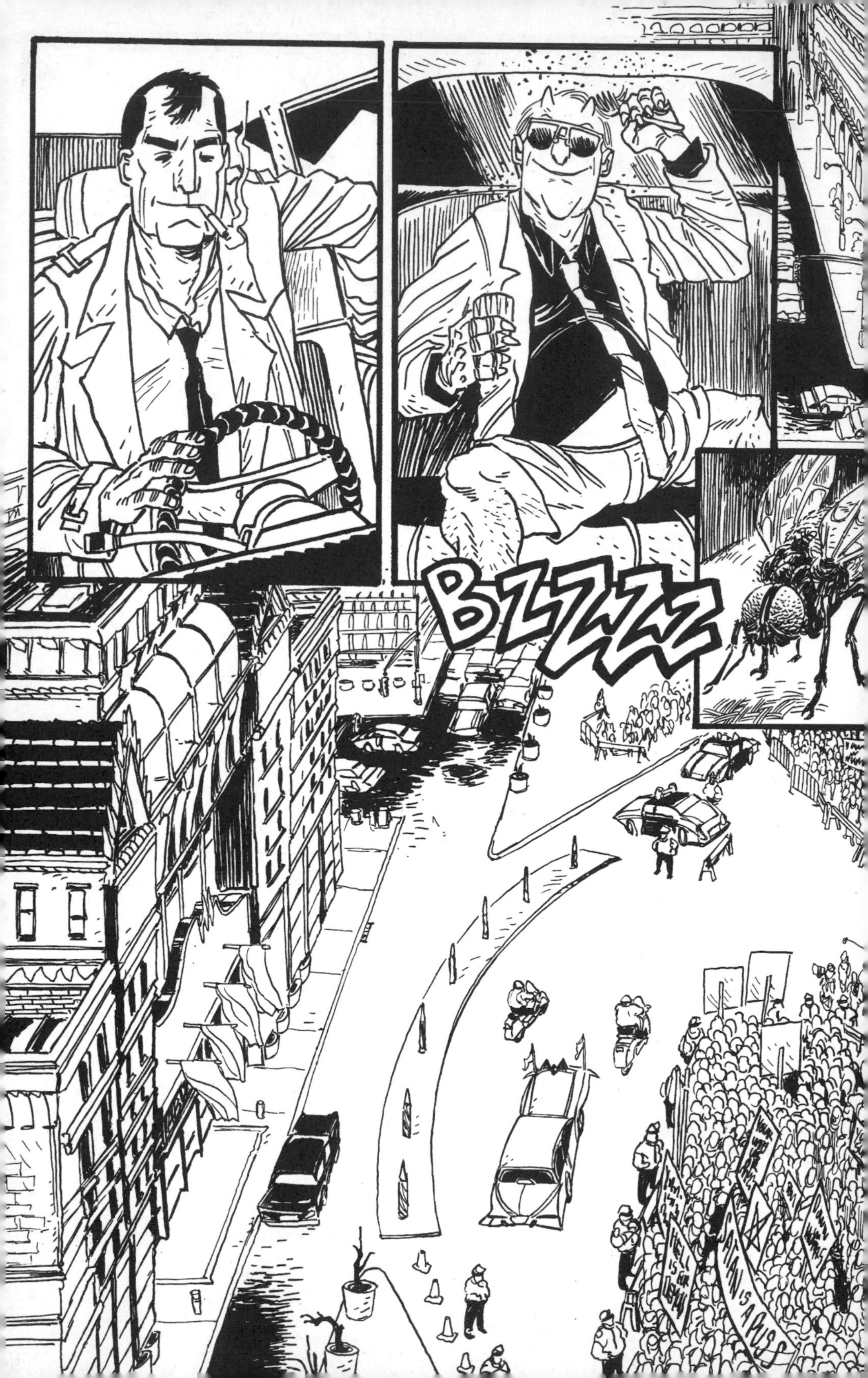
BZZZZ

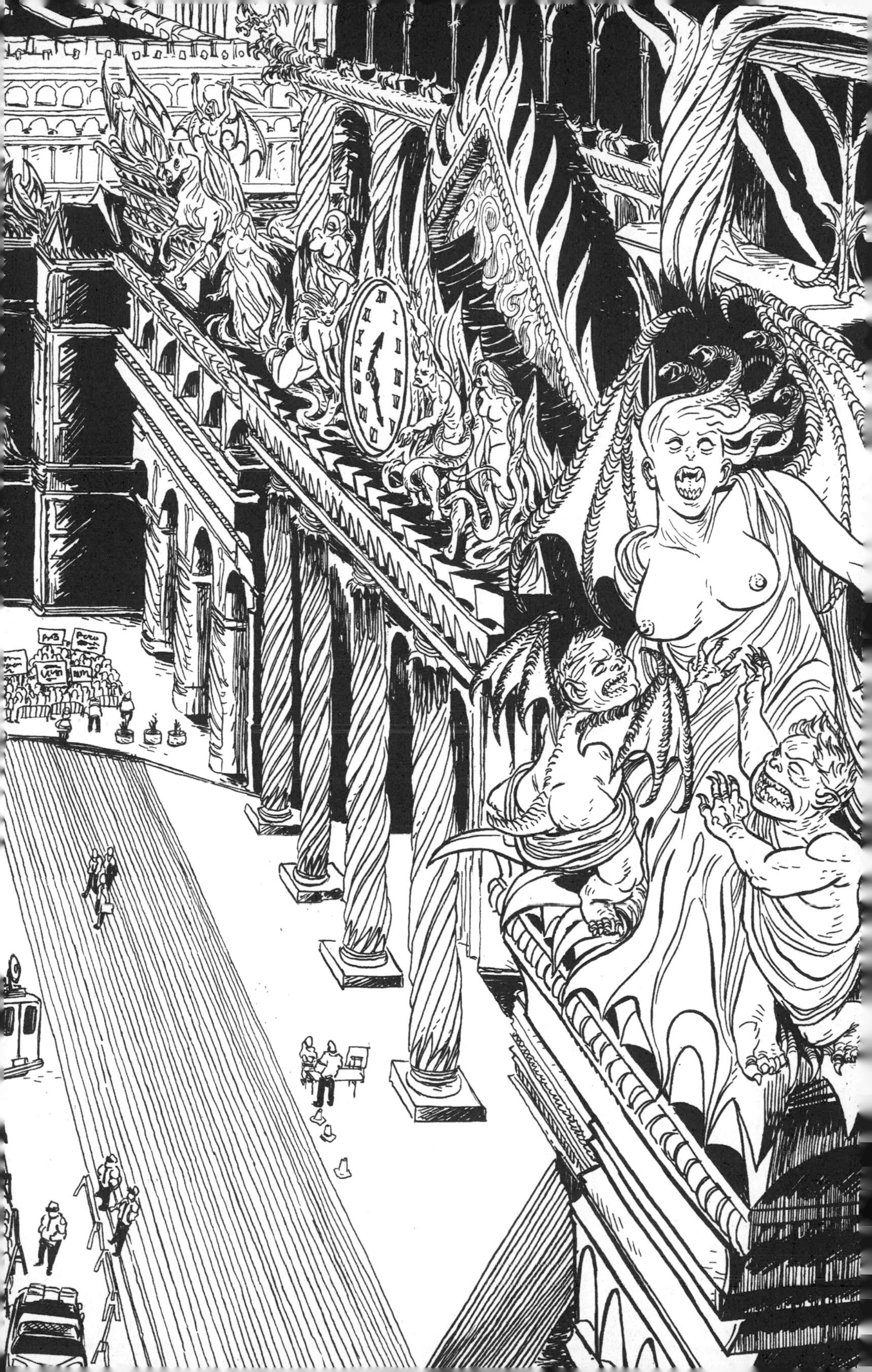

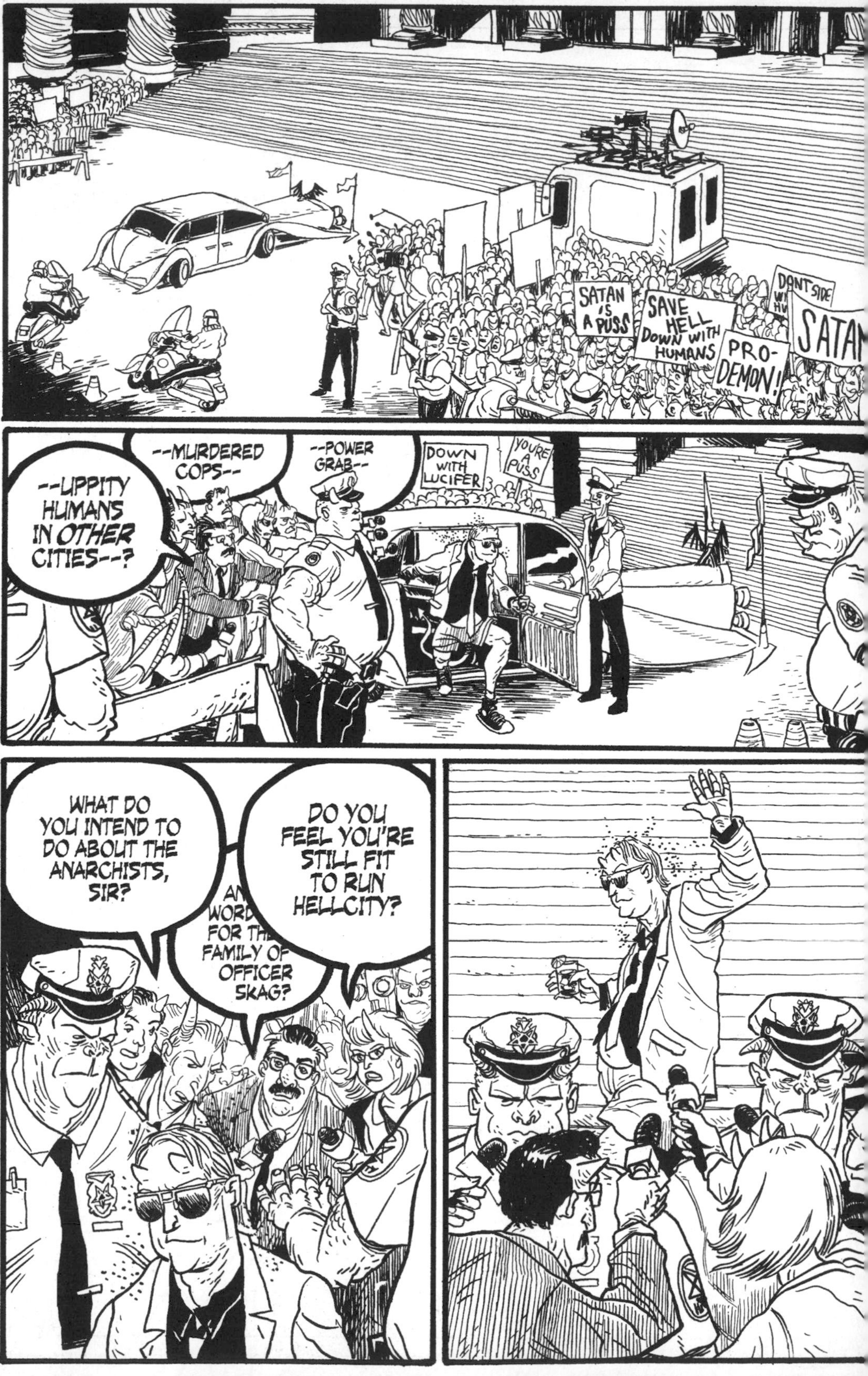
SATAN IS A PUSS
SAVE HELL DOWN WITH HUMANS
PRO-DEMON!
SATAN
DOWN WITH LUCIFER
YOU'RE A PUSS
--UPPITY HUMANS IN *OTHER* CITIES--?
--MURDERED COPS--
--POWER GRAB--
WHAT DO YOU INTEND TO DO ABOUT THE ANARCHISTS, SIR?
DO YOU FEEL YOU'RE STILL FIT TO RUN HELLCITY?
FOR THE FAMILY OF OFFICER SKAG?

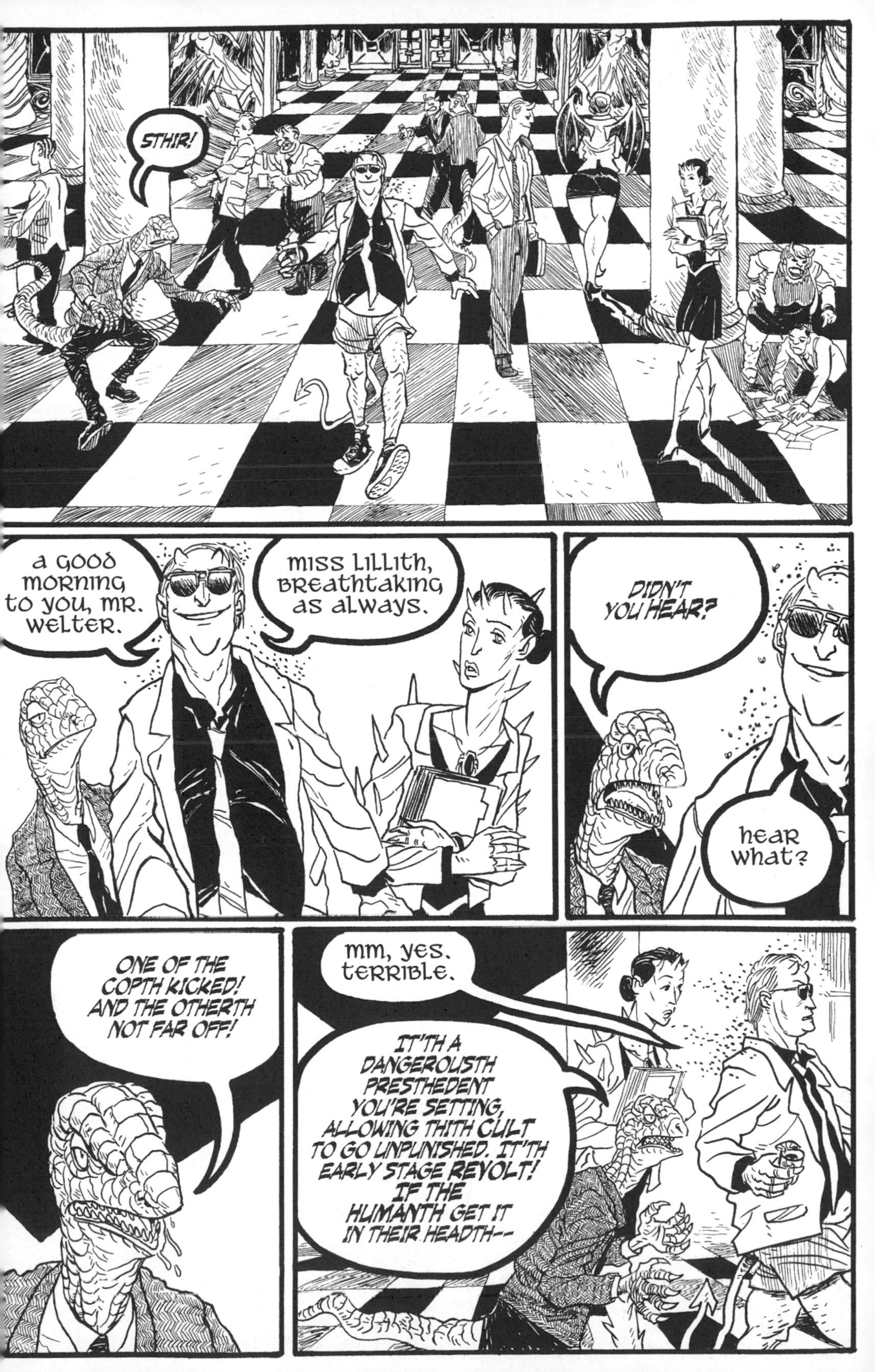
STHIR!
A GOOD MORNING TO YOU, MR. WELTER.
MISS LILLITH, BREATHTAKING AS ALWAYS.
DIDN'T YOU HEAR?
HEAR WHAT?
ONE OF THE COPTH KICKED! AND THE OTHERTH NOT FAR OFF!
MM, YES. TERRIBLE.
IT'TH A DANGEROUSTH PRESTHEDENT YOU'RE SETTING, ALLOWING THITH CULT TO GO UNPUNISHED. IT'TH EARLY STAGE REVOLT! IF THE HUMANTH GET IT IN THEIR HEADTH--

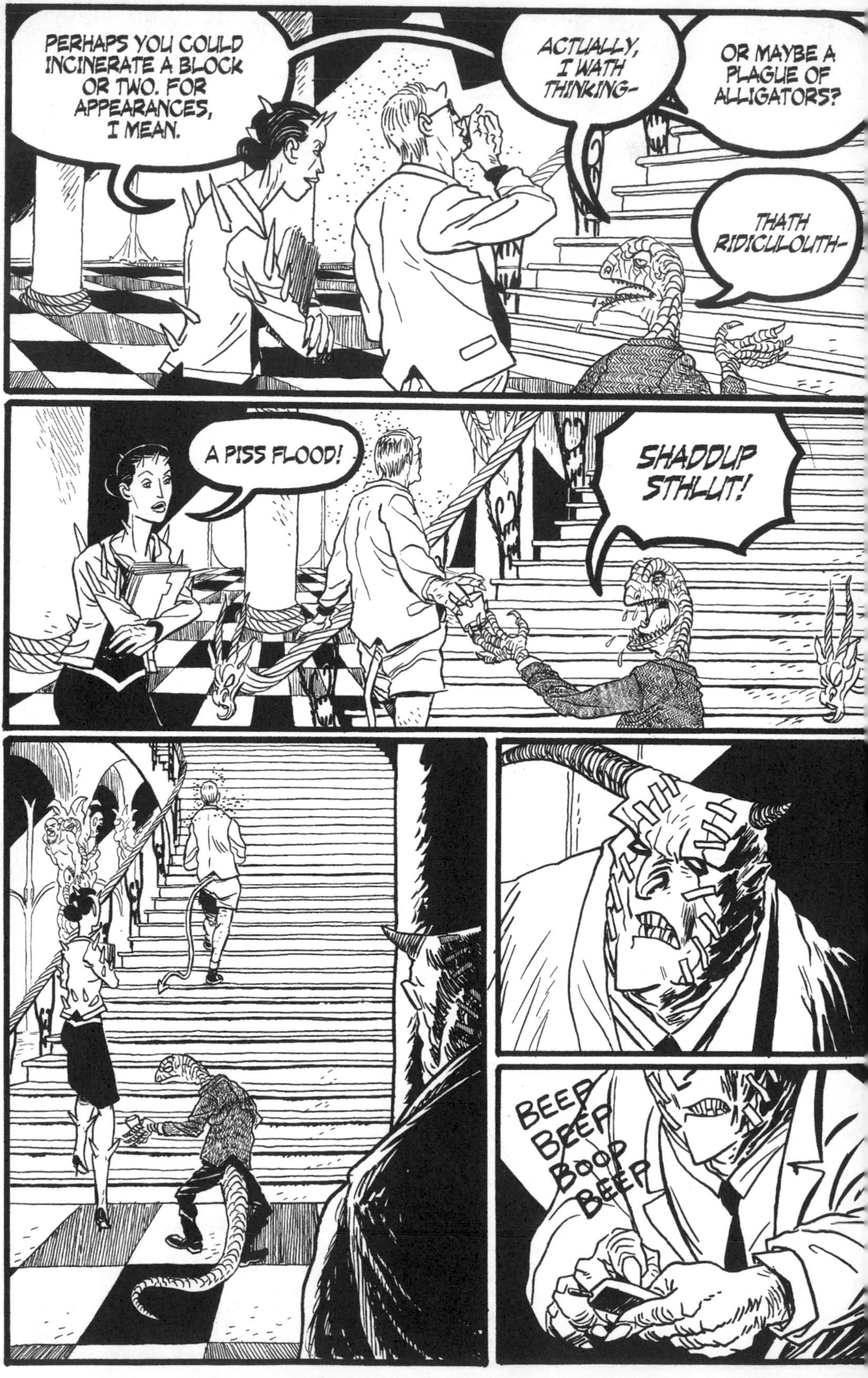
PERHAPS YOU COULD INCINERATE A BLOCK OR TWO. FOR APPEARANCES, I MEAN.
ACTUALLY, I WATH THINKING-
OR MAYBE A PLAGUE OF ALLIGATORS?
THATH RIDICULOUTH-
A PISS FLOOD!
SHADDUP STHLUT!
BEEP BEEP BOOP BEEP

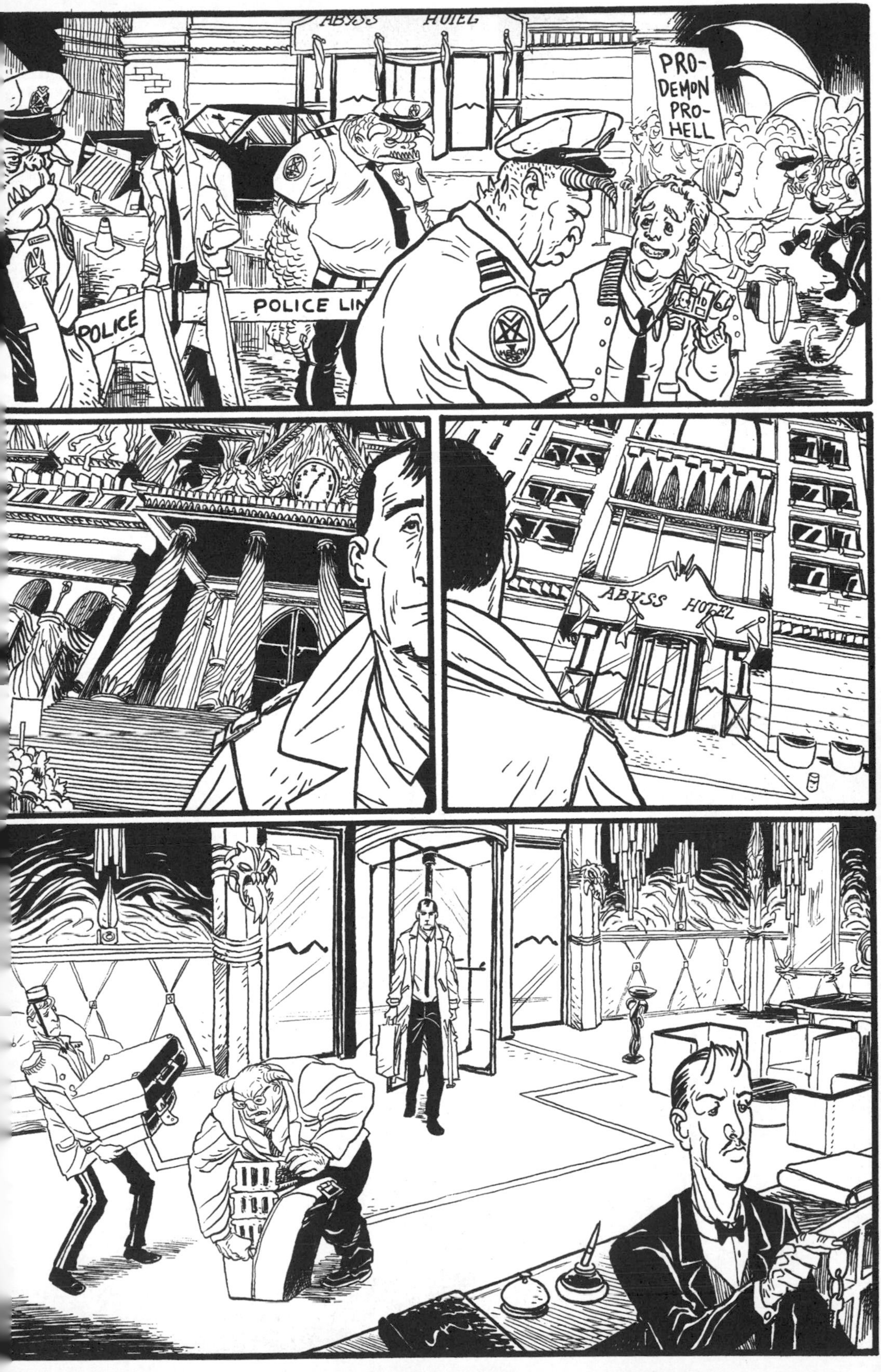
ABYSS HOTEL
PRO-DEMON PRO-HELL
POLICE LIN
POLICE
ABYSS HOTEL

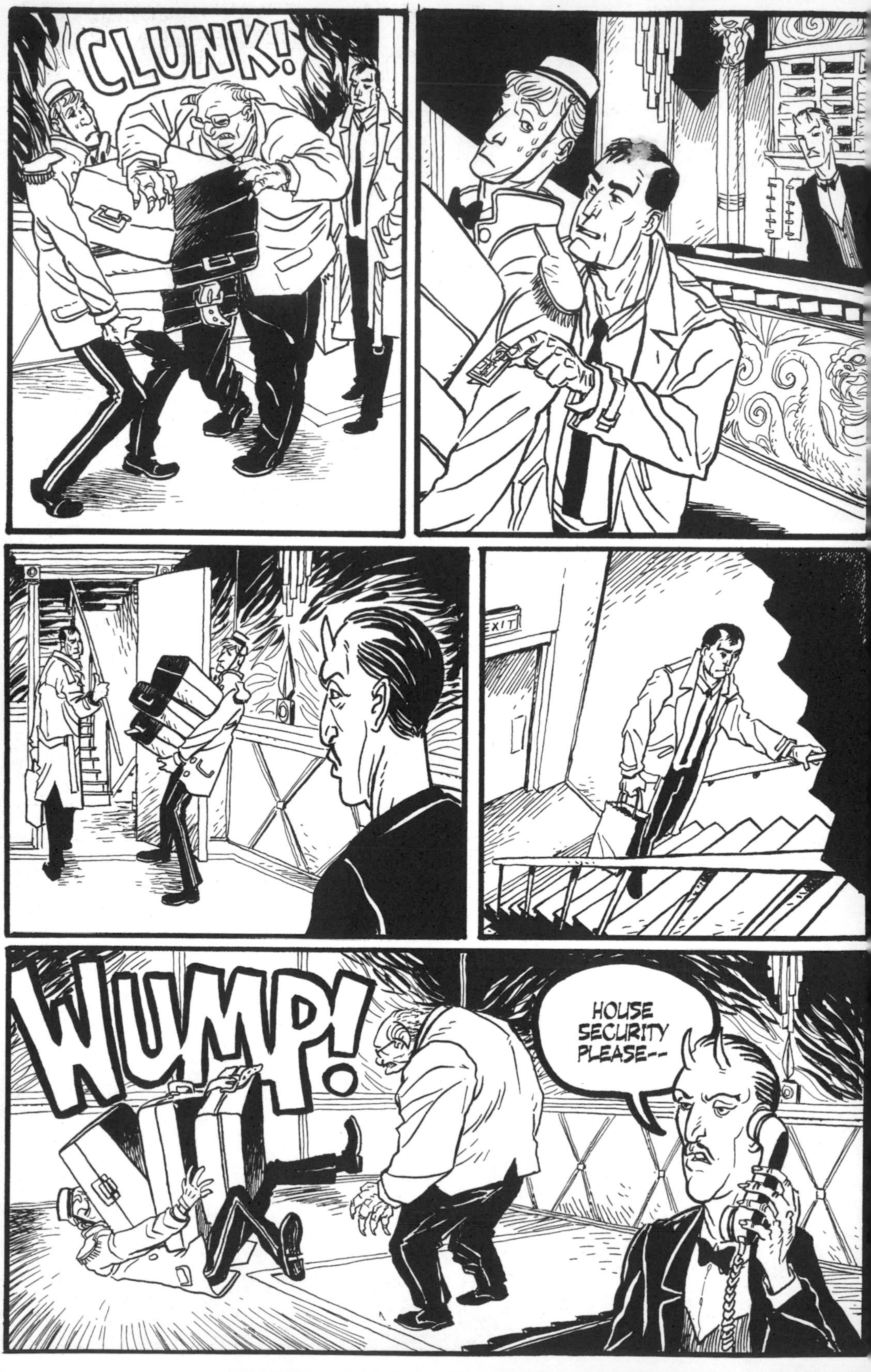
CLUNK!
EXIT
WUMP!
HOUSE SECURITY PLEASE--

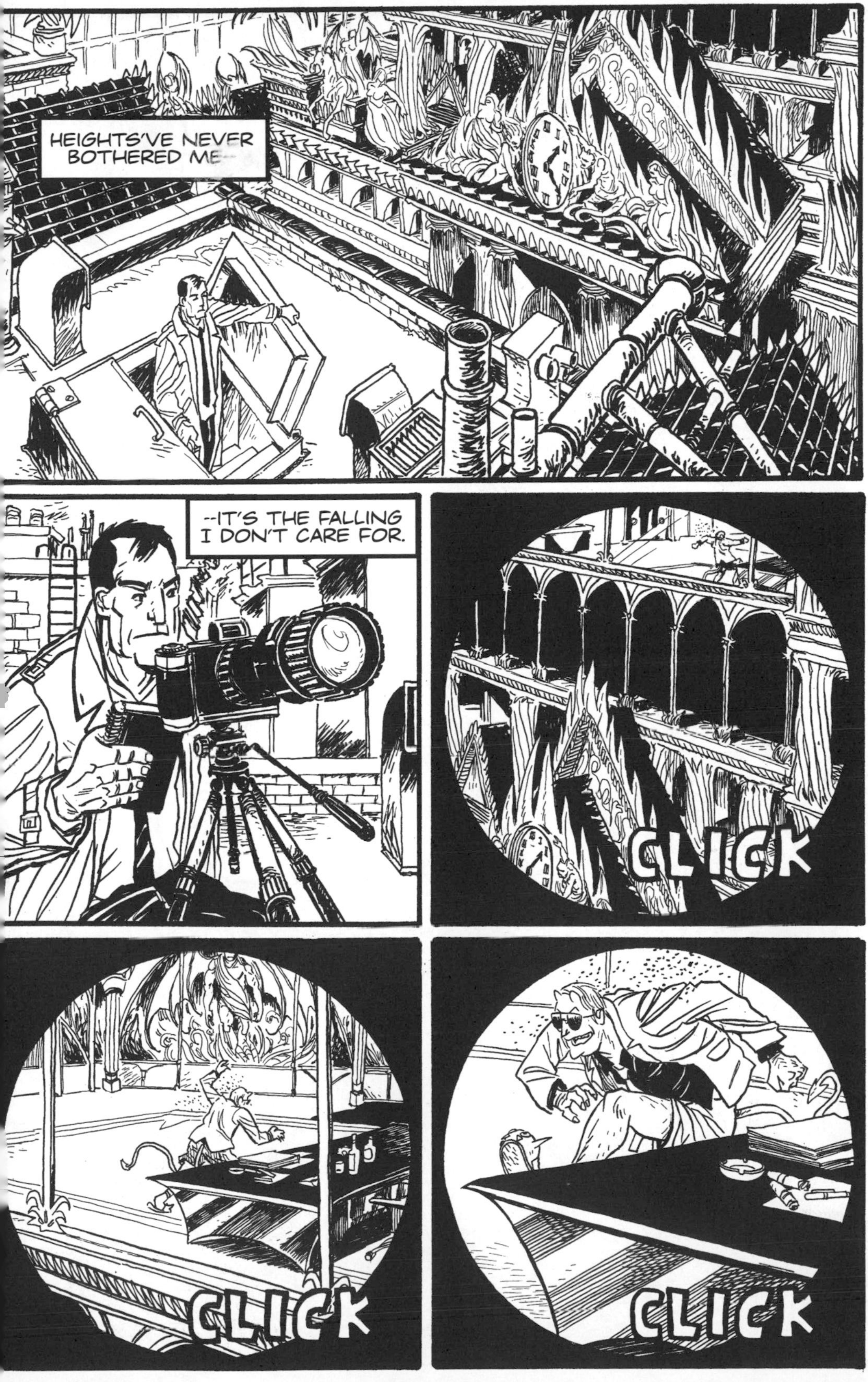
HEIGHTS'VE NEVER BOTHERED ME--
--IT'S THE FALLING I DON'T CARE FOR.
CLICK
CLICK
CLICK

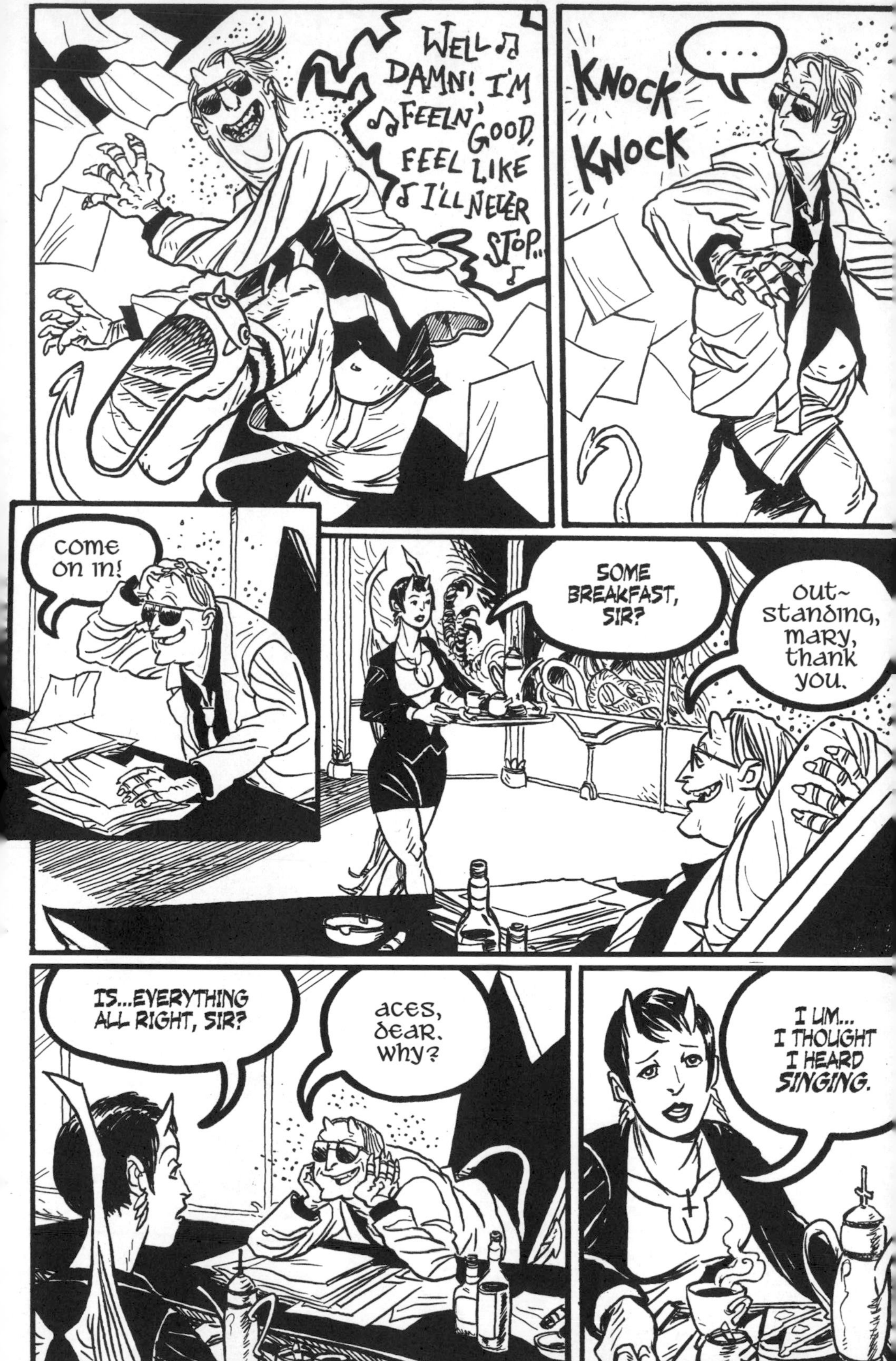

WELL ♫ DAMN! I'M ♫ FEELN' GOOD, FEEL LIKE ♪ I'LL NEVER STOP... ♪
KNOCK KNOCK
....
come on in!
SOME BREAKFAST, SIR?
out~standing, mary, thank you.
IS...EVERYTHING ALL RIGHT, SIR?
aces, dear. why?
I UM... I THOUGHT I HEARD SINGING.

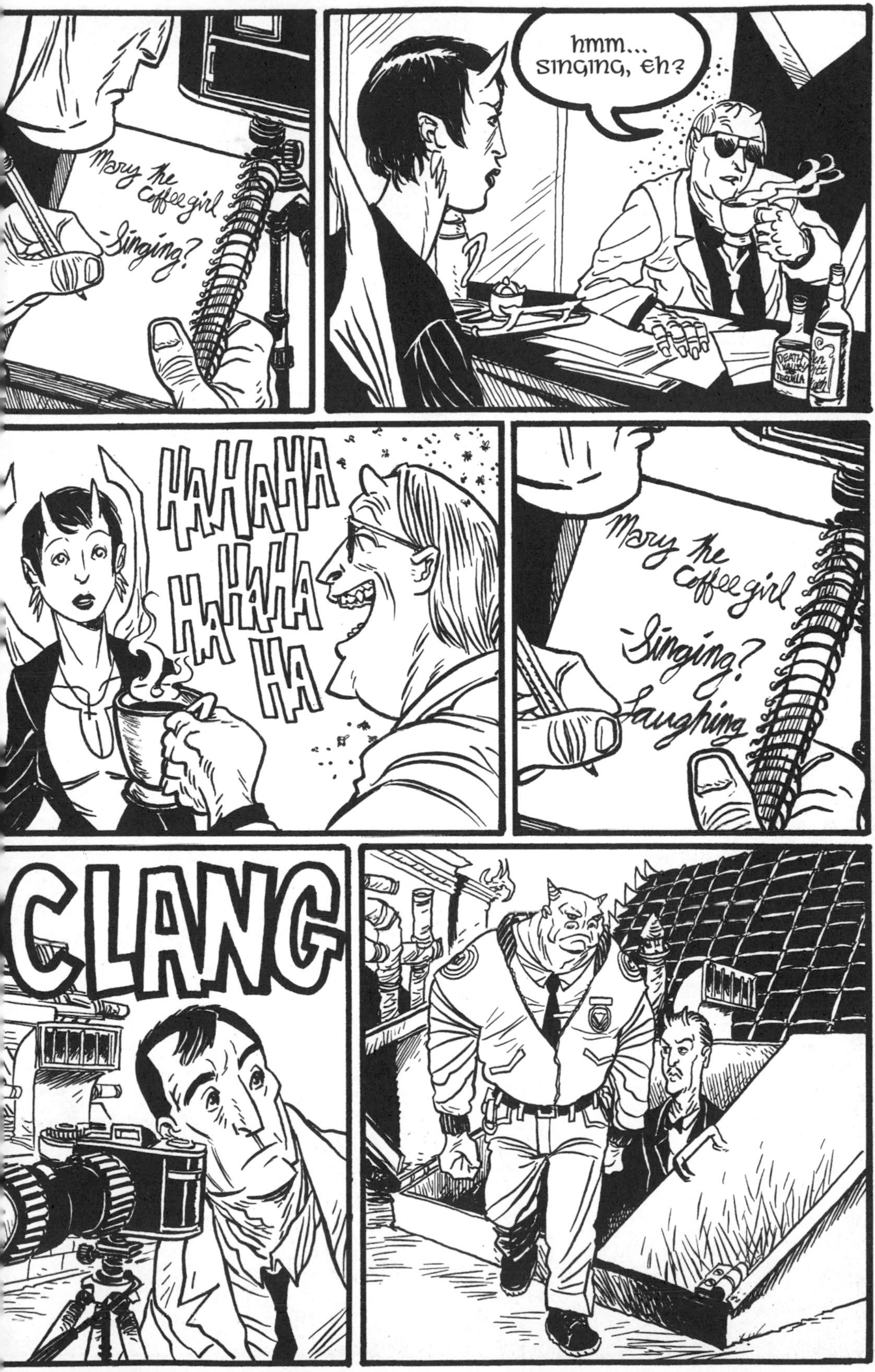
Mary the Coffee girl
-Singing?
hmm... singing, eh?
DEATH VALLEY TEQUILA
HAHAHA HAHAHAHA HA HA
Mary the Coffee girl
-Singing?
-Laughing
CLANG

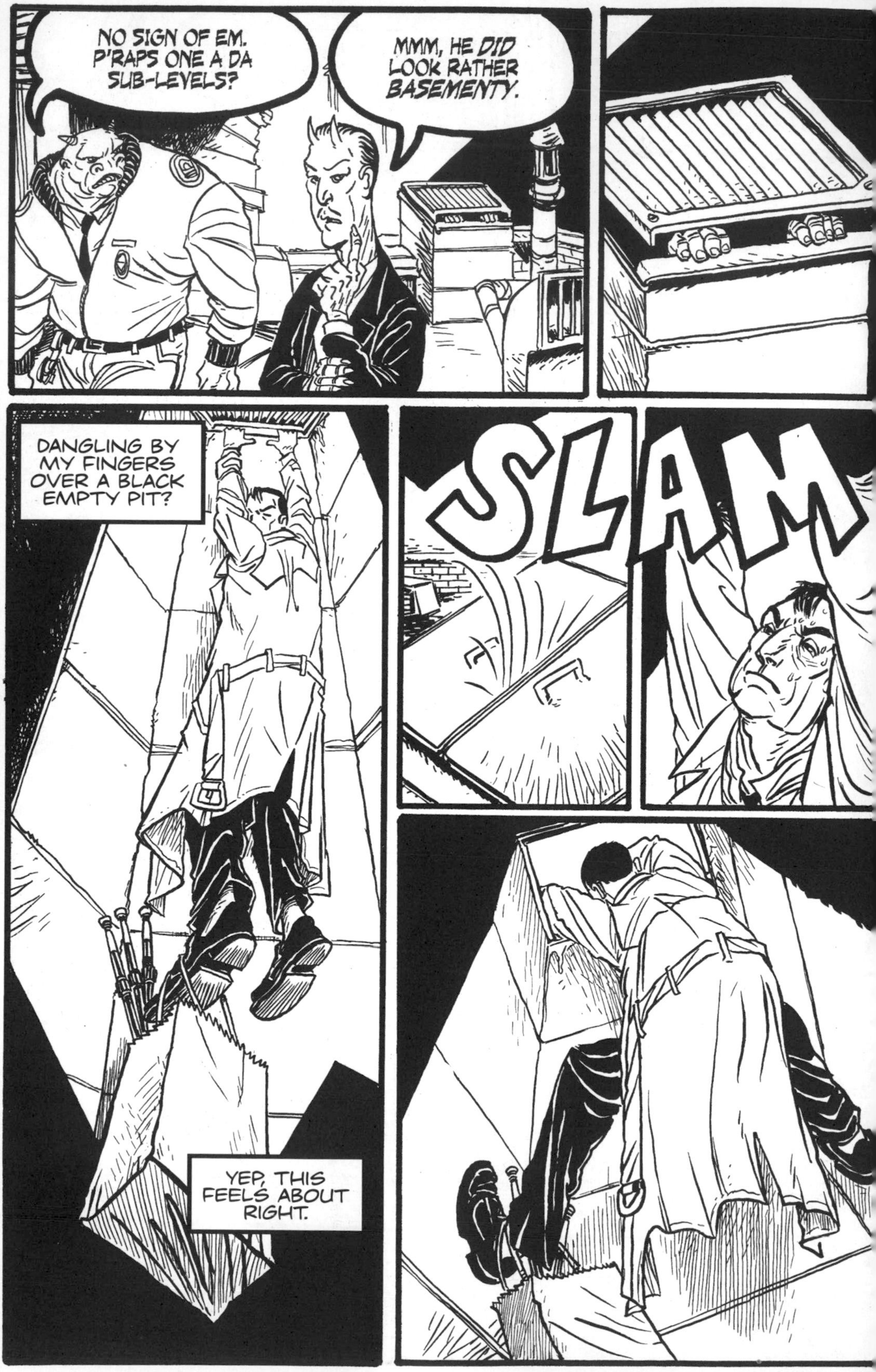
NO SIGN OF EM. P'RAPS ONE A DA SUB-LEVELS?
MMM, HE *DID* LOOK RATHER *BASEMENTY*.
DANGLING BY MY FINGERS OVER A BLACK EMPTY PIT?
YEP, THIS FEELS ABOUT RIGHT.
SLAM

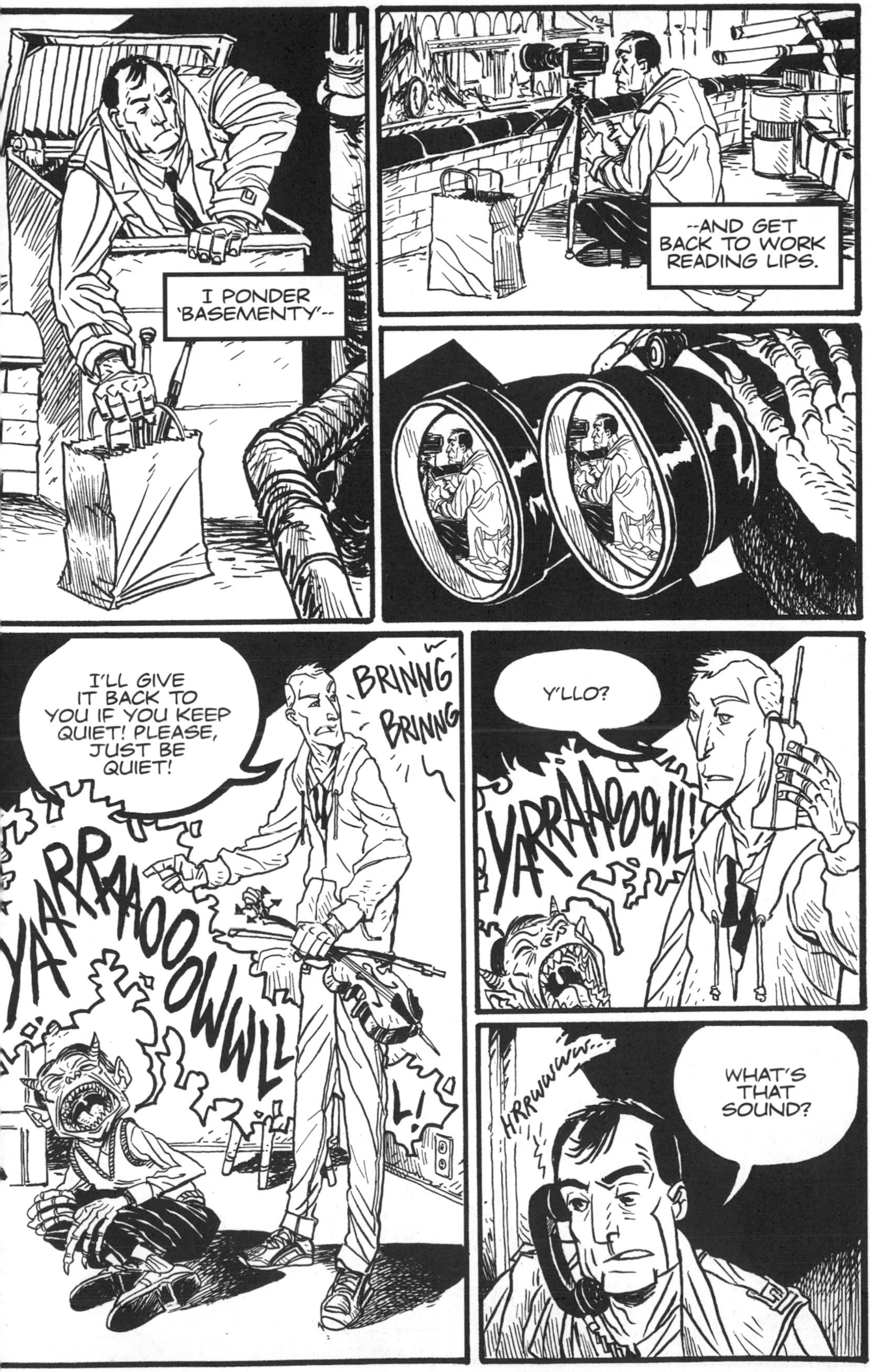
I PONDER 'BASEMENTY'--
--AND GET BACK TO WORK READING LIPS.
I'LL GIVE IT BACK TO YOU IF YOU KEEP QUIET! PLEASE, JUST BE QUIET!
BRINNG
BRINNG
YARRRAAOOOWWLL!
Y'LLO?
YARRAAOOOWL!
HRRWWWW...
WHAT'S THAT SOUND?

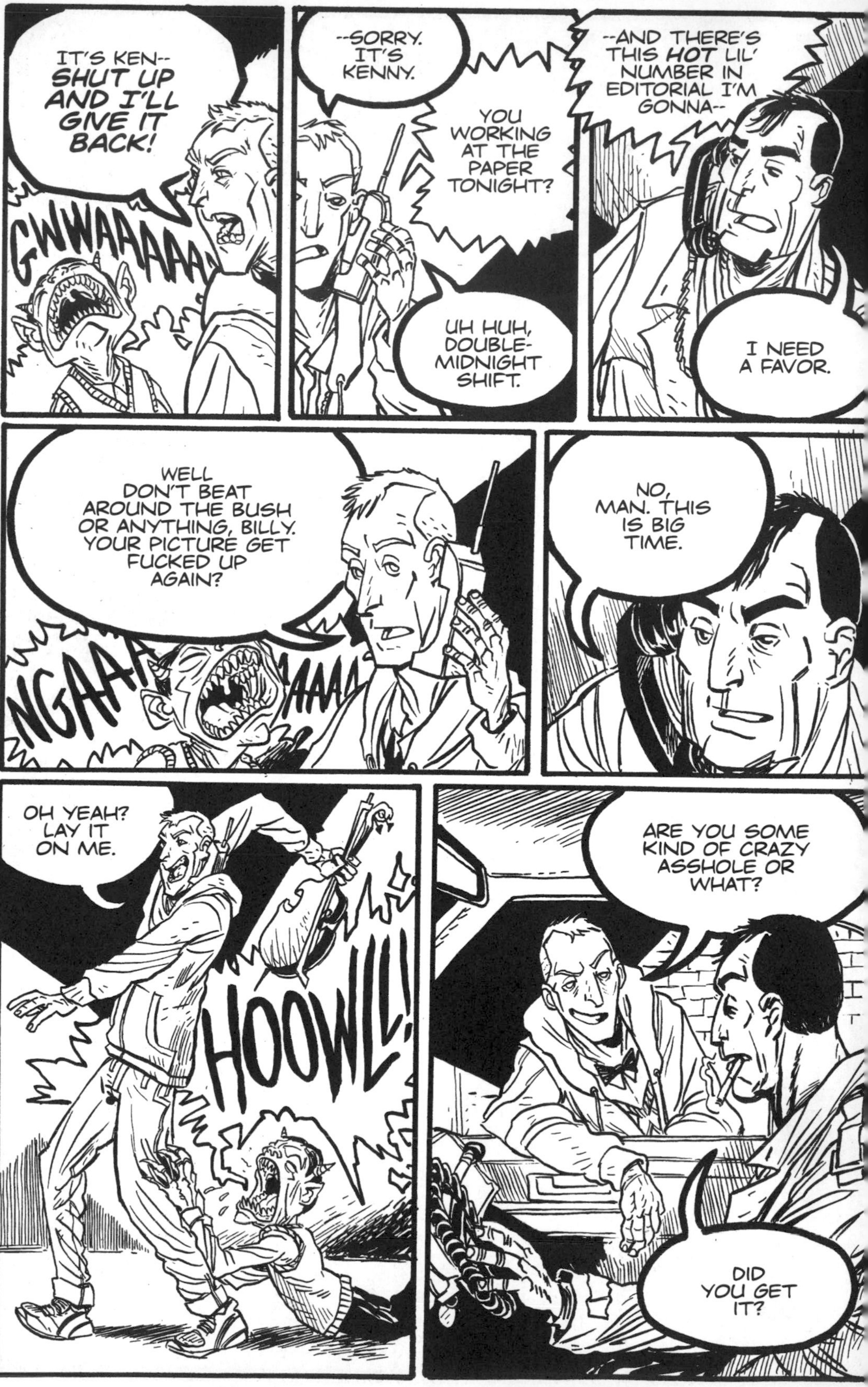
IT'S KEN-- **SHUT UP AND I'LL GIVE IT BACK!**
GWWAAAAAA
--SORRY. IT'S KENNY.
YOU WORKING AT THE PAPER TONIGHT?
UH HUH, DOUBLE-MIDNIGHT SHIFT.
--AND THERE'S THIS **HOT** LIL' NUMBER IN EDITORIAL I'M GONNA--
I NEED A FAVOR.
WELL DON'T BEAT AROUND THE BUSH OR ANYTHING, BILLY. YOUR PICTURE GET FUCKED UP AGAIN?
NGAAAAAAA
NO, MAN. THIS IS BIG TIME.
OH YEAH? LAY IT ON ME.
HOOWL!!
ARE YOU SOME KIND OF CRAZY ASSHOLE OR WHAT?
DID YOU GET IT?

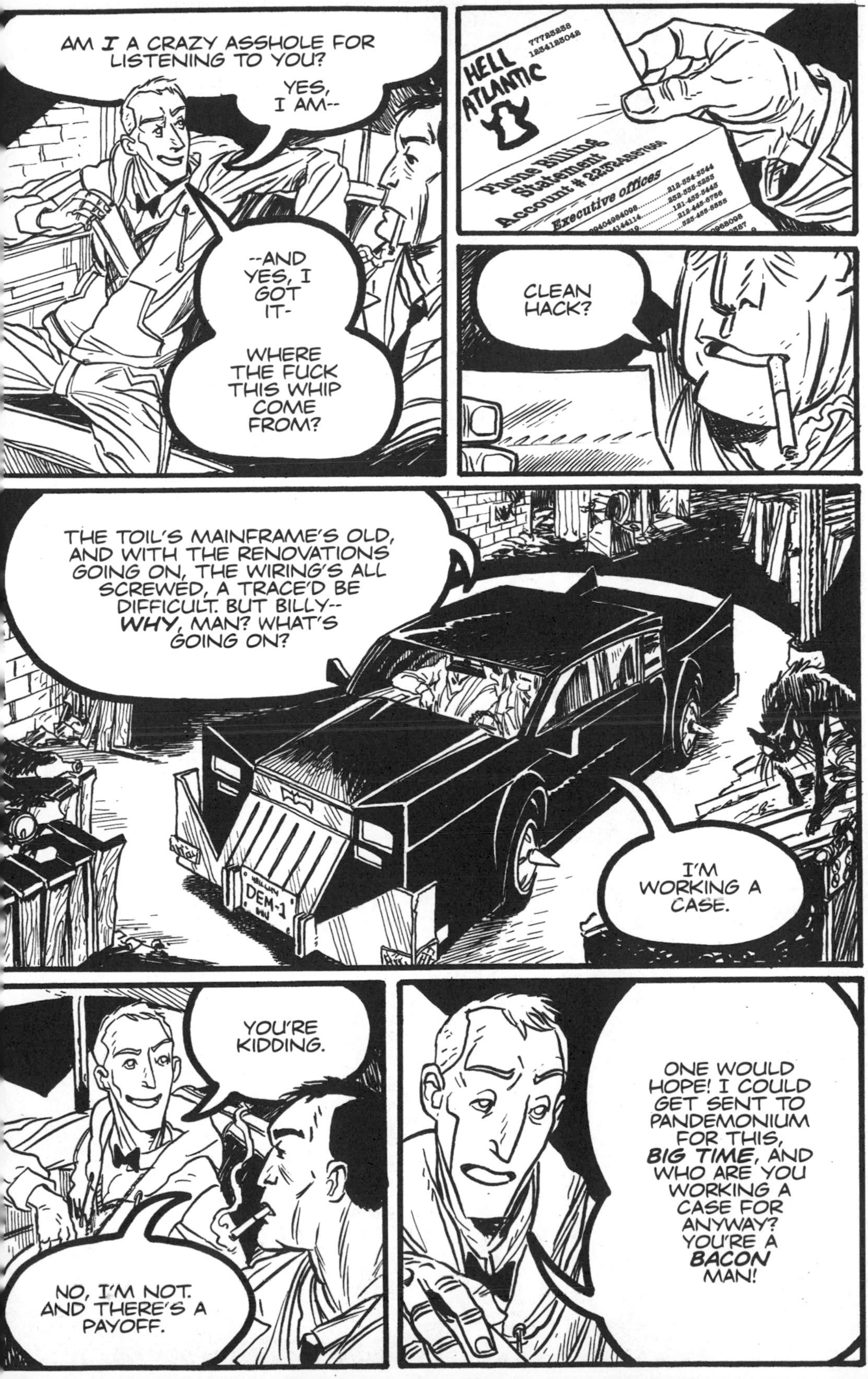
AM *I* A CRAZY ASSHOLE FOR LISTENING TO YOU?
YES, I AM--
--AND YES, I GOT IT-
WHERE THE FUCK THIS WHIP COME FROM?
HELL ATLANTIC
Phone Billing Statement
Executive offices
CLEAN HACK?
THE TOIL'S MAINFRAME'S OLD, AND WITH THE RENOVATIONS GOING ON, THE WIRING'S ALL SCREWED, A TRACE'D BE DIFFICULT. BUT BILLY-- ***WHY***, MAN? WHAT'S GOING ON?
DEM-1
I'M WORKING A CASE.
YOU'RE KIDDING.
NO, I'M NOT. AND THERE'S A PAYOFF.
ONE WOULD HOPE! I COULD GET SENT TO PANDEMONIUM FOR THIS, ***BIG TIME***, AND WHO ARE YOU WORKING A CASE FOR ANYWAY? YOU'RE A ***BACON*** MAN!

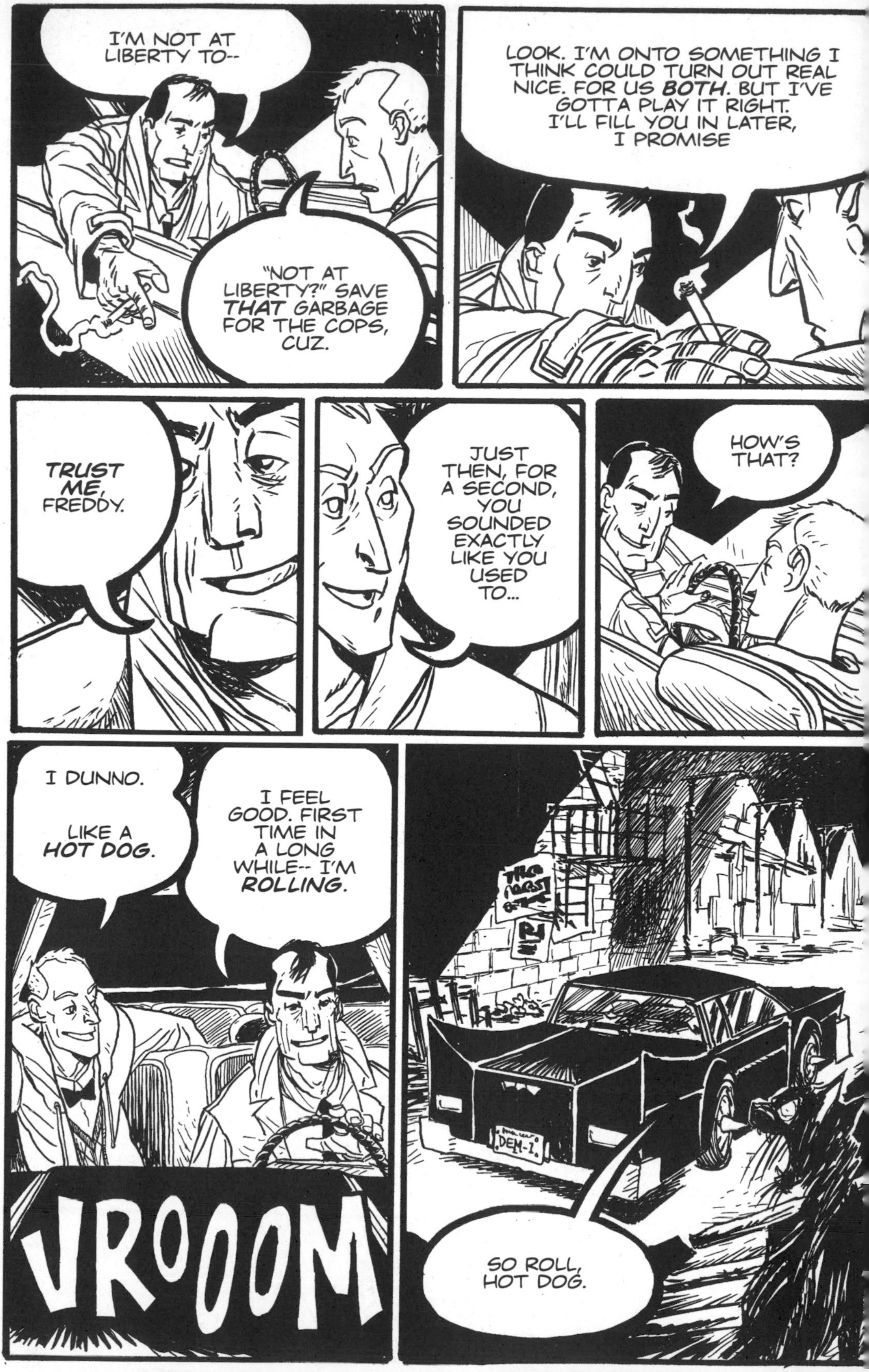
I'M NOT AT LIBERTY TO--
"NOT AT LIBERTY?" SAVE THAT GARBAGE FOR THE COPS, CUZ.
LOOK. I'M ONTO SOMETHING I THINK COULD TURN OUT REAL NICE. FOR US BOTH. BUT I'VE GOTTA PLAY IT RIGHT. I'LL FILL YOU IN LATER, I PROMISE
TRUST ME, FREDDY.
JUST THEN, FOR A SECOND, YOU SOUNDED EXACTLY LIKE YOU USED TO...
HOW'S THAT?
I DUNNO.
LIKE A HOT DOG.
I FEEL GOOD. FIRST TIME IN A LONG WHILE-- I'M ROLLING.
VROOOM
DEM-1
SO ROLL, HOT DOG.

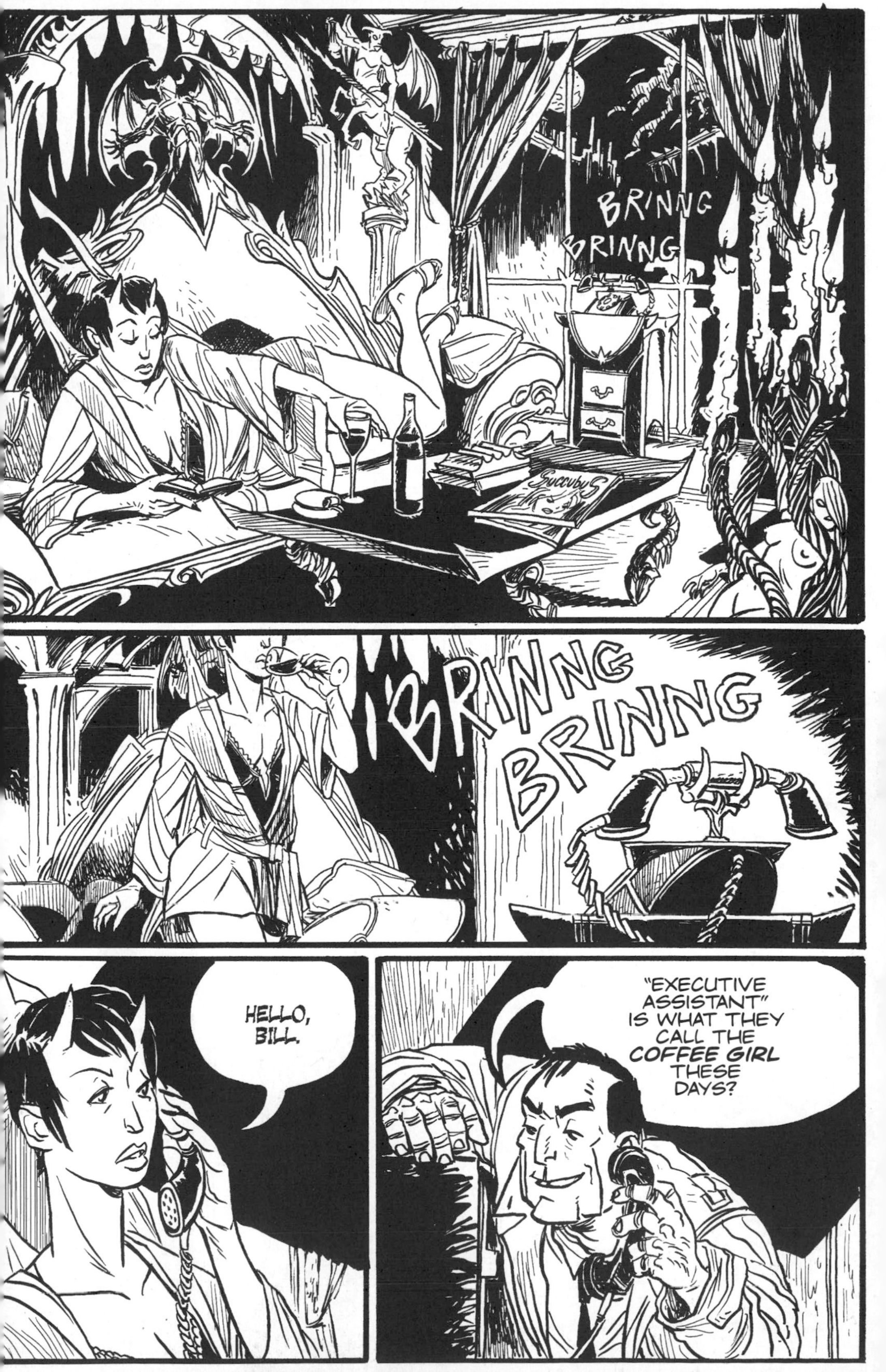
BRINNG
BRINNG
Succubus
BRINNG
BRINNG
HELLO, BILL.
"EXECUTIVE ASSISTANT" IS WHAT THEY CALL THE COFFEE GIRL THESE DAYS?

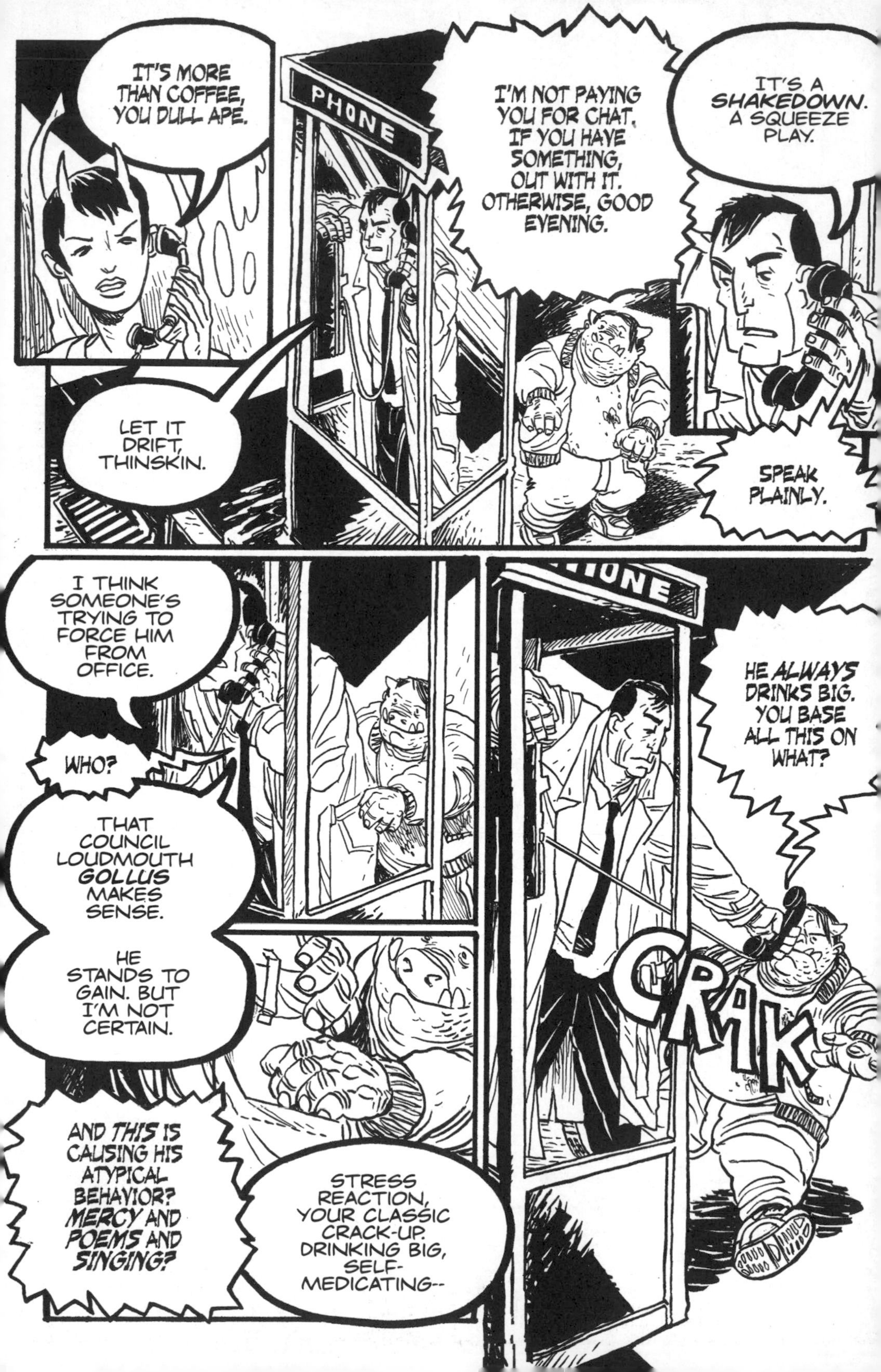
IT'S MORE THAN COFFEE, YOU DULL APE.
I'M NOT PAYING YOU FOR CHAT. IF YOU HAVE SOMETHING, OUT WITH IT. OTHERWISE, GOOD EVENING.
PHONE
IT'S A SHAKEDOWN. A SQUEEZE PLAY.
LET IT DRIFT, THINSKIN.
SPEAK PLAINLY.
I THINK SOMEONE'S TRYING TO FORCE HIM FROM OFFICE.
WHO?
THAT COUNCIL LOUDMOUTH GOLLUS MAKES SENSE.
HE STANDS TO GAIN. BUT I'M NOT CERTAIN.
HE ALWAYS DRINKS BIG. YOU BASE ALL THIS ON WHAT?
CRAK
AND THIS IS CAUSING HIS ATYPICAL BEHAVIOR? MERCY AND POEMS AND SINGING?
STRESS REACTION, YOUR CLASSIC CRACK-UP. DRINKING BIG, SELF-MEDICATING--

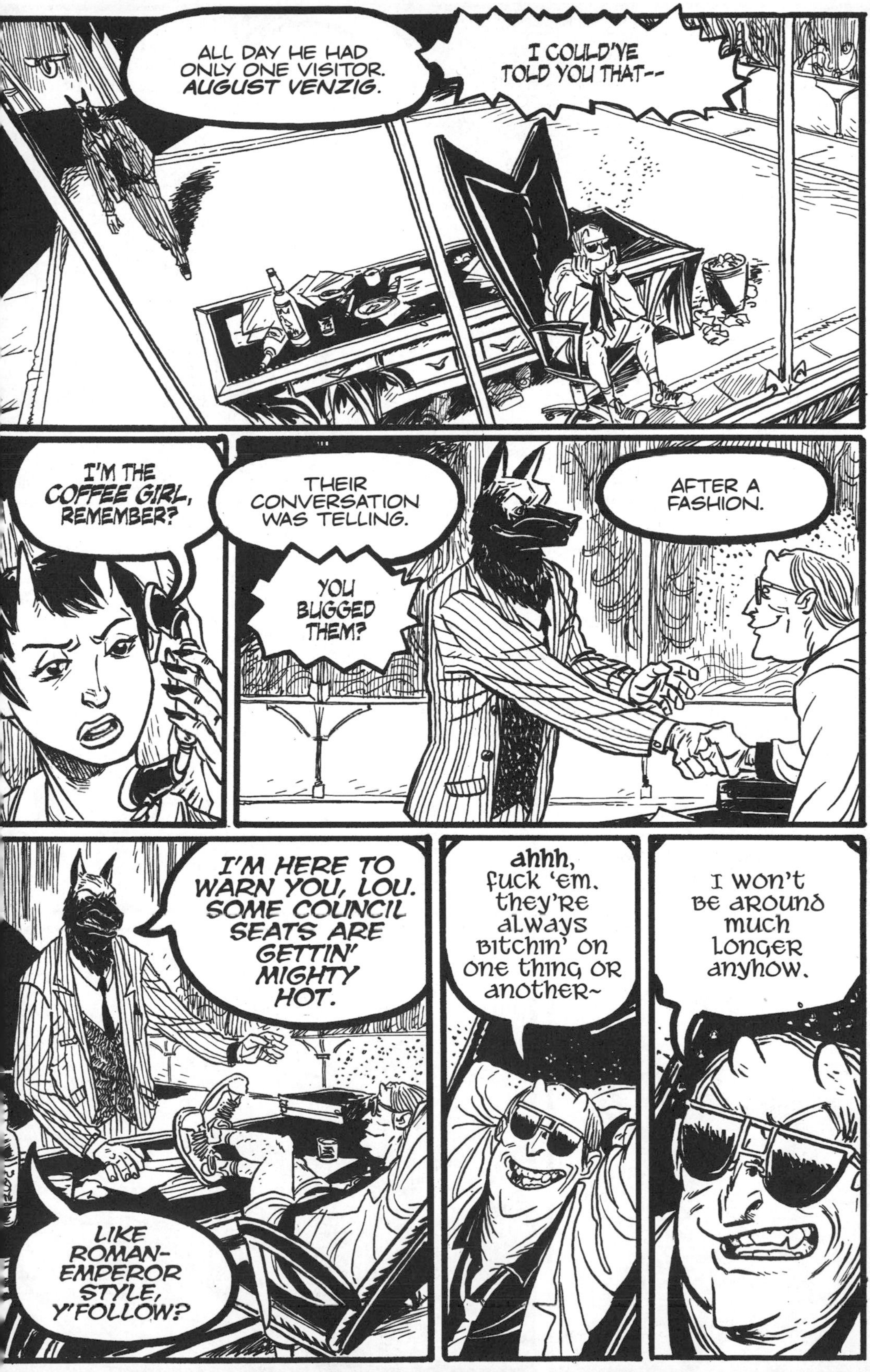
ALL DAY HE HAD ONLY ONE VISITOR. AUGUST VENZIG.
I COULD'VE TOLD YOU THAT--
I'M THE COFFEE GIRL, REMEMBER?
THEIR CONVERSATION WAS TELLING.
YOU BUGGED THEM?
AFTER A FASHION.
I'M HERE TO WARN YOU, LOU. SOME COUNCIL SEATS ARE GETTIN' MIGHTY HOT.
LIKE ROMAN-EMPEROR STYLE, Y'FOLLOW?
ahhh, fuck 'em. they're always bitchin' on one thing or another~
I won't be around much longer anyhow.

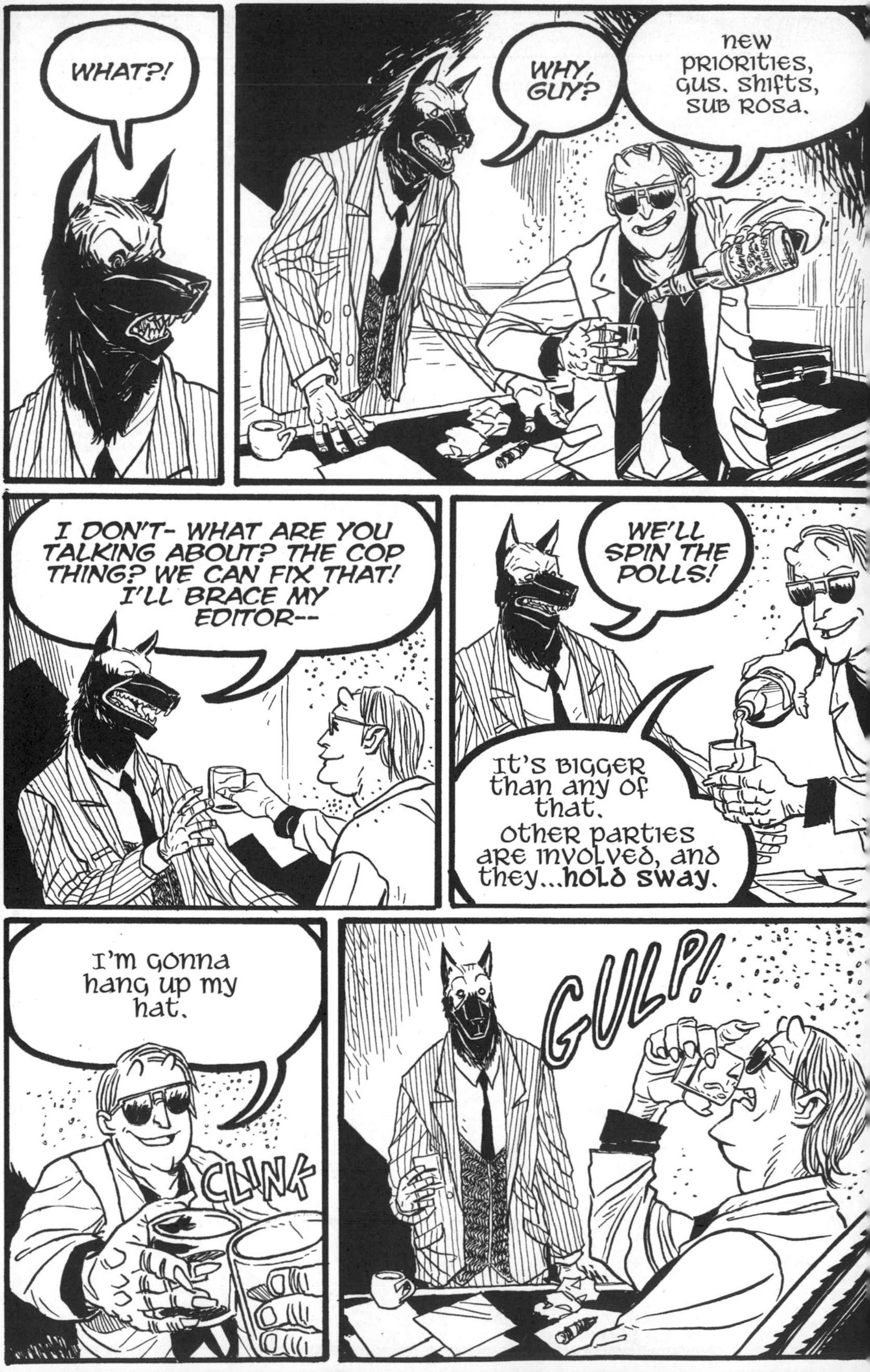
WHAT?!
WHY, GUY?
new priorities, gus. shifts, sub rosa.
I DON'T- WHAT ARE YOU TALKING ABOUT? THE COP THING? WE CAN FIX THAT! I'LL BRACE MY EDITOR--
WE'LL SPIN THE POLLS!
It's BIGGER than any of that. other parties are involved, and they...hold sway.
I'm gonna hang up my hat.
CLINK
GULP!

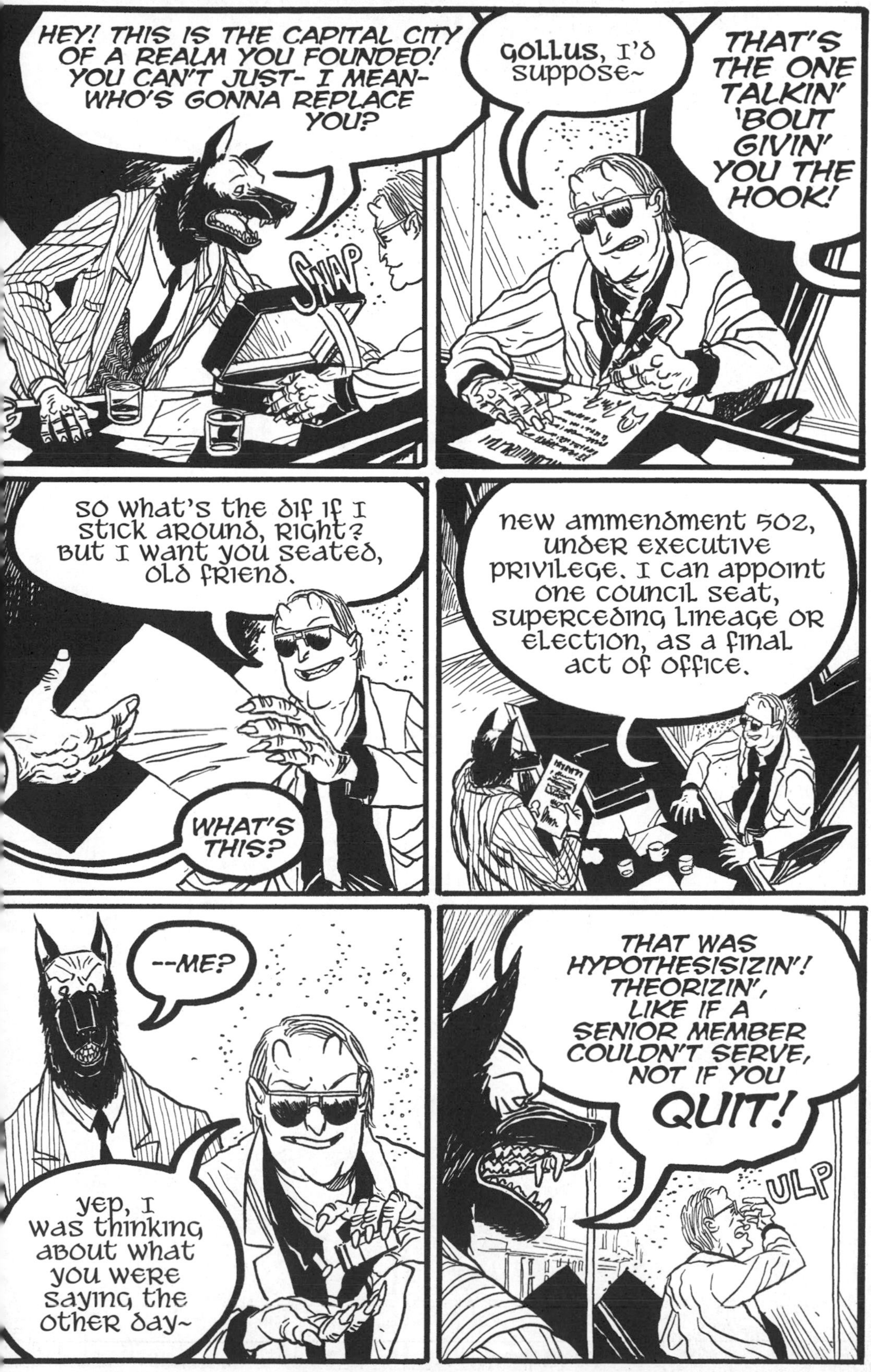
HEY! THIS IS THE CAPITAL CITY OF A REALM YOU FOUNDED! YOU CAN'T JUST- I MEAN- WHO'S GONNA REPLACE YOU?
SNAP
GOLLUS, I'D SUPPOSE~
THAT'S THE ONE TALKIN' 'BOUT GIVIN' YOU THE HOOK!
SO WHAT'S THE DIF IF I STICK AROUND, RIGHT? BUT I WANT YOU SEATED, OLD FRIEND.
WHAT'S THIS?
NEW AMMENDMENT 502, UNDER EXECUTIVE PRIVILEGE. I CAN APPOINT ONE COUNCIL SEAT, SUPERCEDING LINEAGE OR ELECTION, AS A FINAL ACT OF OFFICE.
--ME?
YEP, I WAS THINKING ABOUT WHAT YOU WERE SAYING THE OTHER DAY~
THAT WAS HYPOTHESISIZIN'! THEORIZIN', LIKE IF A SENIOR MEMBER COULDN'T SERVE, NOT IF YOU QUIT!
ULP

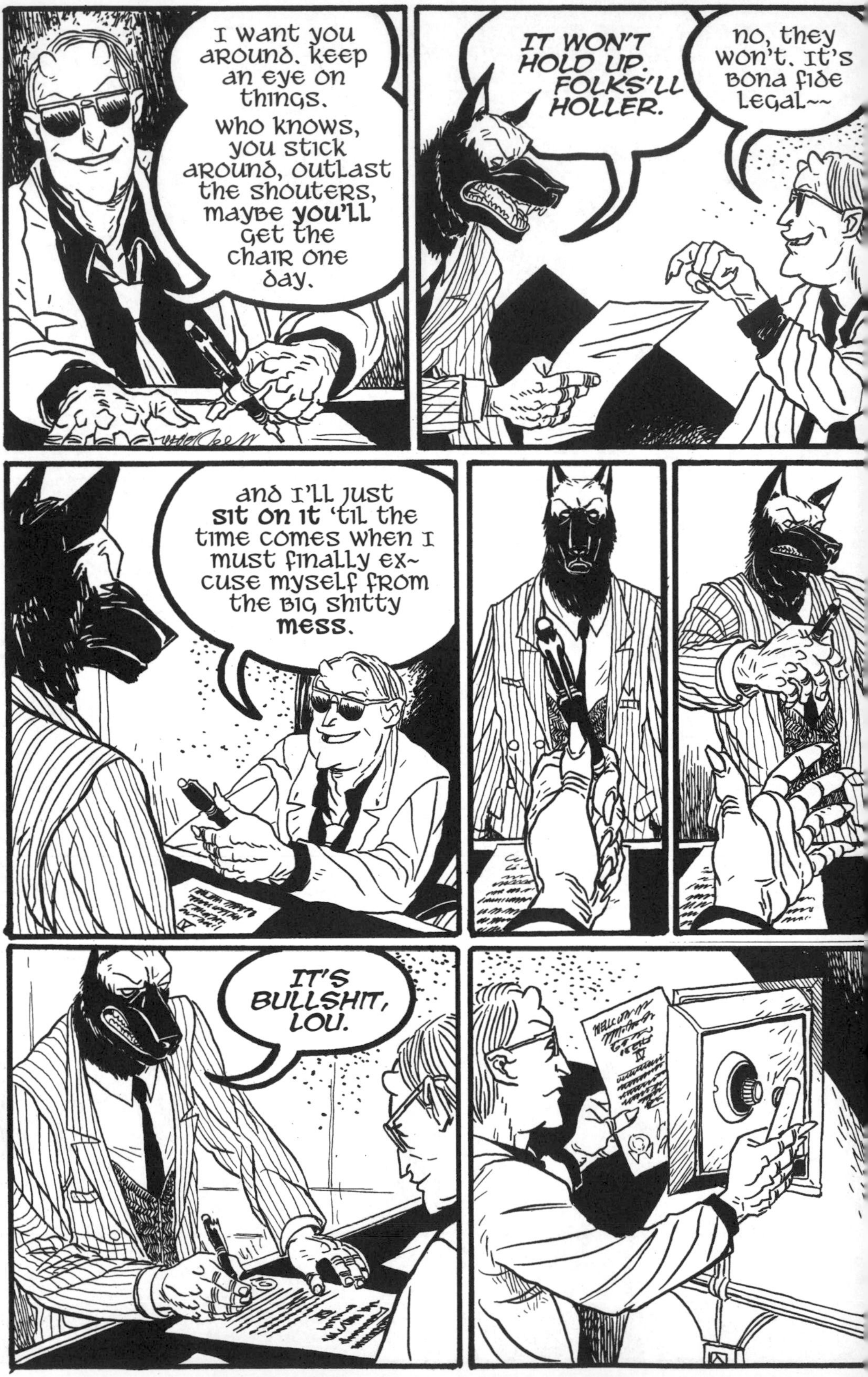
I want you around. keep an eye on things.
who knows, you stick around, outlast the shouters, maybe **you'll** get the chair one day.
IT WON'T HOLD UP. FOLKS'LL HOLLER.
no, they won't. It's bona fide legal~~
and I'll just **sit on it** 'til the time comes when I must finally ex~cuse myself from the big shitty **mess**.
IT'S BULLSHIT, LOU.

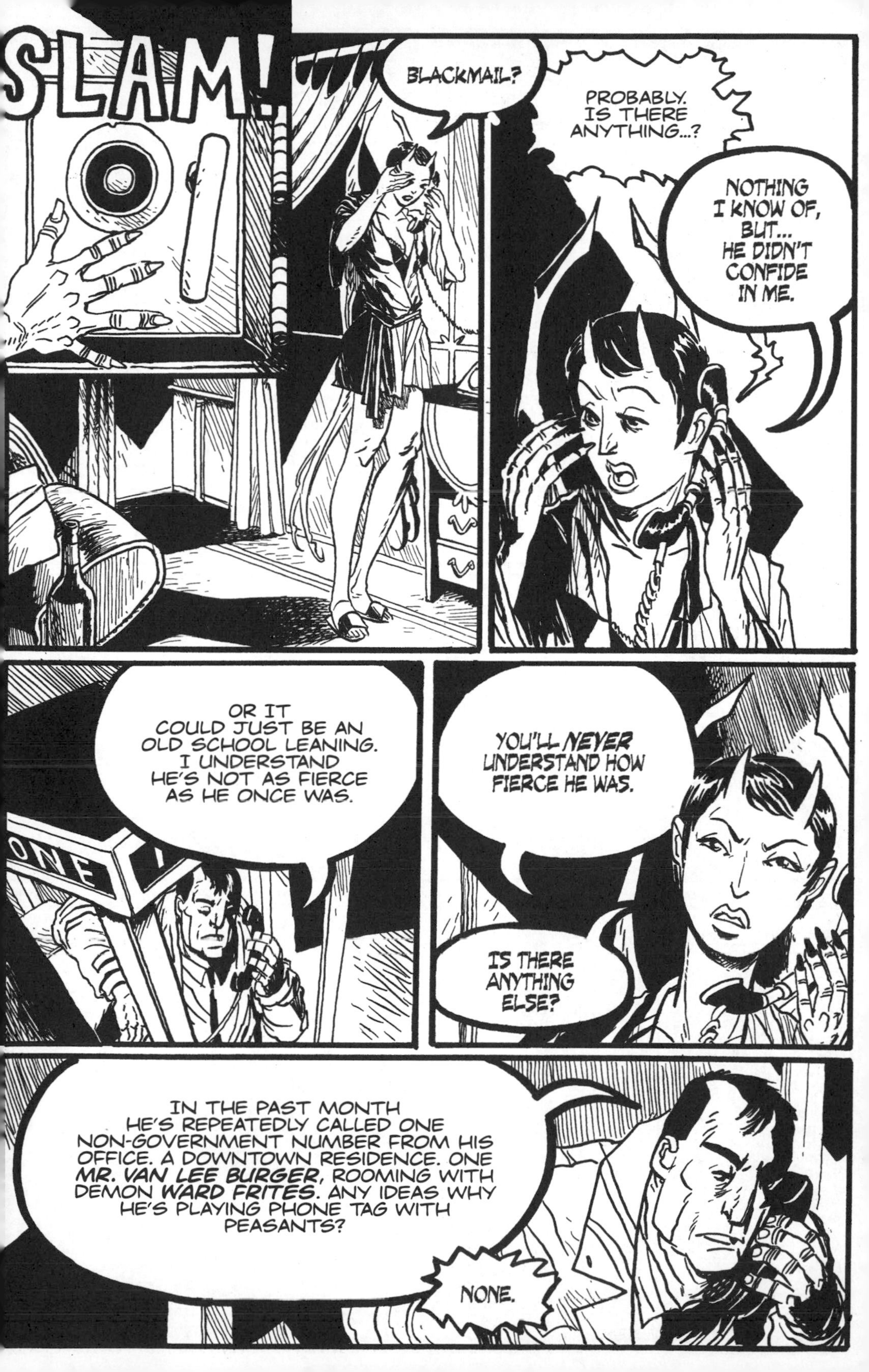
SLAM!
BLACKMAIL?
PROBABLY. IS THERE ANYTHING...?
NOTHING I KNOW OF, BUT... HE DIDN'T CONFIDE IN ME.
OR IT COULD JUST BE AN OLD SCHOOL LEANING. I UNDERSTAND HE'S NOT AS FIERCE AS HE ONCE WAS.
YOU'LL NEVER UNDERSTAND HOW FIERCE HE WAS.
IS THERE ANYTHING ELSE?
IN THE PAST MONTH HE'S REPEATEDLY CALLED ONE NON-GOVERNMENT NUMBER FROM HIS OFFICE. A DOWNTOWN RESIDENCE. ONE MR. VAN LEE BURGER, ROOMING WITH DEMON WARD FRITES. ANY IDEAS WHY HE'S PLAYING PHONE TAG WITH PEASANTS?
NONE.

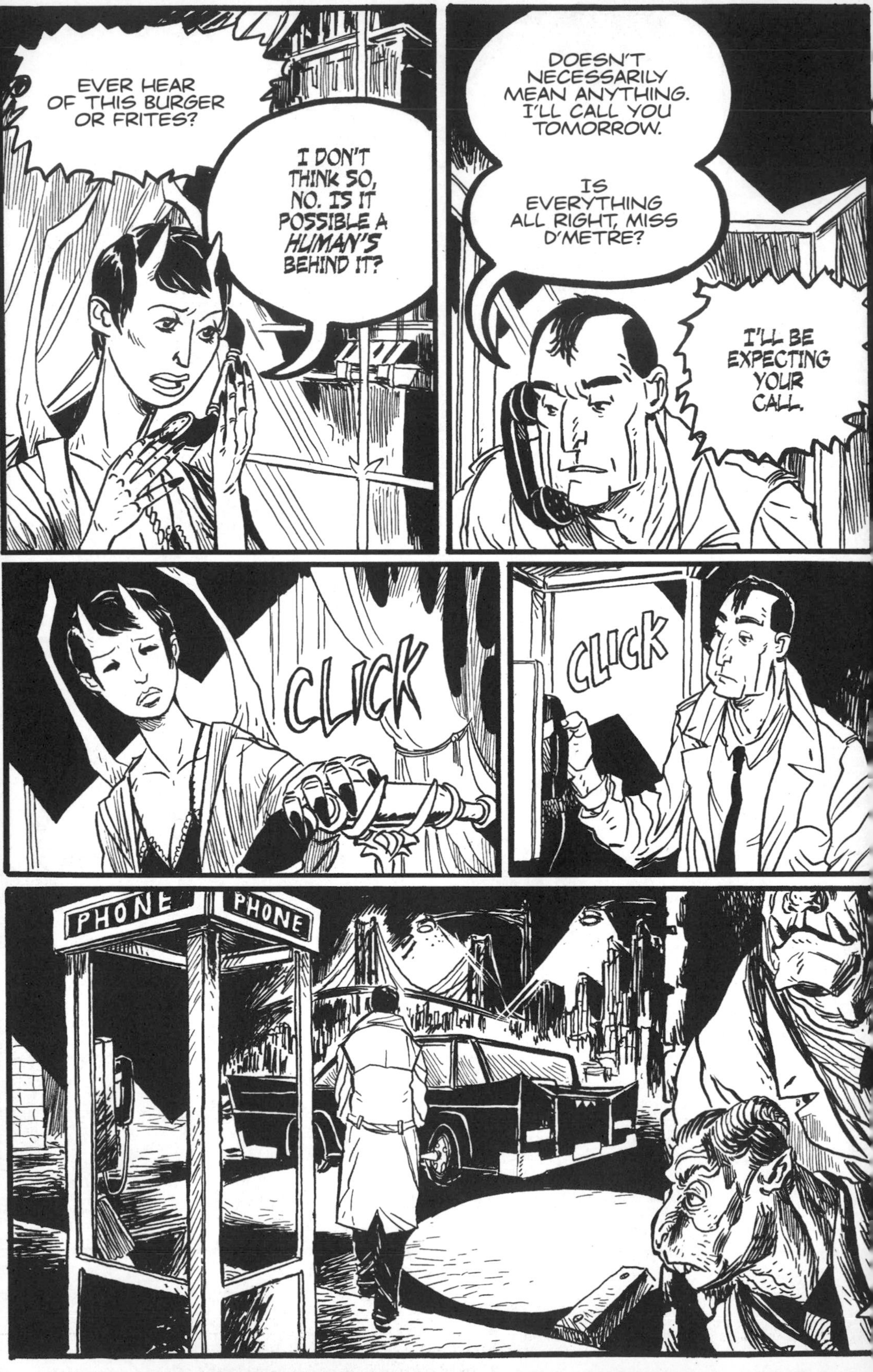
EVER HEAR OF THIS BURGER OR FRITES?
I DON'T THINK SO, NO. IS IT POSSIBLE A *HUMAN'S* BEHIND IT?
DOESN'T NECESSARILY MEAN ANYTHING. I'LL CALL YOU TOMORROW.
IS EVERYTHING ALL RIGHT, MISS D'METRE?
I'LL BE EXPECTING YOUR CALL.
CLICK
CLICK
PHONE
PHONE

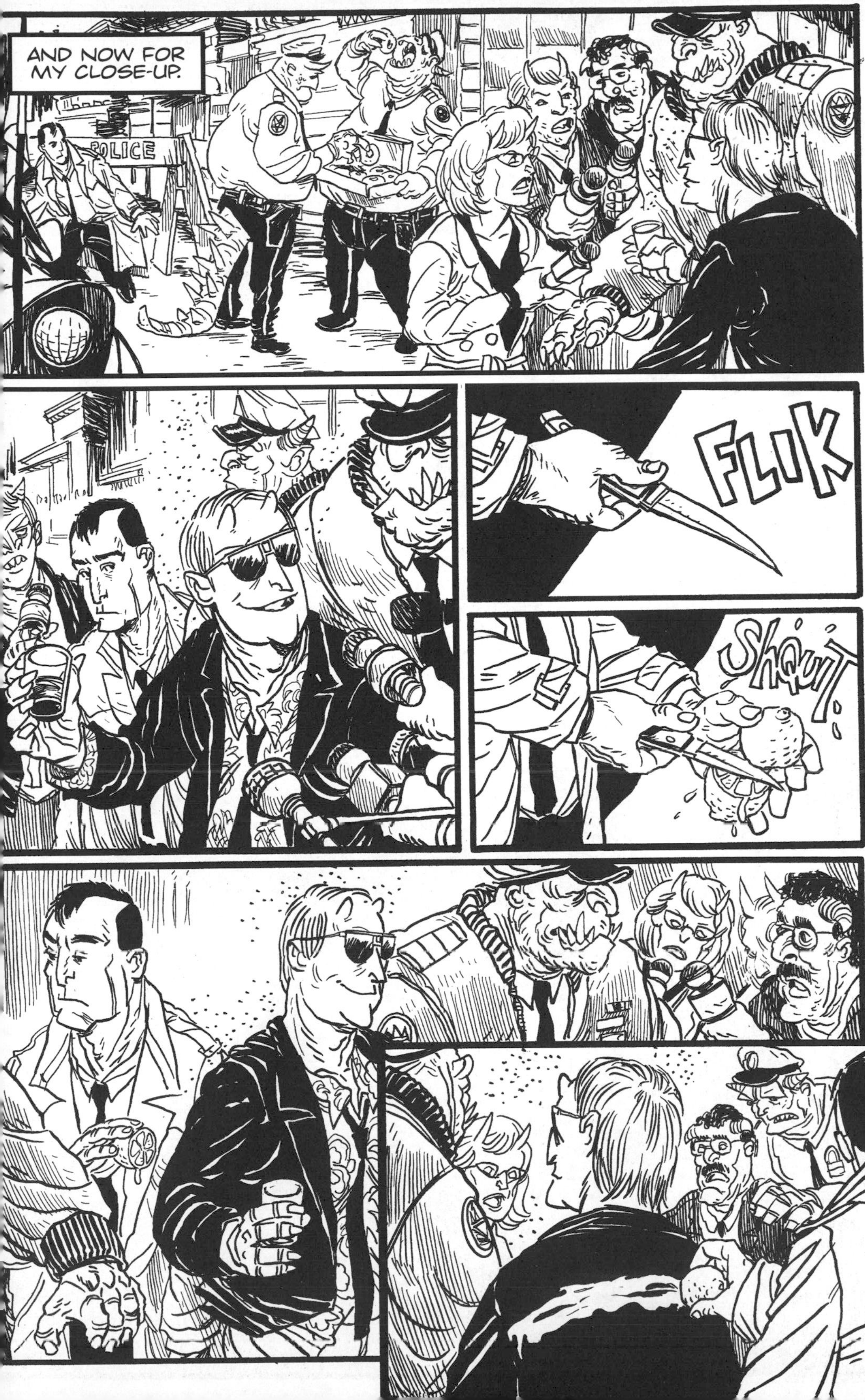
AND NOW FOR MY CLOSE-UP.
POLICE
FLIK
SHQUIT

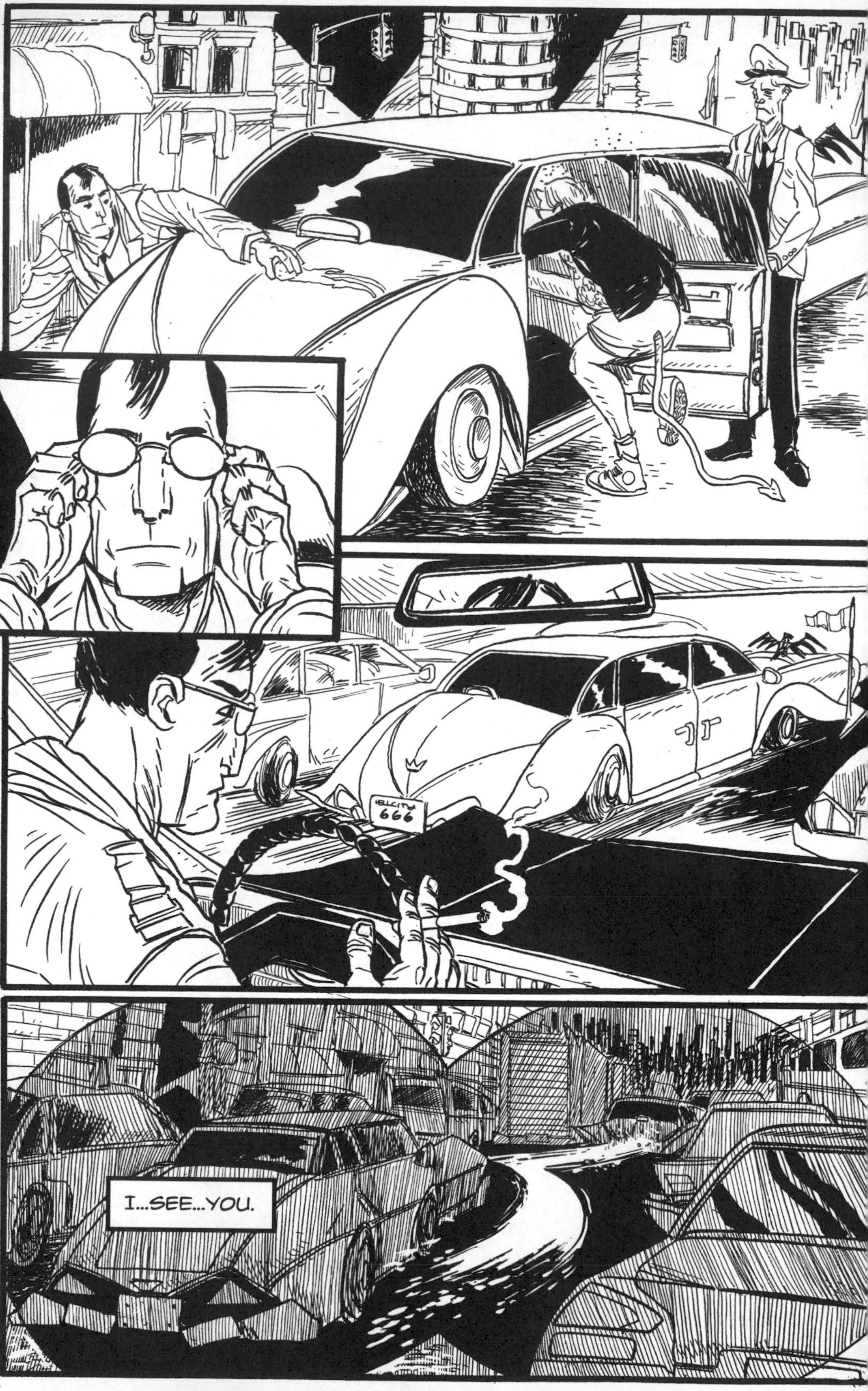
HELLCITY
666
I...SEE...YOU.

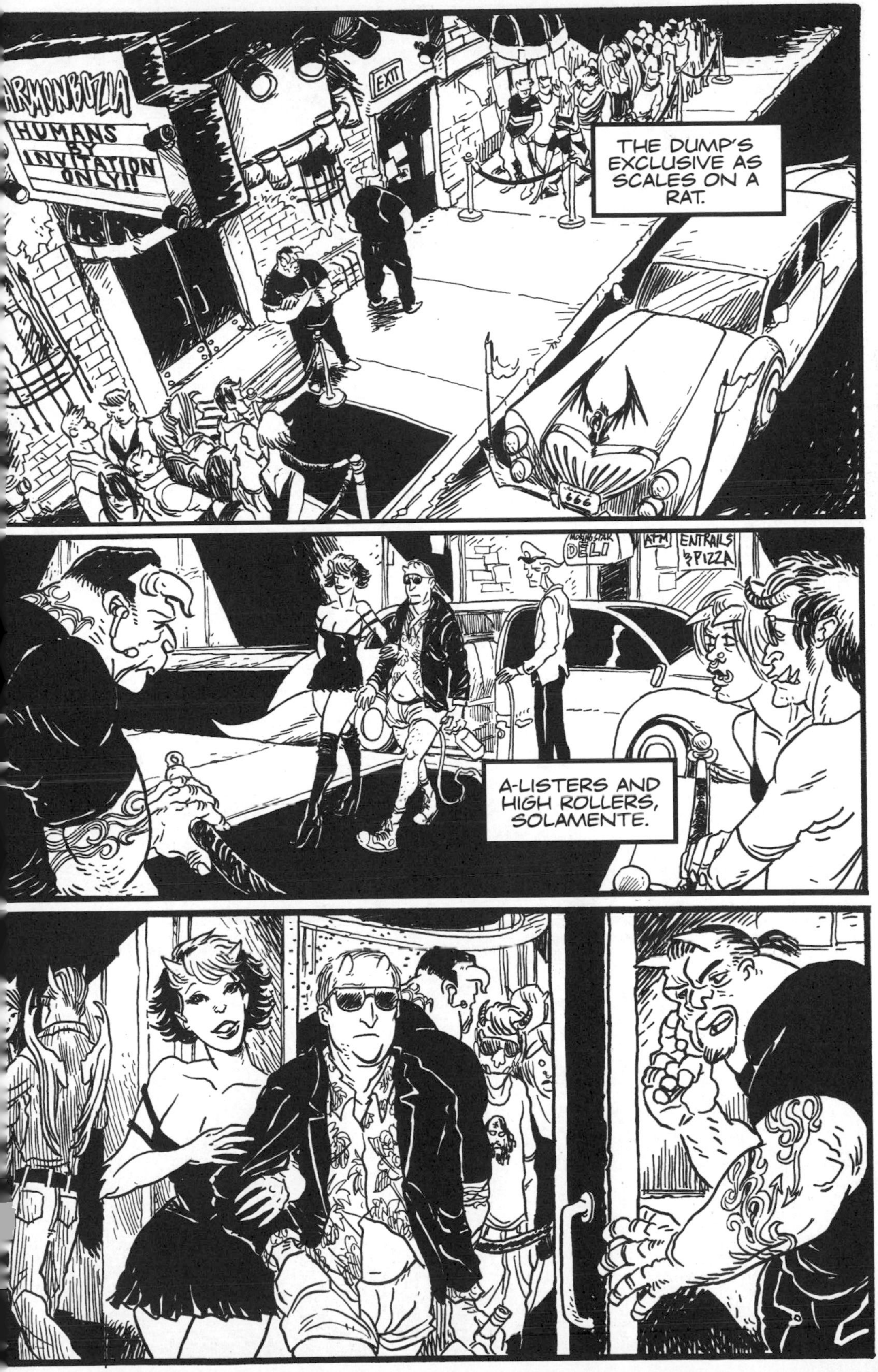
ARMONBOZIA
HUMANS BY INVITATION ONLY!!
EXIT
THE DUMP'S EXCLUSIVE AS SCALES ON A RAT.
666
DELI
ATM
ENTRAILS ½ PIZZA
A-LISTERS AND HIGH ROLLERS, SOLAMENTE.

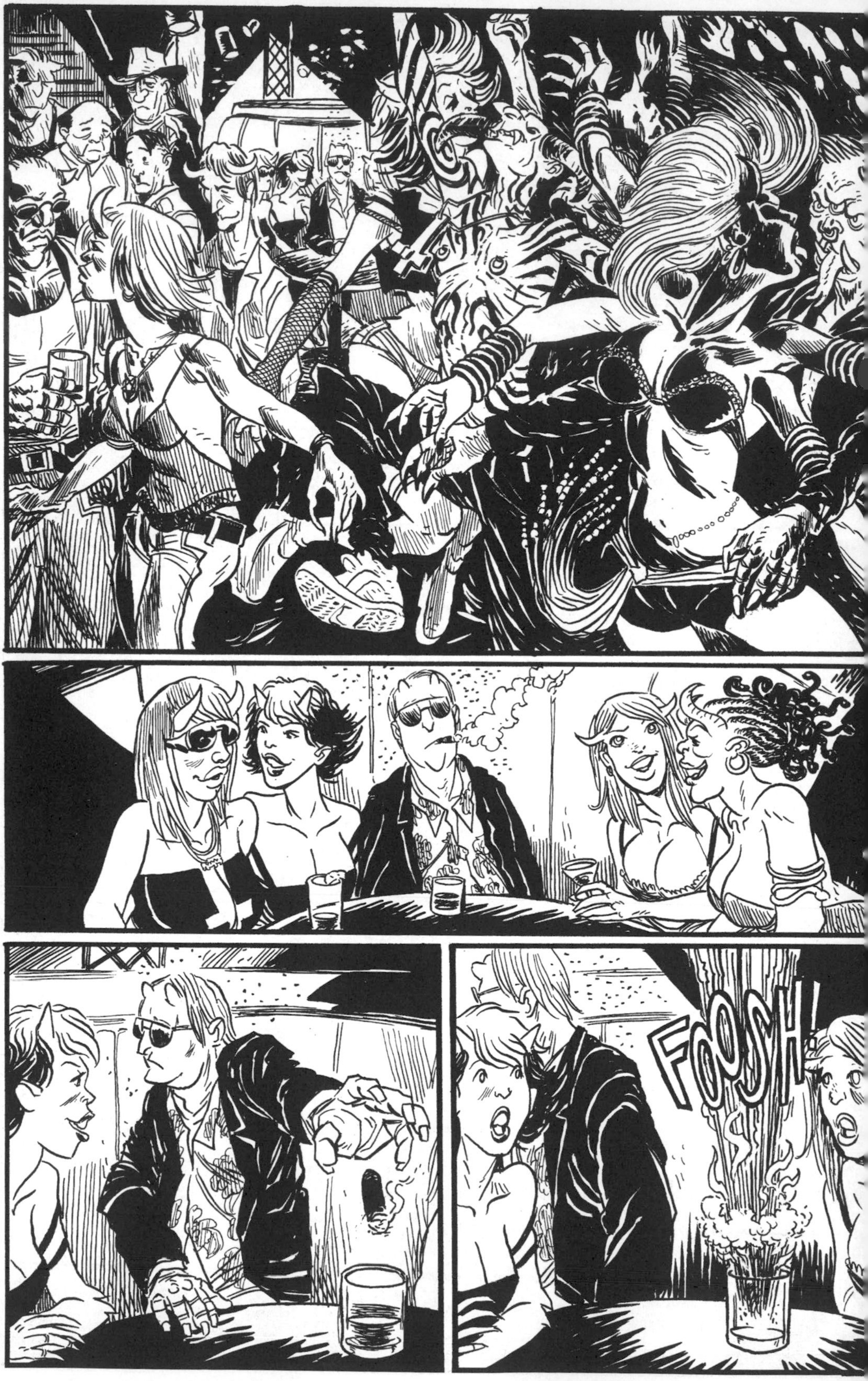
FOOSH!

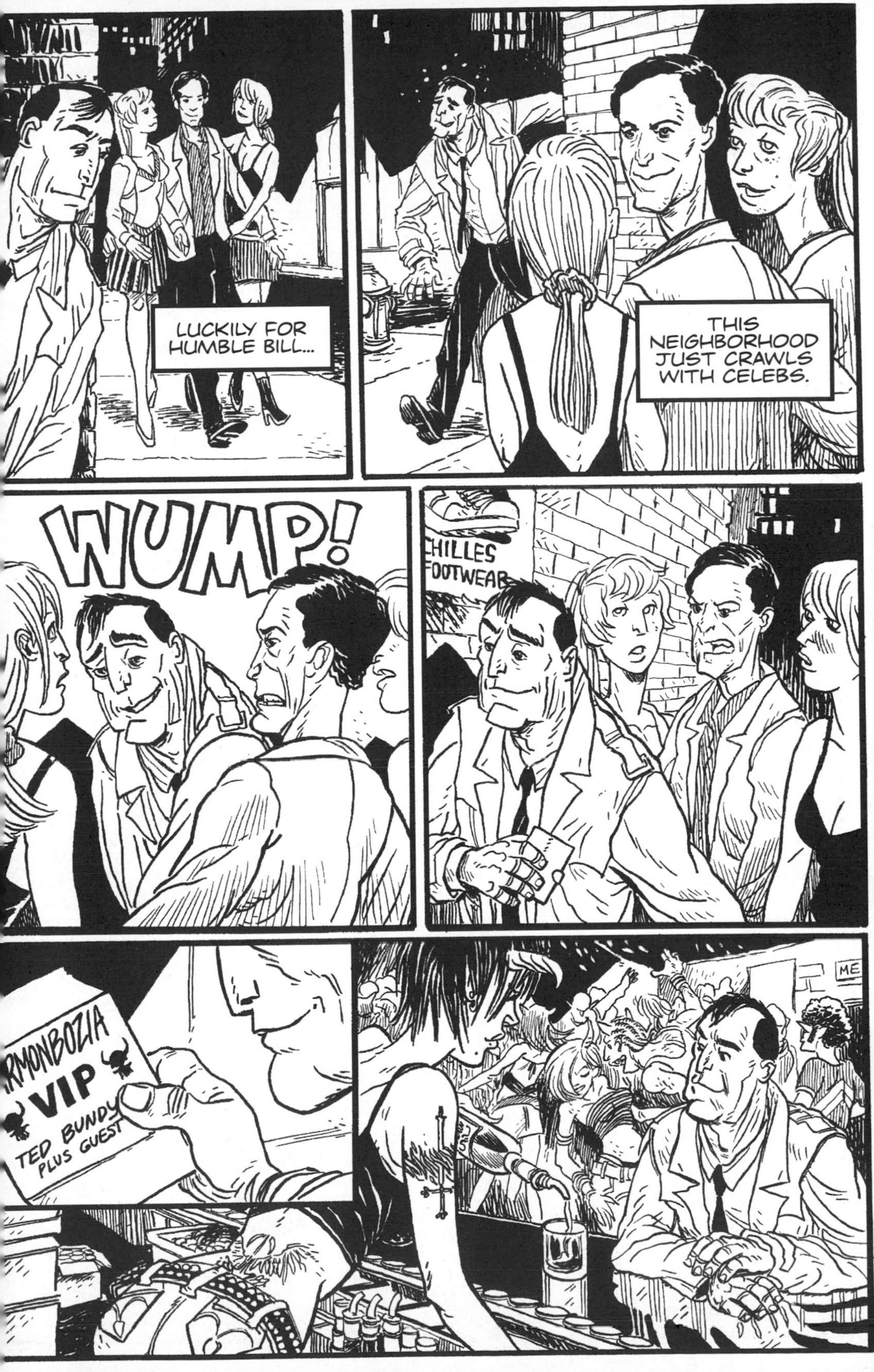

LUCKILY FOR HUMBLE BILL...
THIS NEIGHBORHOOD JUST CRAWLS WITH CELEBS.
WUMP!
CHILLES FOOTWEAR
RMONBOZIA VIP TED BUNDY PLUS GUEST

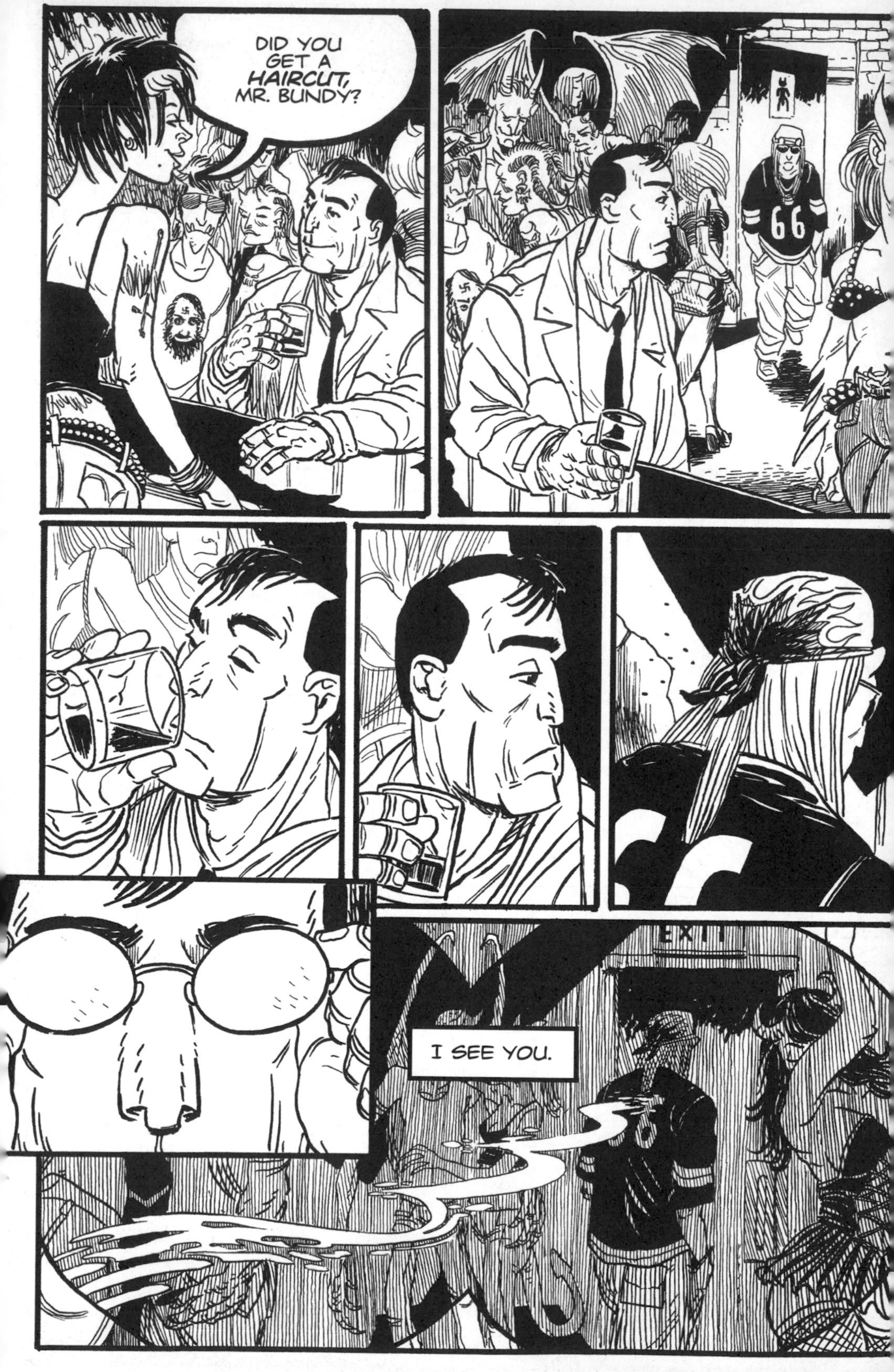
DID YOU GET A HAIRCUT, MR. BUNDY?
66
EXIT
I SEE YOU.

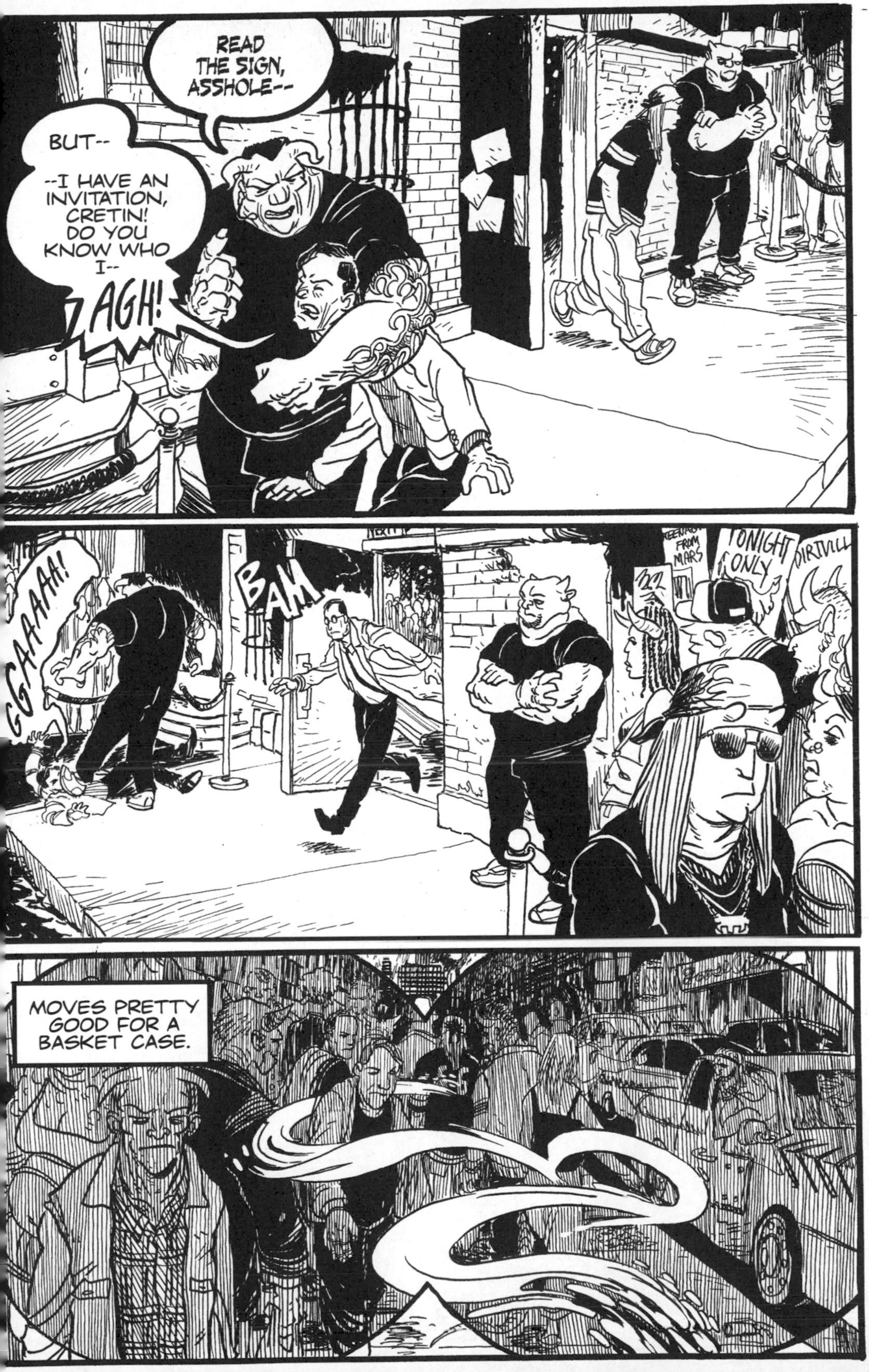
READ THE SIGN, ASSHOLE--
BUT--
--I HAVE AN INVITATION, CRETIN! DO YOU KNOW WHO I--
AGH!
GGAAAAA!
BAM
TEENAGE FROM MARS
TONIGHT ONLY
MOVES PRETTY GOOD FOR A BASKET CASE.

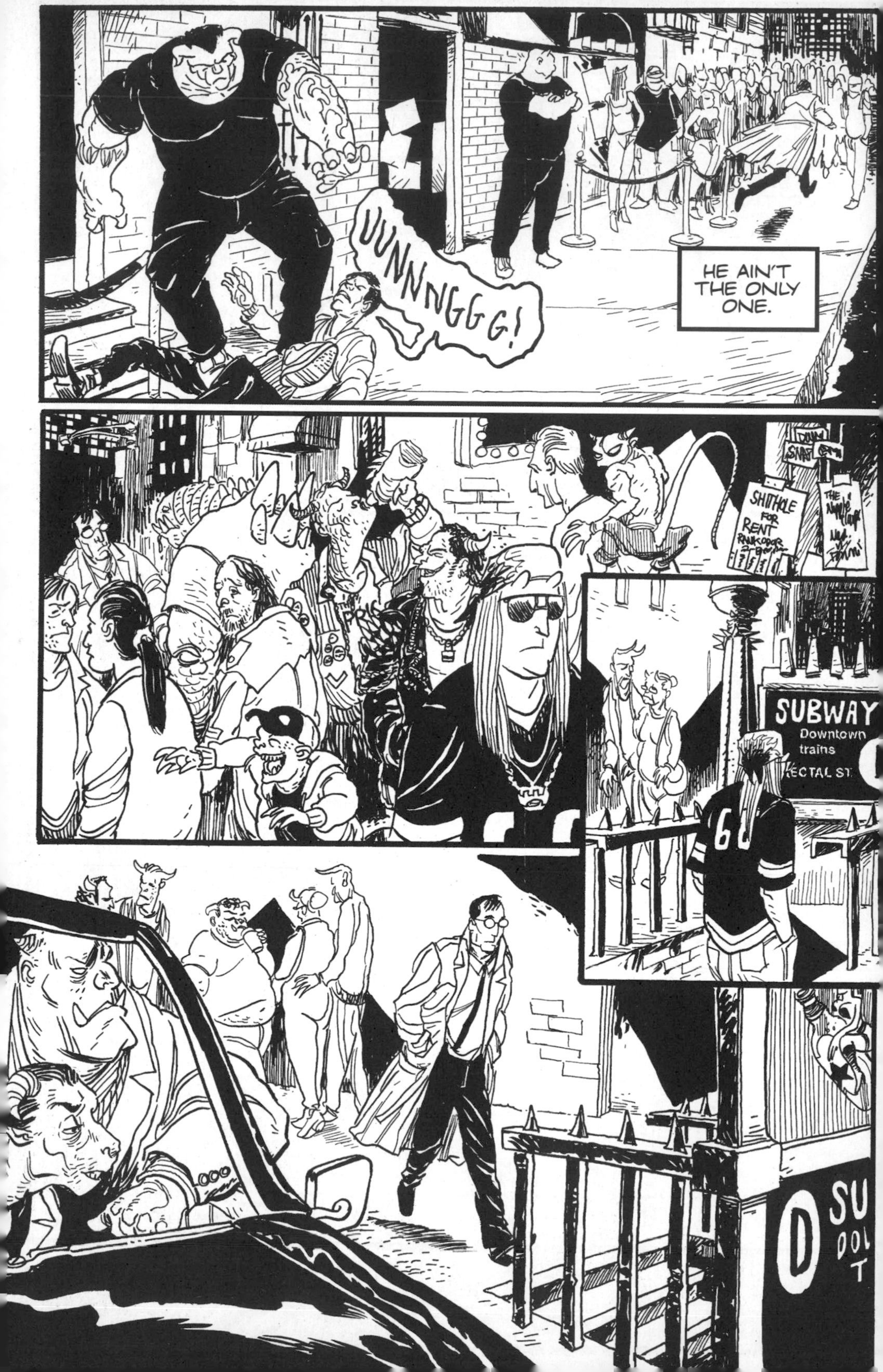
UUNNNGGGG!
HE AIN'T THE ONLY ONE.
SHITHOLE FOR RENT
SUBWAY
Downtown
trains

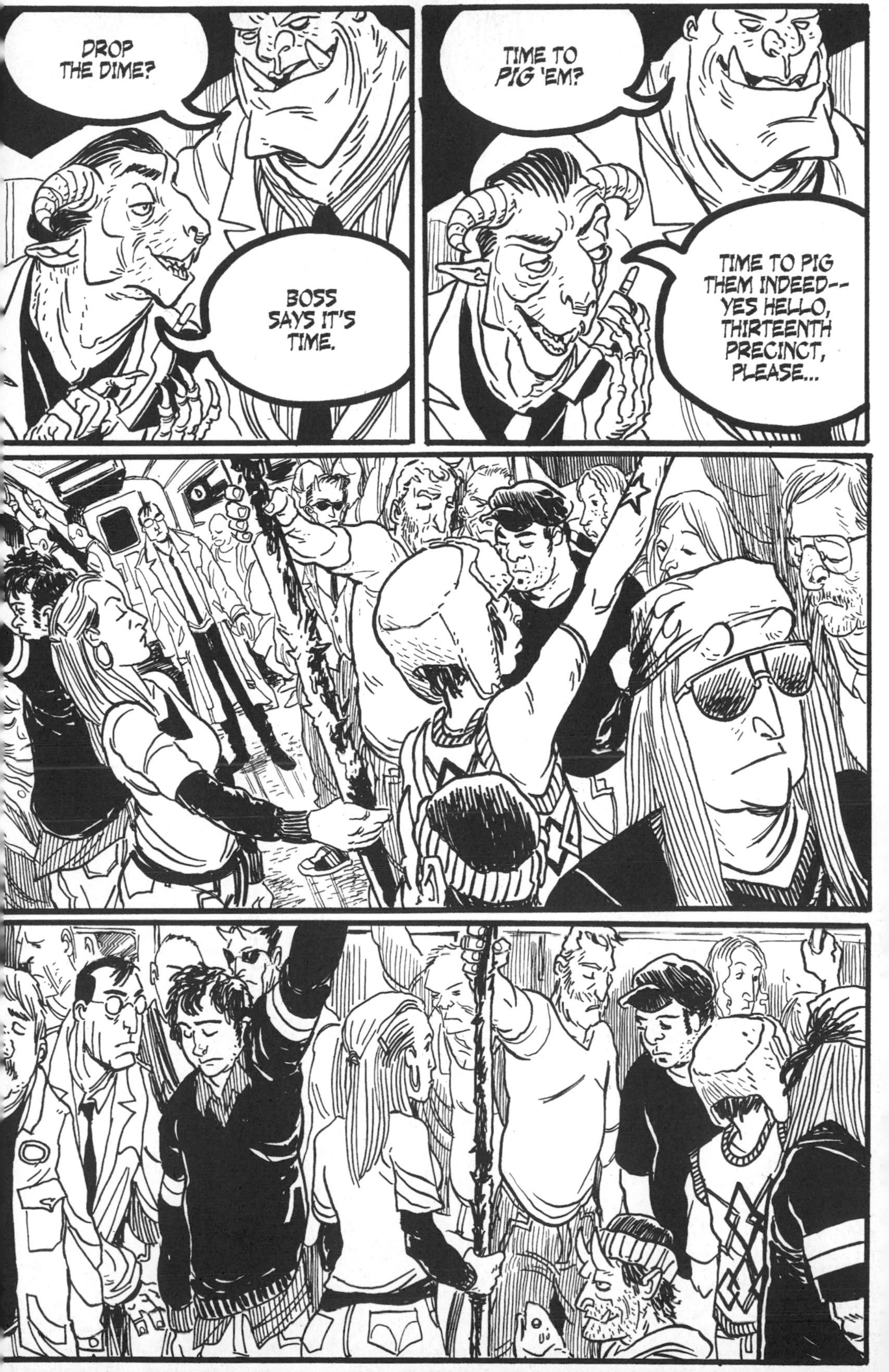
DROP THE DIME?
BOSS SAYS IT'S TIME.
TIME TO *PIG* 'EM?
TIME TO PIG THEM INDEED-- YES HELLO, THIRTEENTH PRECINCT, PLEASE...

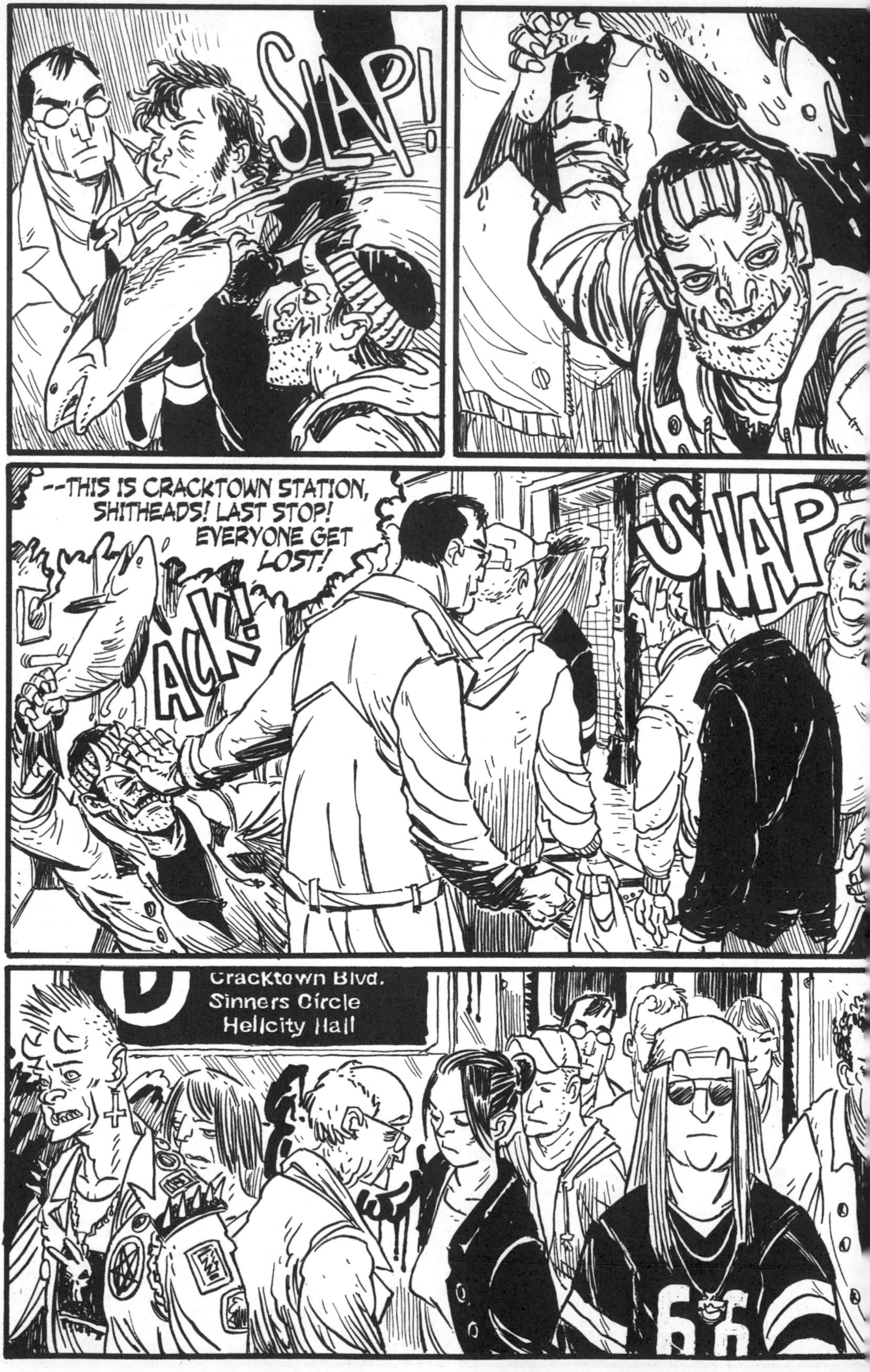

SLAP!
--THIS IS CRACKTOWN STATION, SHITHEADS! LAST STOP! EVERYONE GET LOST!
ACK!
SNAP
Cracktown Blvd.
Sinners Circle
Hellcity Hall

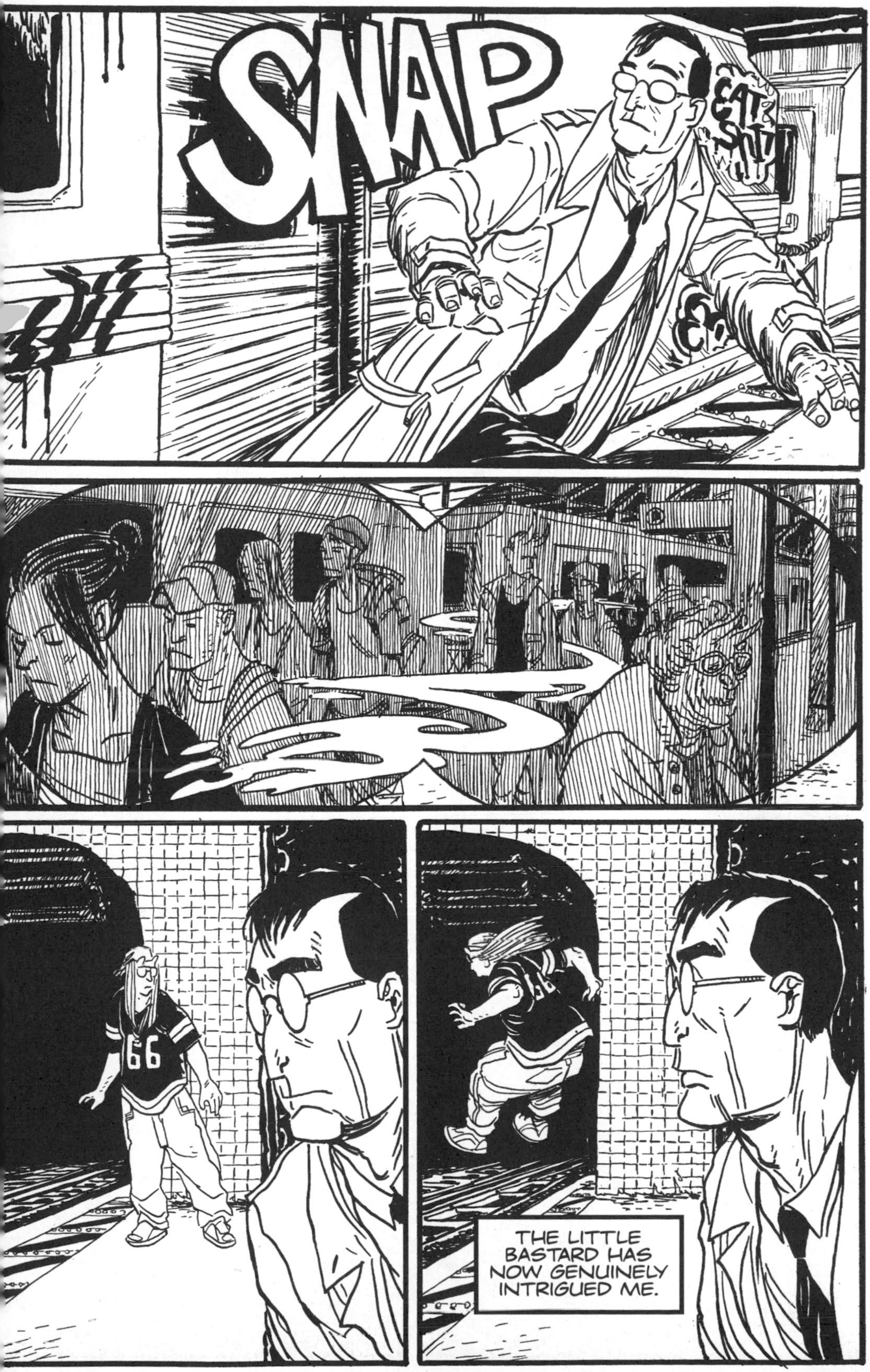
SNAP
EAT SHIT
THE LITTLE BASTARD HAS NOW GENUINELY INTRIGUED ME.

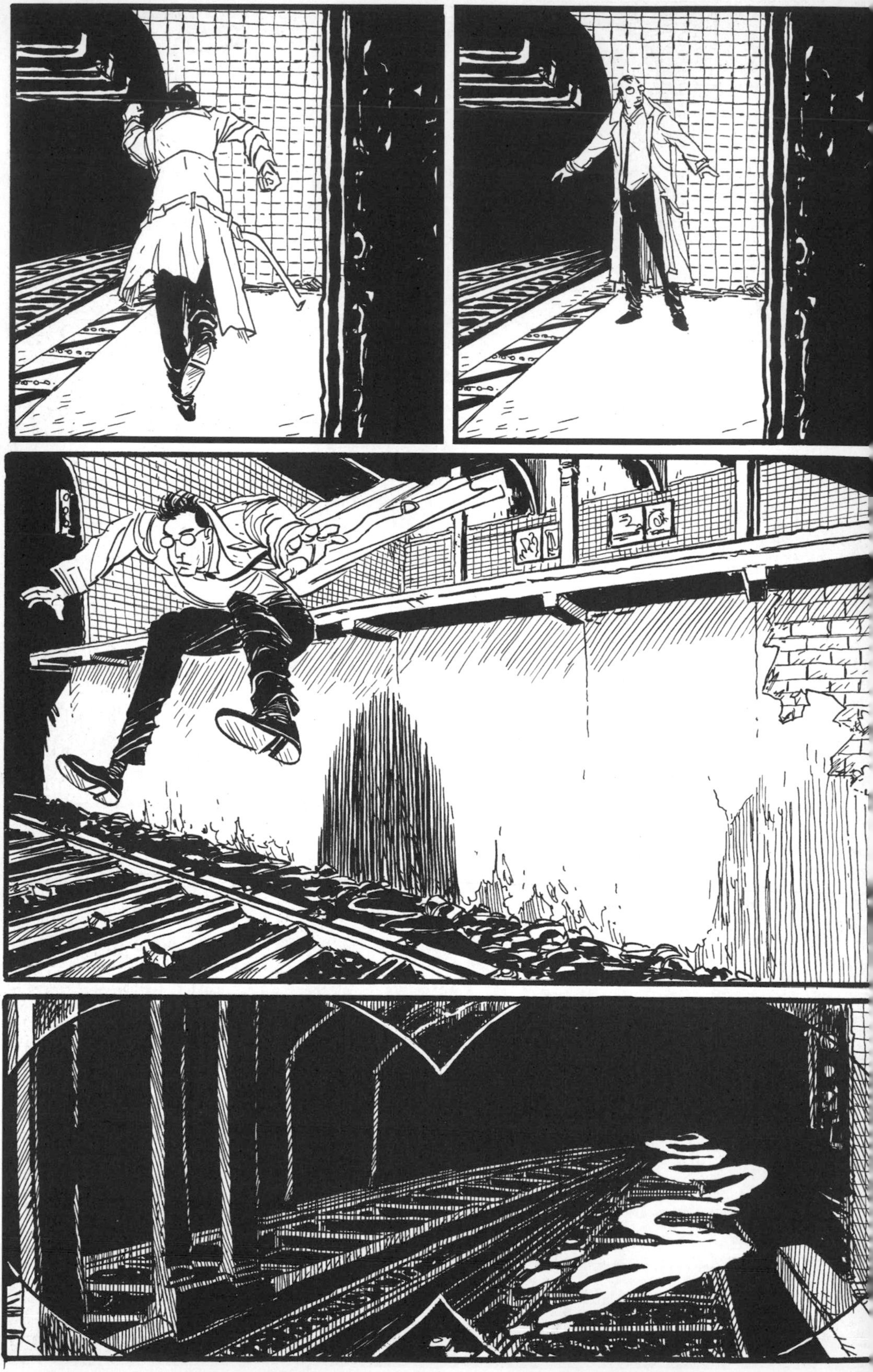

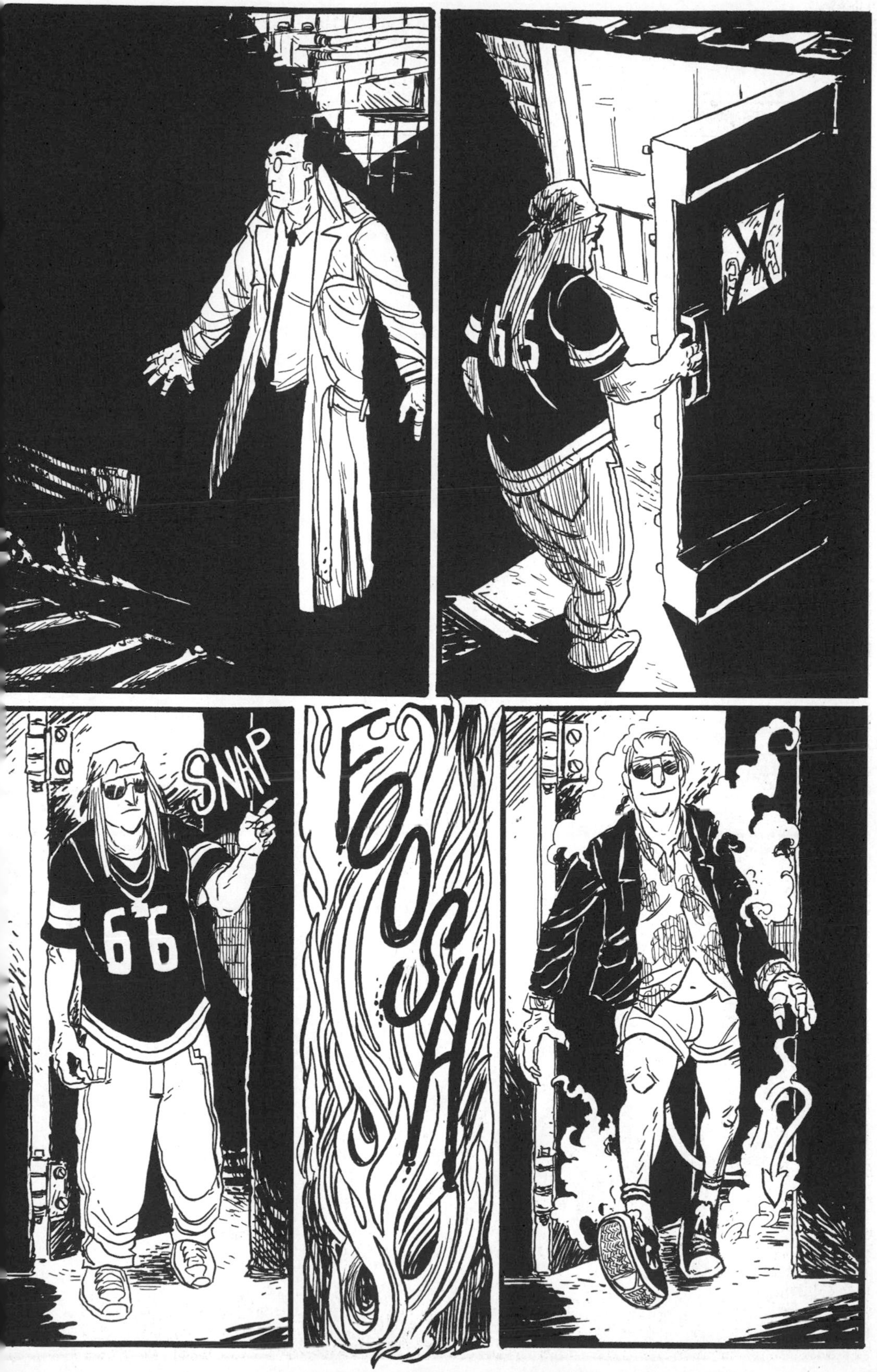
SNAP
FOOSH

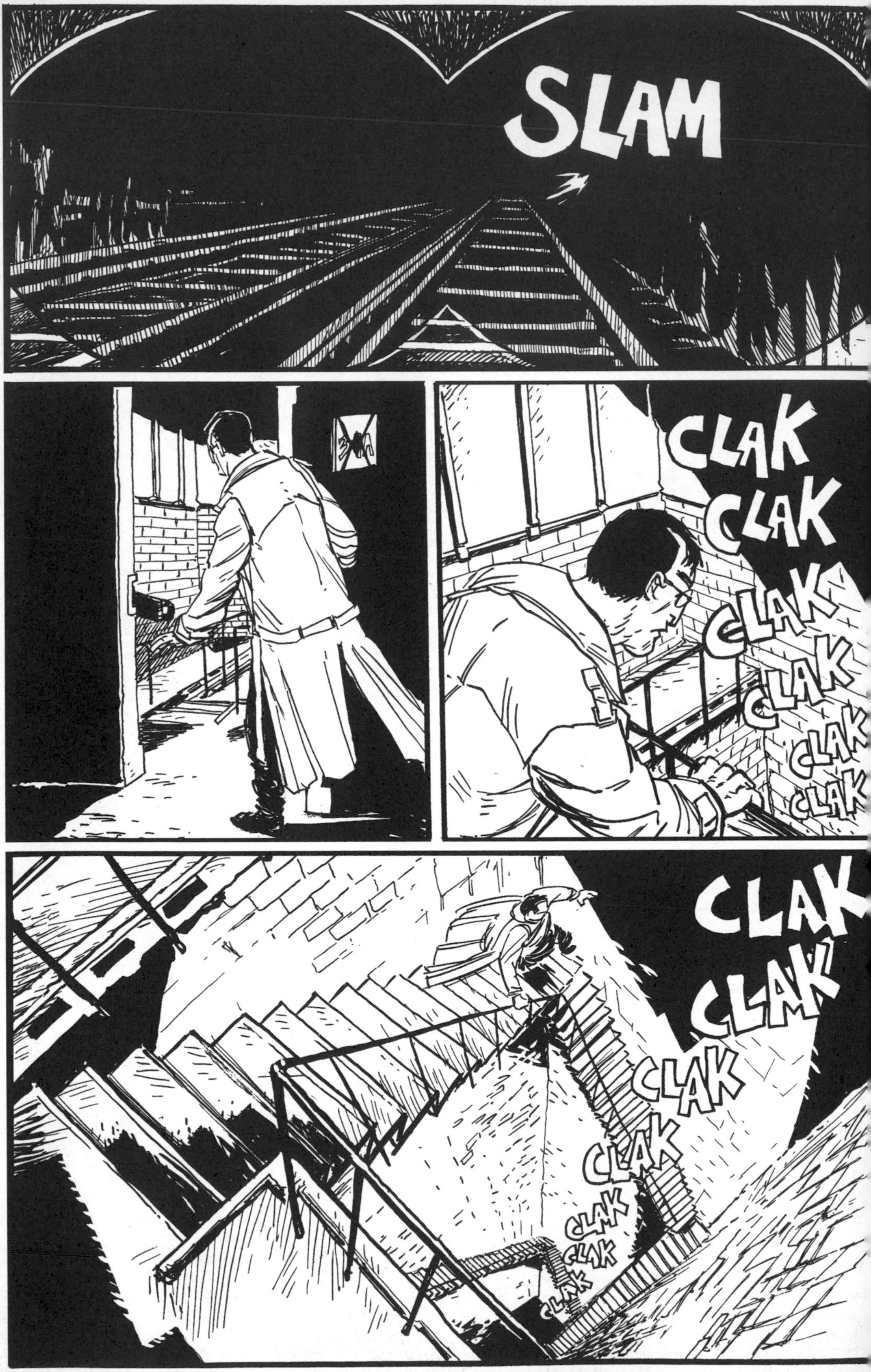
SLAM
CLAK
CLAK
CLAK
CLAK
CLAK
CLAK
CLAK
CLAK
CLAK
CLAK
CLAK
CLAK
CLAK

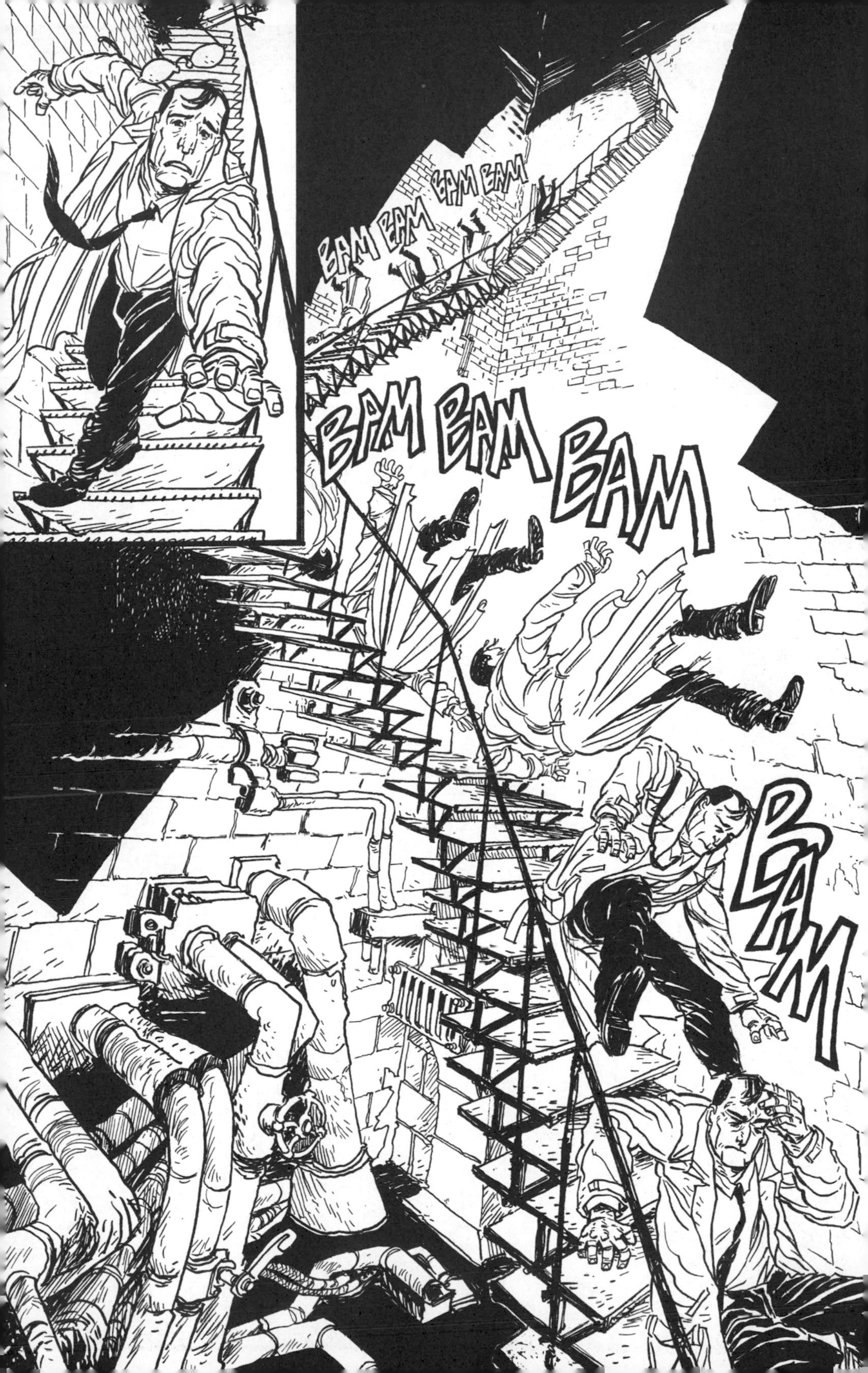
BAM BAM BAM BAM
BAM BAM BAM
BAM

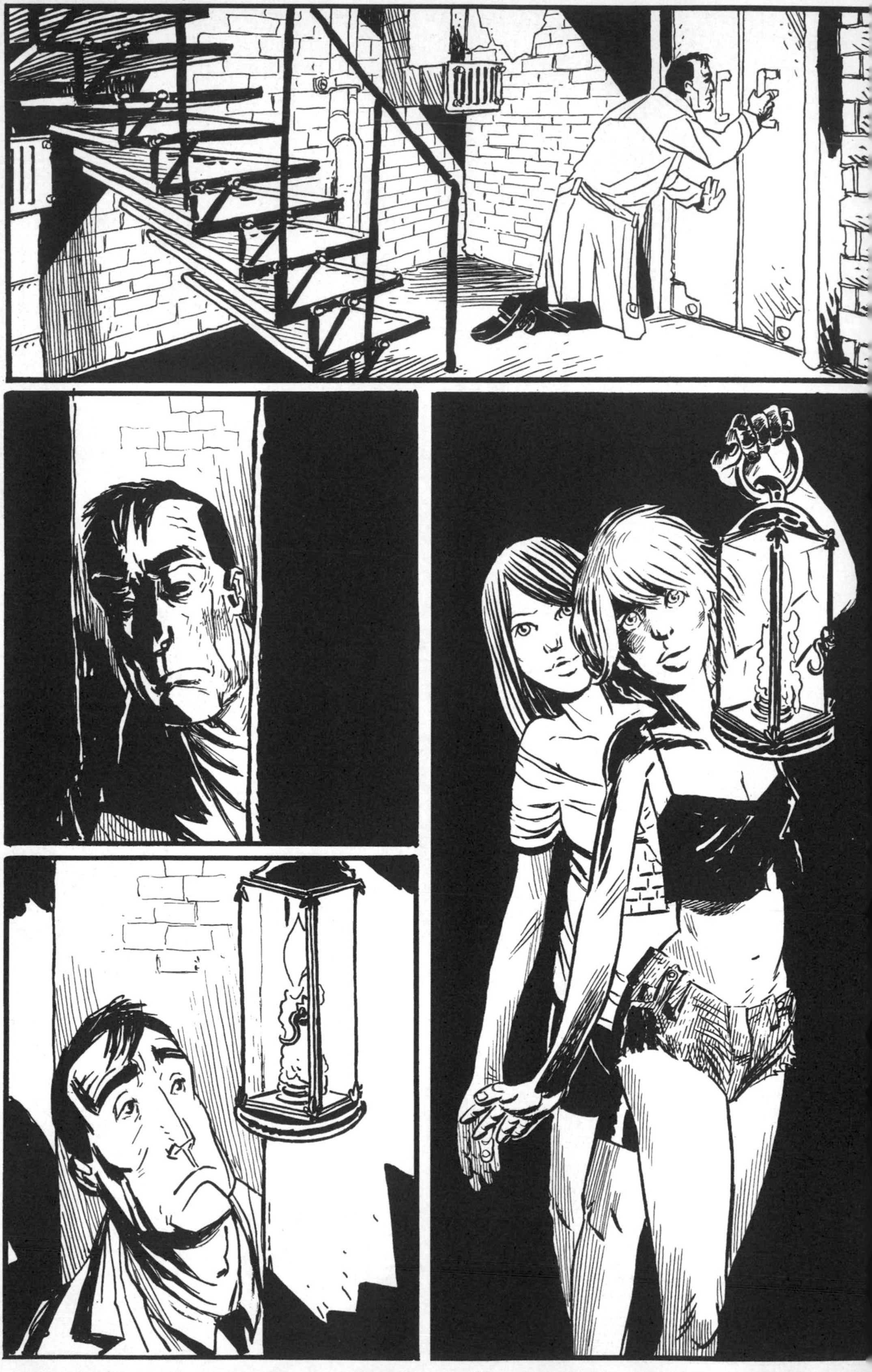

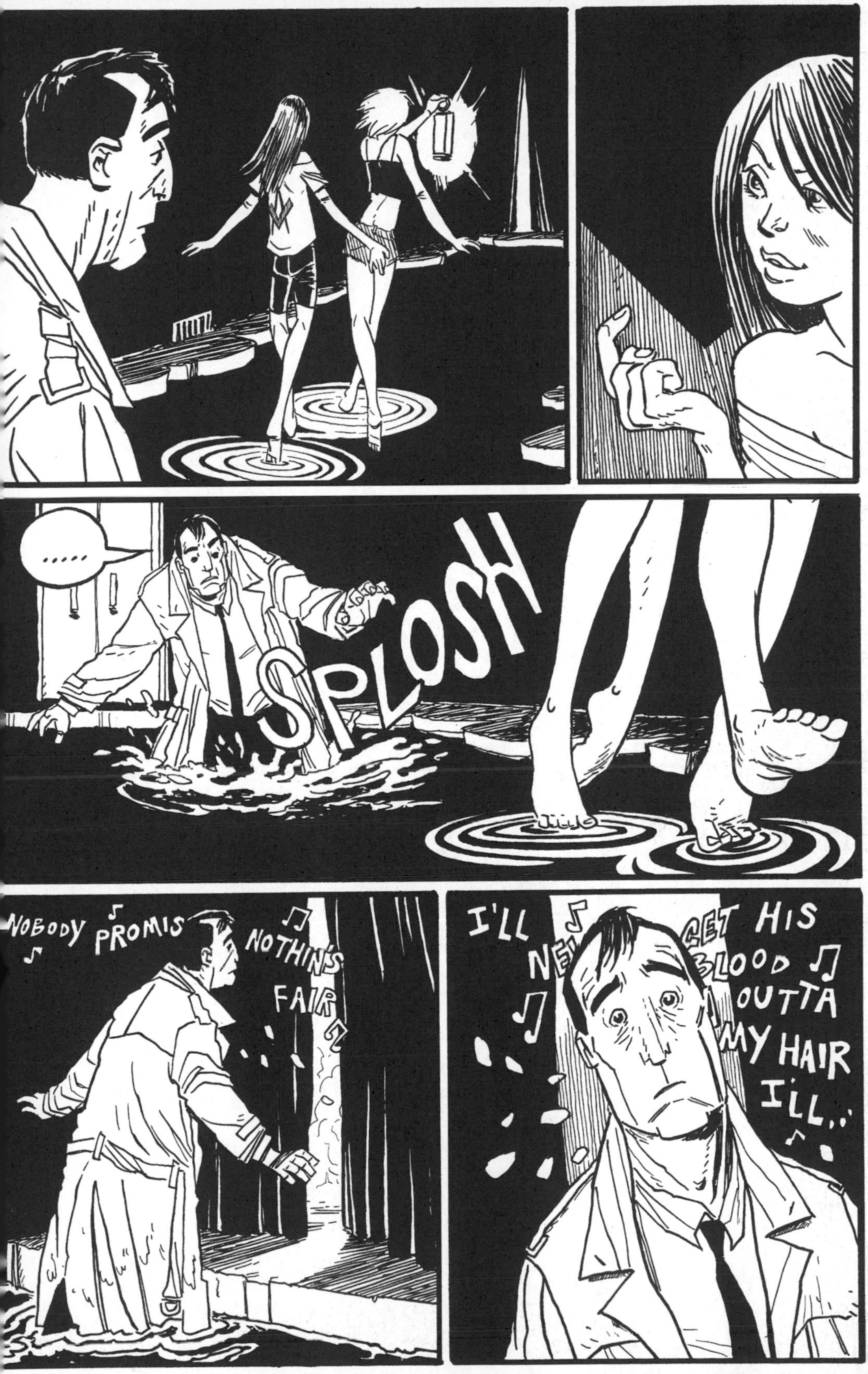
.....
SPLOSH
NOBODY PROMIS NOTHIN'S FAIR
I'LL NE GET HIS BLOOD OUTTA MY HAIR I'LL..

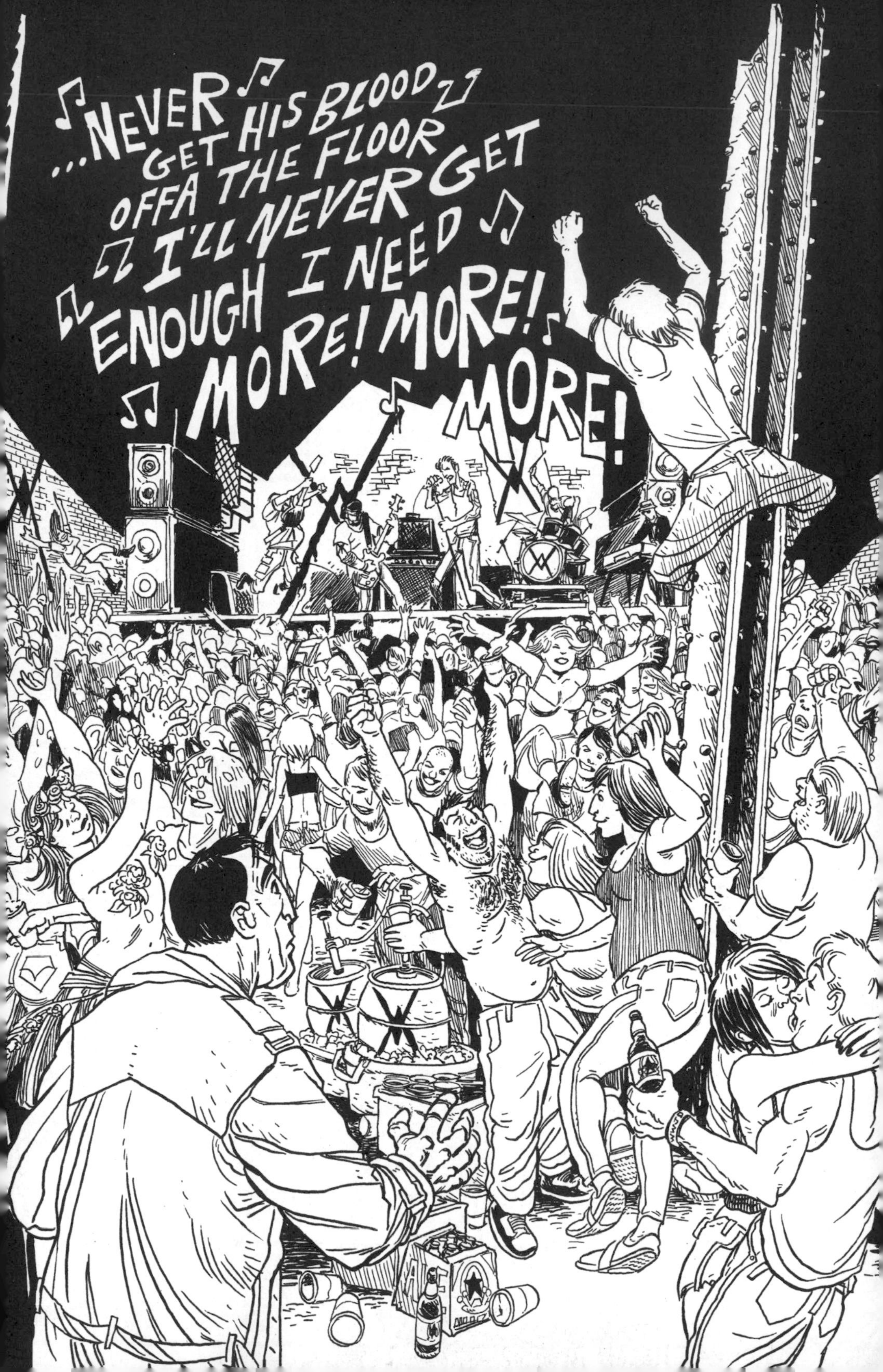
...NEVER GET HIS BLOOD
OFFA THE FLOOR
I'LL NEVER GET
ENOUGH I NEED
MORE! MORE!
MORE!

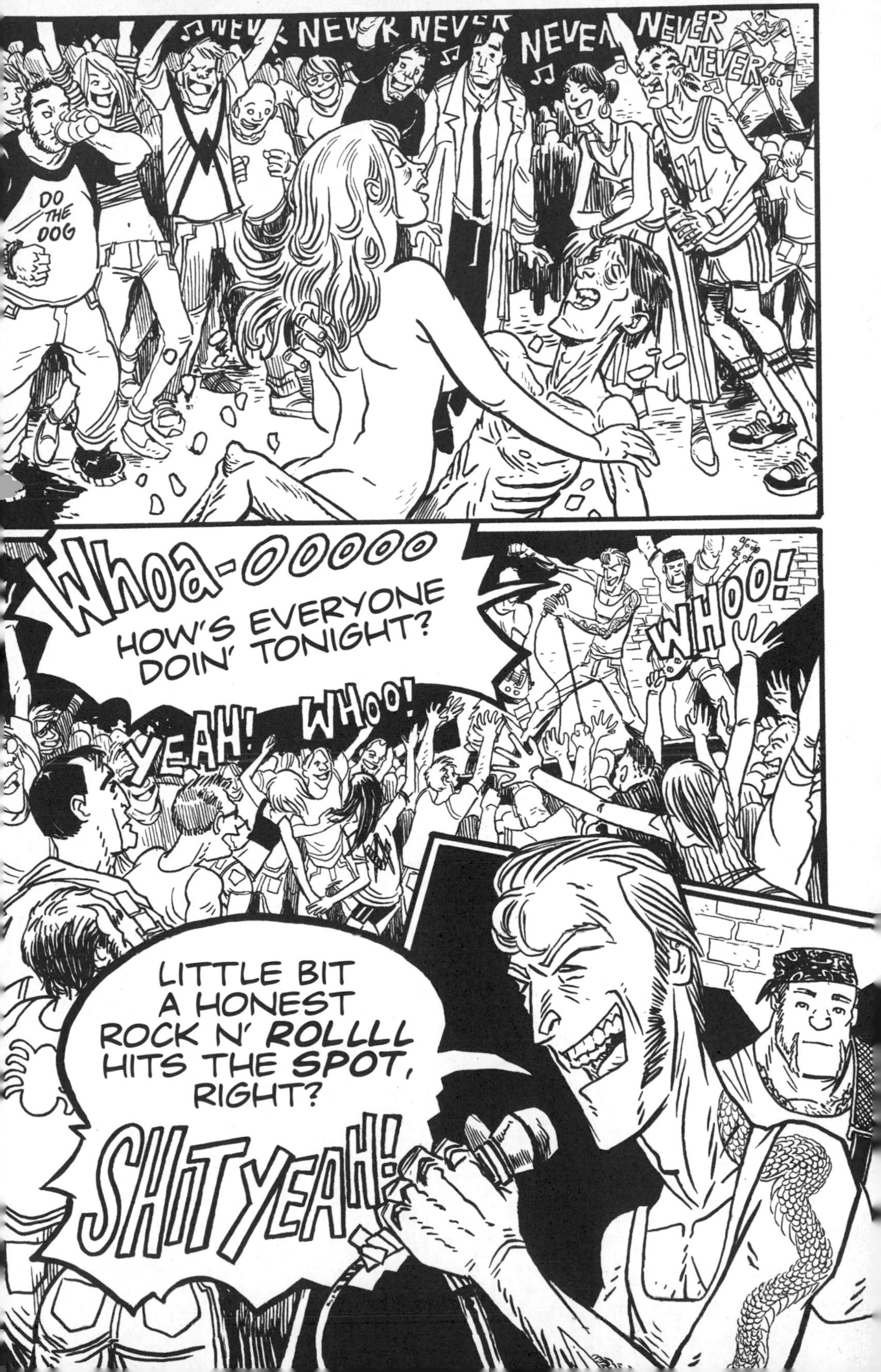
NEVER NEVER NEVER NEVER NEVER NEVER NEVER...
DO THE DOG
11
Whoa-OOOOO
HOW'S EVERYONE DOIN' TONIGHT?
WHOO!
YEAH! WHOO!
LITTLE BIT A HONEST ROCK N' ROLLLL HITS THE SPOT, RIGHT?
SHIT YEAH!

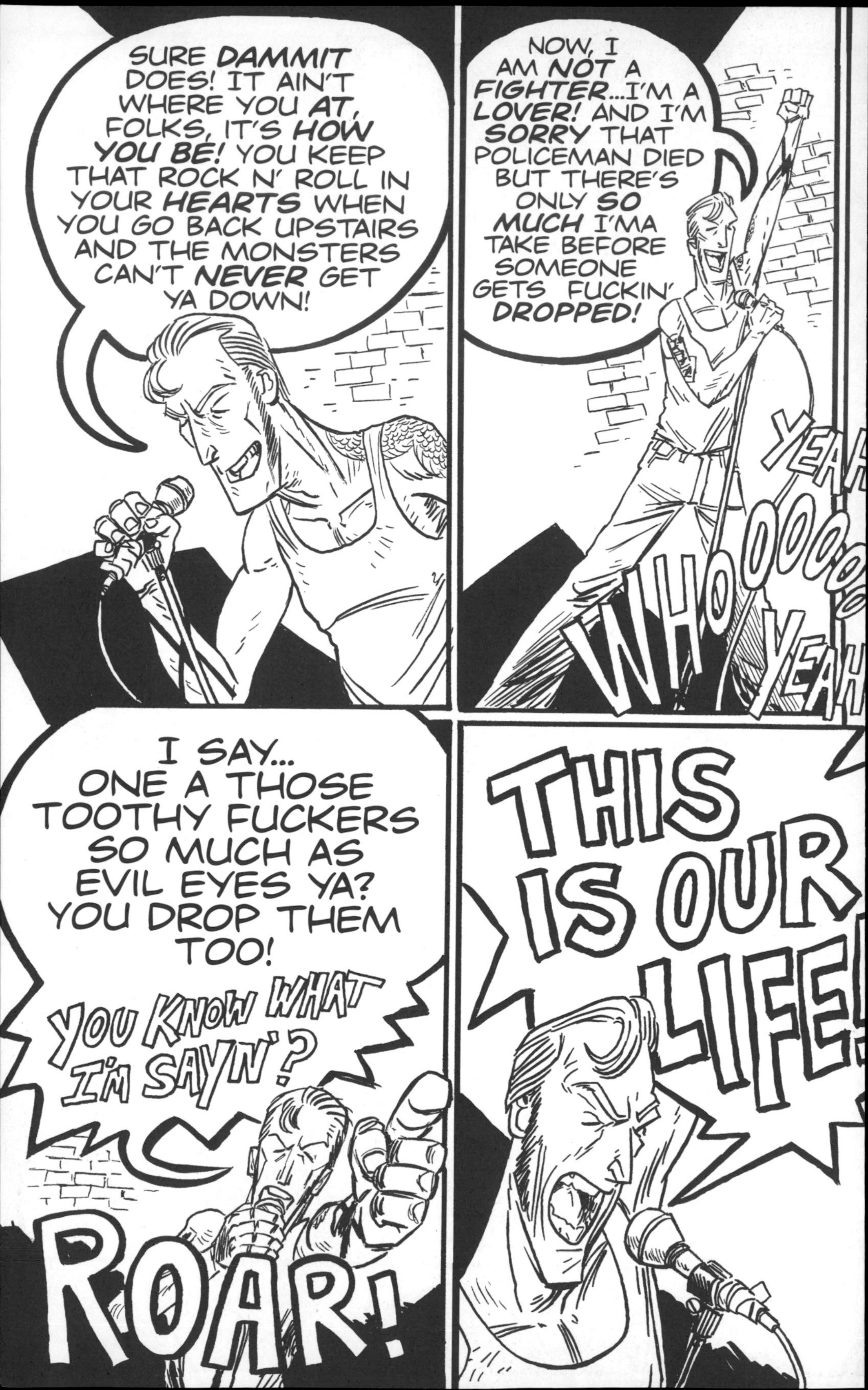
SURE DAMMIT DOES! IT AIN'T WHERE YOU AT, FOLKS, IT'S HOW YOU BE! YOU KEEP THAT ROCK N' ROLL IN YOUR HEARTS WHEN YOU GO BACK UPSTAIRS AND THE MONSTERS CAN'T NEVER GET YA DOWN!
NOW, I AM NOT A FIGHTER...I'M A LOVER! AND I'M SORRY THAT POLICEMAN DIED BUT THERE'S ONLY SO MUCH I'MA TAKE BEFORE SOMEONE GETS FUCKIN' DROPPED!
YEAH
WHOOOOOOO
YEAH
I SAY... ONE A THOSE TOOTHY FUCKERS SO MUCH AS EVIL EYES YA? YOU DROP THEM TOO!
YOU KNOW WHAT I'M SAYN'?
ROAR!
THIS IS OUR LIFE!

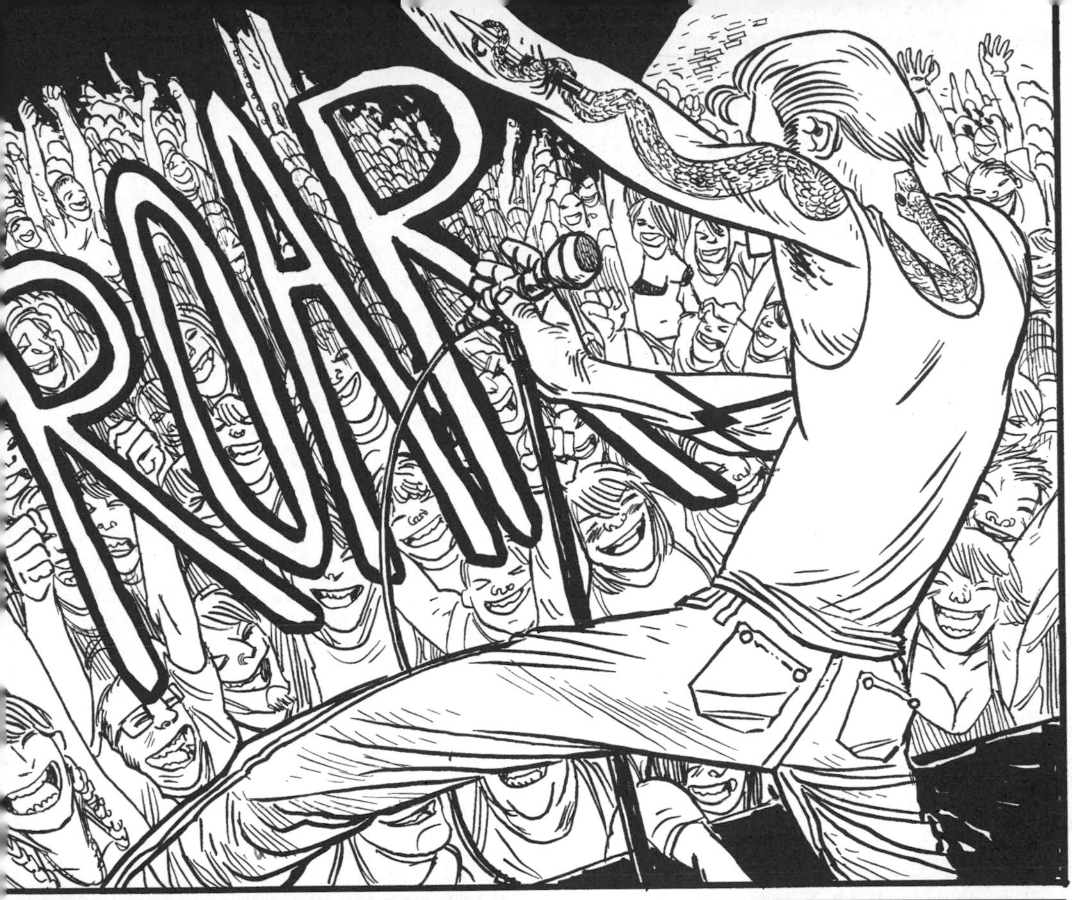
ROAR!

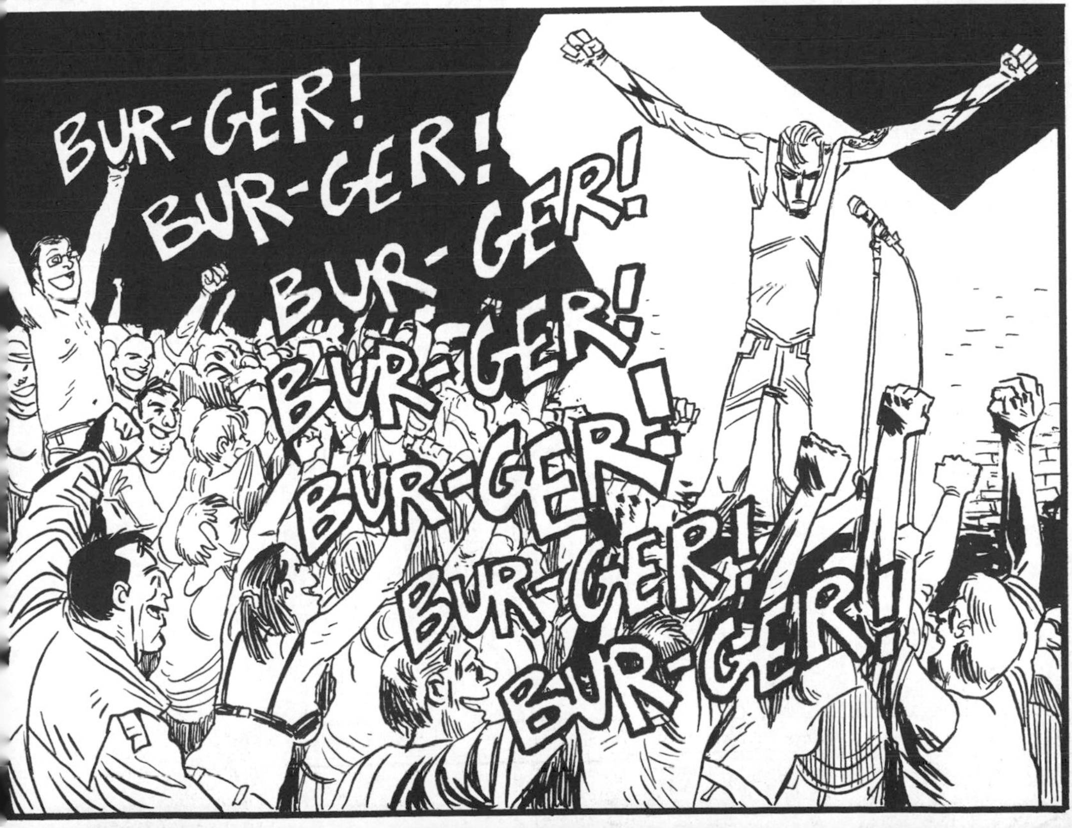
BUR-GER!
BUR-GER!
BUR-GER!
BUR-GER!
BUR-GER!
BUR-GER!
BUR-GER!

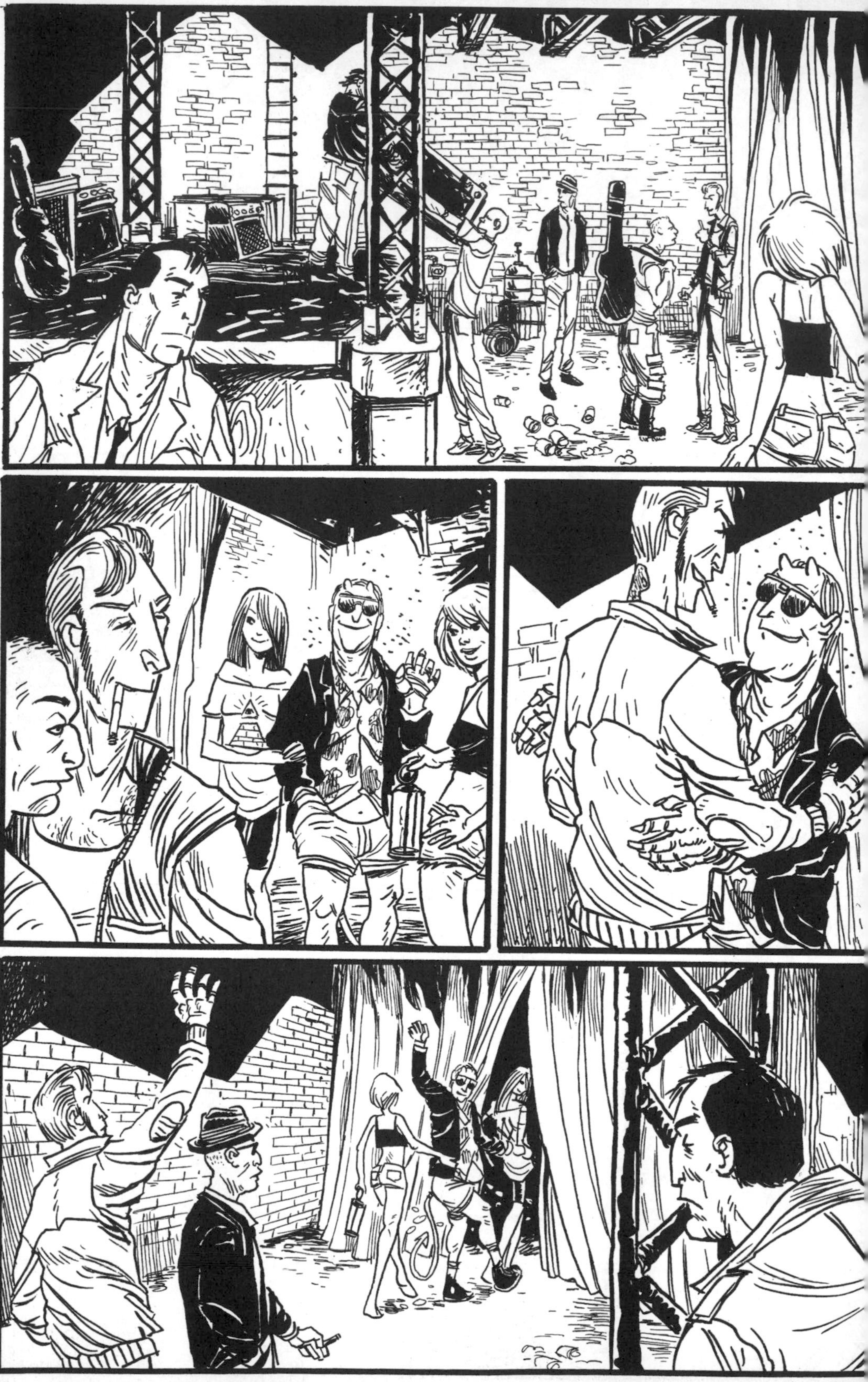

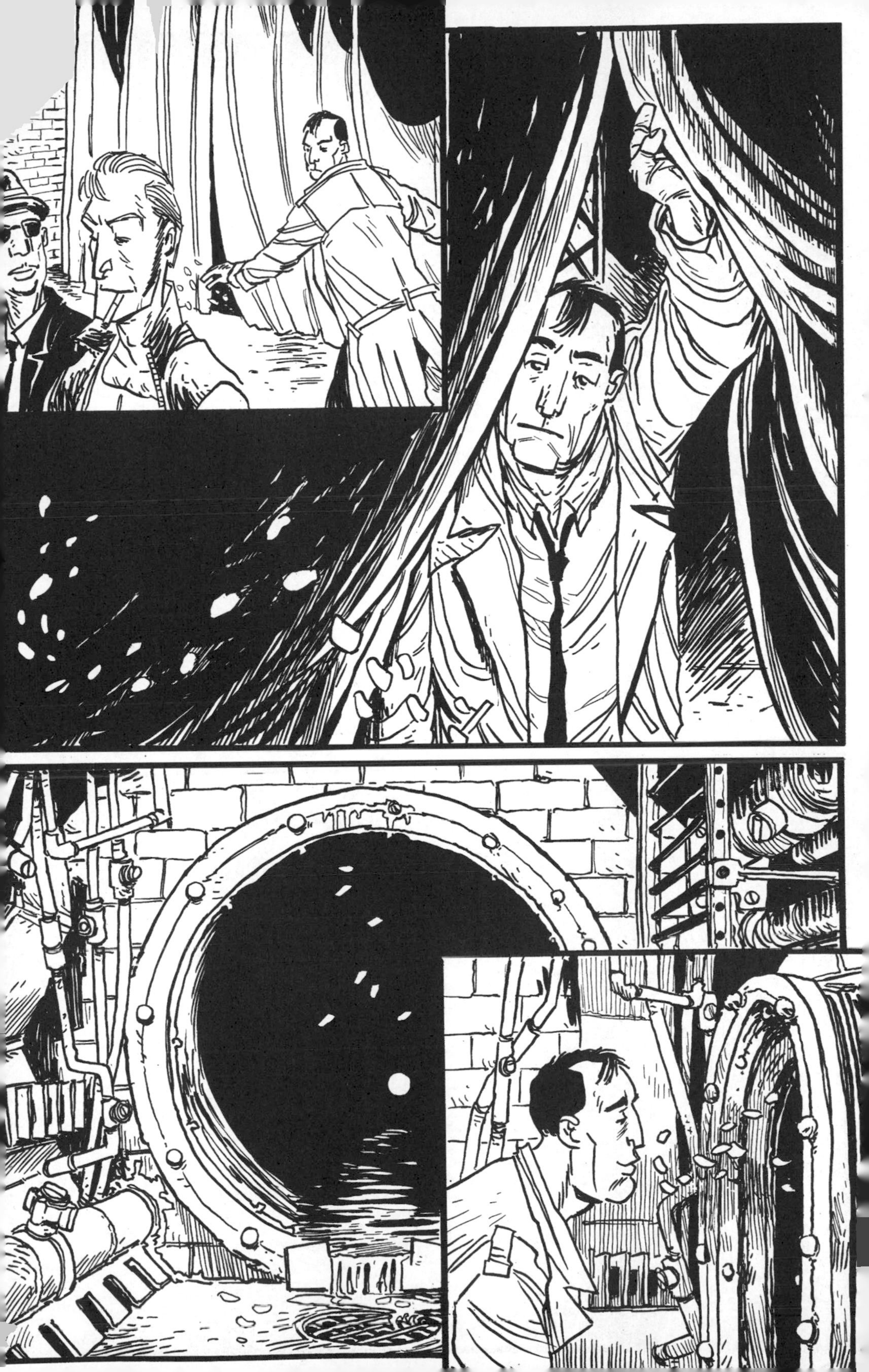

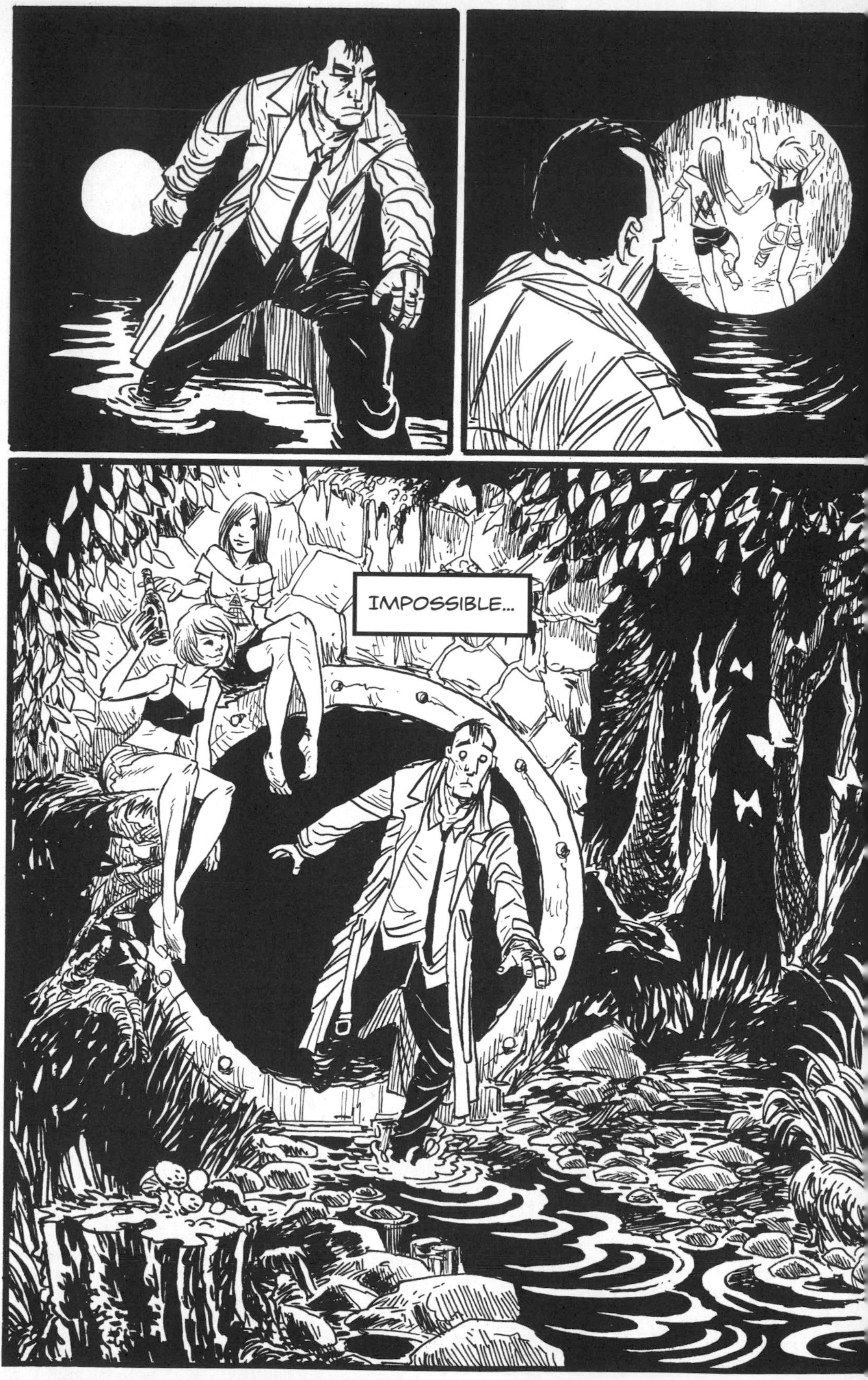
IMPOSSIBLE...

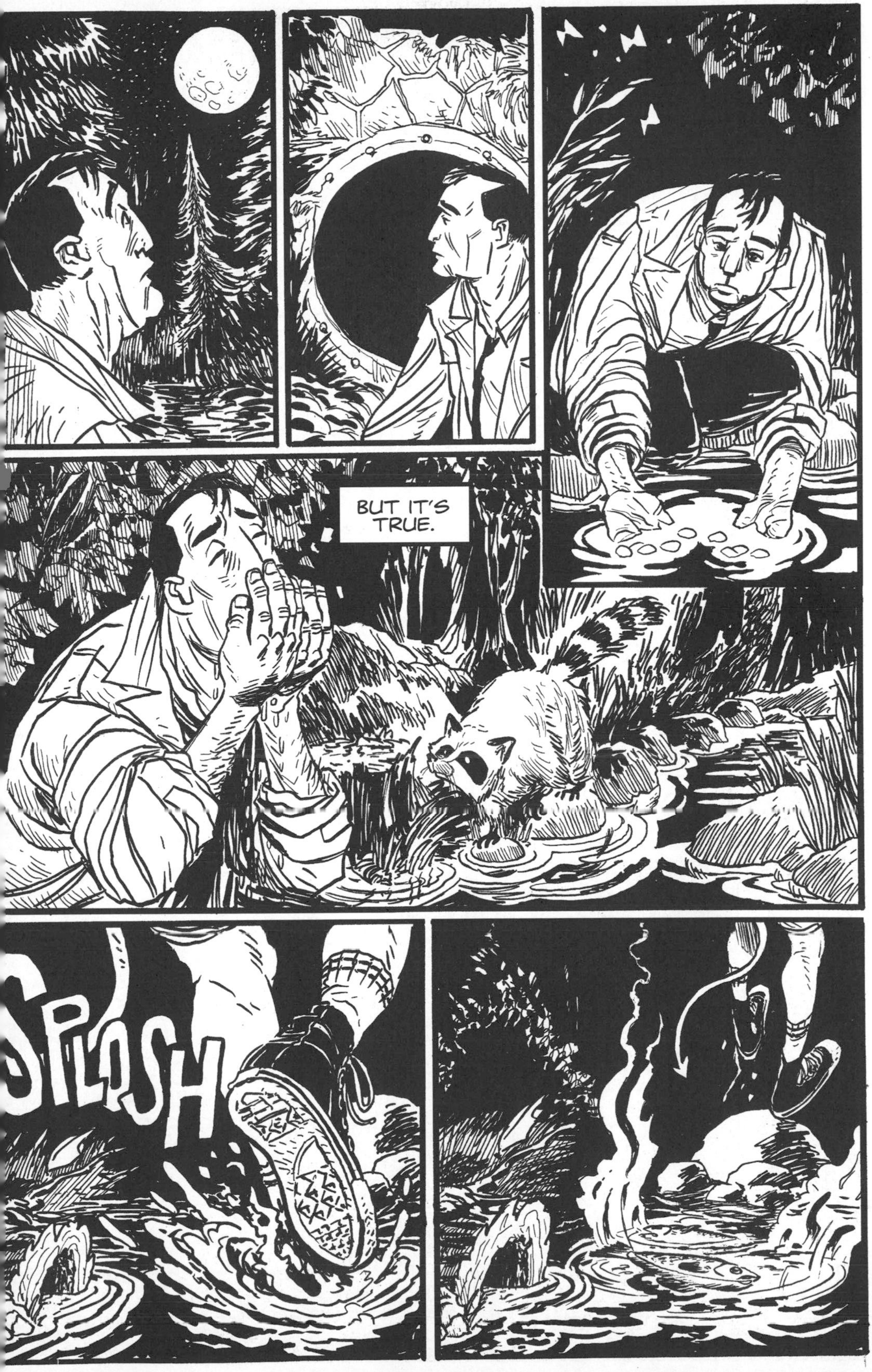
BUT IT'S TRUE.
SPLOSH

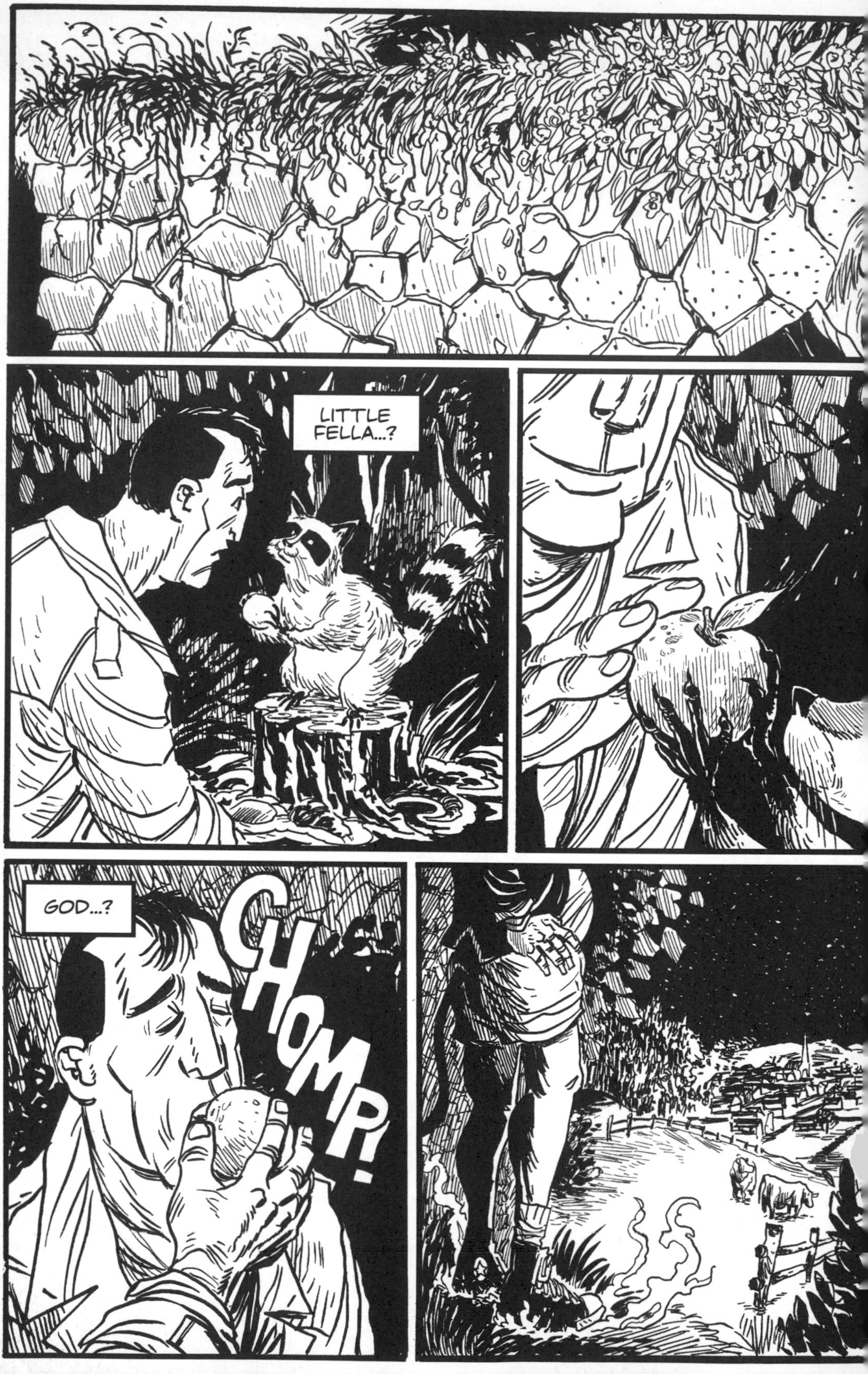
LITTLE FELLA...?
GOD...?
CHOMP!

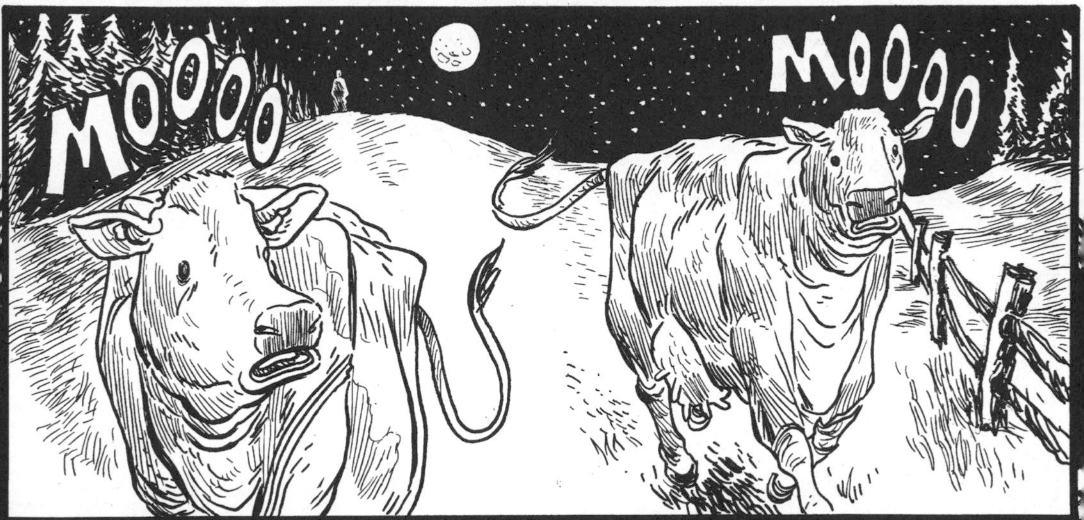
MOOOO
MOOOO

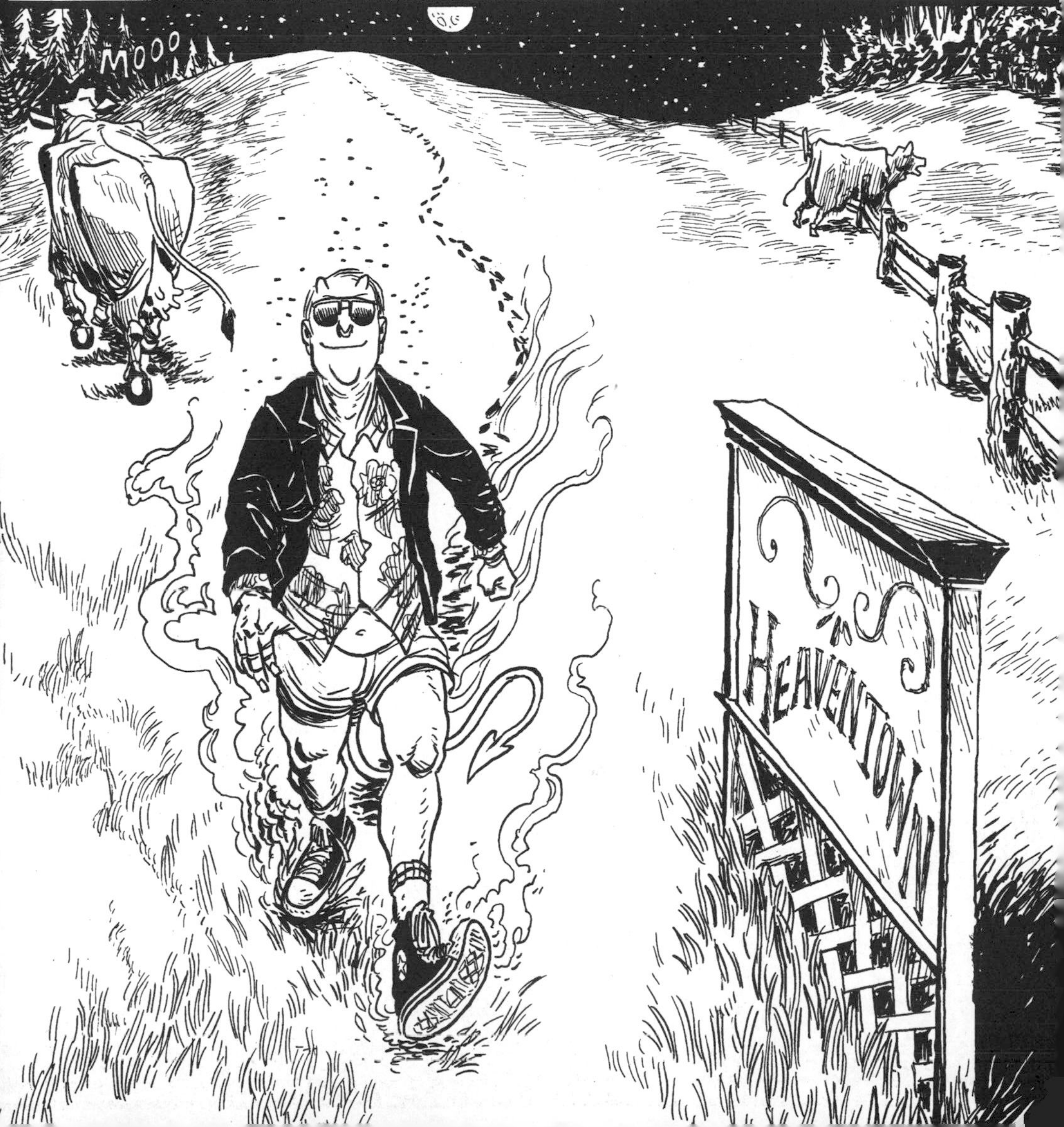
MOOO
HEAVENTOWN

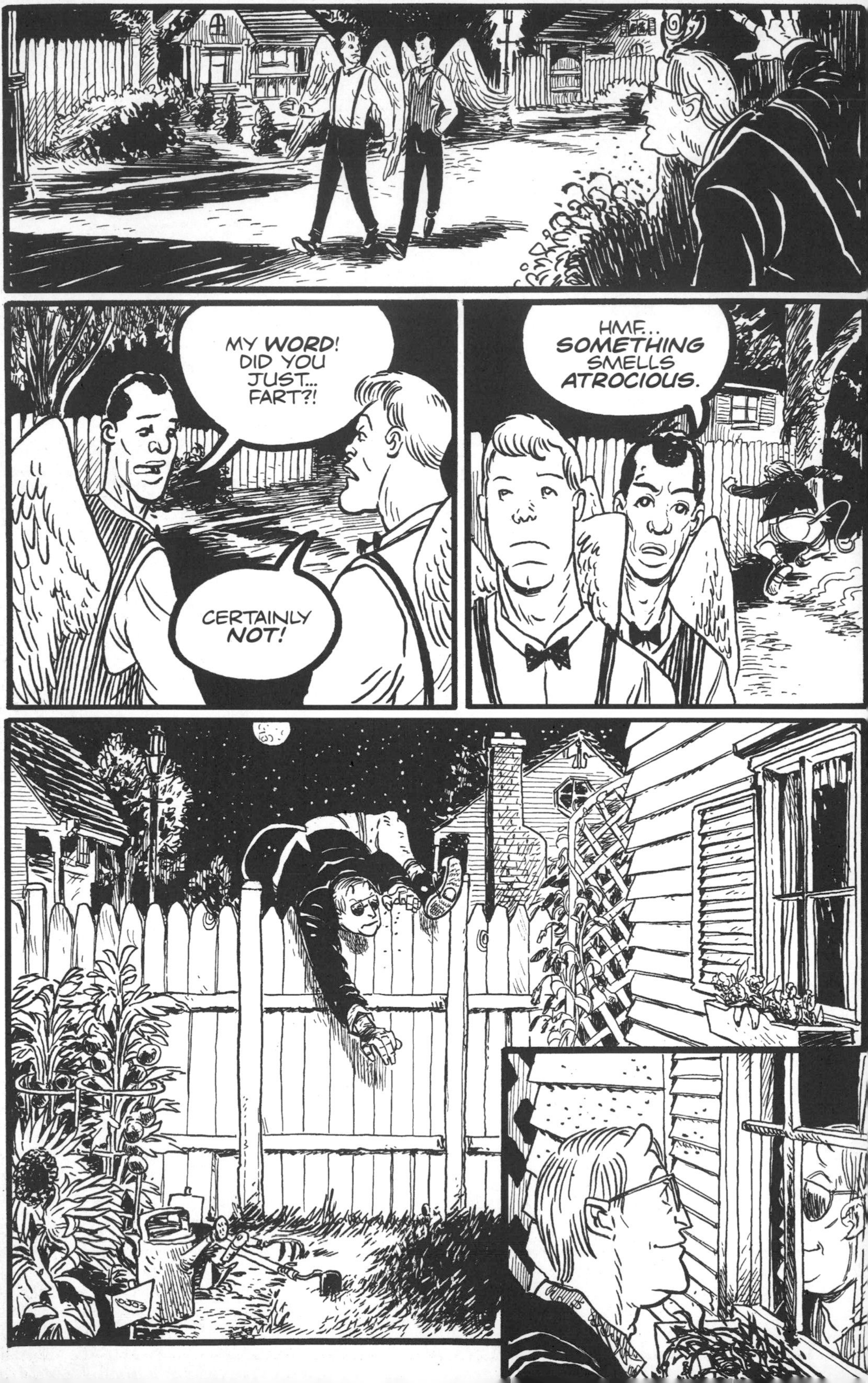

MY WORD! DID YOU JUST... FART?!
CERTAINLY NOT!
HMF... SOMETHING SMELLS ATROCIOUS.

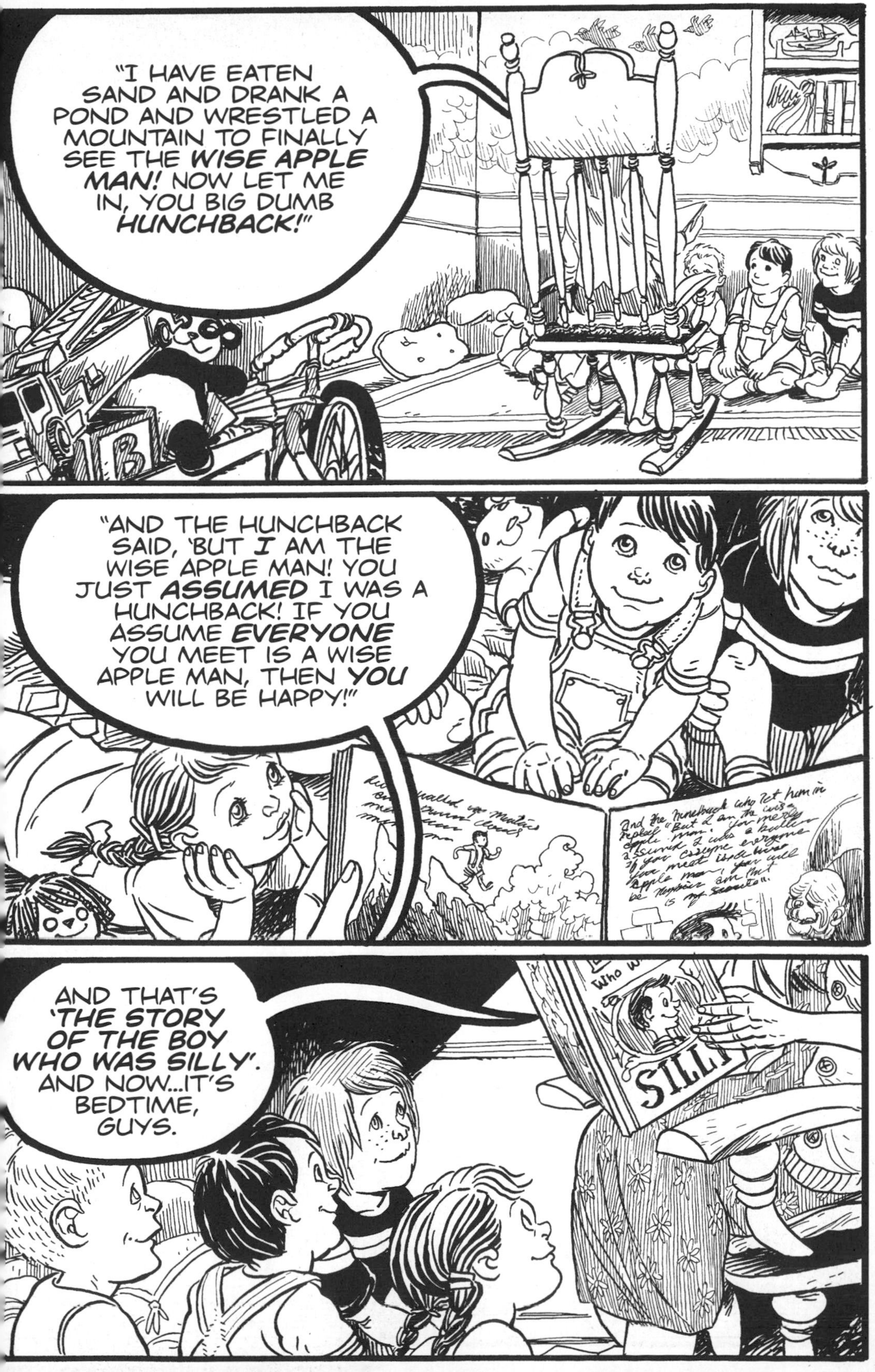
"I HAVE EATEN SAND AND DRANK A POND AND WRESTLED A MOUNTAIN TO FINALLY SEE THE WISE APPLE MAN! NOW LET ME IN, YOU BIG DUMB HUNCHBACK!"
"AND THE HUNCHBACK SAID, 'BUT I AM THE WISE APPLE MAN! YOU JUST ASSUMED I WAS A HUNCHBACK! IF YOU ASSUME EVERYONE YOU MEET IS A WISE APPLE MAN, THEN YOU WILL BE HAPPY!"
AND THAT'S 'THE STORY OF THE BOY WHO WAS SILLY'. AND NOW...IT'S BEDTIME, GUYS.
SILLY

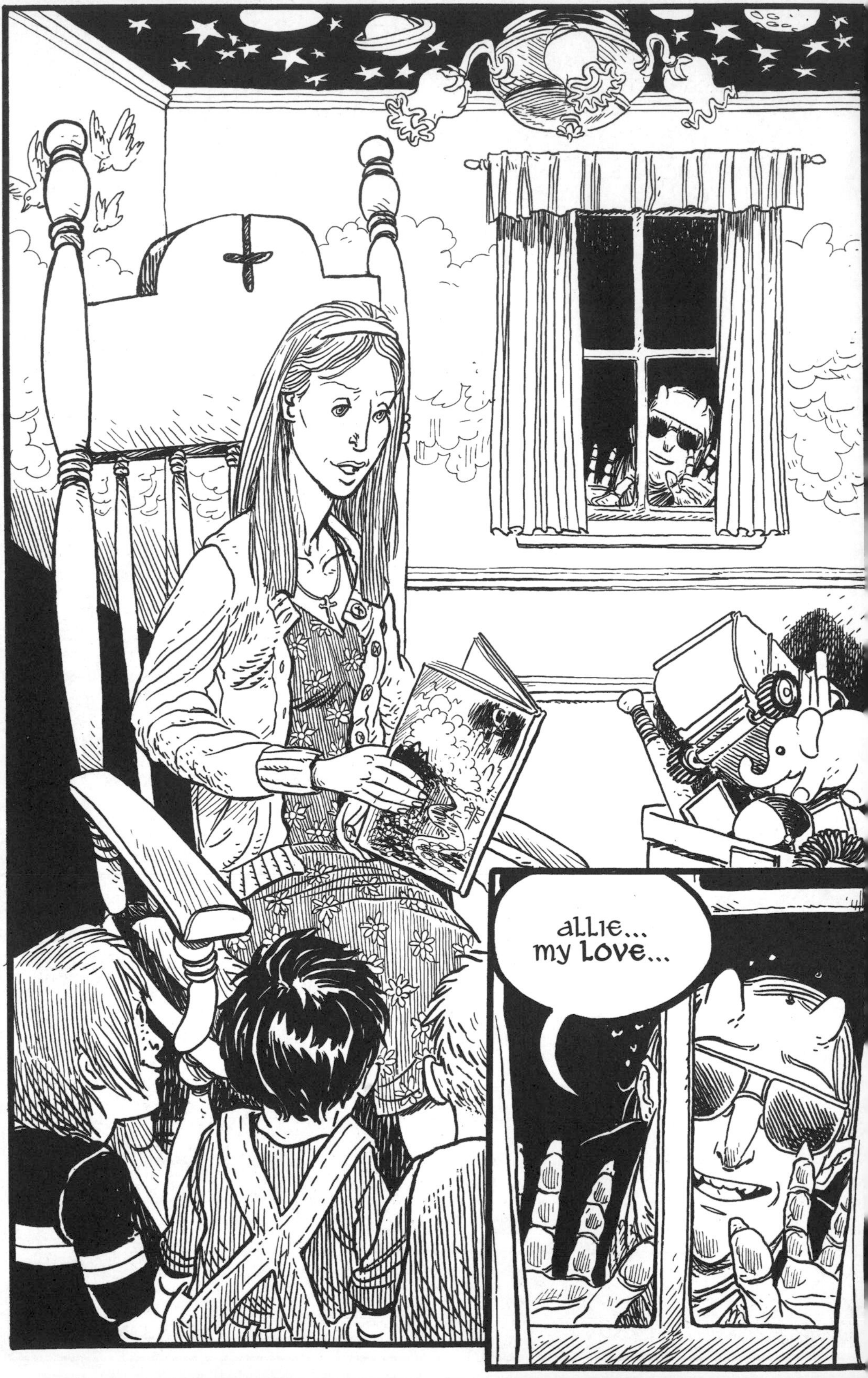
allie... my love...

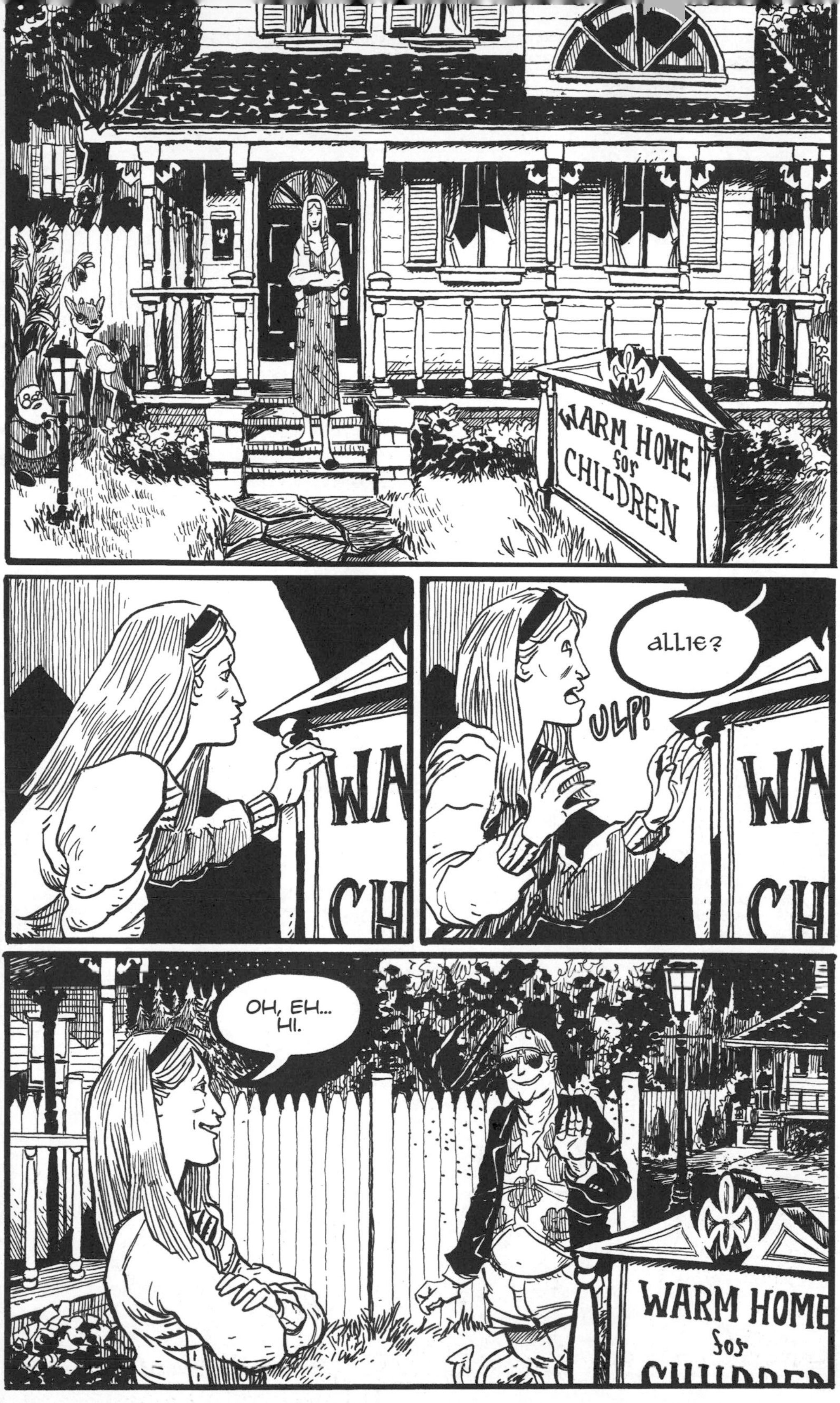
WARM HOME for CHILDREN
allie?
ULP!
OH, EH... HI.
WARM HOME for

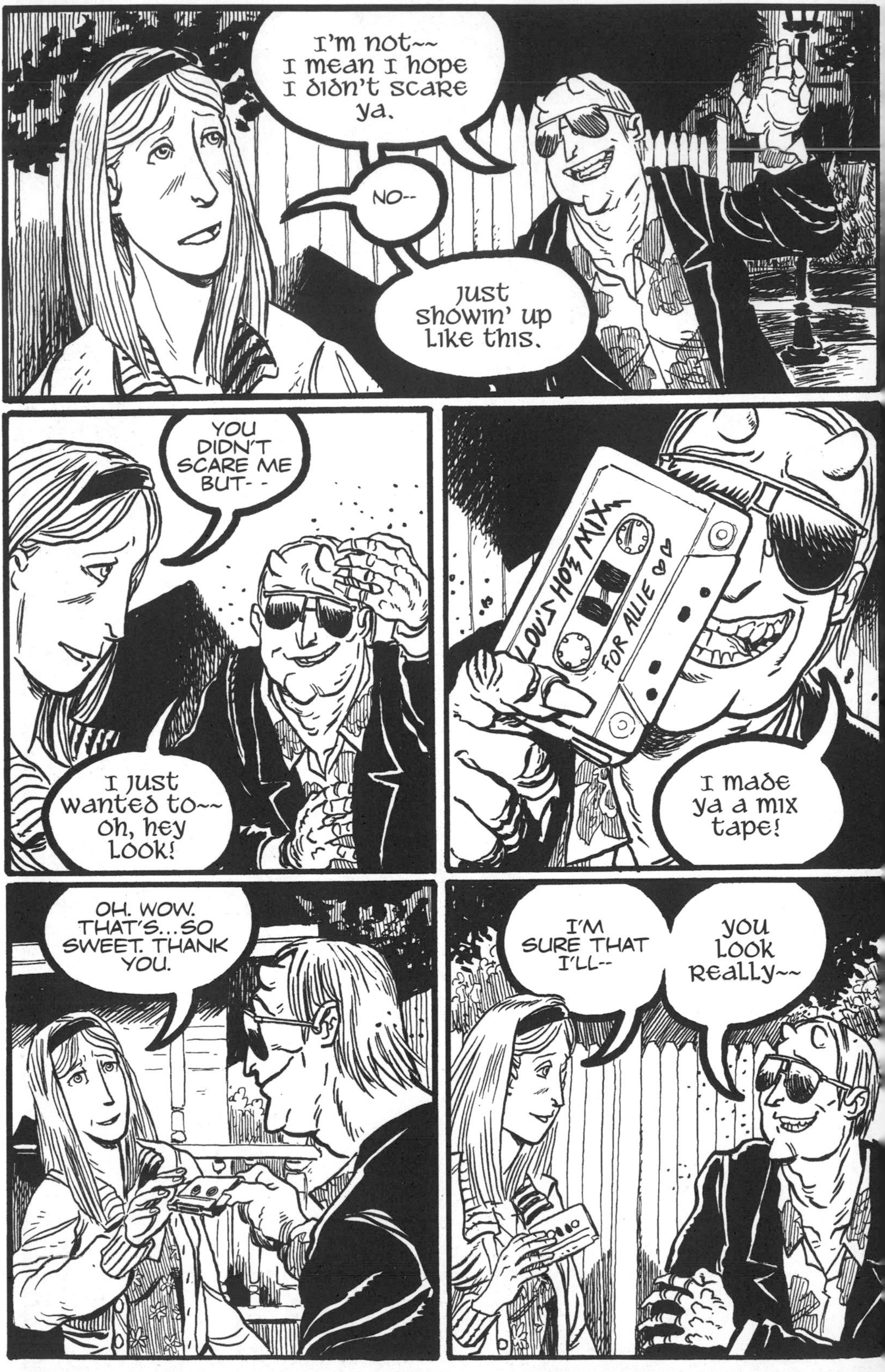
I'm not~~ I mean I hope I didn't scare ya.
NO--
Just showin' up like this.
YOU DIDN'T SCARE ME BUT- -
I just wanted to~~ oh, hey look!
LOU'S HOT MIX
FOR ALLIE
I made ya a mix tape!
OH. WOW. THAT'S...SO SWEET. THANK YOU.
I'M SURE THAT I'LL--
you look Really~~

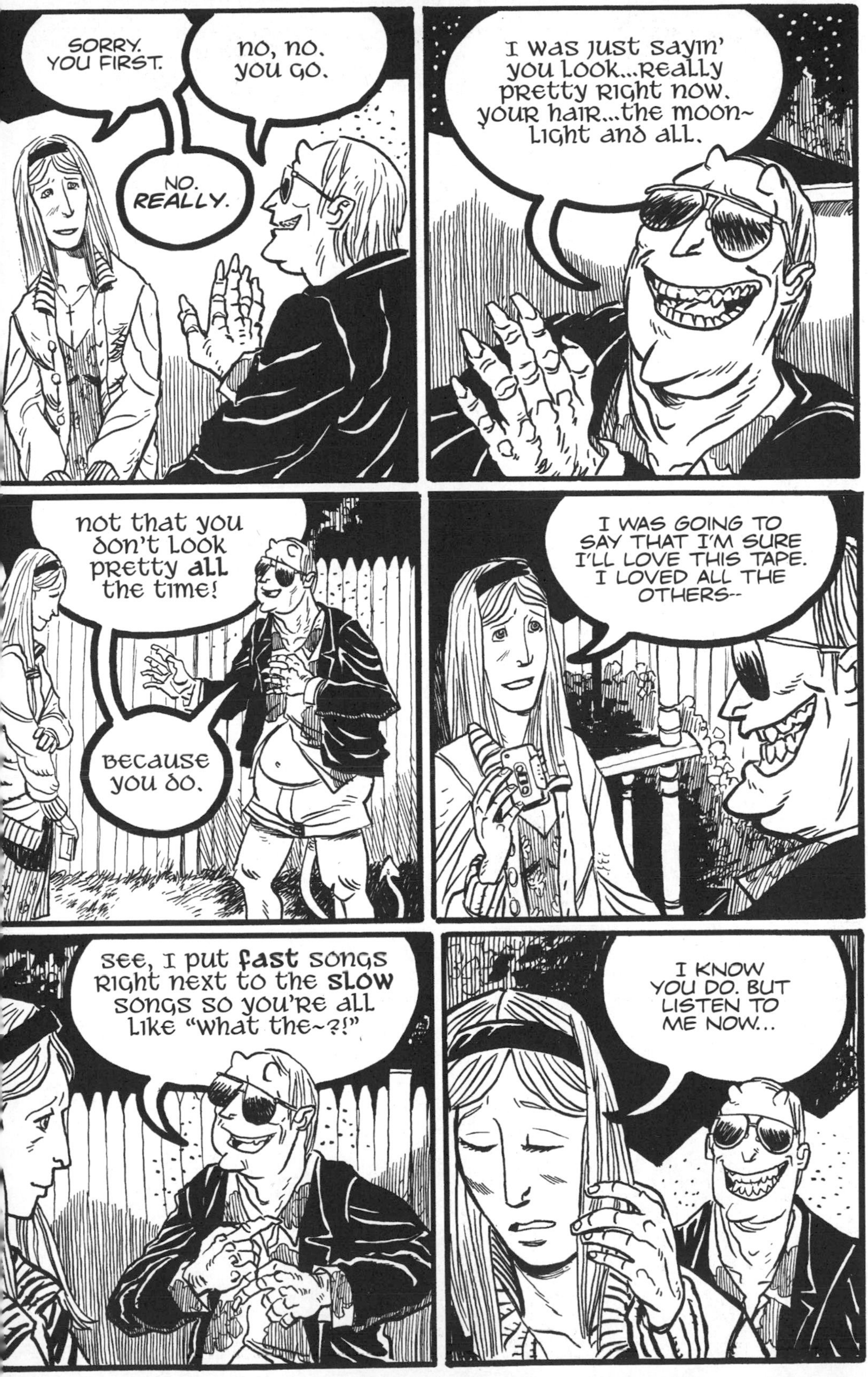
SORRY. YOU FIRST.
no, no. you go.
NO. **REALLY**.
I was just sayin' you look...really pretty right now. your hair...the moon~ light and all.
not that you don't look pretty **all** the time!
BECAUSE you do.
I WAS GOING TO SAY THAT I'M SURE I'LL LOVE THIS TAPE. I LOVED ALL THE OTHERS--
see, I put **fast** songs right next to the **slow** songs so you're all like "what the~?!"
I KNOW YOU DO. BUT LISTEN TO ME NOW...

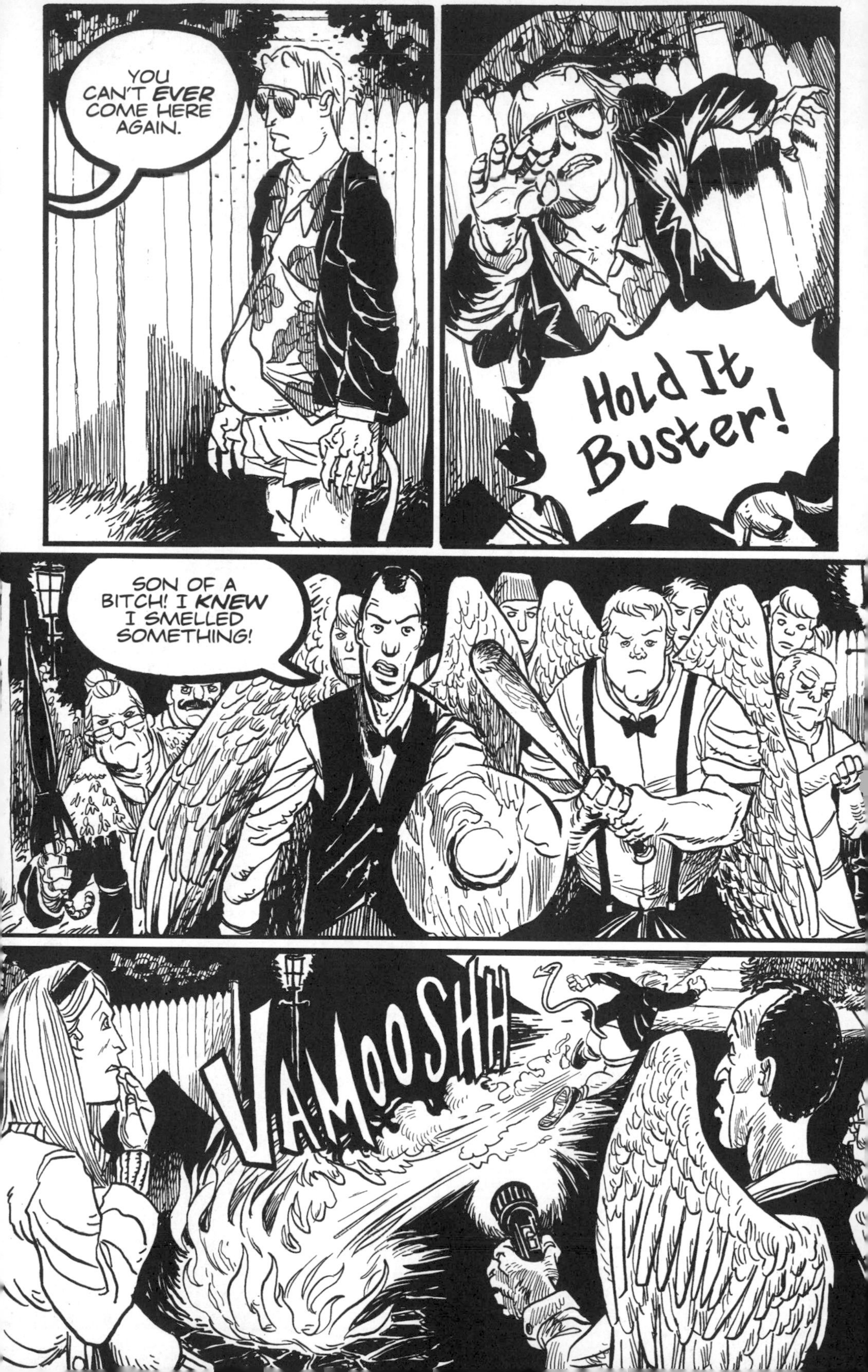
YOU CAN'T EVER COME HERE AGAIN.
Hold It Buster!
SON OF A BITCH! I KNEW I SMELLED SOMETHING!
VAMOOSHH

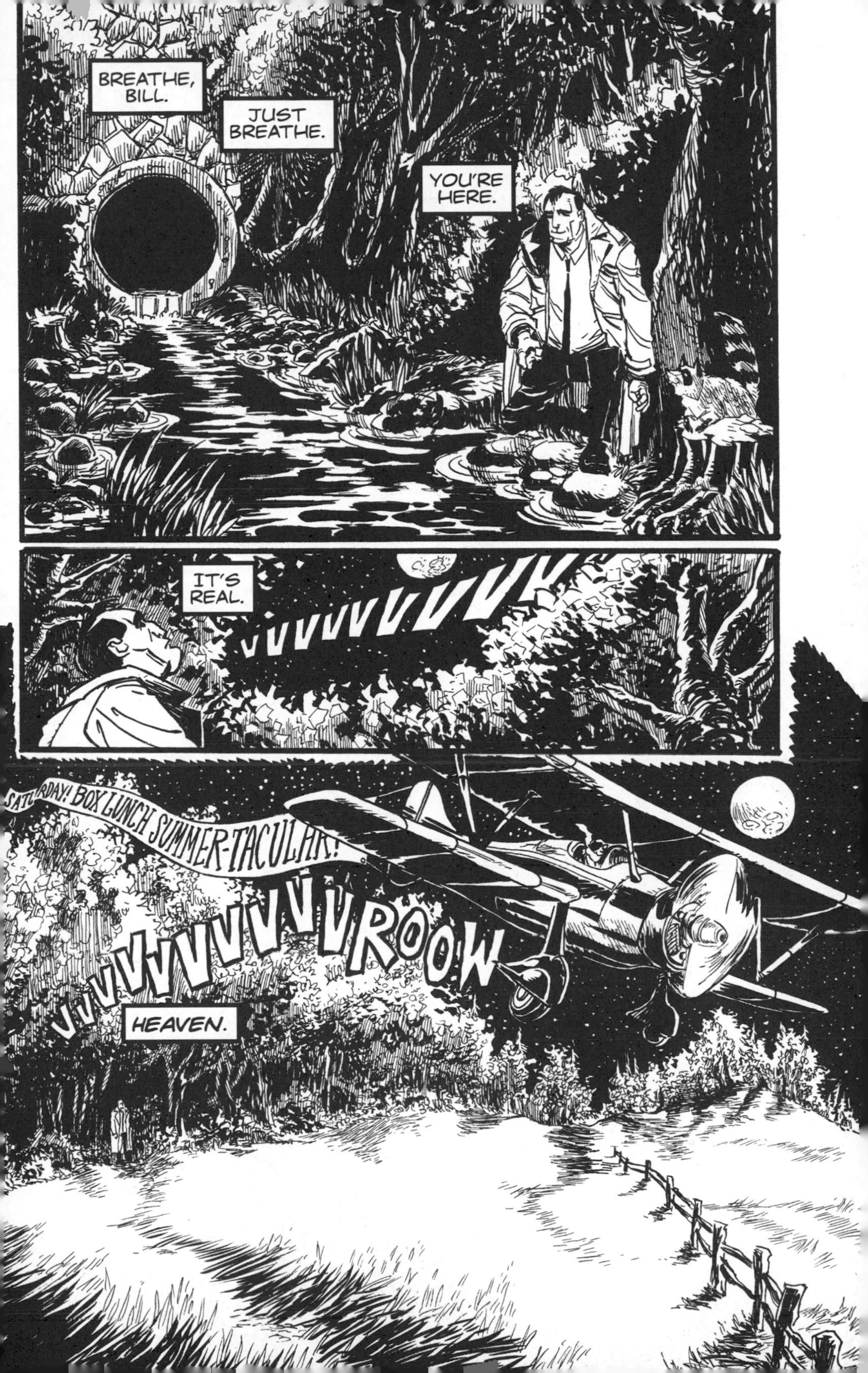
BREATHE, BILL.
JUST BREATHE.
YOU'RE HERE.
IT'S REAL.
VVVVVVVVVVV
SATURDAY! BOX LUNCH SUMMER-TACULAR!
VVVVVVVVVVVROOW
HEAVEN.

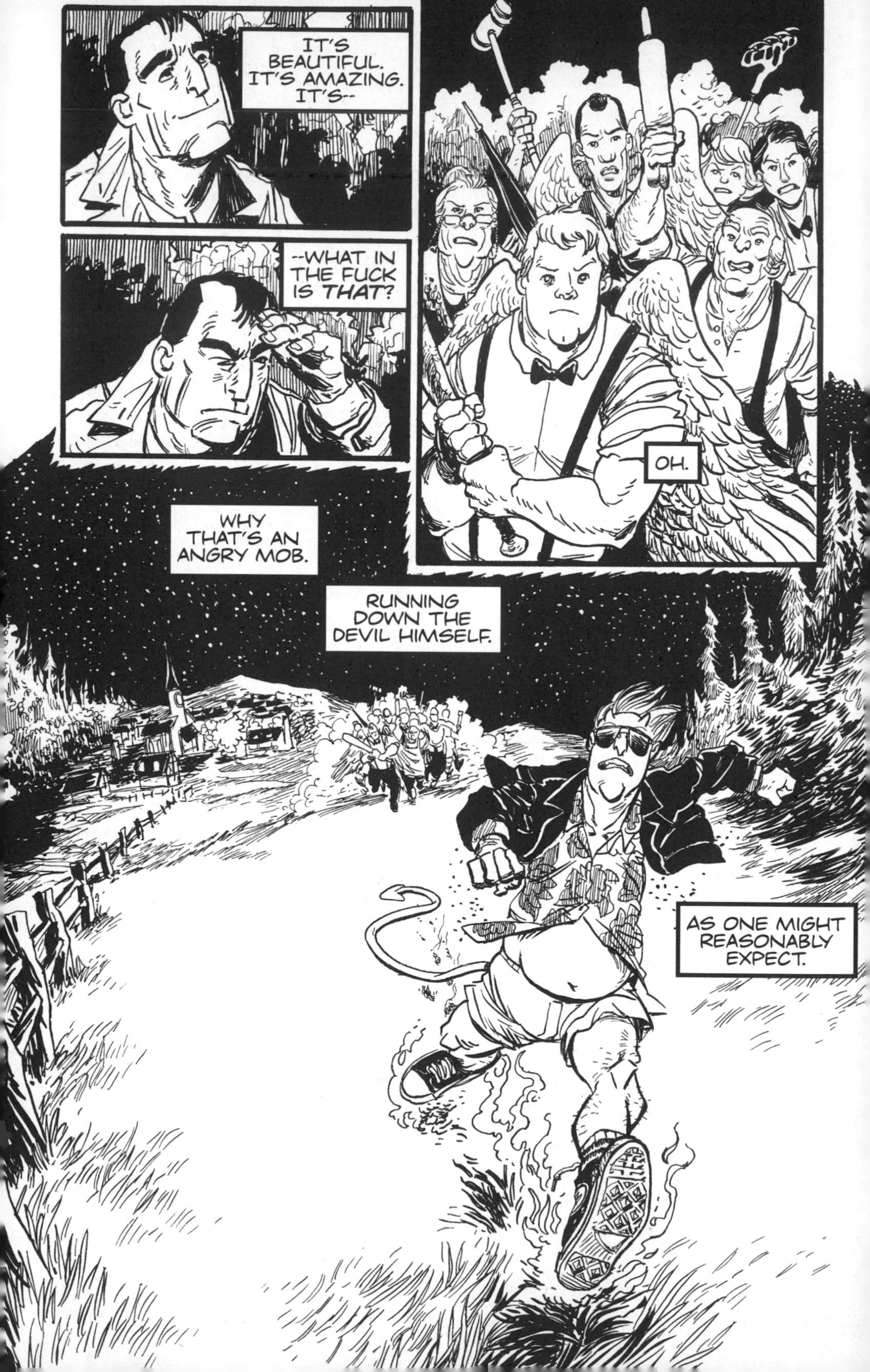
IT'S BEAUTIFUL. IT'S AMAZING. IT'S--
--WHAT IN THE FUCK IS THAT?
OH.
WHY THAT'S AN ANGRY MOB.
RUNNING DOWN THE DEVIL HIMSELF.
AS ONE MIGHT REASONABLY EXPECT.

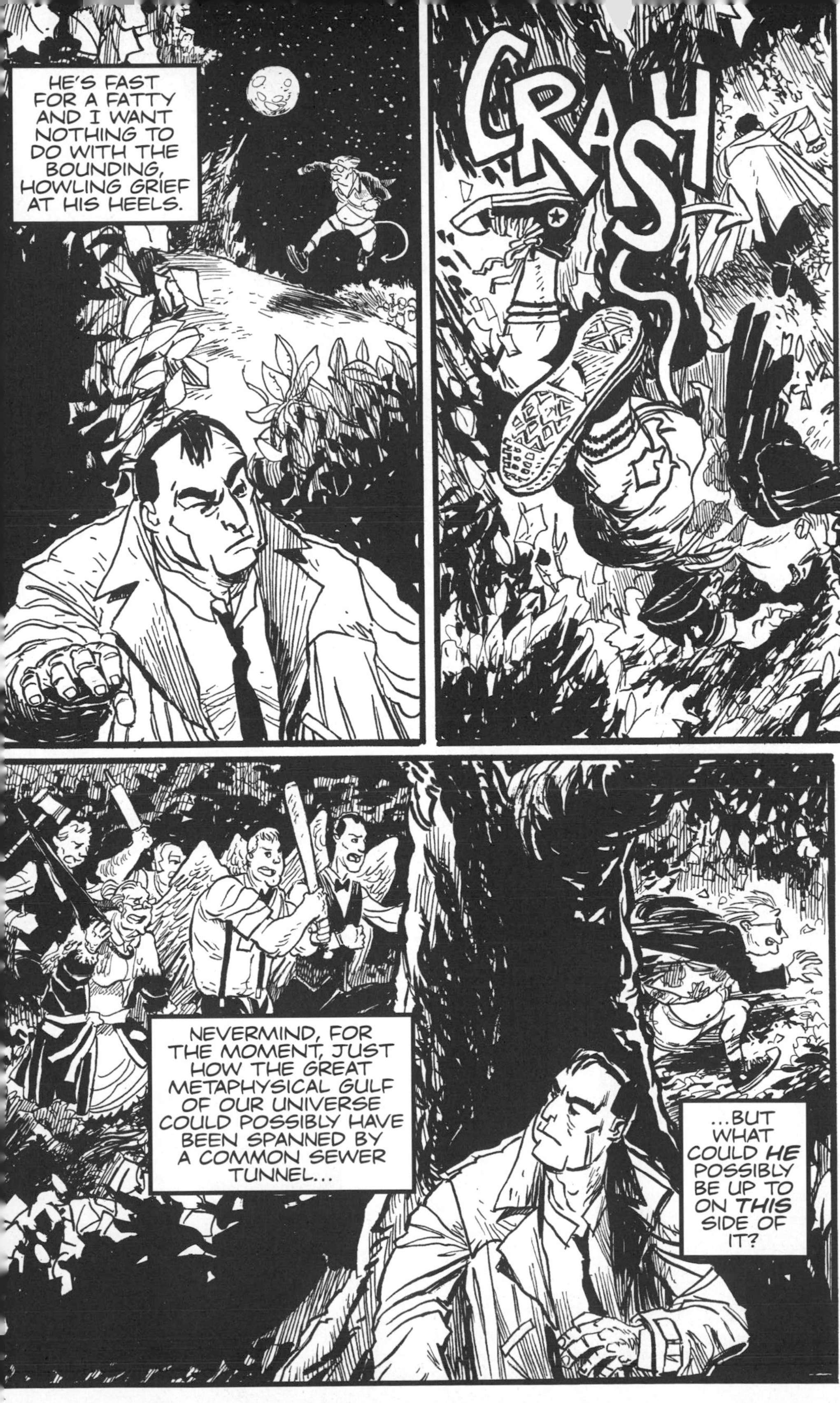
HE'S FAST FOR A FATTY AND I WANT NOTHING TO DO WITH THE BOUNDING, HOWLING GRIEF AT HIS HEELS.
CRASH
NEVERMIND, FOR THE MOMENT, JUST HOW THE GREAT METAPHYSICAL GULF OF OUR UNIVERSE COULD POSSIBLY HAVE BEEN SPANNED BY A COMMON SEWER TUNNEL...
...BUT WHAT COULD *HE* POSSIBLY BE UP TO ON *THIS* SIDE OF IT?

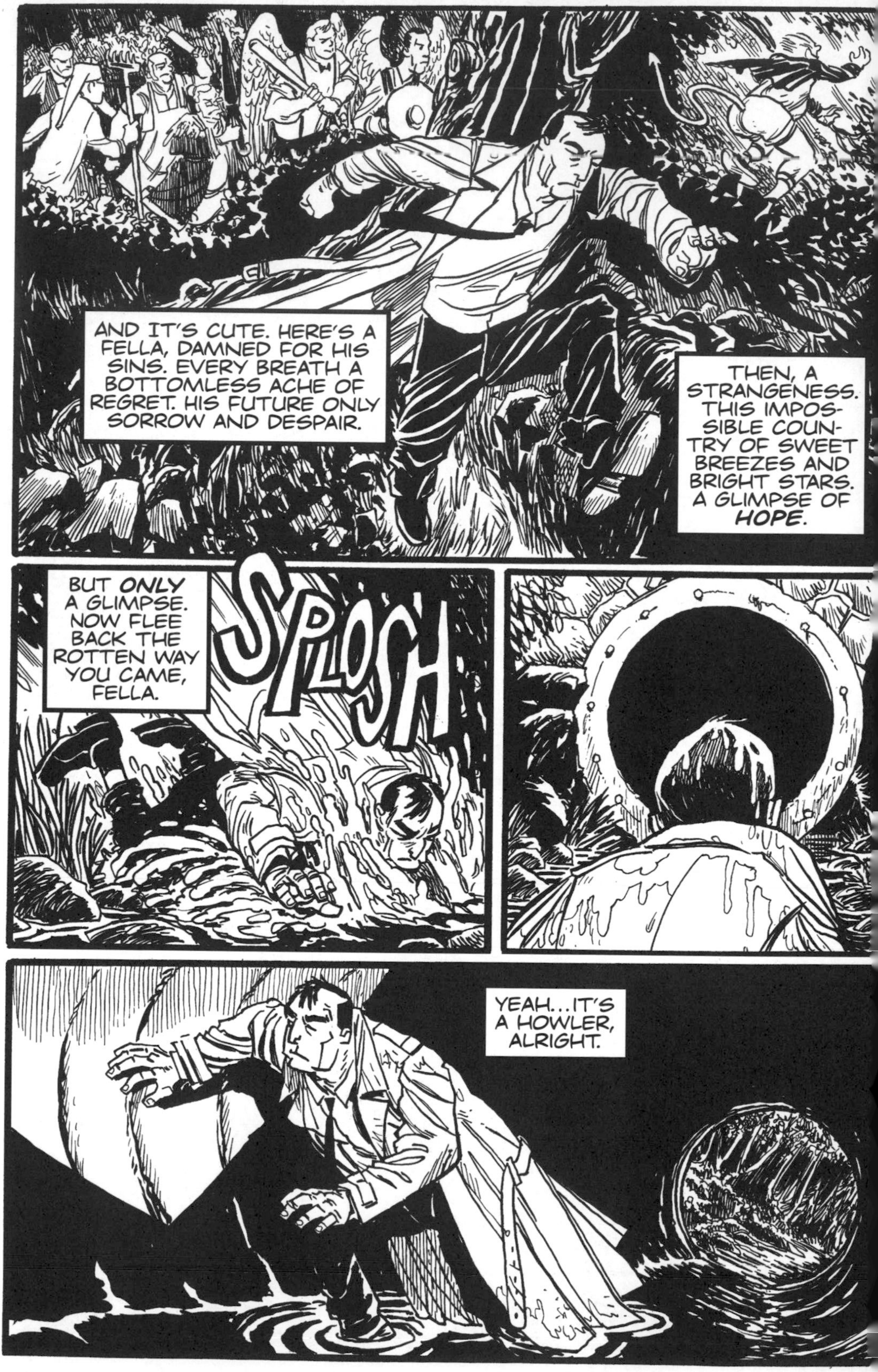
AND IT'S CUTE. HERE'S A FELLA, DAMNED FOR HIS SINS. EVERY BREATH A BOTTOMLESS ACHE OF REGRET. HIS FUTURE ONLY SORROW AND DESPAIR.
THEN, A STRANGENESS. THIS IMPOSSIBLE COUNTRY OF SWEET BREEZES AND BRIGHT STARS. A GLIMPSE OF *HOPE*.
BUT *ONLY* A GLIMPSE. NOW FLEE BACK THE ROTTEN WAY YOU CAME, FELLA.
SPLOSH
YEAH...IT'S A HOWLER, ALRIGHT.

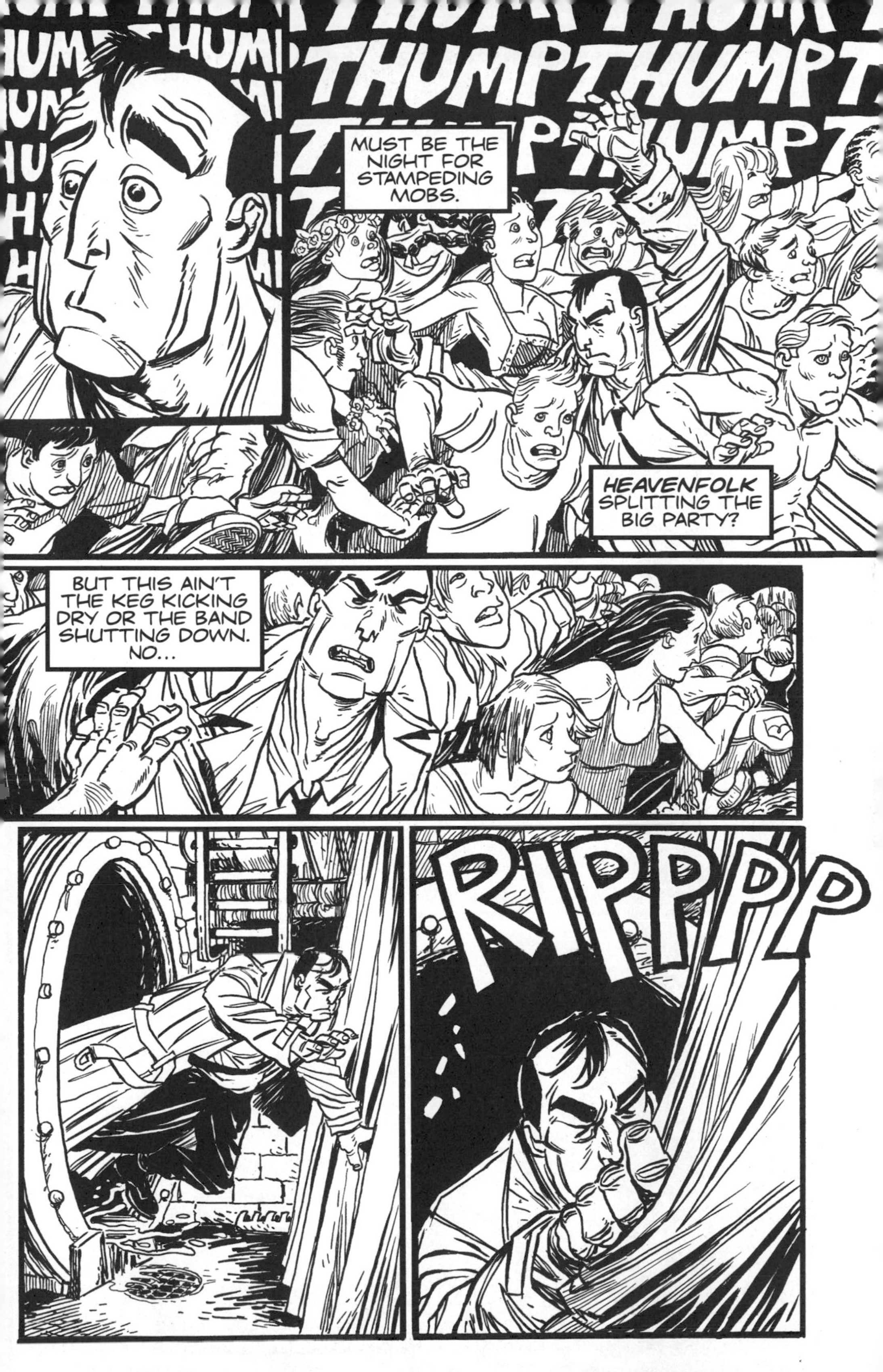
THUMPTHUMPTHUMP
MUST BE THE NIGHT FOR STAMPEDING MOBS.
HEAVENFOLK SPLITTING THE BIG PARTY?
BUT THIS AIN'T THE KEG KICKING DRY OR THE BAND SHUTTING DOWN. NO...
RIPPPP

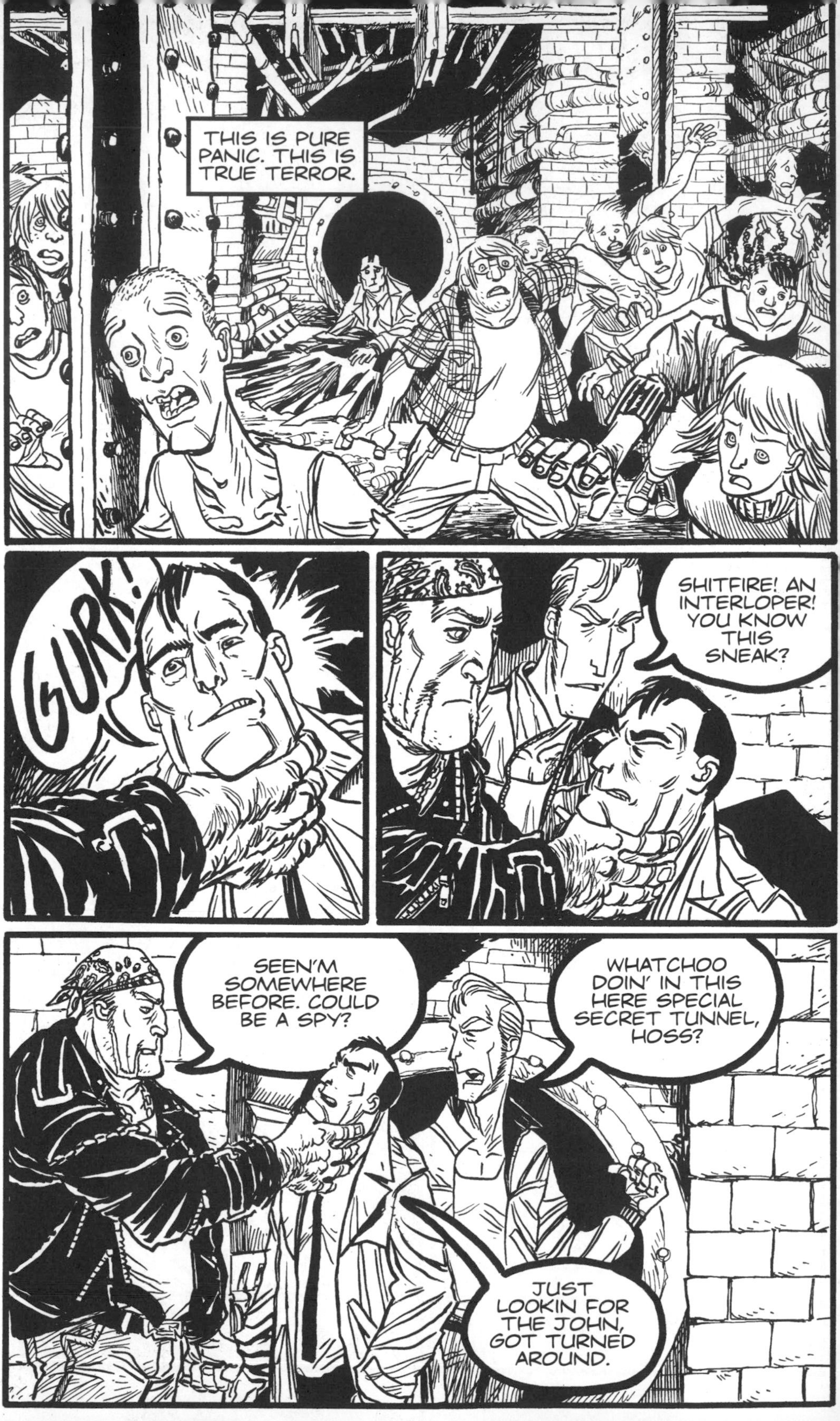
THIS IS PURE PANIC. THIS IS TRUE TERROR.
GURK!
SHITFIRE! AN INTERLOPER! YOU KNOW THIS SNEAK?
SEEN'M SOMEWHERE BEFORE. COULD BE A SPY?
WHATCHOO DOIN' IN THIS HERE SPECIAL SECRET TUNNEL, HOSS?
JUST LOOKIN FOR THE JOHN, GOT TURNED AROUND.

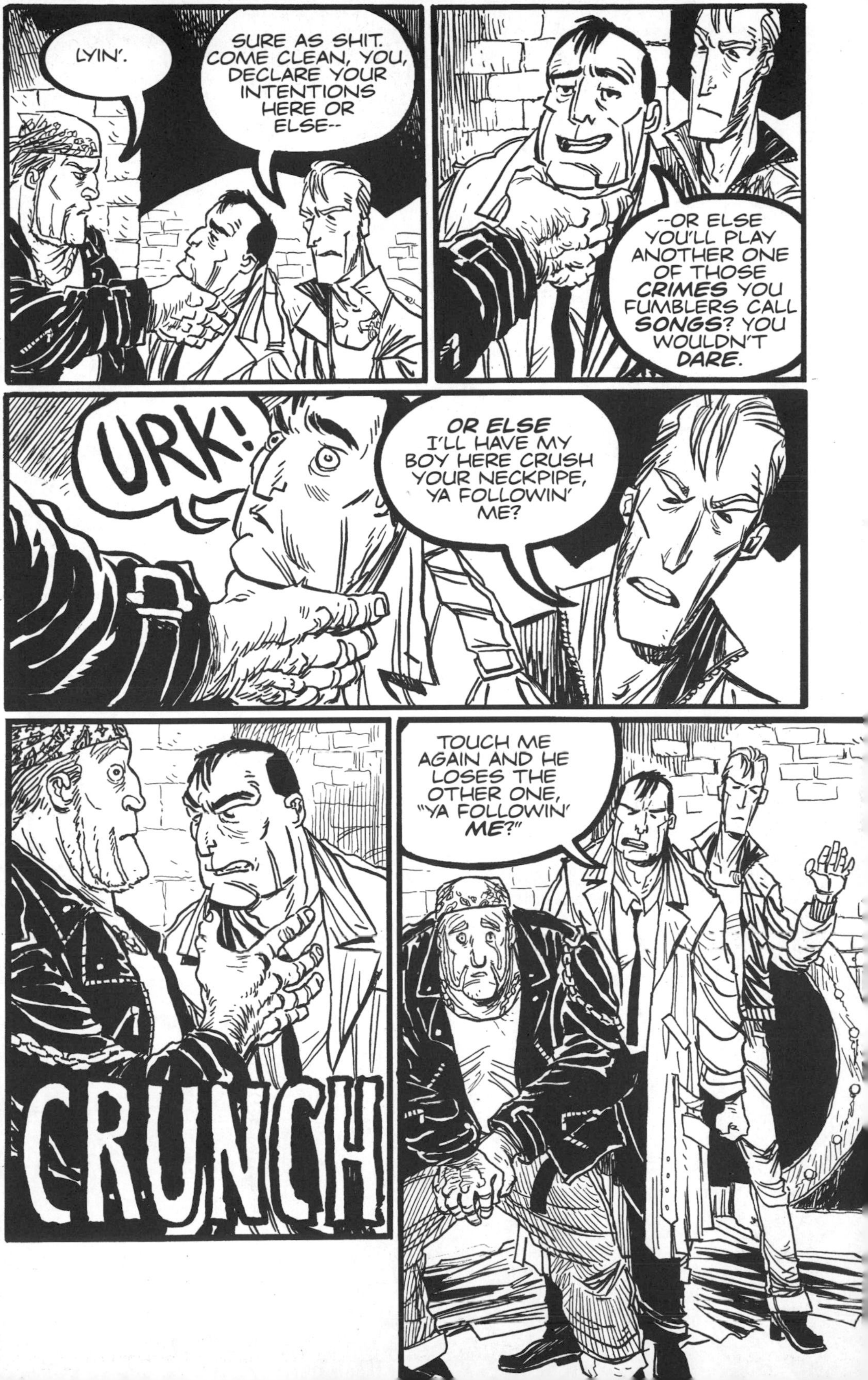
LYIN'.
SURE AS SHIT. COME CLEAN, YOU, DECLARE YOUR INTENTIONS HERE OR ELSE--
--OR ELSE YOU'LL PLAY ANOTHER ONE OF THOSE CRIMES YOU FUMBLERS CALL SONGS? YOU WOULDN'T DARE.
URK!
OR ELSE I'LL HAVE MY BOY HERE CRUSH YOUR NECKPIPE, YA FOLLOWIN' ME?
CRUNCH
TOUCH ME AGAIN AND HE LOSES THE OTHER ONE, "YA FOLLOWIN' ME?"

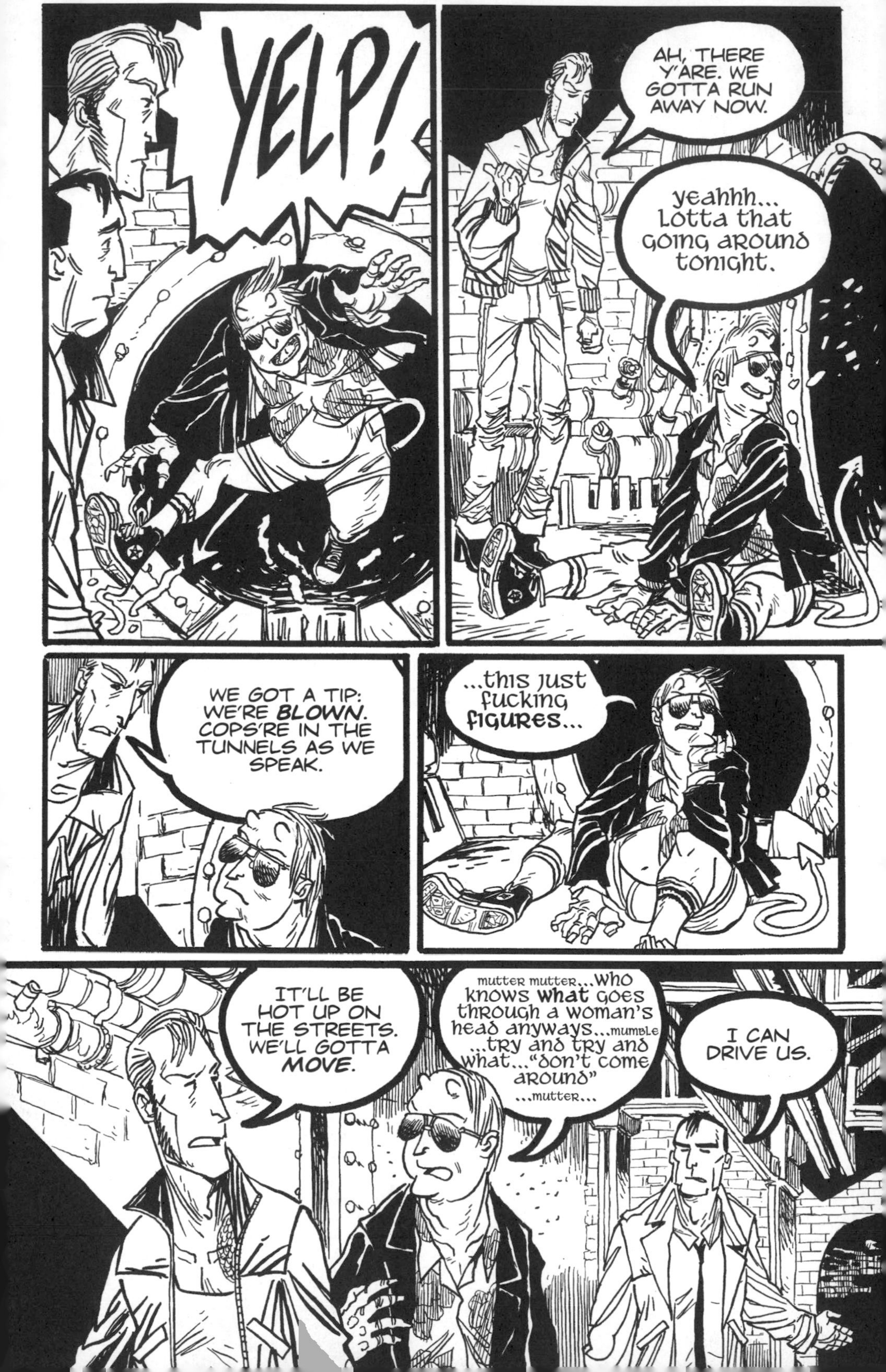
YELP!
AH, THERE Y'ARE. WE GOTTA RUN AWAY NOW.
yeahhh... lotta that going around tonight.
WE GOT A TIP: WE'RE BLOWN. COPS'RE IN THE TUNNELS AS WE SPEAK.
...this just fucking figures...
IT'LL BE HOT UP ON THE STREETS. WE'LL GOTTA MOVE.
mutter mutter...who knows what goes through a woman's head anyways...mumble ...try and try and what..."don't come around" ...mutter...
I CAN DRIVE US.

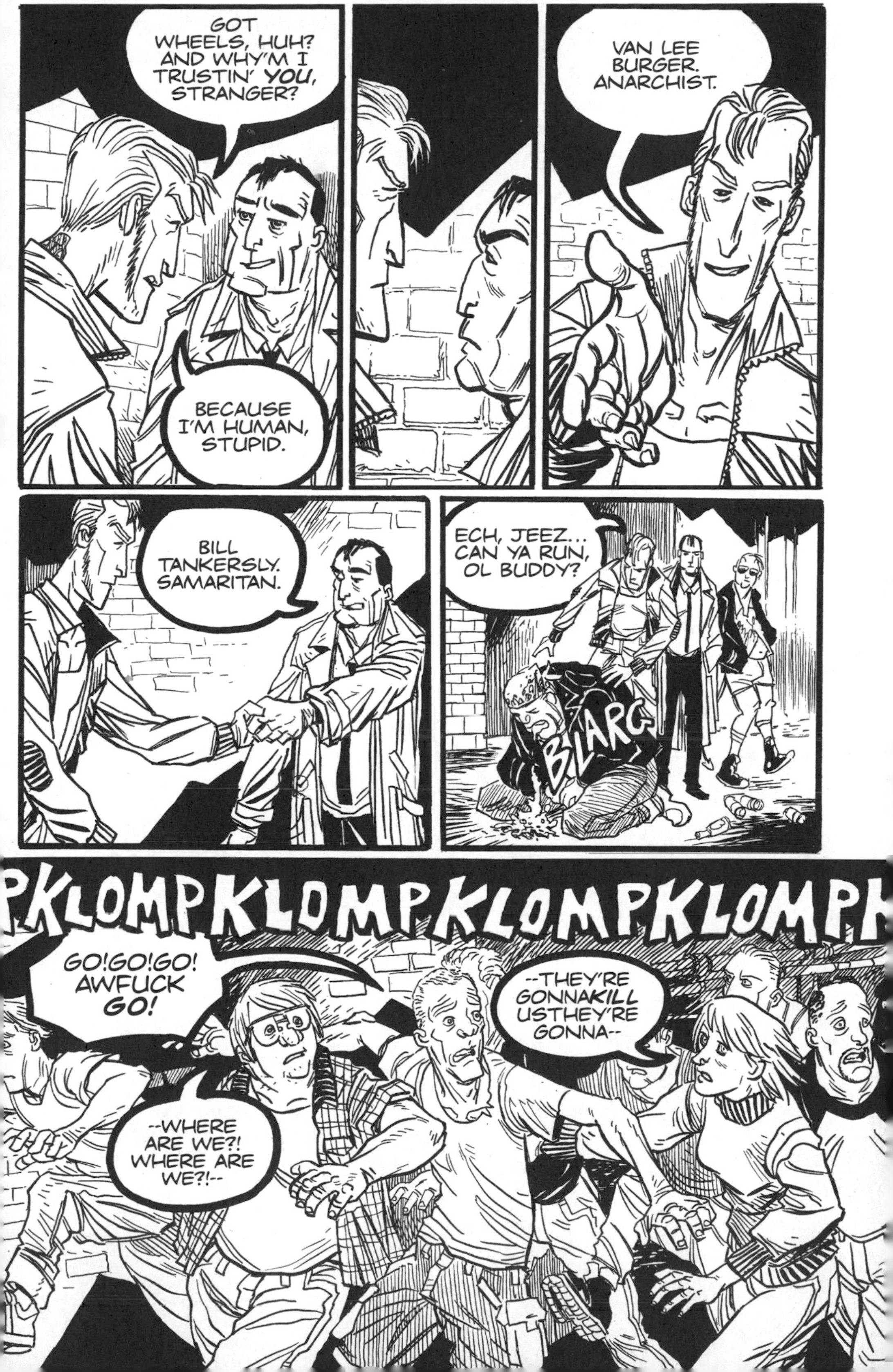

GOT WHEELS, HUH? AND WHY'M I TRUSTIN' *YOU*, STRANGER?
BECAUSE I'M HUMAN, STUPID.
VAN LEE BURGER. ANARCHIST.
BILL TANKERSLY. SAMARITAN.
ECH, JEEZ... CAN YA RUN, OL BUDDY?
BLARG
KLOMPKLOMPKLOMPKLOMP
GO!GO!GO! AWFUCK *GO!*
--THEY'RE GONNA*KILL* USTHEY'RE GONNA--
--WHERE ARE WE?! WHERE ARE WE?!--

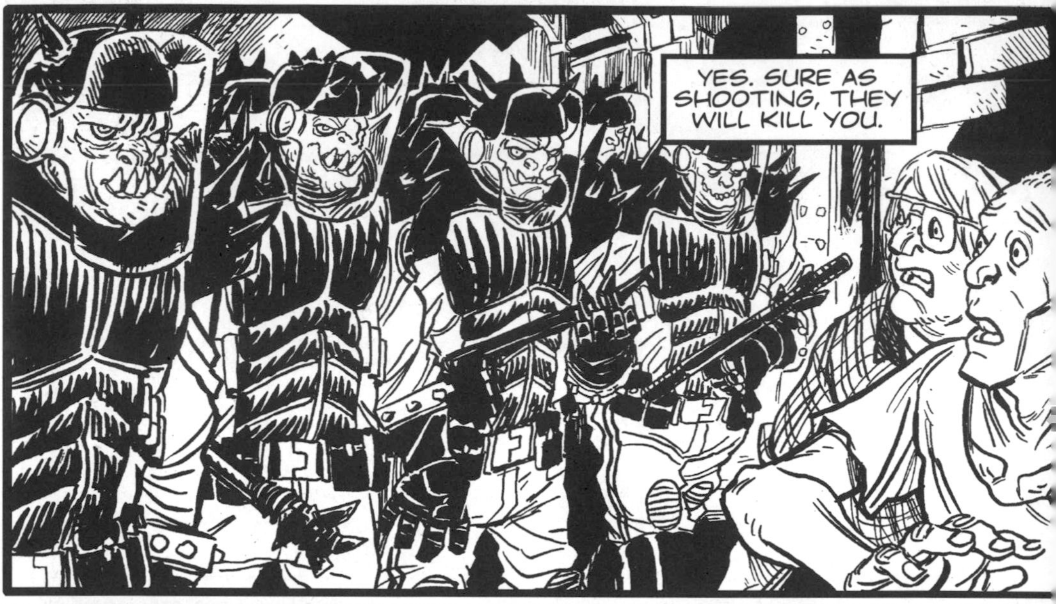
YES. SURE AS SHOOTING, THEY WILL KILL YOU.

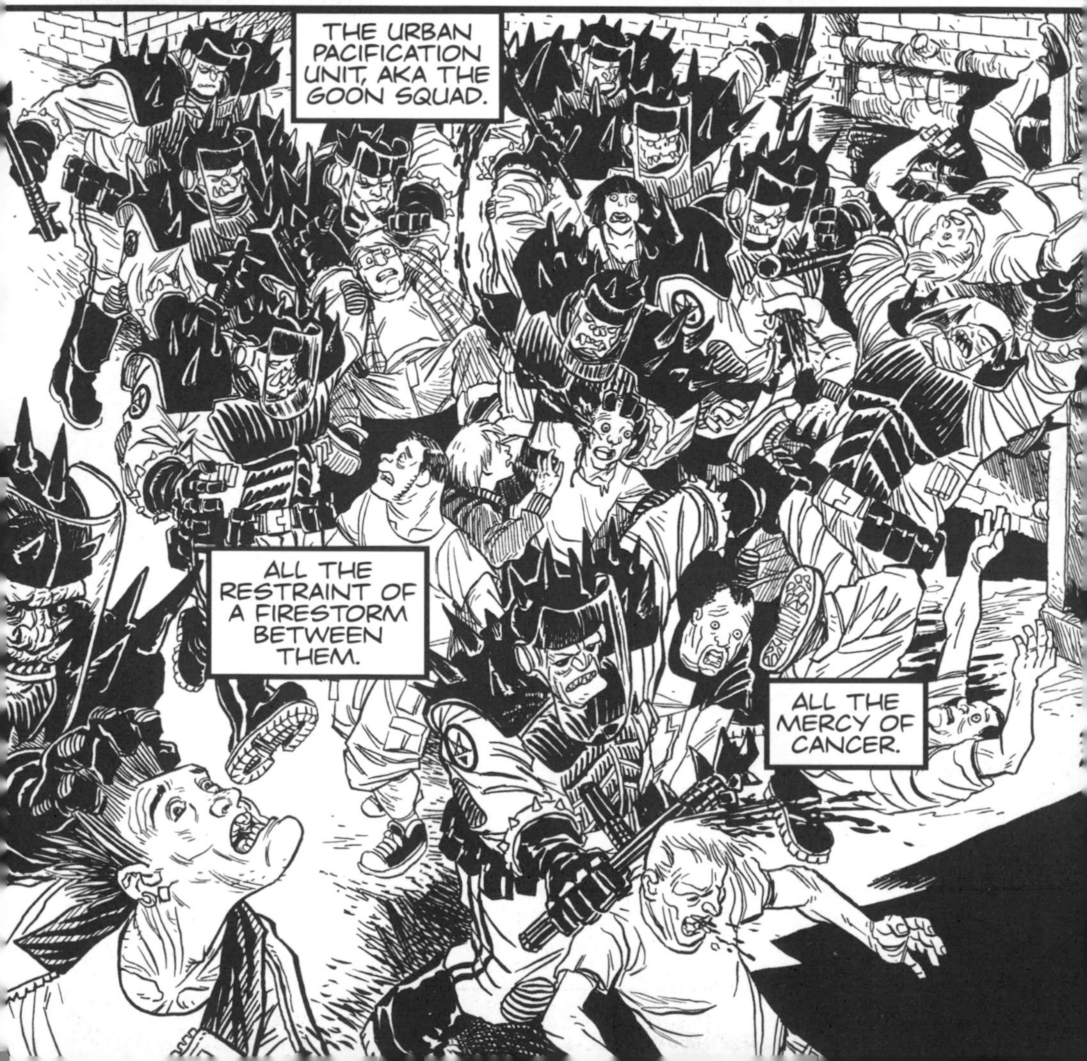
THE URBAN PACIFICATION UNIT, AKA THE GOON SQUAD.
ALL THE RESTRAINT OF A FIRESTORM BETWEEN THEM.
ALL THE MERCY OF CANCER.

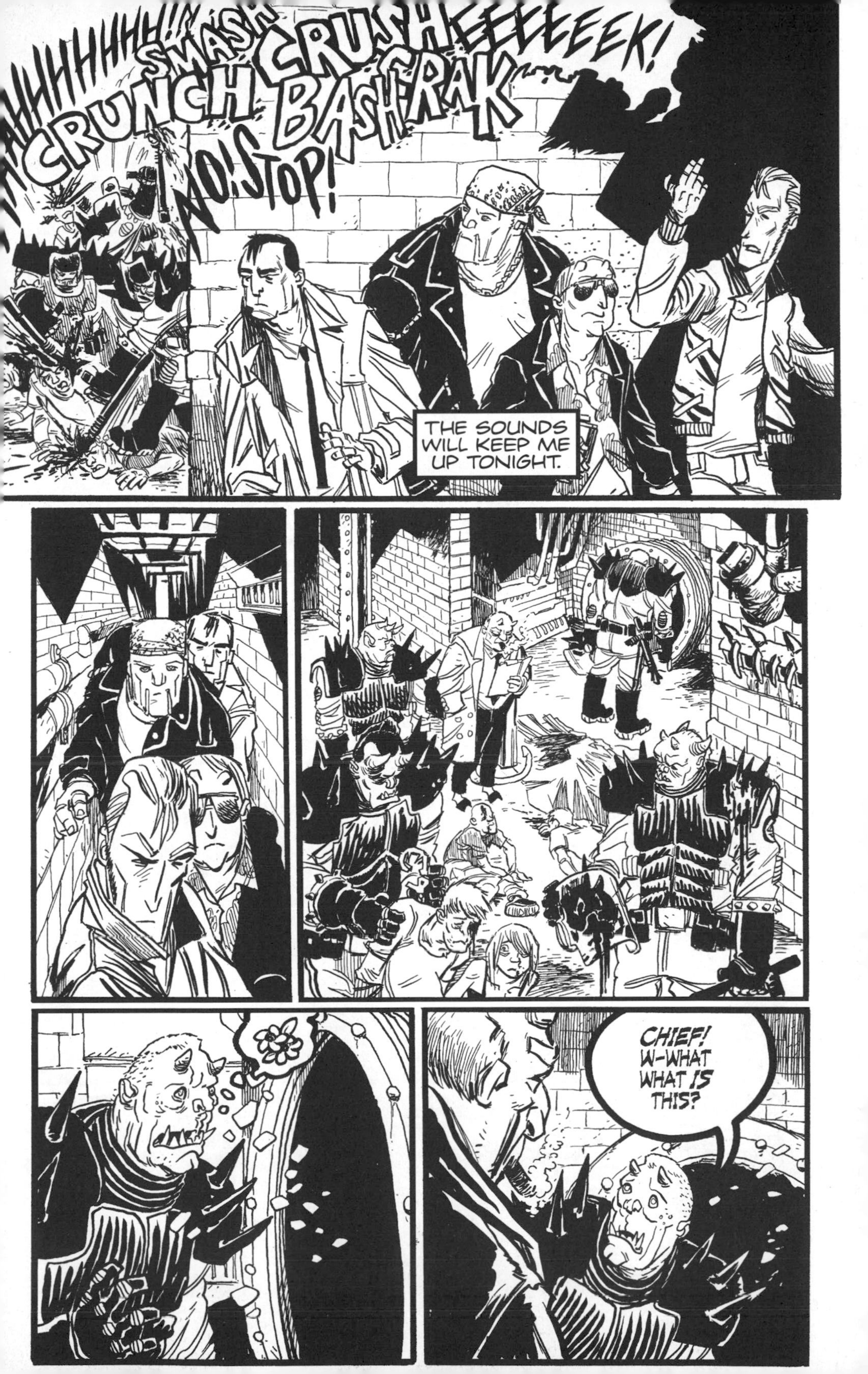
AHHHHHHH!!
SMASH
CRUNCH
CRUSH
EEEEEEEK!
BASH
FRAK
NO! STOP!
THE SOUNDS WILL KEEP ME UP TONIGHT.
CHIEF! W-WHAT WHAT IS THIS?

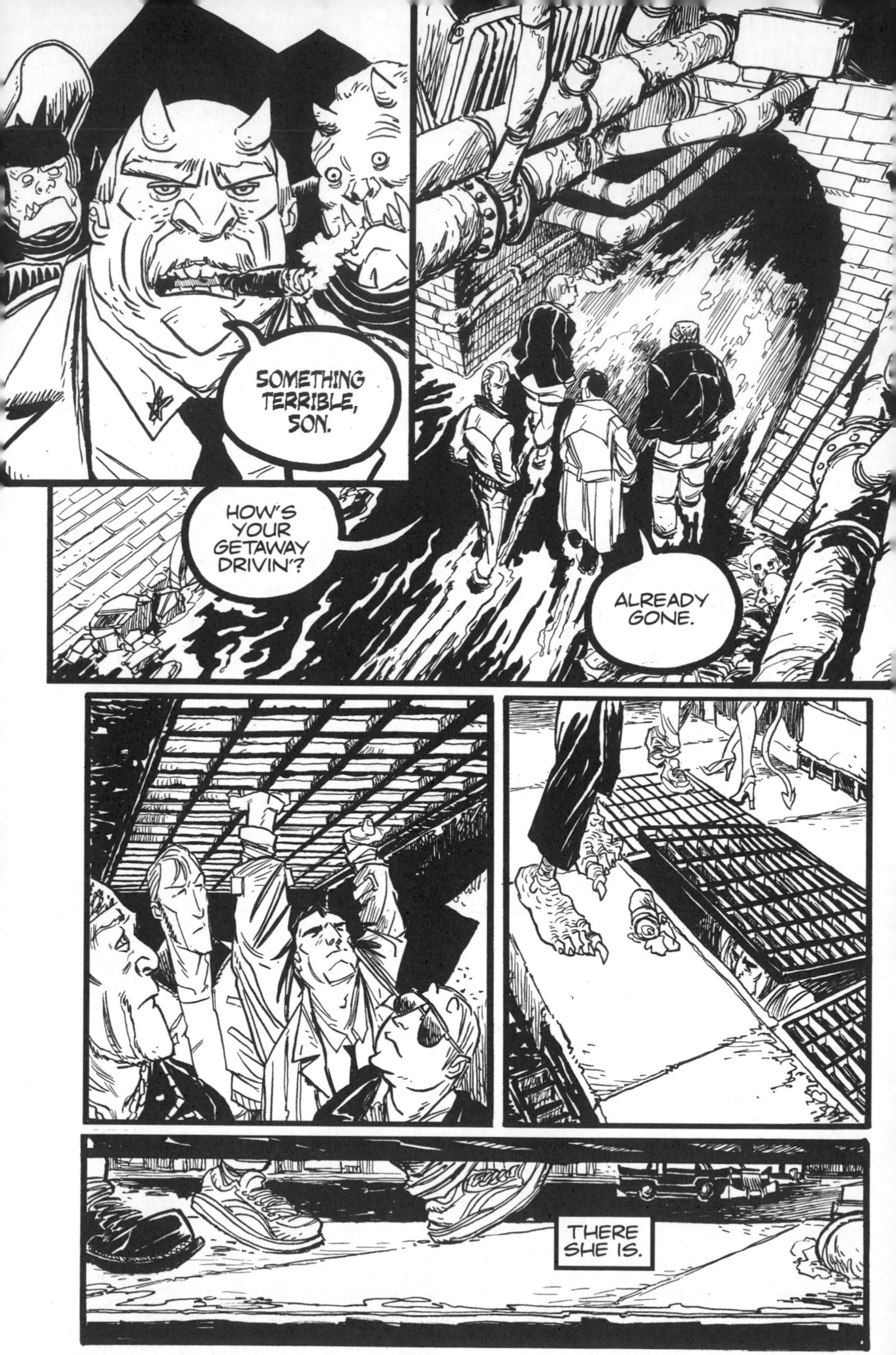
SOMETHING TERRIBLE, SON.
HOW'S YOUR GETAWAY DRIVIN'?
ALREADY GONE.
THERE SHE IS.

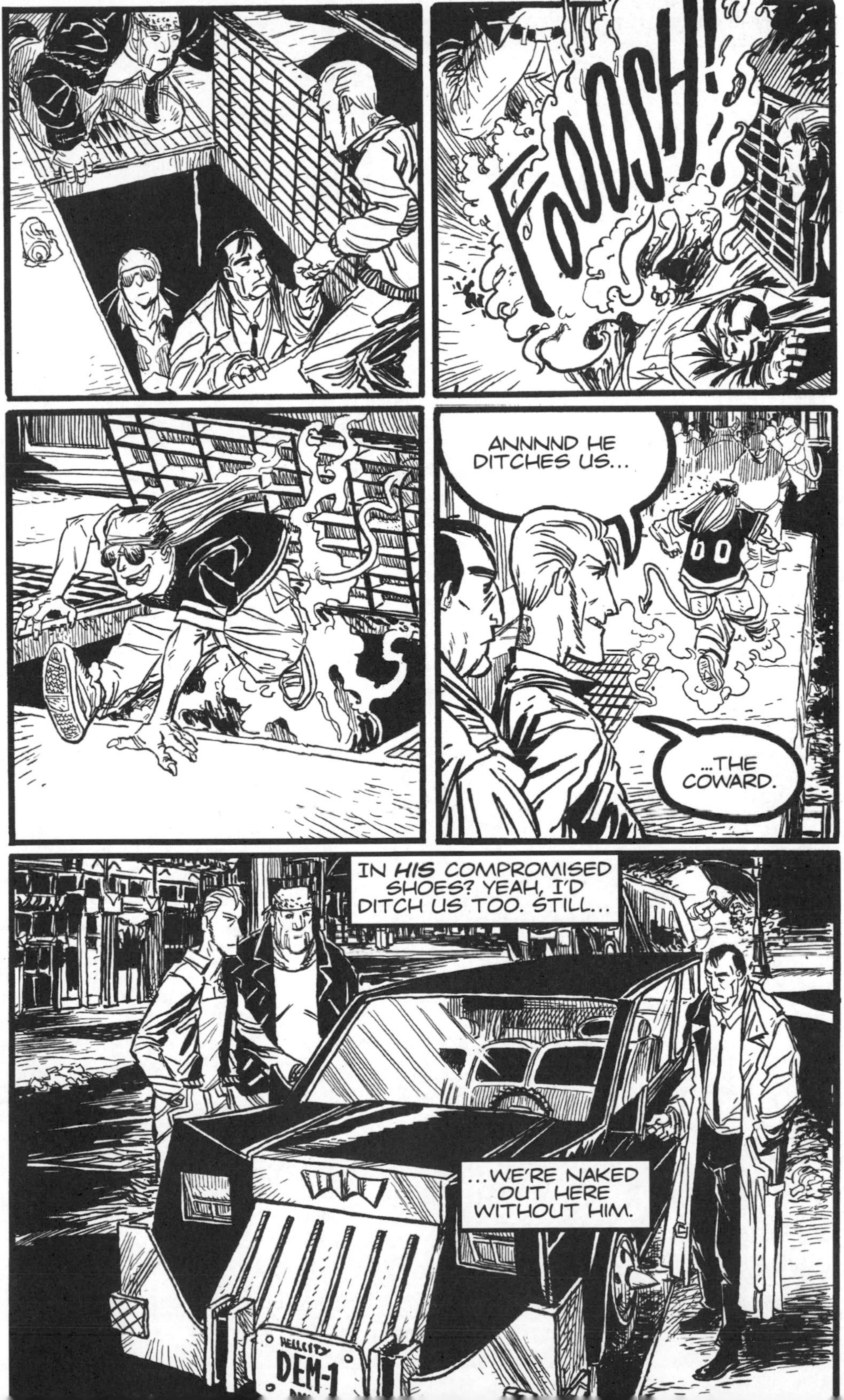
FOOOSH!
ANNNND HE DITCHES US...
...THE COWARD.
IN HIS COMPROMISED SHOES? YEAH, I'D DITCH US TOO. STILL...
...WE'RE NAKED OUT HERE WITHOUT HIM.
HELLCITY
DEM-1

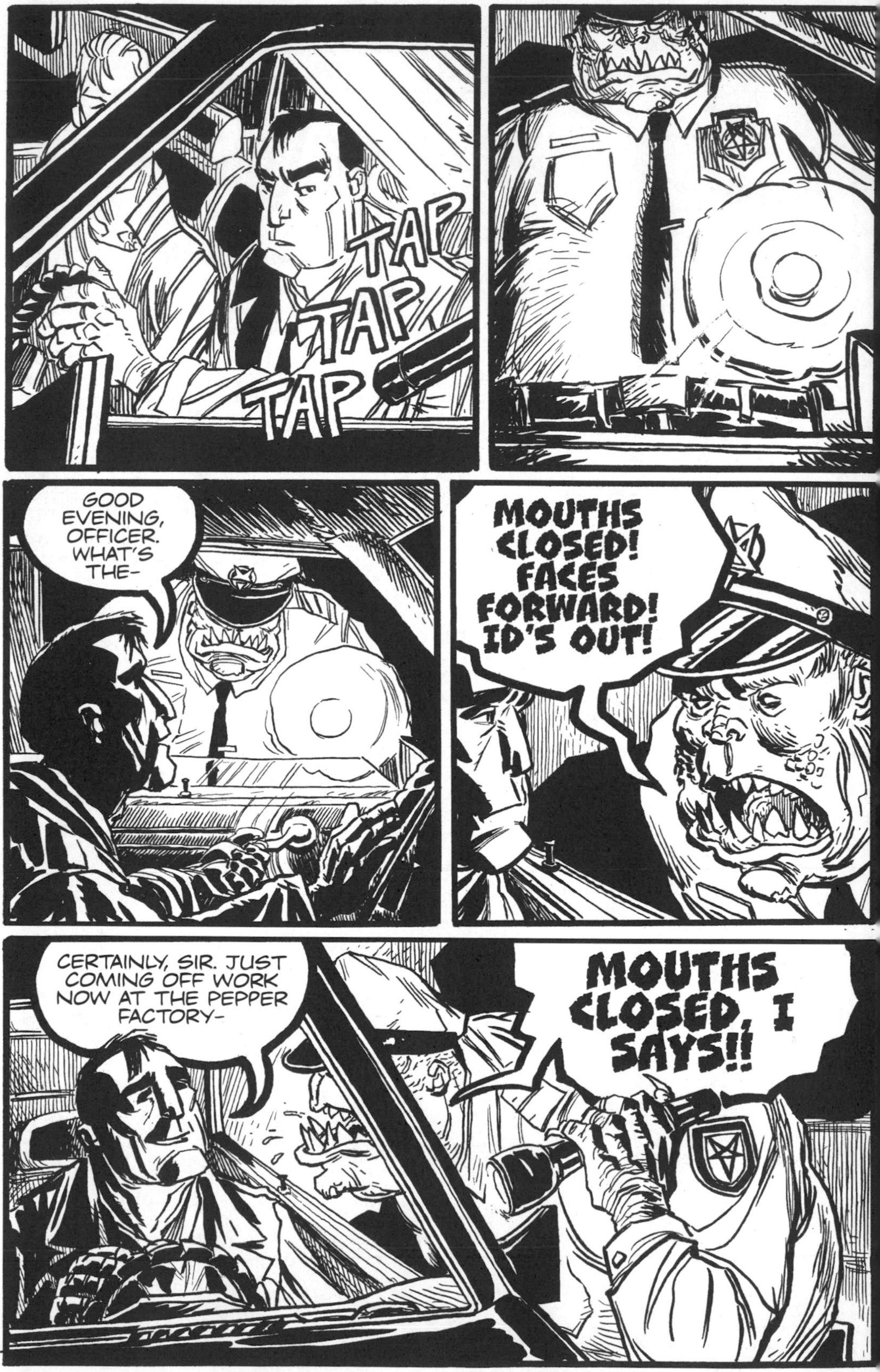
TAP
TAP
TAP
GOOD EVENING, OFFICER. WHAT'S THE-
MOUTHS CLOSED! FACES FORWARD! ID'S OUT!
CERTAINLY, SIR. JUST COMING OFF WORK NOW AT THE PEPPER FACTORY-
MOUTHS CLOSED, I SAYS!!

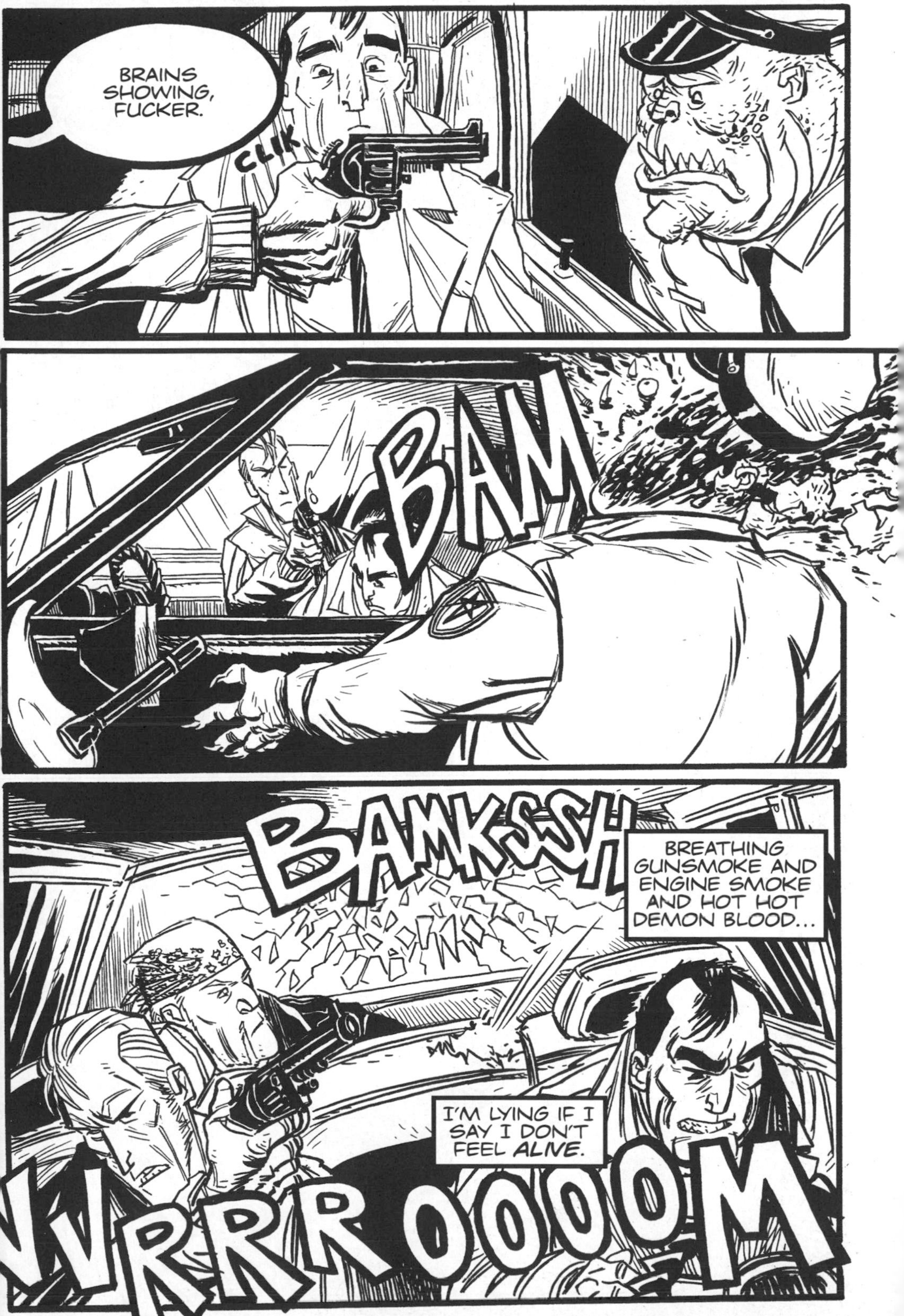
BRAINS SHOWING, FUCKER.
CLIK
BAM
BAMKSSH
BREATHING GUNSMOKE AND ENGINE SMOKE AND HOT HOT DEMON BLOOD...
I'M LYING IF I SAY I DON'T FEEL *ALIVE*.
VRRRROOOOM

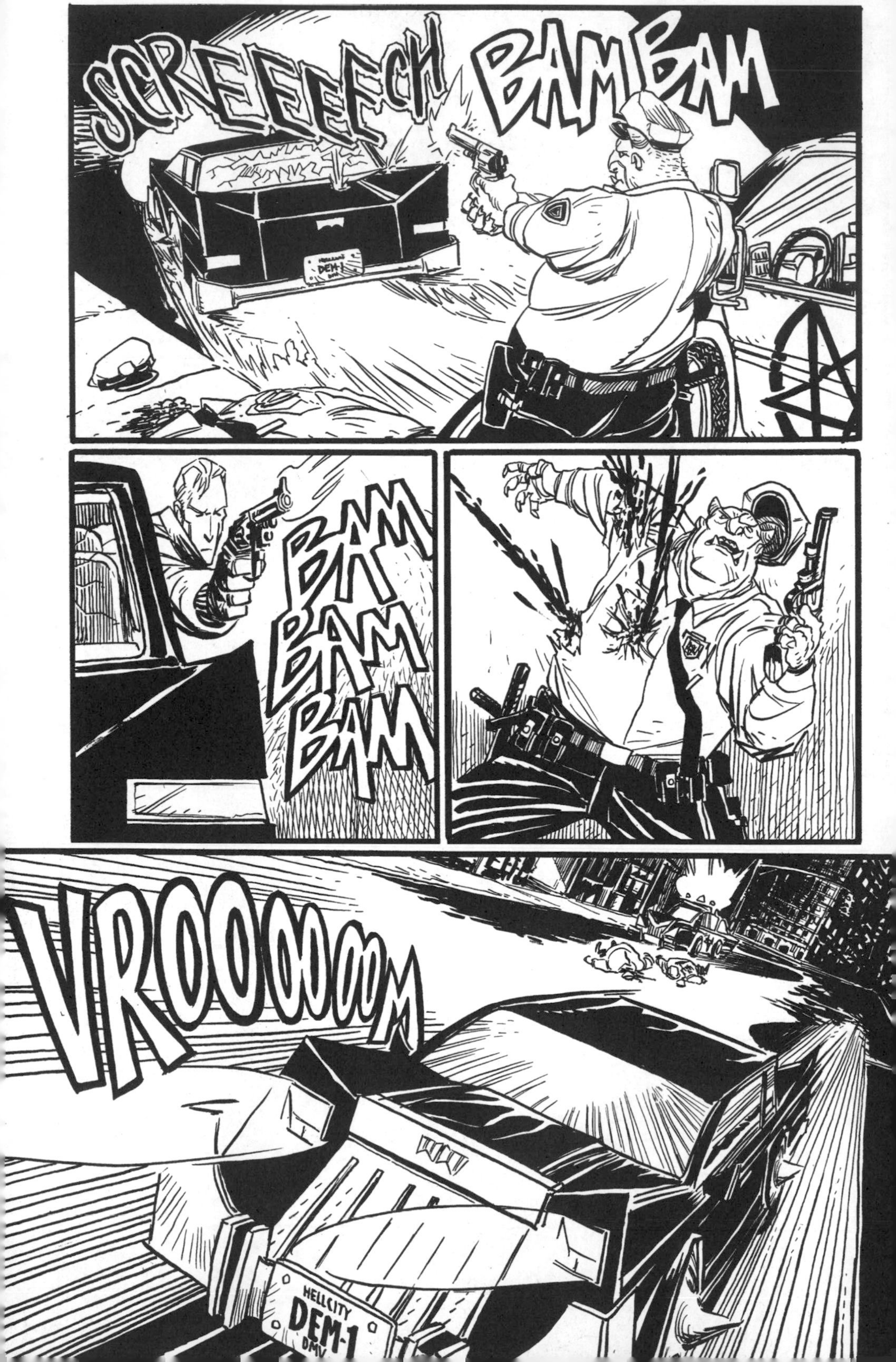
SCREEEECH
BAM BAM
BAM BAM BAM BAM
VROOOOOOM
HELLCITY
DEM-1
DMV

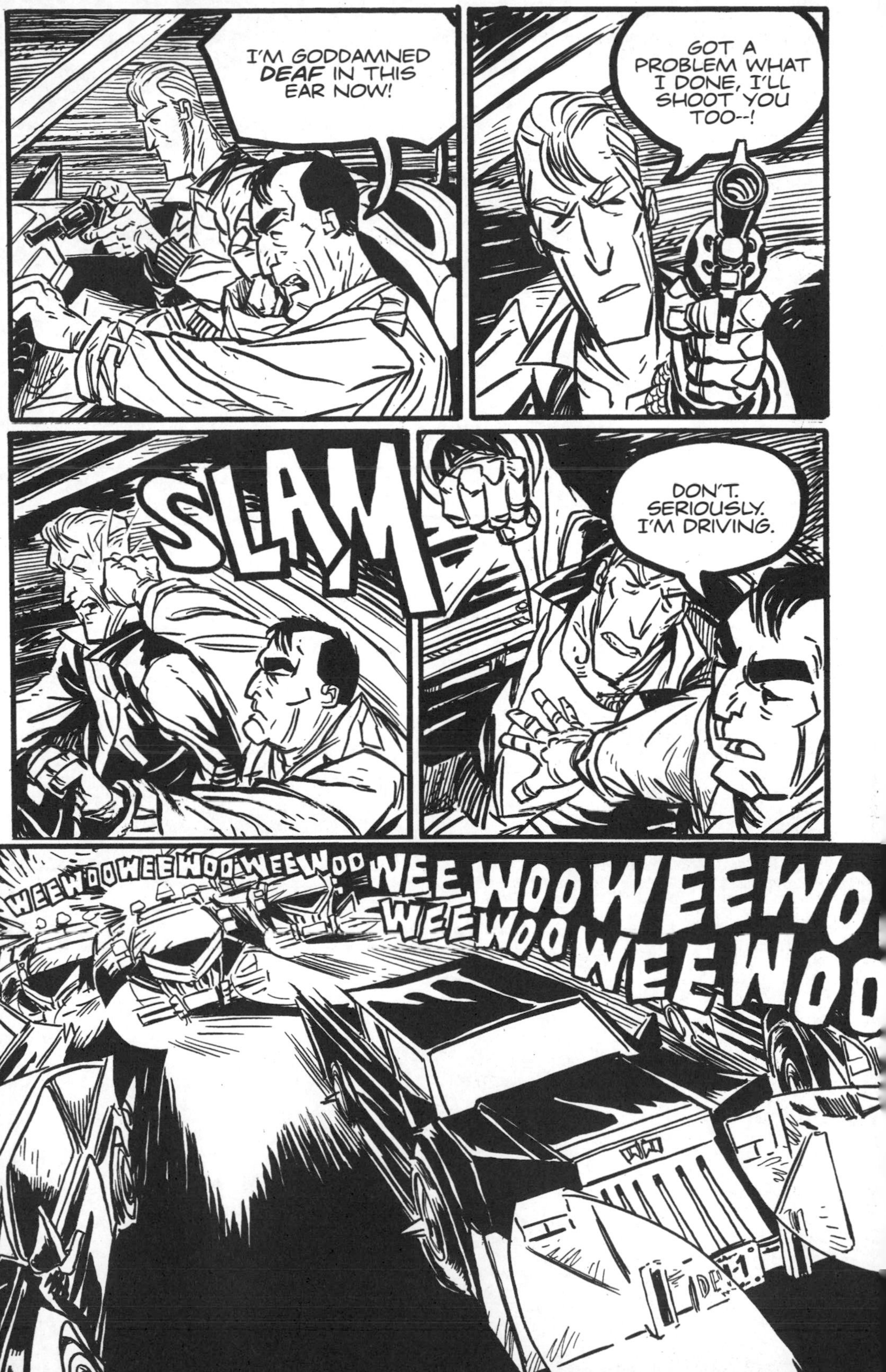
I'M GODDAMNED DEAF IN THIS EAR NOW!
GOT A PROBLEM WHAT I DONE, I'LL SHOOT YOU TOO--!
SLAM
DON'T. SERIOUSLY. I'M DRIVING.
WEEWOOWEEWOOWEEWOO WEE WOO WEEWO
WEEWOO WEEWOO

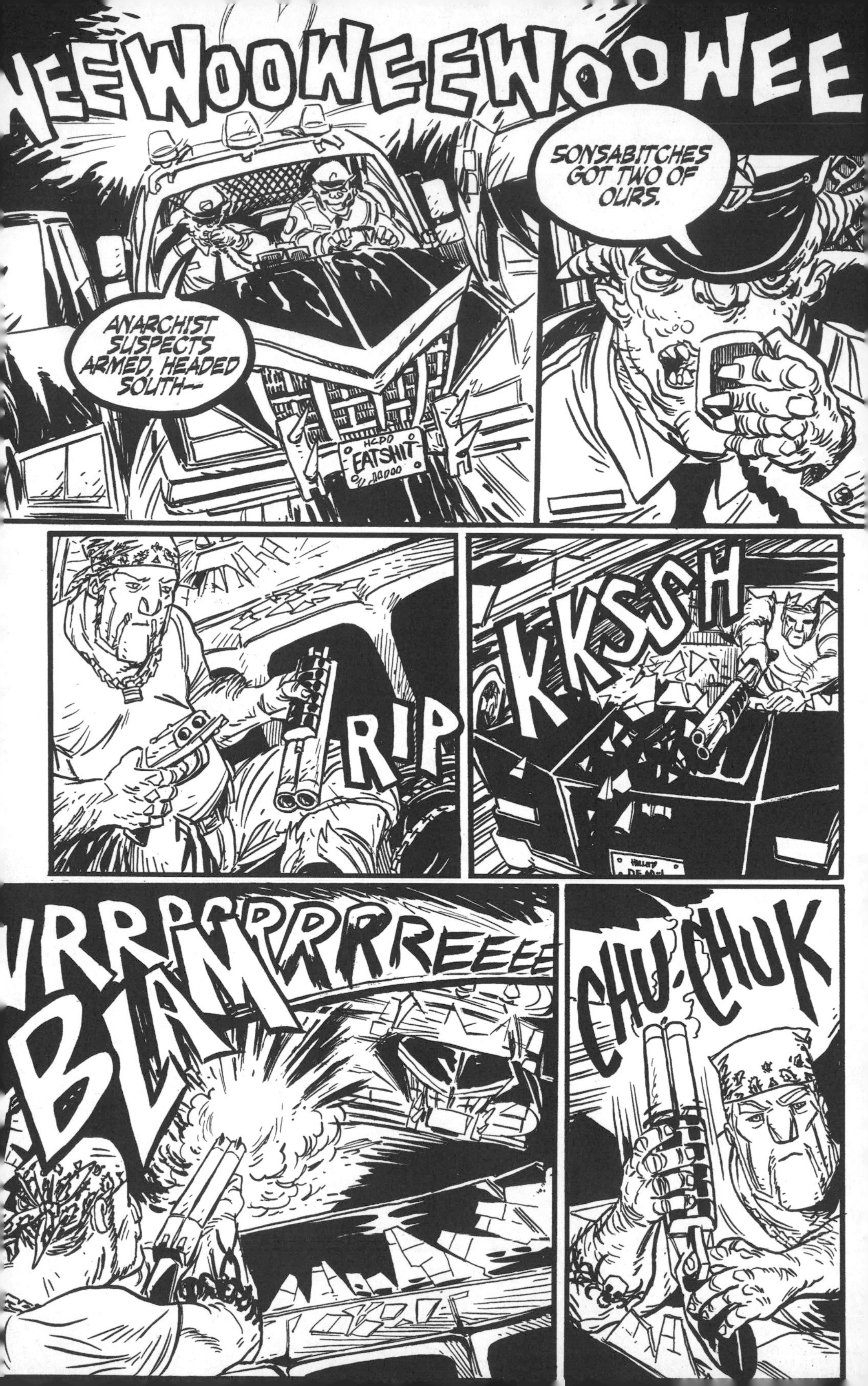
WEEWOOWEEWOOWEE
ANARCHIST SUSPECTS ARMED, HEADED SOUTH--
HCPD
EATSHIT
SONSABITCHES GOT TWO OF OURS.
RIP
KKSSH
VRRRRRRRREEEE
BLAM
CHU-CHUK

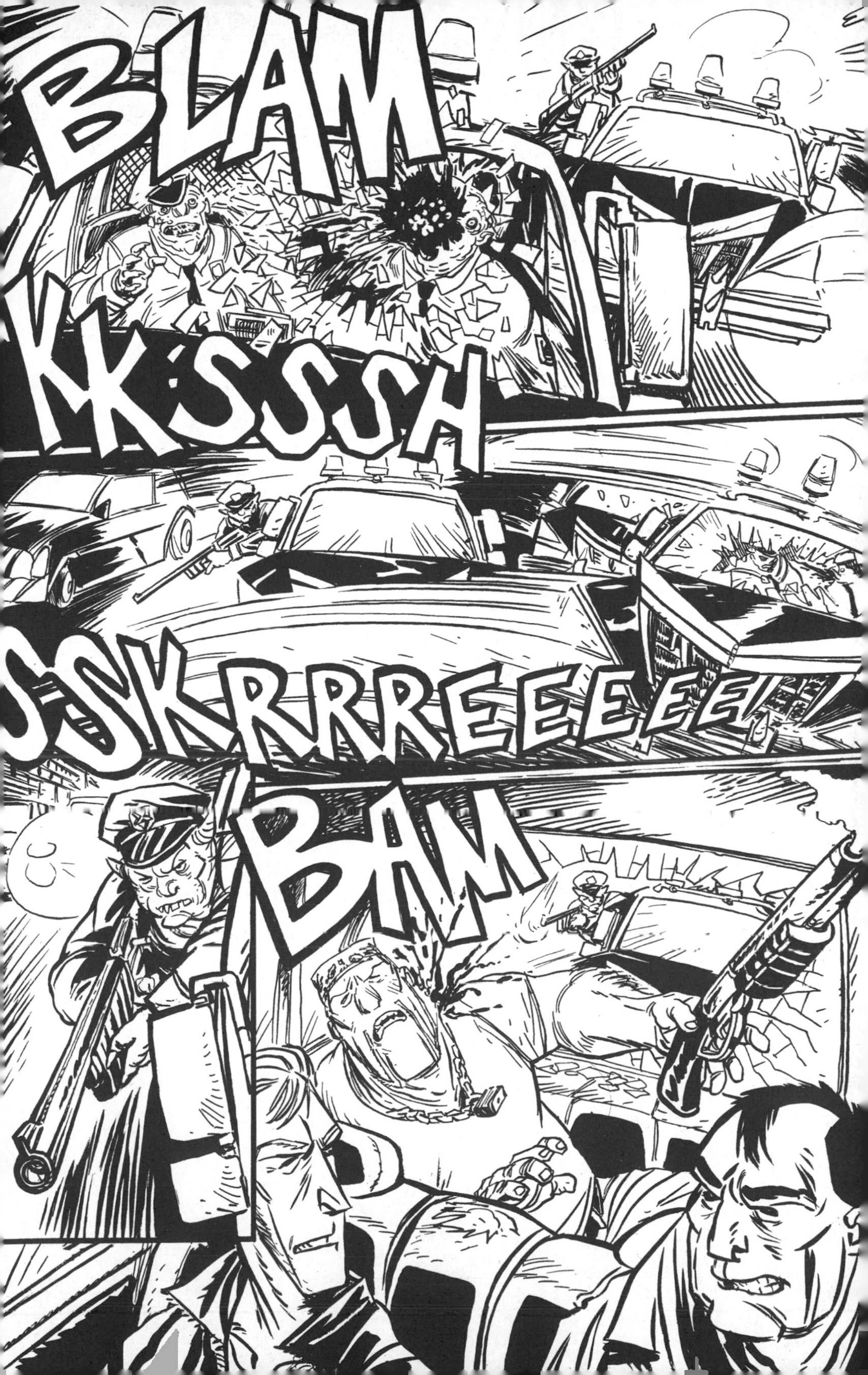
BLAM
KKSSSH
SKRRREEEEEE
BAM

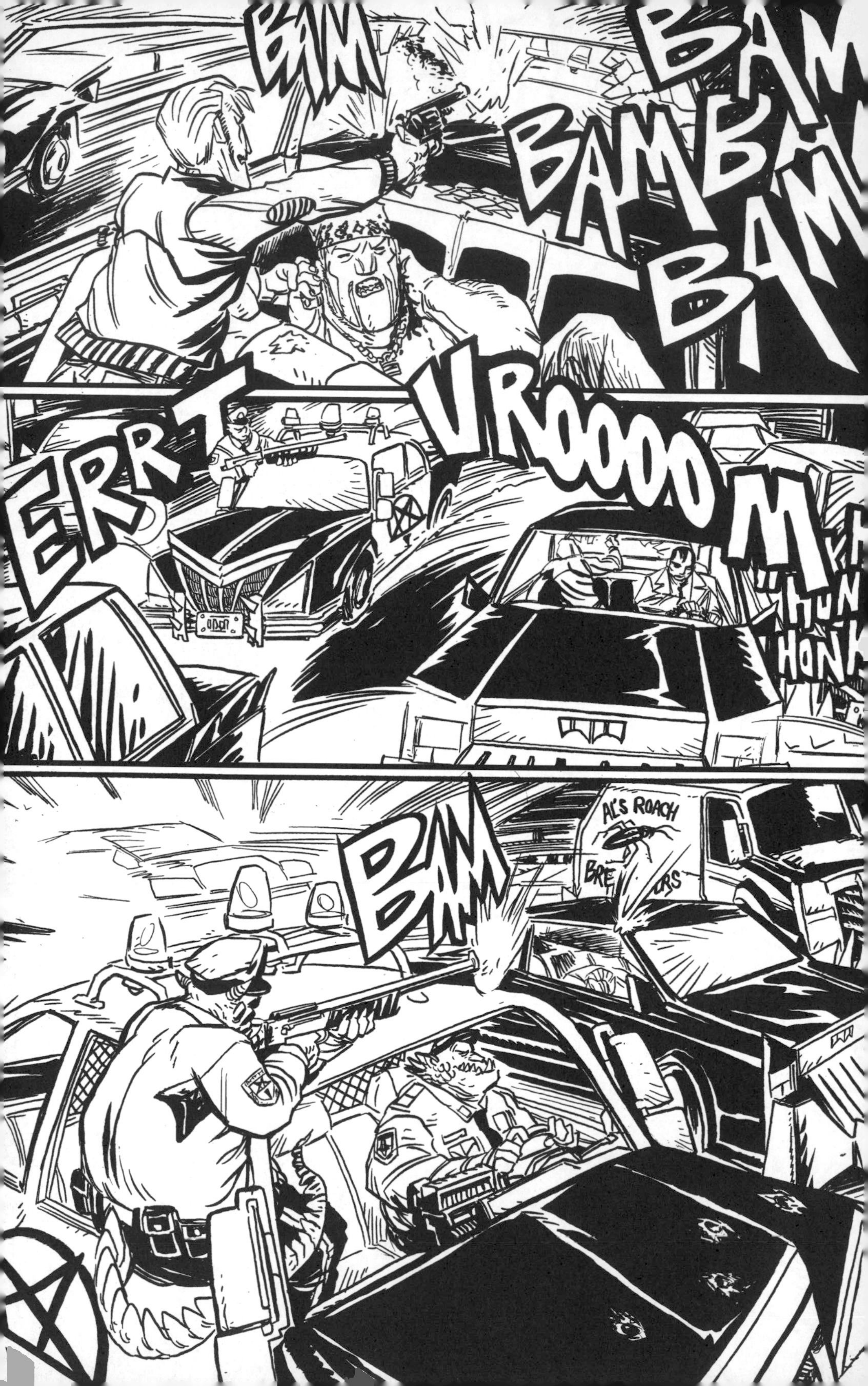

BAM
BAM
BAMBAM
BAM
BAM
ERRT
VROOOOOM
HONK
HONK
AL'S ROACH
BAM
BAM

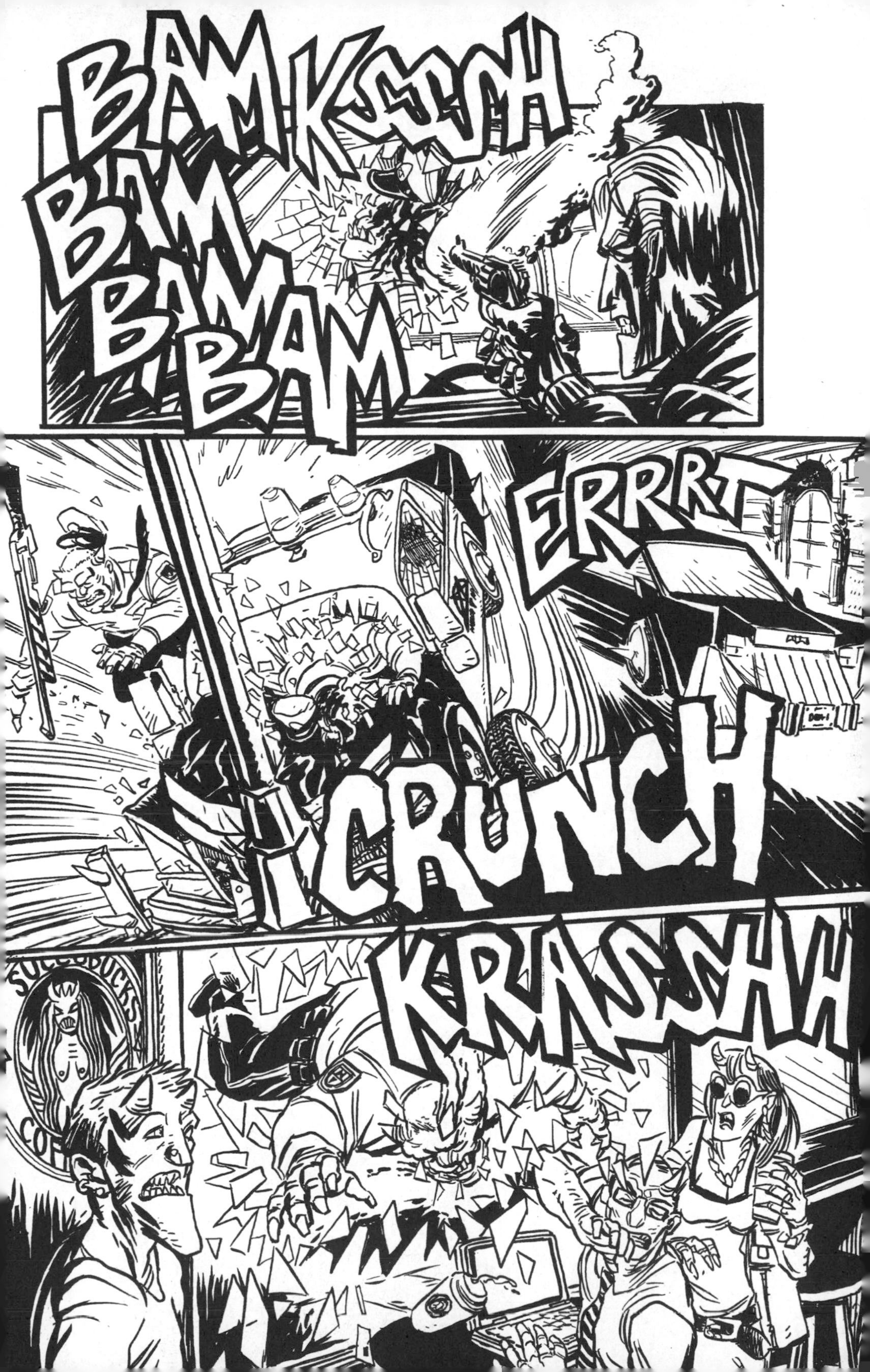
BAM KSSCH
BAM
BAM
BAM
BAM
ERRRT
CRUNCH
KRASSCHH
SUCCUBUCKS
COF

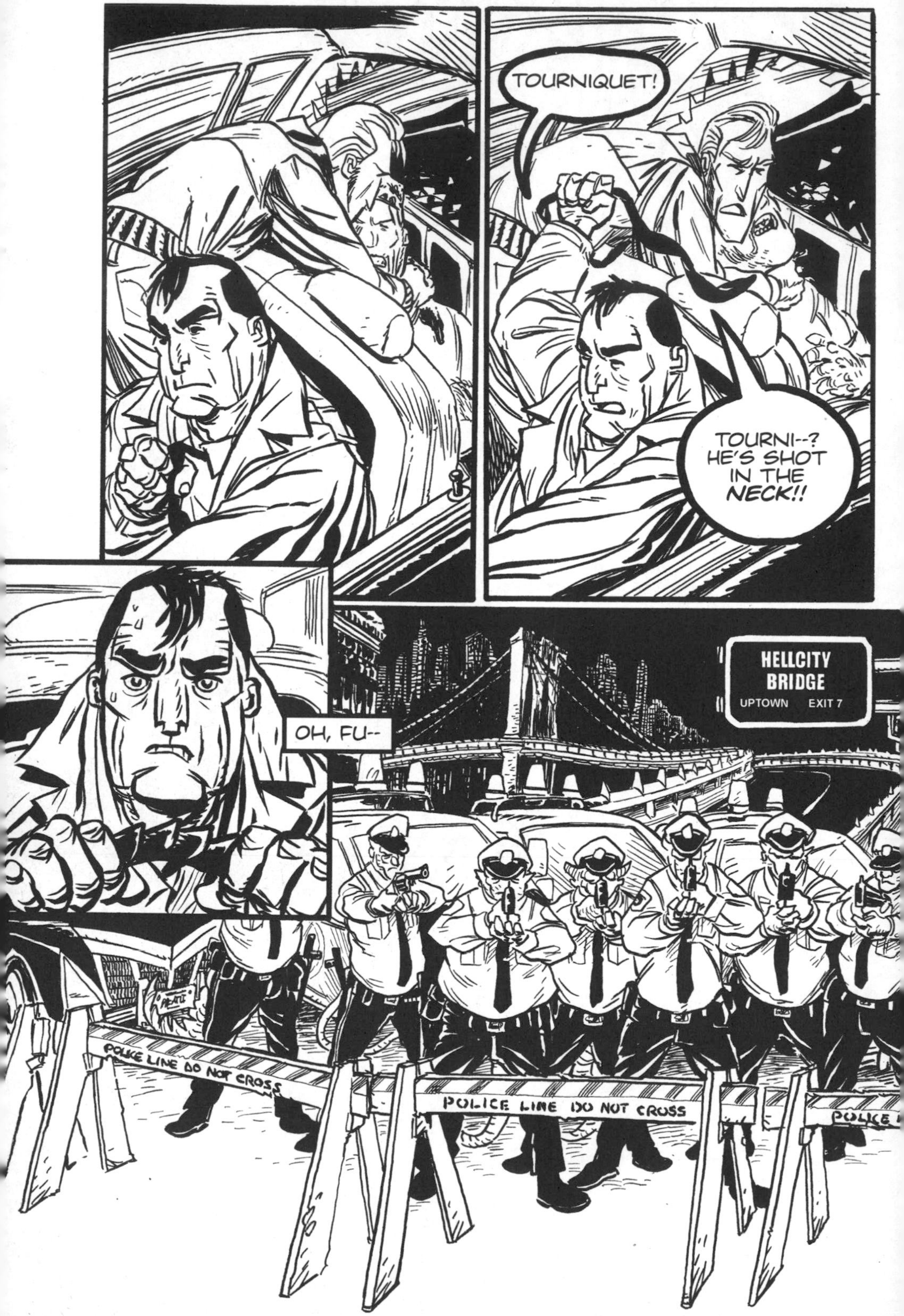
TOURNIQUET!
TOURNI--? HE'S SHOT IN THE NECK!!
OH, FU--
HELLCITY BRIDGE
UPTOWN EXIT 7
POLICE LINE DO NOT CROSS
POLICE LINE DO NOT CROSS

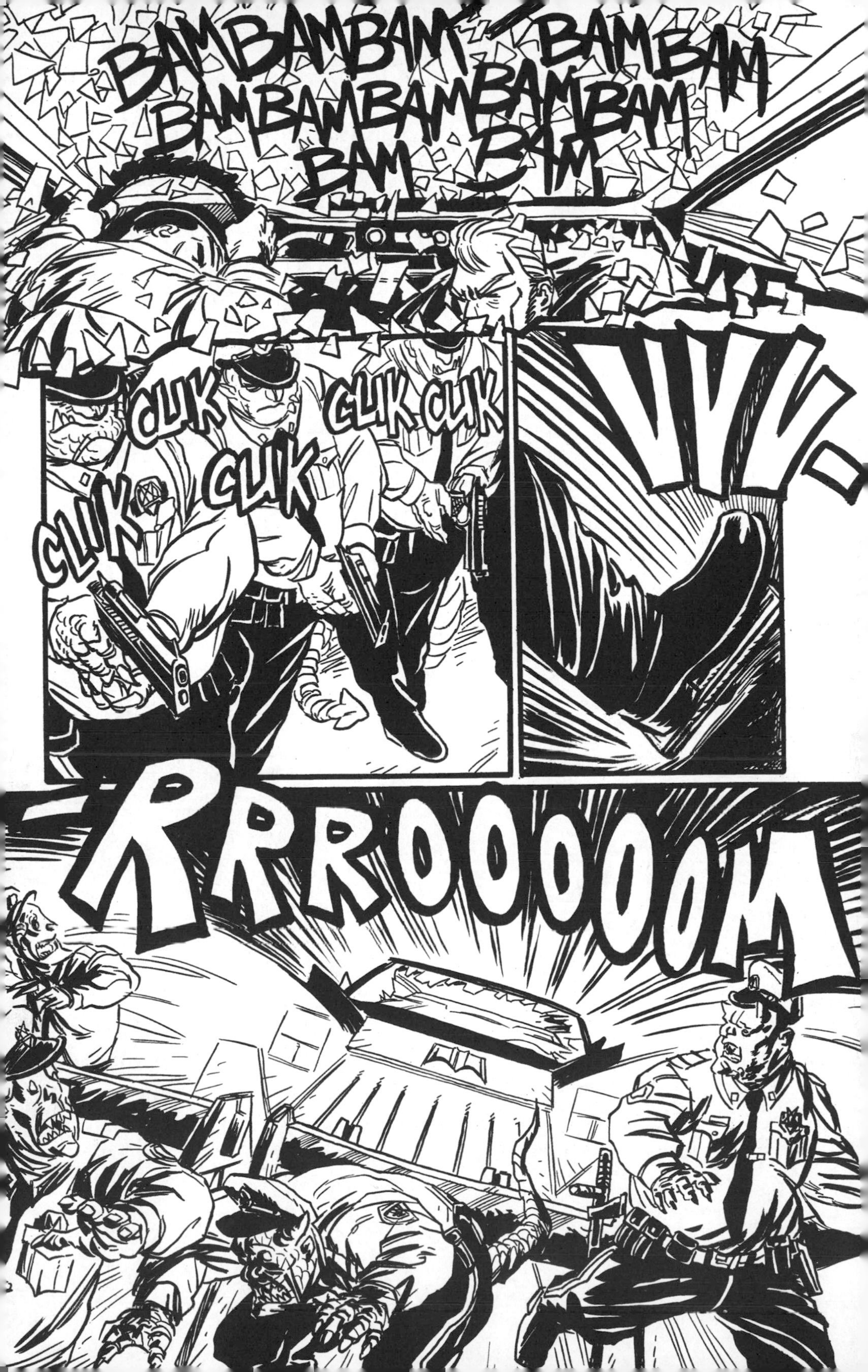
BAMBAMBAM BAMBAM
BAMBAMBAMBAMBAMBAM
BAM BAM
CLIK
CLIK CLIK
CLIK CLIK CLIK
VVV-
RRROOOOOM

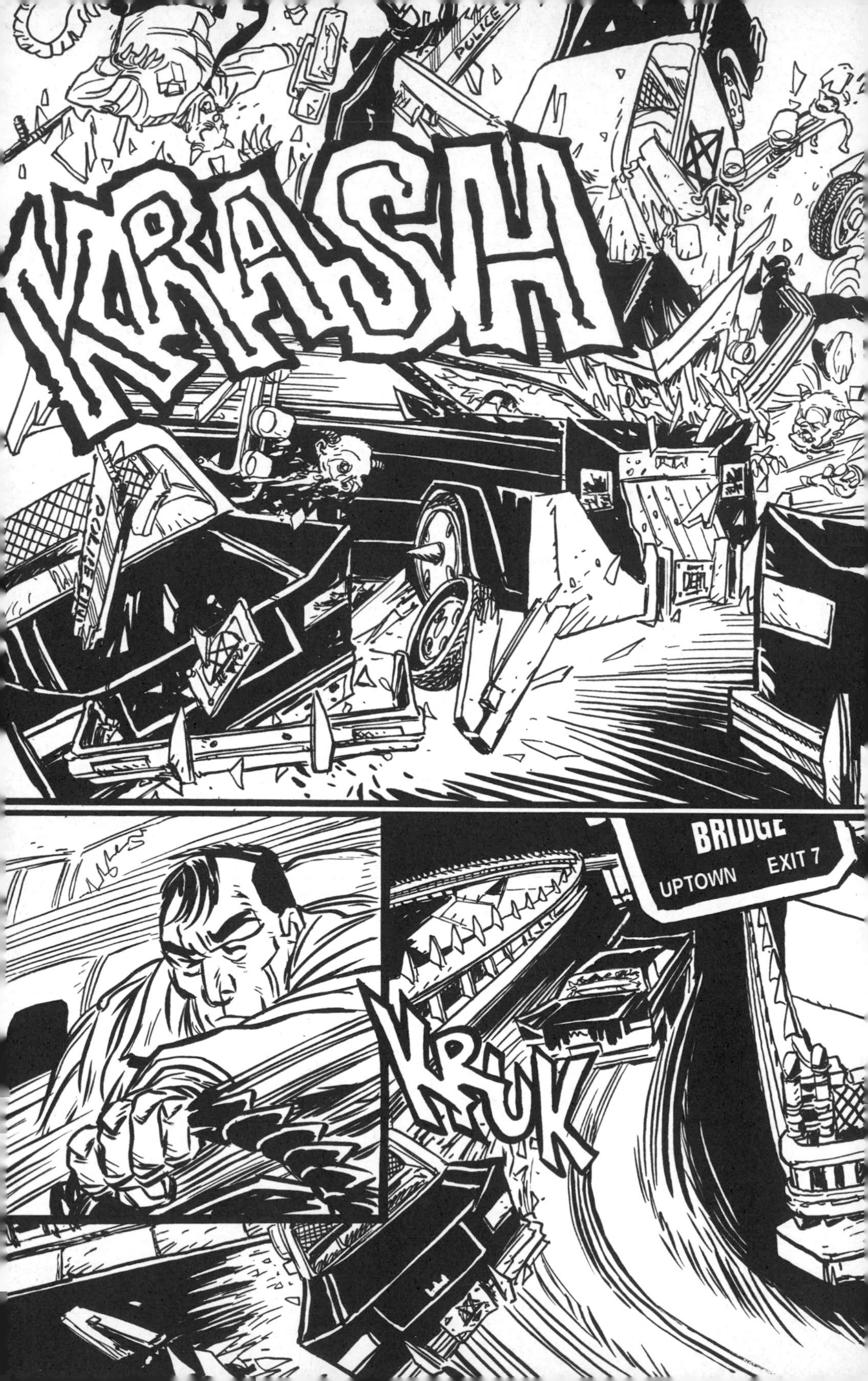
POLICE
KRASH
POLICE
BRIDGE
UPTOWN EXIT 7
KRUK

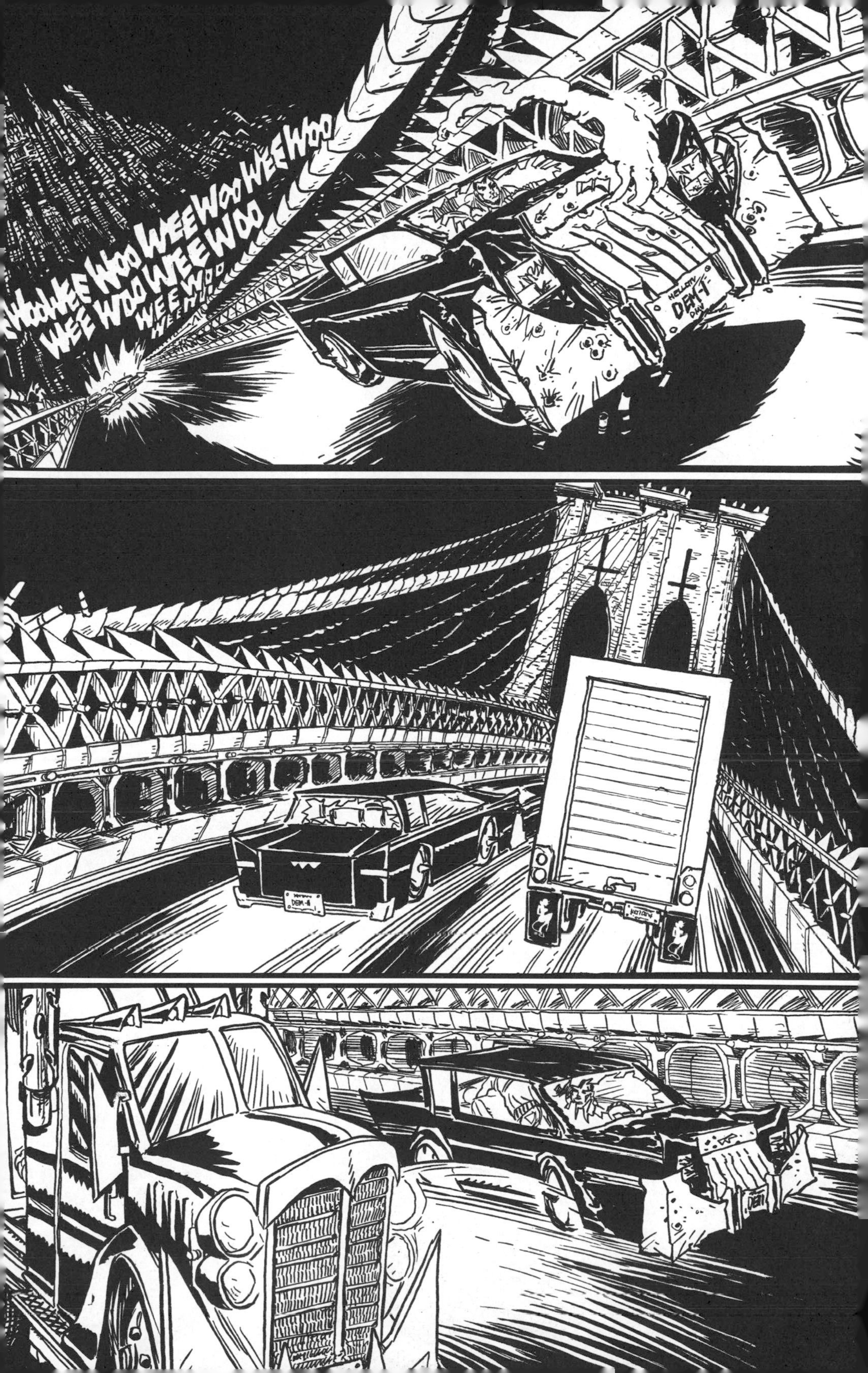
WooWEE Woo WEE Woo WEE Woo
WEE Woo WEE Woo
WEE Woo
DEM-1
DEM-II

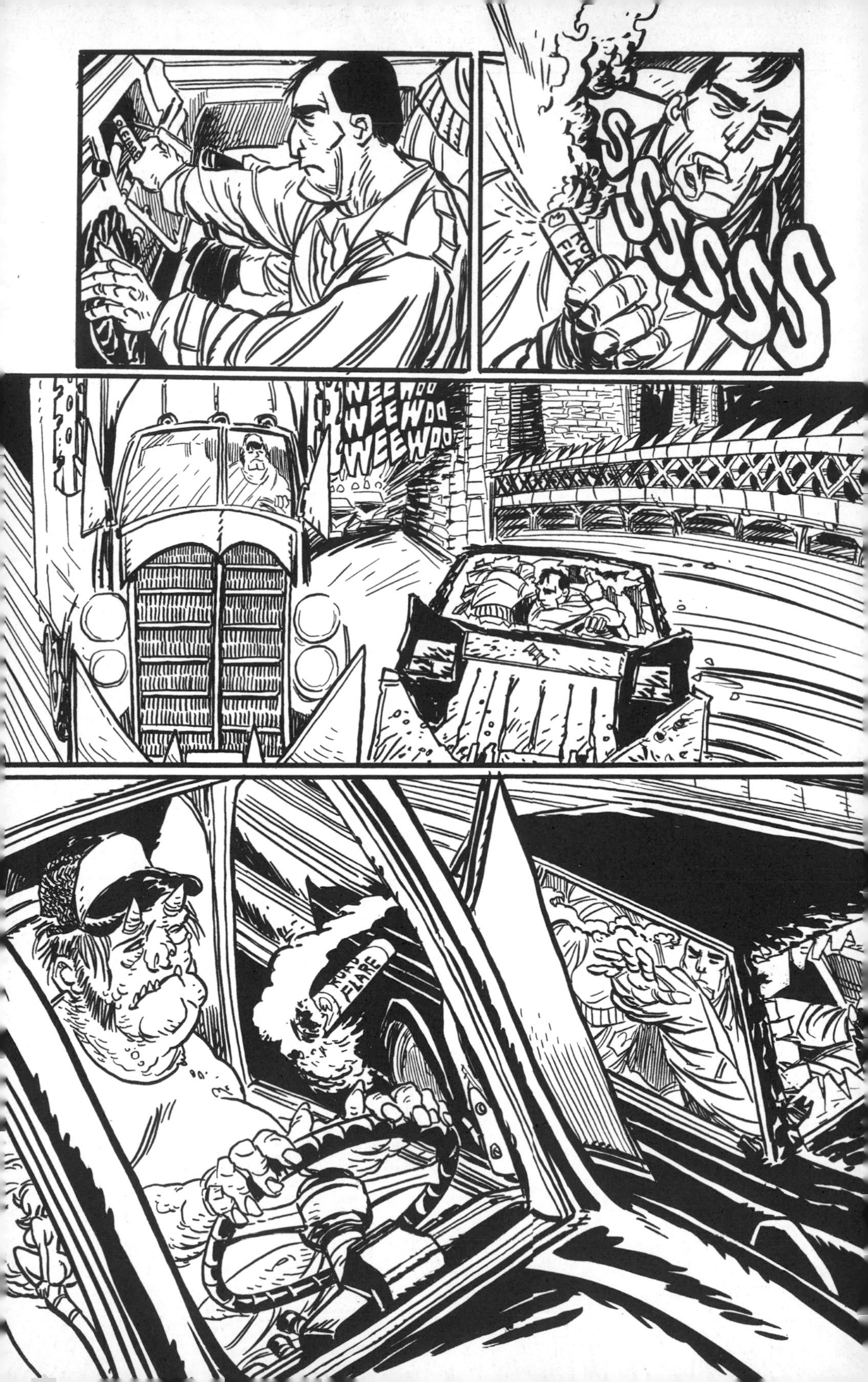
SSSSSS
WEEWOO
WEEWOO
WEEWOO
ROAD FLARE

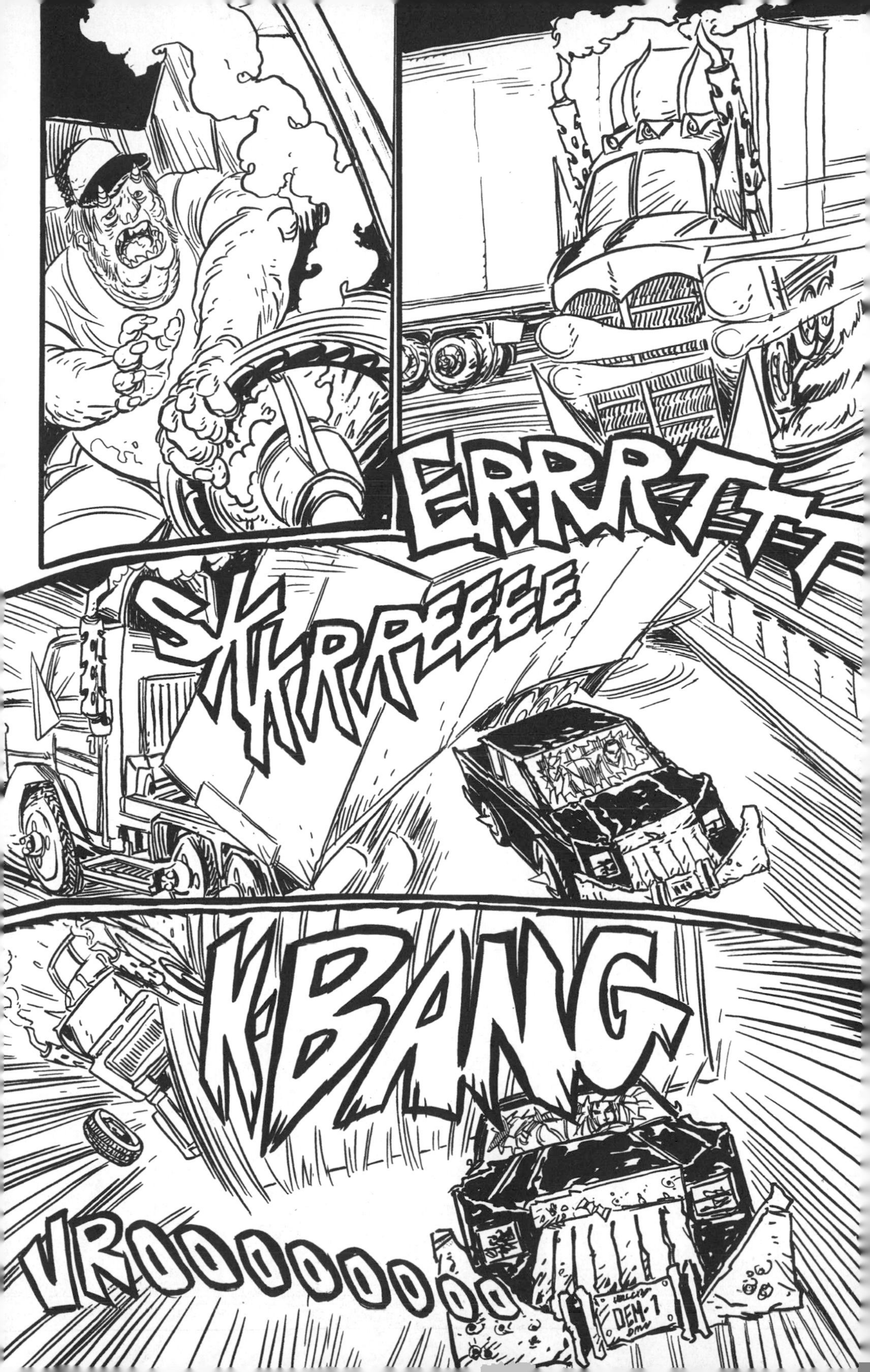
ERRRTTT
SKRREEEE
KBANG
VROOOOOOOOO
DEN-1

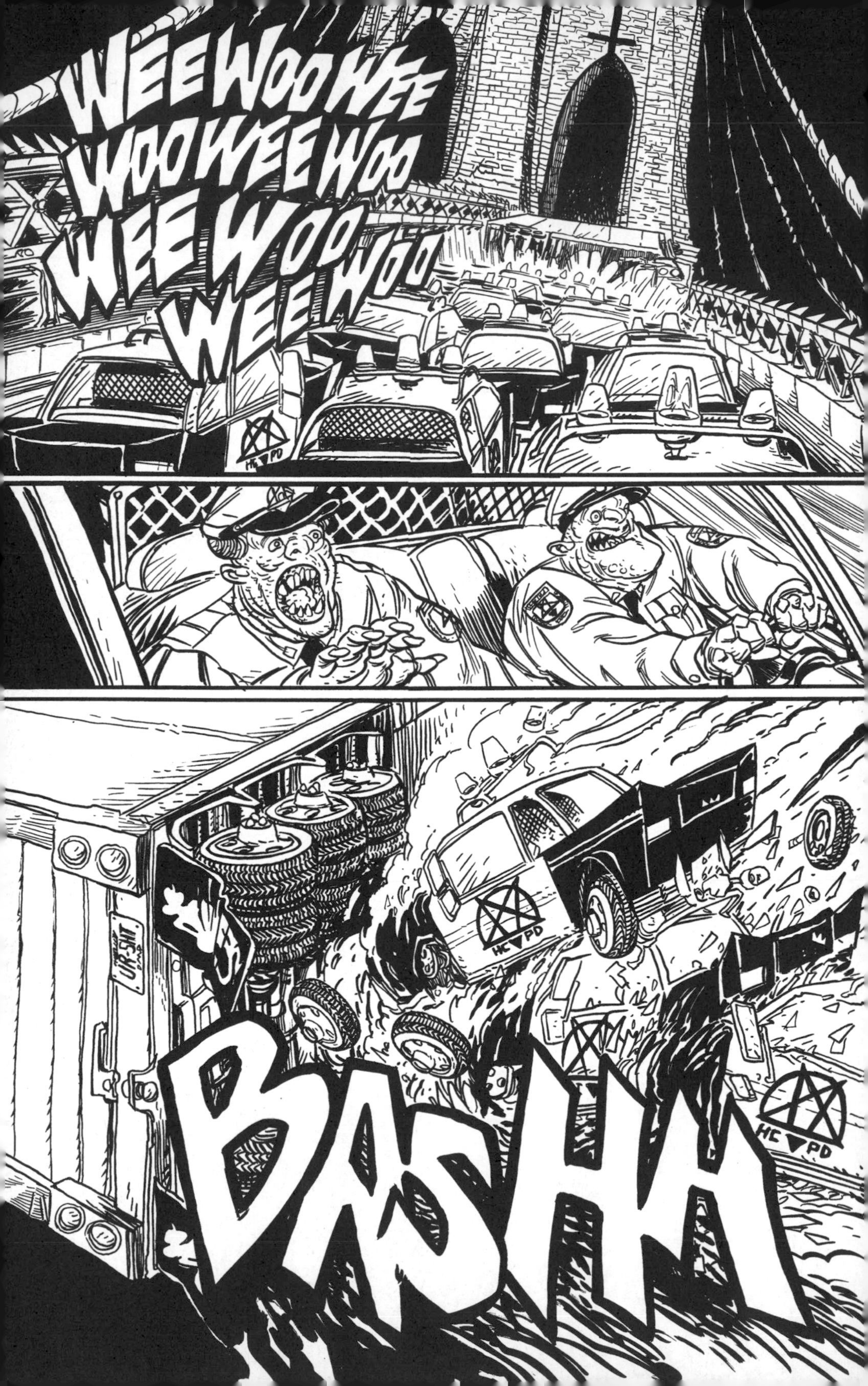

WEE WOO WEE
WOO WEE WOO
WEE WOO
WEE WOO
HC PD
UR-SHIT
HC PD
BASH
HC PD

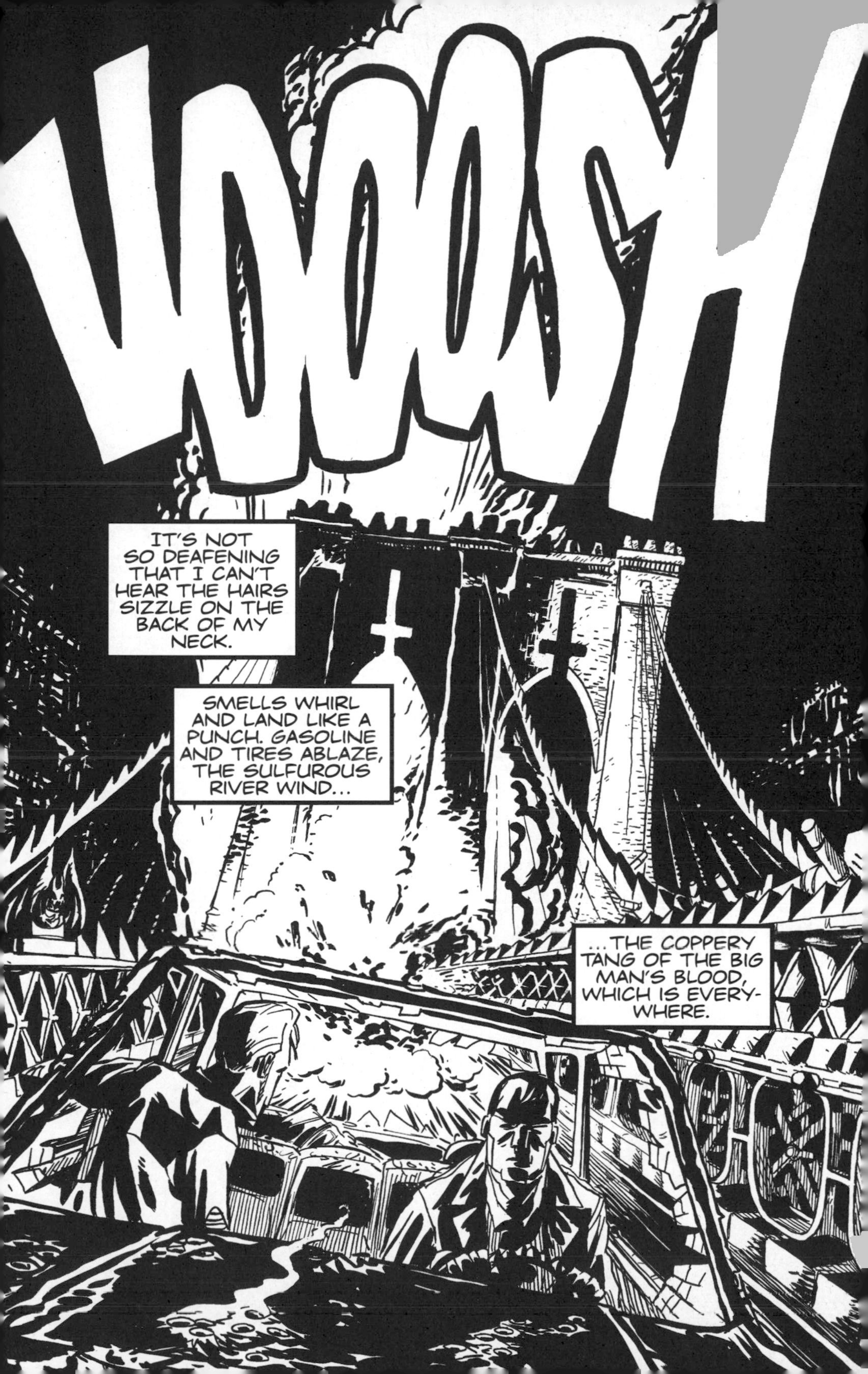
WOOOSH
IT'S NOT SO DEAFENING THAT I CAN'T HEAR THE HAIRS SIZZLE ON THE BACK OF MY NECK.
SMELLS WHIRL AND LAND LIKE A PUNCH. GASOLINE AND TIRES ABLAZE, THE SULFUROUS RIVER WIND...
...THE COPPERY TANG OF THE BIG MAN'S BLOOD, WHICH IS EVERY-WHERE.

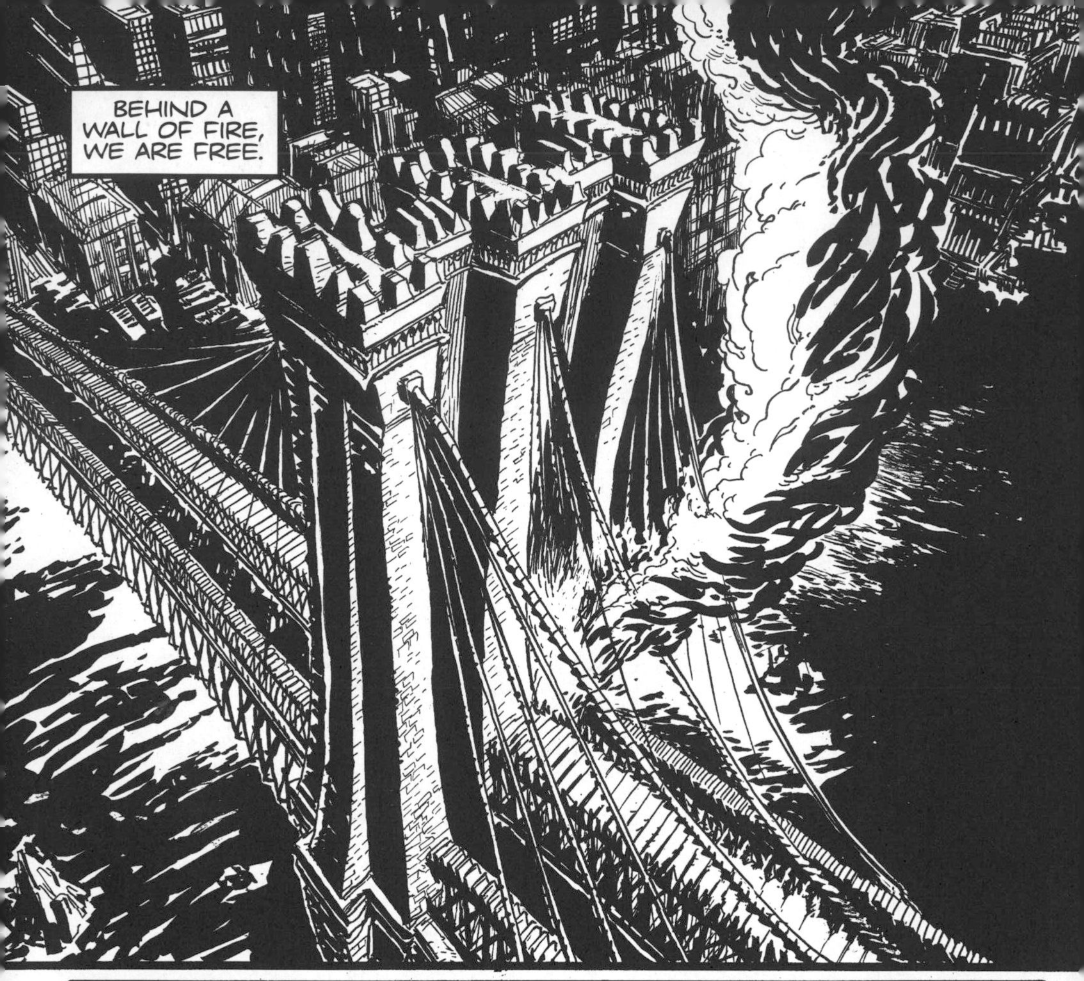
BEHIND A WALL OF FIRE, WE ARE FREE.

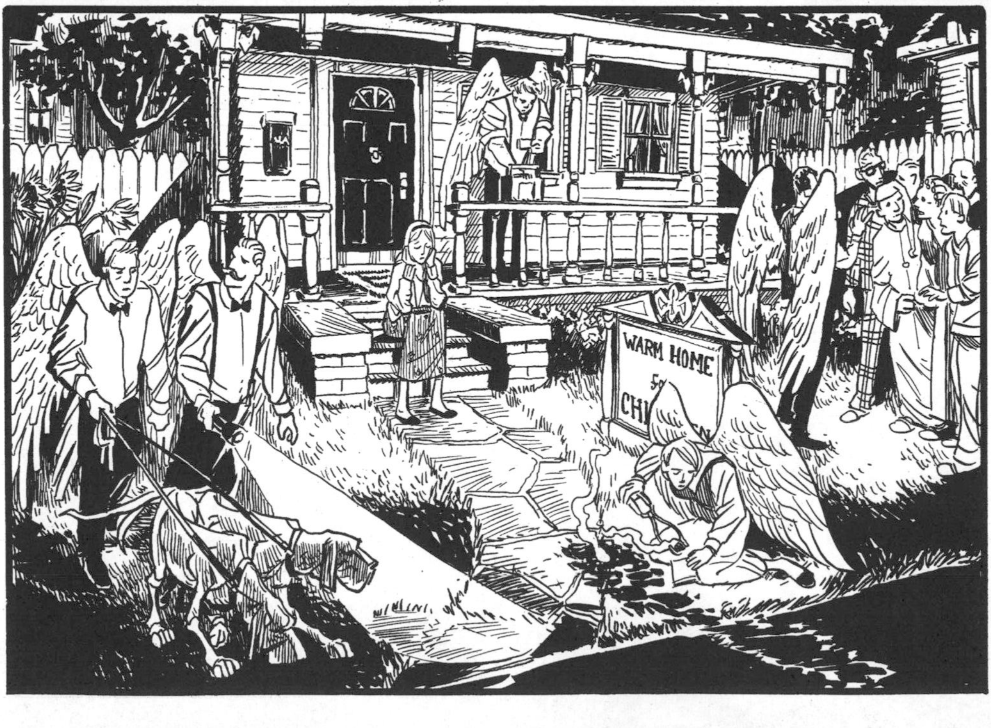
WARM HOME

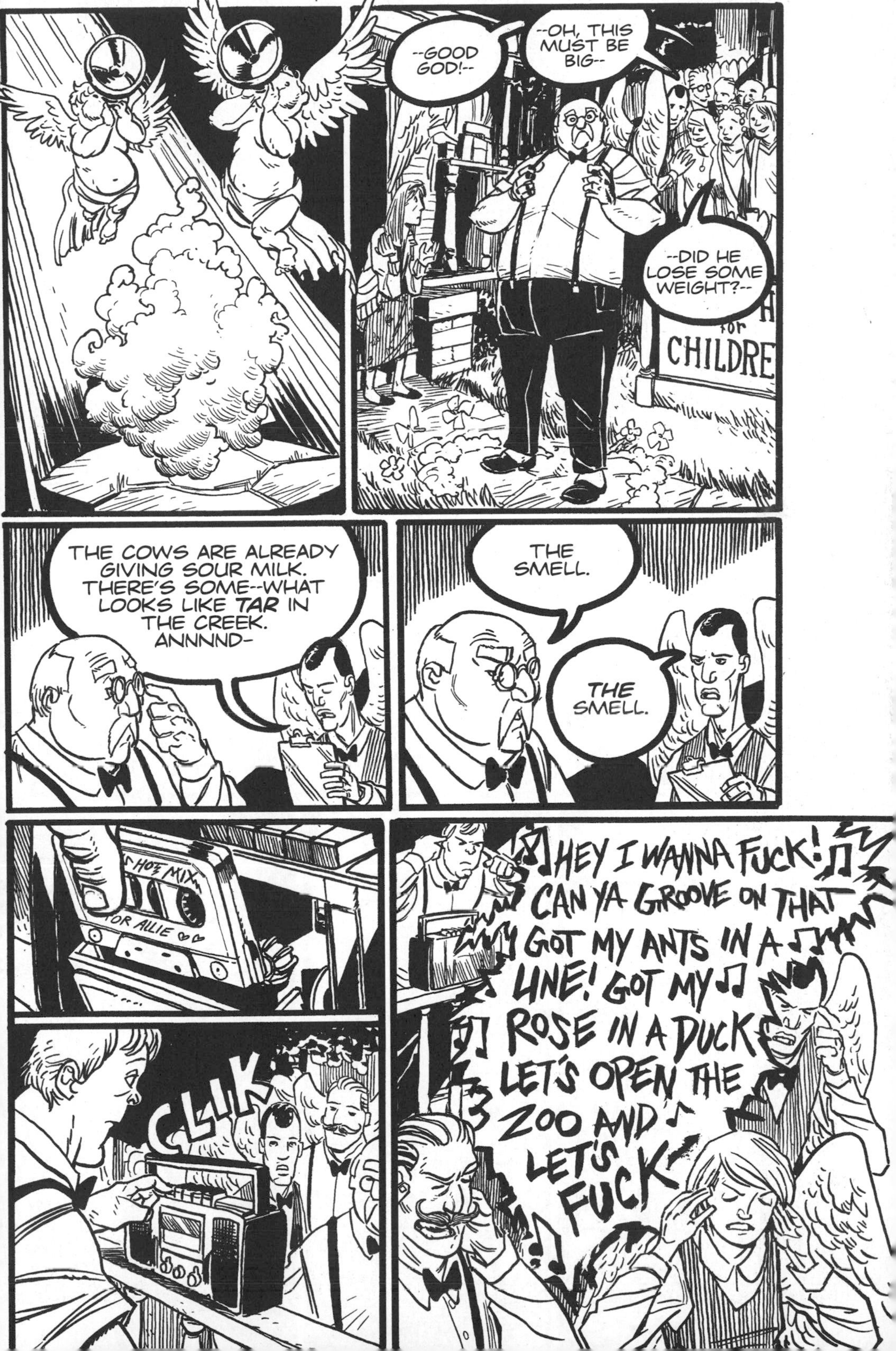
--GOOD GOD!--
--OH, THIS MUST BE BIG--
--DID HE LOSE SOME WEIGHT?--
CHILDRE
THE COWS ARE ALREADY GIVING SOUR MILK. THERE'S SOME--WHAT LOOKS LIKE TAR IN THE CREEK. ANNNND-
THE SMELL.
THE SMELL.
HOT MIX
FOR ALLIE
CLIK
HEY I WANNA FUCK! CAN YA GROOVE ON THAT GOT MY ANTS IN A LINE! GOT MY ROSE IN A DUCK LET'S OPEN THE ZOO AND LET'S FUCK

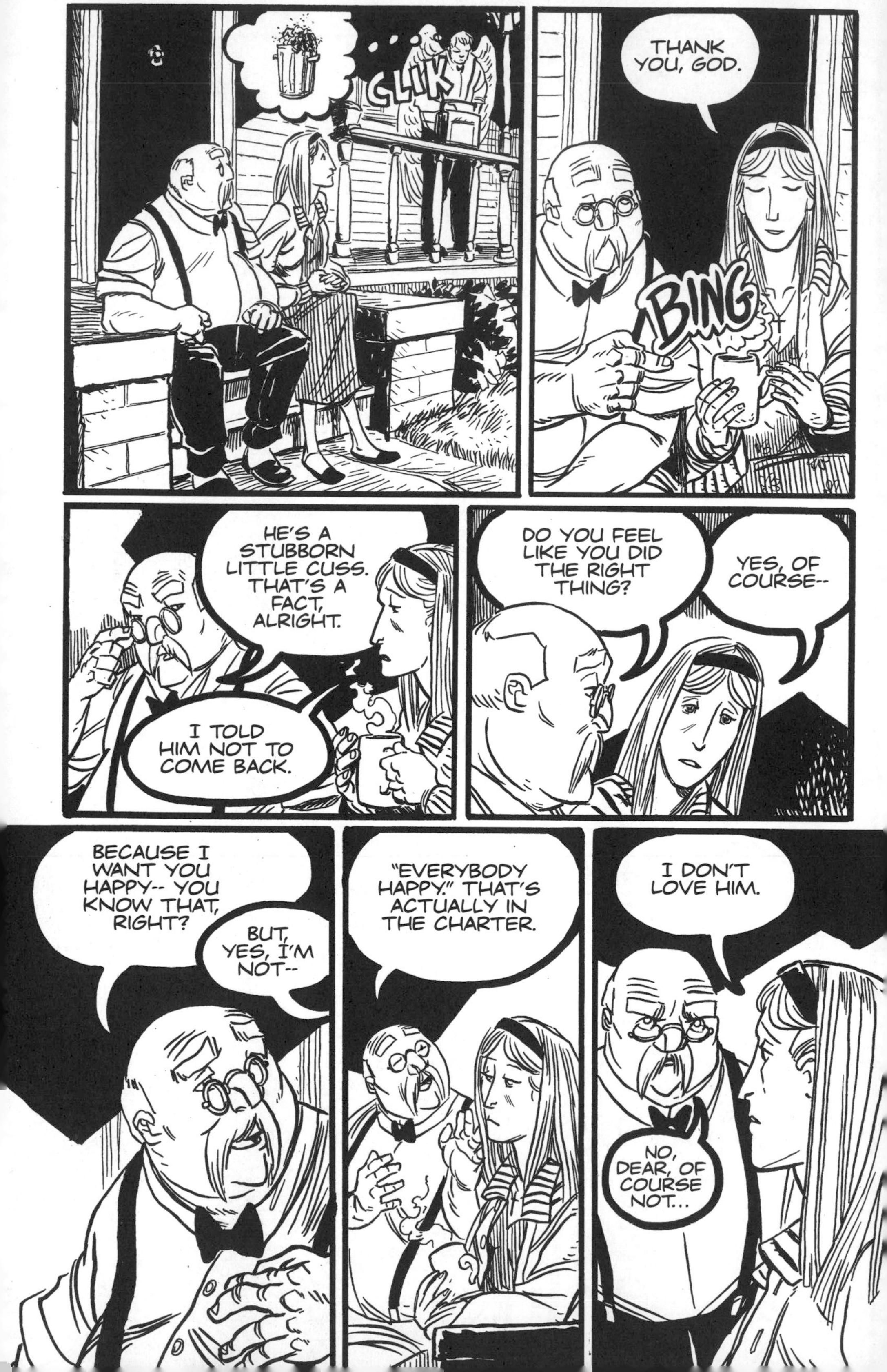
CLIK
THANK YOU, GOD.
BING
HE'S A STUBBORN LITTLE CUSS. THAT'S A FACT, ALRIGHT.
I TOLD HIM NOT TO COME BACK.
DO YOU FEEL LIKE YOU DID THE RIGHT THING?
YES, OF COURSE--
BECAUSE I WANT YOU HAPPY-- YOU KNOW THAT, RIGHT?
BUT, YES, I'M NOT--
"EVERYBODY HAPPY." THAT'S ACTUALLY IN THE CHARTER.
I DON'T LOVE HIM.
NO, DEAR, OF COURSE NOT...

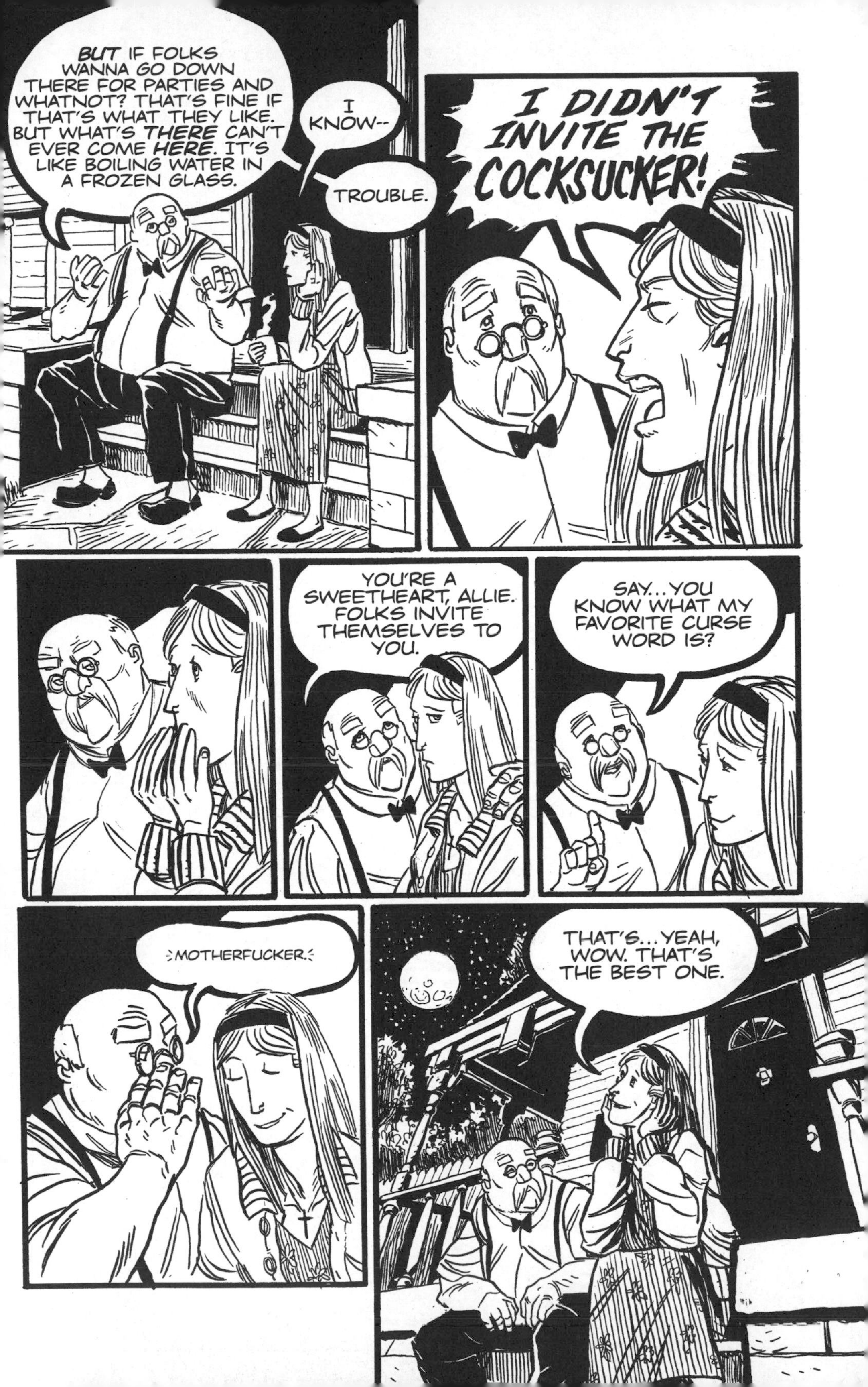
BUT IF FOLKS WANNA GO DOWN THERE FOR PARTIES AND WHATNOT? THAT'S FINE IF THAT'S WHAT THEY LIKE. BUT WHAT'S THERE CAN'T EVER COME HERE. IT'S LIKE BOILING WATER IN A FROZEN GLASS.
I KNOW--
TROUBLE.
I DIDN'T INVITE THE COCKSUCKER!
YOU'RE A SWEETHEART, ALLIE. FOLKS INVITE THEMSELVES TO YOU.
SAY...YOU KNOW WHAT MY FAVORITE CURSE WORD IS?
MOTHERFUCKER.
THAT'S...YEAH, WOW. THAT'S THE BEST ONE.

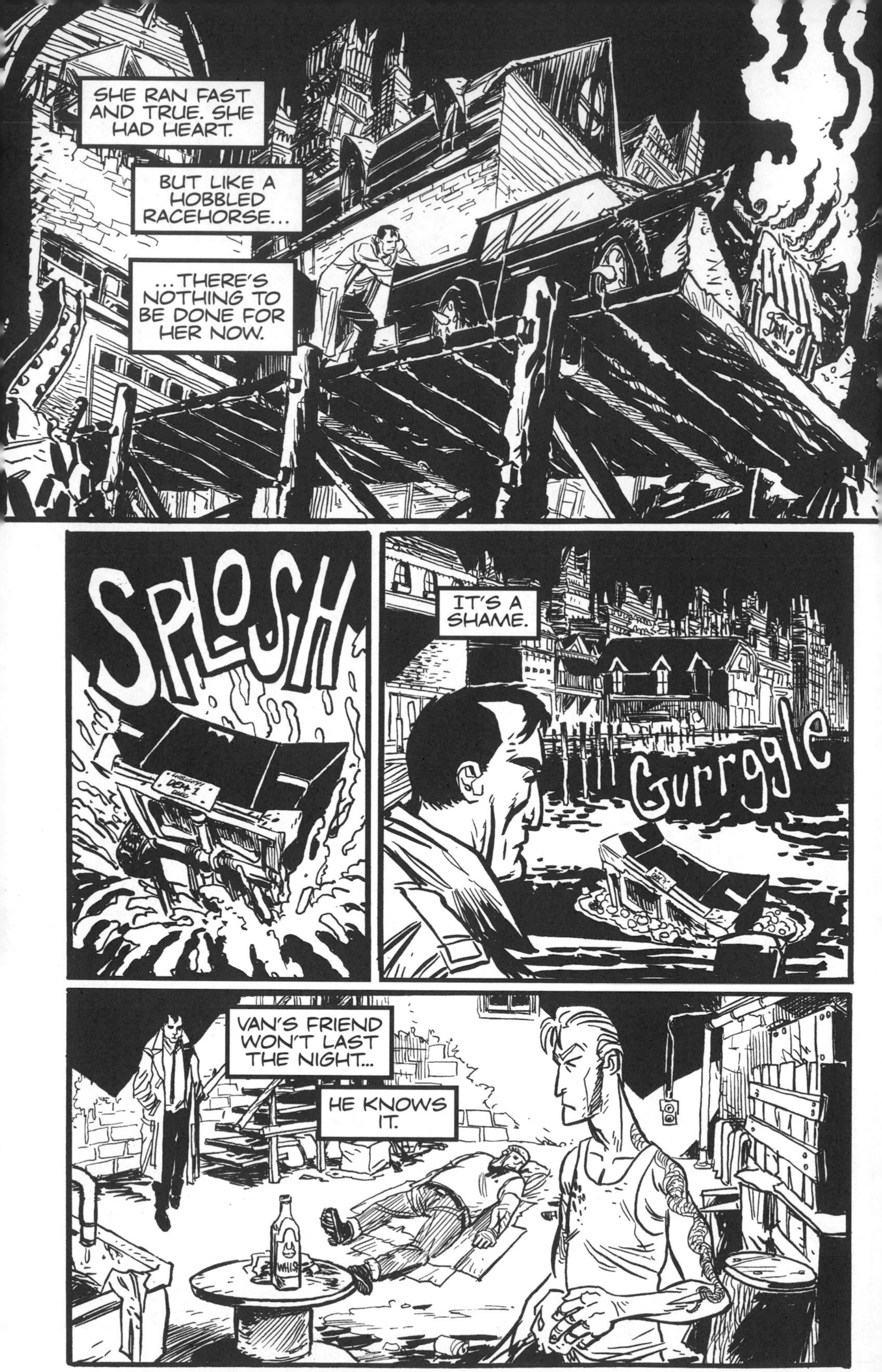
SHE RAN FAST AND TRUE. SHE HAD HEART.
BUT LIKE A HOBBLED RACEHORSE...
...THERE'S NOTHING TO BE DONE FOR HER NOW.
SPLOSH
IT'S A SHAME.
Gurrggle
VAN'S FRIEND WON'T LAST THE NIGHT...
HE KNOWS IT.

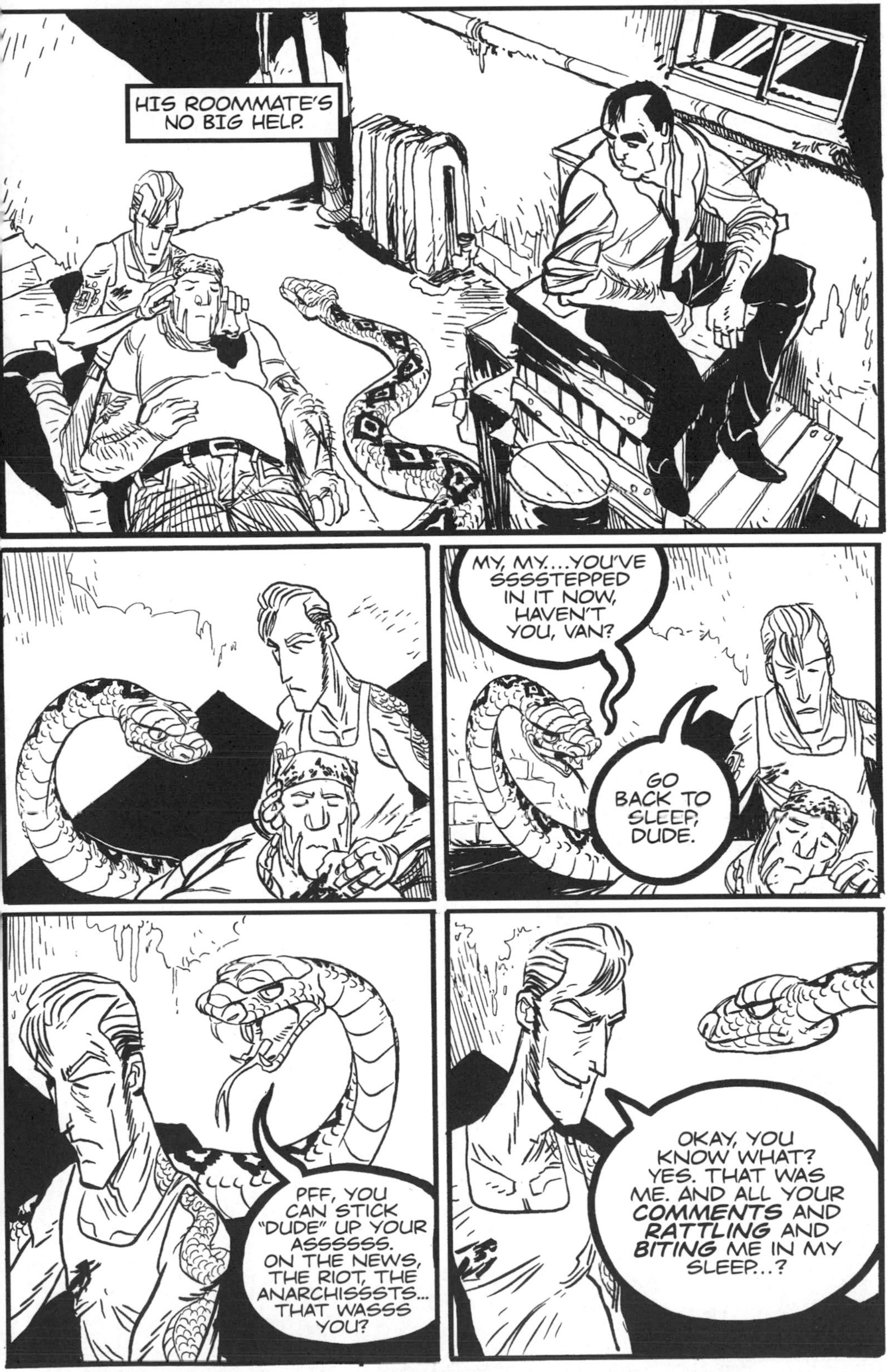
HIS ROOMMATE'S NO BIG HELP.
MY, MY....YOU'VE SSSSTEPPED IN IT NOW, HAVEN'T YOU, VAN?
GO BACK TO SLEEP, DUDE.
PFF, YOU CAN STICK "DUDE" UP YOUR ASSSSSS. ON THE NEWS, THE RIOT, THE ANARCHISSSTS... THAT WASSS YOU?
OKAY, YOU KNOW WHAT? YES. THAT WAS ME. AND ALL YOUR COMMENTS AND RATTLING AND BITING ME IN MY SLEEP...?

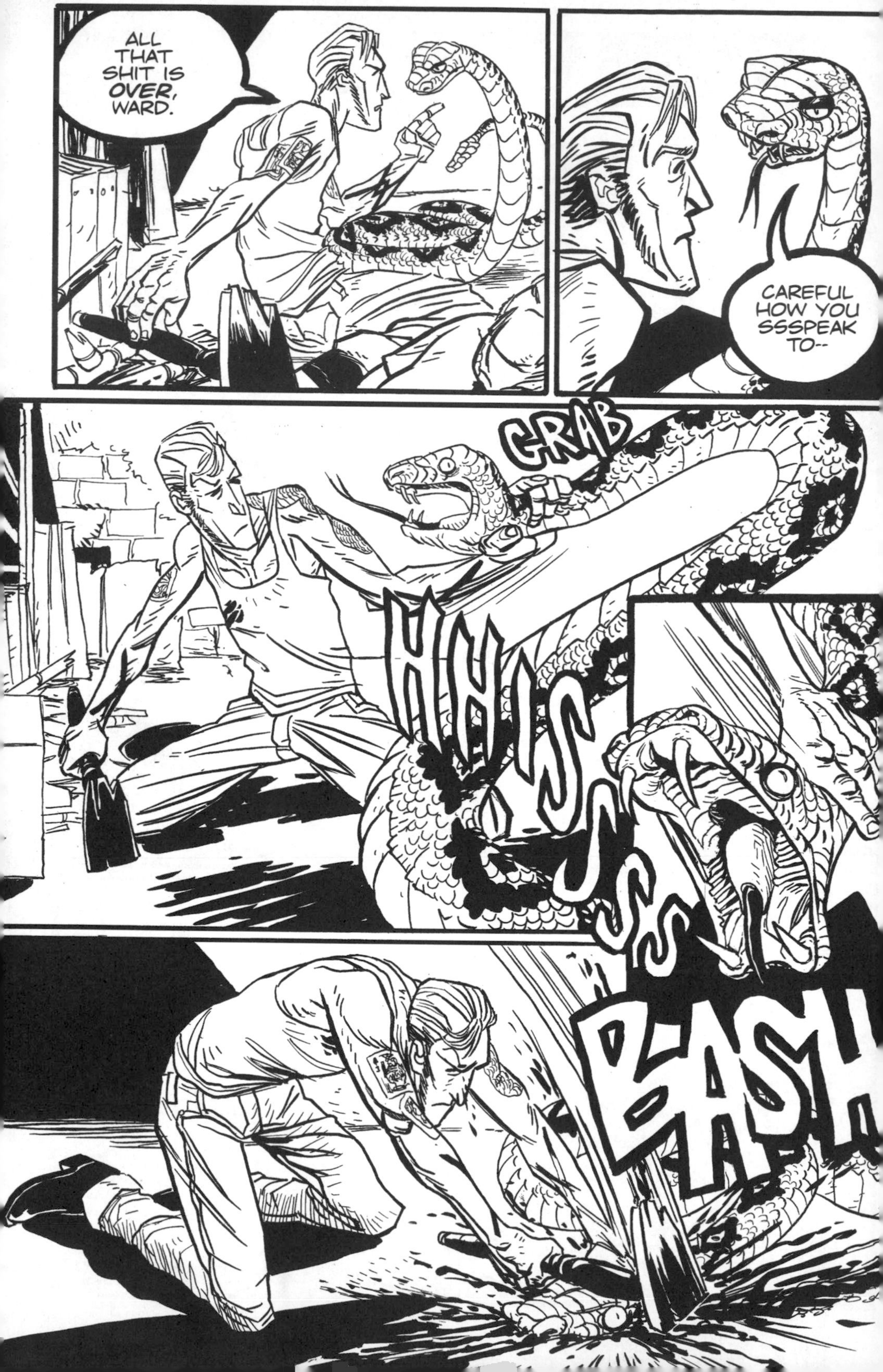
ALL THAT SHIT IS OVER, WARD.
CAREFUL HOW YOU SSSPEAK TO--
GRAB
HHISSSSS
BASH!

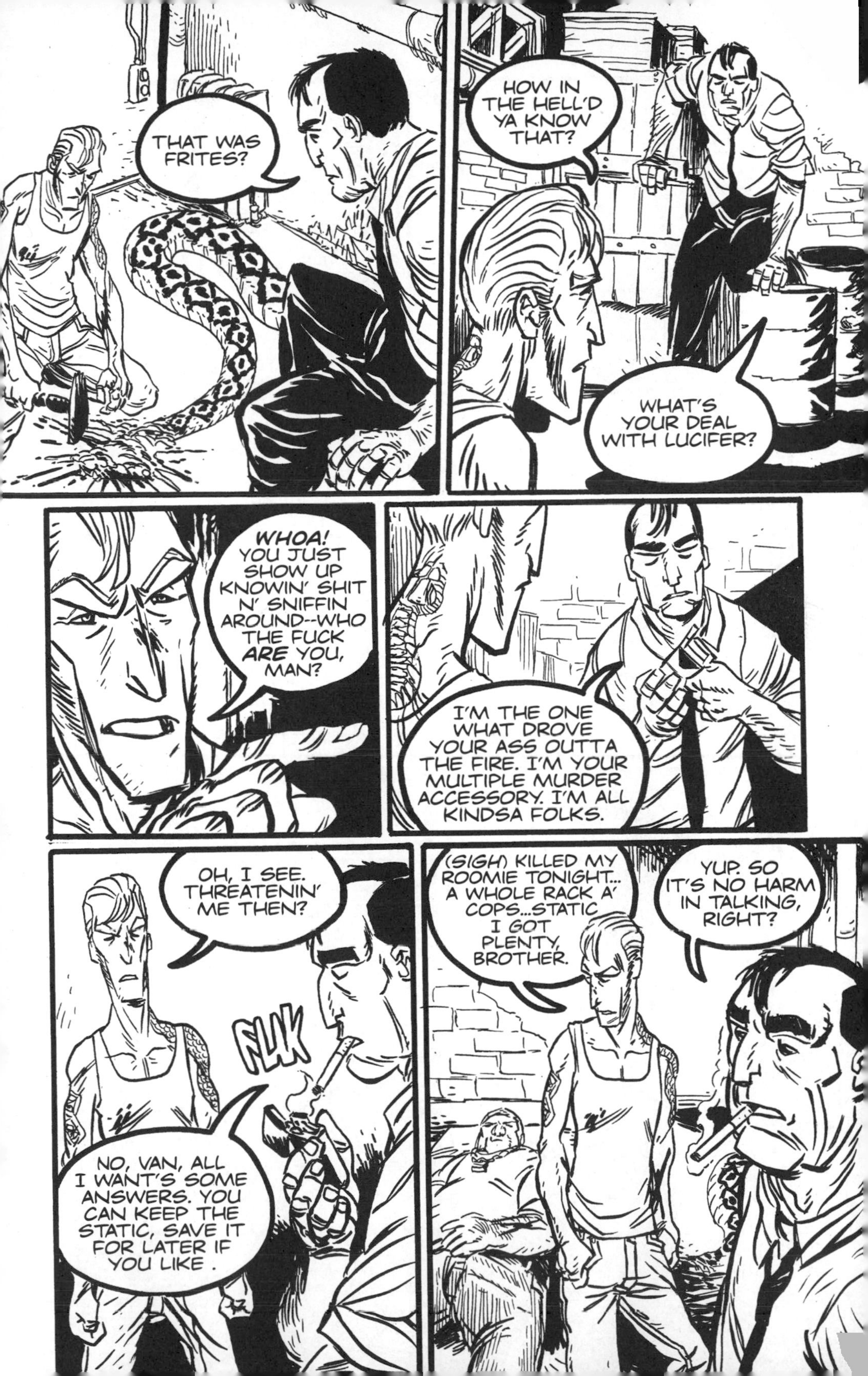
THAT WAS FRITES?
HOW IN THE HELL'D YA KNOW THAT?
WHAT'S YOUR DEAL WITH LUCIFER?
WHOA! YOU JUST SHOW UP KNOWIN' SHIT N' SNIFFIN AROUND--WHO THE FUCK ARE YOU, MAN?
I'M THE ONE WHAT DROVE YOUR ASS OUTTA THE FIRE. I'M YOUR MULTIPLE MURDER ACCESSORY. I'M ALL KINDSA FOLKS.
OH, I SEE. THREATENIN' ME THEN?
FLIK
NO, VAN, ALL I WANT'S SOME ANSWERS. YOU CAN KEEP THE STATIC, SAVE IT FOR LATER IF YOU LIKE.
(SIGH) KILLED MY ROOMIE TONIGHT... A WHOLE RACK A' COPS...STATIC I GOT PLENTY, BROTHER.
YUP. SO IT'S NO HARM IN TALKING, RIGHT?

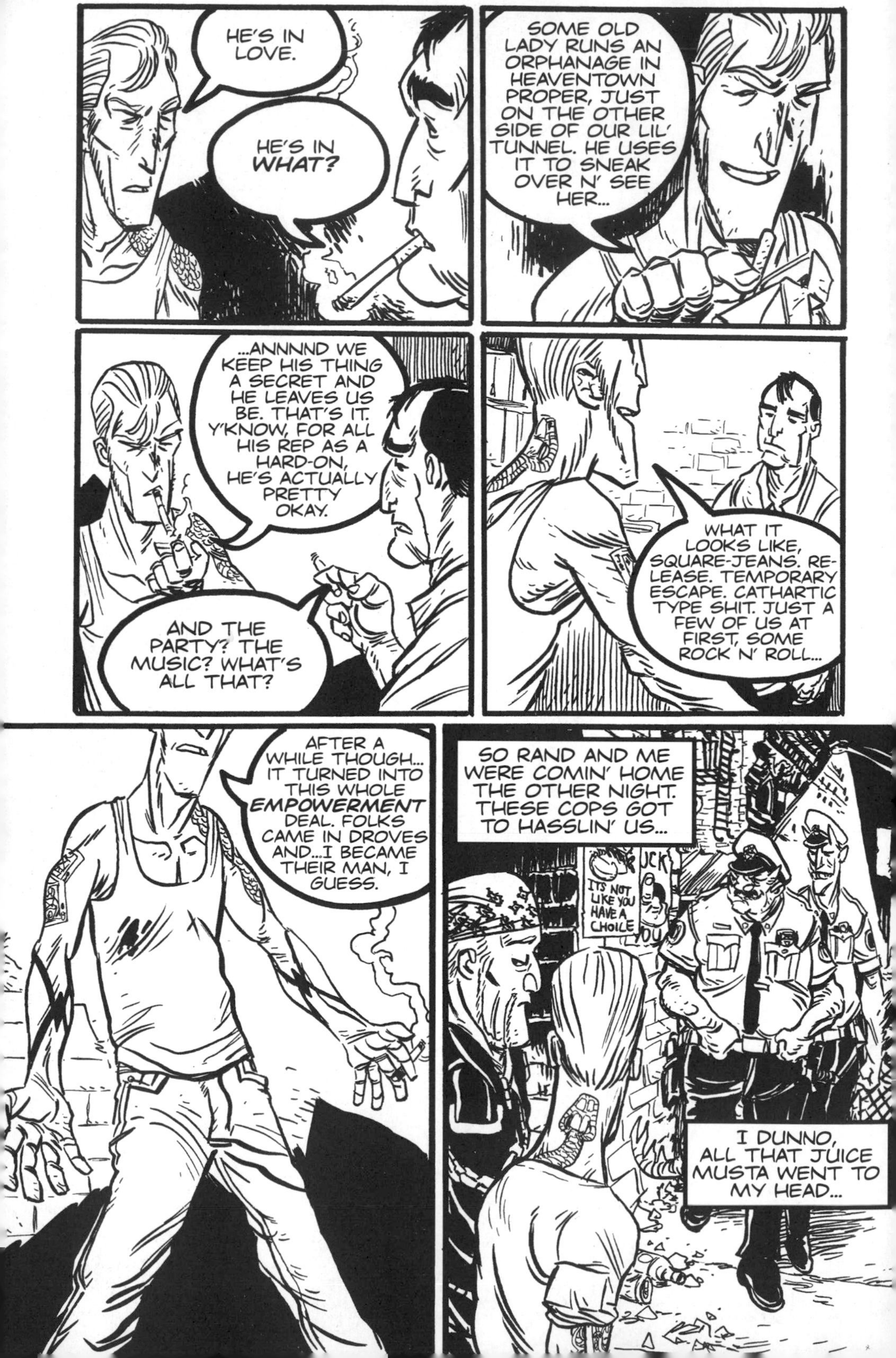
HE'S IN LOVE.
HE'S IN WHAT?
SOME OLD LADY RUNS AN ORPHANAGE IN HEAVENTOWN PROPER, JUST ON THE OTHER SIDE OF OUR LIL' TUNNEL. HE USES IT TO SNEAK OVER N' SEE HER...
...ANNNND WE KEEP HIS THING A SECRET AND HE LEAVES US BE. THAT'S IT. Y'KNOW, FOR ALL HIS REP AS A HARD-ON, HE'S ACTUALLY PRETTY OKAY.
AND THE PARTY? THE MUSIC? WHAT'S ALL THAT?
WHAT IT LOOKS LIKE, SQUARE-JEANS. RE-LEASE. TEMPORARY ESCAPE. CATHARTIC TYPE SHIT. JUST A FEW OF US AT FIRST, SOME ROCK N' ROLL...
AFTER A WHILE THOUGH... IT TURNED INTO THIS WHOLE EMPOWERMENT DEAL. FOLKS CAME IN DROVES AND...I BECAME THEIR MAN, I GUESS.
SO RAND AND ME WERE COMIN' HOME THE OTHER NIGHT. THESE COPS GOT TO HASSLIN' US...
ITS NOT LIKE YOU HAVE A CHOICE
I DUNNO, ALL THAT JUICE MUSTA WENT TO MY HEAD...

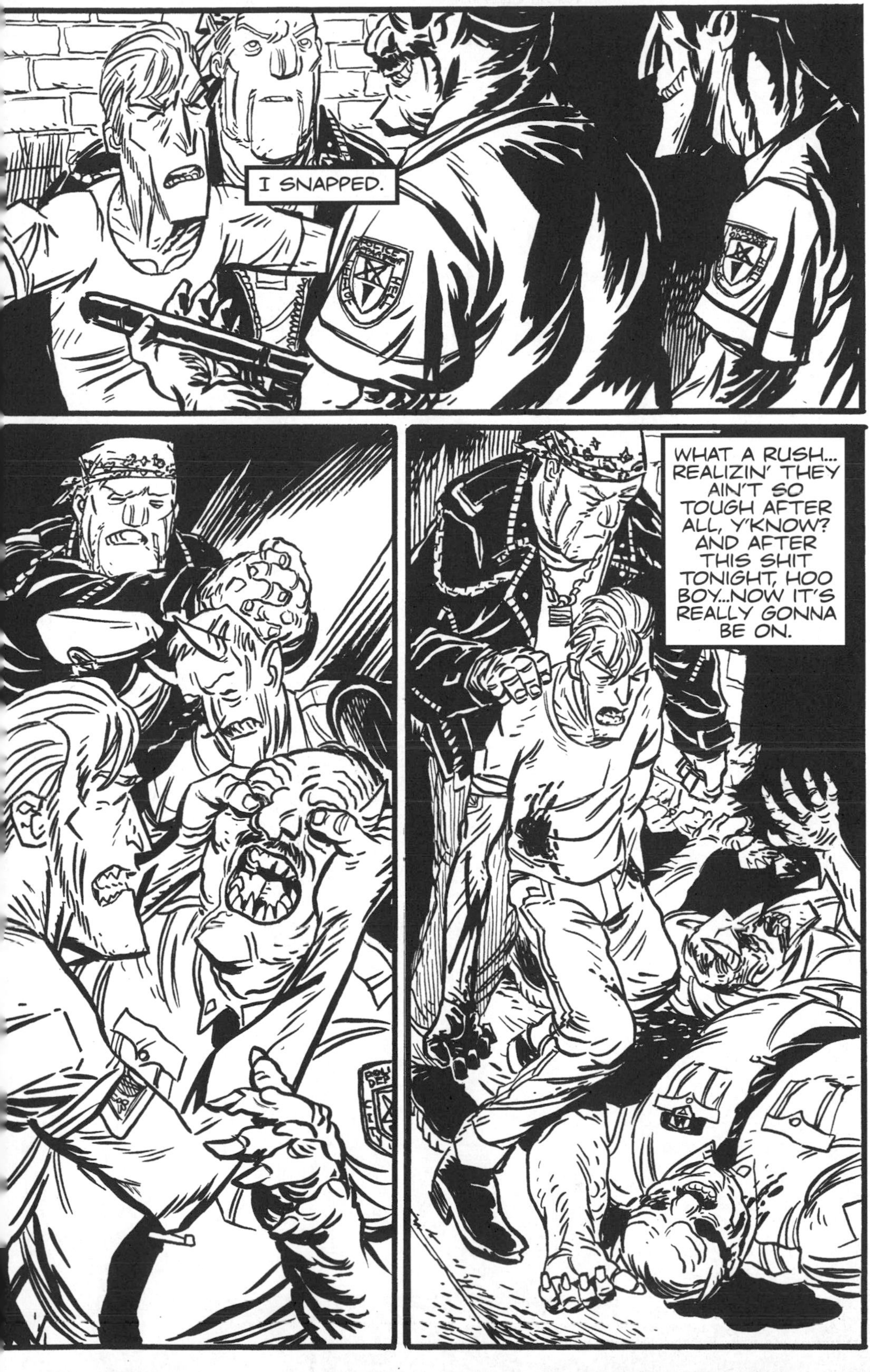
I SNAPPED.
WHAT A RUSH... REALIZIN' THEY AIN'T SO TOUGH AFTER ALL, Y'KNOW? AND AFTER THIS SHIT TONIGHT, HOO BOY...NOW IT'S REALLY GONNA BE ON.

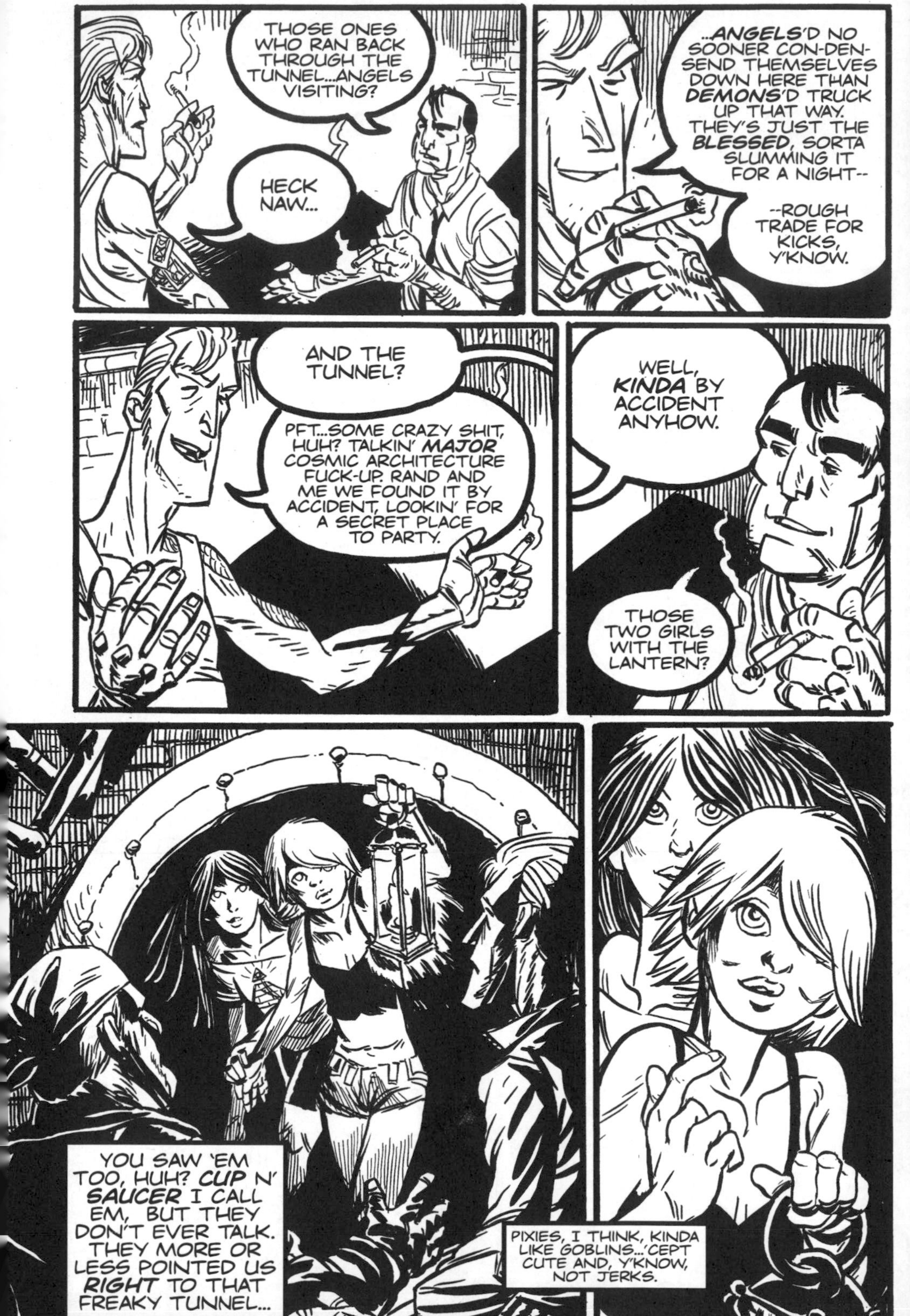
THOSE ONES WHO RAN BACK THROUGH THE TUNNEL...ANGELS VISITING?
HECK NAW...
...ANGELS'D NO SOONER CON-DEN-SEND THEMSELVES DOWN HERE THAN DEMONS'D TRUCK UP THAT WAY. THEY'S JUST THE BLESSED, SORTA SLUMMING IT FOR A NIGHT--
--ROUGH TRADE FOR KICKS, Y'KNOW.
AND THE TUNNEL?
PFT...SOME CRAZY SHIT, HUH? TALKIN' MAJOR COSMIC ARCHITECTURE FUCK-UP. RAND AND ME WE FOUND IT BY ACCIDENT, LOOKIN' FOR A SECRET PLACE TO PARTY.
WELL, KINDA BY ACCIDENT ANYHOW.
THOSE TWO GIRLS WITH THE LANTERN?
YOU SAW 'EM TOO, HUH? CUP N' SAUCER I CALL EM, BUT THEY DON'T EVER TALK. THEY MORE OR LESS POINTED US RIGHT TO THAT FREAKY TUNNEL...
PIXIES, I THINK, KINDA LIKE GOBLINS...'CEPT CUTE AND, Y'KNOW, NOT JERKS.

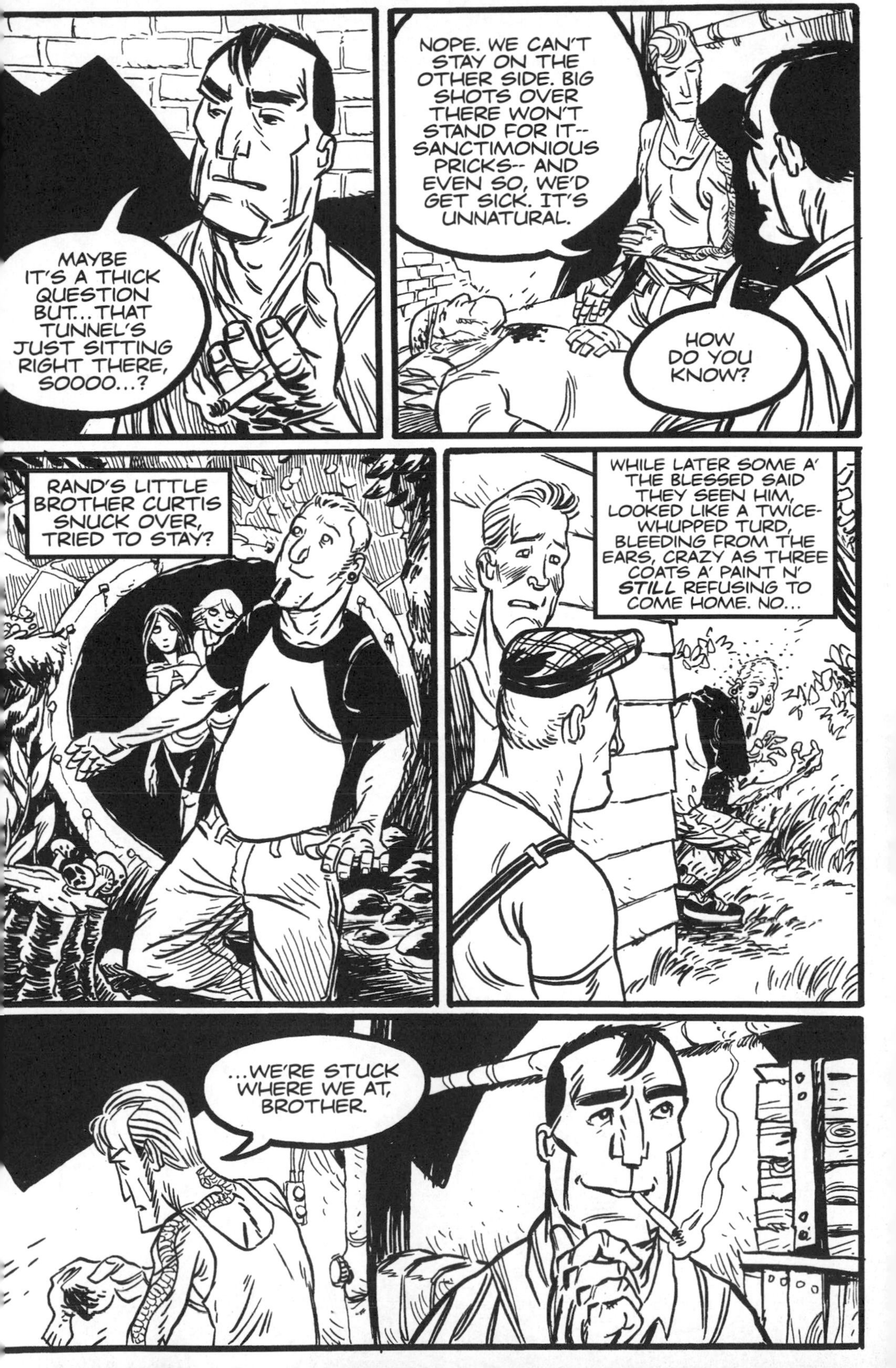

MAYBE IT'S A THICK QUESTION BUT...THAT TUNNEL'S JUST SITTING RIGHT THERE, SOOOO...?
NOPE. WE CAN'T STAY ON THE OTHER SIDE. BIG SHOTS OVER THERE WON'T STAND FOR IT-- SANCTIMONIOUS PRICKS-- AND EVEN SO, WE'D GET SICK. IT'S UNNATURAL.
HOW DO YOU KNOW?
RAND'S LITTLE BROTHER CURTIS SNUCK OVER, TRIED TO STAY?
WHILE LATER SOME A' THE BLESSED SAID THEY SEEN HIM, LOOKED LIKE A TWICE-WHUPPED TURD, BLEEDING FROM THE EARS, CRAZY AS THREE COATS A' PAINT N' STILL REFUSING TO COME HOME. NO...
...WE'RE STUCK WHERE WE AT, BROTHER.

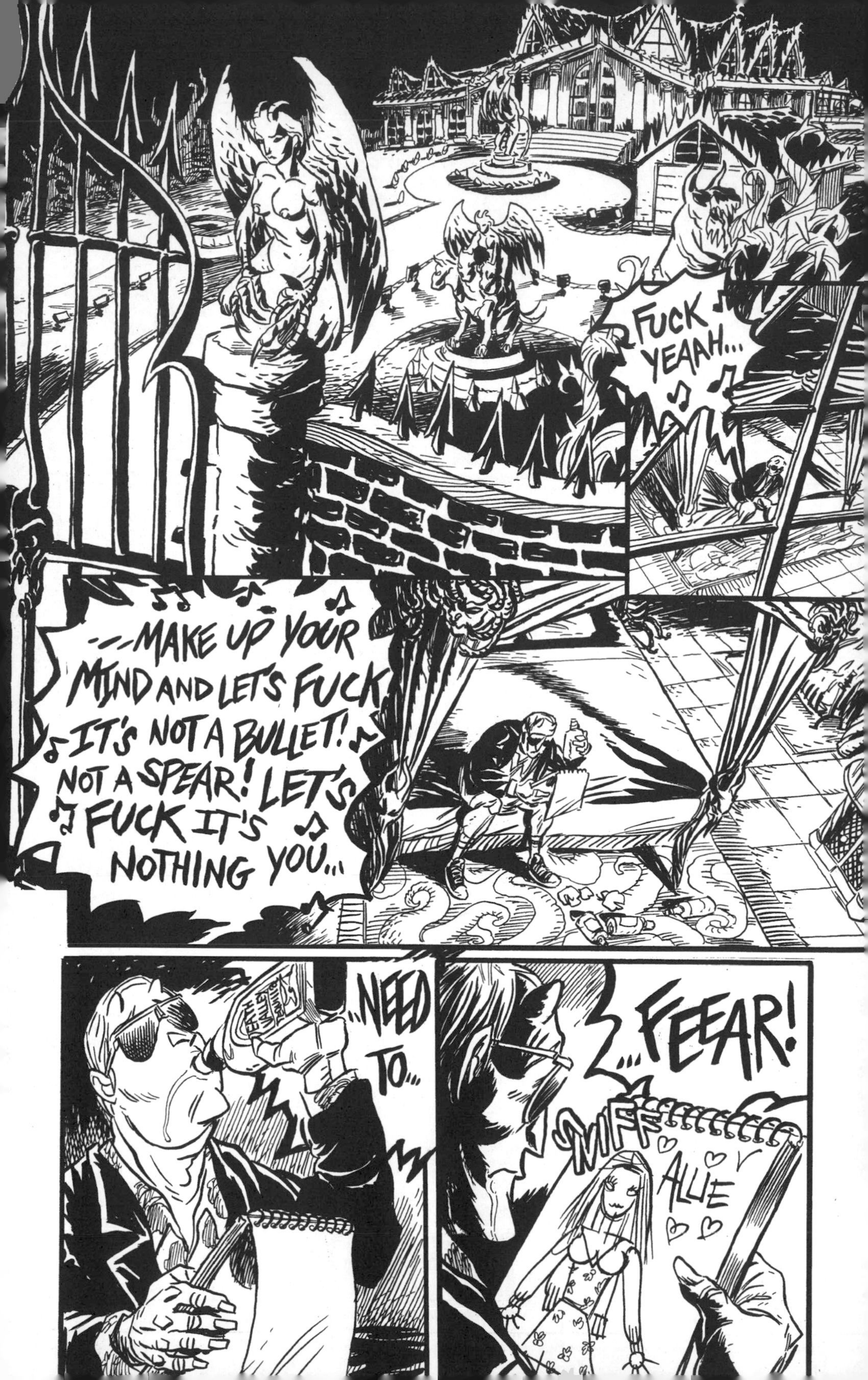
FUCK YEAAH...
--MAKE UP YOUR MIND AND LET'S FUCK IT'S NOT A BULLET! NOT A SPEAR! LET'S FUCK IT'S NOTHING YOU...
...NEED TO...
...FEEAR!
SNIFF
ALLIE

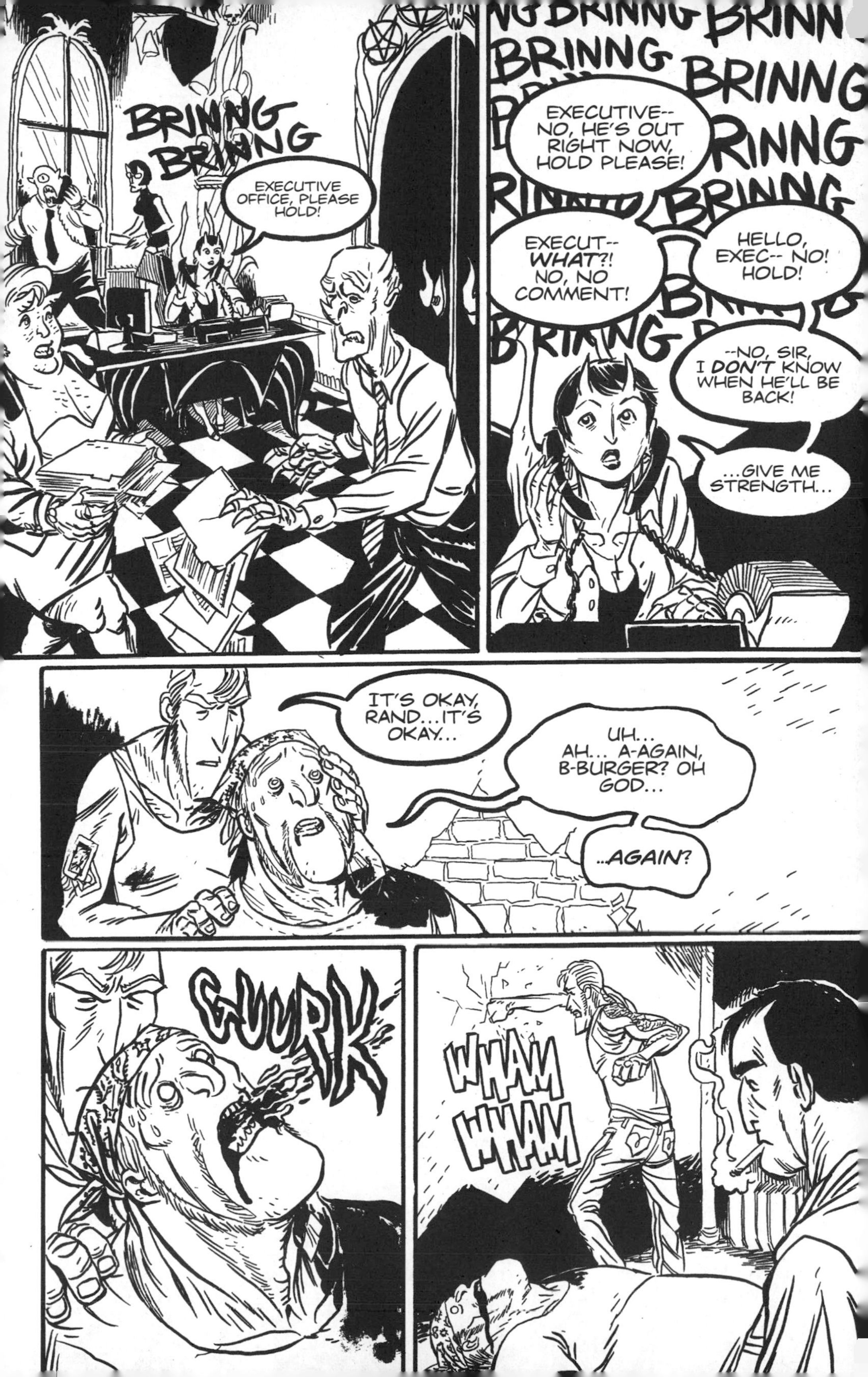
BRINNG BRINNG
EXECUTIVE OFFICE, PLEASE HOLD!
BRINNG BRINNG BRINNG
EXECUTIVE-- NO, HE'S OUT RIGHT NOW, HOLD PLEASE!
EXECUT-- WHAT?! NO, NO COMMENT!
HELLO, EXEC-- NO! HOLD!
--NO, SIR, I DON'T KNOW WHEN HE'LL BE BACK!
...GIVE ME STRENGTH...
IT'S OKAY, RAND...IT'S OKAY...
UH... AH... A-AGAIN, B-BURGER? OH GOD...
...AGAIN?
GUURK
WHAM
WHAM

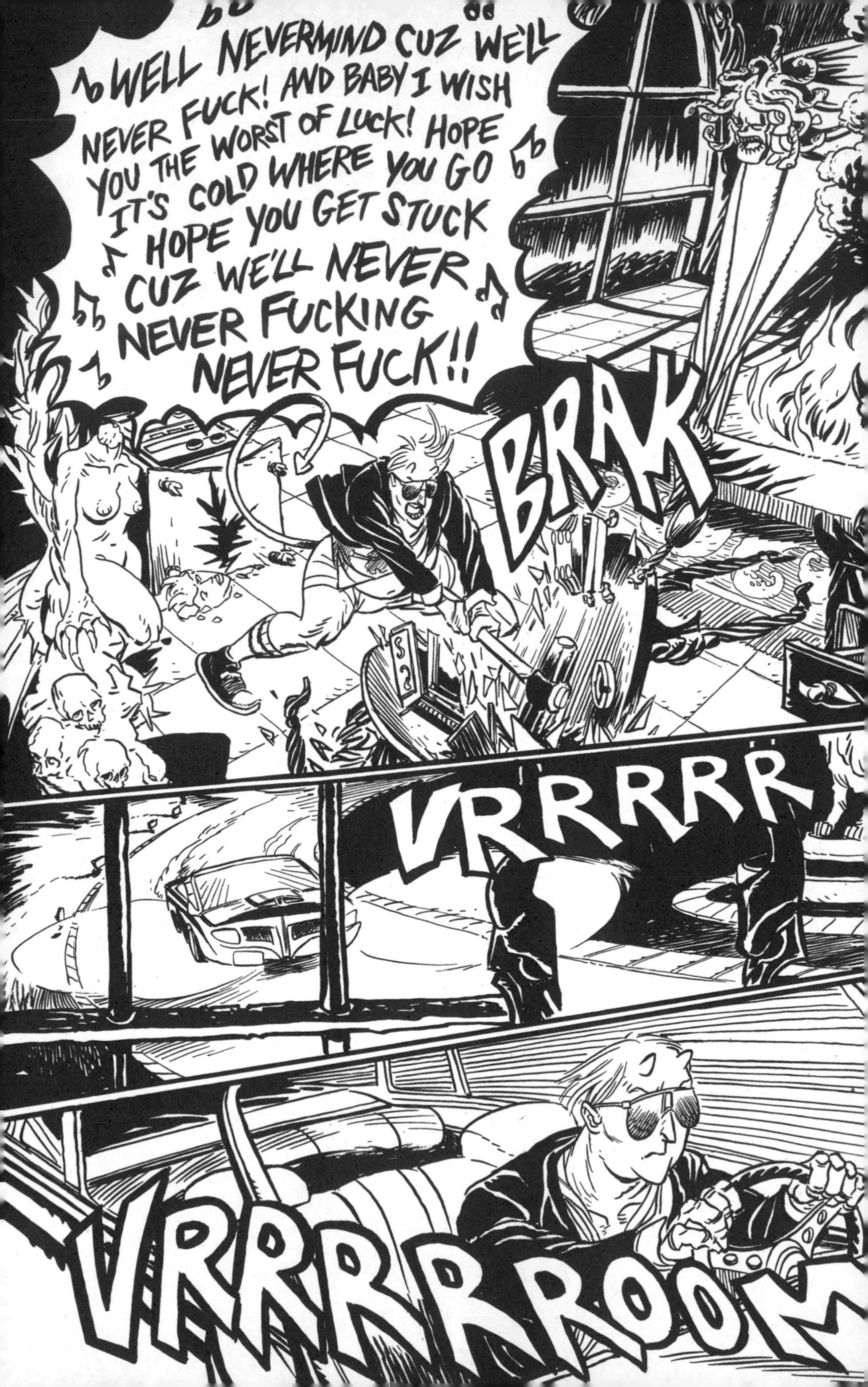
WELL NEVERMIND CUZ WE'LL NEVER FUCK! AND BABY I WISH YOU THE WORST OF LUCK! HOPE IT'S COLD WHERE YOU GO HOPE YOU GET STUCK CUZ WE'LL NEVER NEVER FUCKING NEVER FUCK!!
BRAK
VRRRRR
VRRRRROOM

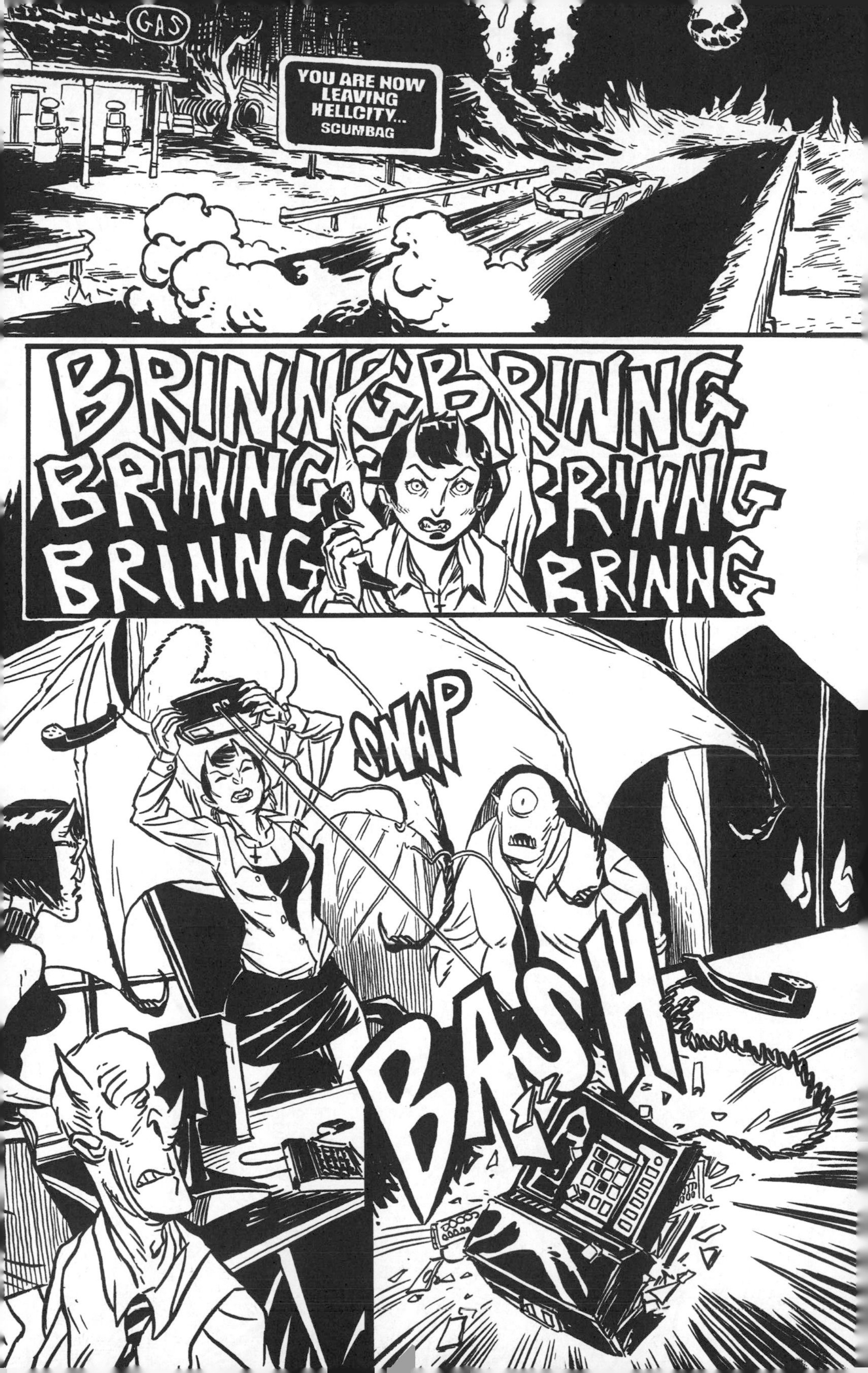
GAS
YOU ARE NOW LEAVING HELLCITY... SCUMBAG
BRINNG BRINNG
BRINNG BRINNG
BRINNG BRINNG
SNAP
BASH

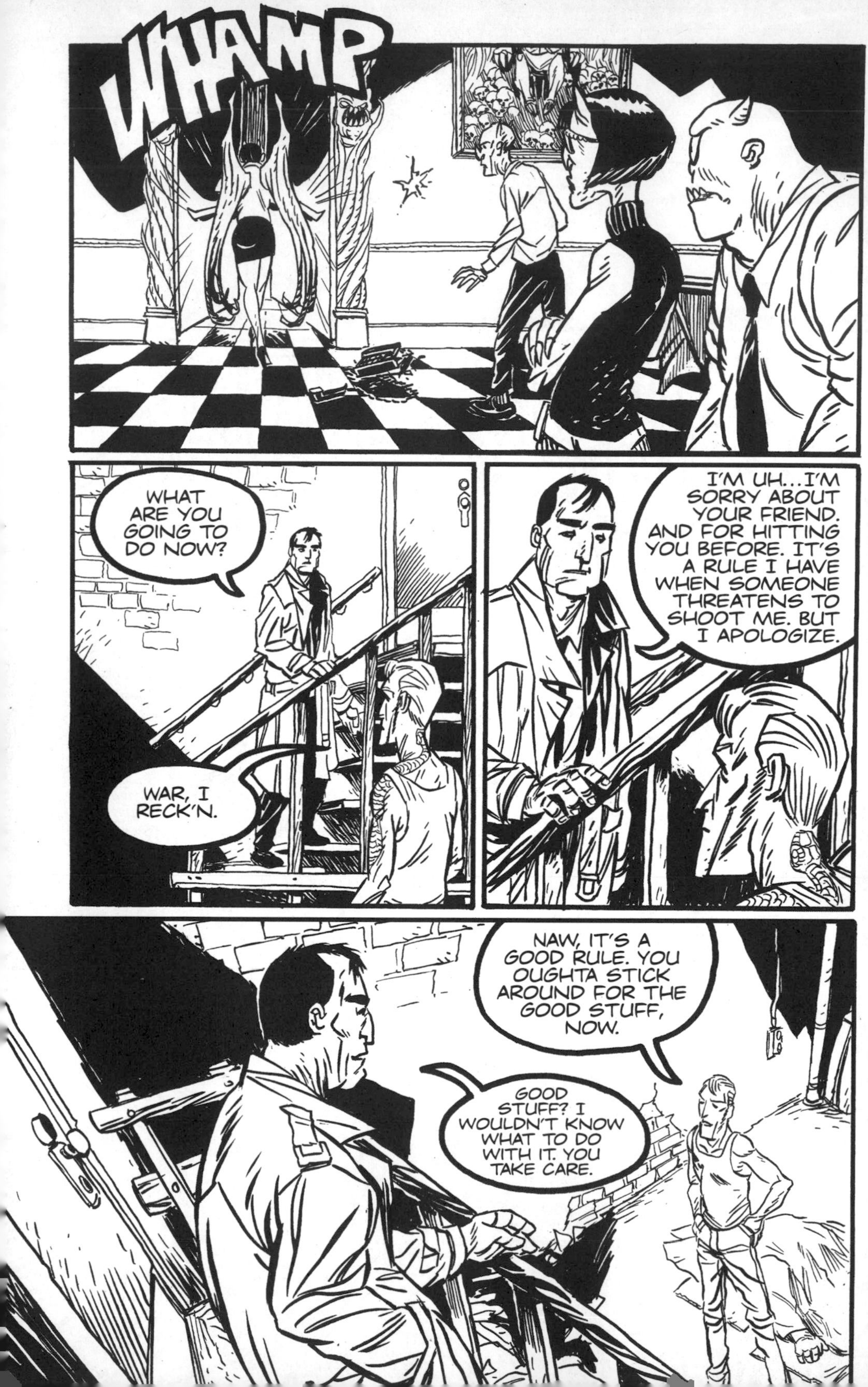
WHAMP
WHAT ARE YOU GOING TO DO NOW?
WAR, I RECK'N.
I'M UH...I'M SORRY ABOUT YOUR FRIEND. AND FOR HITTING YOU BEFORE. IT'S A RULE I HAVE WHEN SOMEONE THREATENS TO SHOOT ME. BUT I APOLOGIZE.
NAW, IT'S A GOOD RULE. YOU OUGHTA STICK AROUND FOR THE GOOD STUFF, NOW.
GOOD STUFF? I WOULDN'T KNOW WHAT TO DO WITH IT. YOU TAKE CARE.

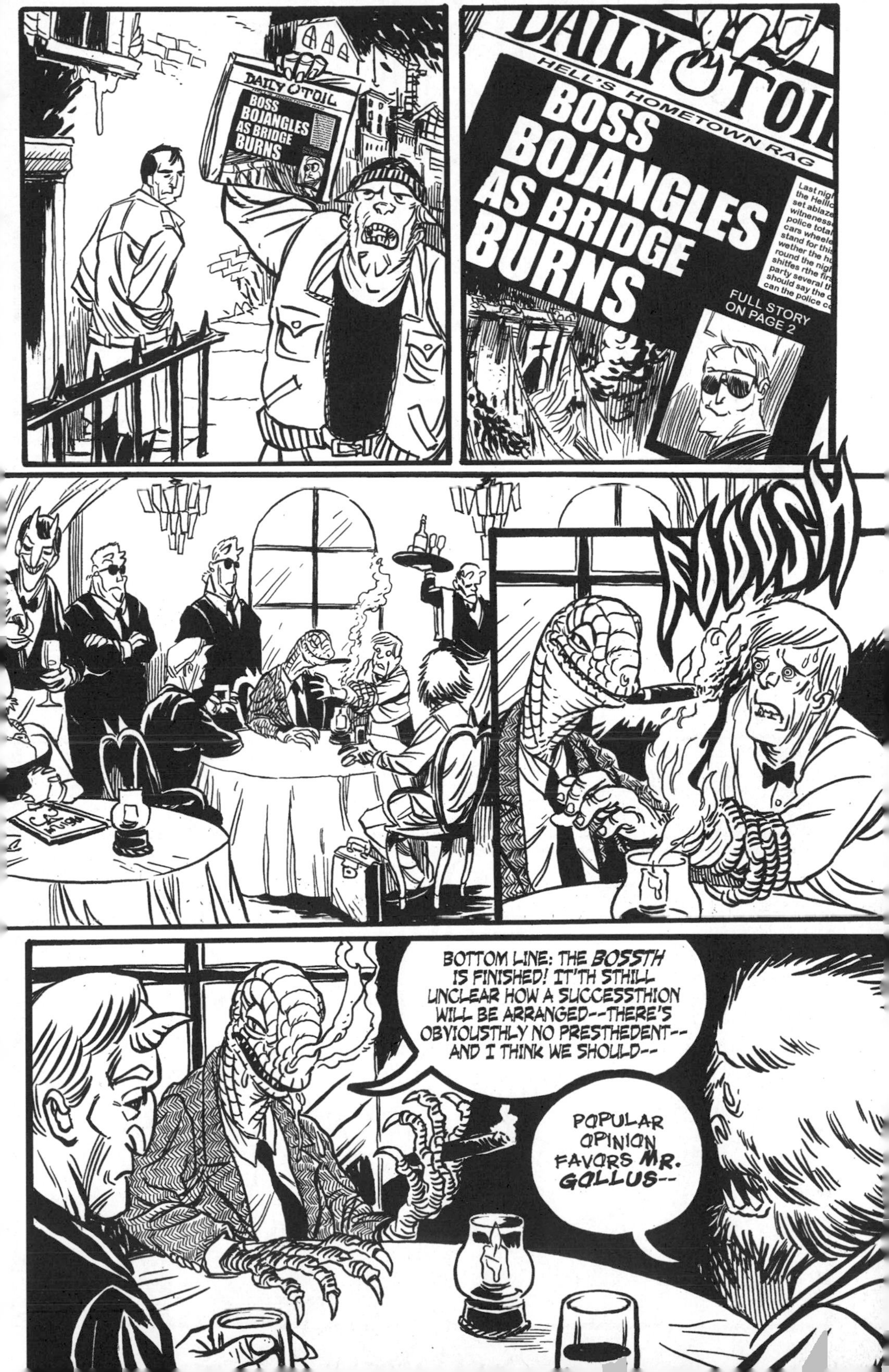
DAILY TOIL
HELL'S HOMETOWN RAG
BOSS BOJANGLES AS BRIDGE BURNS
FULL STORY ON PAGE 2
BOTTOM LINE: THE BOSSTH IS FINISHED! IT'TH STHILL UNCLEAR HOW A SUCCESSTHION WILL BE ARRANGED--THERE'S OBVIOUSTHLY NO PRESTHEDENT--AND I THINK WE SHOULD--
POPULAR OPINION FAVORS MR. GOLLUS--

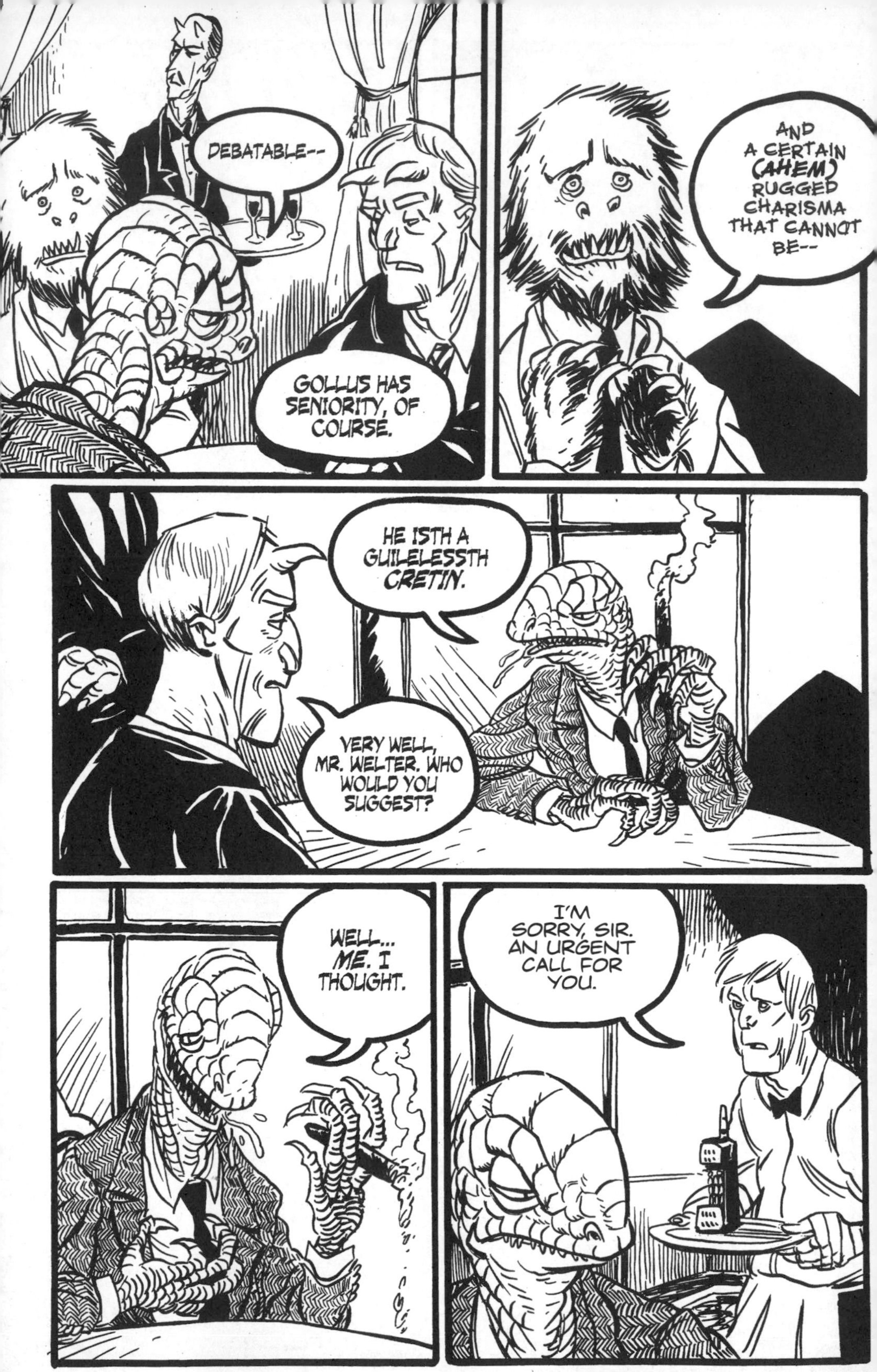
DEBATABLE--
GOLLUS HAS SENIORITY, OF COURSE.
AND A CERTAIN (AHEM) RUGGED CHARISMA THAT CANNOT BE--
HE ISTH A GUILELESSTH CRETIN.
VERY WELL, MR. WELTER. WHO WOULD YOU SUGGEST?
WELL... ME. I THOUGHT.
I'M SORRY, SIR. AN URGENT CALL FOR YOU.

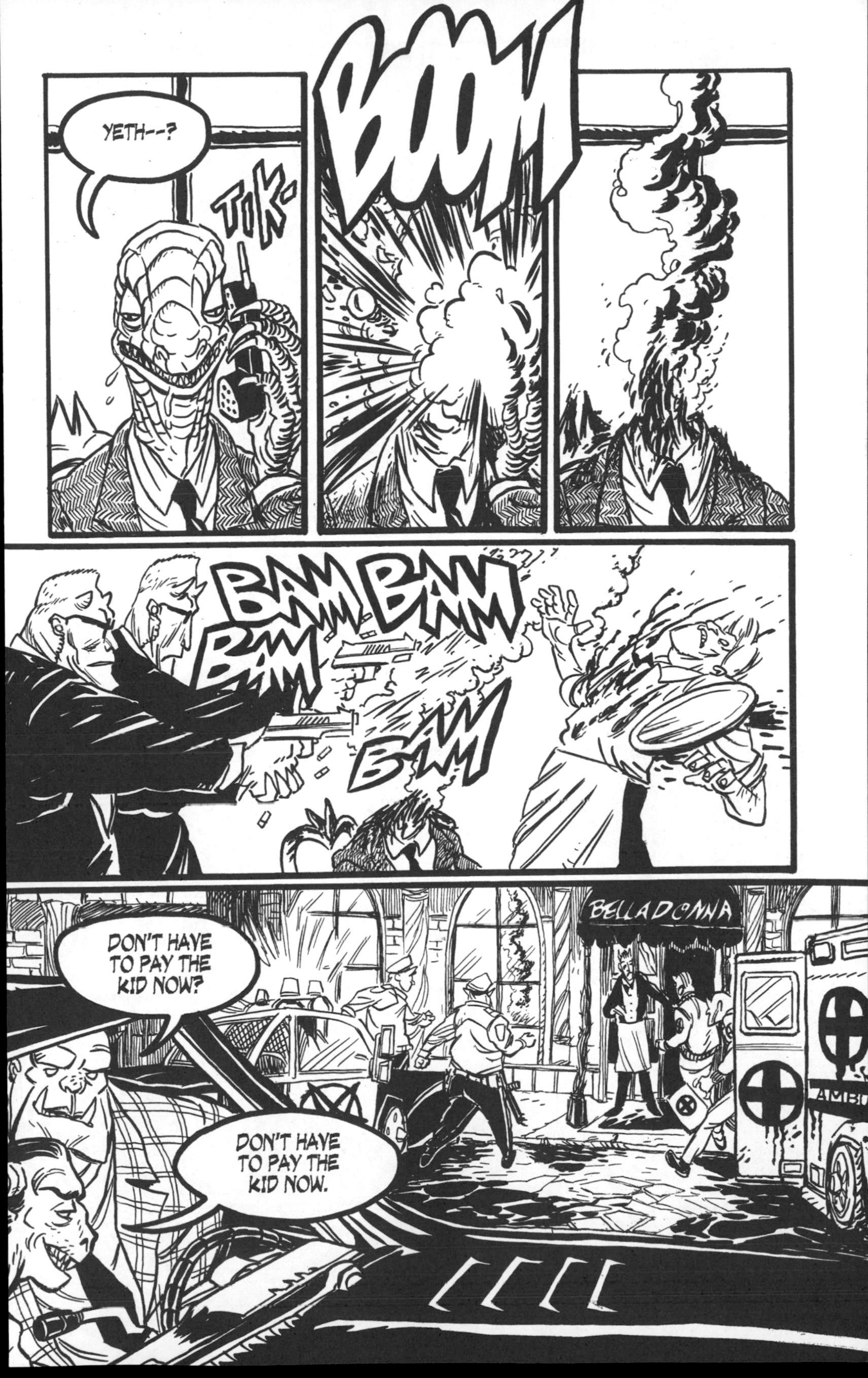
YETH--?
TIK-
BOOM
BAM BAM
BAM
BAM
BELLADONNA
DON'T HAVE TO PAY THE KID NOW?
DON'T HAVE TO PAY THE KID NOW.

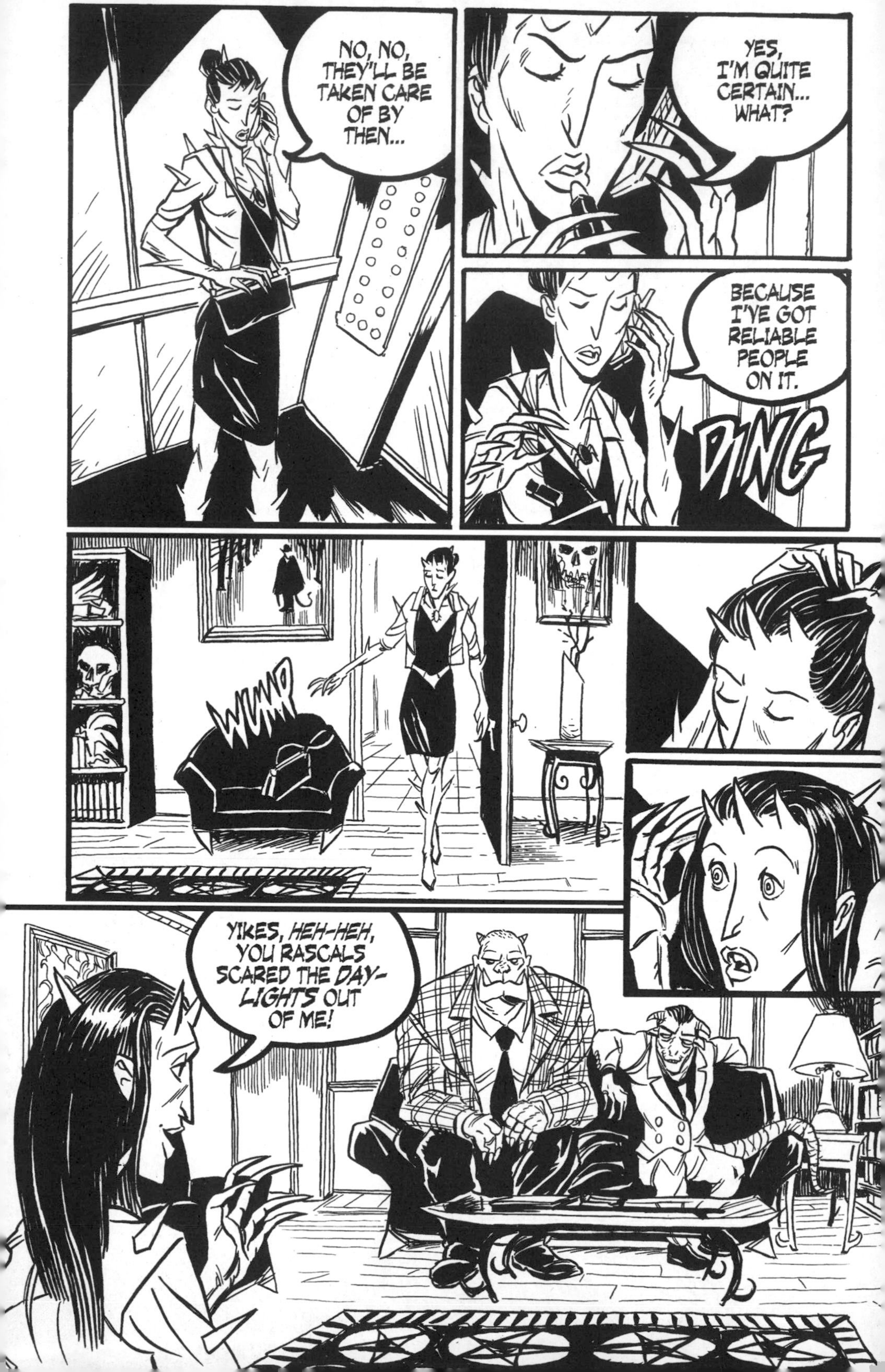
NO, NO, THEY'LL BE TAKEN CARE OF BY THEN...
YES, I'M QUITE CERTAIN... WHAT?
BECAUSE I'VE GOT RELIABLE PEOPLE ON IT.
DING
WUMP
YIKES, HEH-HEH, YOU RASCALS SCARED THE DAY-LIGHTS OUT OF ME!

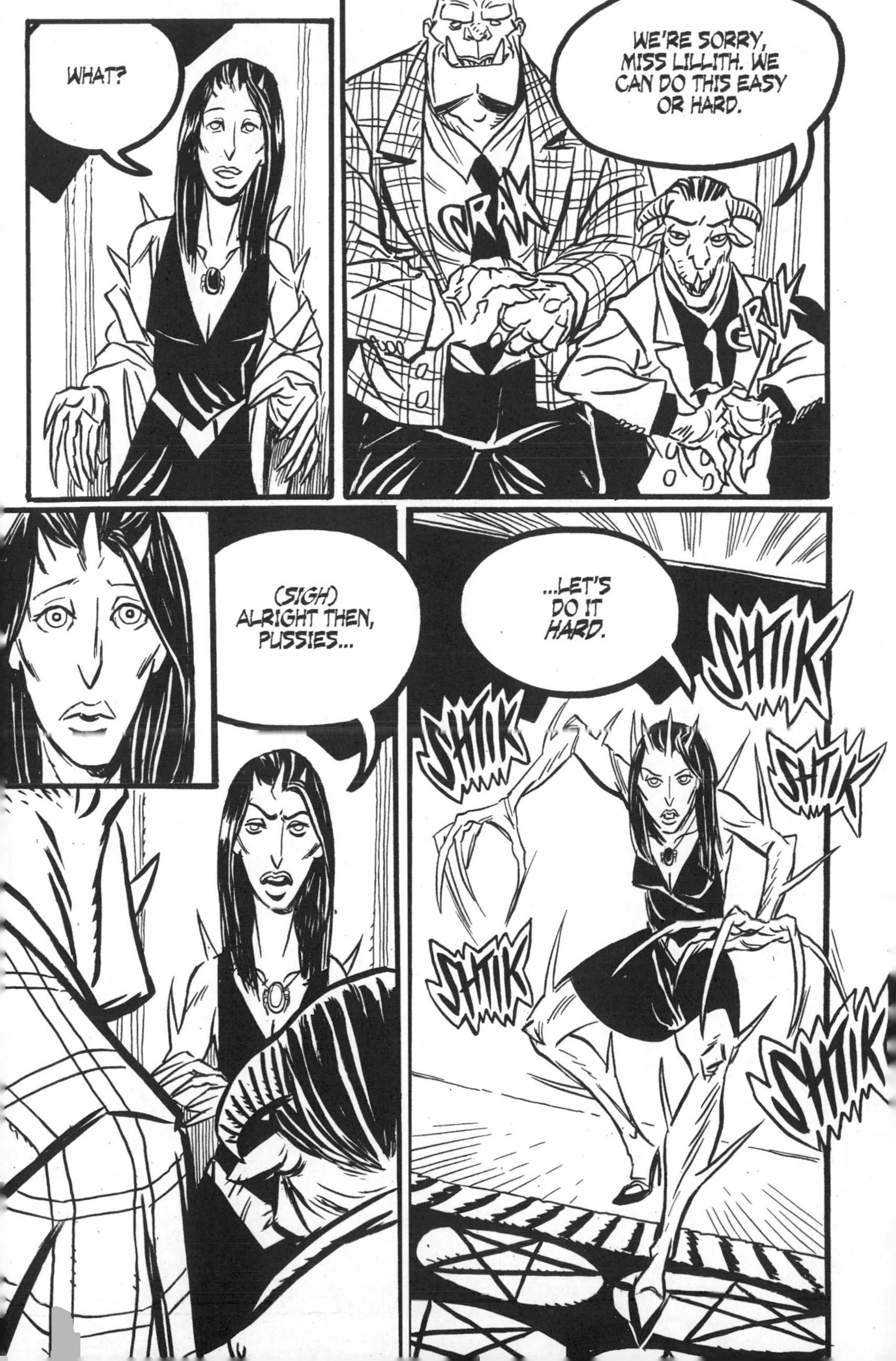
WHAT?
WE'RE SORRY, MISS LILLITH. WE CAN DO THIS EASY OR HARD.
CRAK
CRIK
(SIGH) ALRIGHT THEN, PUSSIES...
...LET'S DO IT HARD.
SHIK
SHIK
SHIK
SHIK
SHIK

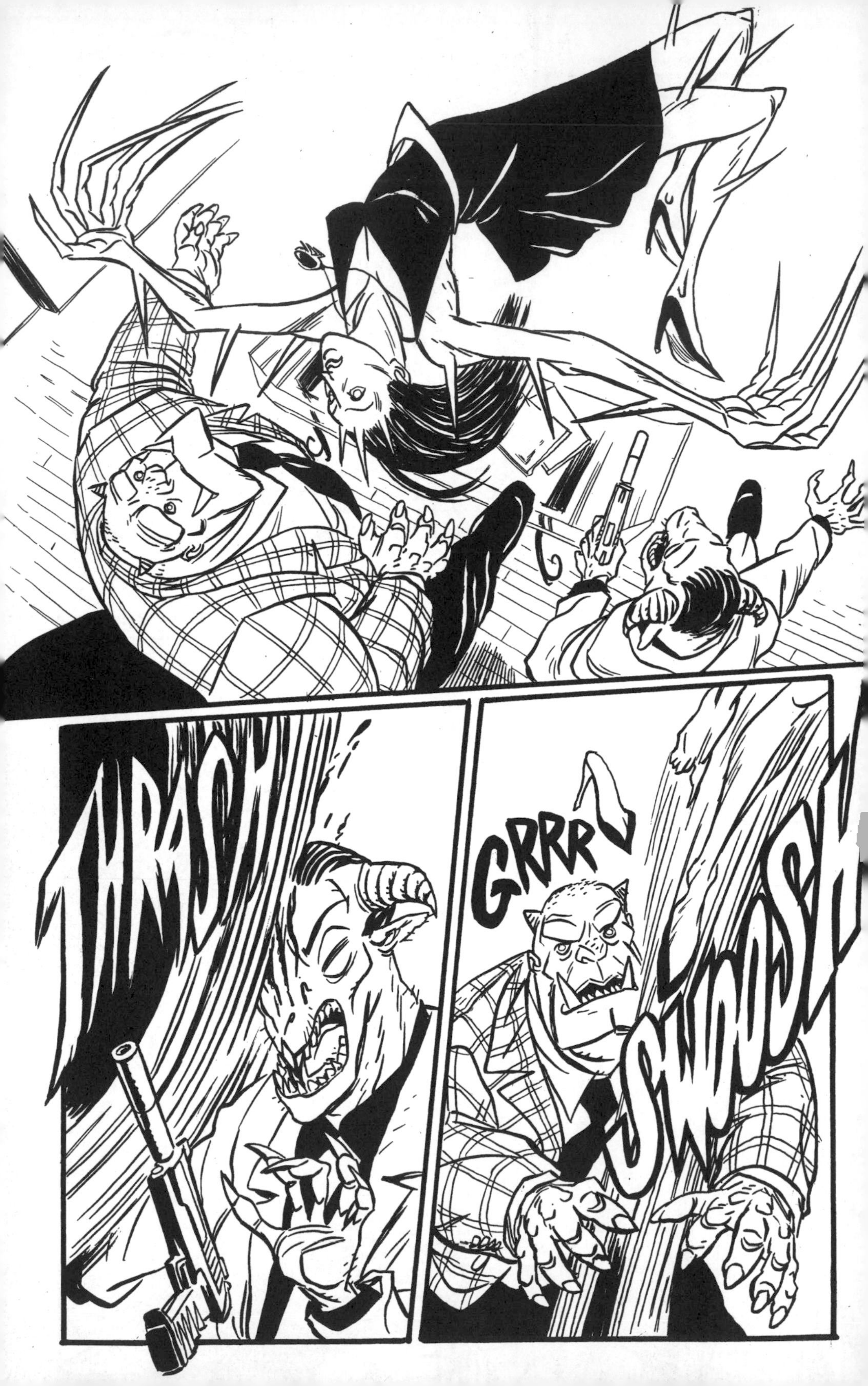
THRASH
GRRR
SWOOSH

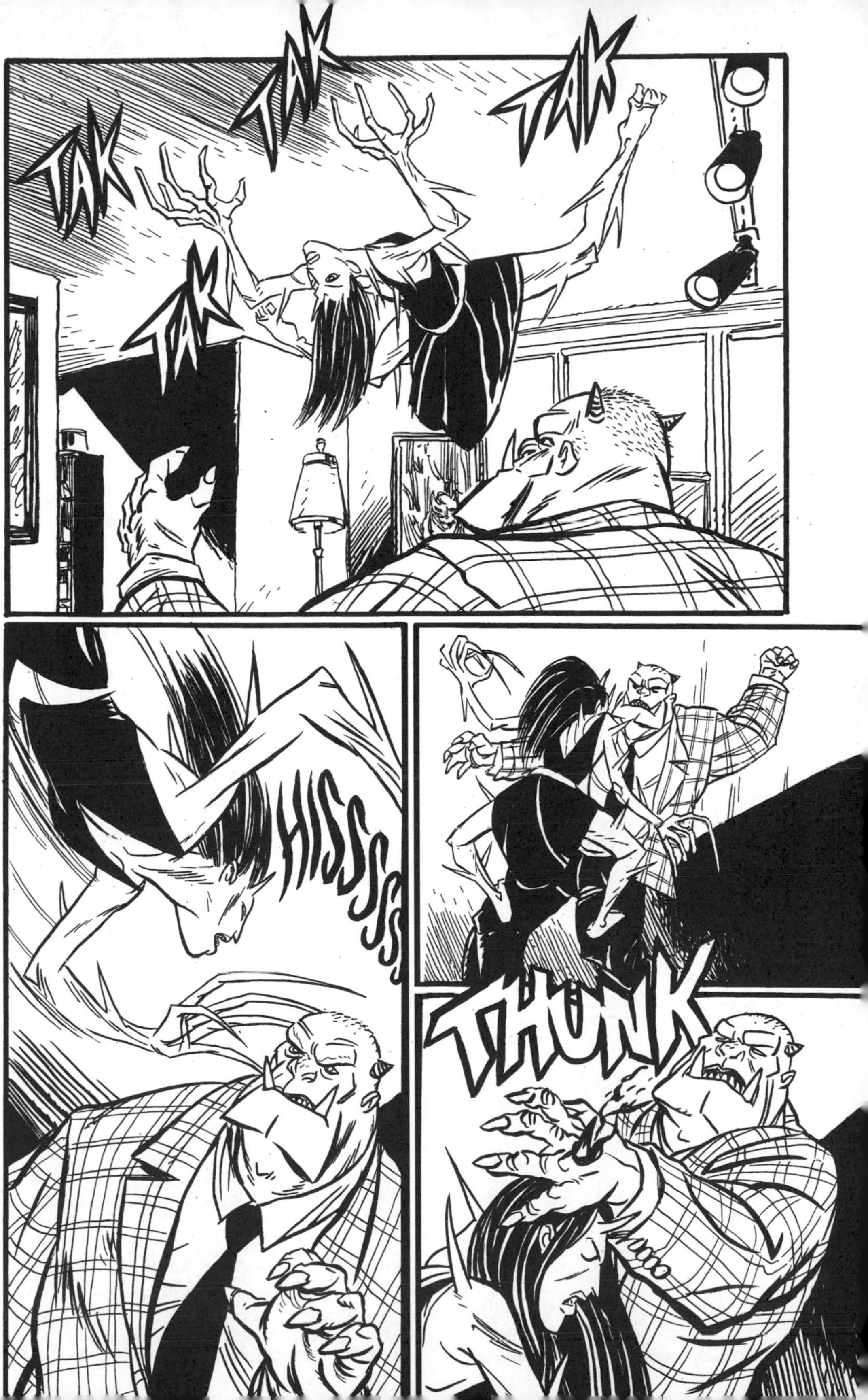
TAK
TAK
TAK
TAK
HISSSSSS
THUNK

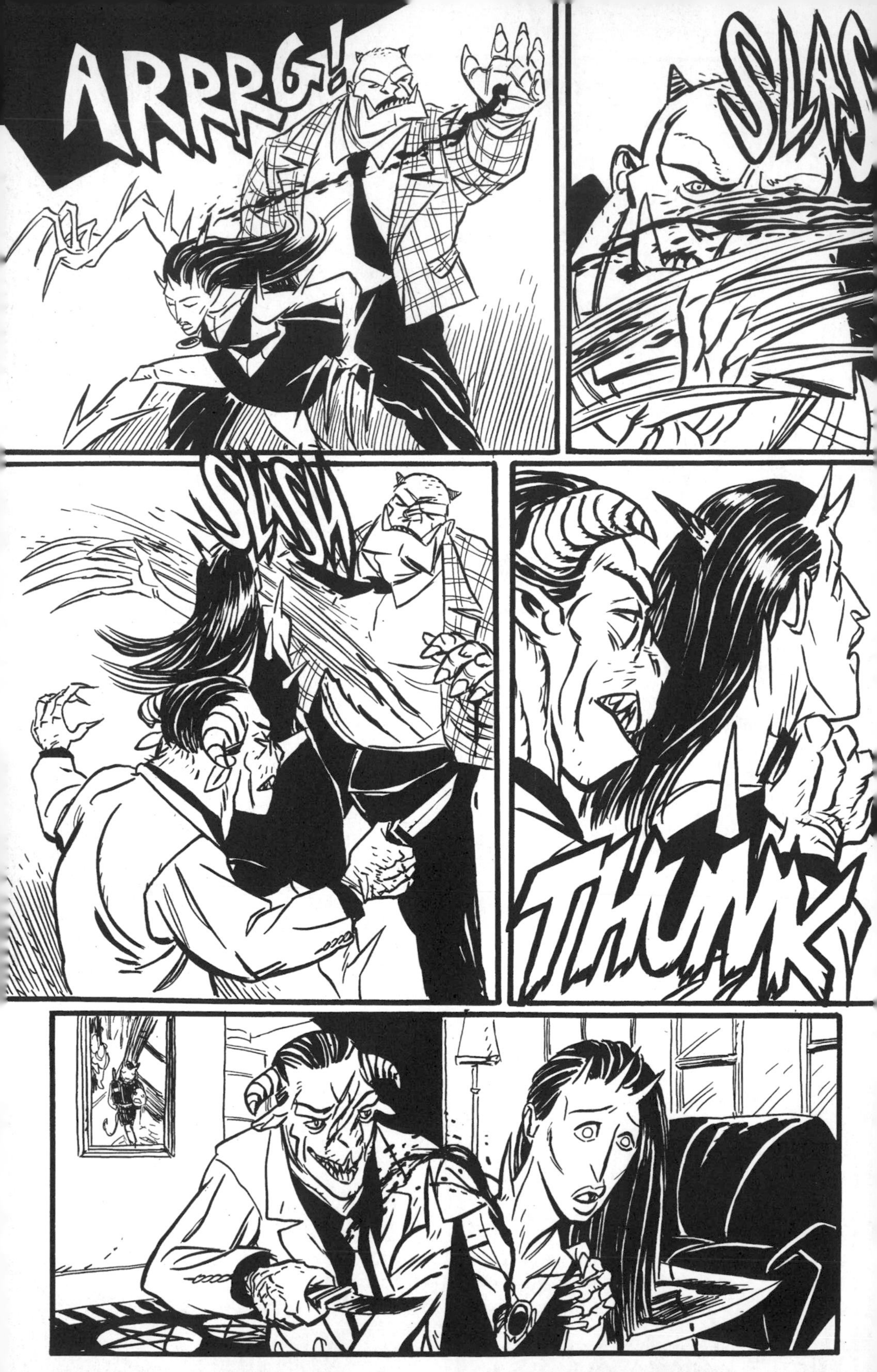
ARRRG!
SLAS
SLASH
THUNK

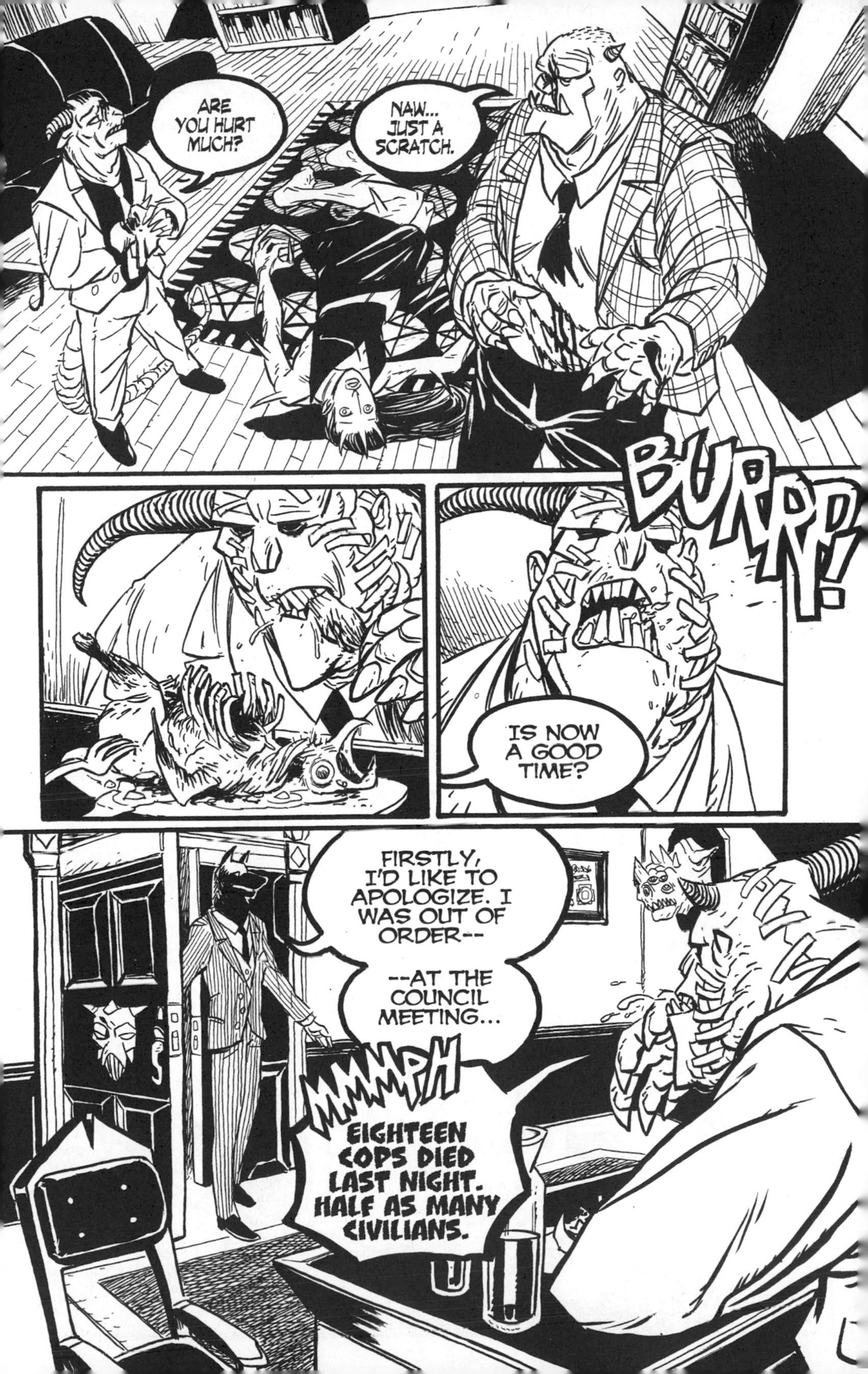
ARE YOU HURT MUCH?
NAW... JUST A SCRATCH.
BURRP!
IS NOW A GOOD TIME?
FIRSTLY, I'D LIKE TO APOLOGIZE. I WAS OUT OF ORDER--
--AT THE COUNCIL MEETING...
MMMMPH
EIGHTEEN COPS DIED LAST NIGHT. HALF AS MANY CIVILIANS.

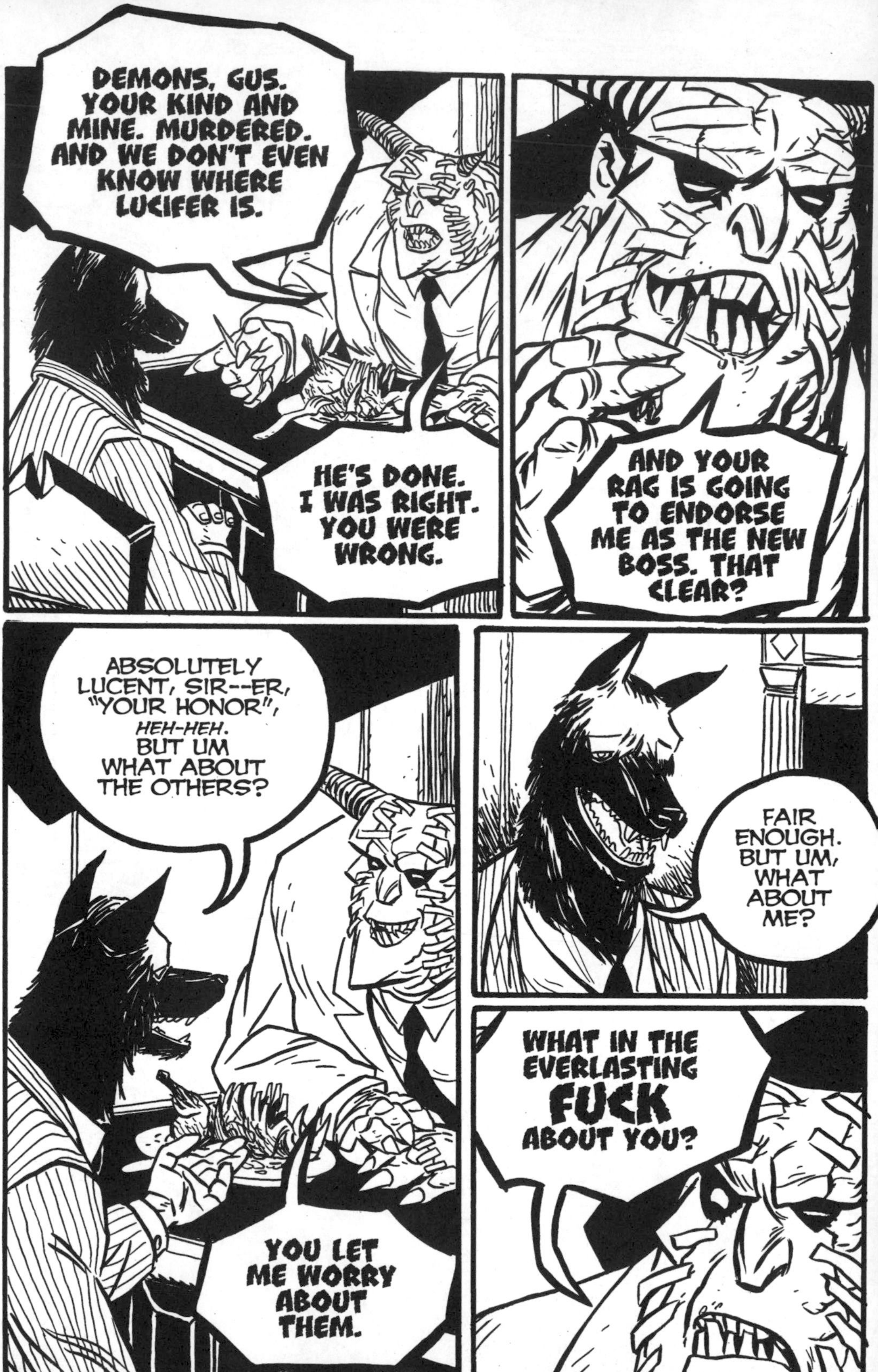
DEMONS, GUS. YOUR KIND AND MINE. MURDERED. AND WE DON'T EVEN KNOW WHERE LUCIFER IS.
HE'S DONE. I WAS RIGHT. YOU WERE WRONG.
AND YOUR RAG IS GOING TO ENDORSE ME AS THE NEW BOSS. THAT CLEAR?
ABSOLUTELY LUCENT, SIR--ER, "YOUR HONOR", HEH-HEH. BUT UM WHAT ABOUT THE OTHERS?
YOU LET ME WORRY ABOUT THEM.
FAIR ENOUGH. BUT UM, WHAT ABOUT ME?
WHAT IN THE EVERLASTING FUCK ABOUT YOU?

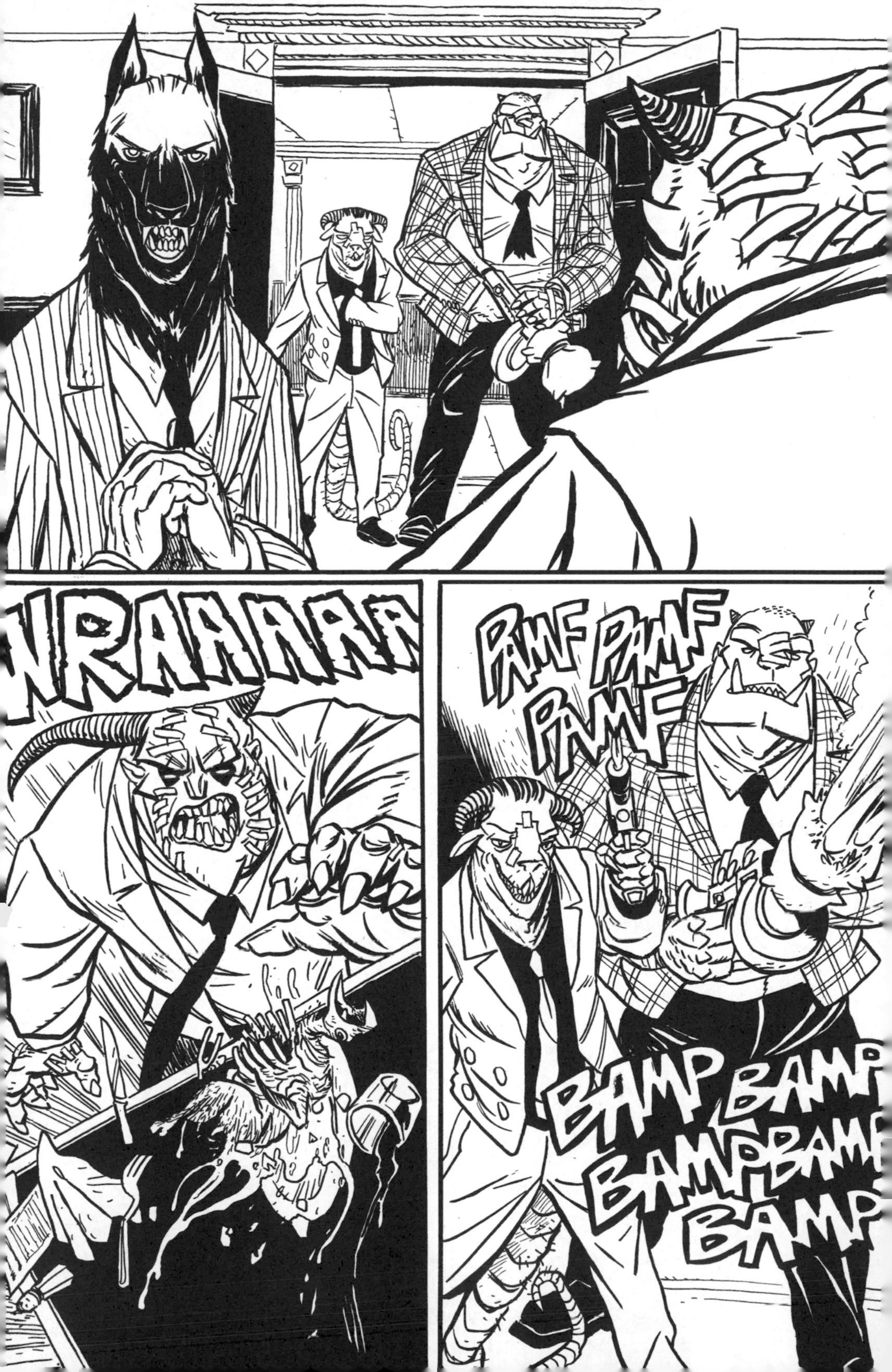

NRAAAARRR
PAMF PAMF
PAMF
BAMP BAMP
BAMPBAMP
BAMP

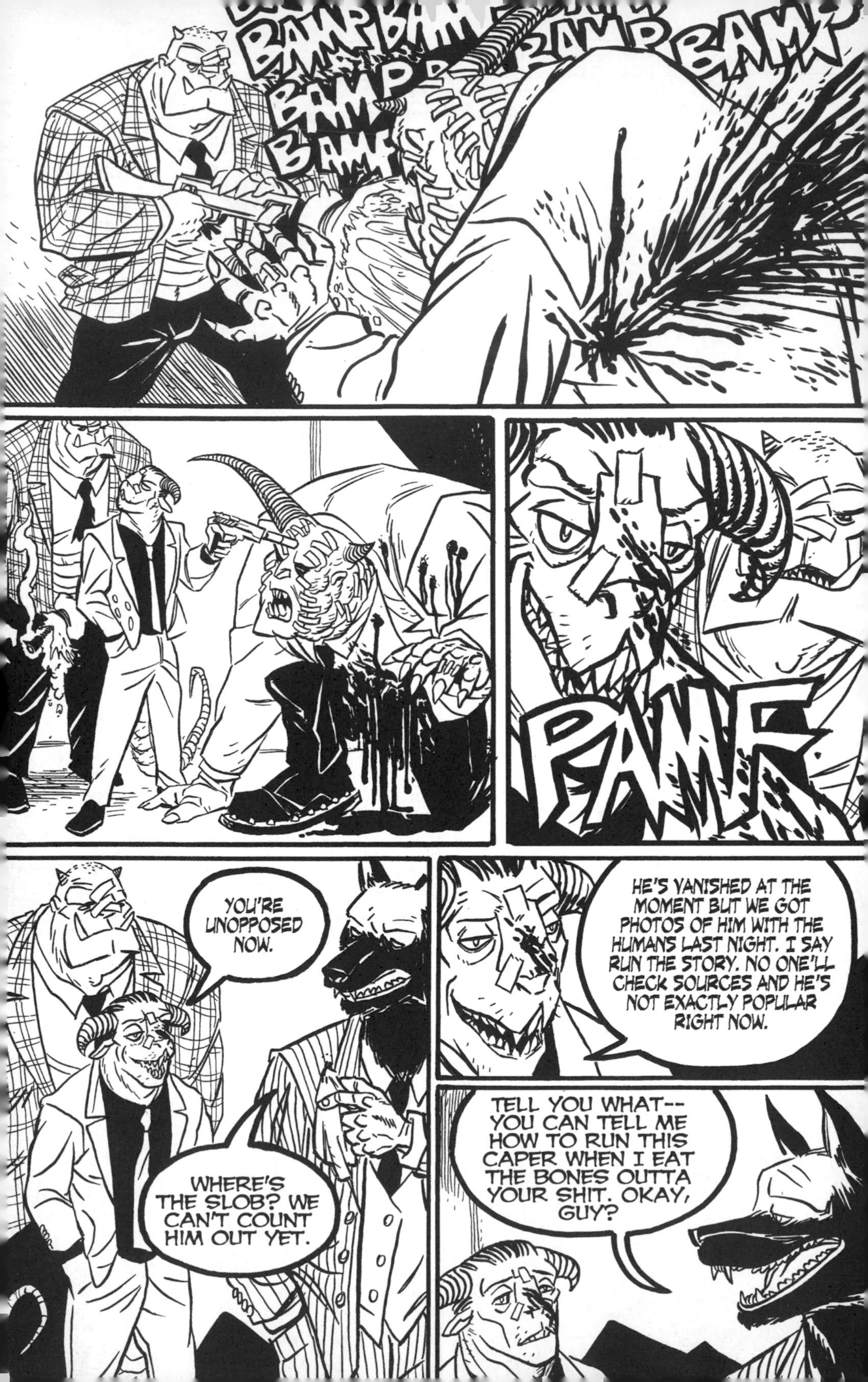
BAM BAM BAMP BAMP BAMP BAMP BAM BAM
PAMF
YOU'RE UNOPPOSED NOW.
WHERE'S THE SLOB? WE CAN'T COUNT HIM OUT YET.
HE'S VANISHED AT THE MOMENT BUT WE GOT PHOTOS OF HIM WITH THE HUMANS LAST NIGHT. I SAY RUN THE STORY. NO ONE'LL CHECK SOURCES AND HE'S NOT EXACTLY POPULAR RIGHT NOW.
TELL YOU WHAT-- YOU CAN TELL ME HOW TO RUN THIS CAPER WHEN I EAT THE BONES OUTTA YOUR SHIT. OKAY, GUY?

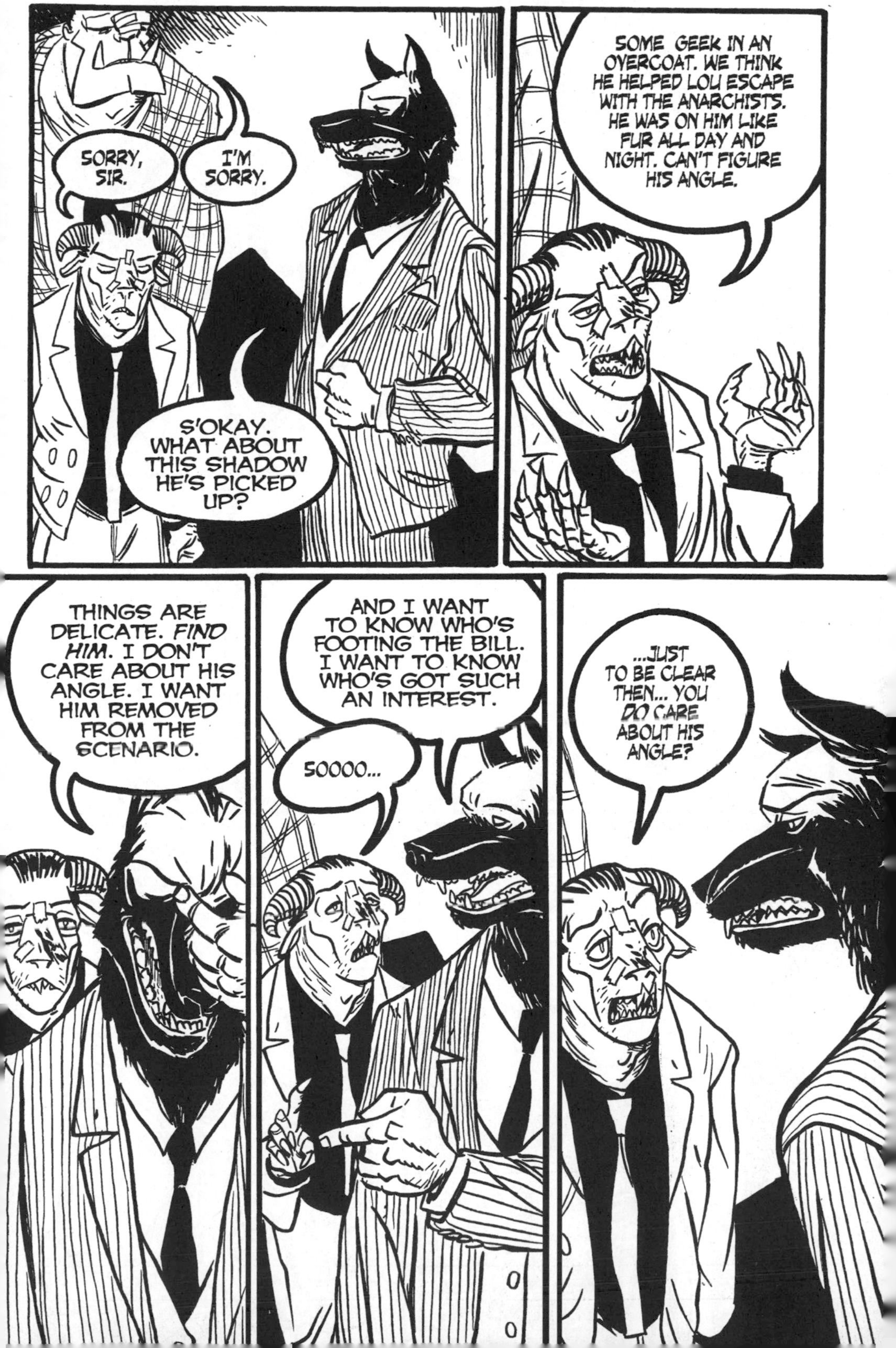
SORRY, SIR.
I'M SORRY.
S'OKAY. WHAT ABOUT THIS SHADOW HE'S PICKED UP?
SOME GEEK IN AN OVERCOAT. WE THINK HE HELPED LOU ESCAPE WITH THE ANARCHISTS. HE WAS ON HIM LIKE FUR ALL DAY AND NIGHT. CAN'T FIGURE HIS ANGLE.
THINGS ARE DELICATE. FIND HIM. I DON'T CARE ABOUT HIS ANGLE. I WANT HIM REMOVED FROM THE SCENARIO.
AND I WANT TO KNOW WHO'S FOOTING THE BILL. I WANT TO KNOW WHO'S GOT SUCH AN INTEREST.
SOOOO...
...JUST TO BE CLEAR THEN... YOU DO CARE ABOUT HIS ANGLE?

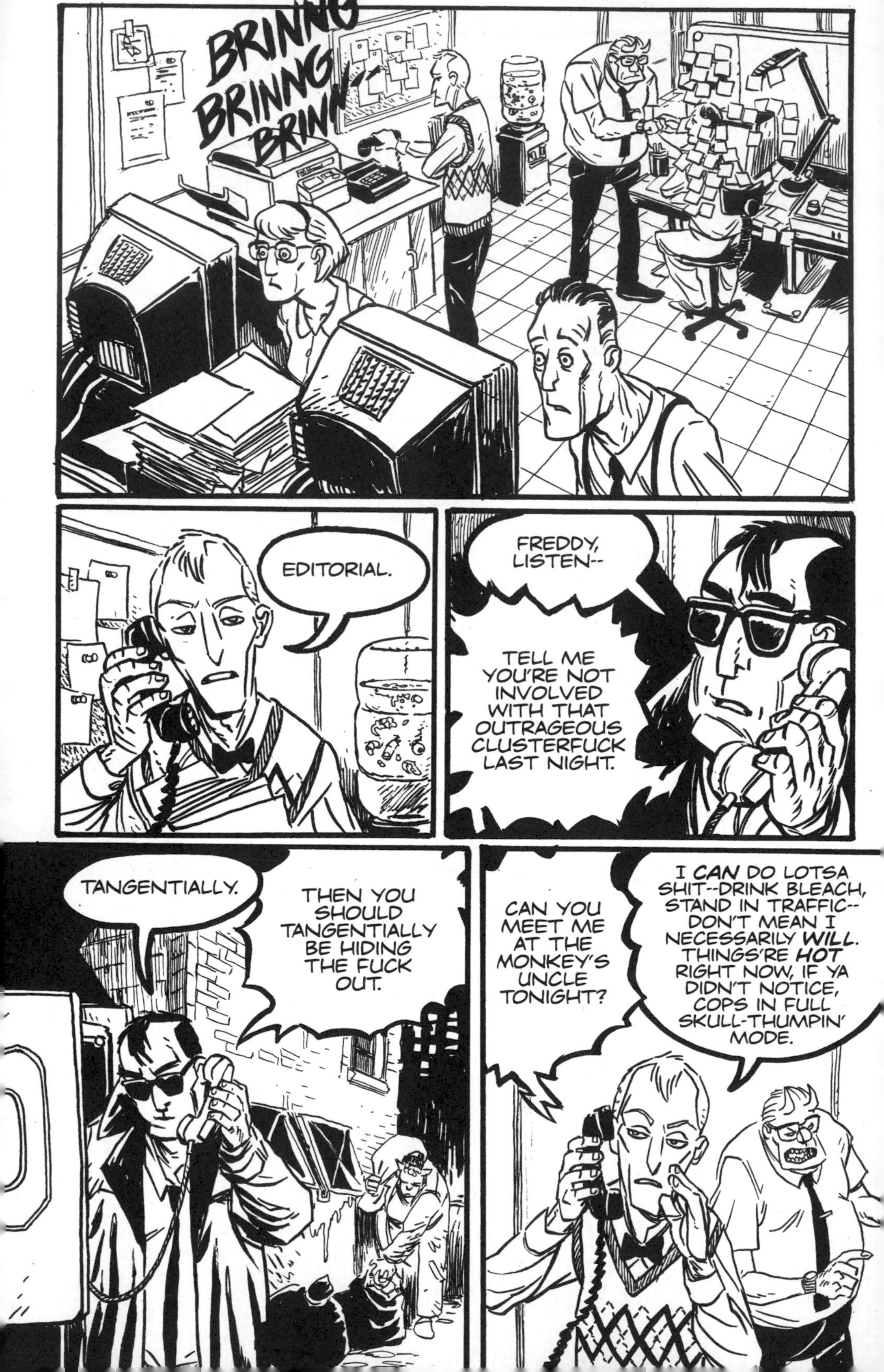
BRINNG BRINNG BRINN
EDITORIAL.
FREDDY, LISTEN--
TELL ME YOU'RE NOT INVOLVED WITH THAT OUTRAGEOUS CLUSTERFUCK LAST NIGHT.
TANGENTIALLY.
THEN YOU SHOULD TANGENTIALLY BE HIDING THE FUCK OUT.
CAN YOU MEET ME AT THE MONKEY'S UNCLE TONIGHT?
I CAN DO LOTSA SHIT--DRINK BLEACH, STAND IN TRAFFIC--DON'T MEAN I NECESSARILY WILL. THINGS'RE HOT RIGHT NOW, IF YA DIDN'T NOTICE, COPS IN FULL SKULL-THUMPIN' MODE.

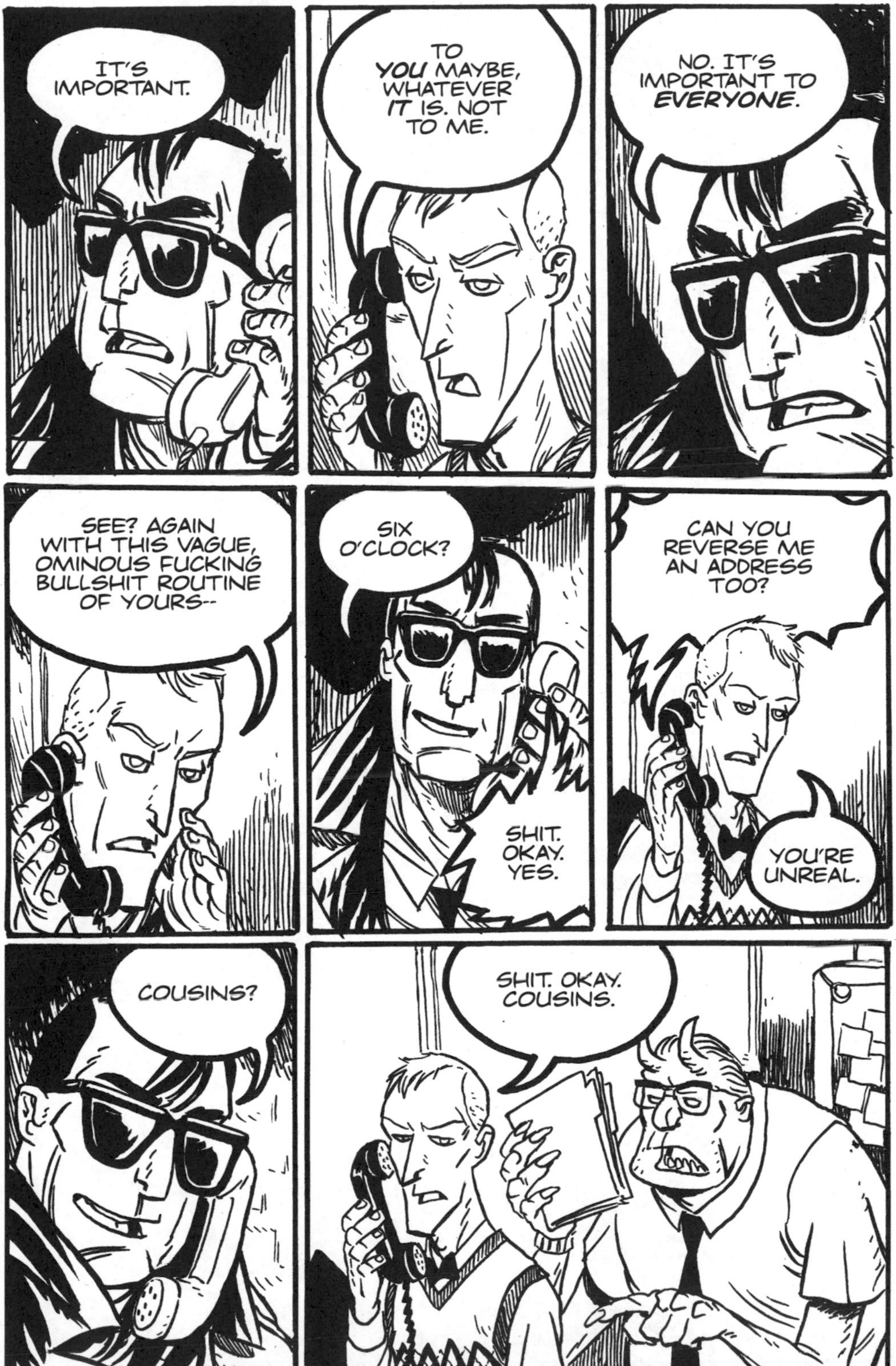
IT'S IMPORTANT.
TO *YOU* MAYBE, WHATEVER *IT* IS. NOT TO ME.
NO. IT'S IMPORTANT TO *EVERYONE*.
SEE? AGAIN WITH THIS VAGUE, OMINOUS FUCKING BULLSHIT ROUTINE OF YOURS--
SIX O'CLOCK?
SHIT. OKAY. YES.
CAN YOU REVERSE ME AN ADDRESS TOO?
YOU'RE UNREAL.
COUSINS?
SHIT. OKAY. COUSINS.

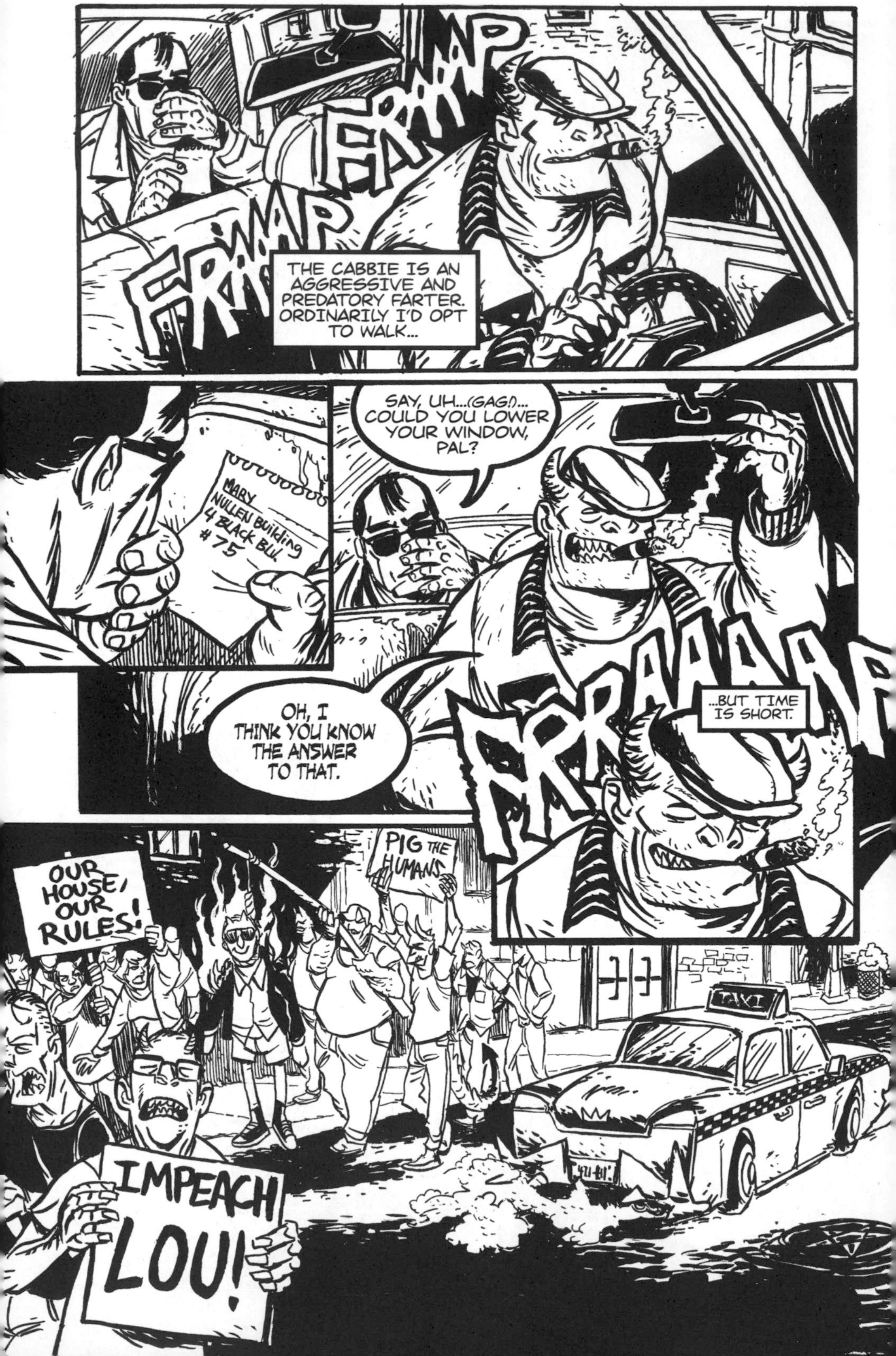
FRAMP
FRAAP
FRAMP
THE CABBIE IS AN AGGRESSIVE AND PREDATORY FARTER. ORDINARILY I'D OPT TO WALK...
MARY
NULLEN Building
4 BLACK BLV.
#75
SAY, UH...(GAG!)... COULD YOU LOWER YOUR WINDOW, PAL?
OH, I THINK YOU KNOW THE ANSWER TO THAT.
FRAAAAP
...BUT TIME IS SHORT.
OUR HOUSE, OUR RULES!
PIG THE HUMANS
TAXI
IMPEACH LOU!

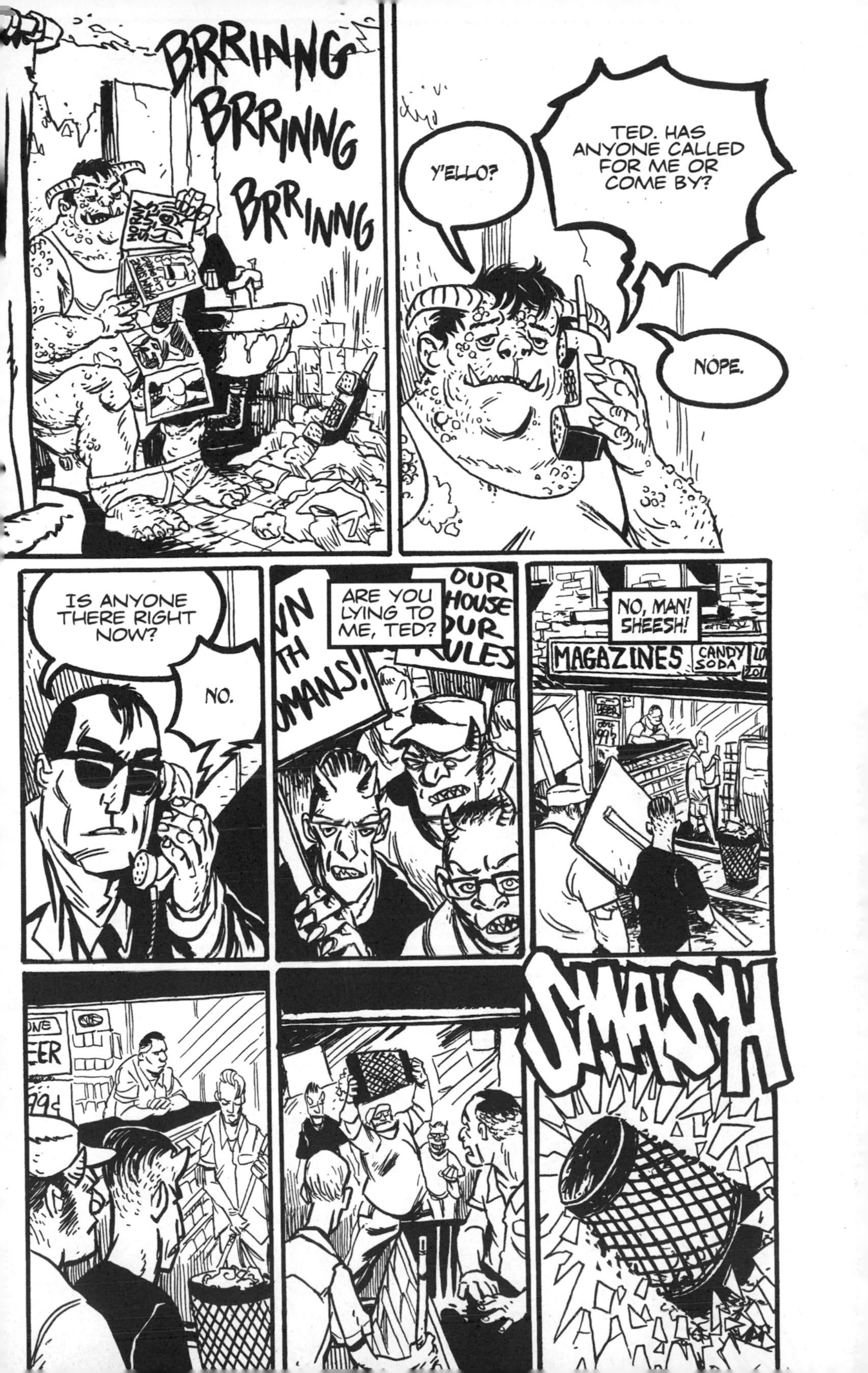
BRRINNG
BRRINNG
BRRINNG
Y'ELLO?
TED. HAS ANYONE CALLED FOR ME OR COME BY?
NOPE.
IS ANYONE THERE RIGHT NOW?
NO.
ARE YOU LYING TO ME, TED?
OUR HOUSE OUR RULES
NO, MAN! SHEESH!
MAGAZINES
CANDY SODA
SMASH

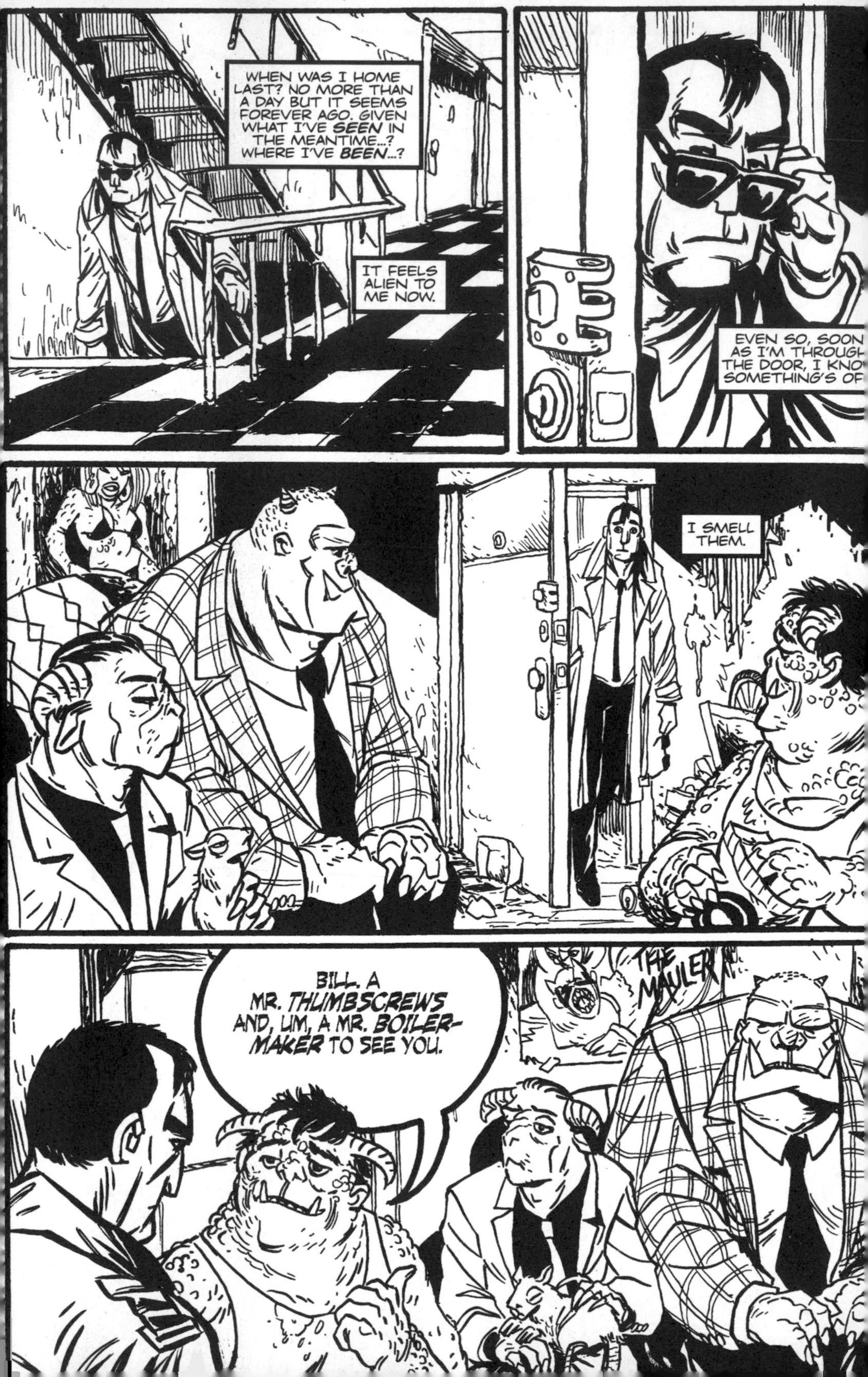
WHEN WAS I HOME LAST? NO MORE THAN A DAY BUT IT SEEMS FOREVER AGO. GIVEN WHAT I'VE SEEN IN THE MEANTIME...? WHERE I'VE BEEN...?
IT FEELS ALIEN TO ME NOW.
EVEN SO, SOON AS I'M THROUGH THE DOOR, I KNO SOMETHING'S OF
I SMELL THEM.
BILL. A MR. THUMBSCREWS AND, UM, A MR. BOILER-MAKER TO SEE YOU.
THE MAULER

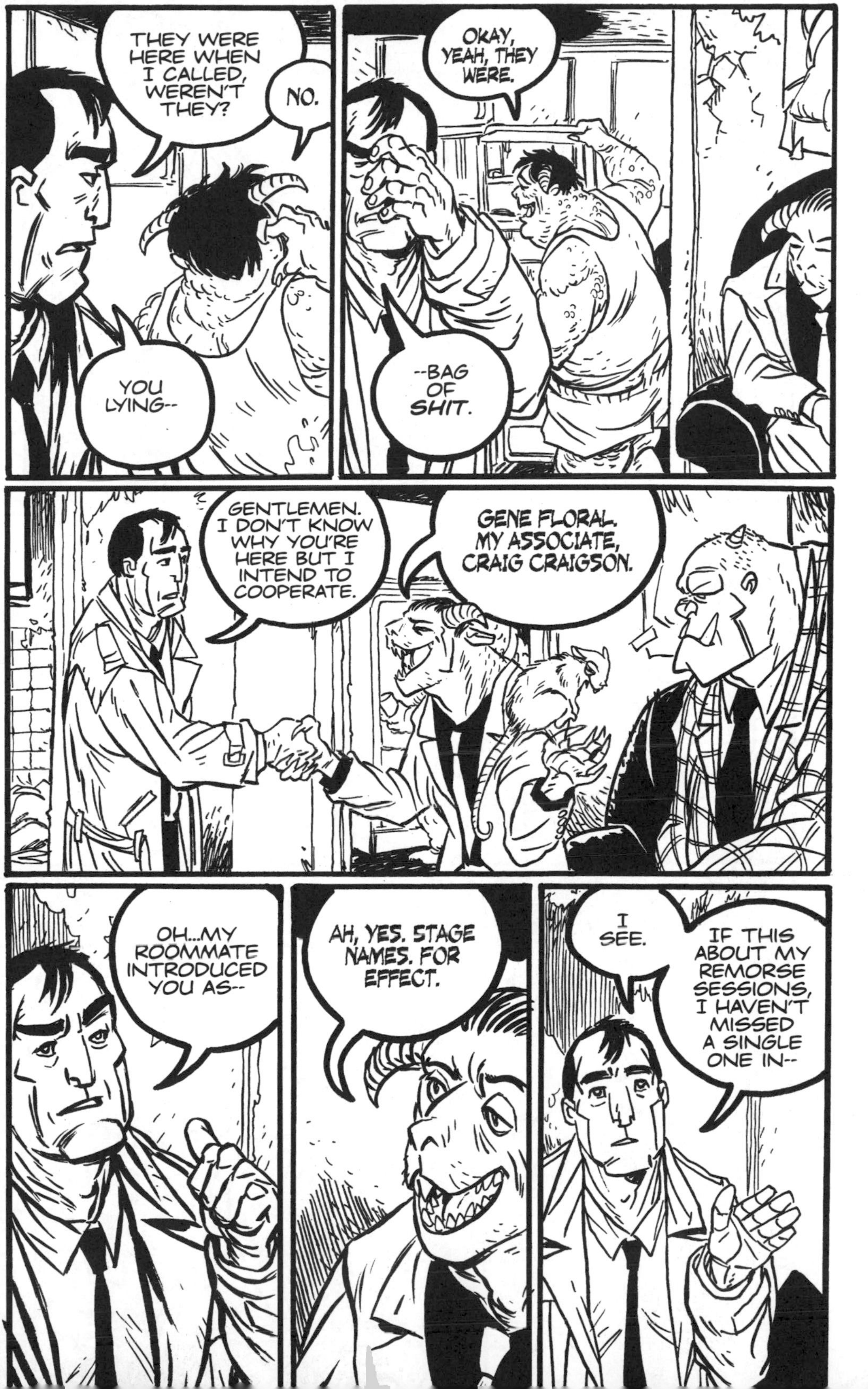
THEY WERE HERE WHEN I CALLED, WEREN'T THEY?
NO.
YOU LYING--
OKAY, YEAH, THEY WERE.
--BAG OF SHIT.
GENTLEMEN. I DON'T KNOW WHY YOU'RE HERE BUT I INTEND TO COOPERATE.
GENE FLORAL. MY ASSOCIATE, CRAIG CRAIGSON.
OH...MY ROOMMATE INTRODUCED YOU AS--
AH, YES. STAGE NAMES. FOR EFFECT.
I SEE.
IF THIS ABOUT MY REMORSE SESSIONS, I HAVEN'T MISSED A SINGLE ONE IN--

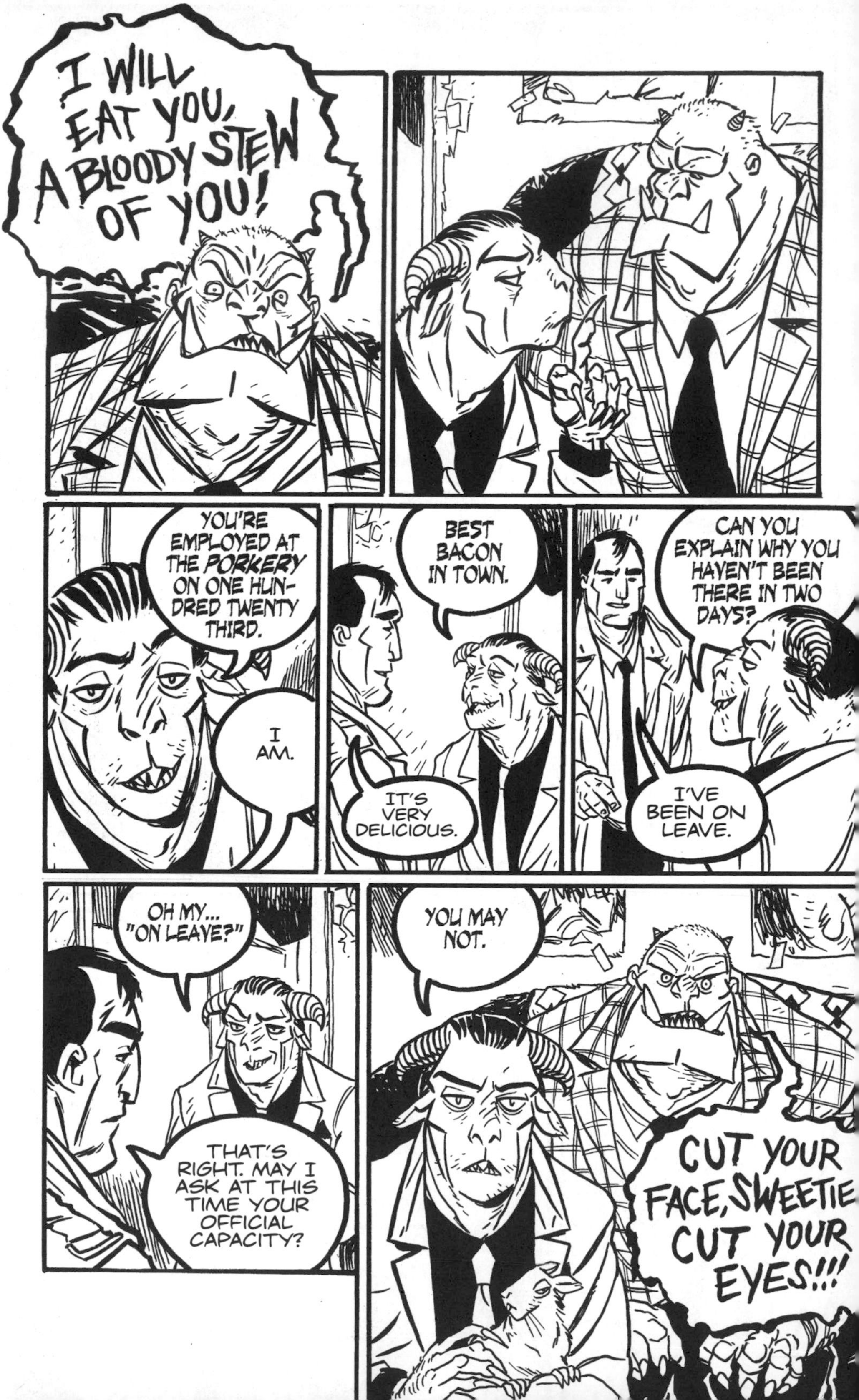
I WILL EAT YOU, A BLOODY STEW OF YOU!
YOU'RE EMPLOYED AT THE *PORKERY* ON ONE HUNDRED TWENTY THIRD.
I AM.
BEST BACON IN TOWN.
IT'S VERY DELICIOUS.
CAN YOU EXPLAIN WHY YOU HAVEN'T BEEN THERE IN TWO DAYS?
I'VE BEEN ON LEAVE.
OH MY... "ON LEAVE?"
THAT'S RIGHT. MAY I ASK AT THIS TIME YOUR OFFICIAL CAPACITY?
YOU MAY NOT.
CUT YOUR FACE, SWEETIE CUT YOUR EYES!!!

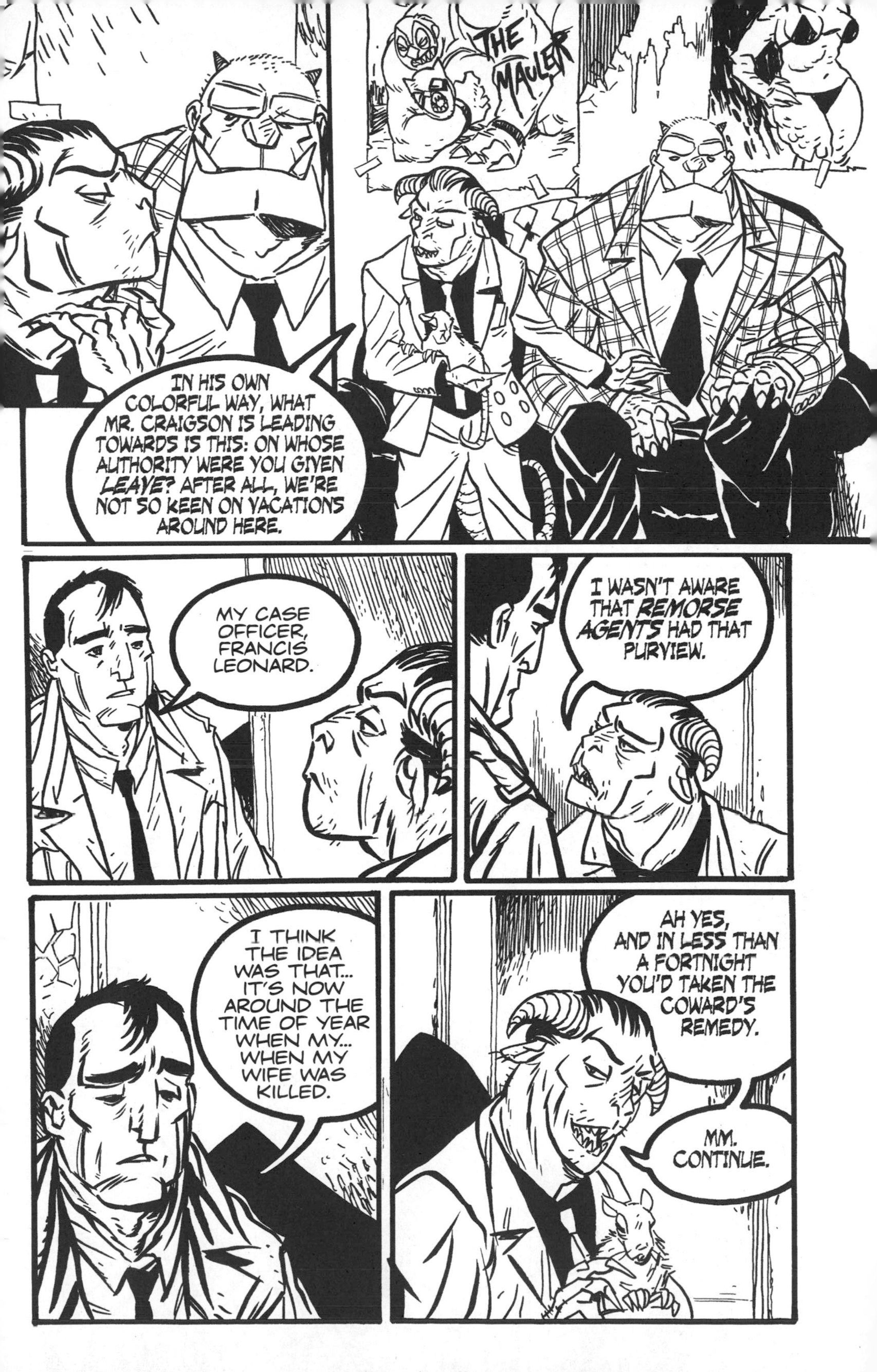
THE MAULER
IN HIS OWN COLORFUL WAY, WHAT MR. CRAIGSON IS LEADING TOWARDS IS THIS: ON WHOSE AUTHORITY WERE YOU GIVEN LEAVE? AFTER ALL, WE'RE NOT SO KEEN ON VACATIONS AROUND HERE.
MY CASE OFFICER, FRANCIS LEONARD.
I WASN'T AWARE THAT REMORSE AGENTS HAD THAT PURVIEW.
I THINK THE IDEA WAS THAT... IT'S NOW AROUND THE TIME OF YEAR WHEN MY... WHEN MY WIFE WAS KILLED.
AH YES, AND IN LESS THAN A FORTNIGHT YOU'D TAKEN THE COWARD'S REMEDY.
MM. CONTINUE.

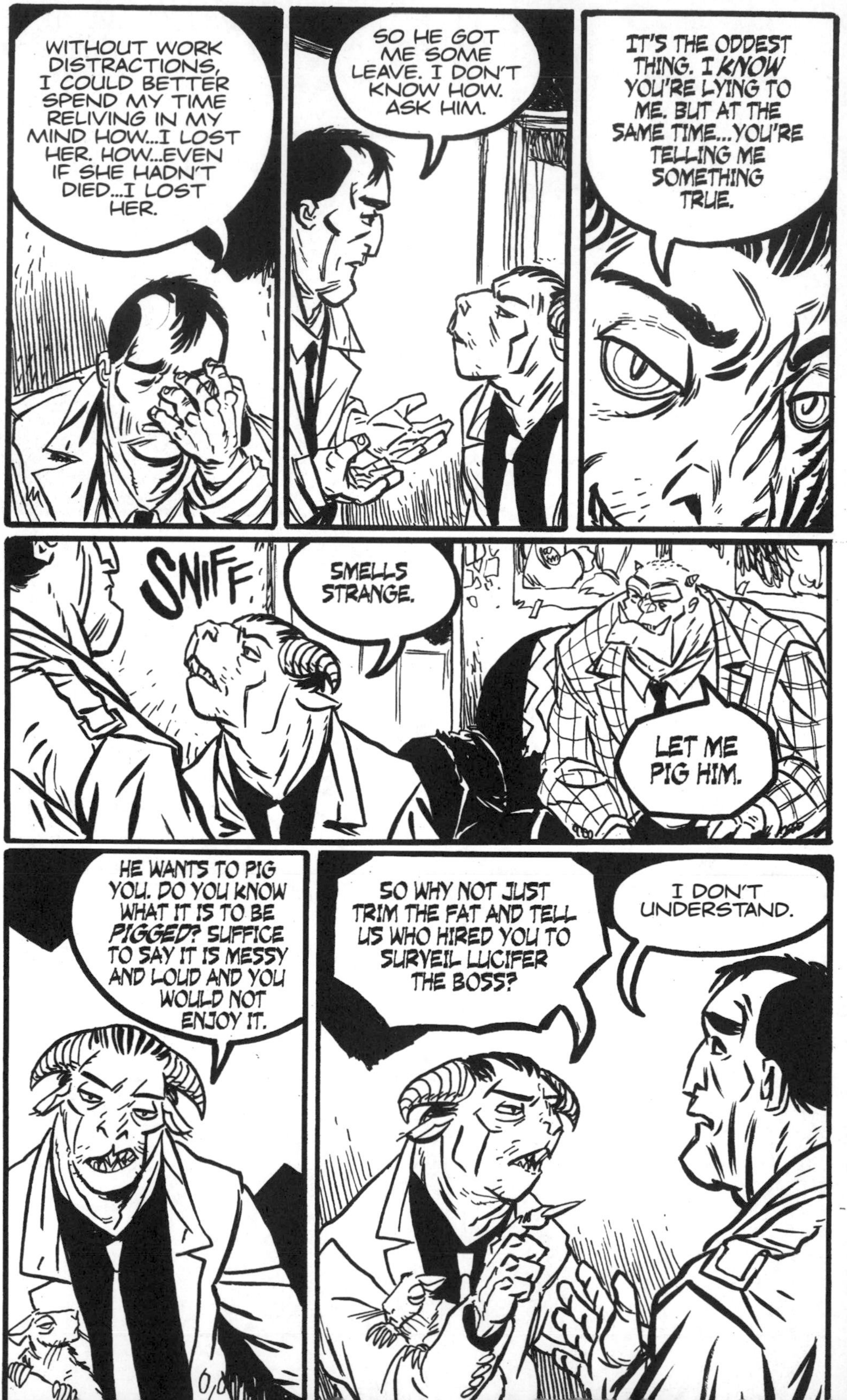
WITHOUT WORK DISTRACTIONS, I COULD BETTER SPEND MY TIME RELIVING IN MY MIND HOW...I LOST HER. HOW...EVEN IF SHE HADN'T DIED...I LOST HER.
SO HE GOT ME SOME LEAVE. I DON'T KNOW HOW. ASK HIM.
IT'S THE ODDEST THING. I KNOW YOU'RE LYING TO ME. BUT AT THE SAME TIME...YOU'RE TELLING ME SOMETHING TRUE.
SNIFFF
SMELLS STRANGE.
LET ME PIG HIM.
HE WANTS TO PIG YOU. DO YOU KNOW WHAT IT IS TO BE PIGGED? SUFFICE TO SAY IT IS MESSY AND LOUD AND YOU WOULD NOT ENJOY IT.
SO WHY NOT JUST TRIM THE FAT AND TELL US WHO HIRED YOU TO SURVEIL LUCIFER THE BOSS?
I DON'T UNDERSTAND.

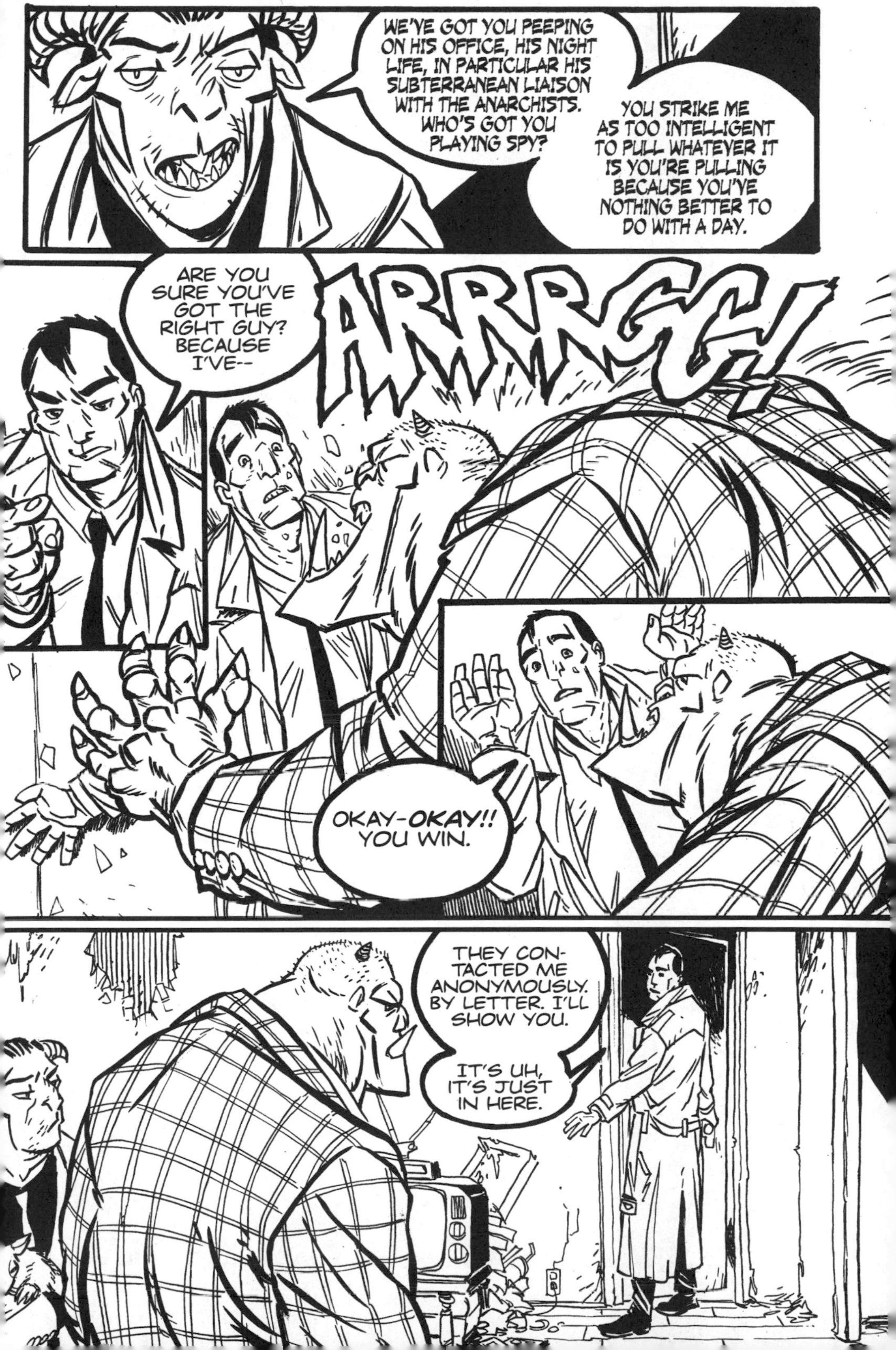

WE'VE GOT YOU PEEPING ON HIS OFFICE, HIS NIGHT LIFE, IN PARTICULAR HIS SUBTERRANEAN LIAISON WITH THE ANARCHISTS. WHO'S GOT YOU PLAYING SPY?
YOU STRIKE ME AS TOO INTELLIGENT TO PULL WHATEVER IT IS YOU'RE PULLING BECAUSE YOU'VE NOTHING BETTER TO DO WITH A DAY.
ARE YOU SURE YOU'VE GOT THE RIGHT GUY? BECAUSE I'VE--
ARRRGGH!
OKAY-**OKAY**!! YOU WIN.
THEY CONTACTED ME ANONYMOUSLY. BY LETTER. I'LL SHOW YOU.
IT'S UH, IT'S JUST IN HERE.

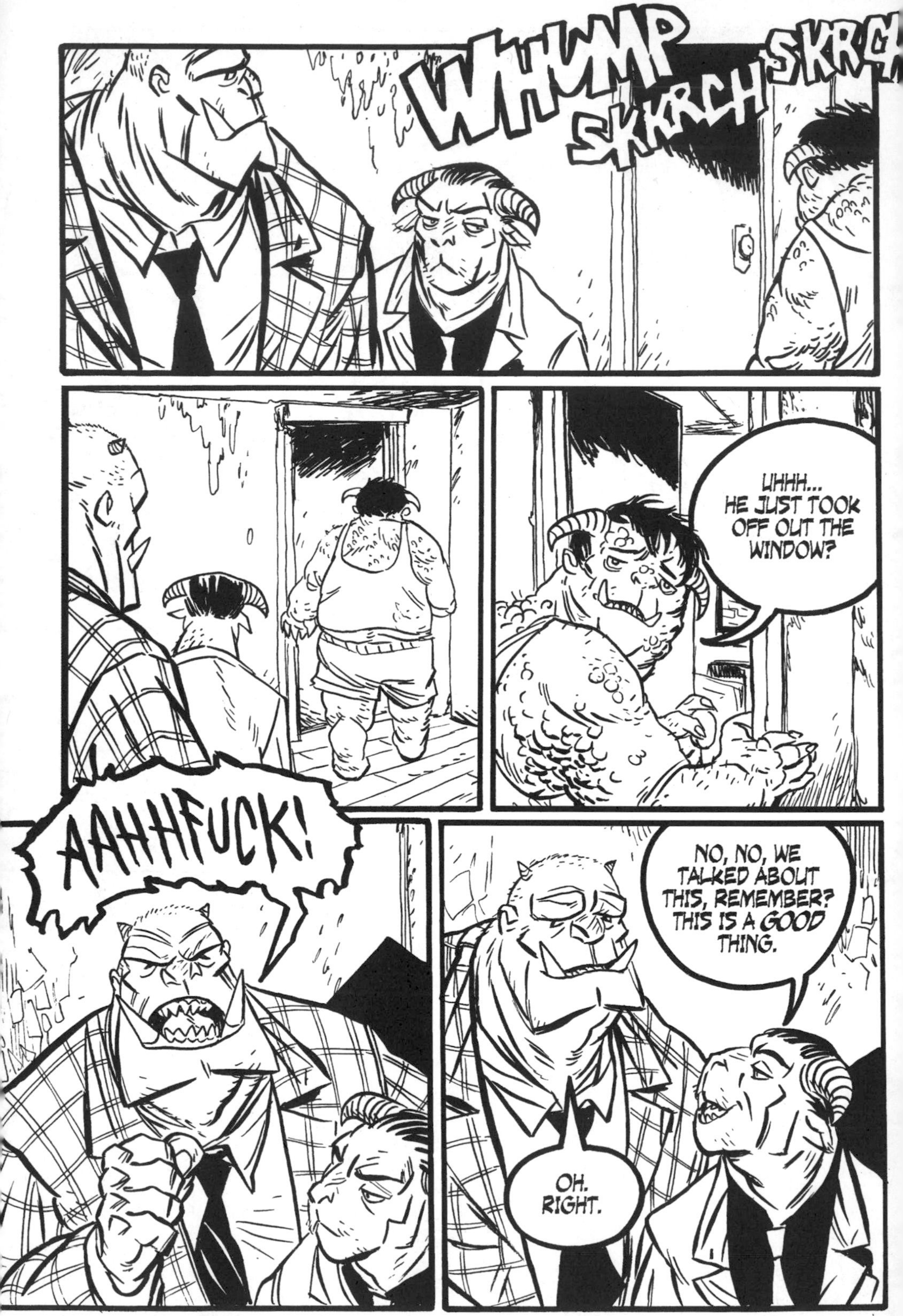
WHUMP
SKRCH
SKRCH
UHHH... HE JUST TOOK OFF OUT THE WINDOW?
AAHHFUCK!
NO, NO, WE TALKED ABOUT THIS, REMEMBER? THIS IS A *GOOD* THING.
OH. RIGHT.

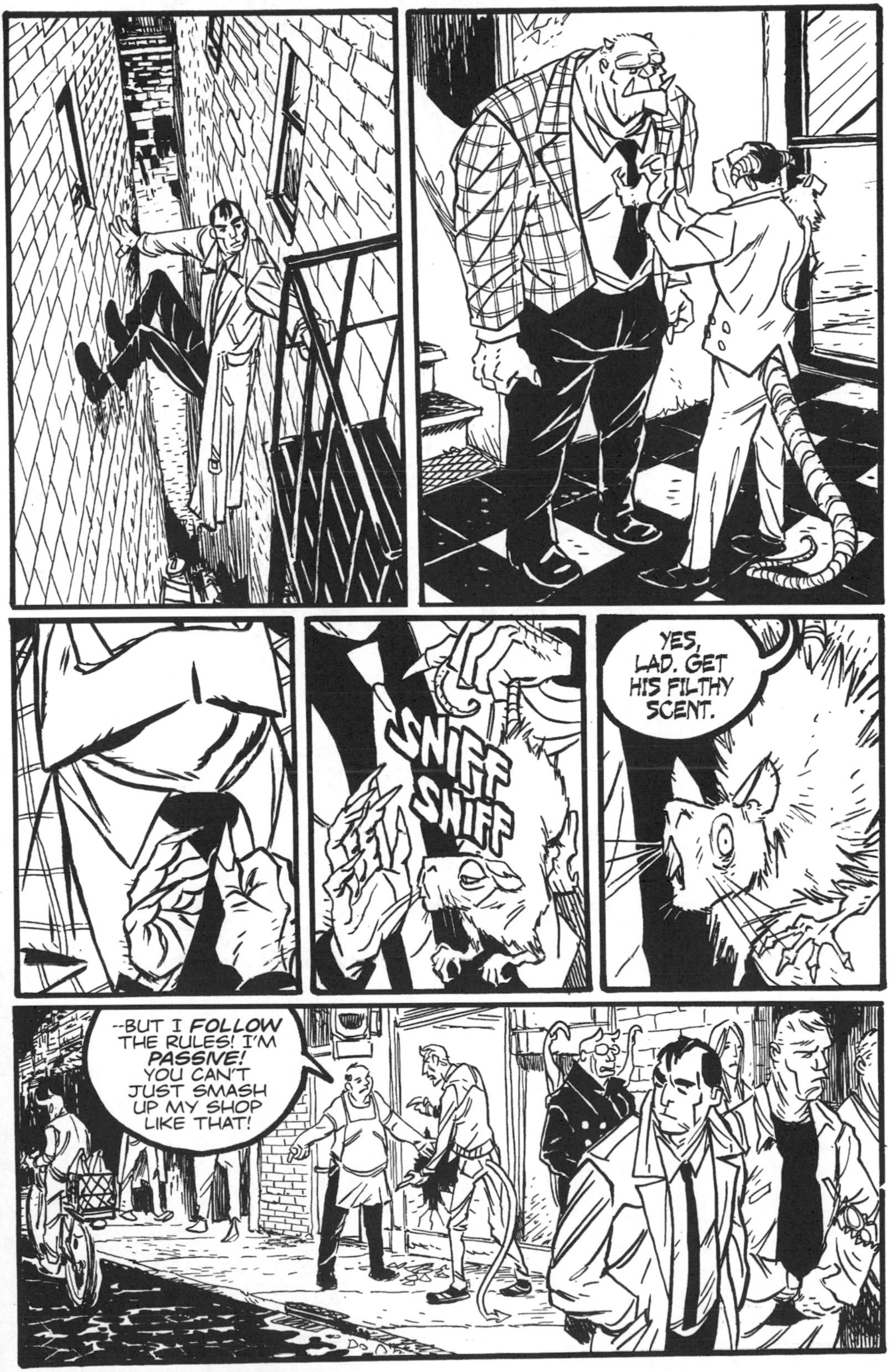
SNIFF SNIFF
YES, LAD. GET HIS FILTHY SCENT.
--BUT I FOLLOW THE RULES! I'M PASSIVE! YOU CAN'T JUST SMASH UP MY SHOP LIKE THAT!

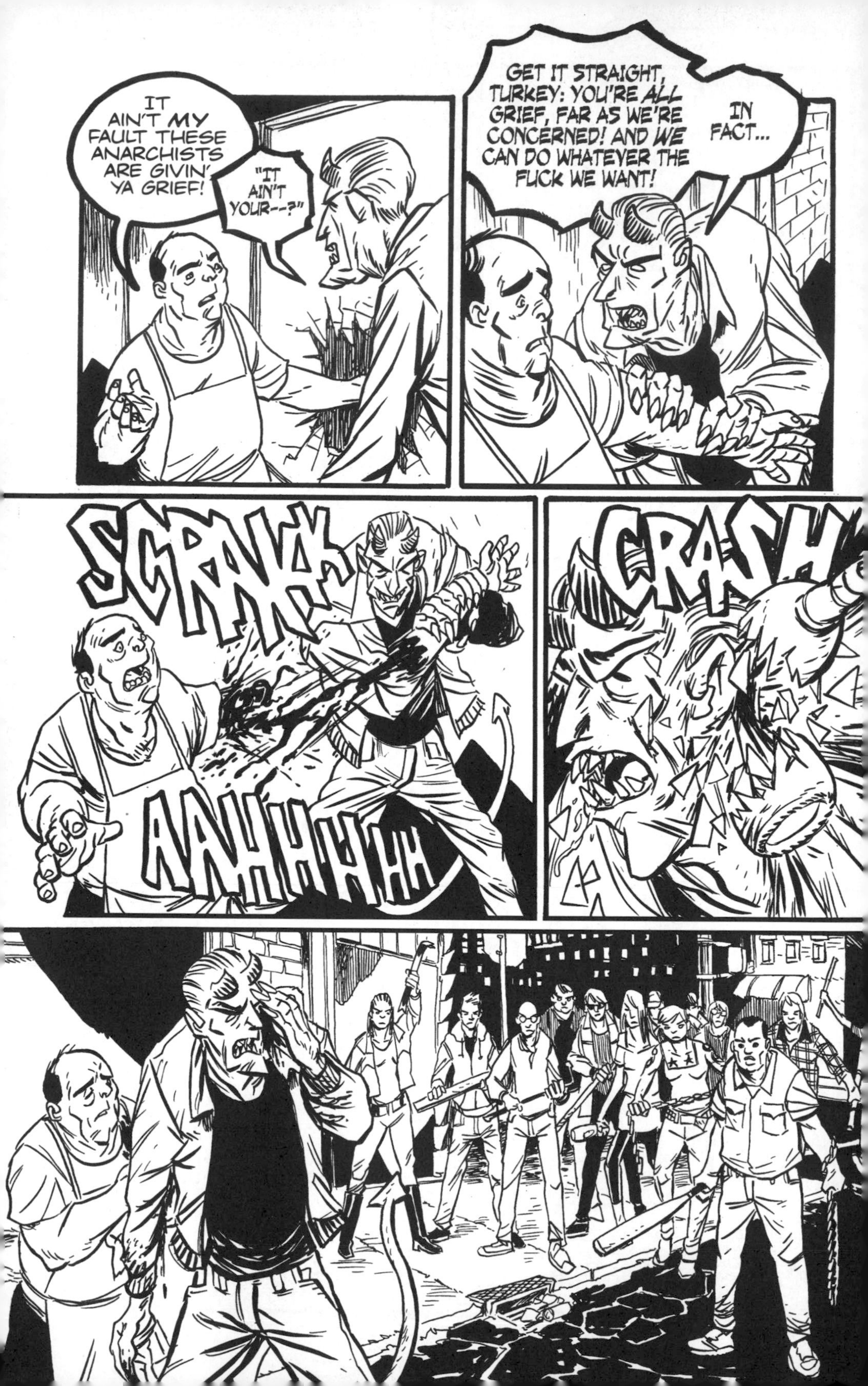
IT AIN'T MY FAULT THESE ANARCHISTS ARE GIVIN' YA GRIEF!
"IT AIN'T YOUR--?"
GET IT STRAIGHT, TURKEY: YOU'RE ALL GRIEF, FAR AS WE'RE CONCERNED! AND WE CAN DO WHATEVER THE FUCK WE WANT!
IN FACT...
SCRAKK
AAHHHHHH
CRASH

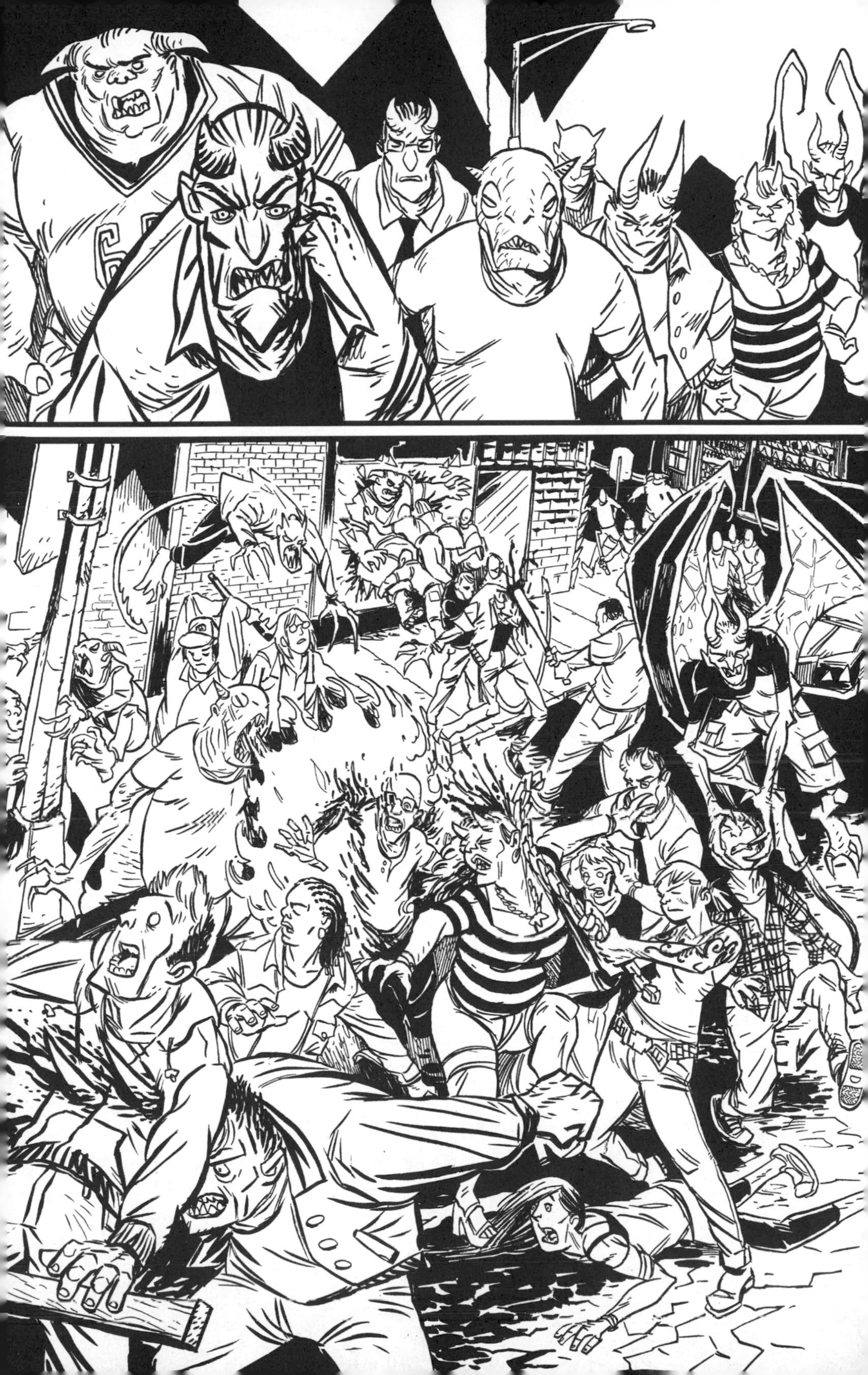

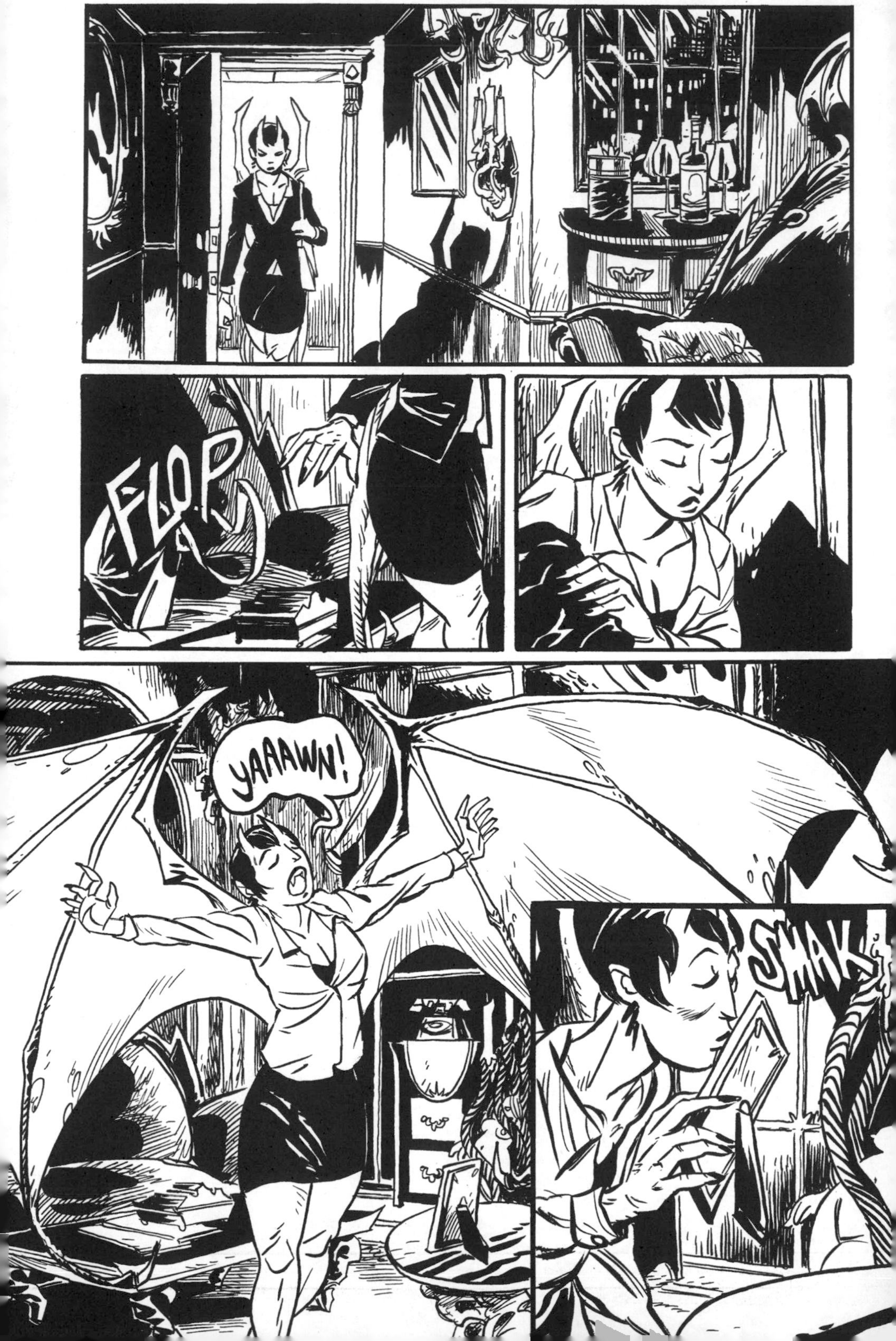
FLOP
YAAAWN!
SMAK

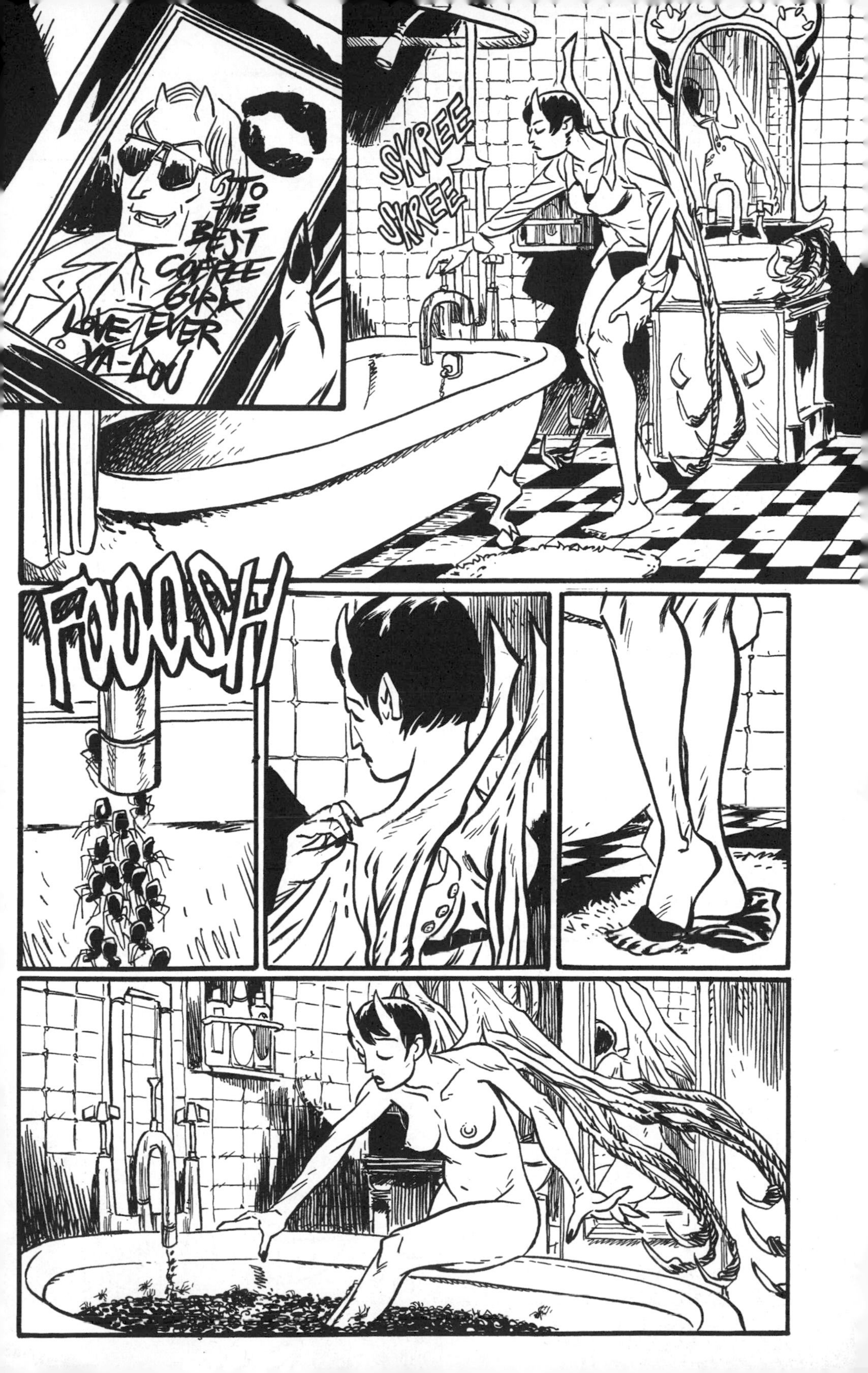
TO THE BEST COFFEE GIRL
LOVE EVER
YA-DOU
SKREE
SKREE
FOOOSH

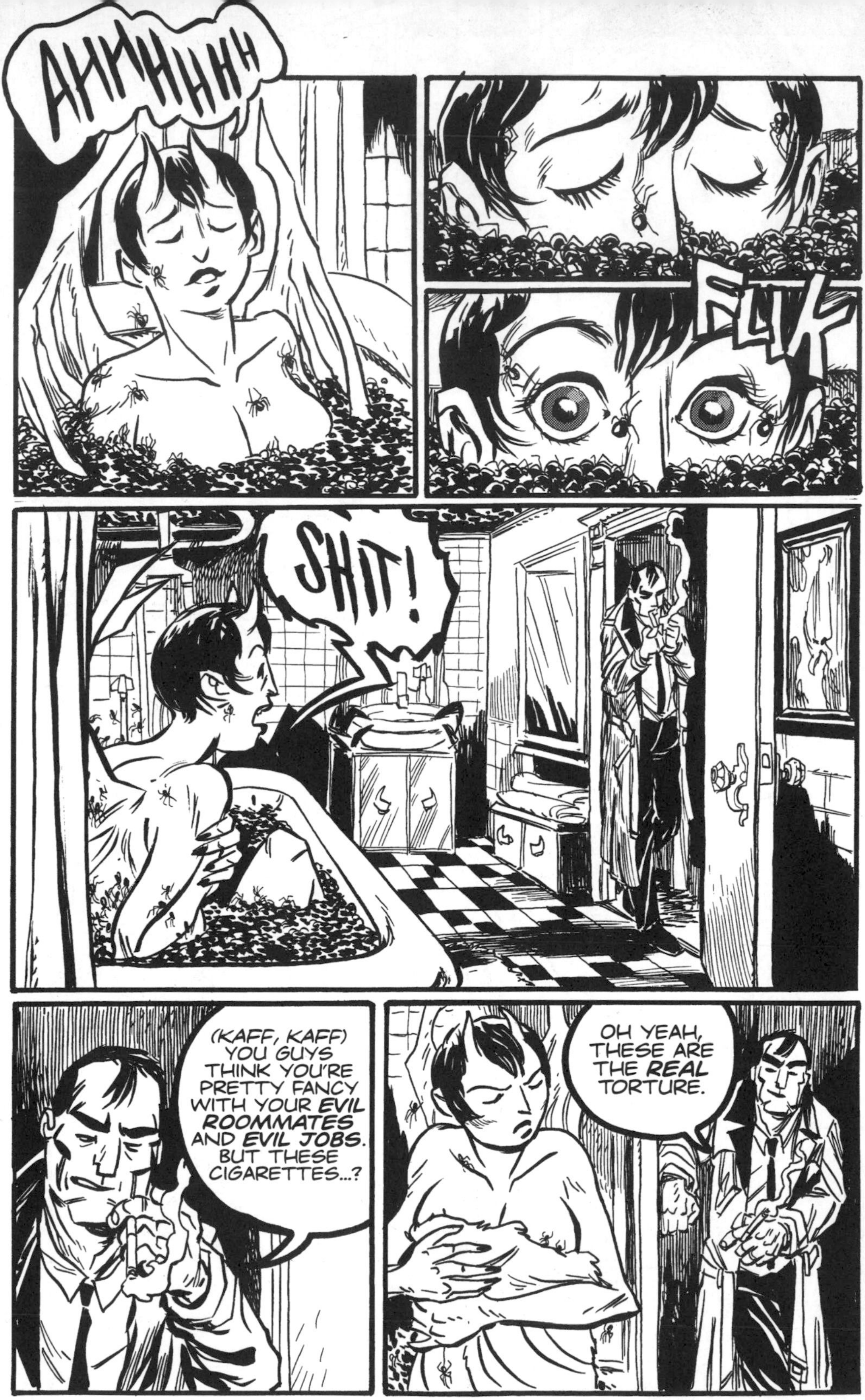
AHHHHHHH
FLIK
SHIT!
(KAFF, KAFF) YOU GUYS THINK YOU'RE PRETTY FANCY WITH YOUR EVIL ROOMMATES AND EVIL JOBS. BUT THESE CIGARETTES...?
OH YEAH, THESE ARE THE REAL TORTURE.

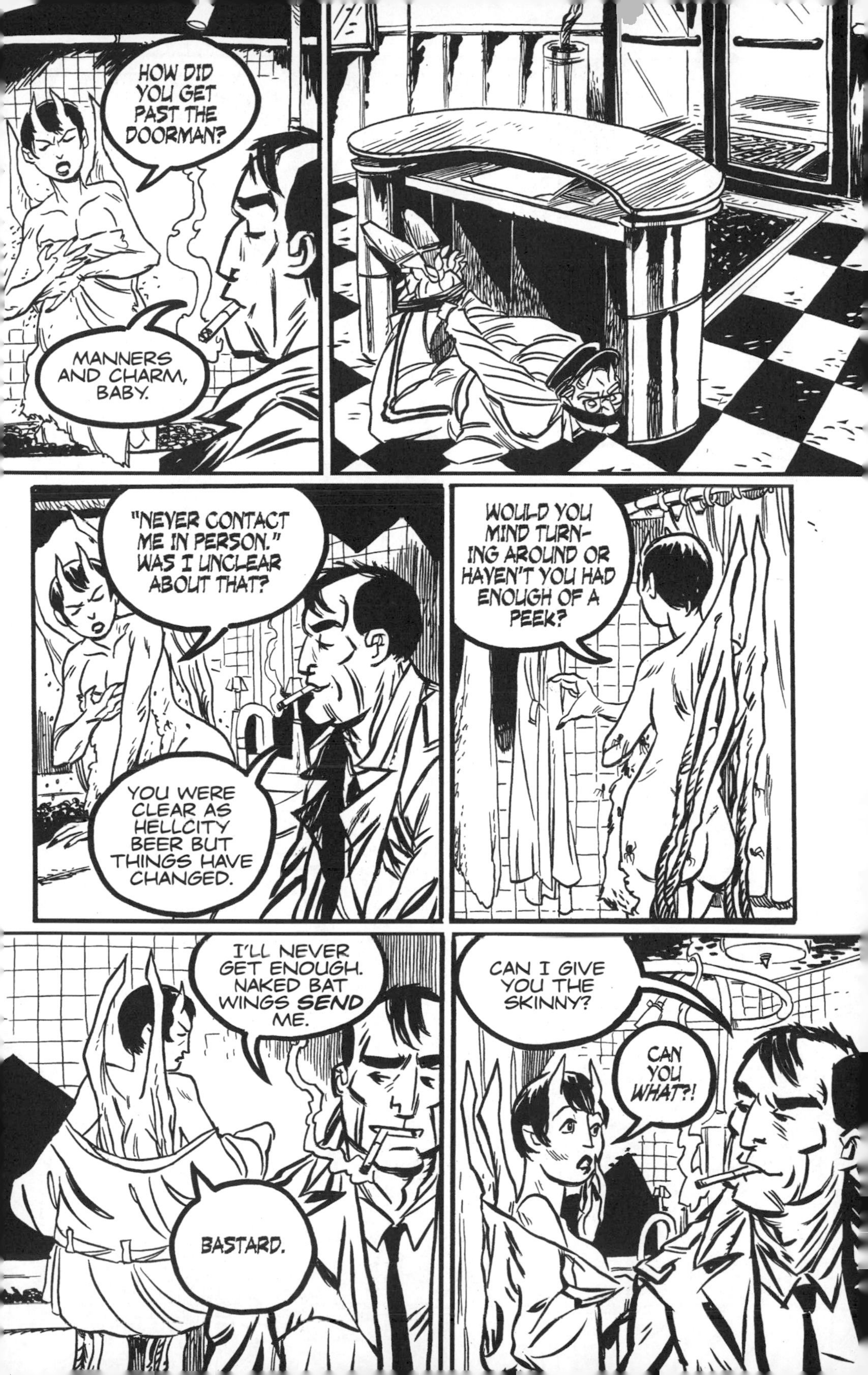
HOW DID YOU GET PAST THE DOORMAN?
MANNERS AND CHARM, BABY.
"NEVER CONTACT ME IN PERSON." WAS I UNCLEAR ABOUT THAT?
YOU WERE CLEAR AS HELLCITY BEER BUT THINGS HAVE CHANGED.
WOULD YOU MIND TURN-ING AROUND OR HAVEN'T YOU HAD ENOUGH OF A PEEK?
I'LL NEVER GET ENOUGH. NAKED BAT WINGS SEND ME.
BASTARD.
CAN I GIVE YOU THE SKINNY?
CAN YOU WHAT?!

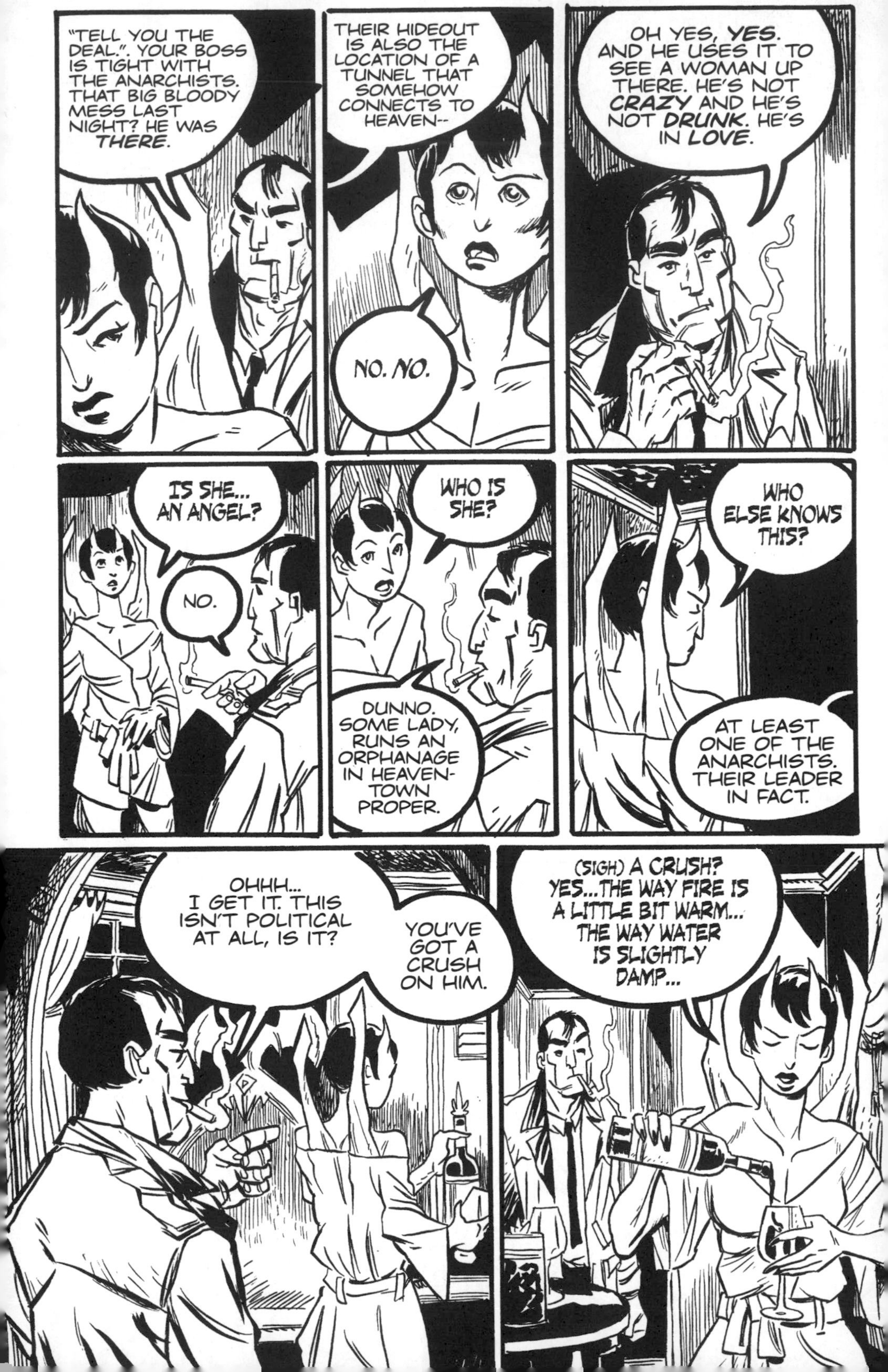
"TELL YOU THE DEAL.". YOUR BOSS IS TIGHT WITH THE ANARCHISTS. THAT BIG BLOODY MESS LAST NIGHT? HE WAS *THERE*.
THEIR HIDEOUT IS ALSO THE LOCATION OF A TUNNEL THAT SOMEHOW CONNECTS TO HEAVEN--
NO. *NO.*
OH YES, ***YES***. AND HE USES IT TO SEE A WOMAN UP THERE. HE'S NOT ***CRAZY*** AND HE'S NOT ***DRUNK***. HE'S IN ***LOVE***.
IS SHE... AN ANGEL?
NO.
WHO IS SHE?
DUNNO. SOME LADY, RUNS AN ORPHANAGE IN HEAVEN-TOWN PROPER.
WHO ELSE KNOWS THIS?
AT LEAST ONE OF THE ANARCHISTS. THEIR LEADER IN FACT.
OHHH... I GET IT. THIS ISN'T POLITICAL AT ALL, IS IT?
YOU'VE GOT A CRUSH ON HIM.
(SIGH) A CRUSH? YES...THE WAY FIRE IS A LITTLE BIT WARM... THE WAY WATER IS SLIGHTLY DAMP...

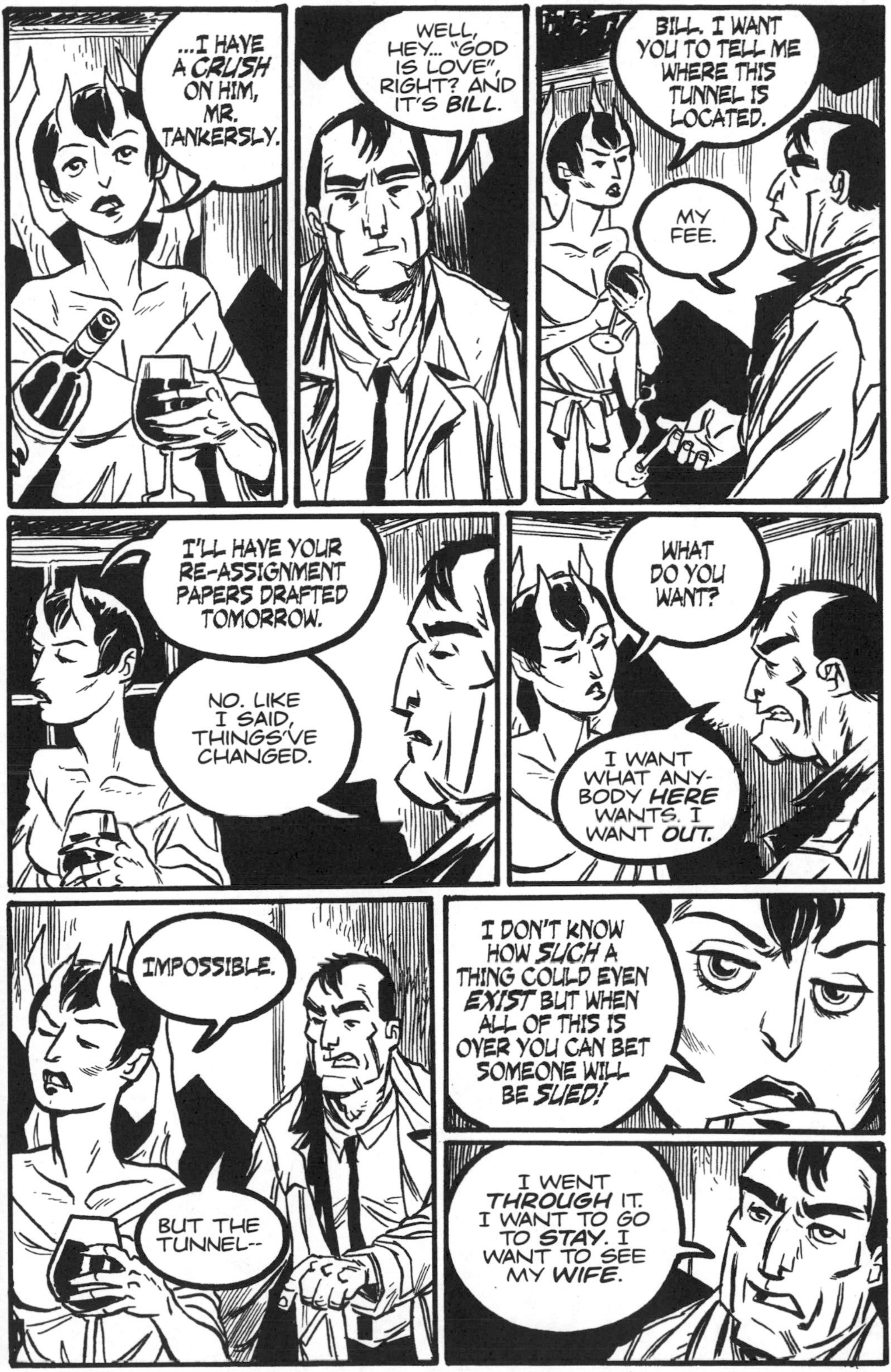
...I HAVE A CRUSH ON HIM, MR. TANKERSLY.
WELL, HEY... "GOD IS LOVE", RIGHT? AND IT'S BILL.
BILL. I WANT YOU TO TELL ME WHERE THIS TUNNEL IS LOCATED.
MY FEE.
I'LL HAVE YOUR RE-ASSIGNMENT PAPERS DRAFTED TOMORROW.
NO. LIKE I SAID, THINGS'VE CHANGED.
WHAT DO YOU WANT?
I WANT WHAT ANY-BODY HERE WANTS. I WANT OUT.
IMPOSSIBLE.
BUT THE TUNNEL--
I DON'T KNOW HOW SUCH A THING COULD EVEN EXIST BUT WHEN ALL OF THIS IS OVER YOU CAN BET SOMEONE WILL BE SUED!
I WENT THROUGH IT. I WANT TO GO TO STAY. I WANT TO SEE MY WIFE.

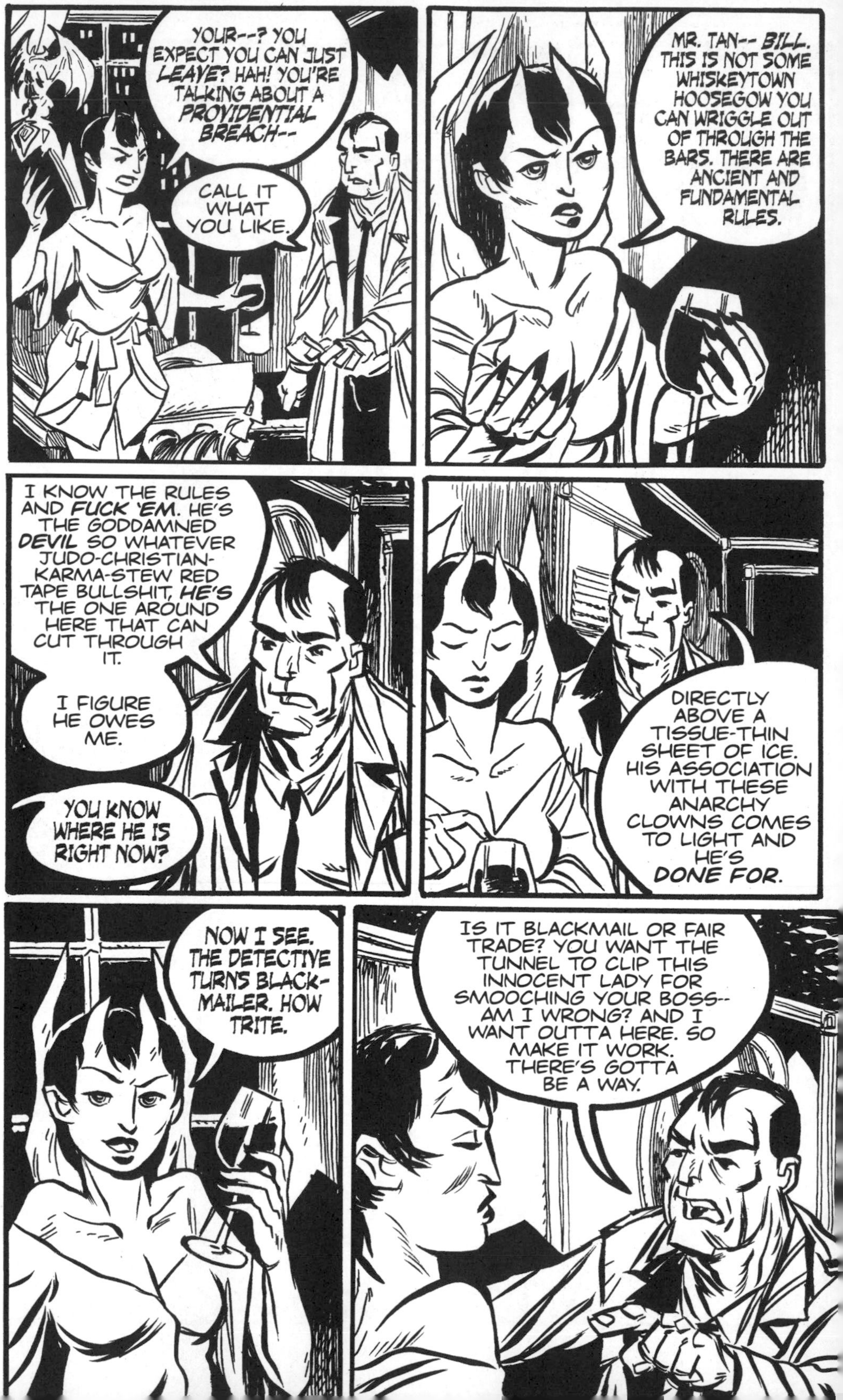
YOUR--? YOU EXPECT YOU CAN JUST LEAVE? HAH! YOU'RE TALKING ABOUT A PROVIDENTIAL BREACH--
CALL IT WHAT YOU LIKE.
MR. TAN-- BILL. THIS IS NOT SOME WHISKEYTOWN HOOSEGOW YOU CAN WRIGGLE OUT OF THROUGH THE BARS. THERE ARE ANCIENT AND FUNDAMENTAL RULES.
I KNOW THE RULES AND FUCK 'EM. HE'S THE GODDAMNED DEVIL SO WHATEVER JUDO-CHRISTIAN-KARMA-STEW RED TAPE BULLSHIT, HE'S THE ONE AROUND HERE THAT CAN CUT THROUGH IT.
I FIGURE HE OWES ME.
YOU KNOW WHERE HE IS RIGHT NOW?
DIRECTLY ABOVE A TISSUE-THIN SHEET OF ICE. HIS ASSOCIATION WITH THESE ANARCHY CLOWNS COMES TO LIGHT AND HE'S DONE FOR.
NOW I SEE. THE DETECTIVE TURNS BLACK-MAILER. HOW TRITE.
IS IT BLACKMAIL OR FAIR TRADE? YOU WANT THE TUNNEL TO CLIP THIS INNOCENT LADY FOR SMOOCHING YOUR BOSS-- AM I WRONG? AND I WANT OUTTA HERE. SO MAKE IT WORK. THERE'S GOTTA BE A WAY.

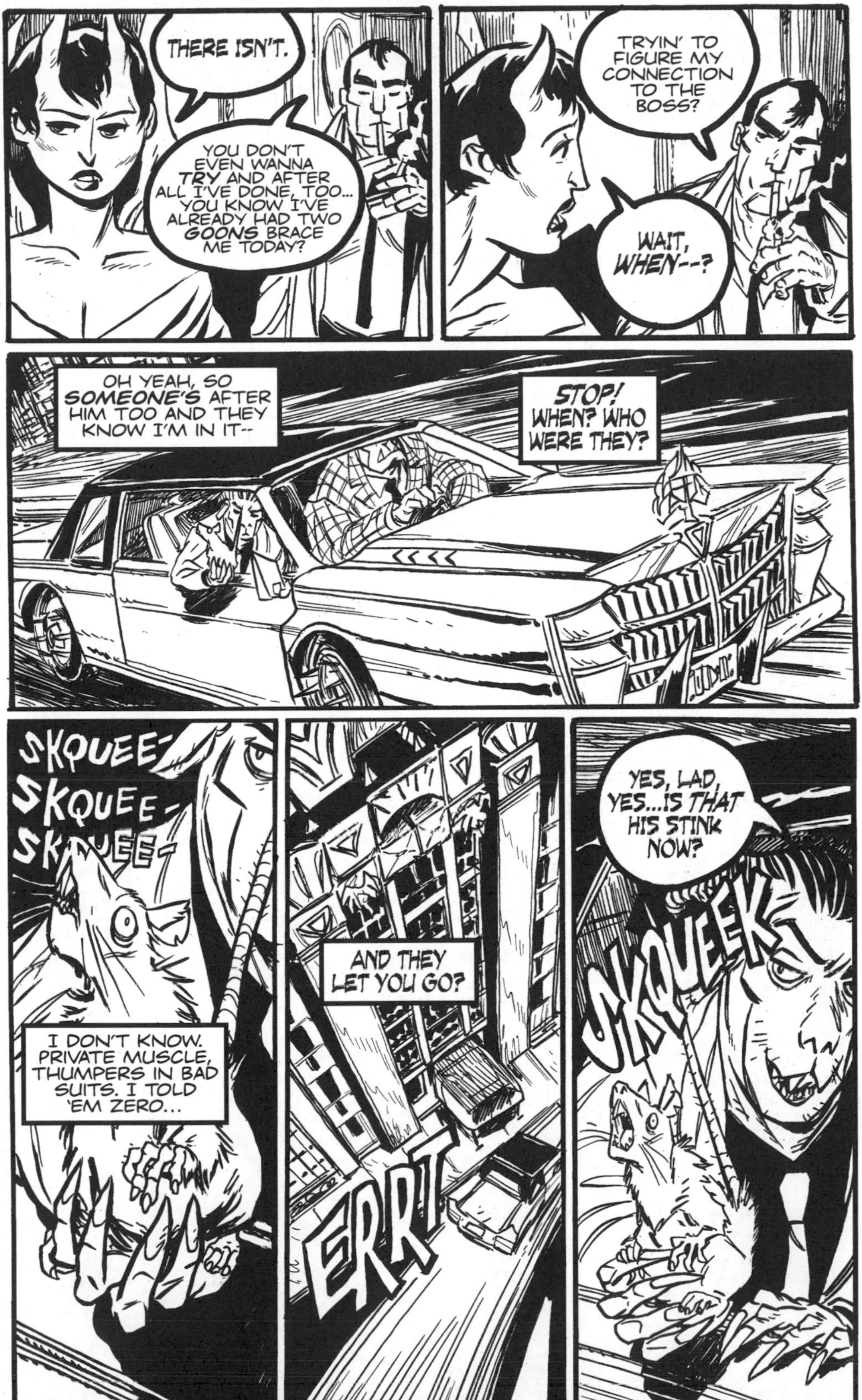
THERE ISN'T.
YOU DON'T EVEN WANNA TRY AND AFTER ALL I'VE DONE, TOO... YOU KNOW I'VE ALREADY HAD TWO GOONS BRACE ME TODAY?
TRYIN' TO FIGURE MY CONNECTION TO THE BOSS?
WAIT, WHEN--?
OH YEAH, SO SOMEONE'S AFTER HIM TOO AND THEY KNOW I'M IN IT--
STOP! WHEN? WHO WERE THEY?
SKQUEE-
SKQUEE-
SKQUEE-
I DON'T KNOW. PRIVATE MUSCLE, THUMPERS IN BAD SUITS. I TOLD 'EM ZERO...
AND THEY LET YOU GO?
ERRT
YES, LAD, YES...IS THAT HIS STINK NOW?
SKQUEEK

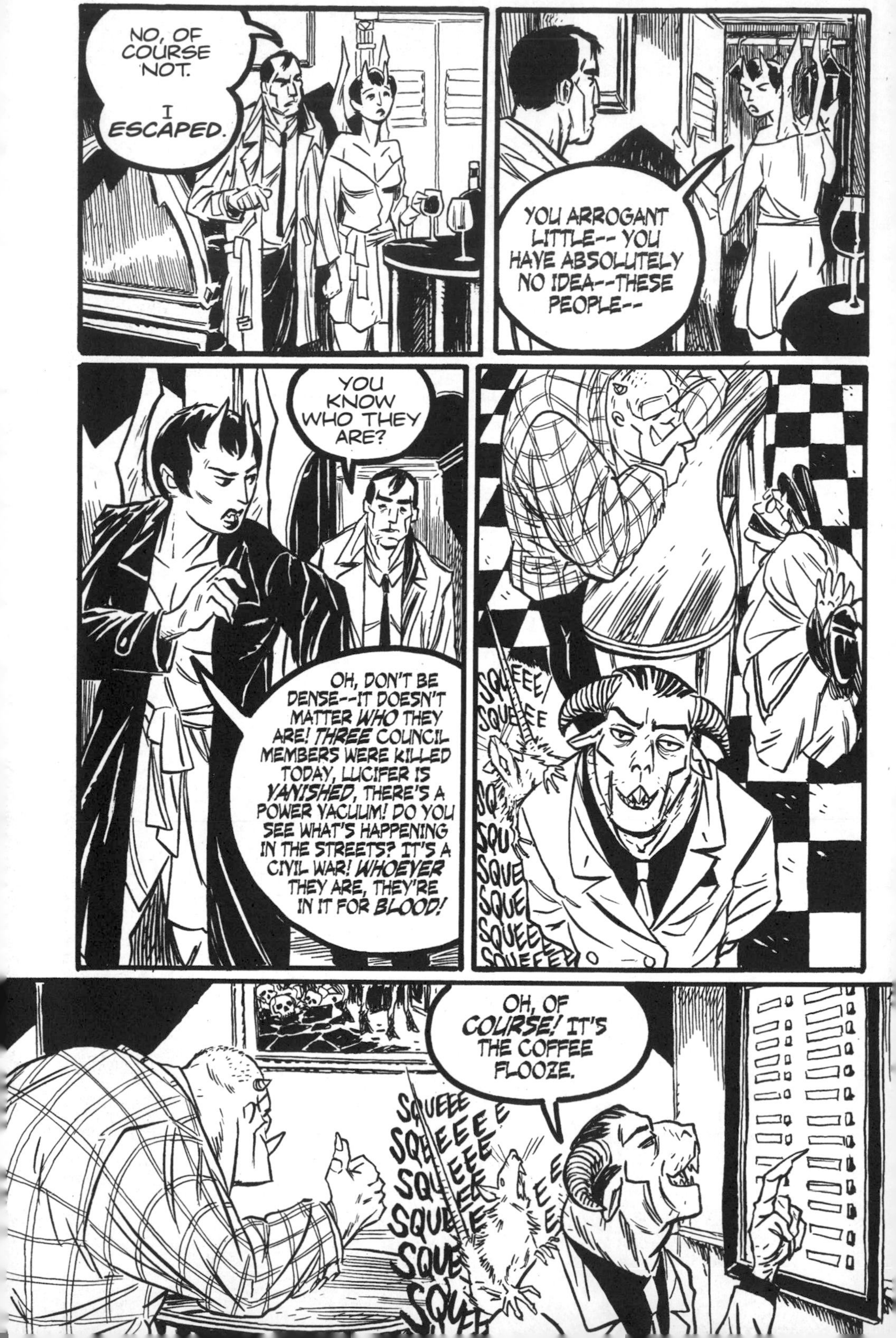
NO, OF COURSE NOT.
I ESCAPED.
YOU ARROGANT LITTLE-- YOU HAVE ABSOLUTELY NO IDEA--THESE PEOPLE--
YOU KNOW WHO THEY ARE?
OH, DON'T BE DENSE--IT DOESN'T MATTER WHO THEY ARE! THREE COUNCIL MEMBERS WERE KILLED TODAY, LUCIFER IS VANISHED, THERE'S A POWER VACUUM! DO YOU SEE WHAT'S HAPPENING IN THE STREETS? IT'S A CIVIL WAR! WHOEVER THEY ARE, THEY'RE IN IT FOR BLOOD!
SQUEEE SQUEEE SQ SQU SQUE SQUE SQUEE SQUEEE
OH, OF COURSE! IT'S THE COFFEE FLOOZE.
SQUEEE SQUEEEE SQUEEE SQUEE SQUE SQUE

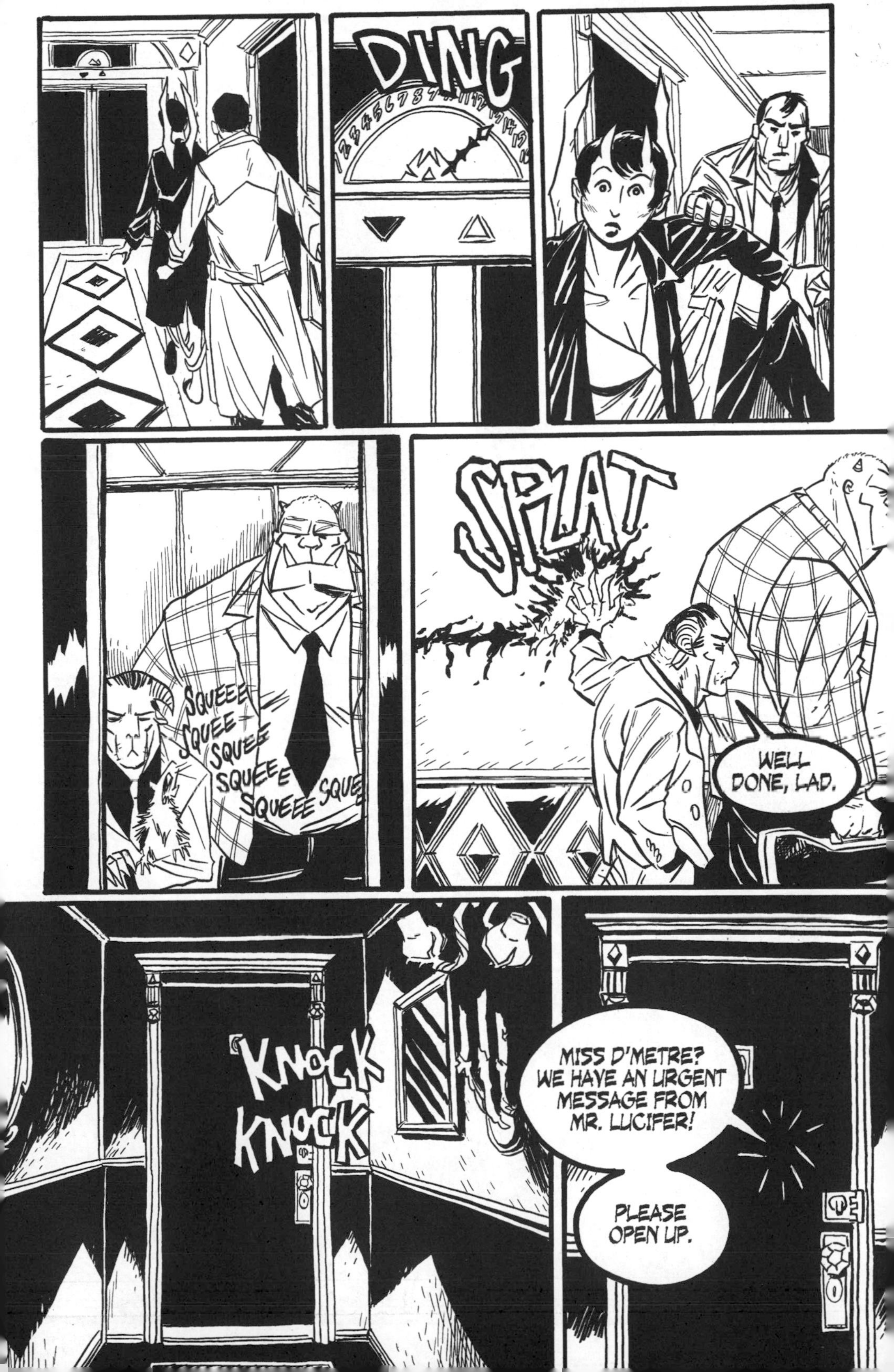
DING
SQUEEE SQUEE SQUEE SQUEEE SQUEEE SQUE
SPLAT
WELL DONE, LAD.
KNOCK KNOCK
MISS D'METRE? WE HAVE AN URGENT MESSAGE FROM MR. LUCIFER!
PLEASE OPEN UP.

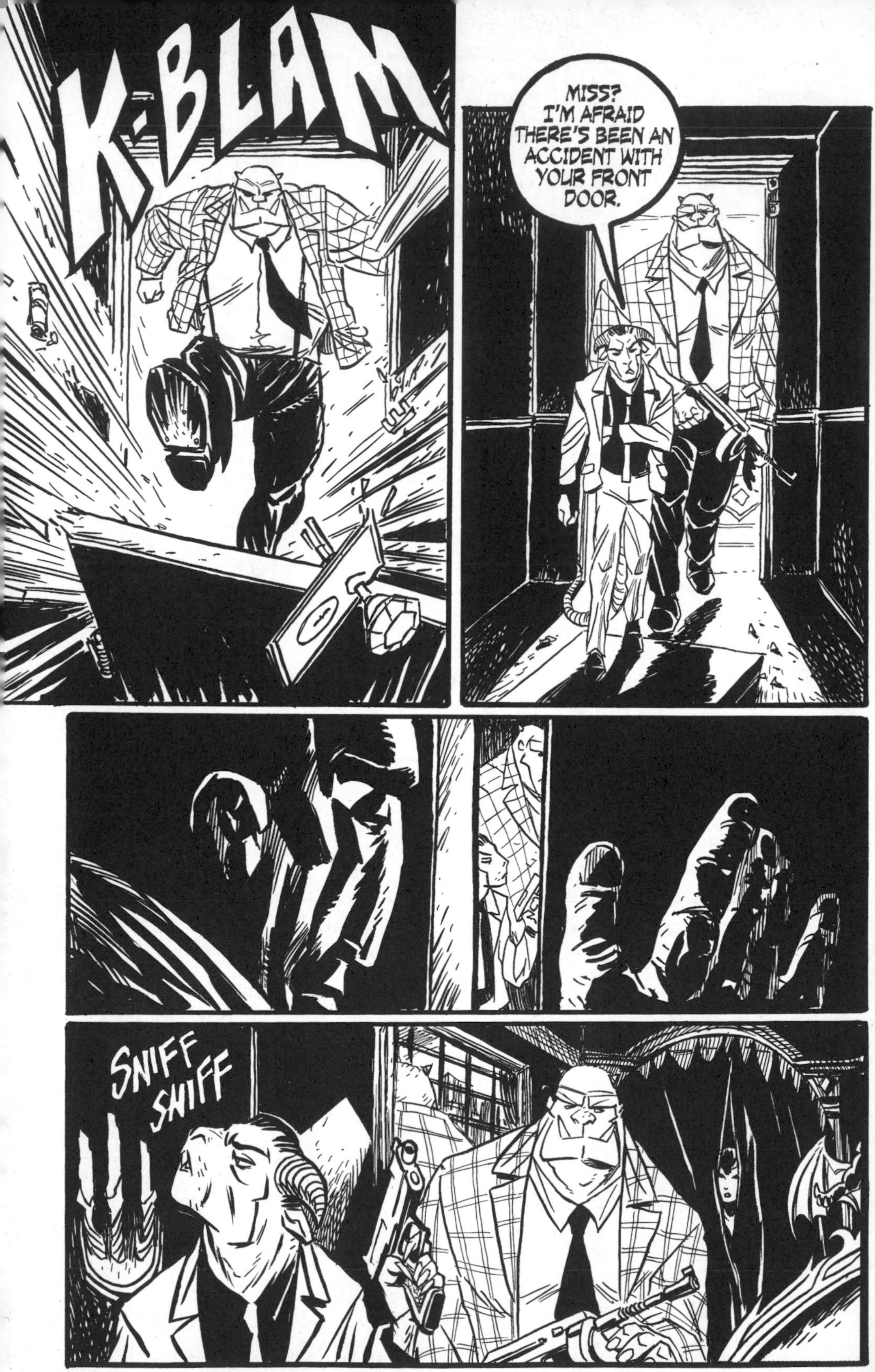
K-BLAM
MISS? I'M AFRAID THERE'S BEEN AN ACCIDENT WITH YOUR FRONT DOOR.
SNIFF SNIFF

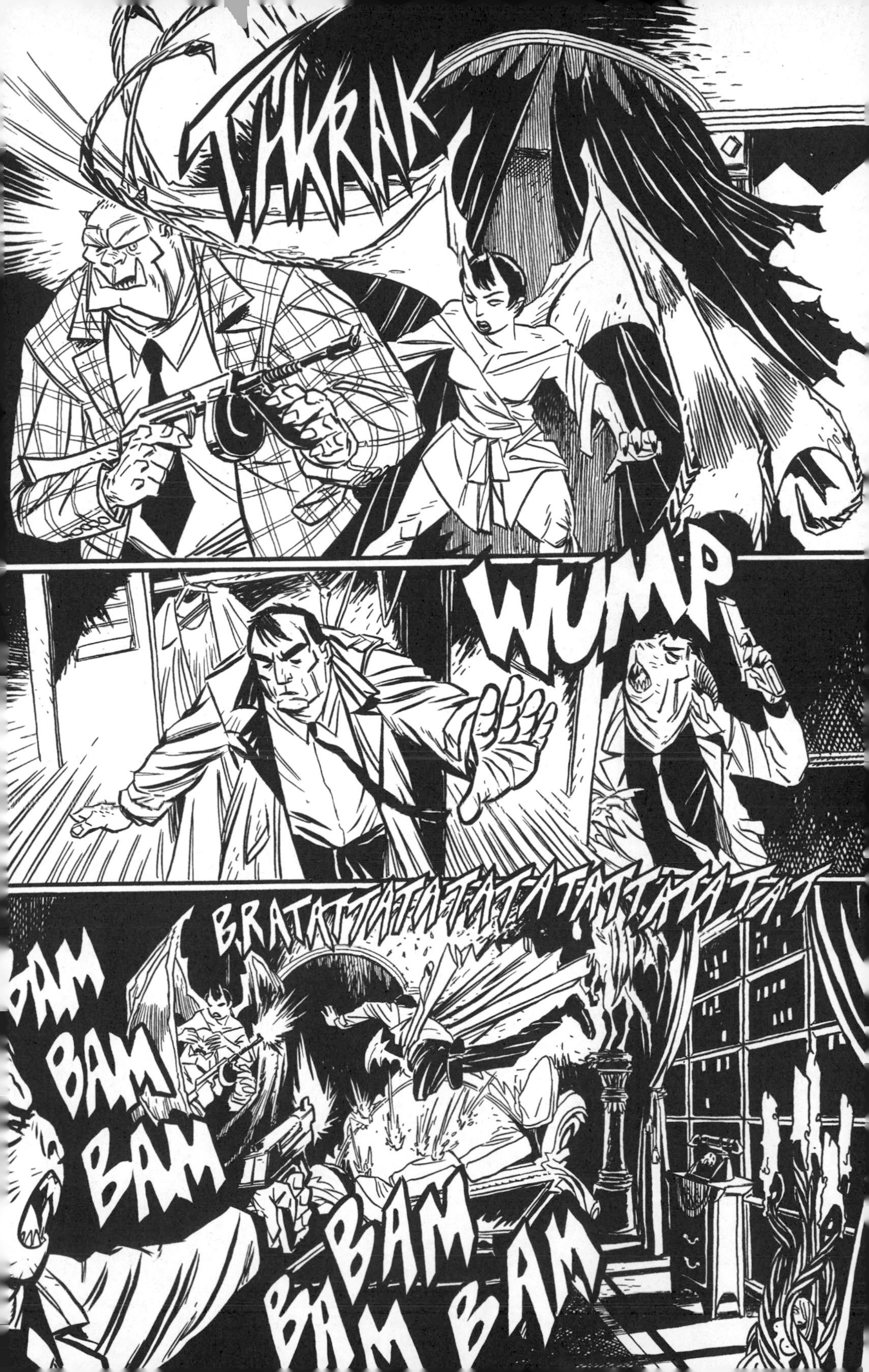
THRAK
WUMP
BRATATTATATATATATATTATATATAT
BAM
BAM
BAM
BAM
BAM
BAM

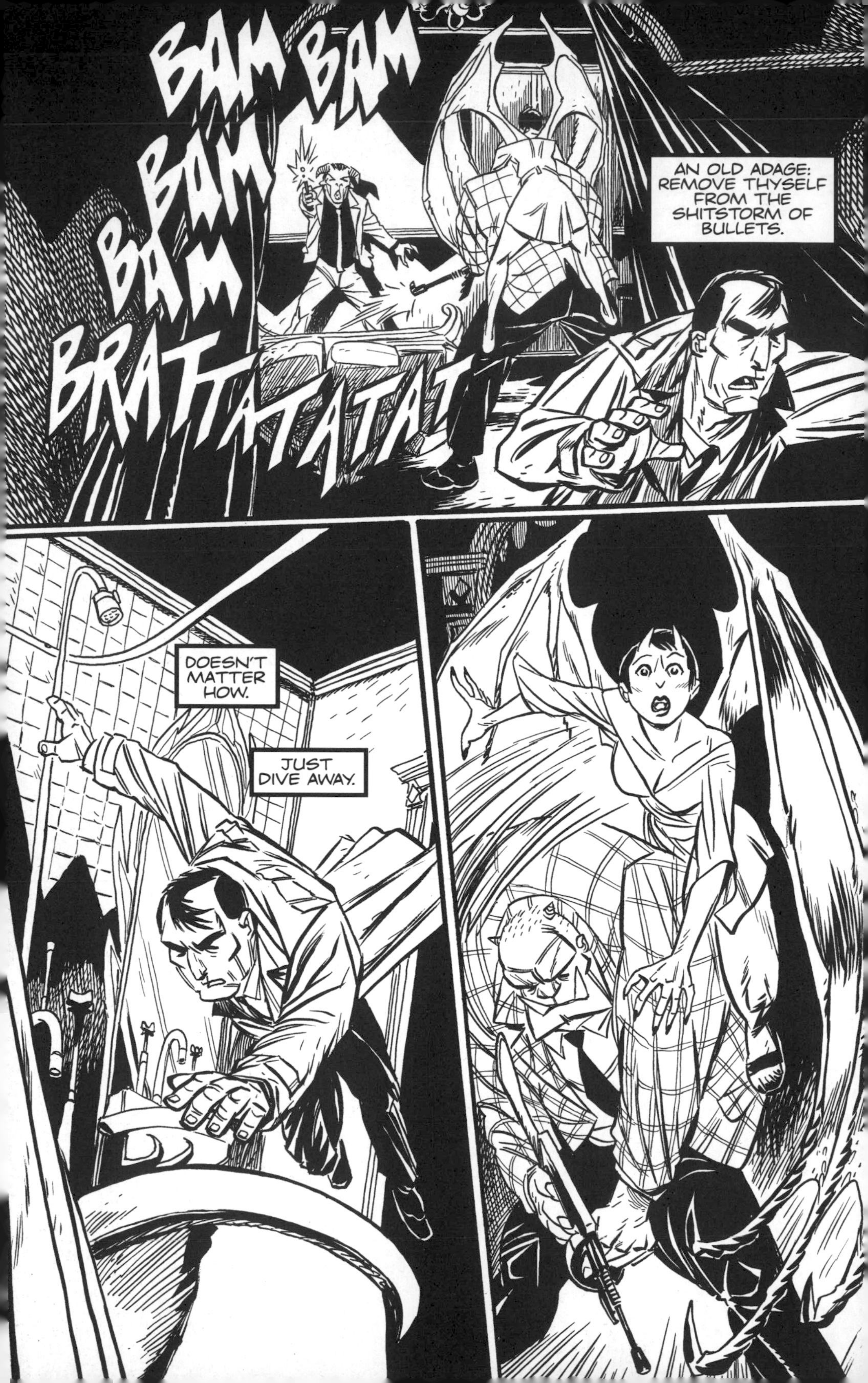
BAM BAM BAM BAM
BAM BAM
BRATTATATAT
AN OLD ADAGE: REMOVE THYSELF FROM THE SHITSTORM OF BULLETS.
DOESN'T MATTER HOW.
JUST DIVE AWAY.

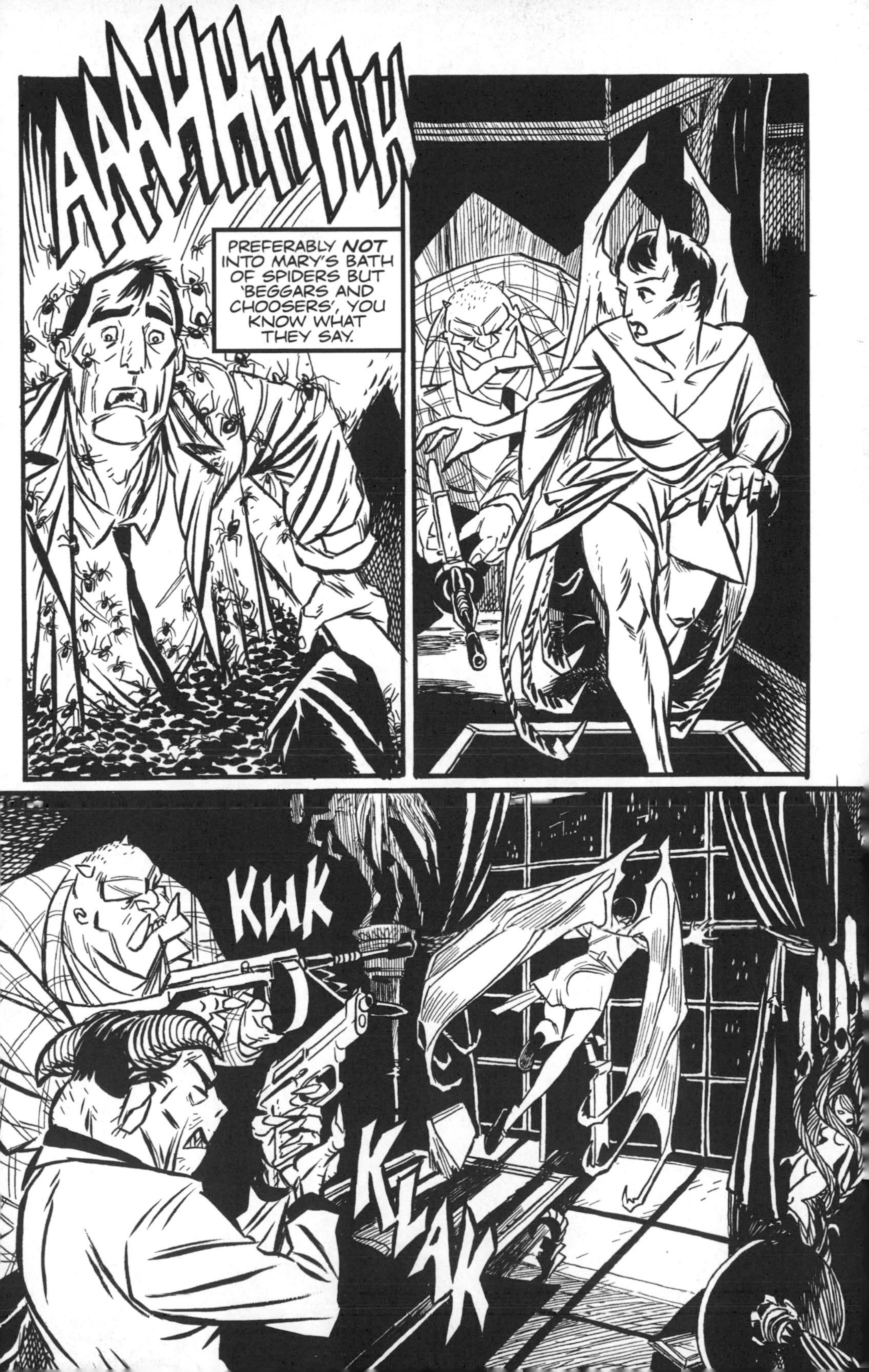
AAAHHHHHK
PREFERABLY NOT INTO MARY'S BATH OF SPIDERS BUT 'BEGGARS AND CHOOSERS', YOU KNOW WHAT THEY SAY.
KWK
KZAK

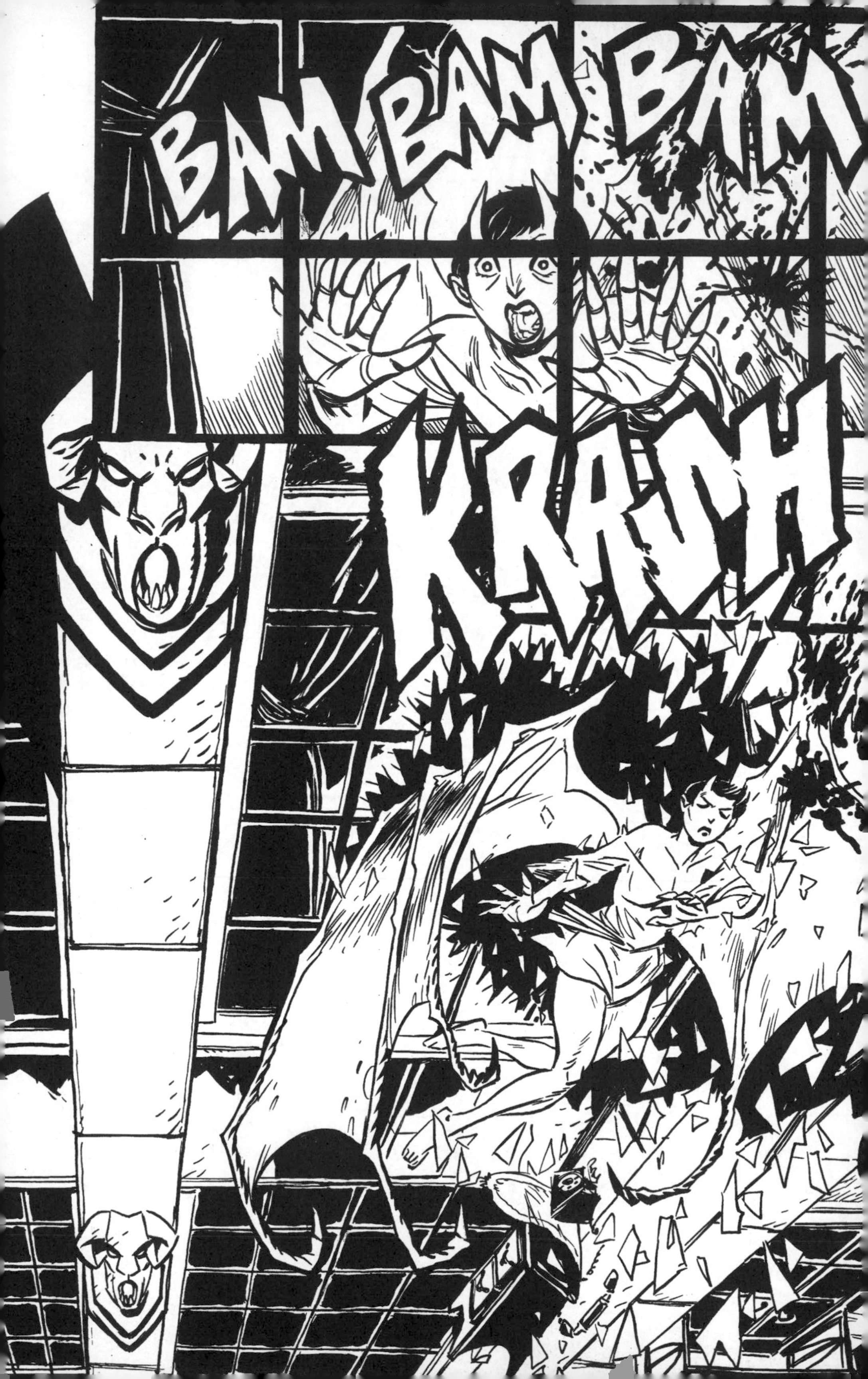
BAM BAM BAM
KRACH

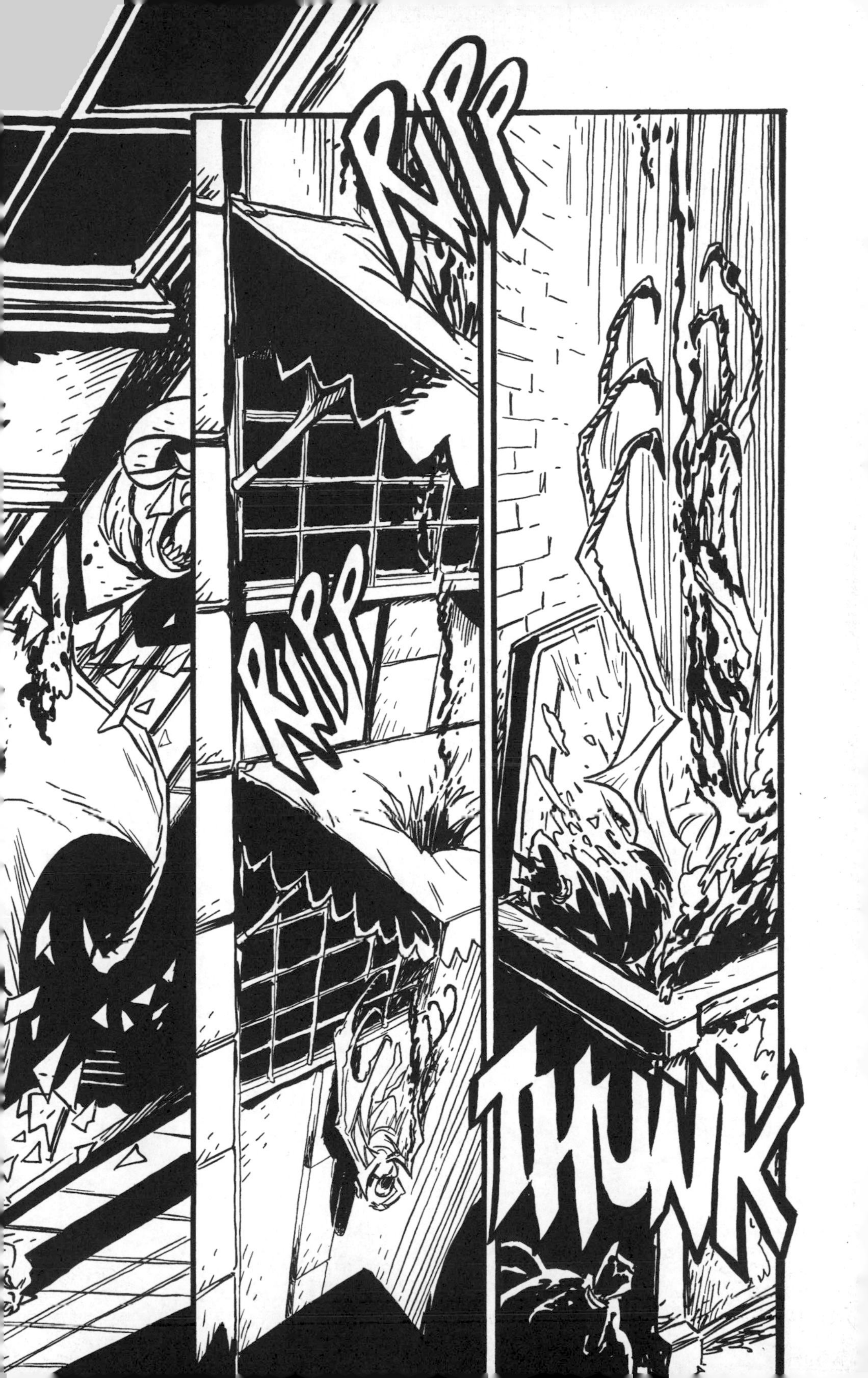
RIPP
RIPP
THUNK

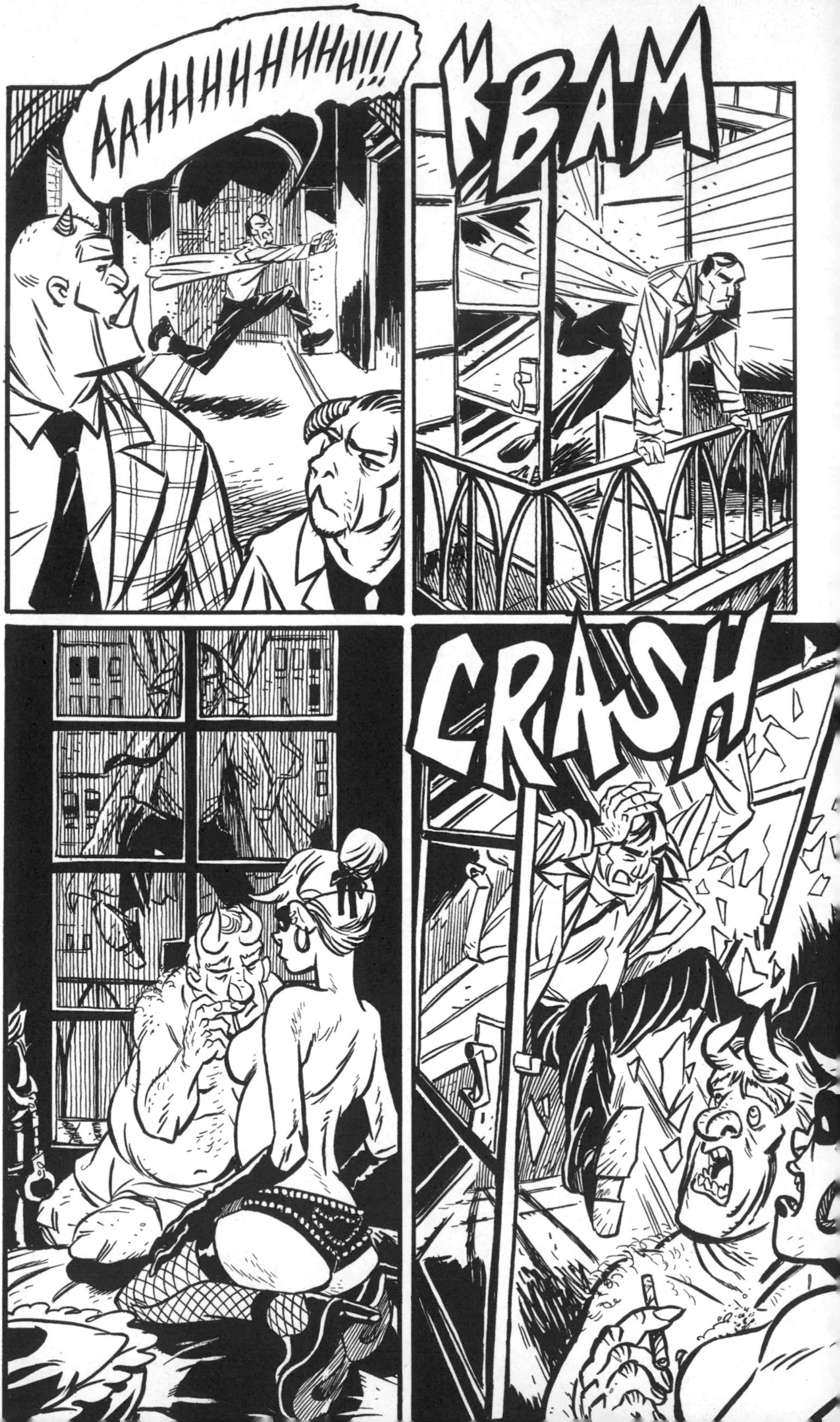
AAHHHHHHHHH!!!
KBAM
CRASH

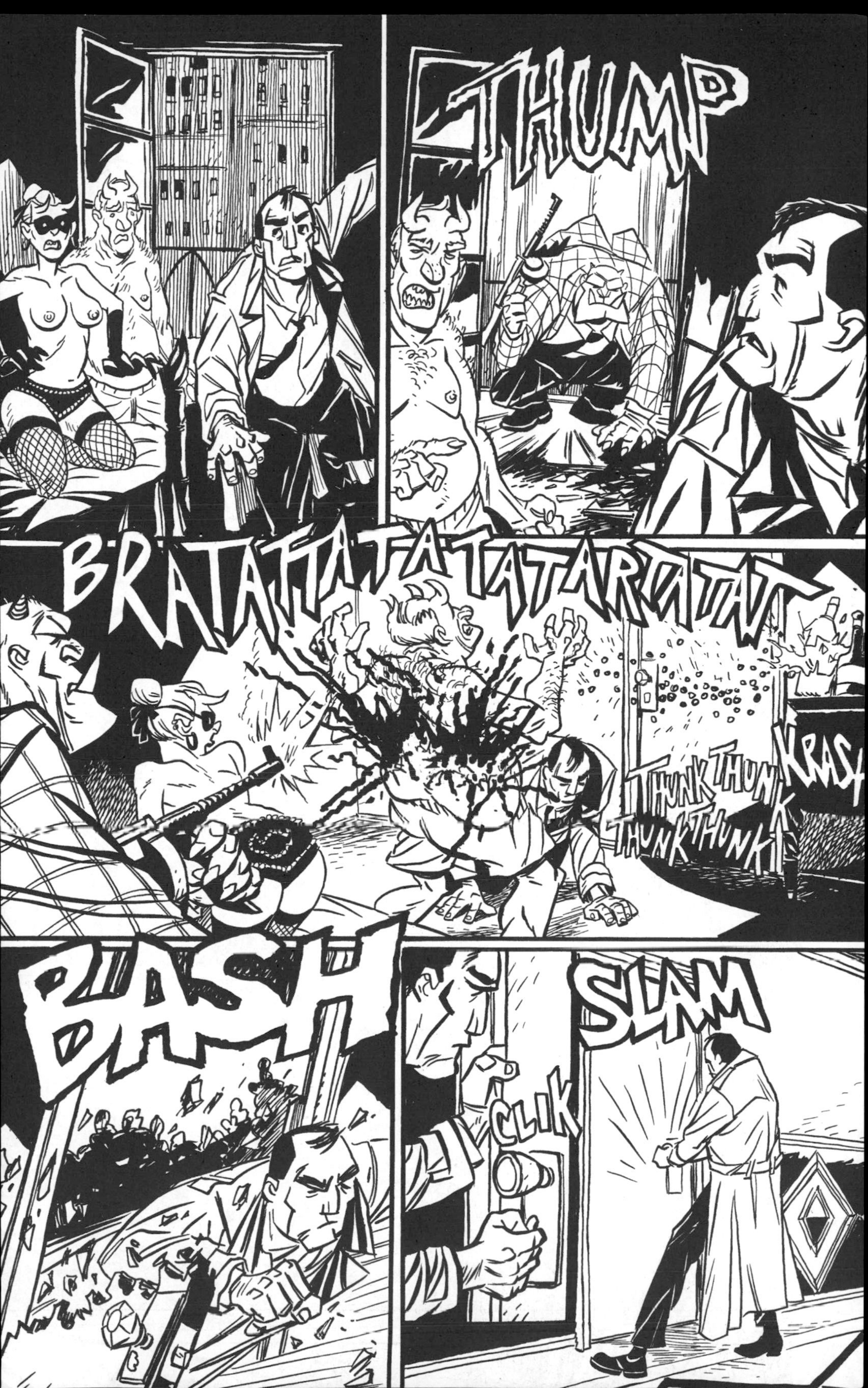
THUMP
BRATATTATATATARTATATT
THUNK THUNK
THUNK THUNK
KRASH
BASH
CLIK
SLAM

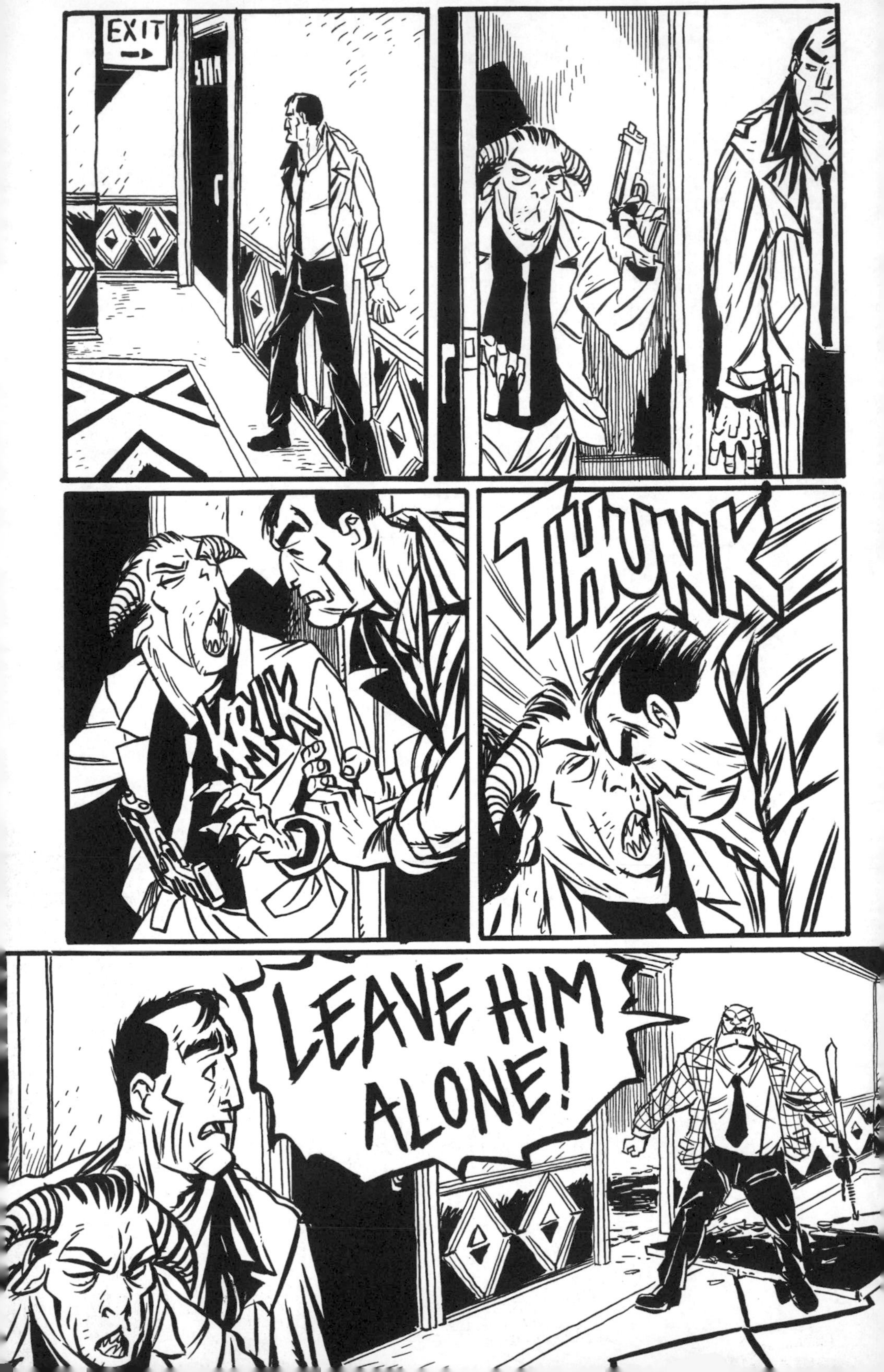
EXIT
THUNK
LEAVE HIM ALONE!

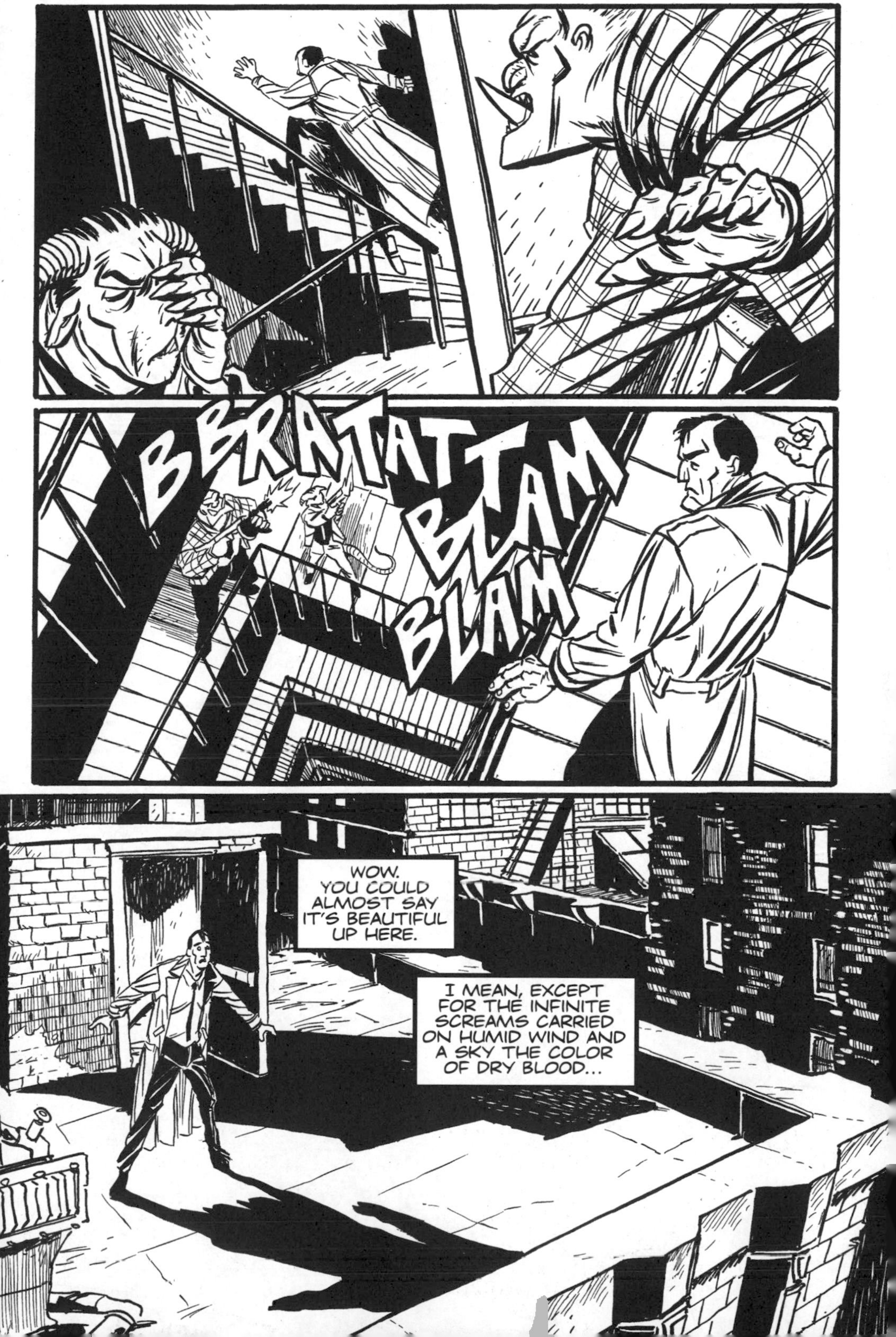
BBRATATTAM
BLAM
BLAM
WOW. YOU COULD ALMOST SAY IT'S BEAUTIFUL UP HERE.
I MEAN, EXCEPT FOR THE INFINITE SCREAMS CARRIED ON HUMID WIND AND A SKY THE COLOR OF DRY BLOOD...

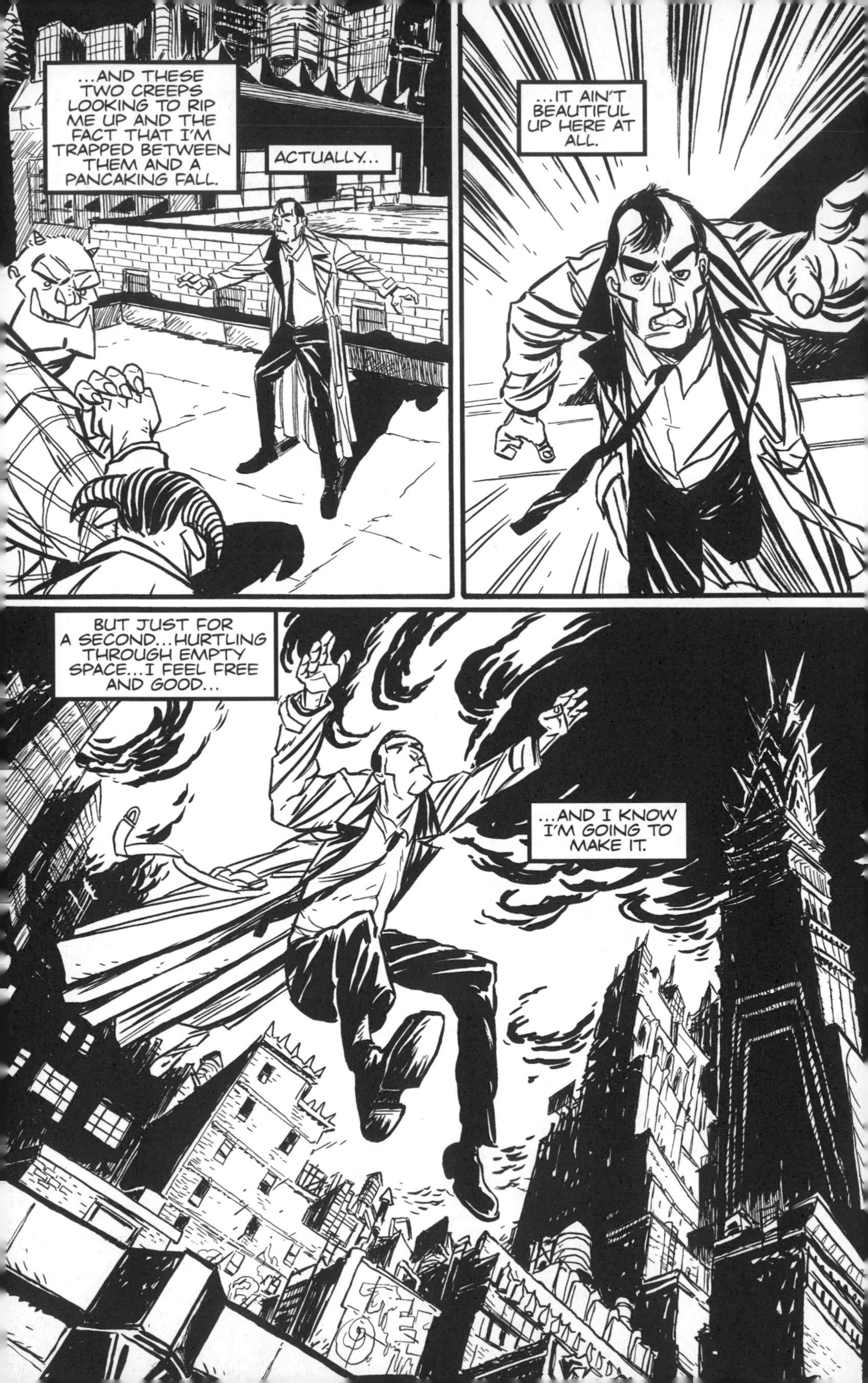
...AND THESE TWO CREEPS LOOKING TO RIP ME UP AND THE FACT THAT I'M TRAPPED BETWEEN THEM AND A PANCAKING FALL.
ACTUALLY...
...IT AIN'T BEAUTIFUL UP HERE AT ALL.
BUT JUST FOR A SECOND...HURTLING THROUGH EMPTY SPACE...I FEEL FREE AND GOOD...
...AND I KNOW I'M GOING TO MAKE IT.

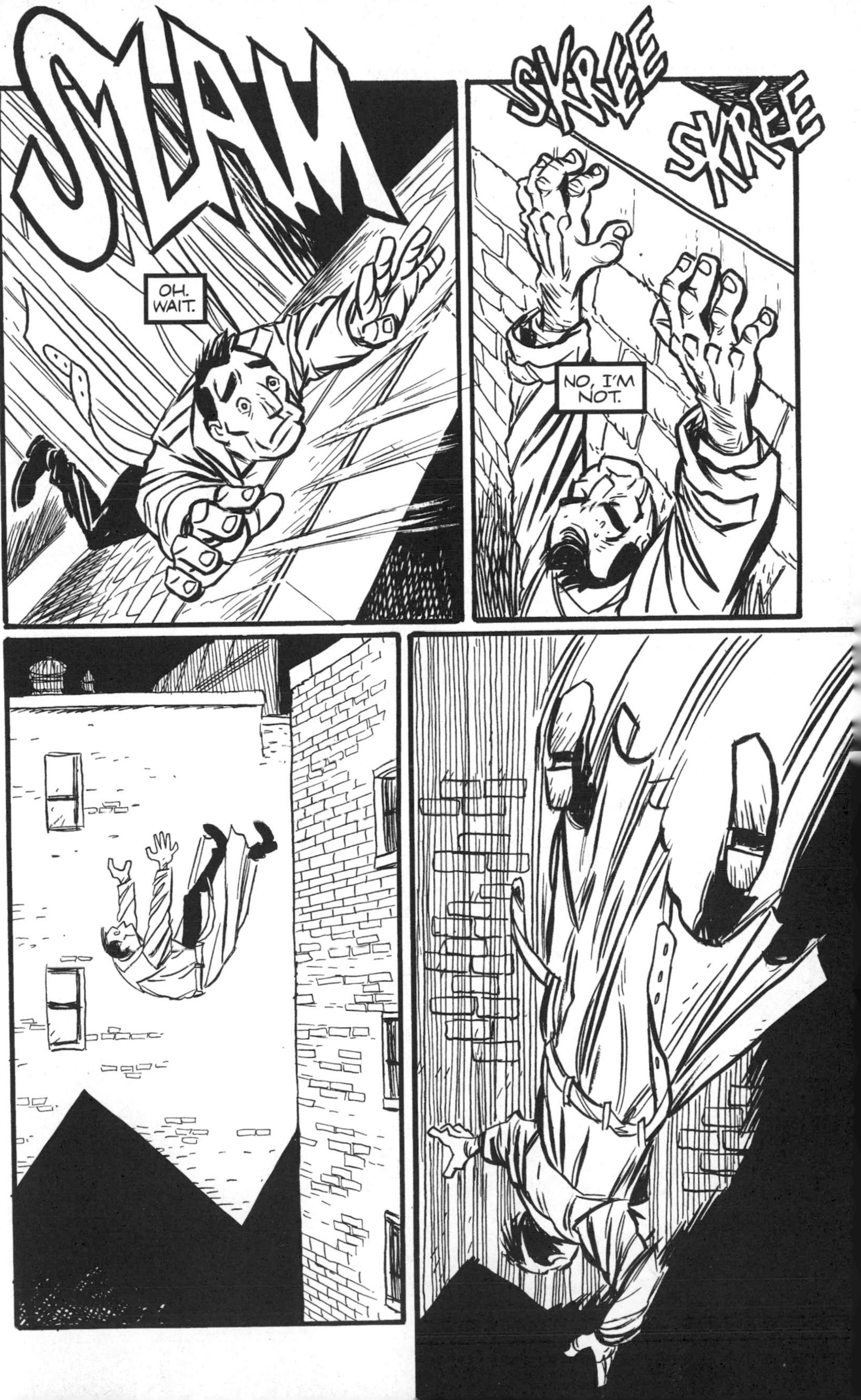
SLAM
OH. WAIT.
SKREE
SKREE
NO, I'M NOT.

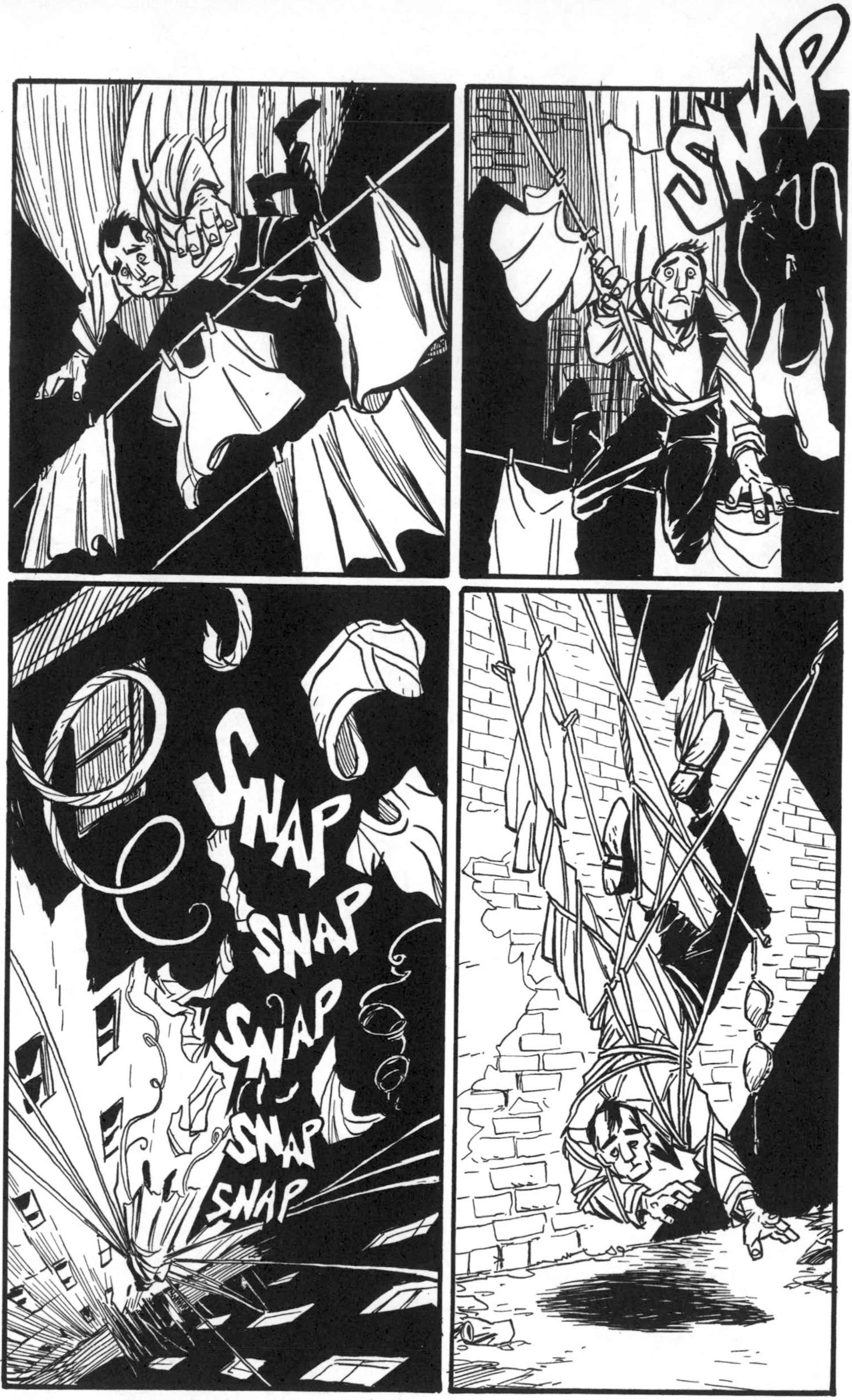
SNAP
SNAP
SNAP
SNAP
SNAP
SNAP

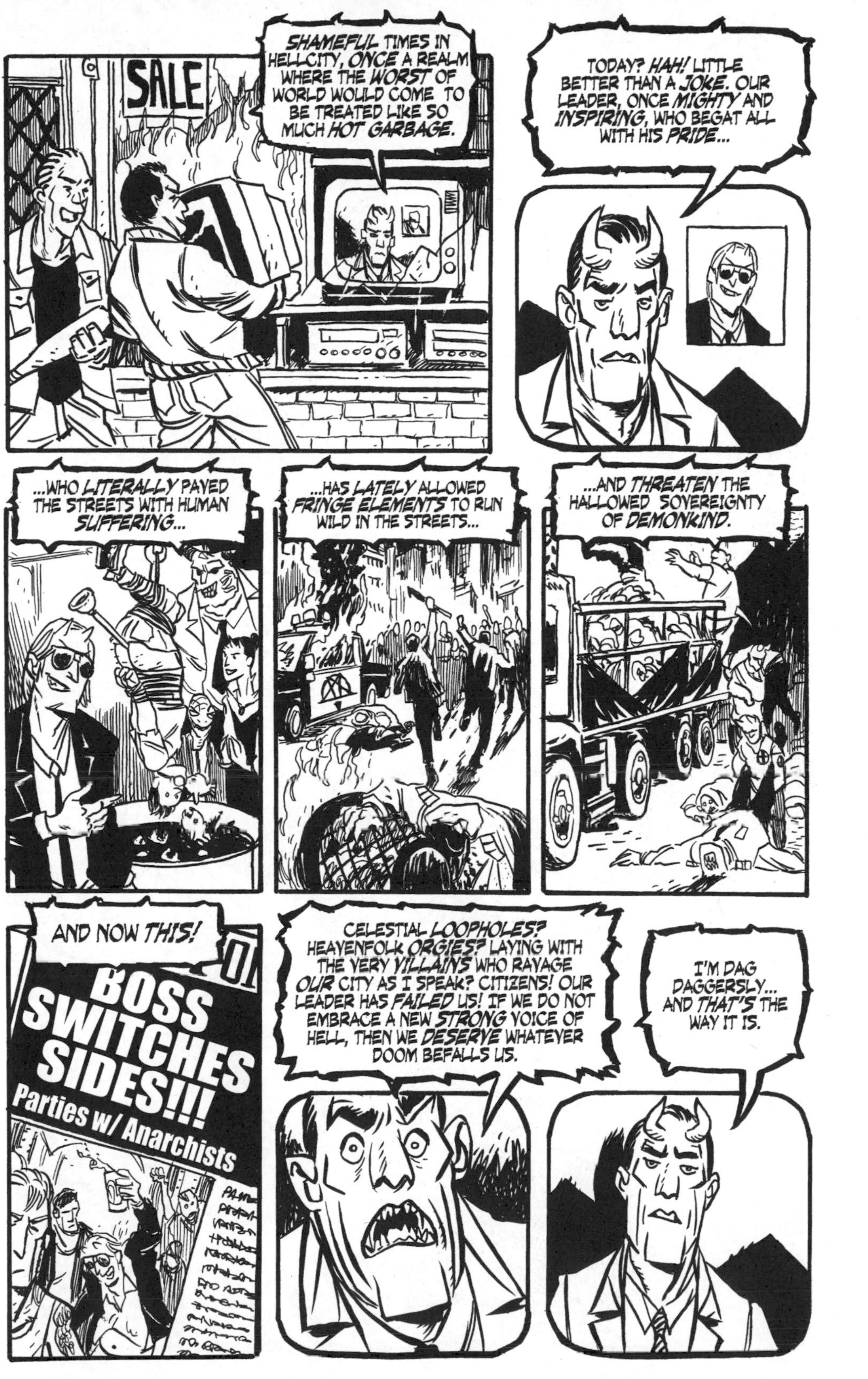
SALE
SHAMEFUL TIMES IN HELLCITY, ONCE A REALM WHERE THE WORST OF WORLD WOULD COME TO BE TREATED LIKE SO MUCH HOT GARBAGE.
TODAY? HAH! LITTLE BETTER THAN A JOKE. OUR LEADER, ONCE MIGHTY AND INSPIRING, WHO BEGAT ALL WITH HIS PRIDE...
...WHO LITERALLY PAVED THE STREETS WITH HUMAN SUFFERING...
...HAS LATELY ALLOWED FRINGE ELEMENTS TO RUN WILD IN THE STREETS...
...AND THREATEN THE HALLOWED SOVEREIGNTY OF DEMONKIND.
AND NOW THIS!
BOSS SWITCHES SIDES!!!
Parties w/ Anarchists
CELESTIAL LOOPHOLES? HEAVENFOLK ORGIES? LAYING WITH THE VERY VILLAINS WHO RAVAGE OUR CITY AS I SPEAK? CITIZENS! OUR LEADER HAS FAILED US! IF WE DO NOT EMBRACE A NEW STRONG VOICE OF HELL, THEN WE DESERVE WHATEVER DOOM BEFALLS US.
I'M DAG DAGGERSLY... AND THAT'S THE WAY IT IS.

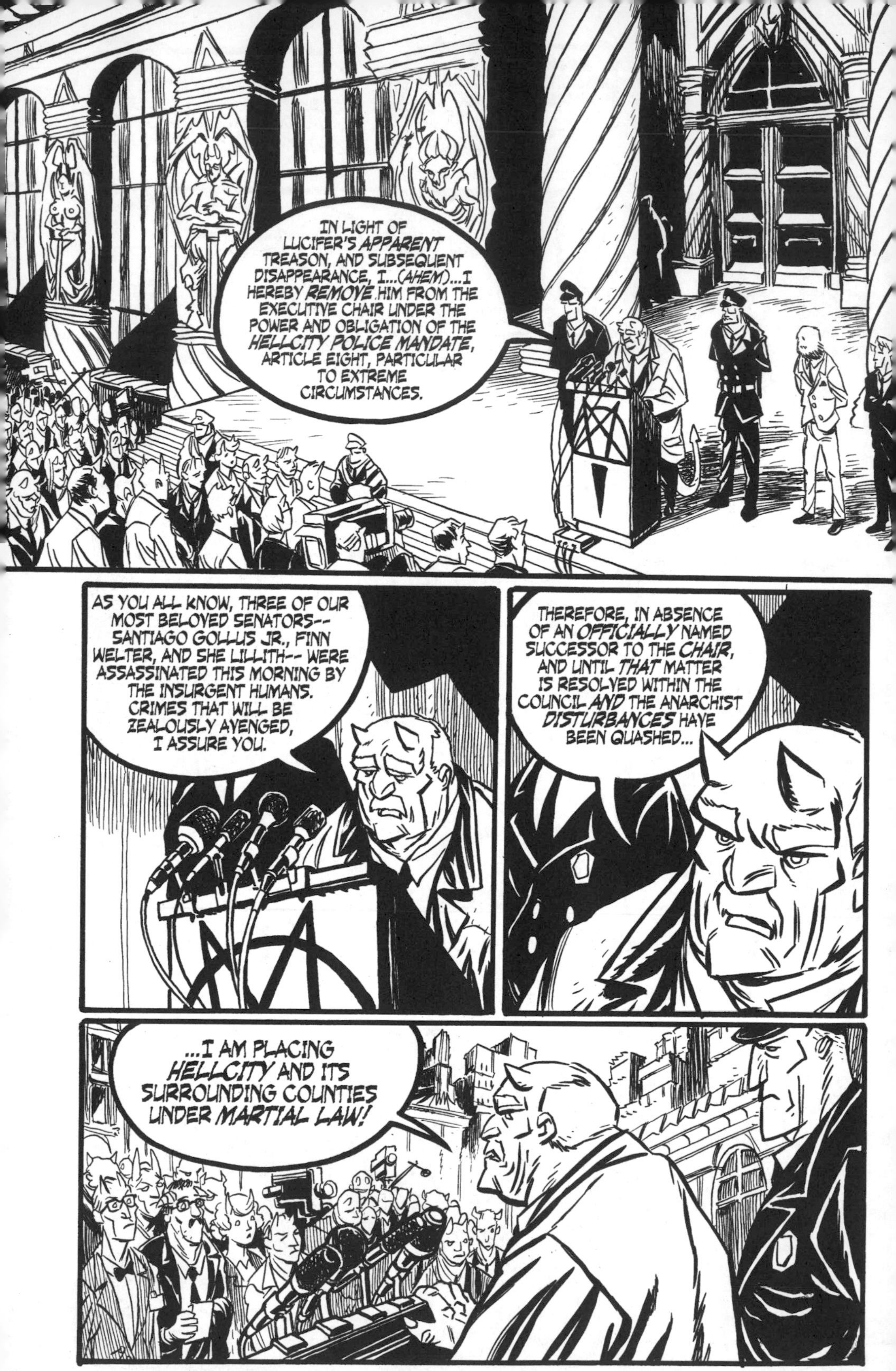
IN LIGHT OF LUCIFER'S APPARENT TREASON, AND SUBSEQUENT DISAPPEARANCE, I...(AHEM)...I HEREBY REMOVE HIM FROM THE EXECUTIVE CHAIR UNDER THE POWER AND OBLIGATION OF THE HELLCITY POLICE MANDATE, ARTICLE EIGHT, PARTICULAR TO EXTREME CIRCUMSTANCES.
AS YOU ALL KNOW, THREE OF OUR MOST BELOVED SENATORS--SANTIAGO GOLLUS JR., FINN WELTER, AND SHE LILLITH-- WERE ASSASSINATED THIS MORNING BY THE INSURGENT HUMANS. CRIMES THAT WILL BE ZEALOUSLY AVENGED, I ASSURE YOU.
THEREFORE, IN ABSENCE OF AN OFFICIALLY NAMED SUCCESSOR TO THE CHAIR, AND UNTIL THAT MATTER IS RESOLVED WITHIN THE COUNCIL AND THE ANARCHIST DISTURBANCES HAVE BEEN QUASHED...
...I AM PLACING HELLCITY AND ITS SURROUNDING COUNTIES UNDER MARTIAL LAW!

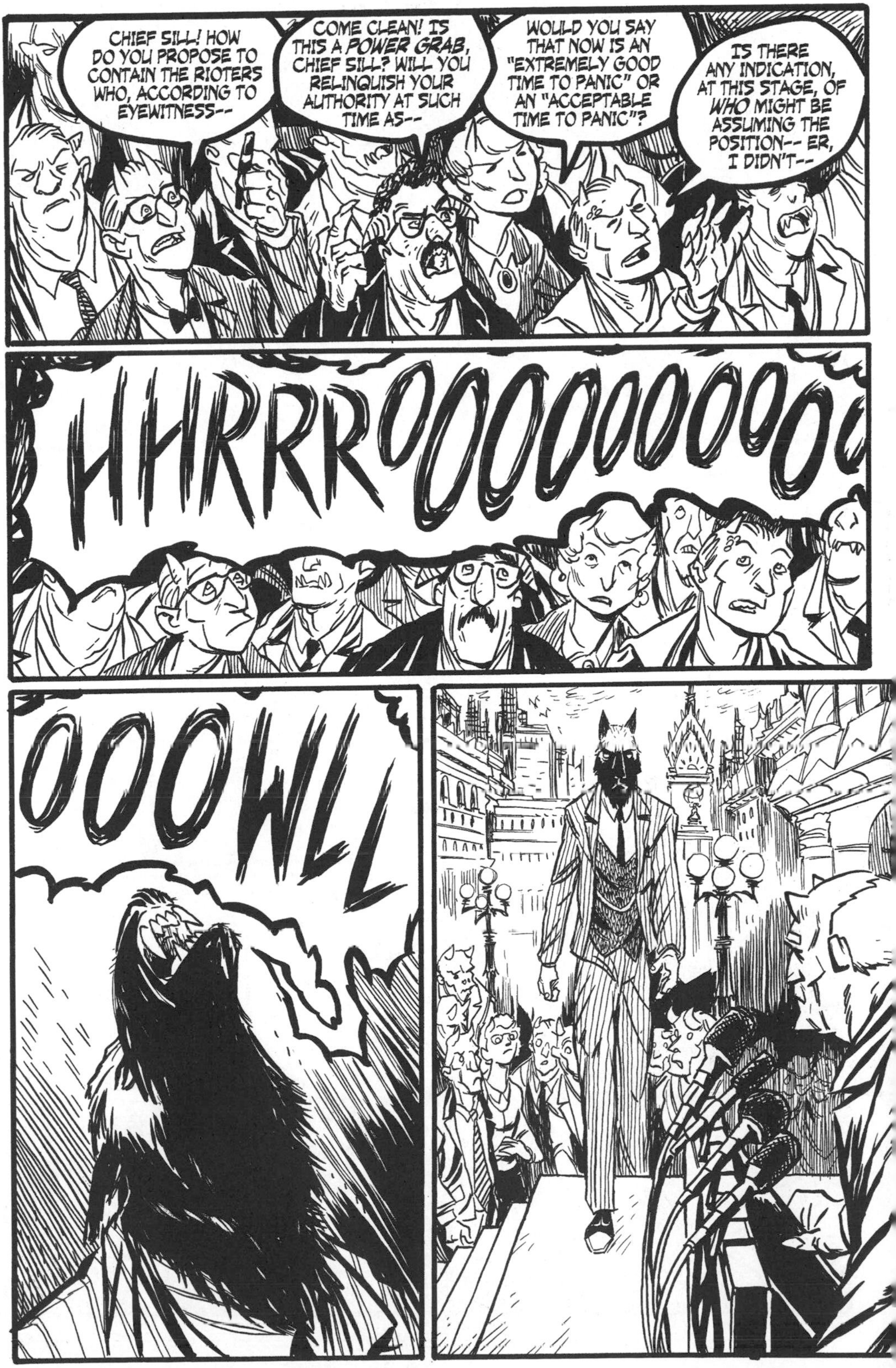
CHIEF SILL! HOW DO YOU PROPOSE TO CONTAIN THE RIOTERS WHO, ACCORDING TO EYEWITNESS--
COME CLEAN! IS THIS A *POWER GRAB*, CHIEF SILL? WILL YOU RELINQUISH YOUR AUTHORITY AT SUCH TIME AS--
WOULD YOU SAY THAT NOW IS AN "EXTREMELY GOOD TIME TO PANIC" OR AN "ACCEPTABLE TIME TO PANIC"?
IS THERE ANY INDICATION, AT THIS STAGE, OF *WHO* MIGHT BE ASSUMING THE POSITION-- ER, I DIDN'T--
HHRRROOOOOOOOOO
OOOWLL

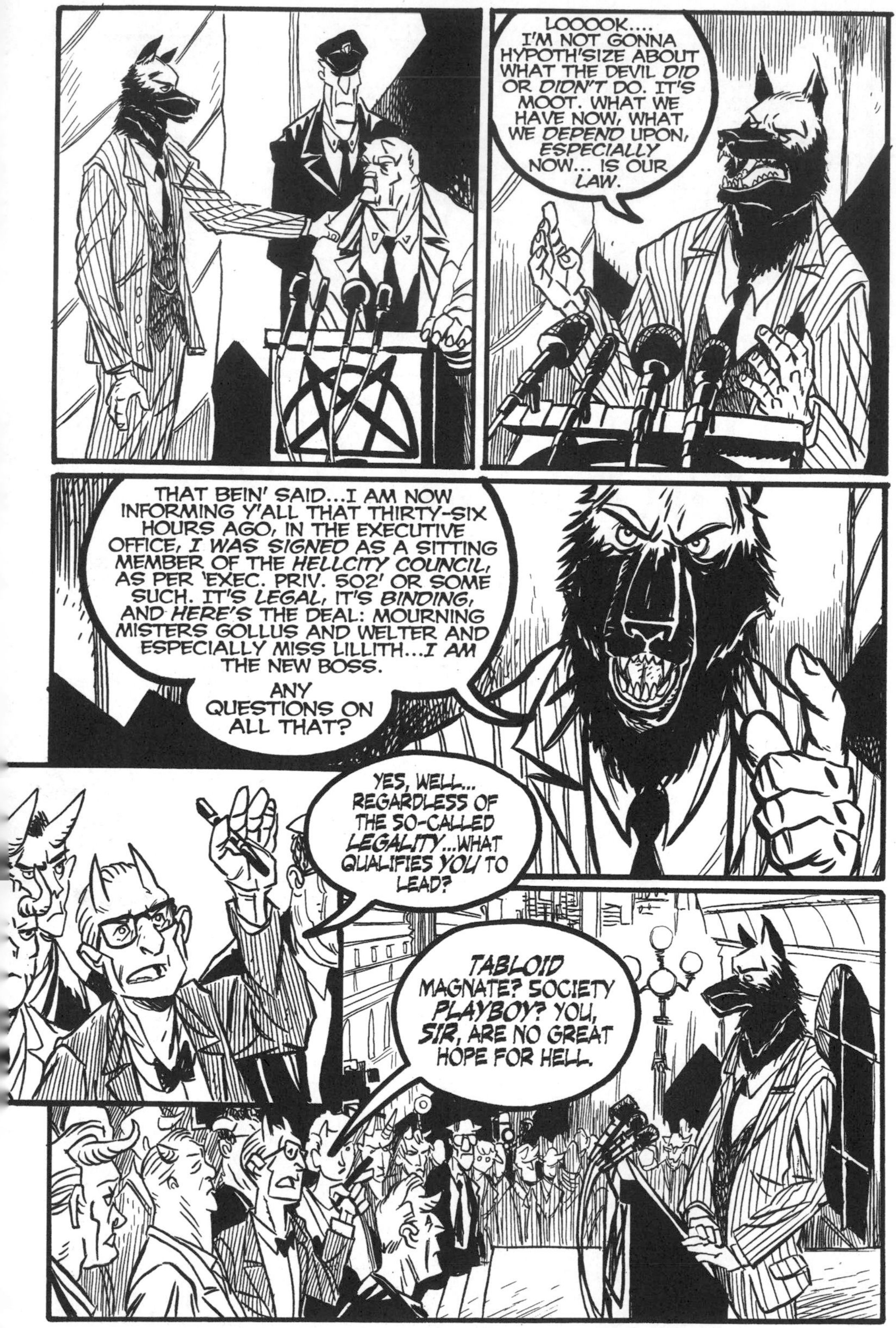
LOOOOK.... I'M NOT GONNA HYPOTH'SIZE ABOUT WHAT THE DEVIL DID OR DIDN'T DO. IT'S MOOT. WHAT WE HAVE NOW, WHAT WE DEPEND UPON, ESPECIALLY NOW... IS OUR LAW.
THAT BEIN' SAID...I AM NOW INFORMING Y'ALL THAT THIRTY-SIX HOURS AGO, IN THE EXECUTIVE OFFICE, I WAS SIGNED AS A SITTING MEMBER OF THE HELLCITY COUNCIL, AS PER 'EXEC. PRIV. 502' OR SOME SUCH. IT'S LEGAL, IT'S BINDING, AND HERE'S THE DEAL: MOURNING MISTERS GOLLUS AND WELTER AND ESPECIALLY MISS LILLITH...I AM THE NEW BOSS.
ANY QUESTIONS ON ALL THAT?
YES, WELL... REGARDLESS OF THE SO-CALLED LEGALITY...WHAT QUALIFIES YOU TO LEAD?
TABLOID MAGNATE? SOCIETY PLAYBOY? YOU, SIR, ARE NO GREAT HOPE FOR HELL.

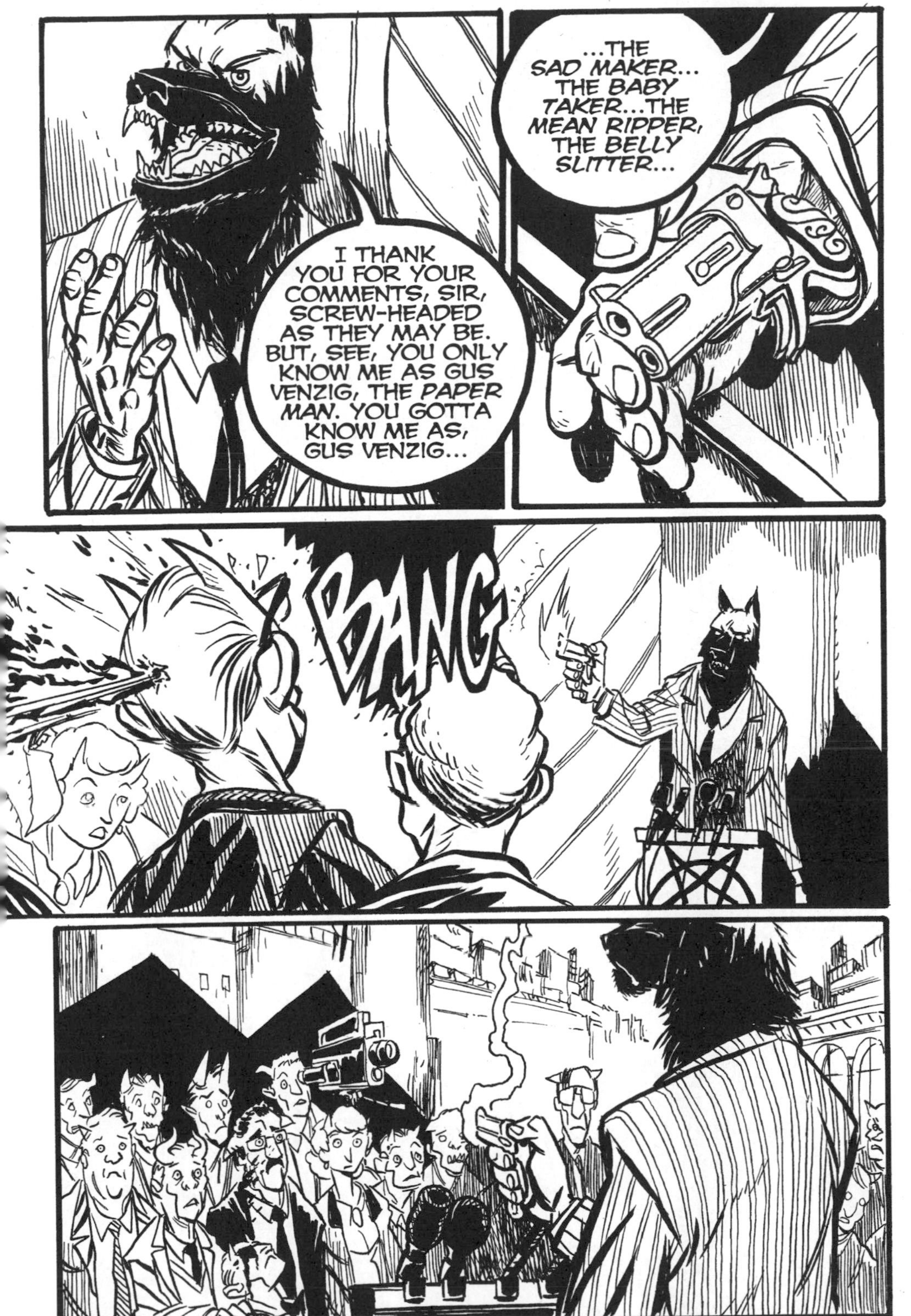
I THANK YOU FOR YOUR COMMENTS, SIR, SCREW-HEADED AS THEY MAY BE. BUT, SEE, YOU ONLY KNOW ME AS GUS VENZIG, THE *PAPER MAN*. YOU GOTTA KNOW ME AS, GUS VENZIG...
...THE *SAD MAKER*... THE *BABY TAKER*...THE *MEAN RIPPER*, THE *BELLY SLITTER*...
BANG

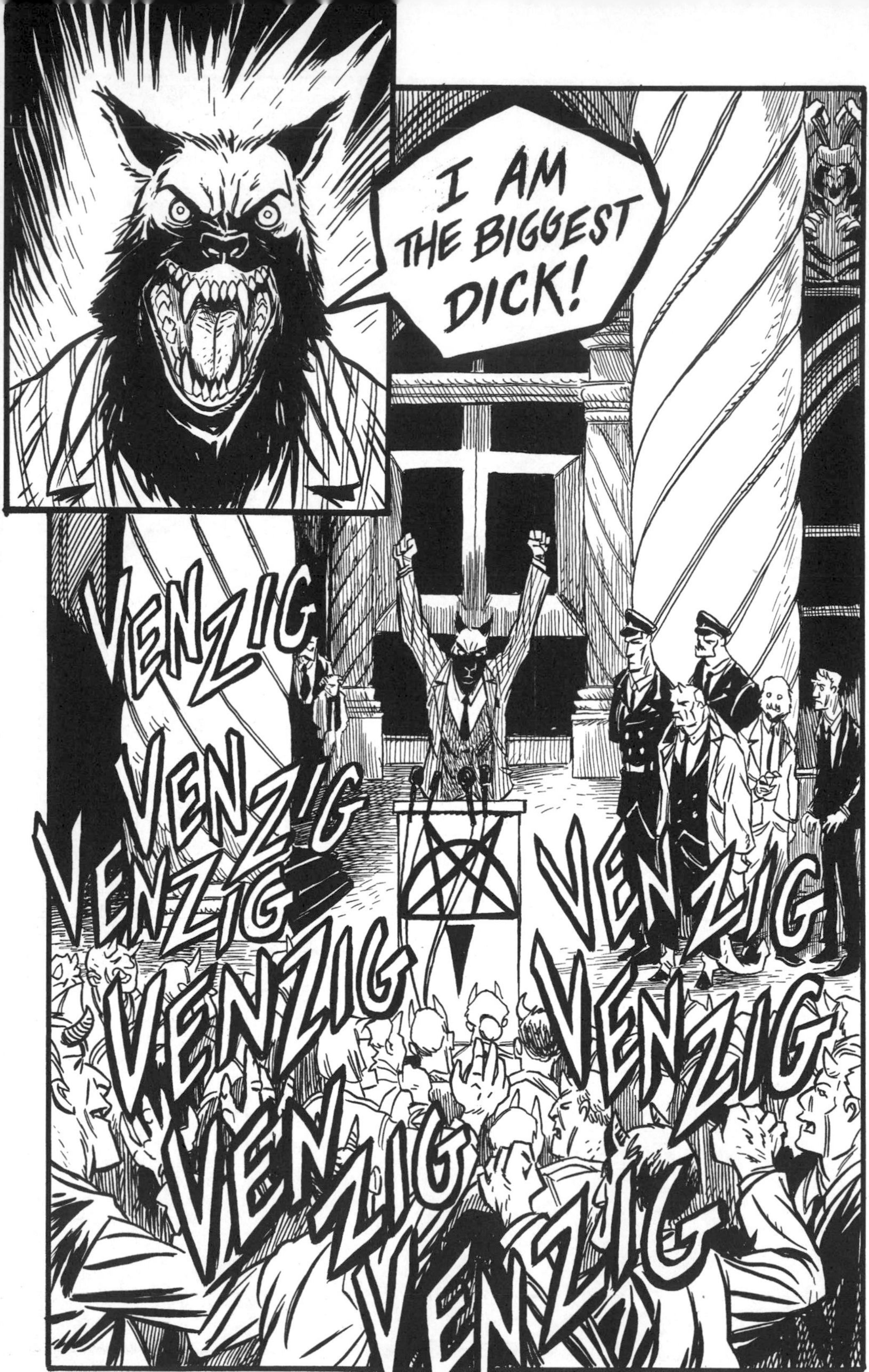
I AM THE BIGGEST DICK!
VENZIG
VENZIG
VENZIG
VENZIG
VENZIG
VENZIG
VENZIG
VENZIG

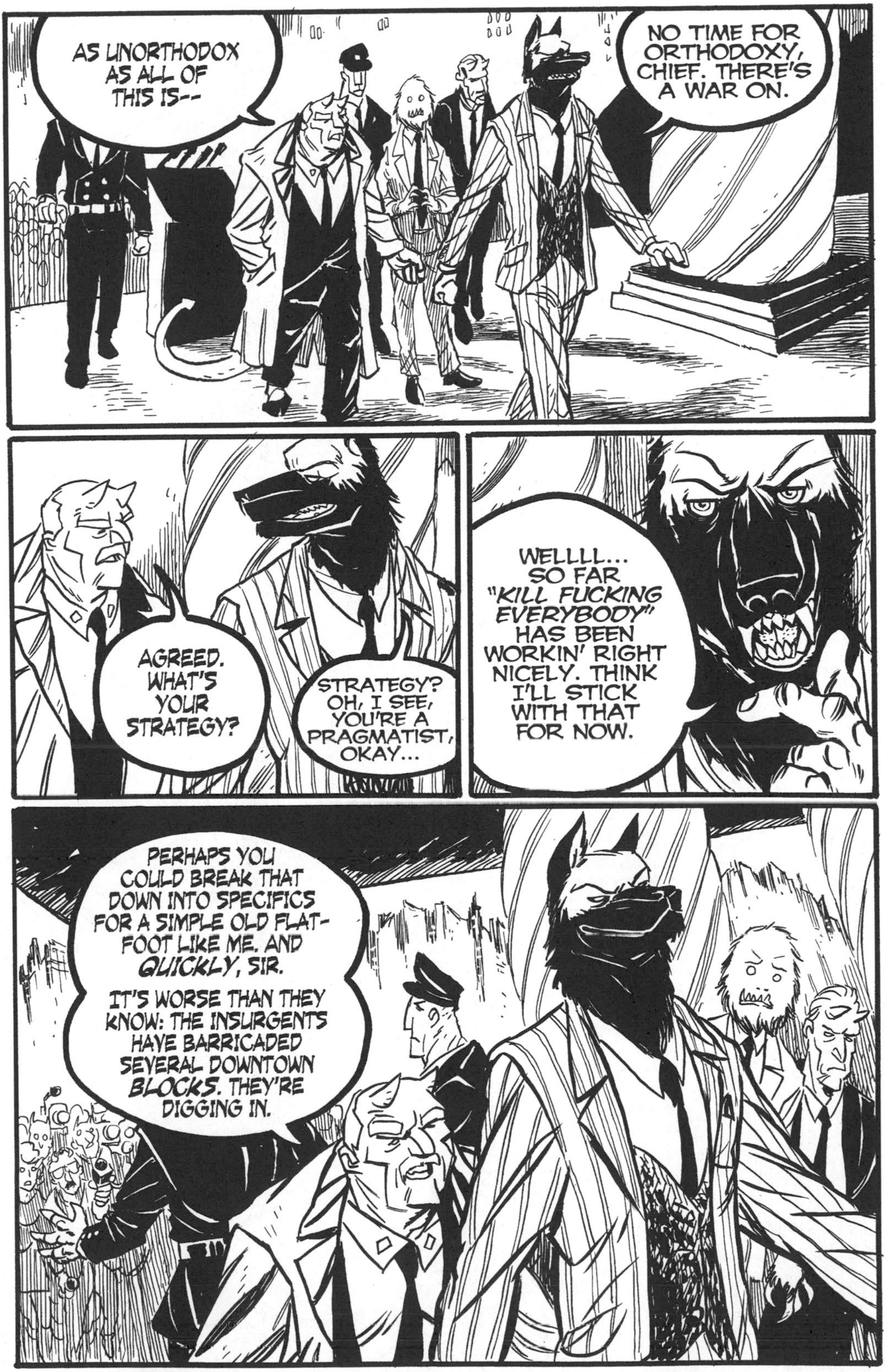
AS UNORTHODOX AS ALL OF THIS IS--
NO TIME FOR ORTHODOXY, CHIEF. THERE'S A WAR ON.
AGREED. WHAT'S YOUR STRATEGY?
STRATEGY? OH, I SEE, YOU'RE A PRAGMATIST, OKAY...
WELLLL... SO FAR "KILL FUCKING EVERYBODY" HAS BEEN WORKIN' RIGHT NICELY. THINK I'LL STICK WITH THAT FOR NOW.
PERHAPS YOU COULD BREAK THAT DOWN INTO SPECIFICS FOR A SIMPLE OLD FLAT-FOOT LIKE ME. AND QUICKLY, SIR.
IT'S WORSE THAN THEY KNOW: THE INSURGENTS HAVE BARRICADED SEVERAL DOWNTOWN BLOCKS. THEY'RE DIGGING IN.

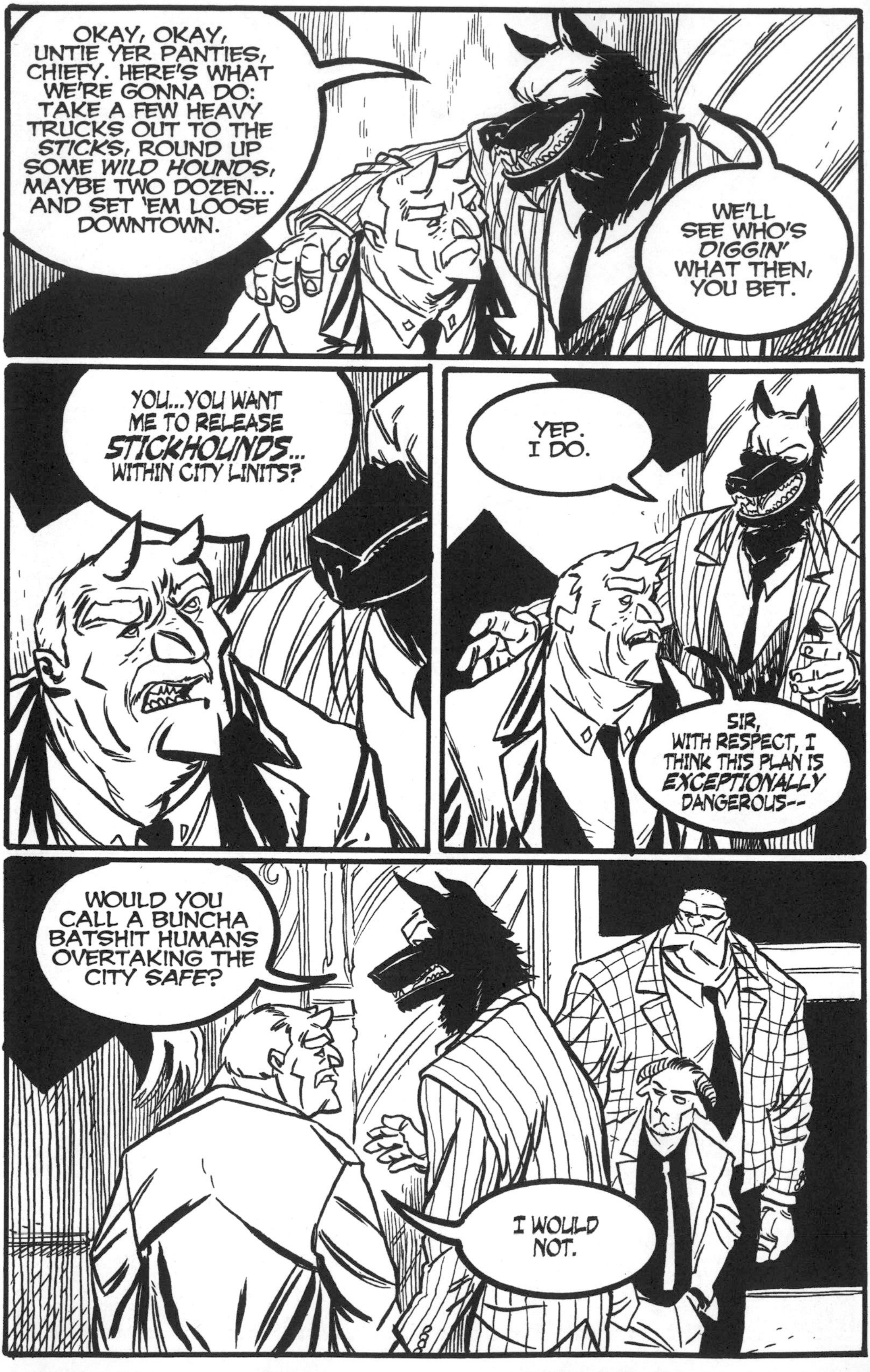
OKAY, OKAY, UNTIE YER PANTIES, CHIEFY. HERE'S WHAT WE'RE GONNA DO: TAKE A FEW HEAVY TRUCKS OUT TO THE STICKS, ROUND UP SOME WILD HOUNDS, MAYBE TWO DOZEN... AND SET 'EM LOOSE DOWNTOWN.
WE'LL SEE WHO'S DIGGIN' WHAT THEN, YOU BET.
YOU...YOU WANT ME TO RELEASE STICKHOUNDS... WITHIN CITY LIMITS?
YEP. I DO.
SIR, WITH RESPECT, I THINK THIS PLAN IS EXCEPTIONALLY DANGEROUS--
WOULD YOU CALL A BUNCHA BATSHIT HUMANS OVERTAKING THE CITY SAFE?
I WOULD NOT.

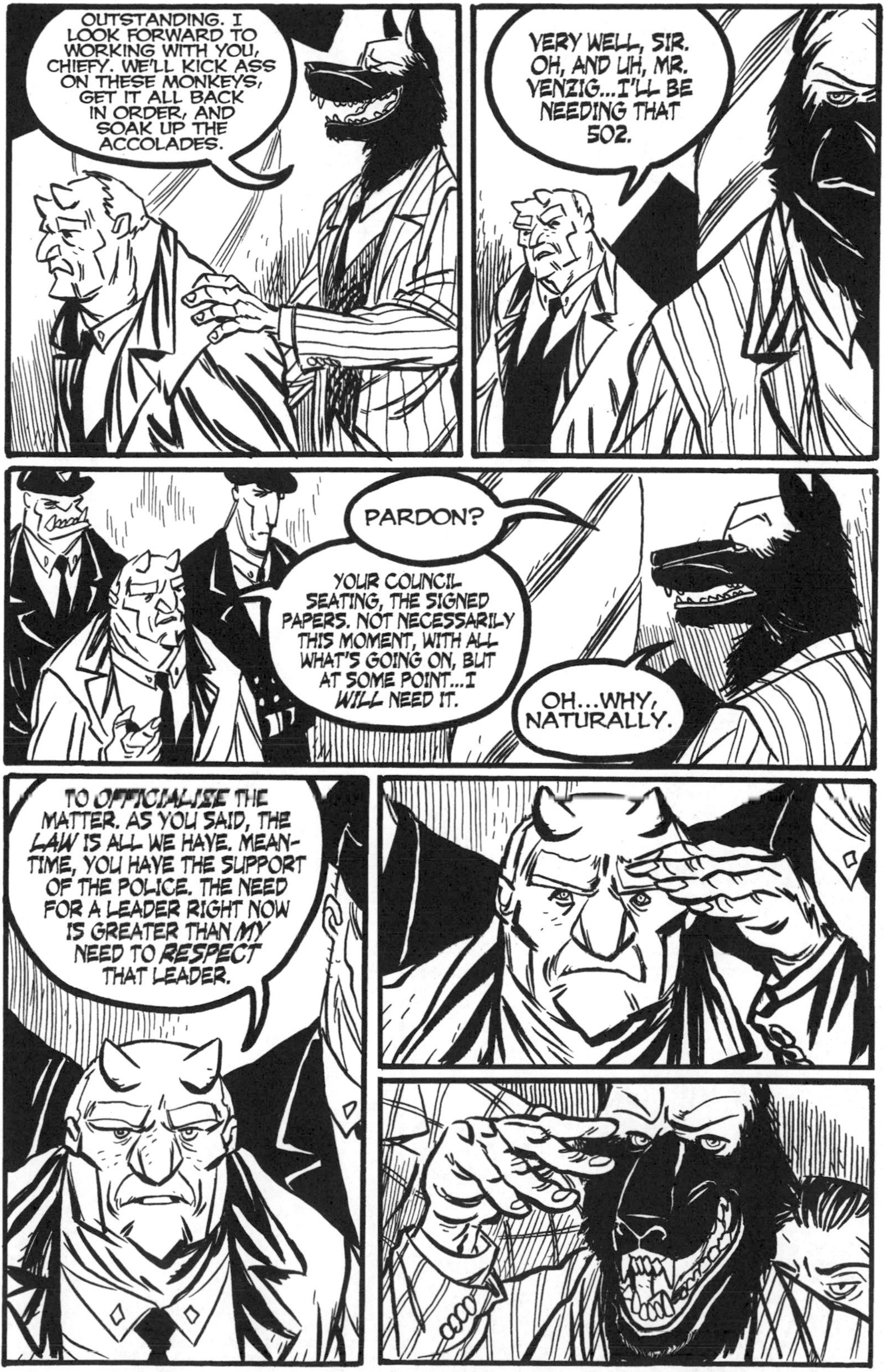
OUTSTANDING. I LOOK FORWARD TO WORKING WITH YOU, CHIEFY. WE'LL KICK ASS ON THESE MONKEYS, GET IT ALL BACK IN ORDER, AND SOAK UP THE ACCOLADES.
VERY WELL, SIR. OH, AND UH, MR. VENZIG...I'LL BE NEEDING THAT 502.
PARDON?
YOUR COUNCIL SEATING, THE SIGNED PAPERS. NOT NECESSARILY THIS MOMENT, WITH ALL WHAT'S GOING ON, BUT AT SOME POINT...I WILL NEED IT.
OH...WHY, NATURALLY.
TO OFFICIALISE THE MATTER. AS YOU SAID, THE LAW IS ALL WE HAVE. MEANTIME, YOU HAVE THE SUPPORT OF THE POLICE. THE NEED FOR A LEADER RIGHT NOW IS GREATER THAN MY NEED TO RESPECT THAT LEADER.

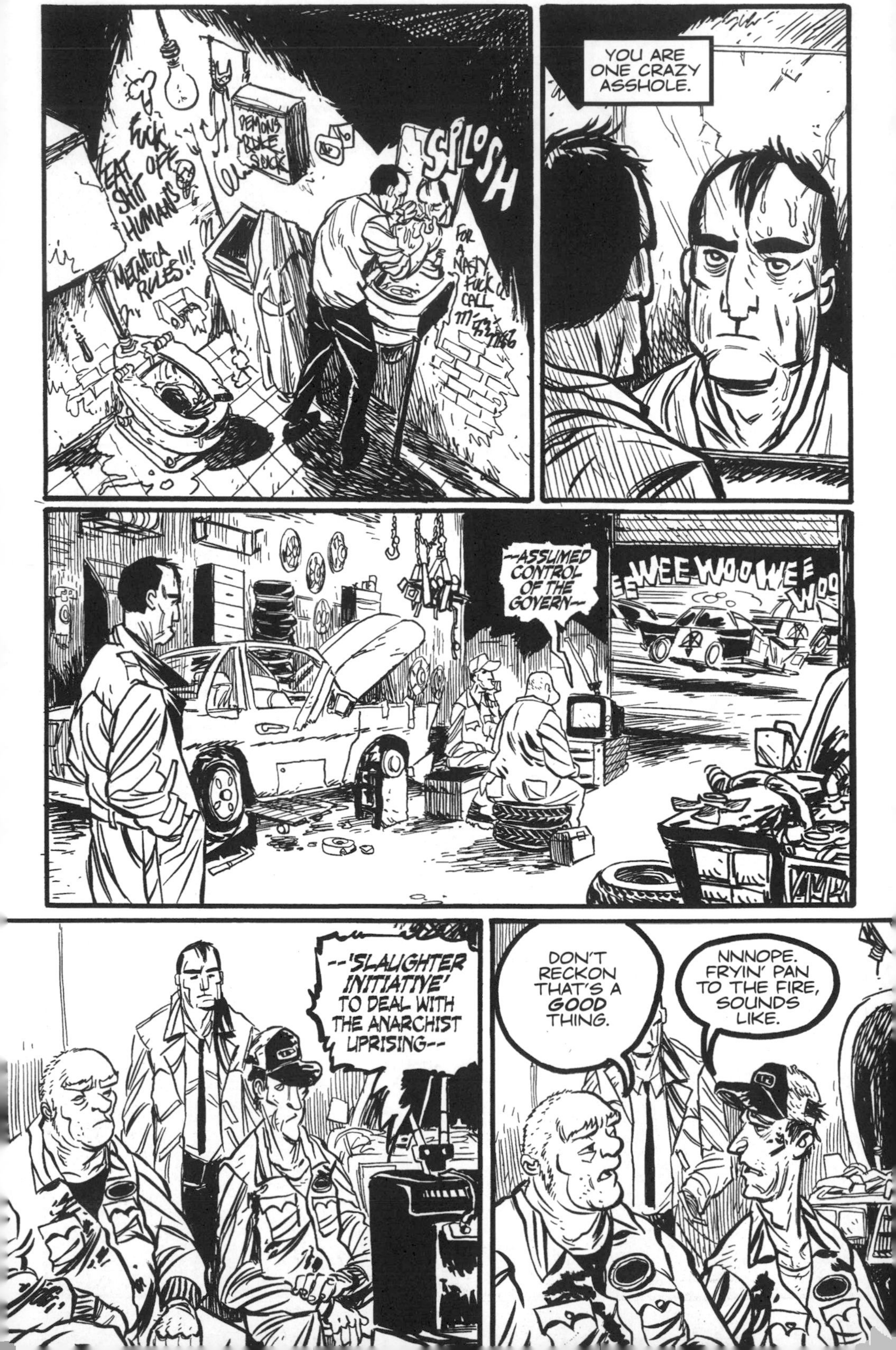
FUCK
EAT SHIT OFF HUMANS
METALLICA RULES!!!
SPLOSH
FOR A NASTY FUCK CALL
YOU ARE ONE CRAZY ASSHOLE.
--ASSUMED CONTROL OF THE GOVERN--
WEE WOO WEE WOO
--'SLAUGHTER INITIATIVE' TO DEAL WITH THE ANARCHIST UPRISING--
DON'T RECKON THAT'S A *GOOD* THING.
NNNOPE. FRYIN' PAN TO THE FIRE, SOUNDS LIKE.

THERE A PHONE I COULD USE, FELLAS?

SOMETHING THE TELEVISION SAID RINGS A BELL: "OBSCURE CONSTITUTIONAL CLAUSE."

THAT'S MY LEVERAGE POINT NOW THAT THE DEVIL'S NO GOOD FOR A SQUEEZE.

BRIIING BRIINNG BRIING BRIINNG

CRAZY I MAY BE...

...BUT STUPID I AM NOT.

EH-EXECUTIVE?

YES, THIS IS POLICY DIRECTOR JOHNSON, CUSTOMER RELATIONS FROM SWOFFORD SECURITY CORP. I'M DOING A VERY ROUTINE CHECK WITH OUR TOP TIER CLIENTS AND THEIR SECURABLES. CAN YOU WORK WITH ME ON THIS ONE, SON?

OH, I UH... OKAY?

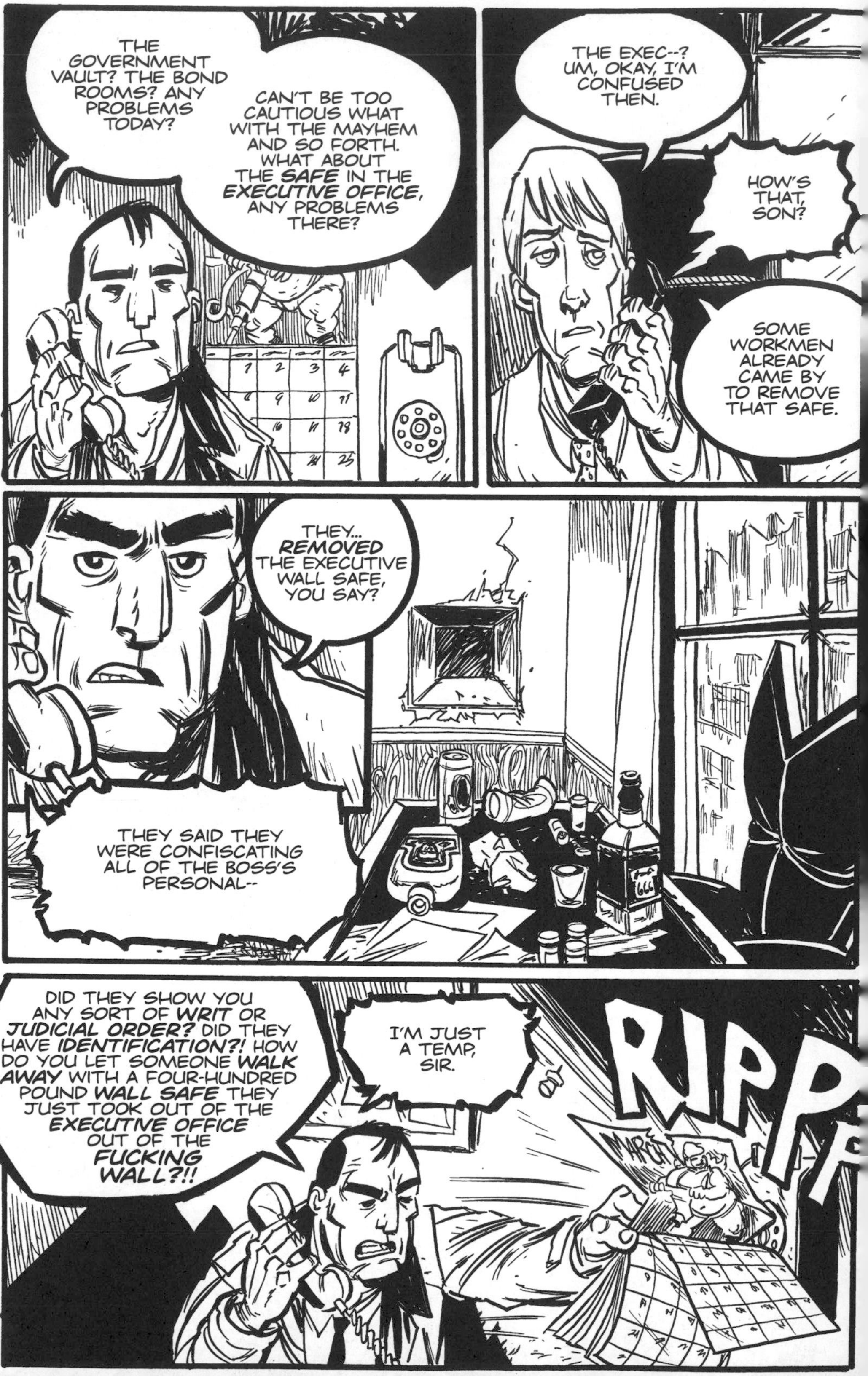
THE GOVERNMENT VAULT? THE BOND ROOMS? ANY PROBLEMS TODAY?
CAN'T BE TOO CAUTIOUS WHAT WITH THE MAYHEM AND SO FORTH. WHAT ABOUT THE SAFE IN THE EXECUTIVE OFFICE, ANY PROBLEMS THERE?
THE EXEC--? UM, OKAY, I'M CONFUSED THEN.
HOW'S THAT, SON?
SOME WORKMEN ALREADY CAME BY TO REMOVE THAT SAFE.
THEY... REMOVED THE EXECUTIVE WALL SAFE, YOU SAY?
THEY SAID THEY WERE CONFISCATING ALL OF THE BOSS'S PERSONAL--
DID THEY SHOW YOU ANY SORT OF WRIT OR JUDICIAL ORDER? DID THEY HAVE IDENTIFICATION?! HOW DO YOU LET SOMEONE WALK AWAY WITH A FOUR-HUNDRED POUND WALL SAFE THEY JUST TOOK OUT OF THE EXECUTIVE OFFICE OUT OF THE FUCKING WALL?!!
I'M JUST A TEMP, SIR.
RIPPP

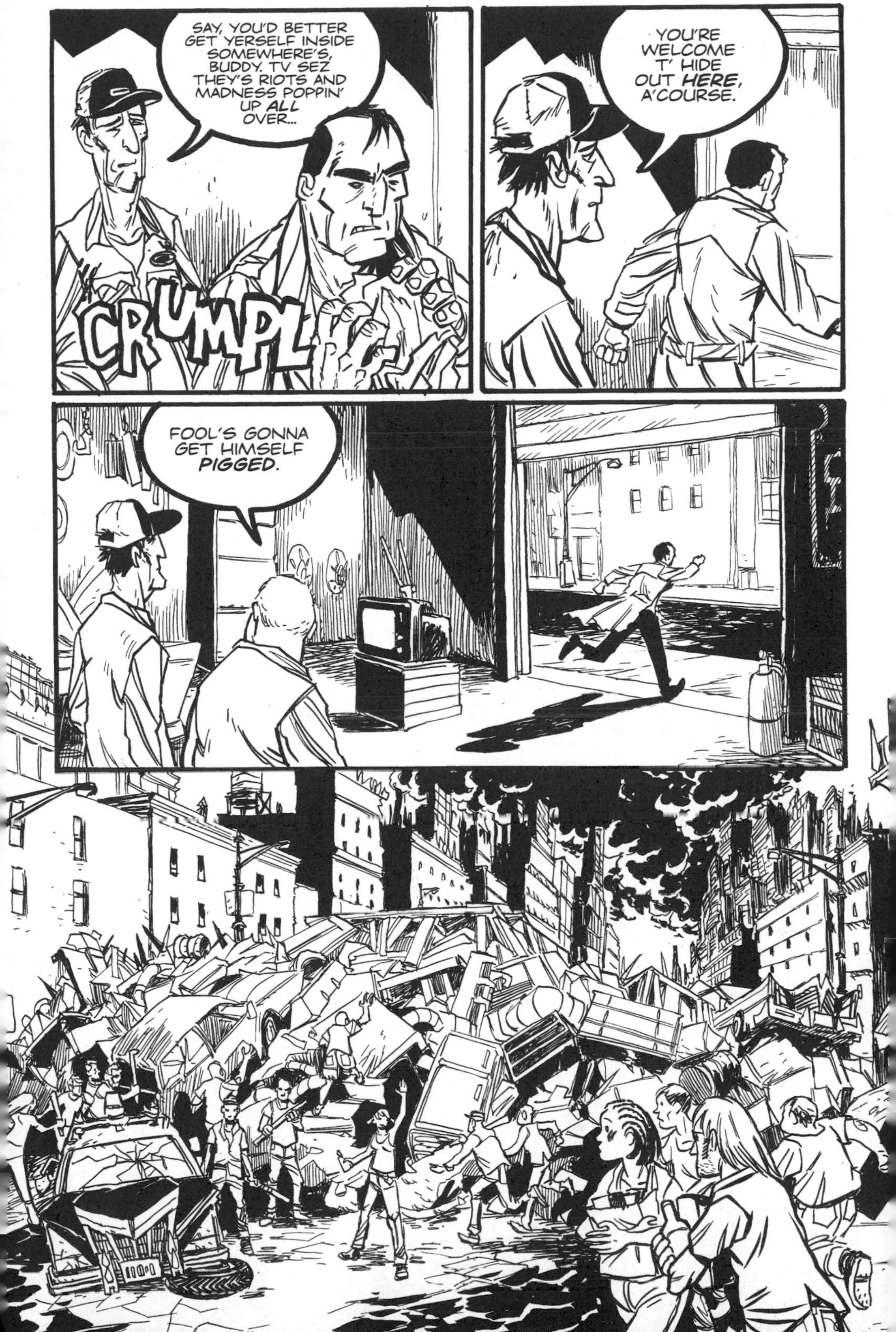
SAY, YOU'D BETTER GET YERSELF INSIDE SOMEWHERE'S, BUDDY. TV SEZ THEY'S RIOTS AND MADNESS POPPIN' UP ALL OVER...
CRUMPL
YOU'RE WELCOME T' HIDE OUT HERE, A'COURSE.
FOOL'S GONNA GET HIMSELF PIGGED.

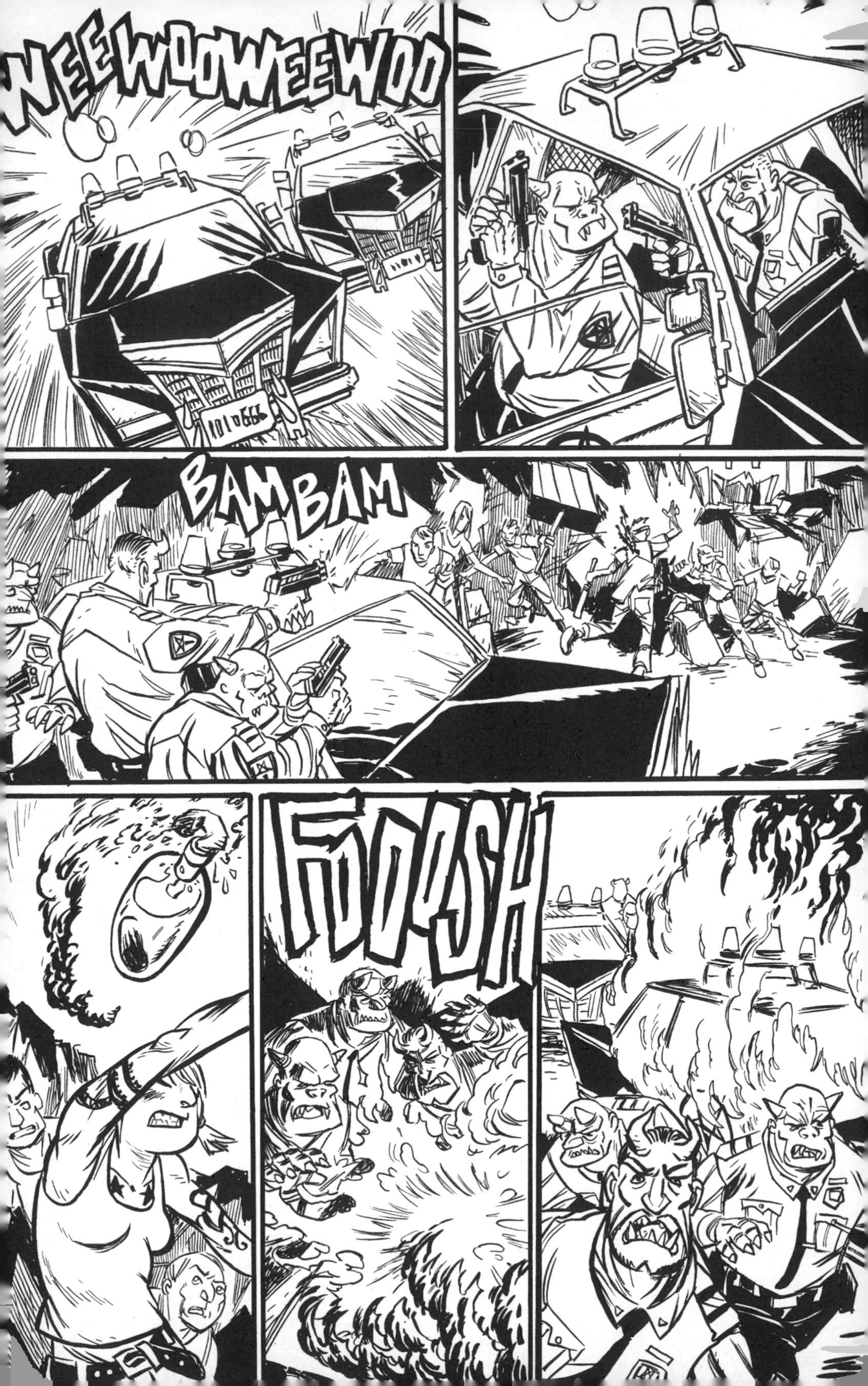
WEEWOOWEEWOO
BAMBAM
FOOOSH

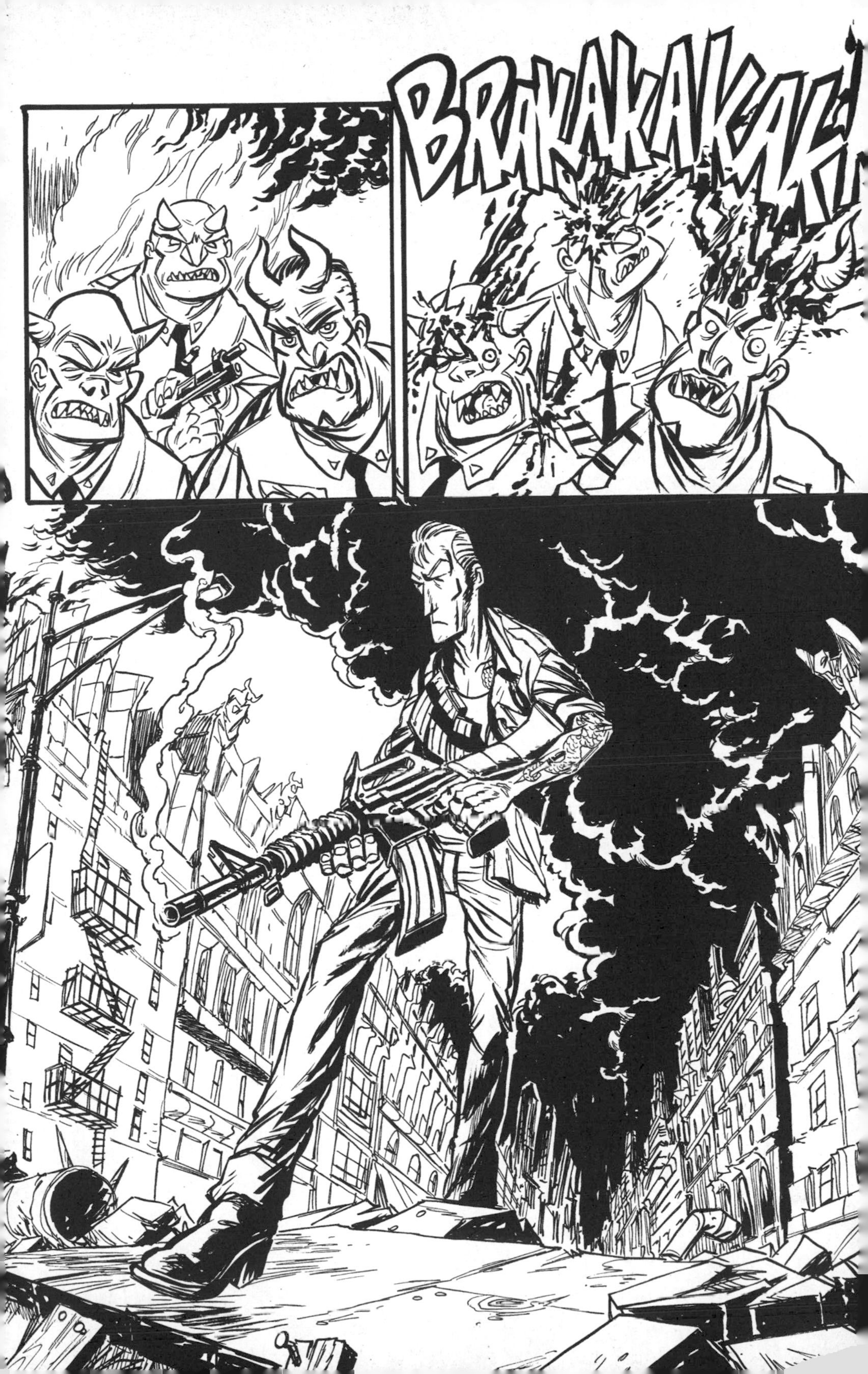
BRAKAKAKAK!

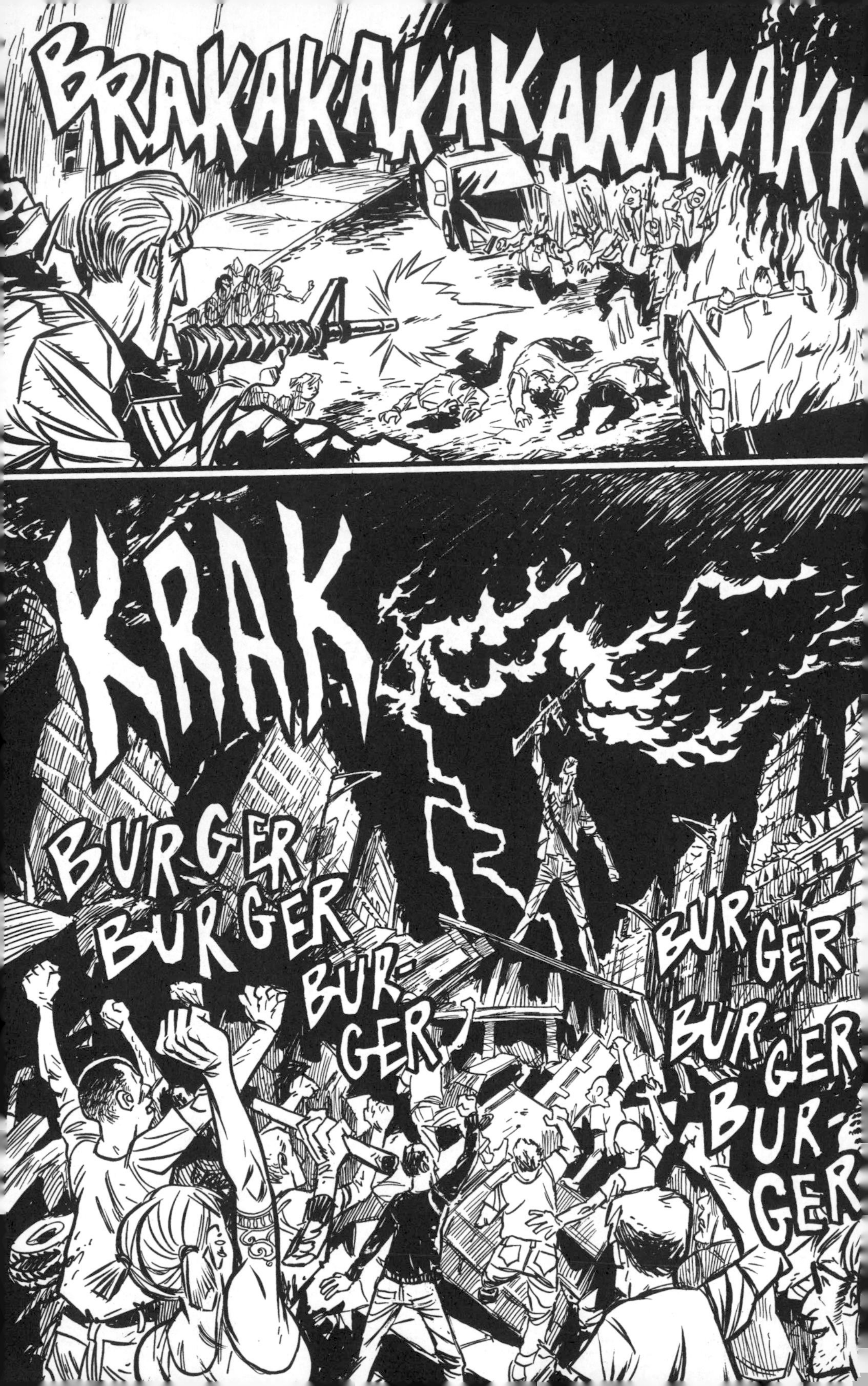
BRAKAKAKAKAKAKAKK
KRAK
BURGER BURGER BURGER
BURGER BURGER BURGER

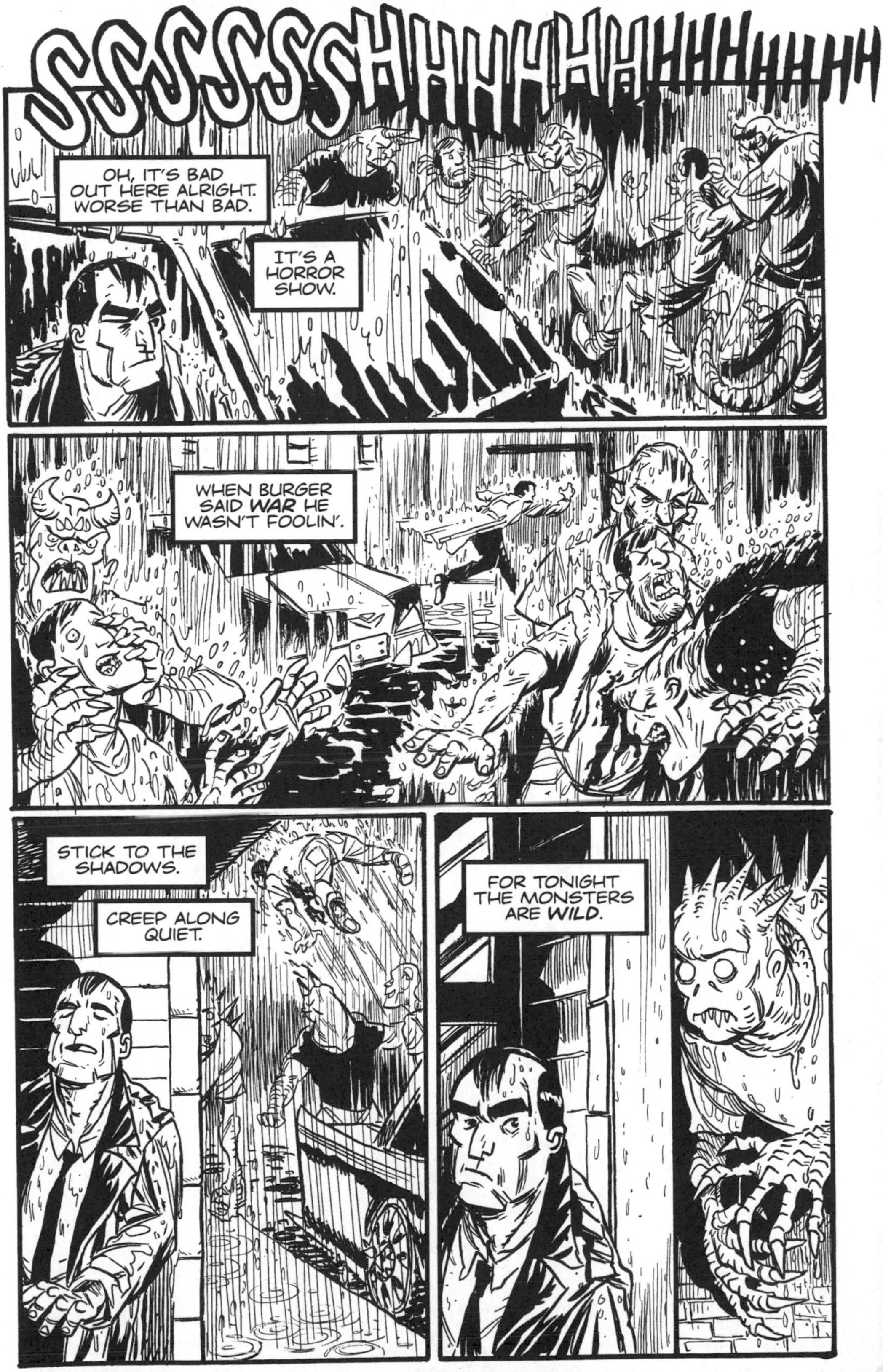
SSSSSSHHHHHHHHHHHHH
OH, IT'S BAD OUT HERE ALRIGHT. WORSE THAN BAD.
IT'S A HORROR SHOW.
WHEN BURGER SAID WAR HE WASN'T FOOLIN'.
STICK TO THE SHADOWS.
CREEP ALONG QUIET.
FOR TONIGHT THE MONSTERS ARE WILD.

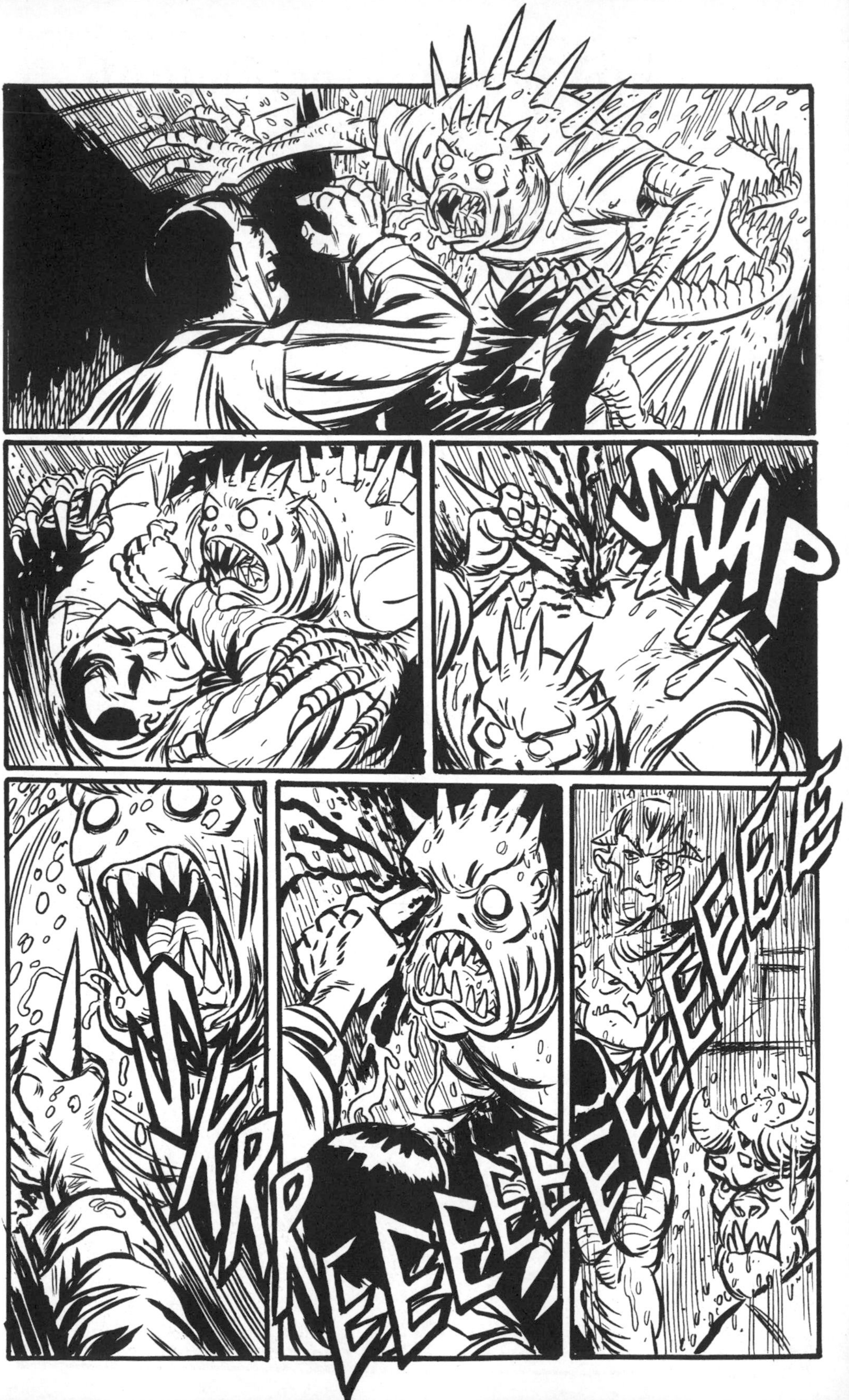

SNAP
SKRREEEEEEEEEEEEEEEE

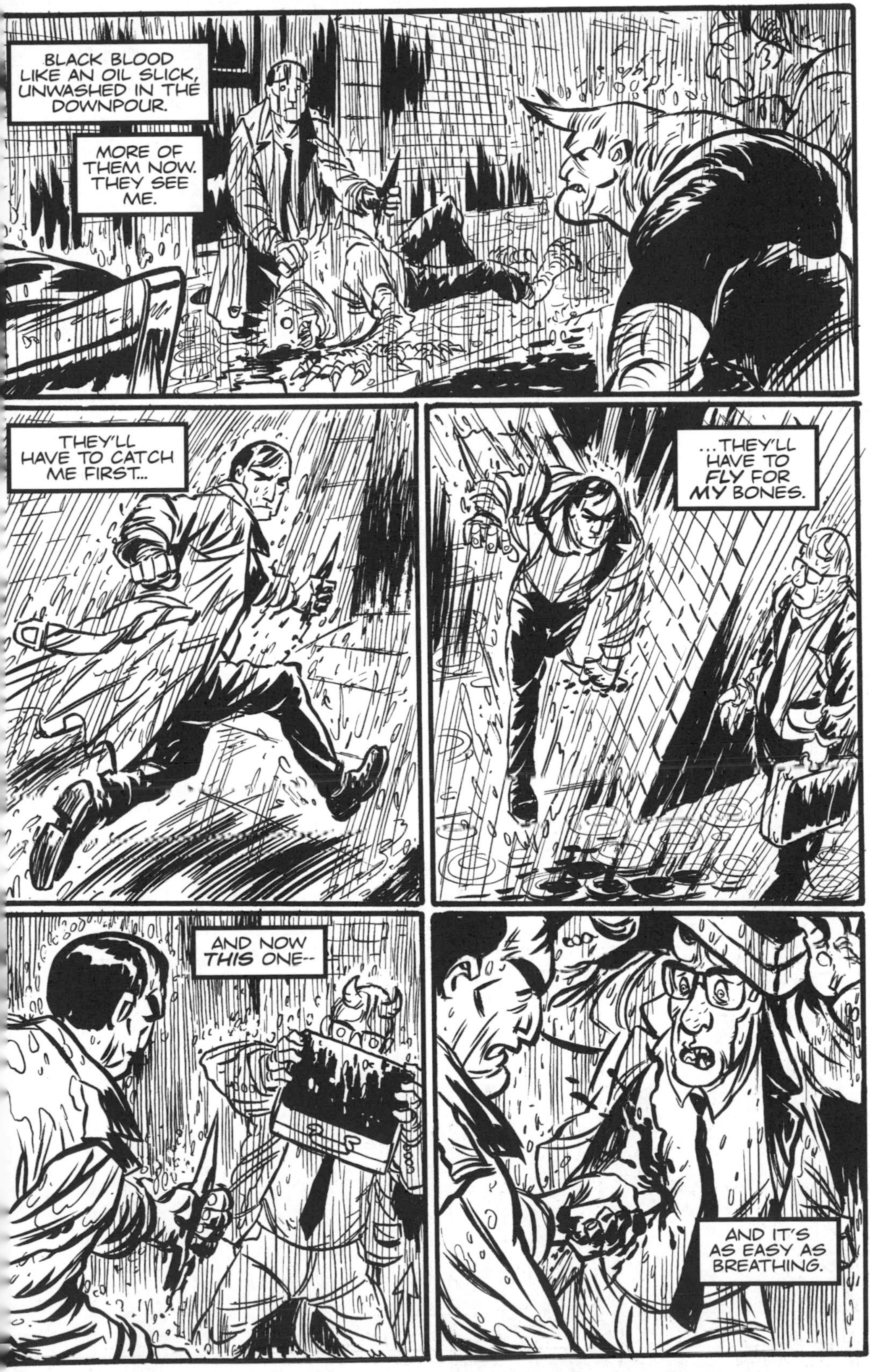
BLACK BLOOD LIKE AN OIL SLICK, UNWASHED IN THE DOWNPOUR.
MORE OF THEM NOW. THEY SEE ME.
THEY'LL HAVE TO CATCH ME FIRST...
...THEY'LL HAVE TO FLY FOR MY BONES.
AND NOW THIS ONE--
AND IT'S AS EASY AS BREATHING.

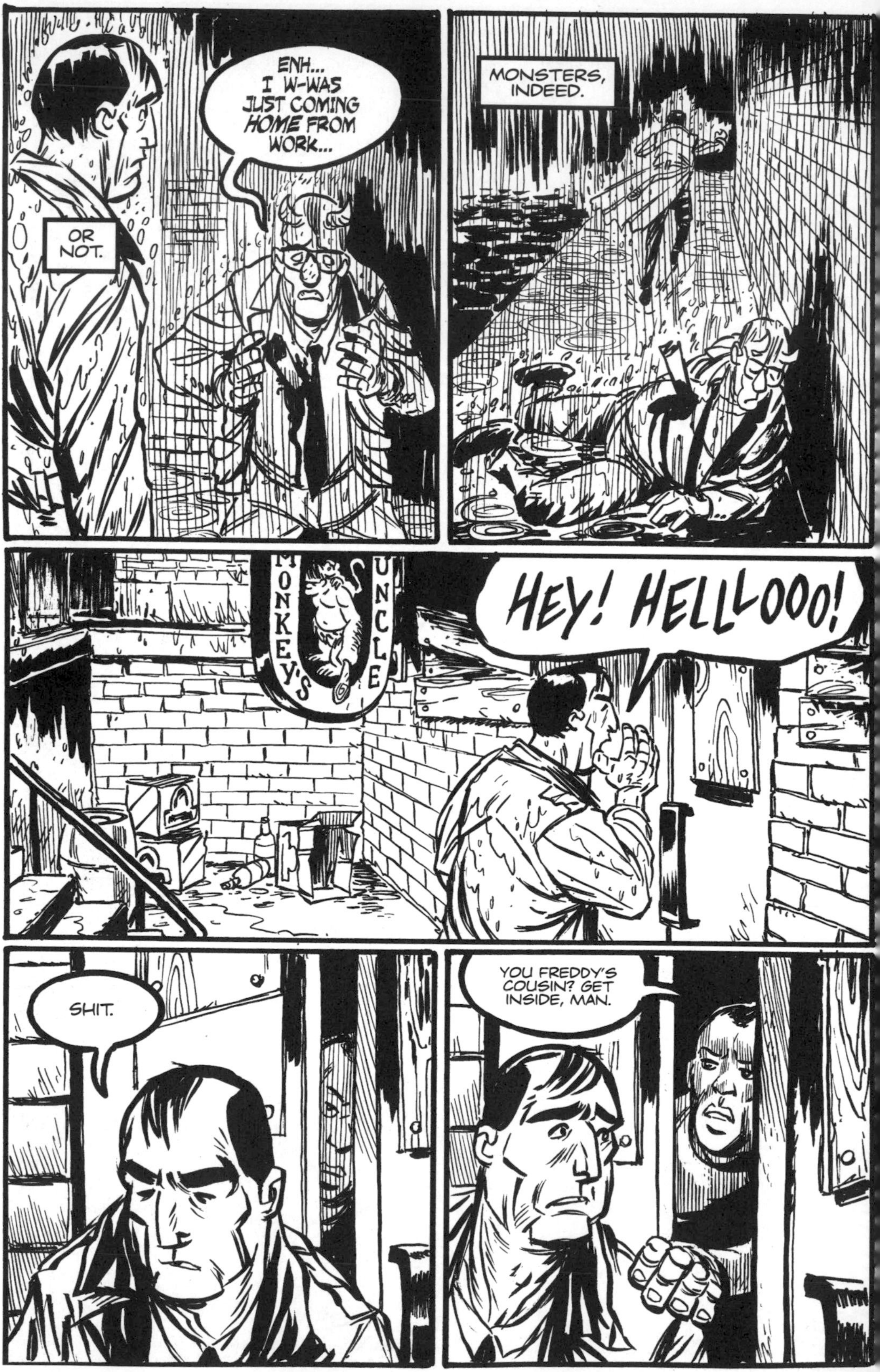
ENH... I W-WAS JUST COMING HOME FROM WORK...
OR NOT.
MONSTERS, INDEED.
MONKEY'S UNCLE
HEY! HELLLOOO!
SHIT.
YOU FREDDY'S COUSIN? GET INSIDE, MAN.

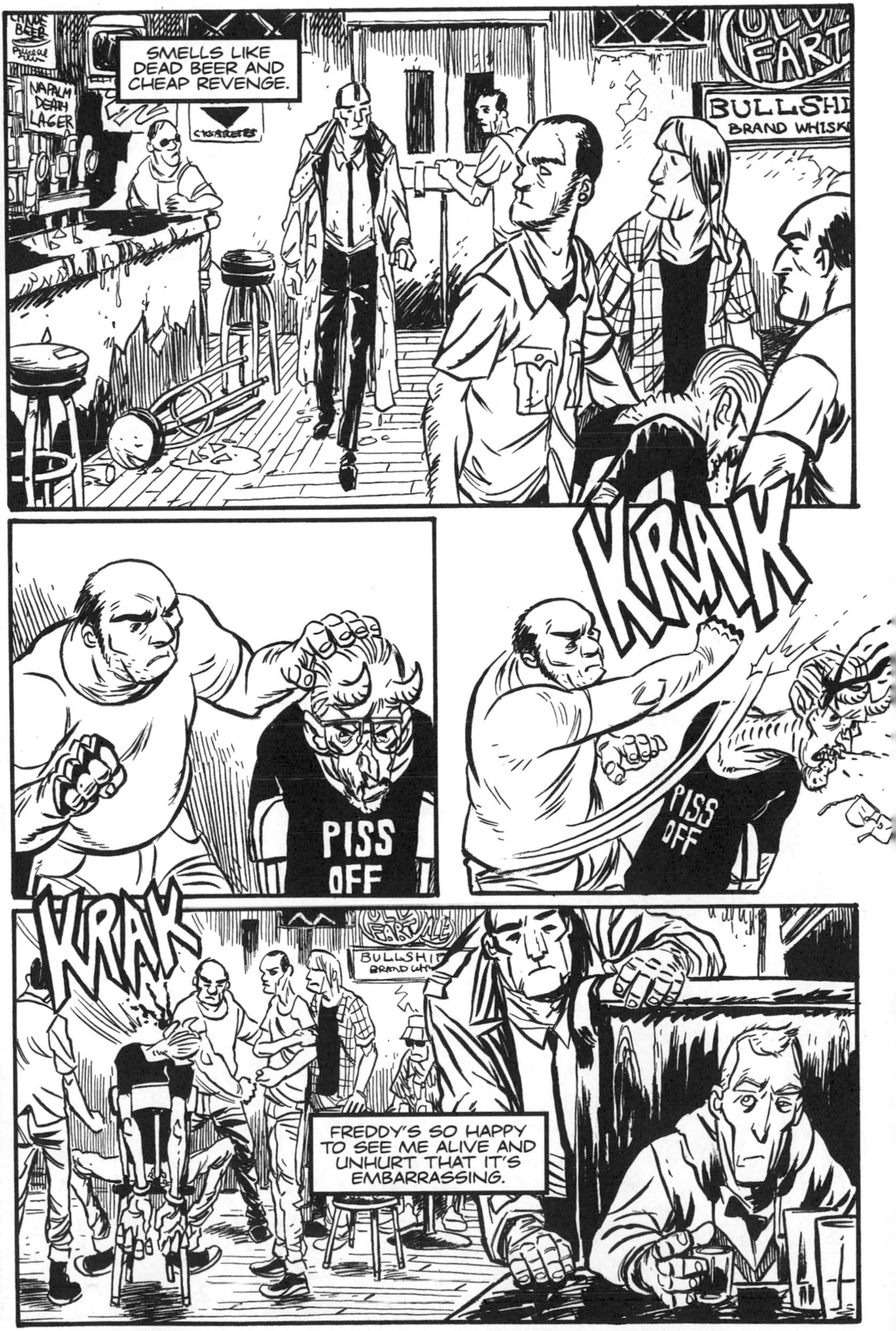
SMELLS LIKE DEAD BEER AND CHEAP REVENGE.
NAPALM DEATH LAGER
CIGARETTES
FART
BULLSHI
BRAND WHISK
KRAK
PISS OFF
PISS OFF
KRAK
BULLSHI
FREDDY'S SO HAPPY TO SEE ME ALIVE AND UNHURT THAT IT'S EMBARRASSING.

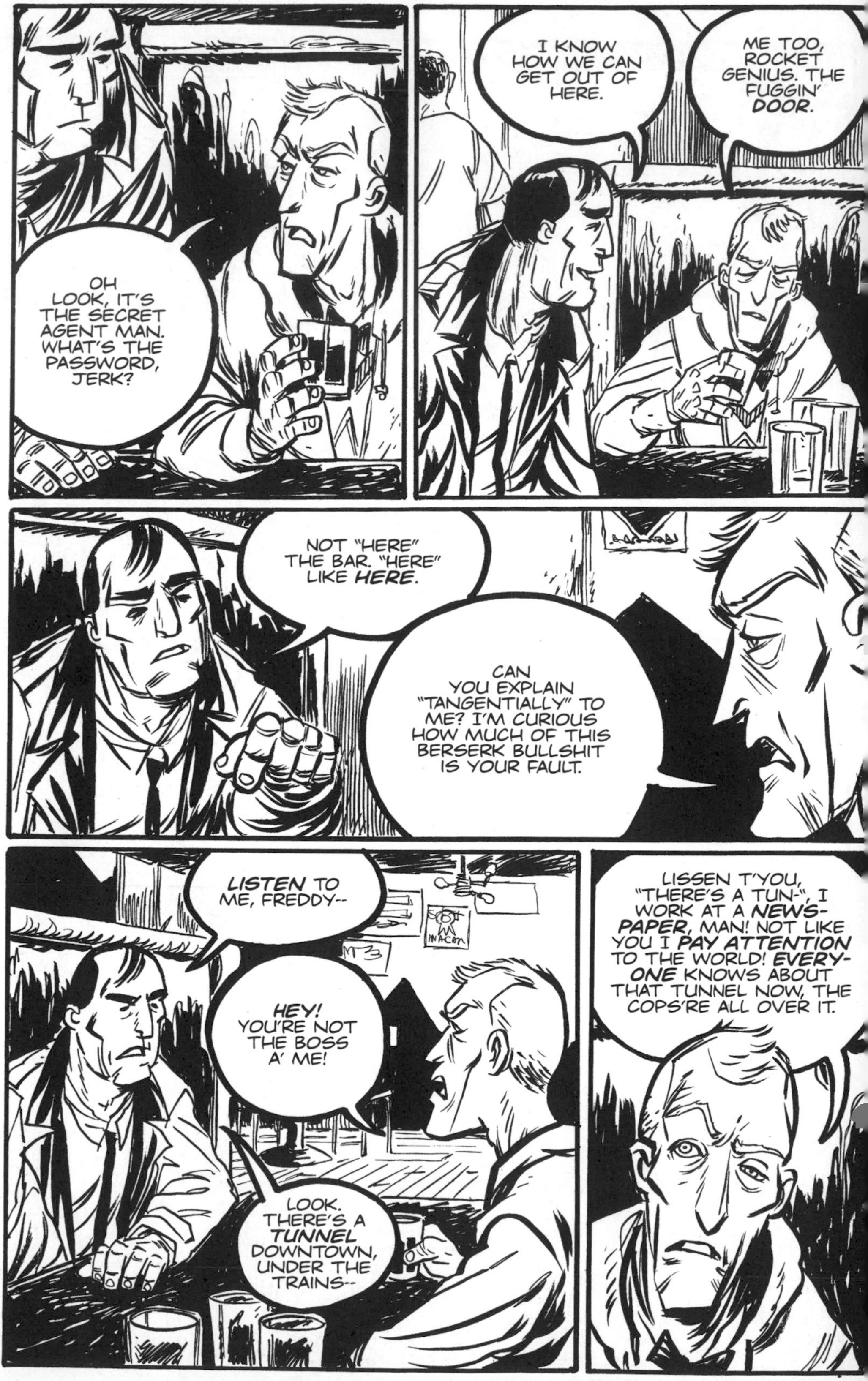
OH LOOK, IT'S THE SECRET AGENT MAN. WHAT'S THE PASSWORD, JERK?
I KNOW HOW WE CAN GET OUT OF HERE.
ME TOO, ROCKET GENIUS. THE FUGGIN' DOOR.
NOT "HERE" THE BAR. "HERE" LIKE HERE.
CAN YOU EXPLAIN "TANGENTIALLY" TO ME? I'M CURIOUS HOW MUCH OF THIS BERSERK BULLSHIT IS YOUR FAULT.
LISTEN TO ME, FREDDY--
HEY! YOU'RE NOT THE BOSS A' ME!
LOOK. THERE'S A TUNNEL DOWNTOWN, UNDER THE TRAINS--
LISSEN T'YOU, "THERE'S A TUN-", I WORK AT A NEWS-PAPER, MAN! NOT LIKE YOU I PAY ATTENTION TO THE WORLD! EVERY-ONE KNOWS ABOUT THAT TUNNEL NOW, THE COPS'RE ALL OVER IT.

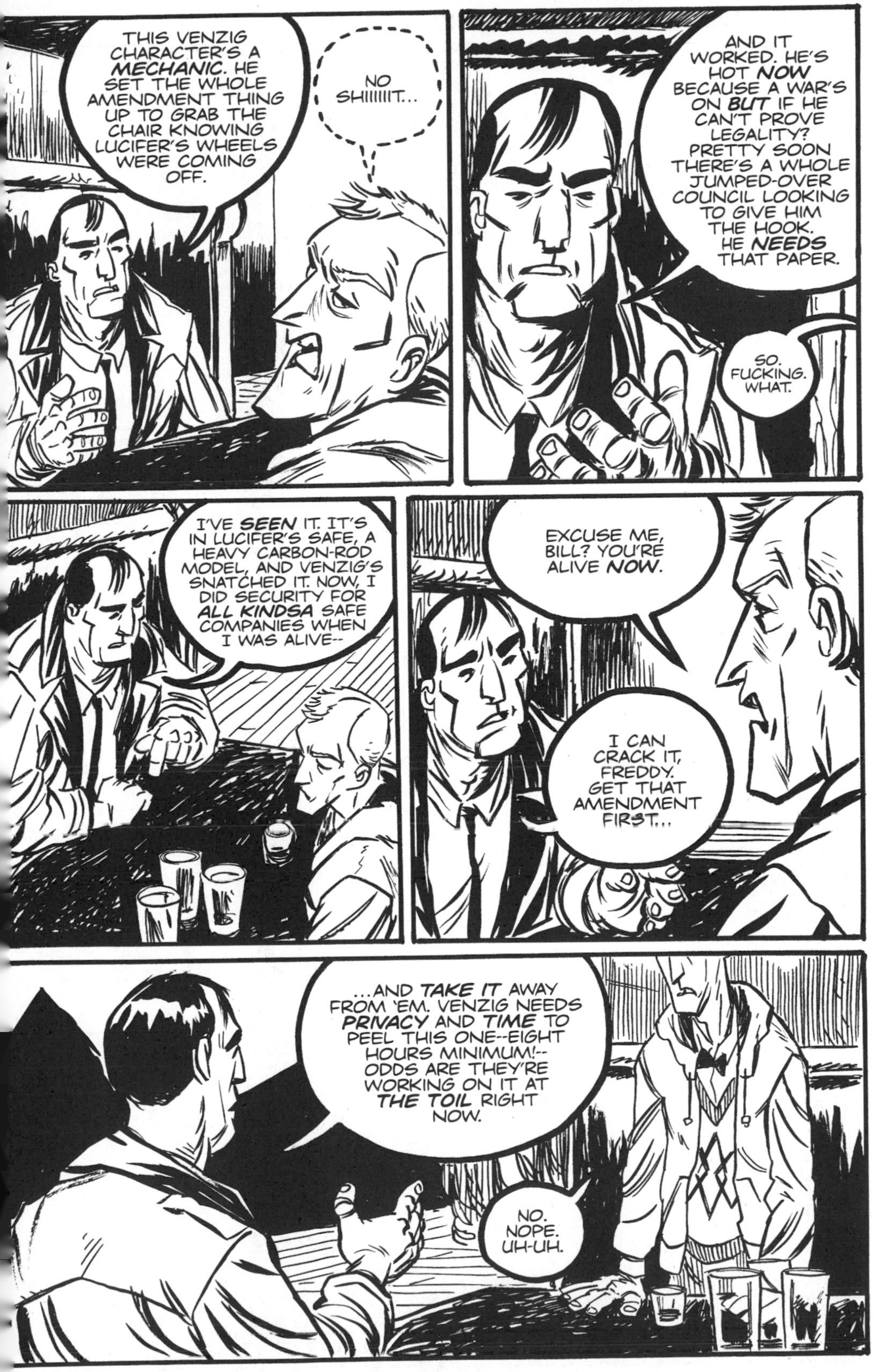
THIS VENZIG CHARACTER'S A MECHANIC. HE SET THE WHOLE AMENDMENT THING UP TO GRAB THE CHAIR KNOWING LUCIFER'S WHEELS WERE COMING OFF.
NO SHIIIIIIT...
AND IT WORKED. HE'S HOT NOW BECAUSE A WAR'S ON BUT IF HE CAN'T PROVE LEGALITY? PRETTY SOON THERE'S A WHOLE JUMPED-OVER COUNCIL LOOKING TO GIVE HIM THE HOOK. HE NEEDS THAT PAPER.
SO. FUCKING. WHAT.
I'VE SEEN IT. IT'S IN LUCIFER'S SAFE, A HEAVY CARBON-ROD MODEL, AND VENZIG'S SNATCHED IT. NOW, I DID SECURITY FOR ALL KINDSA SAFE COMPANIES WHEN I WAS ALIVE--
EXCUSE ME, BILL? YOU'RE ALIVE NOW.
I CAN CRACK IT, FREDDY. GET THAT AMENDMENT FIRST...
...AND TAKE IT AWAY FROM 'EM. VENZIG NEEDS PRIVACY AND TIME TO PEEL THIS ONE--EIGHT HOURS MINIMUM!--ODDS ARE THEY'RE WORKING ON IT AT THE TOIL RIGHT NOW.
NO. NOPE. UH-UH.

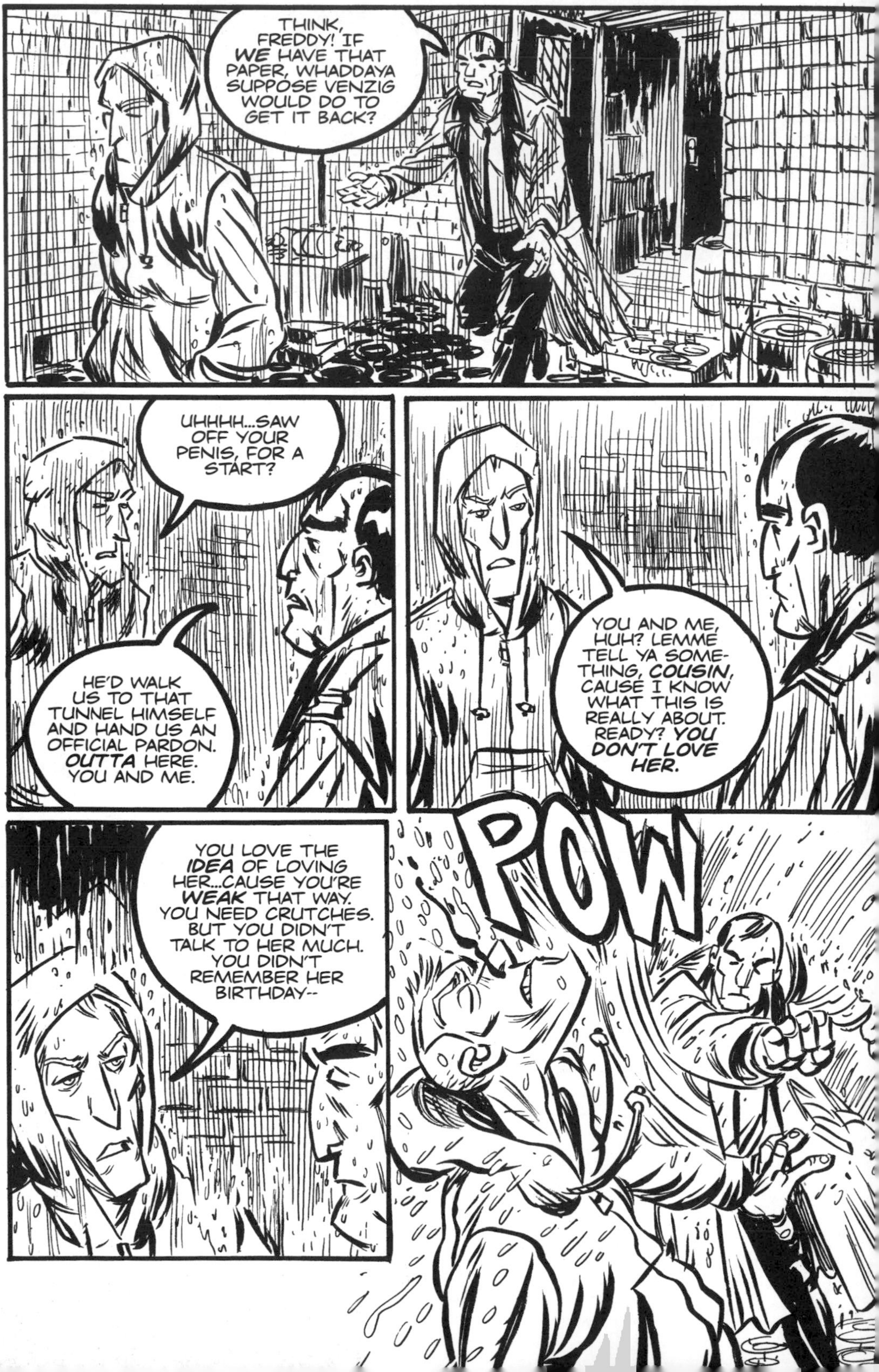
THINK, FREDDY! IF WE HAVE THAT PAPER, WHADDAYA SUPPOSE VENZIG WOULD DO TO GET IT BACK?
UHHHH...SAW OFF YOUR PENIS, FOR A START?
HE'D WALK US TO THAT TUNNEL HIMSELF AND HAND US AN OFFICIAL PARDON. OUTTA HERE. YOU AND ME.
YOU AND ME, HUH? LEMME TELL YA SOME-THING, COUSIN, CAUSE I KNOW WHAT THIS IS REALLY ABOUT. READY? YOU DON'T LOVE HER.
YOU LOVE THE IDEA OF LOVING HER...CAUSE YOU'RE WEAK THAT WAY. YOU NEED CRUTCHES. BUT YOU DIDN'T TALK TO HER MUCH. YOU DIDN'T REMEMBER HER BIRTHDAY--
POW

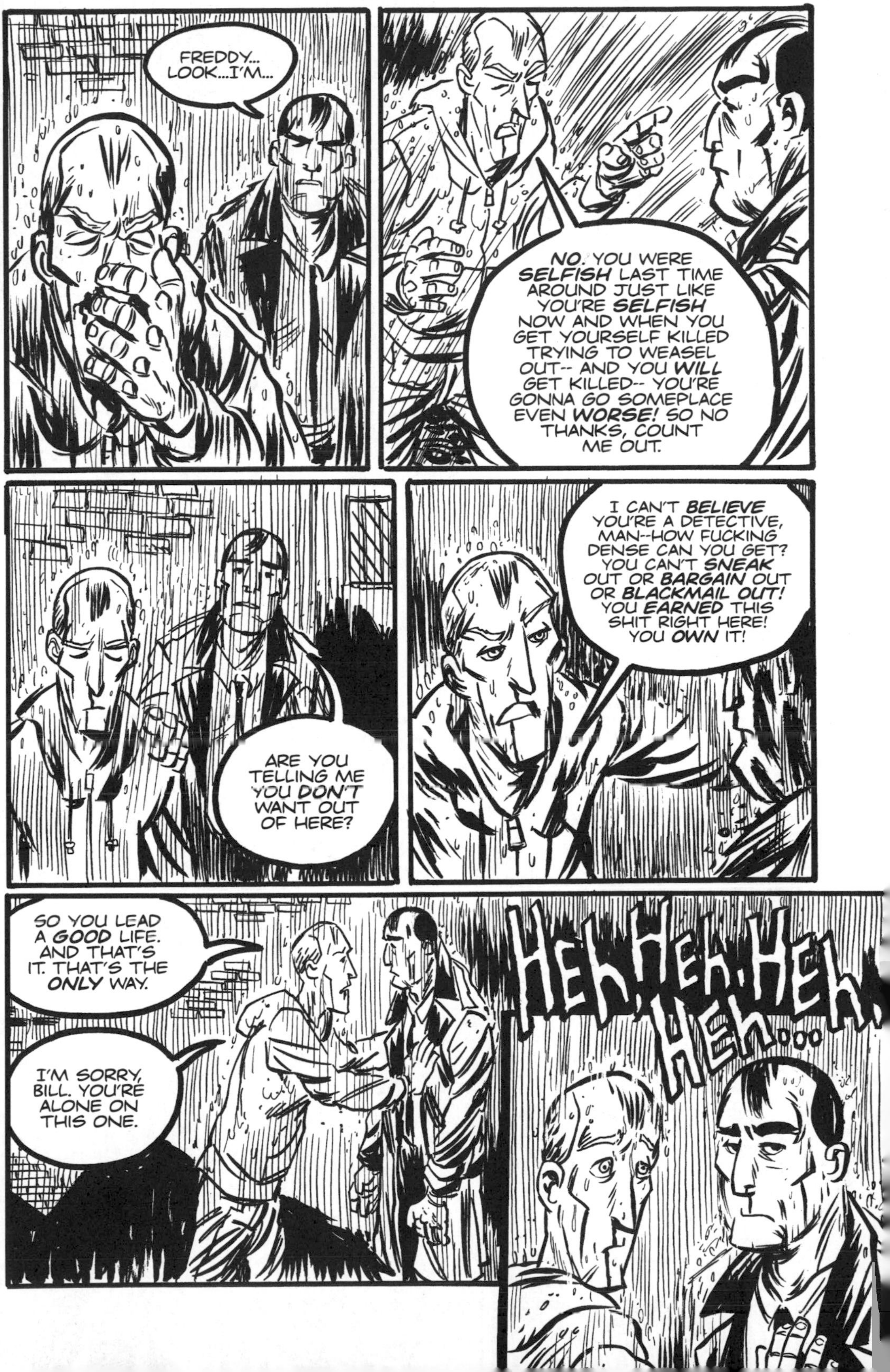
FREDDY... LOOK...I'M...
NO. YOU WERE SELFISH LAST TIME AROUND JUST LIKE YOU'RE SELFISH NOW AND WHEN YOU GET YOURSELF KILLED TRYING TO WEASEL OUT-- AND YOU WILL GET KILLED-- YOU'RE GONNA GO SOMEPLACE EVEN WORSE! SO NO THANKS, COUNT ME OUT.
ARE YOU TELLING ME YOU DON'T WANT OUT OF HERE?
I CAN'T BELIEVE YOU'RE A DETECTIVE, MAN--HOW FUCKING DENSE CAN YOU GET? YOU CAN'T SNEAK OUT OR BARGAIN OUT OR BLACKMAIL OUT! YOU EARNED THIS SHIT RIGHT HERE! YOU OWN IT!
SO YOU LEAD A GOOD LIFE. AND THAT'S IT. THAT'S THE ONLY WAY.
I'M SORRY, BILL. YOU'RE ALONE ON THIS ONE.
HEH.HEH.HEH.HEH. HEH...

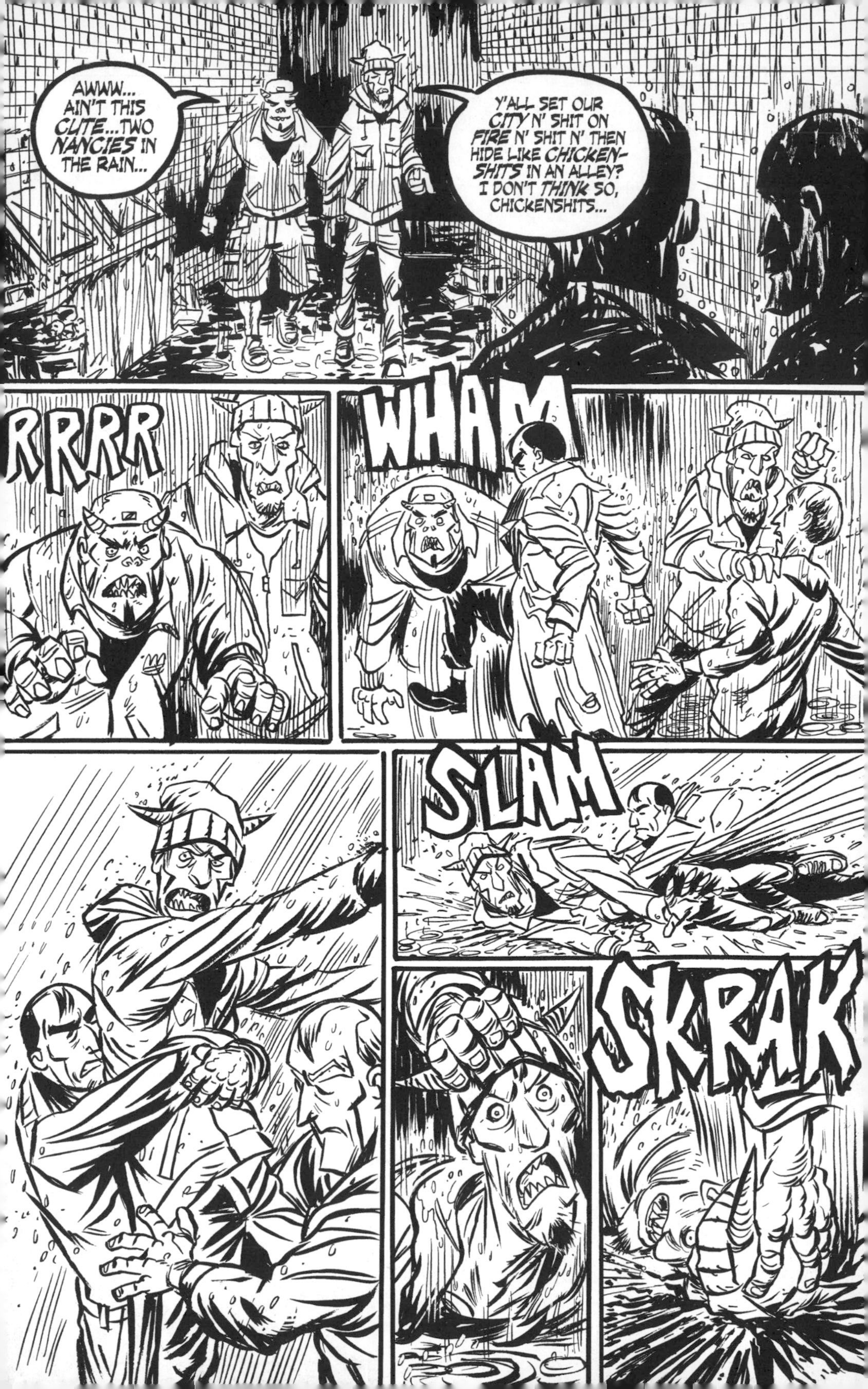
AWWW... AIN'T THIS CUTE...TWO NANCIES IN THE RAIN...
Y'ALL SET OUR CITY N' SHIT ON FIRE N' SHIT N' THEN HIDE LIKE CHICKEN-SHITS IN AN ALLEY? I DON'T THINK SO, CHICKENSHITS...
RRRR
WHAM
SLAM
SKRAK

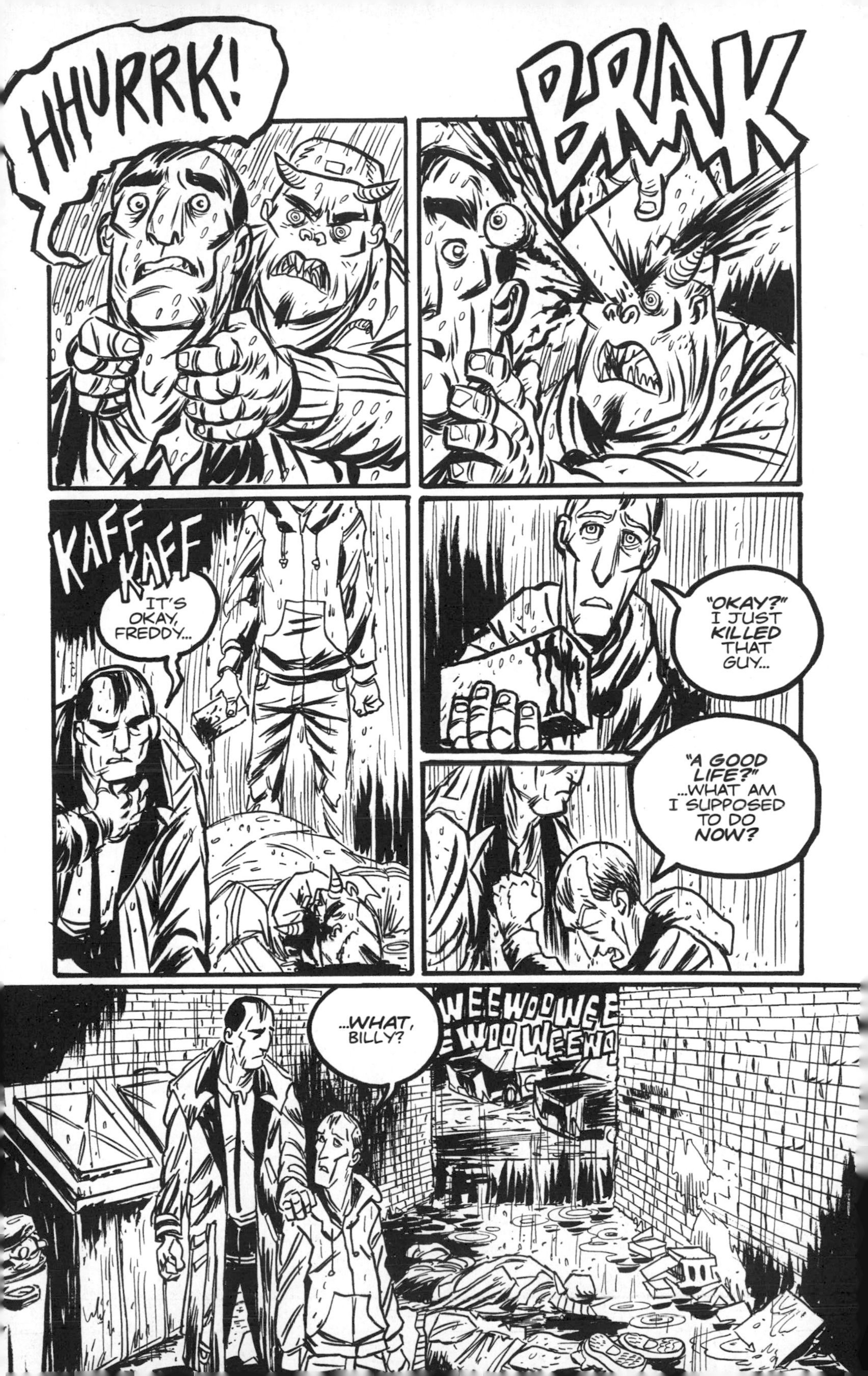

HHURRK!
BRAK
KAFF KAFF
IT'S OKAY, FREDDY...
"OKAY?" I JUST KILLED THAT GUY...
"A GOOD LIFE?" ...WHAT AM I SUPPOSED TO DO NOW?
...WHAT, BILLY?
WEEWOOWEE WOOWEEWO

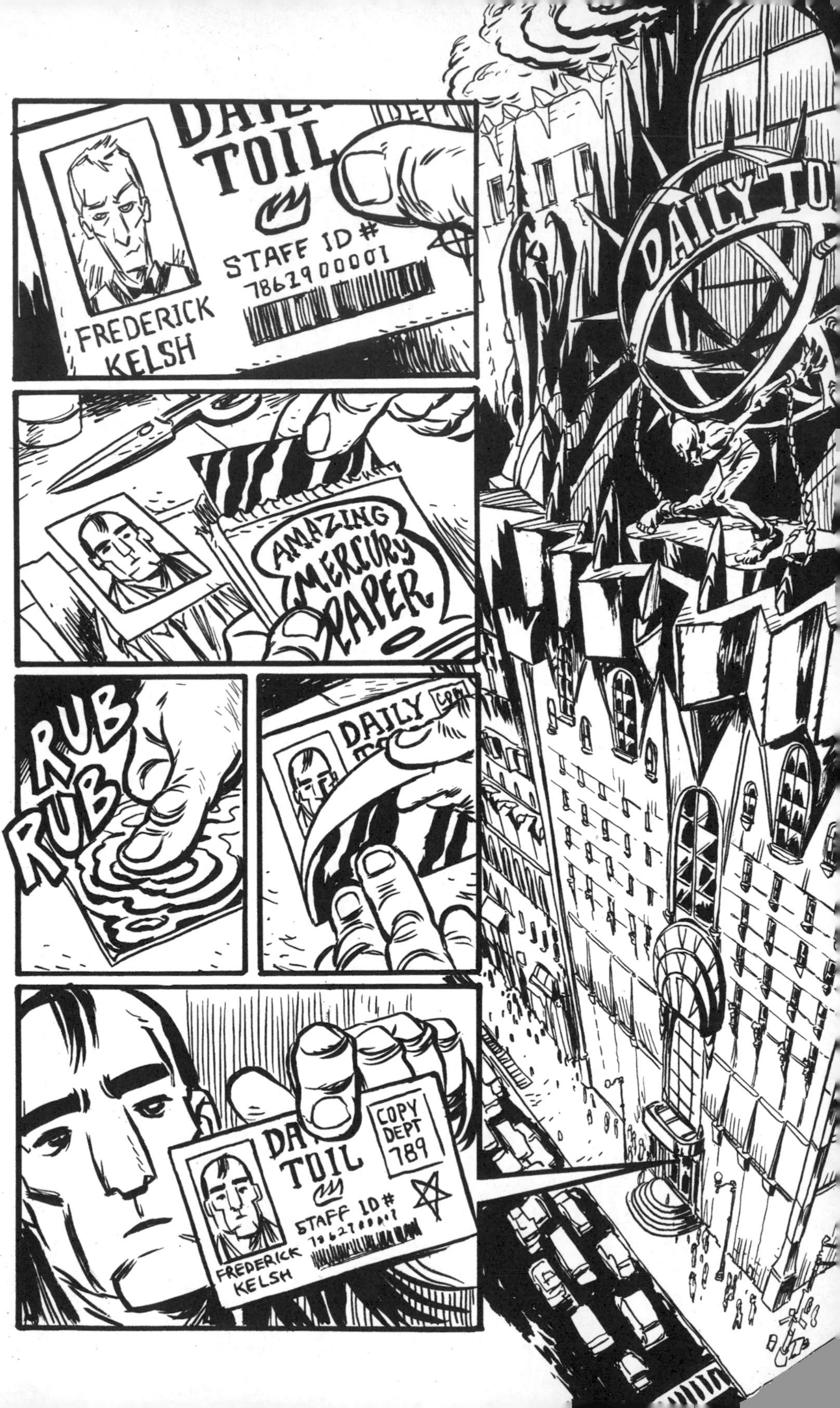
TOIL
STAFF ID #
7862900001
FREDERICK
KELSH
AMAZING
MERCURY
PAPER
RUB
RUB
DAILY
TOIL
COPY
DEPT
789
STAFF ID #
FREDERICK
KELSH
DAILY TO

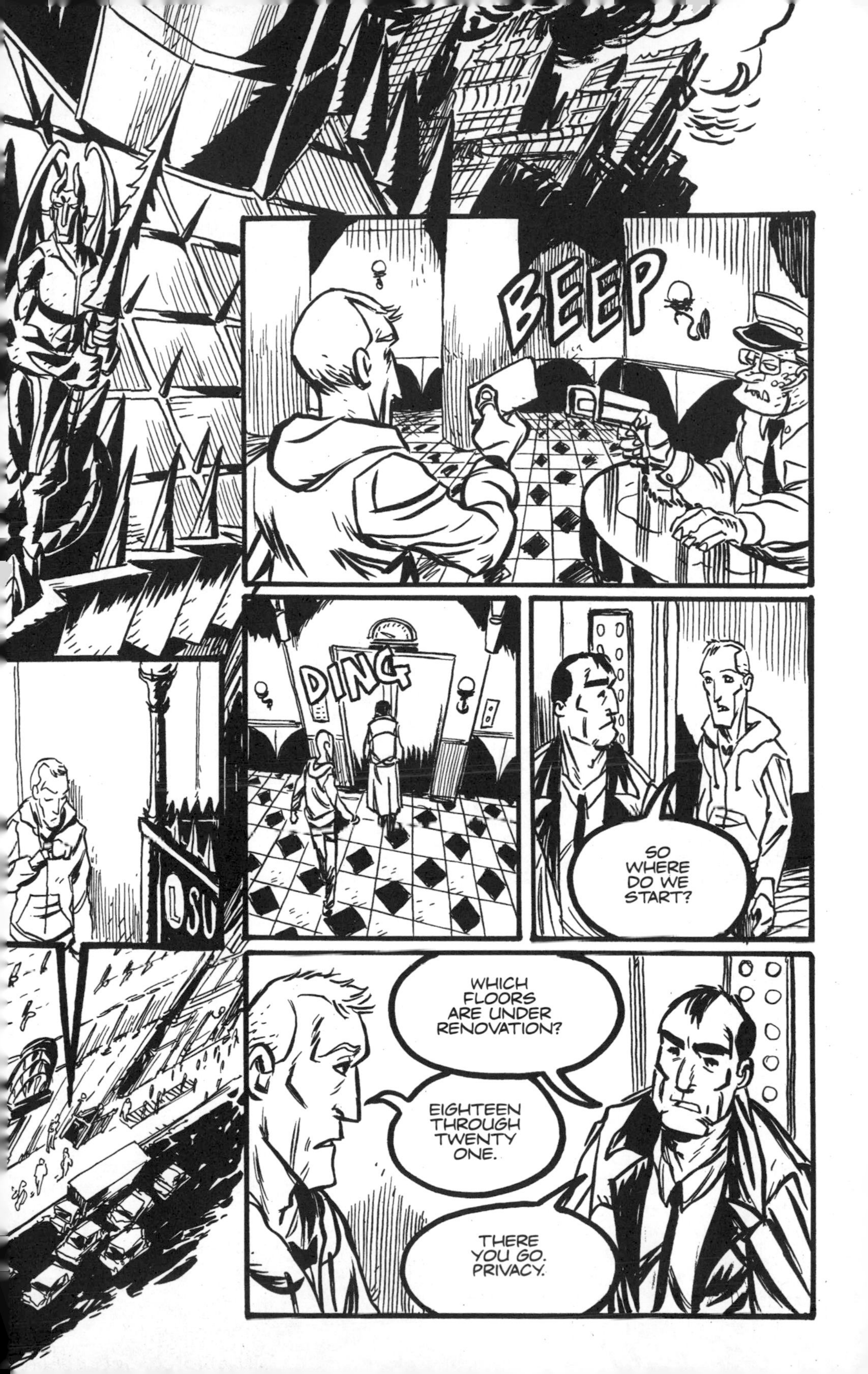
BEEP
DING
SO WHERE DO WE START?
WHICH FLOORS ARE UNDER RENOVATION?
EIGHTEEN THROUGH TWENTY ONE.
THERE YOU GO. PRIVACY.

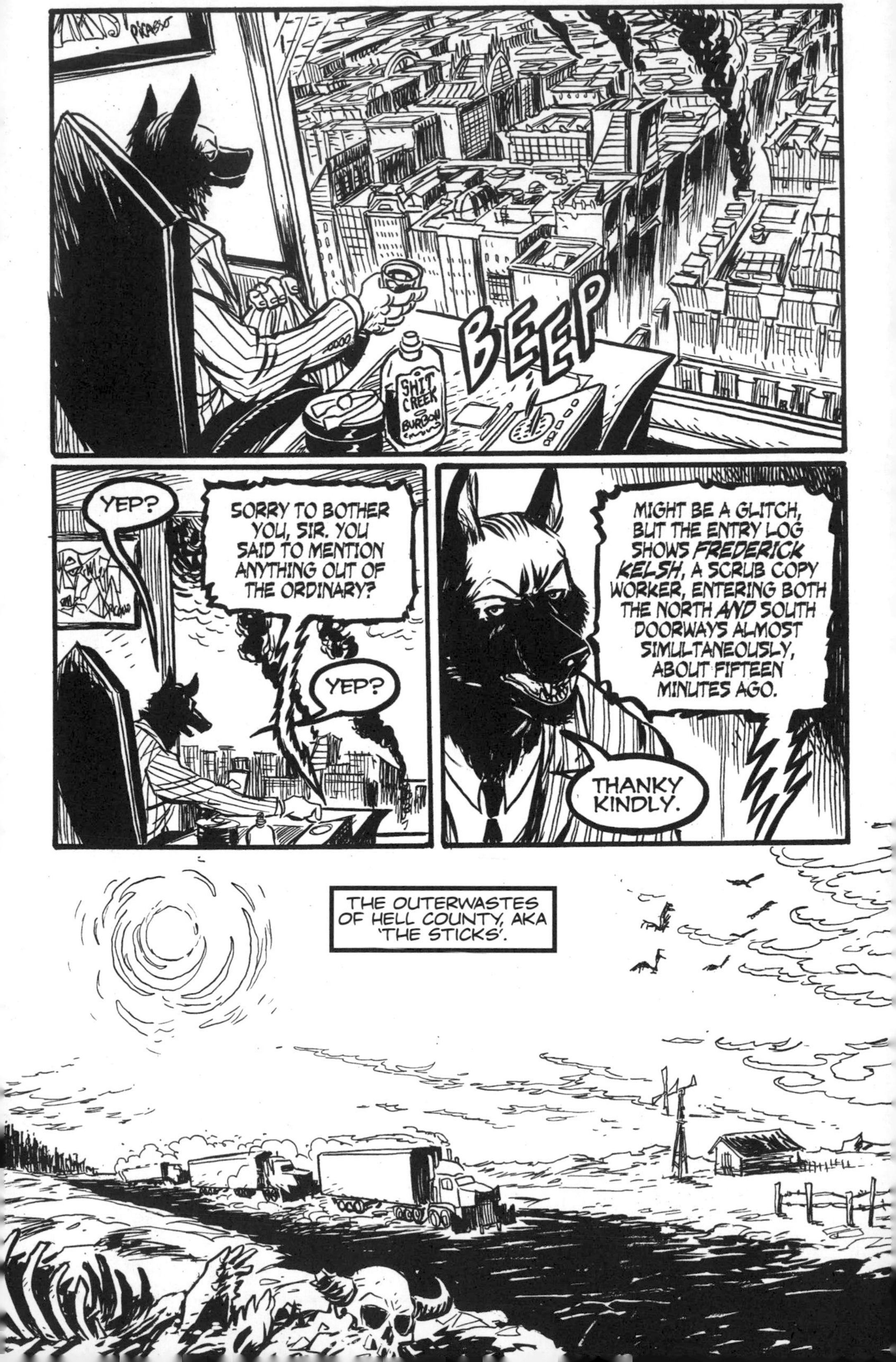
PICASSO
SHIT CREEK BURBON
BEEP
YEP?
SORRY TO BOTHER YOU, SIR. YOU SAID TO MENTION ANYTHING OUT OF THE ORDINARY?
YEP?
MIGHT BE A GLITCH, BUT THE ENTRY LOG SHOWS FREDERICK KELSH, A SCRUB COPY WORKER, ENTERING BOTH THE NORTH AND SOUTH DOORWAYS ALMOST SIMULTANEOUSLY, ABOUT FIFTEEN MINUTES AGO.
THANKY KINDLY.
THE OUTERWASTES OF HELL COUNTY, AKA 'THE STICKS'.

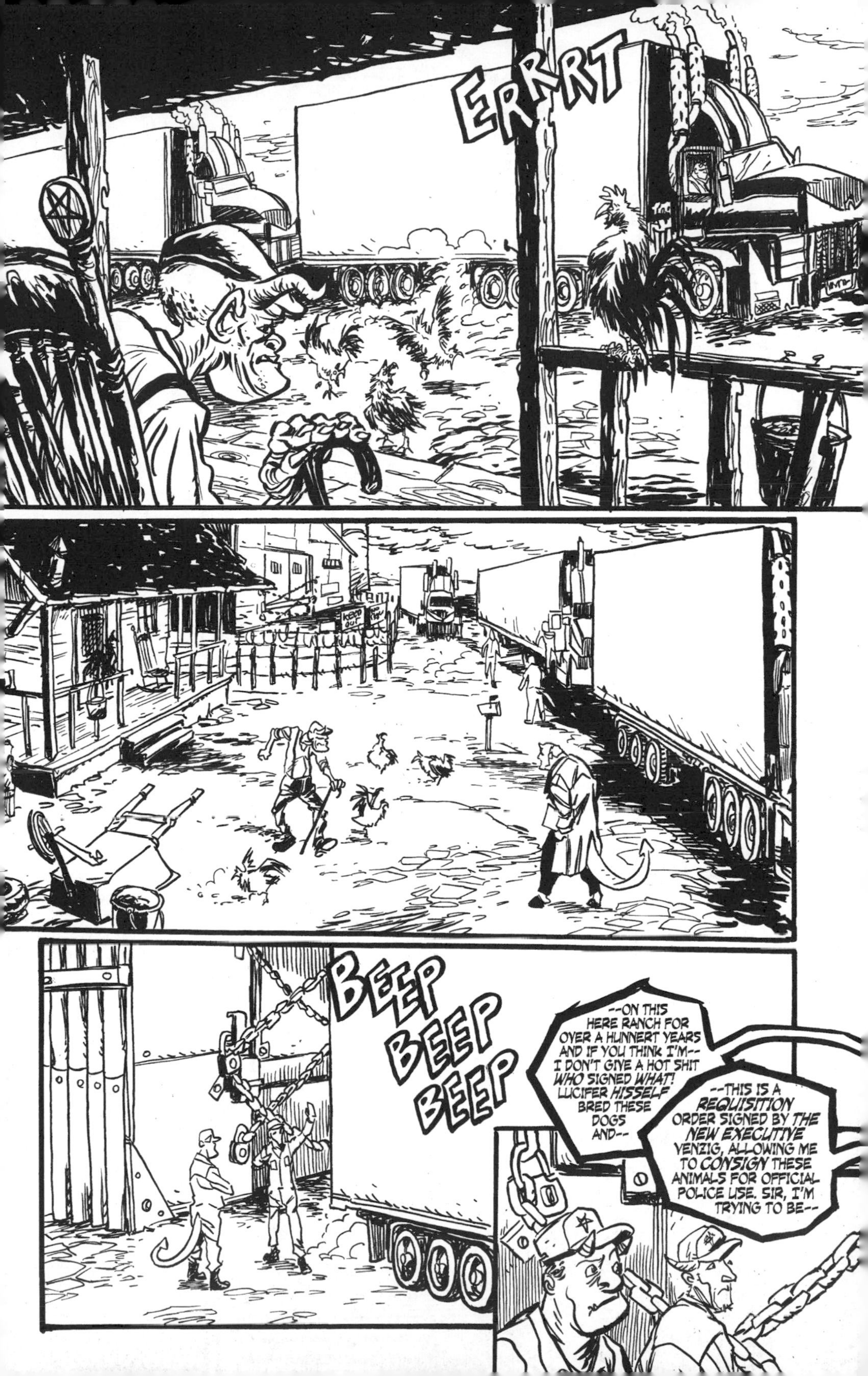
ERRRT
BEEP
BEEP
BEEP
--ON THIS HERE RANCH FOR OVER A HUNNERT YEARS AND IF YOU THINK I'M-- I DON'T GIVE A HOT SHIT *WHO* SIGNED *WHAT*! LUCIFER *HISSELF* BRED THESE DOGS AND--
--THIS IS A *REQUISITION* ORDER SIGNED BY *THE NEW EXECUTIVE* VENZIG, ALLOWING ME TO *CONSIGN* THESE ANIMALS FOR OFFICIAL POLICE USE. SIR, I'M TRYING TO BE--

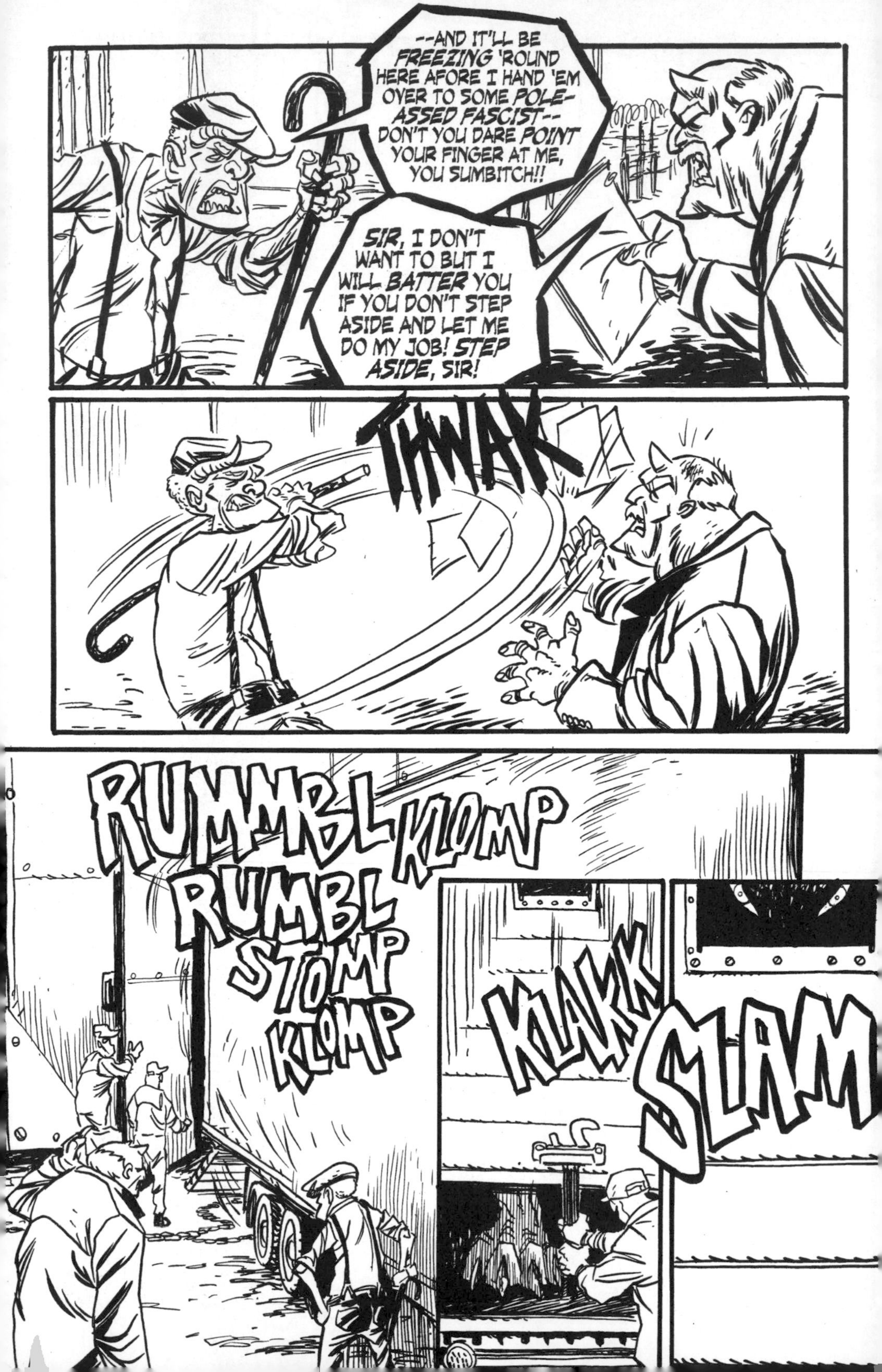
--AND IT'LL BE FREEZING 'ROUND HERE AFORE I HAND 'EM OVER TO SOME POLE-ASSED FASCIST-- DON'T YOU DARE POINT YOUR FINGER AT ME, YOU SUMBITCH!!
SIR, I DON'T WANT TO BUT I WILL BATTER YOU IF YOU DON'T STEP ASIDE AND LET ME DO MY JOB! STEP ASIDE, SIR!
THWAK
RUMMBL
KLOMP
RUMBL
STOMP
KLOMP
KLAKK
SLAM

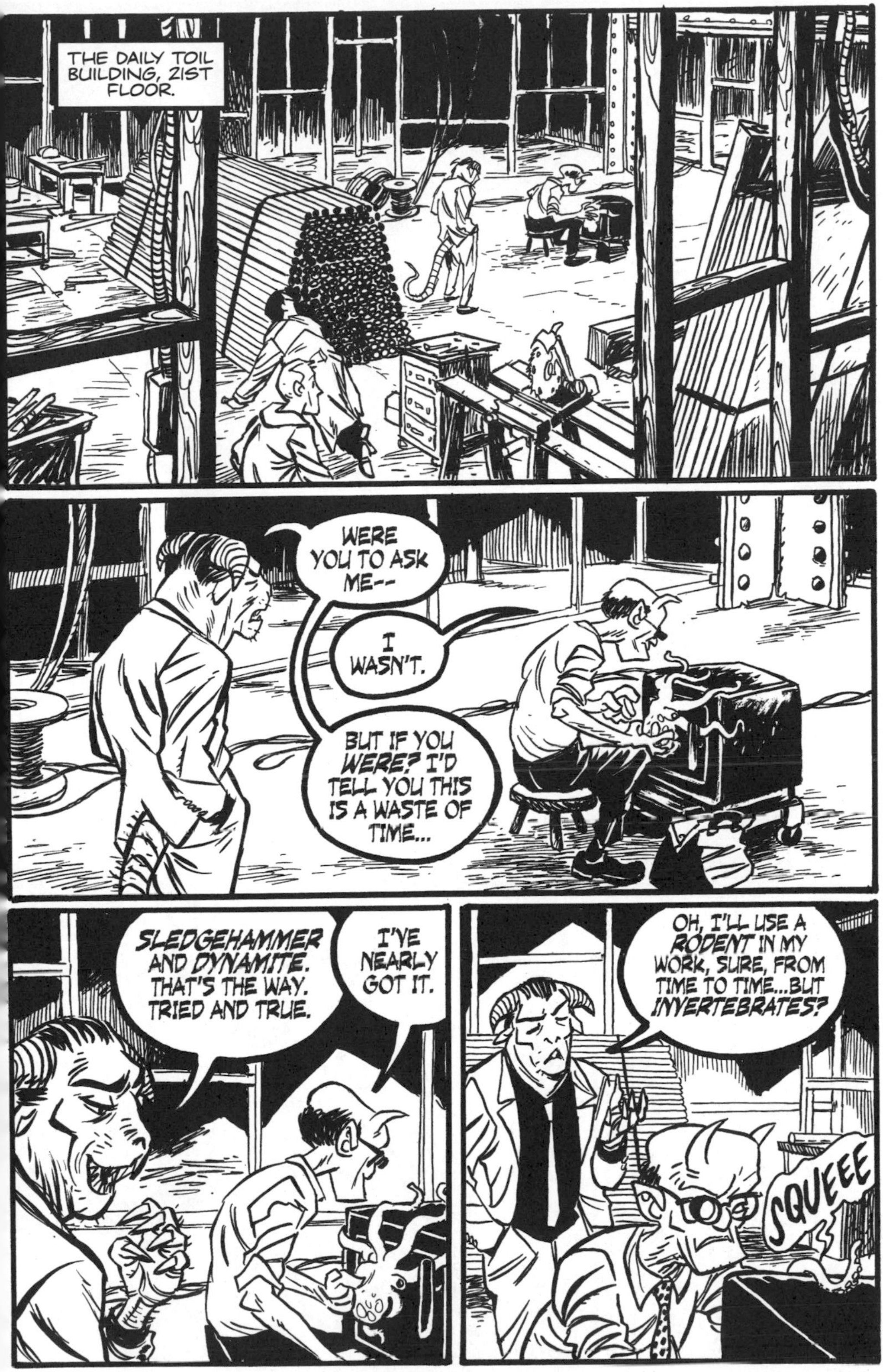
THE DAILY TOIL BUILDING, 21ST FLOOR.
WERE YOU TO ASK ME--
I WASN'T.
BUT IF YOU *WERE?* I'D TELL YOU THIS IS A WASTE OF TIME...
SLEDGEHAMMER AND *DYNAMITE*. THAT'S THE WAY. TRIED AND TRUE.
I'VE NEARLY GOT IT.
OH, I'LL USE A *RODENT* IN MY WORK, SURE, FROM TIME TO TIME...BUT *INVERTEBRATES?*
SQUEEE

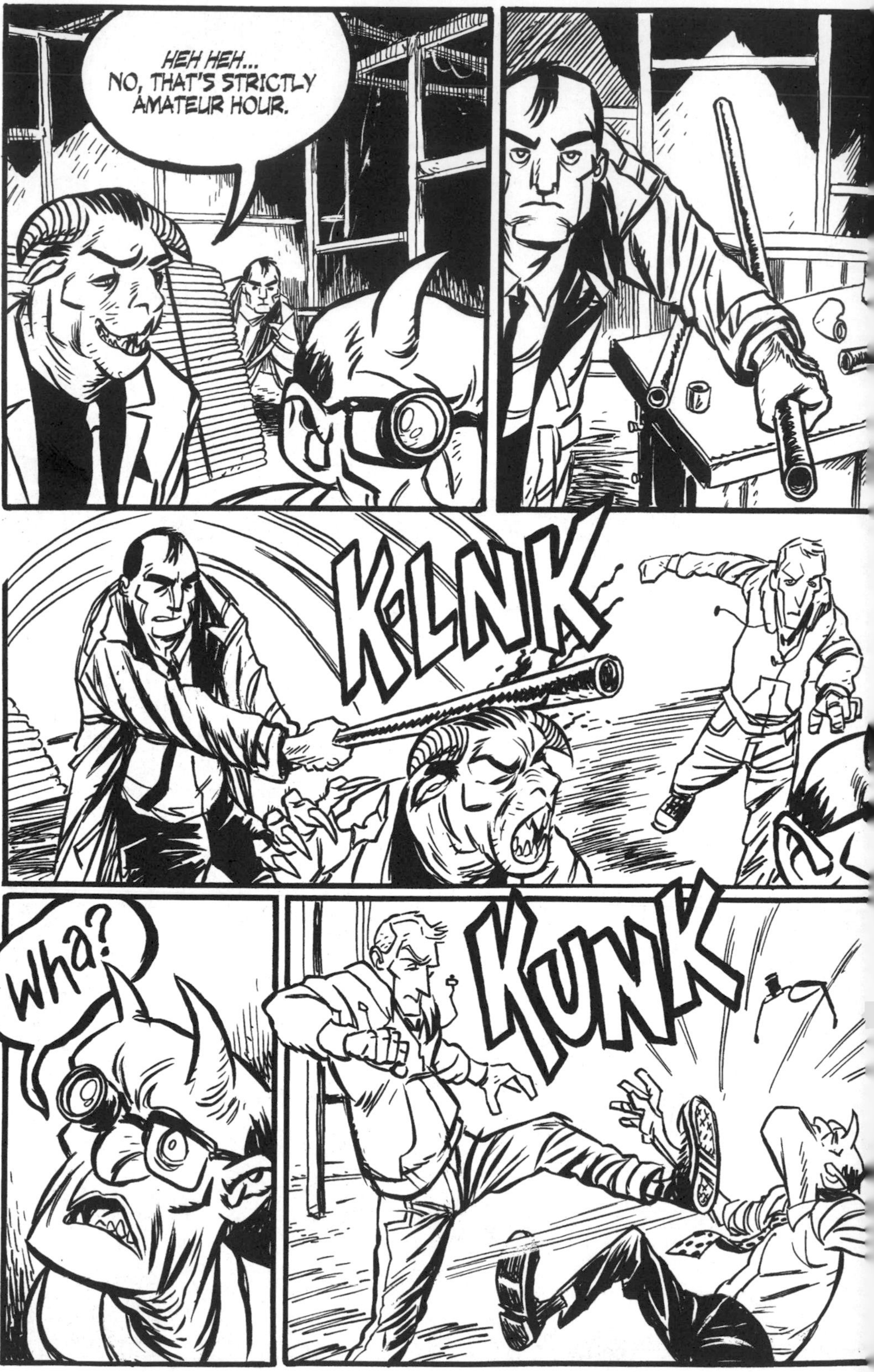
HEH HEH... NO, THAT'S STRICTLY AMATEUR HOUR.
K-LNK
wha?
KUNK

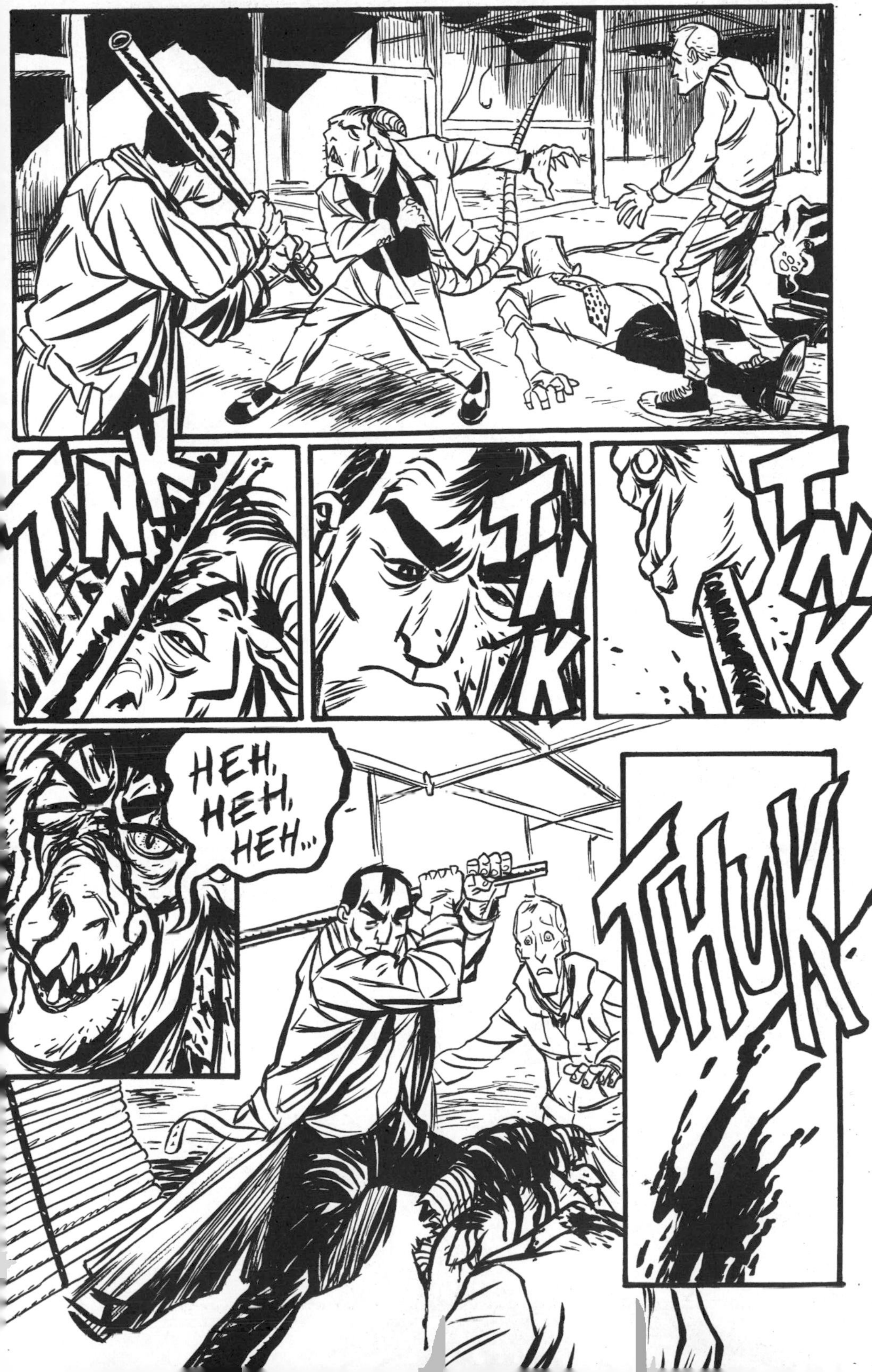
TNK
TNK
TNK
HEH, HEH, HEH...
THUK

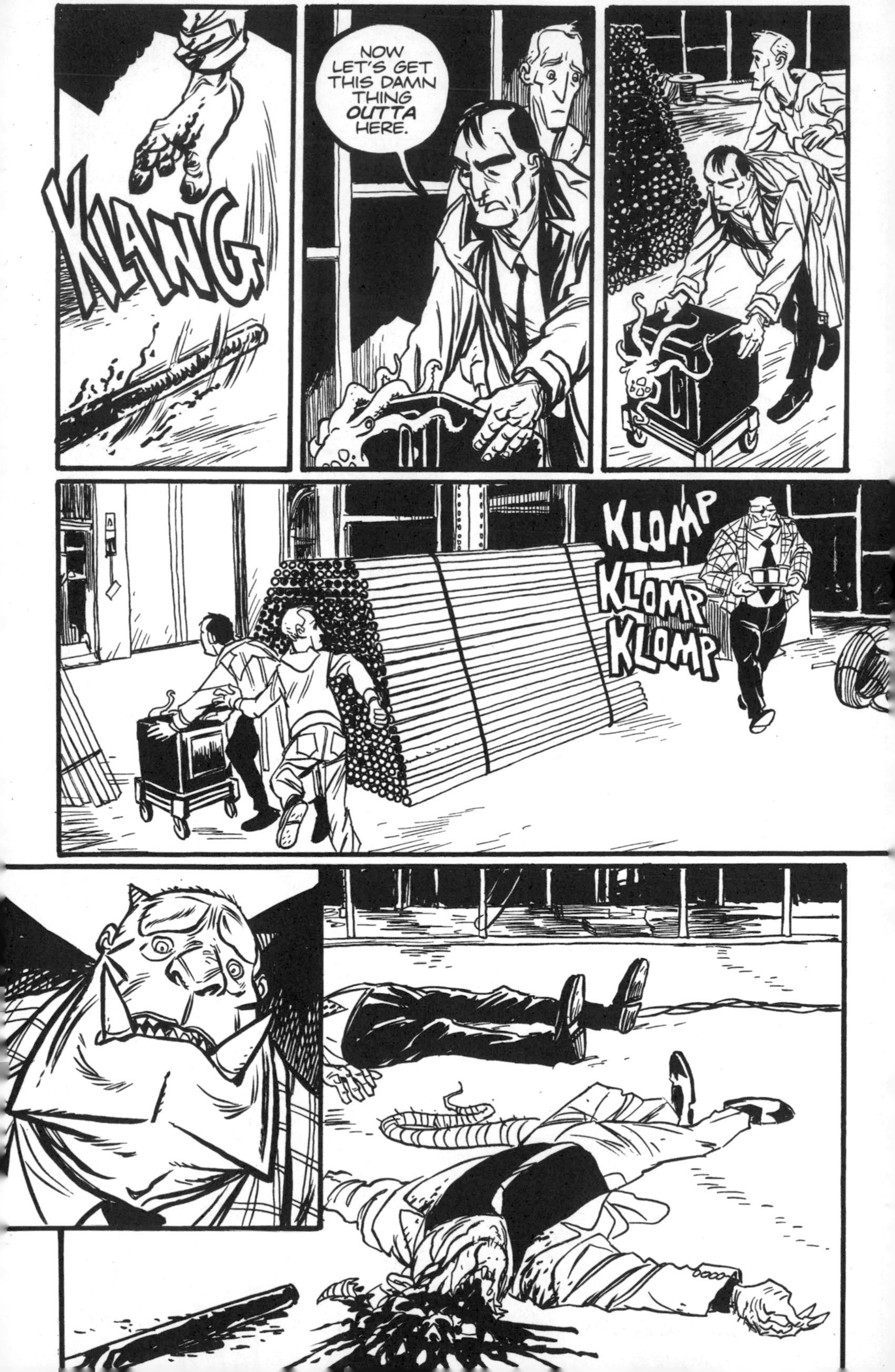
KLANG
NOW LET'S GET THIS DAMN THING *OUTTA* HERE.
KLOMP
KLOMP
KLOMP

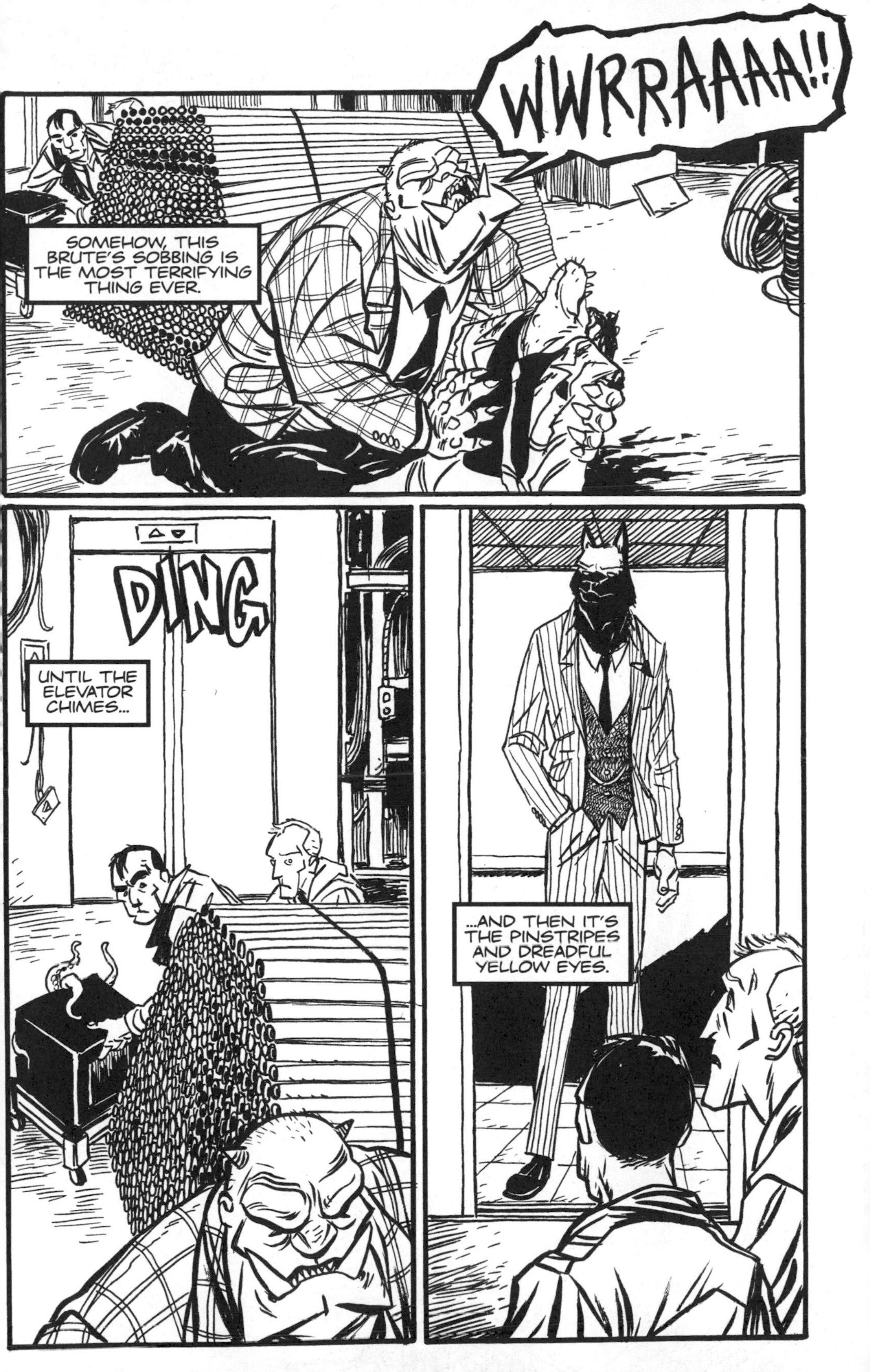
WWRRAAAA!!
SOMEHOW, THIS BRUTE'S SOBBING IS THE MOST TERRIFYING THING EVER.
DING
UNTIL THE ELEVATOR CHIMES...
...AND THEN IT'S THE PINSTRIPES AND DREADFUL YELLOW EYES.

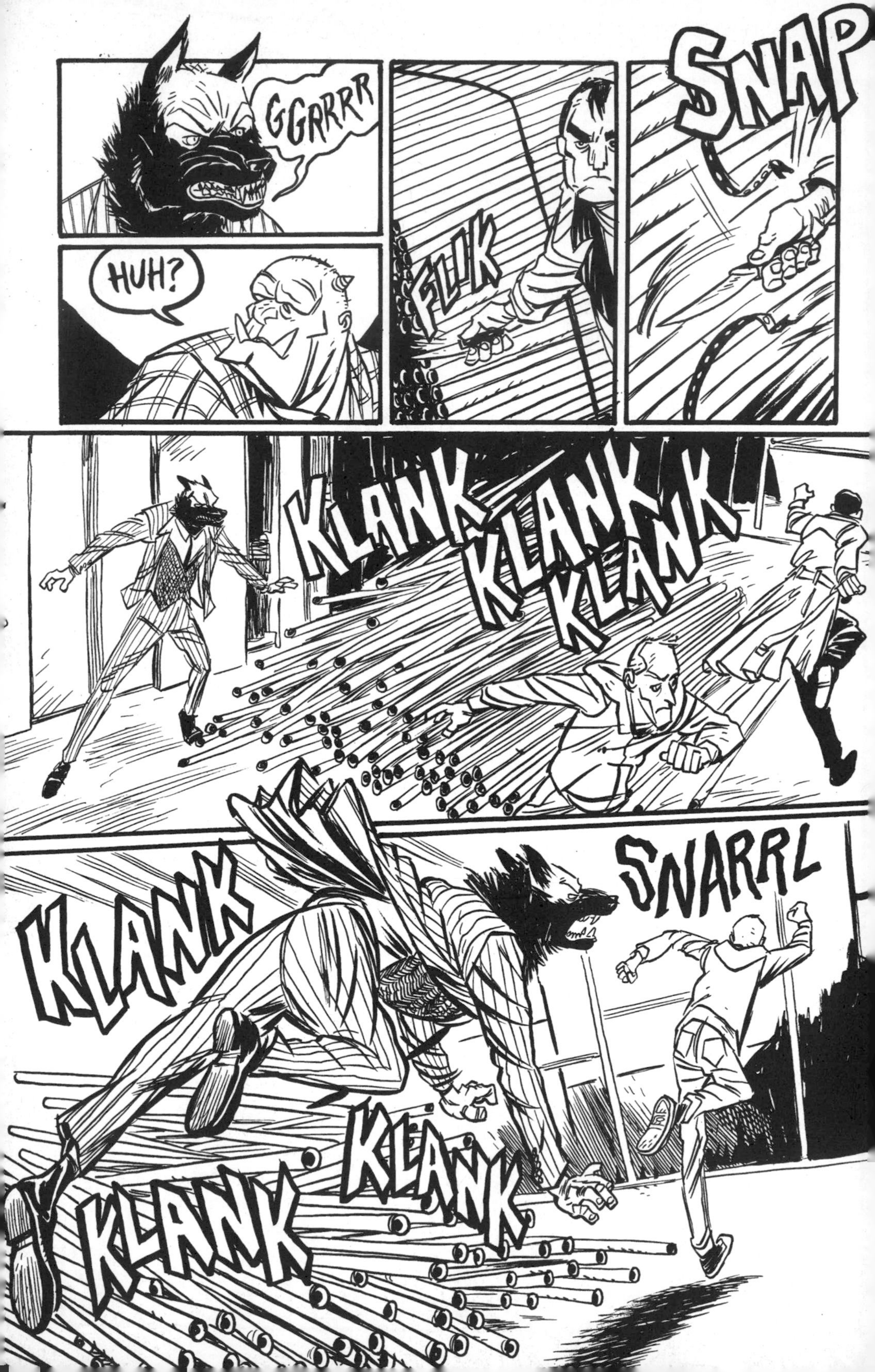
GGRRRR
HUH?
FLIK
SNAP
KLANK
KLANK
KLANK
KLANK
SNARRL
KLANK
KLANK

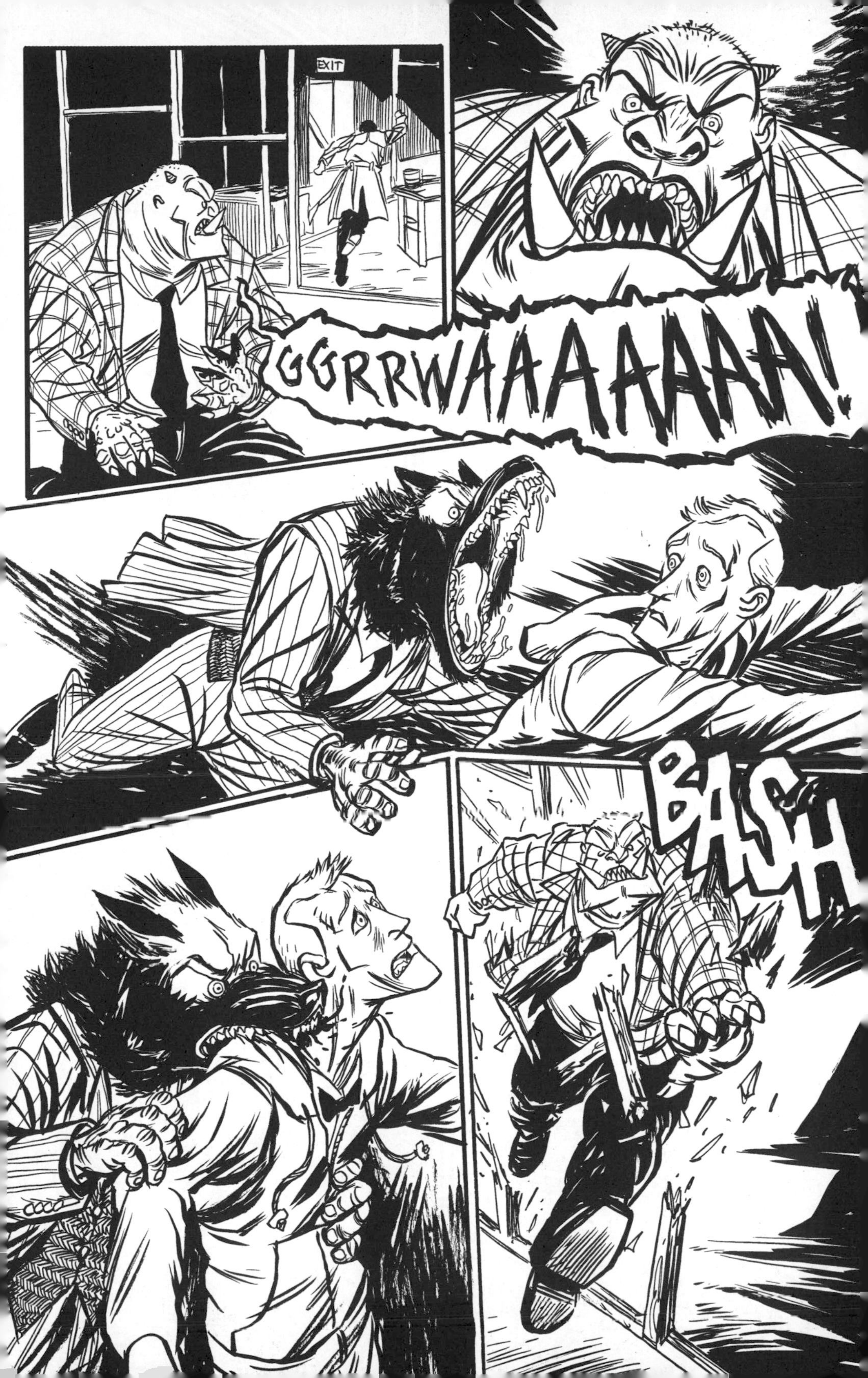
EXIT
GGRRWAAAAAAA!
BASH

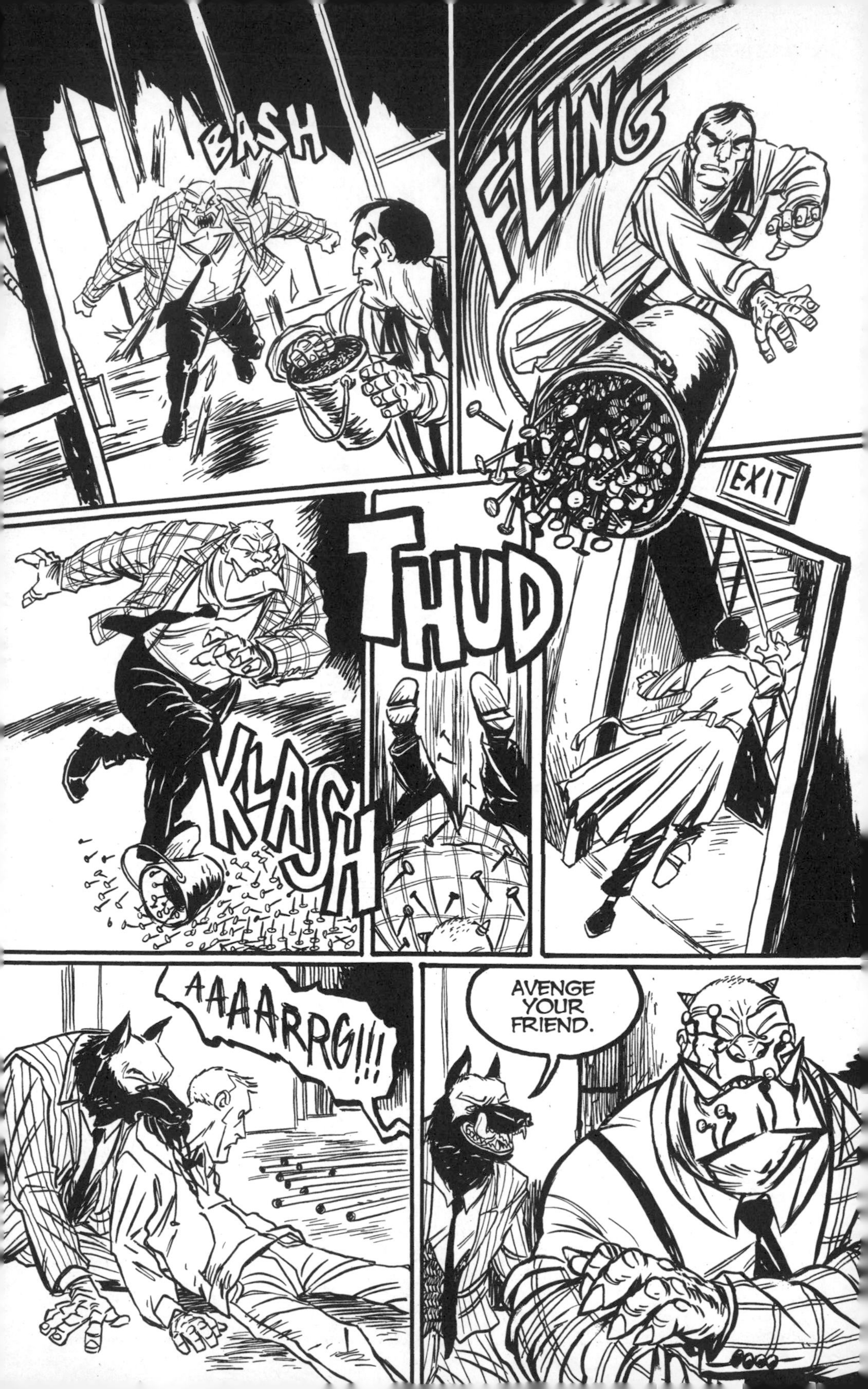
BASH
FLING
EXIT
THUD
KLASH
AAAARRG!!!
AVENGE YOUR FRIEND.

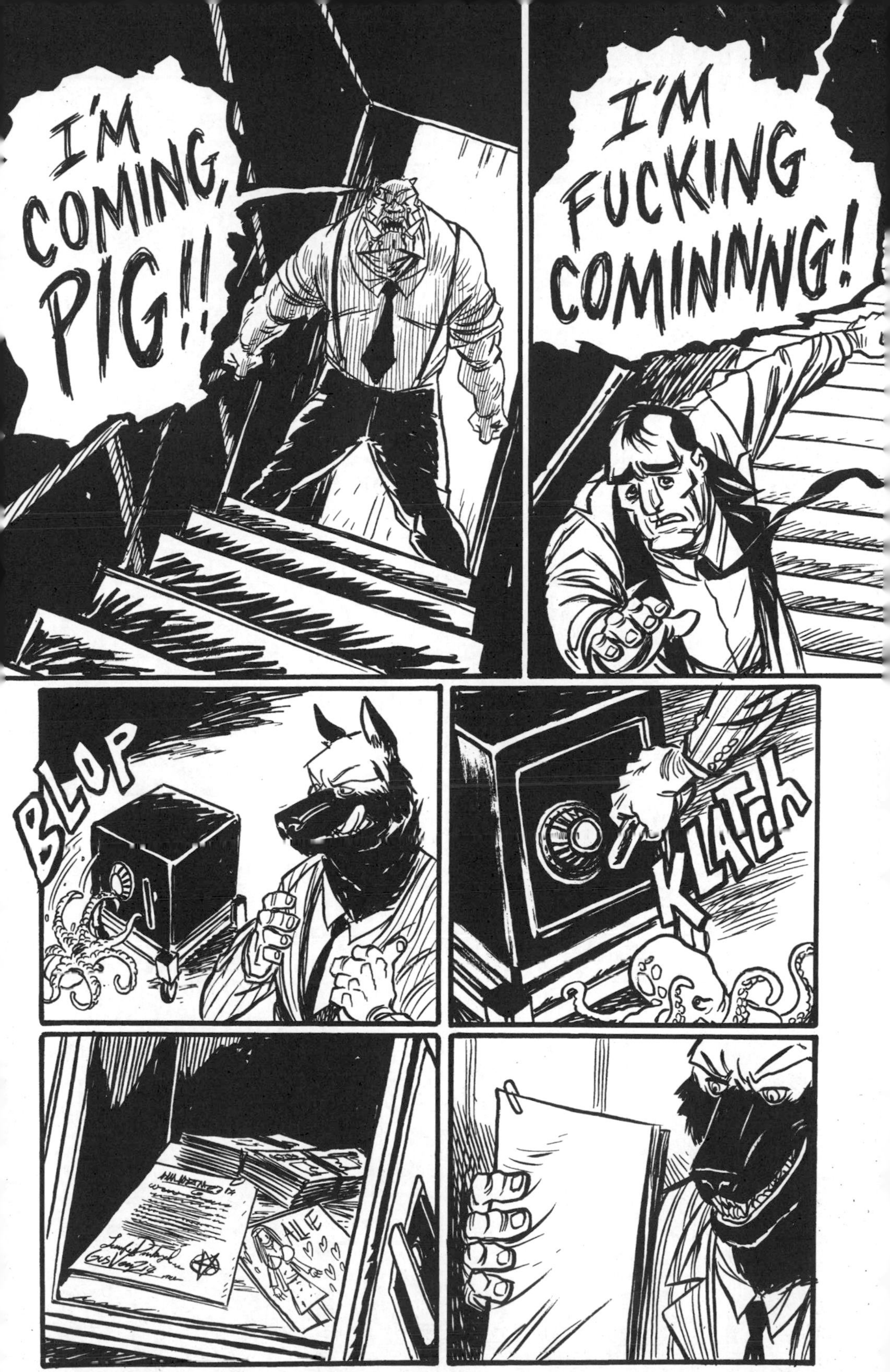
I'M COMING, PIG!!
I'M FUCKING COMINNNG!
BLOP
KLATCH
ALLIE

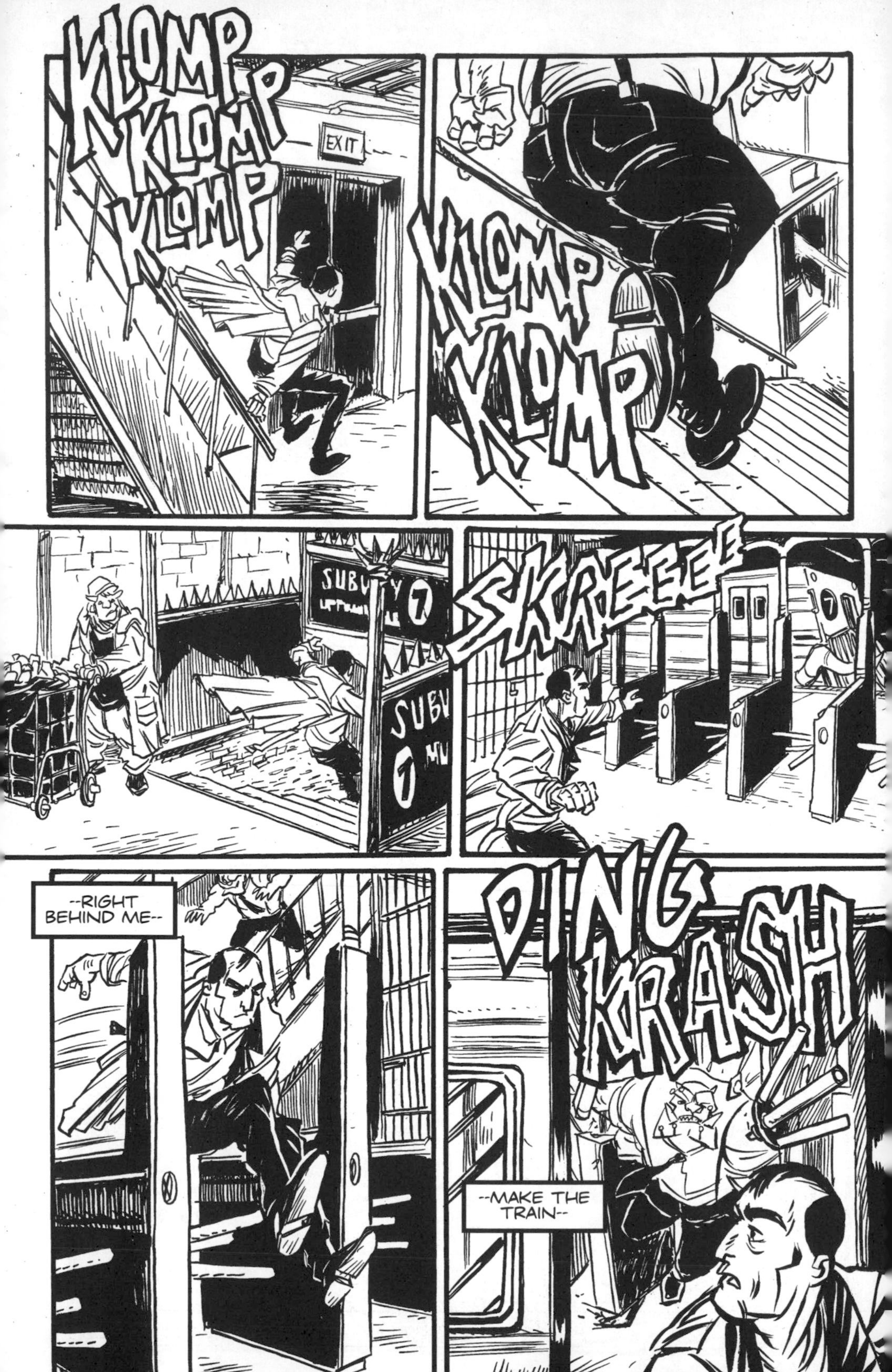
KLOMP KLOMP KLOMP
EXIT
KLOMP KLOMP
SKREEEE
--RIGHT BEHIND ME--
DING KRASH
--MAKE THE TRAIN--

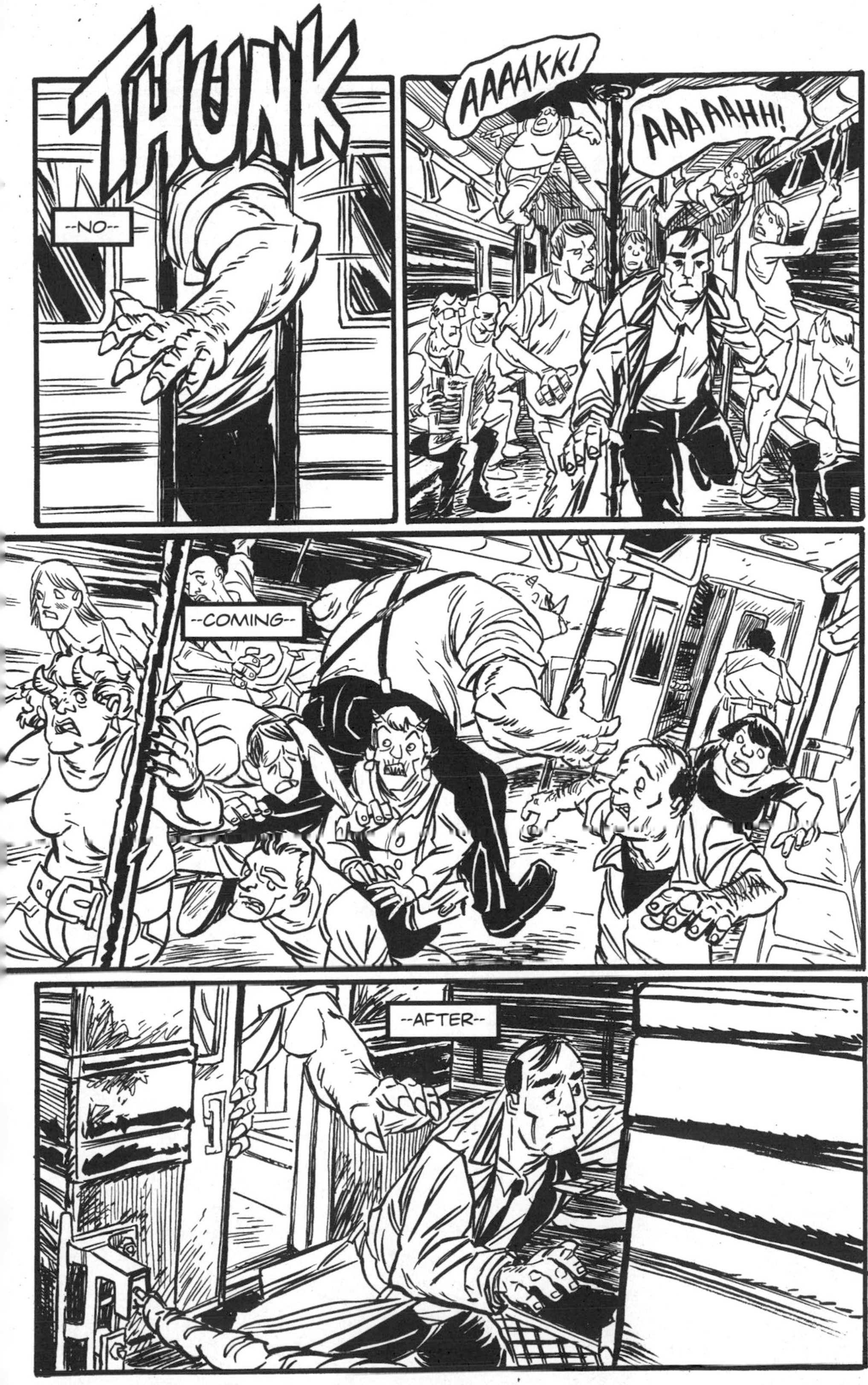
THUNK
--NO--
AAAAKK!
AAAAHH!
--COMING--
--AFTER--

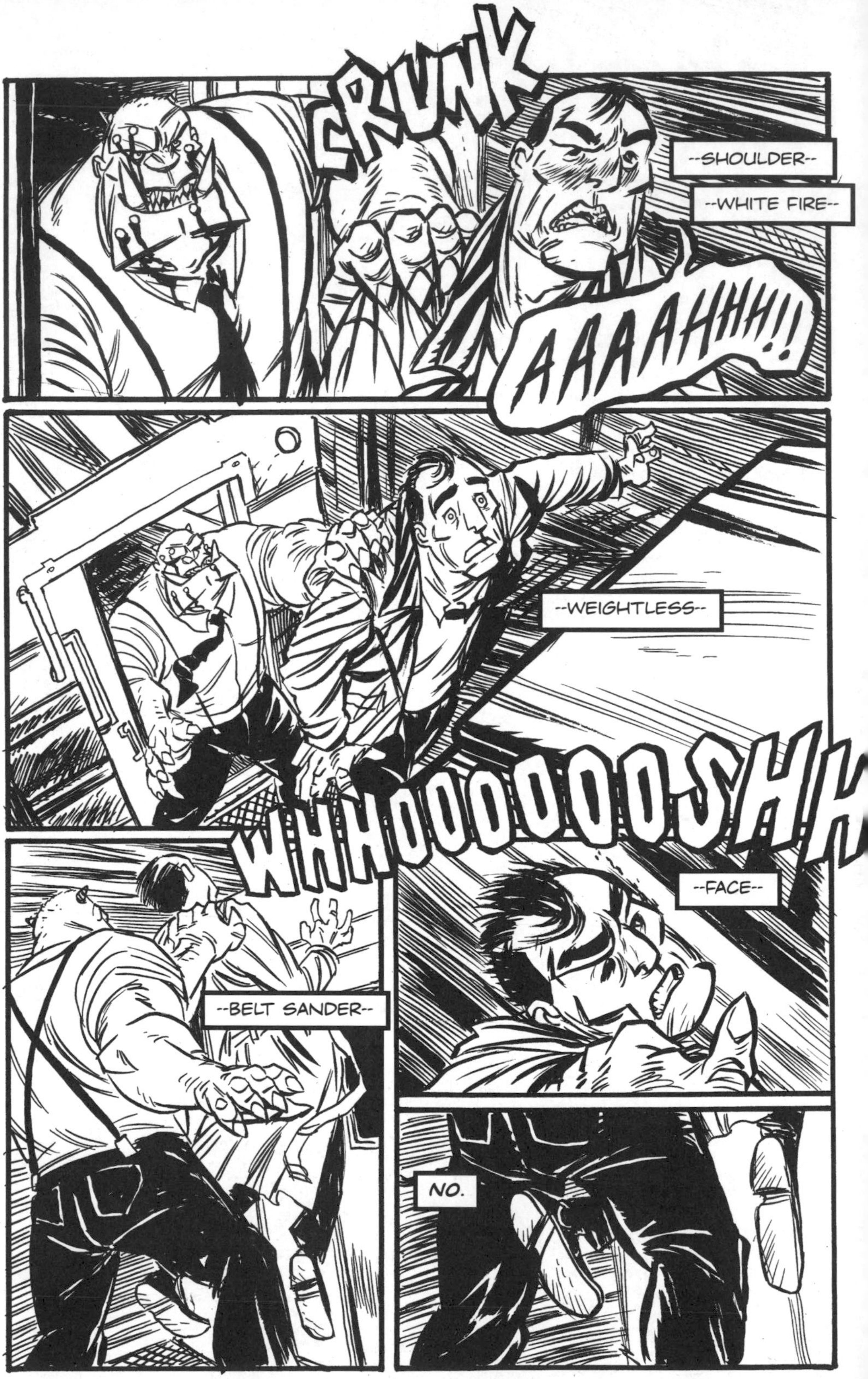
CRUNK
--SHOULDER--
--WHITE FIRE--
AAAAHHH!!
--WEIGHTLESS--
WHHOOOOOOOOSHH
--BELT SANDER--
--FACE--
NO.

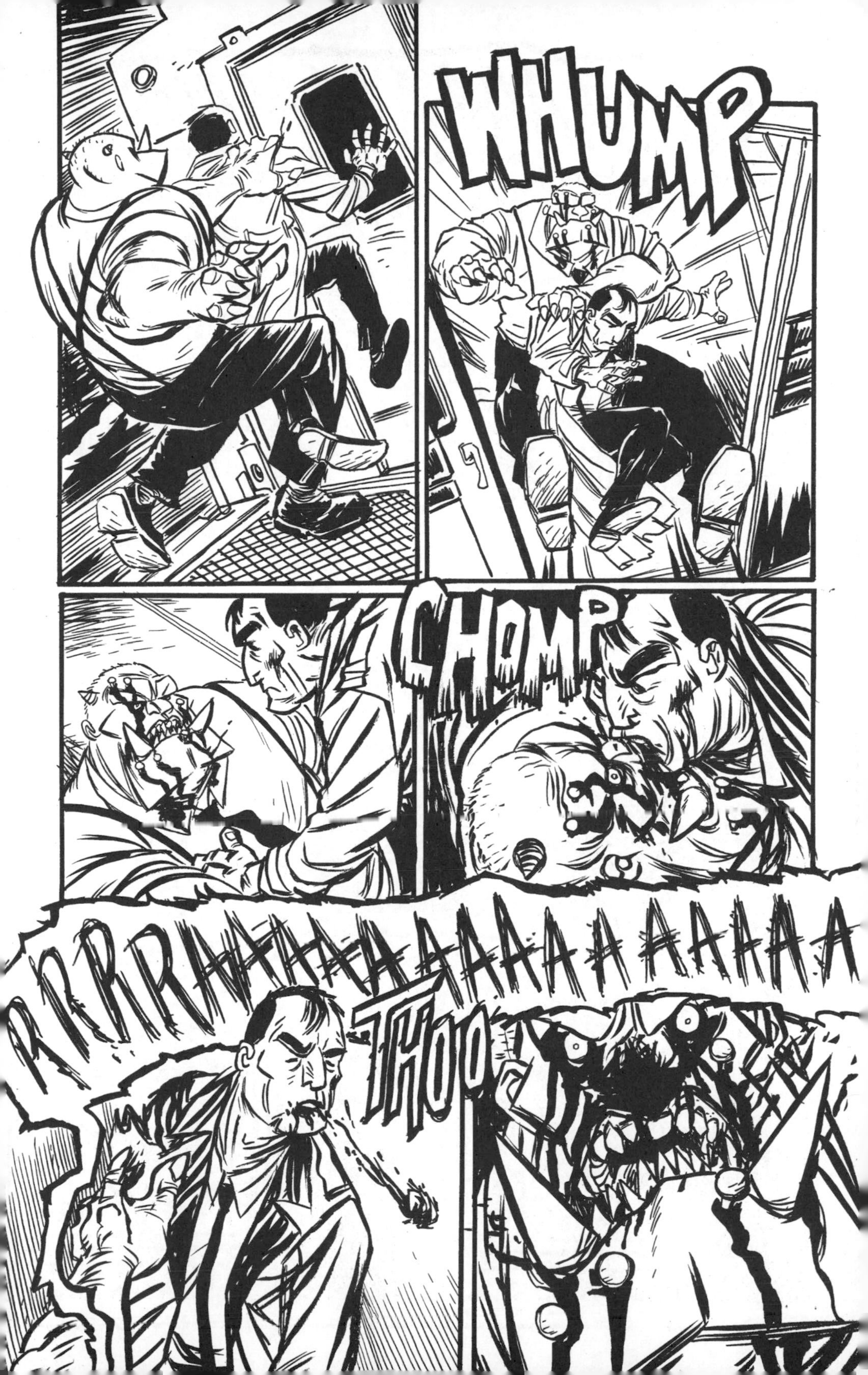
WHUMP
CHOMP
RRRRRAAAAAAAAAAAAAAAA
THOO

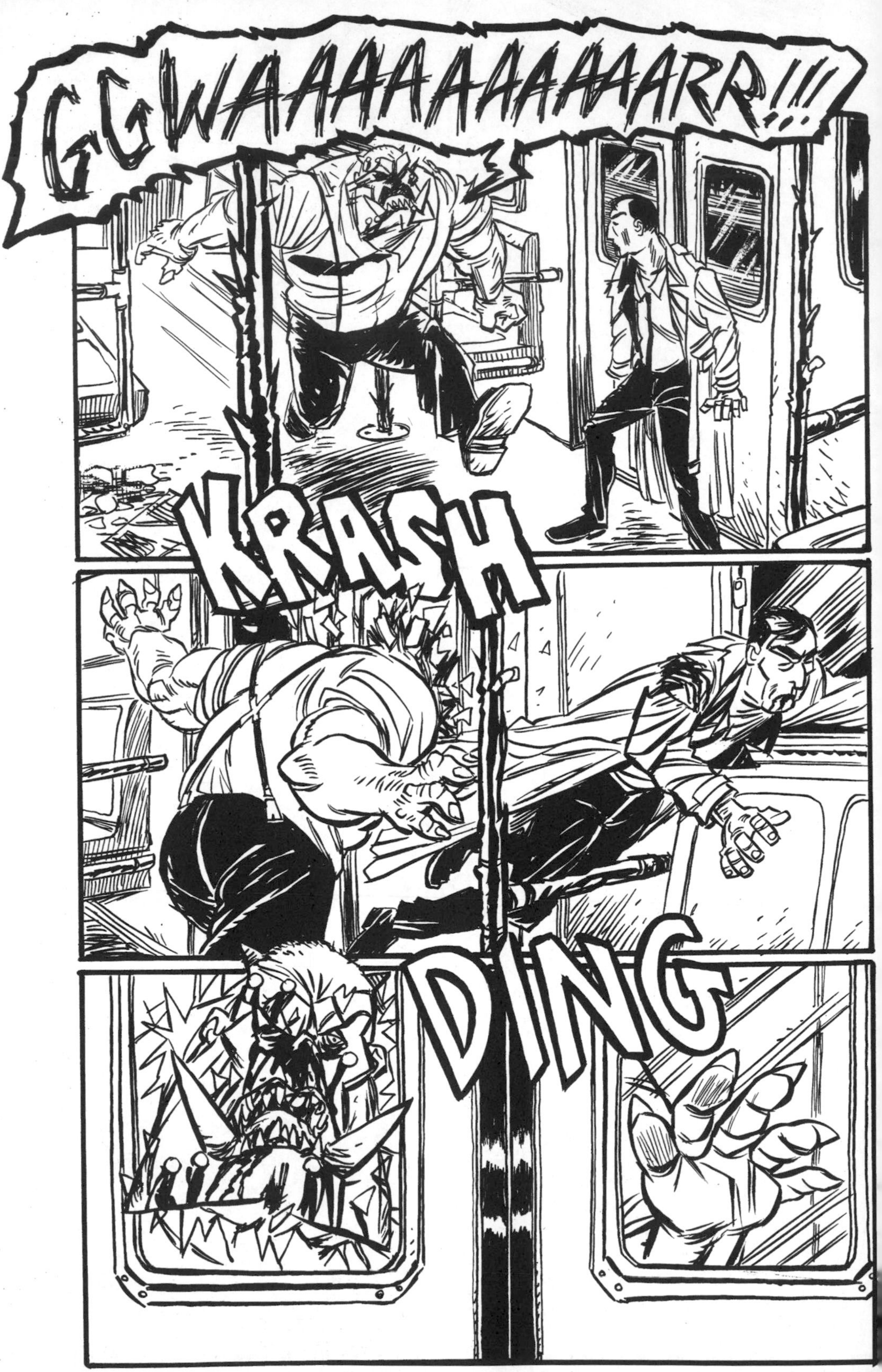
GGWAAAAAAAAAARR!!!
KRASH
DING

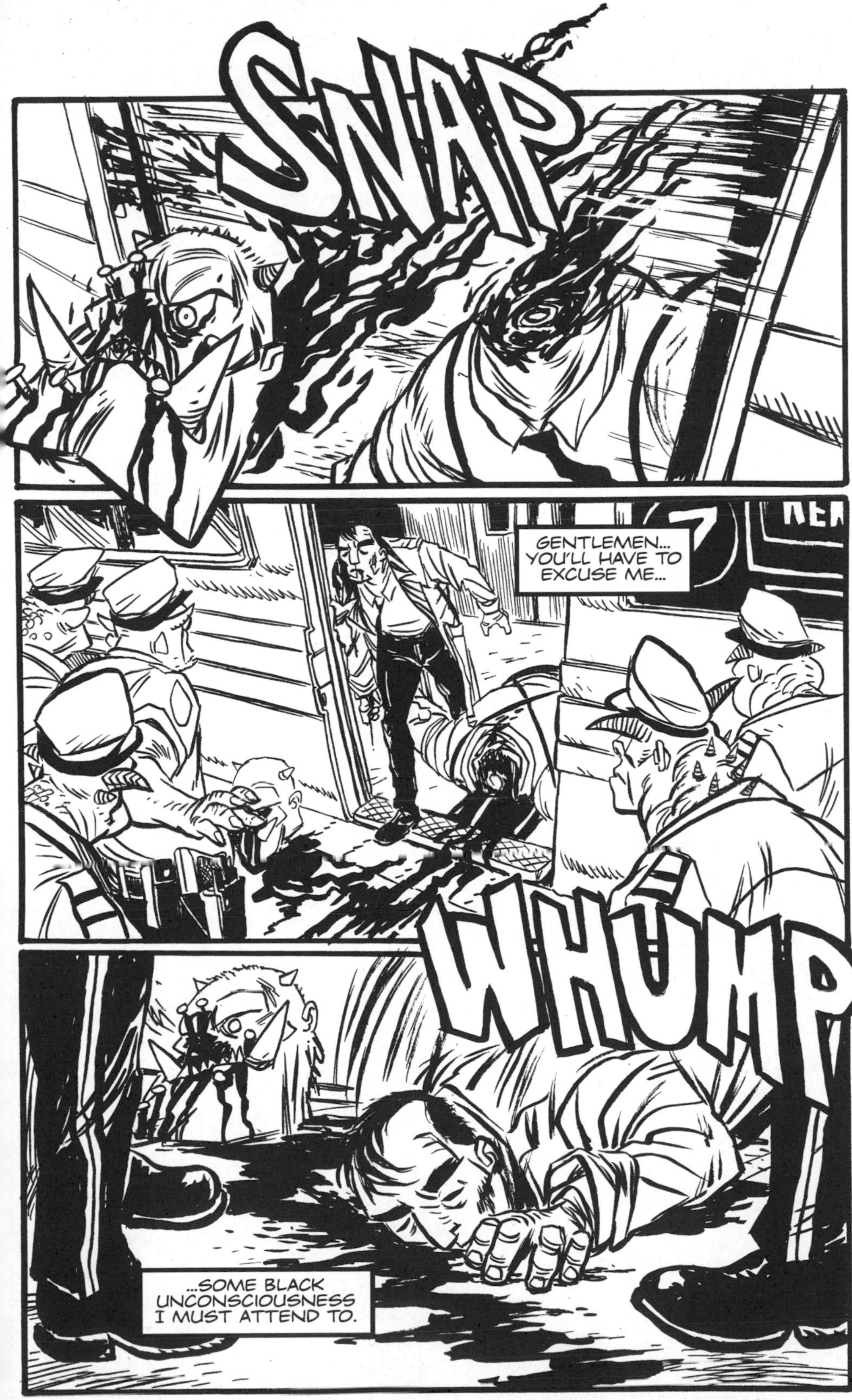
SNAP
GENTLEMEN... YOU'LL HAVE TO EXCUSE ME...
WHUMP
...SOME BLACK UNCONSCIOUSNESS I MUST ATTEND TO.

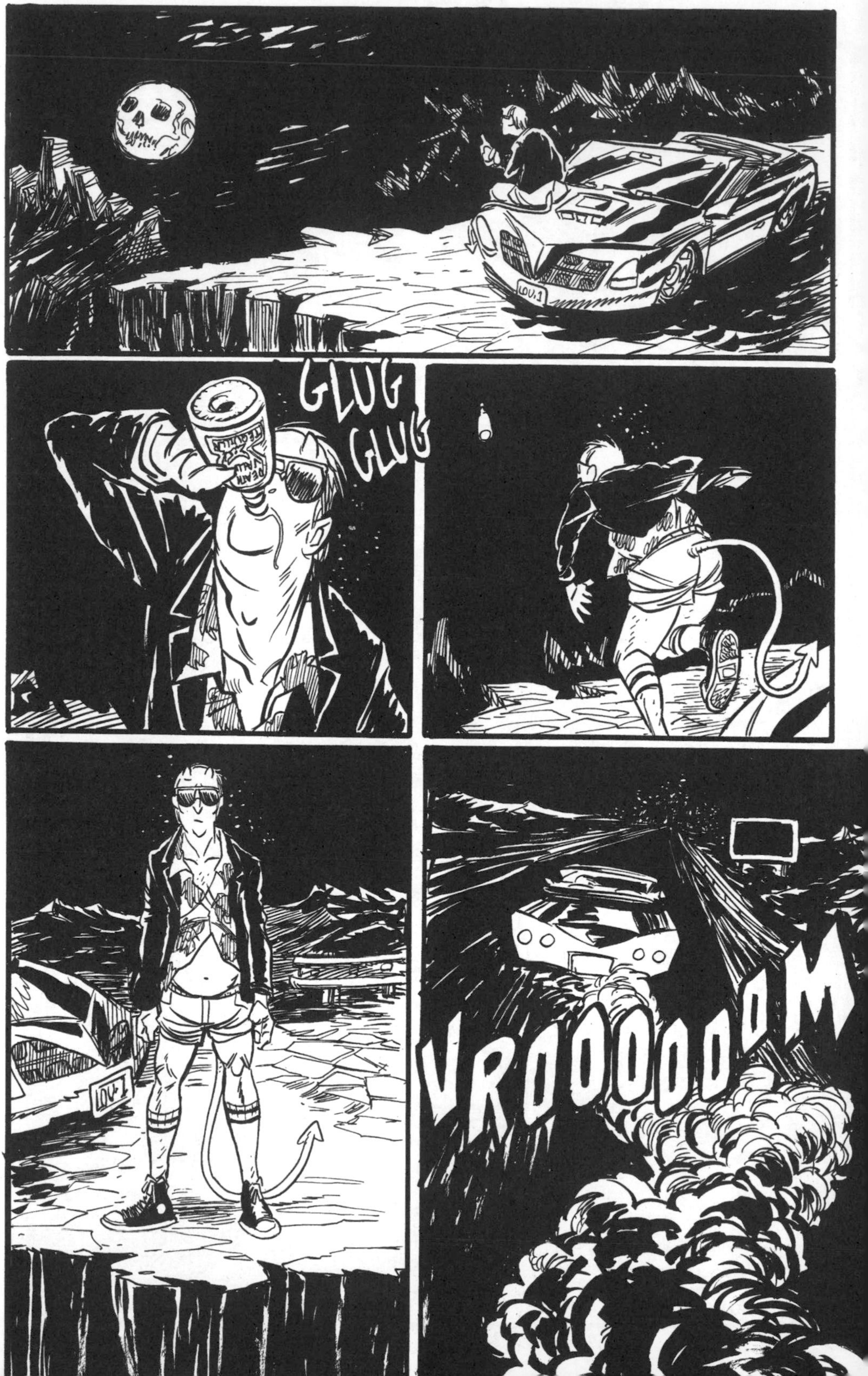
LOV.1
GLUG
GLUG
LOV-1
VROOOOOOM

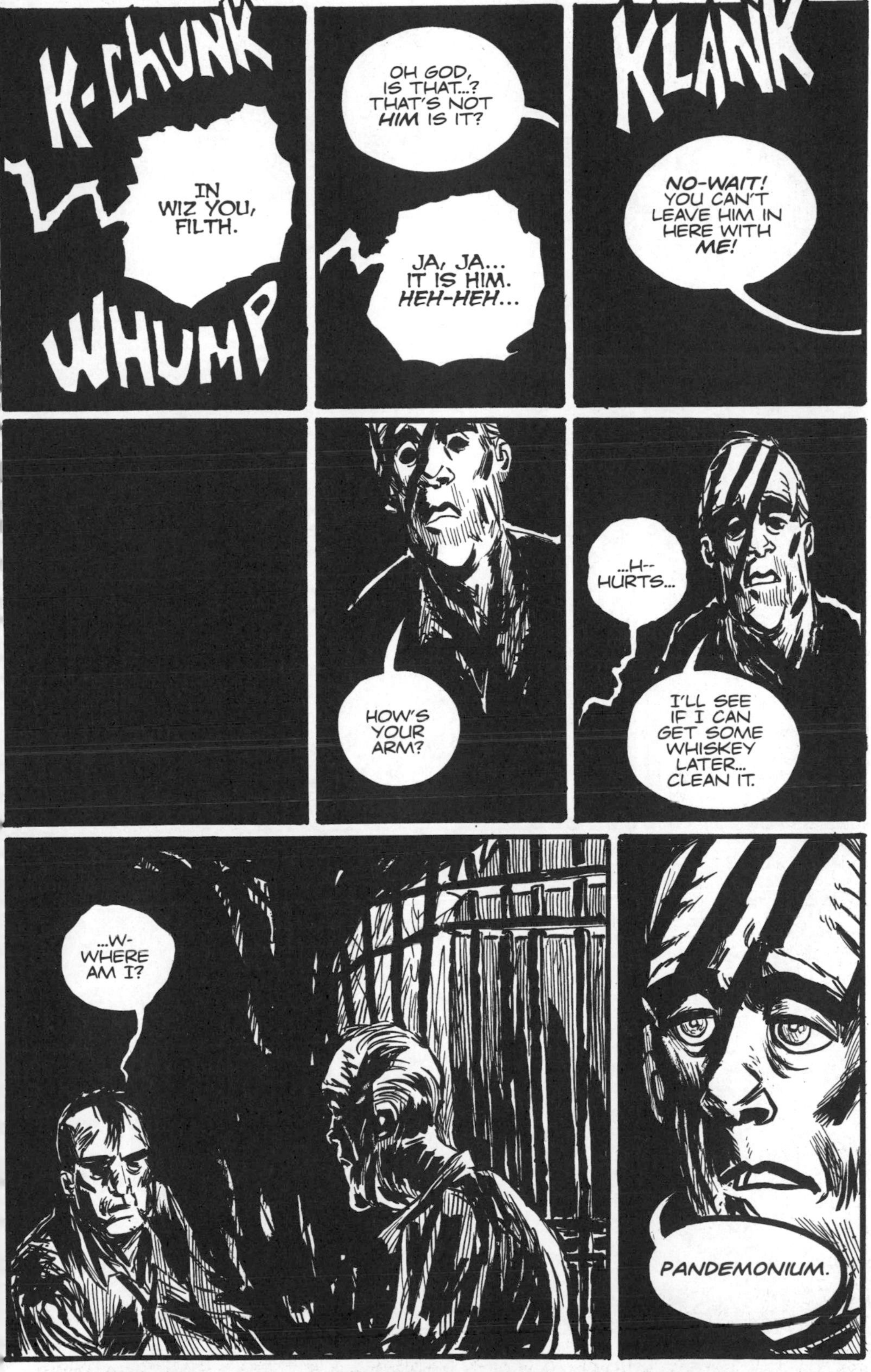
K-CHUNK
IN WIZ YOU, FILTH.
WHUMP
OH GOD, IS THAT...? THAT'S NOT HIM IS IT?
JA, JA... IT IS HIM. HEH-HEH...
KLANK
NO-WAIT! YOU CAN'T LEAVE HIM IN HERE WITH ME!
HOW'S YOUR ARM?
...H-HURTS...
I'LL SEE IF I CAN GET SOME WHISKEY LATER... CLEAN IT.
...W-WHERE AM I?
PANDEMONIUM.

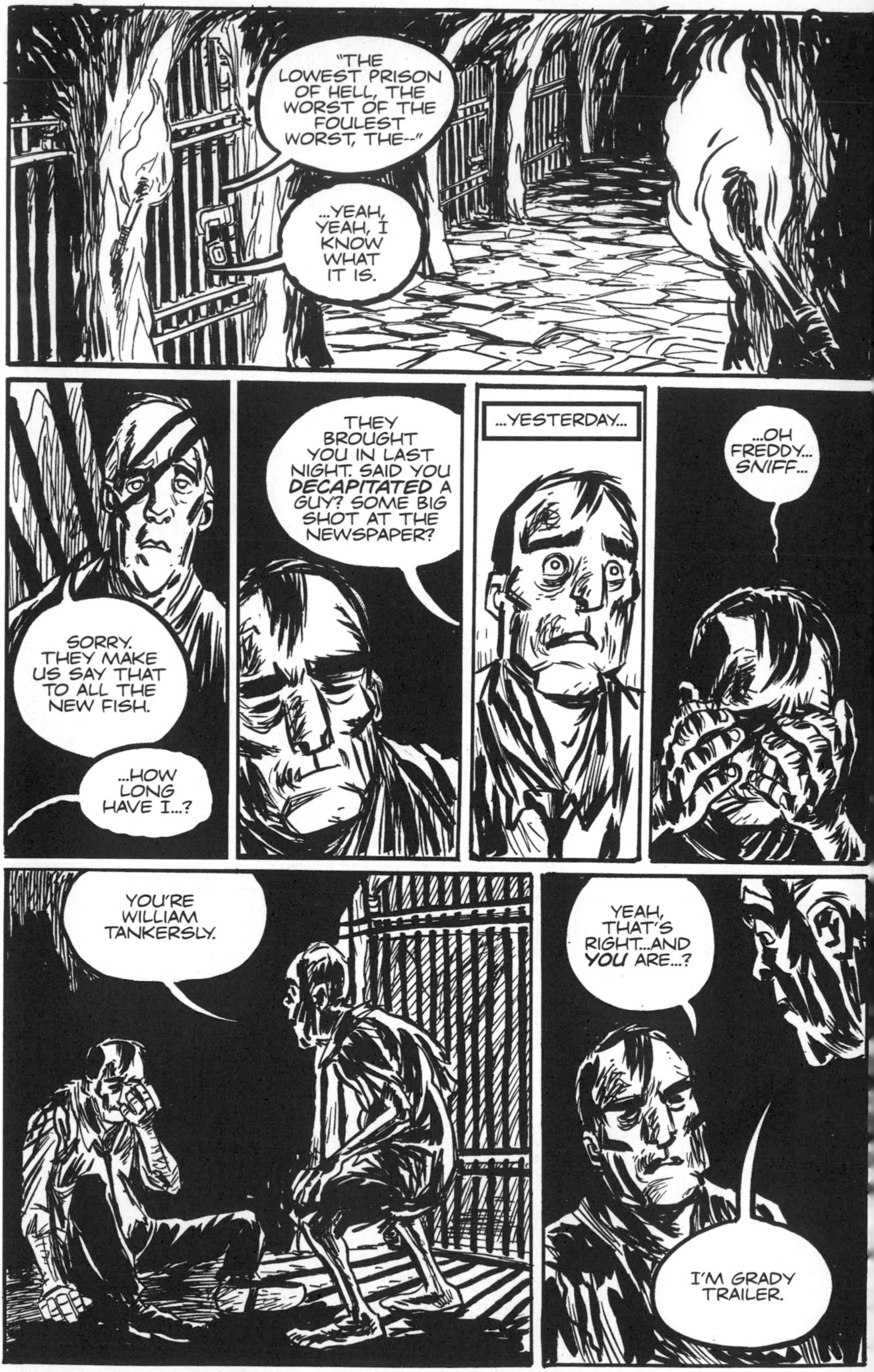
"THE LOWEST PRISON OF HELL, THE WORST OF THE FOULEST WORST, THE--"
...YEAH, YEAH, I KNOW WHAT IT IS.
SORRY. THEY MAKE US SAY THAT TO ALL THE NEW FISH.
...HOW LONG HAVE I...?
THEY BROUGHT YOU IN LAST NIGHT. SAID YOU *DECAPITATED* A GUY? SOME BIG SHOT AT THE NEWSPAPER?
...YESTERDAY...
...OH FREDDY... SNIFF...
YOU'RE WILLIAM TANKERSLY.
YEAH, THAT'S RIGHT...AND *YOU* ARE...?
I'M GRADY TRAILER.

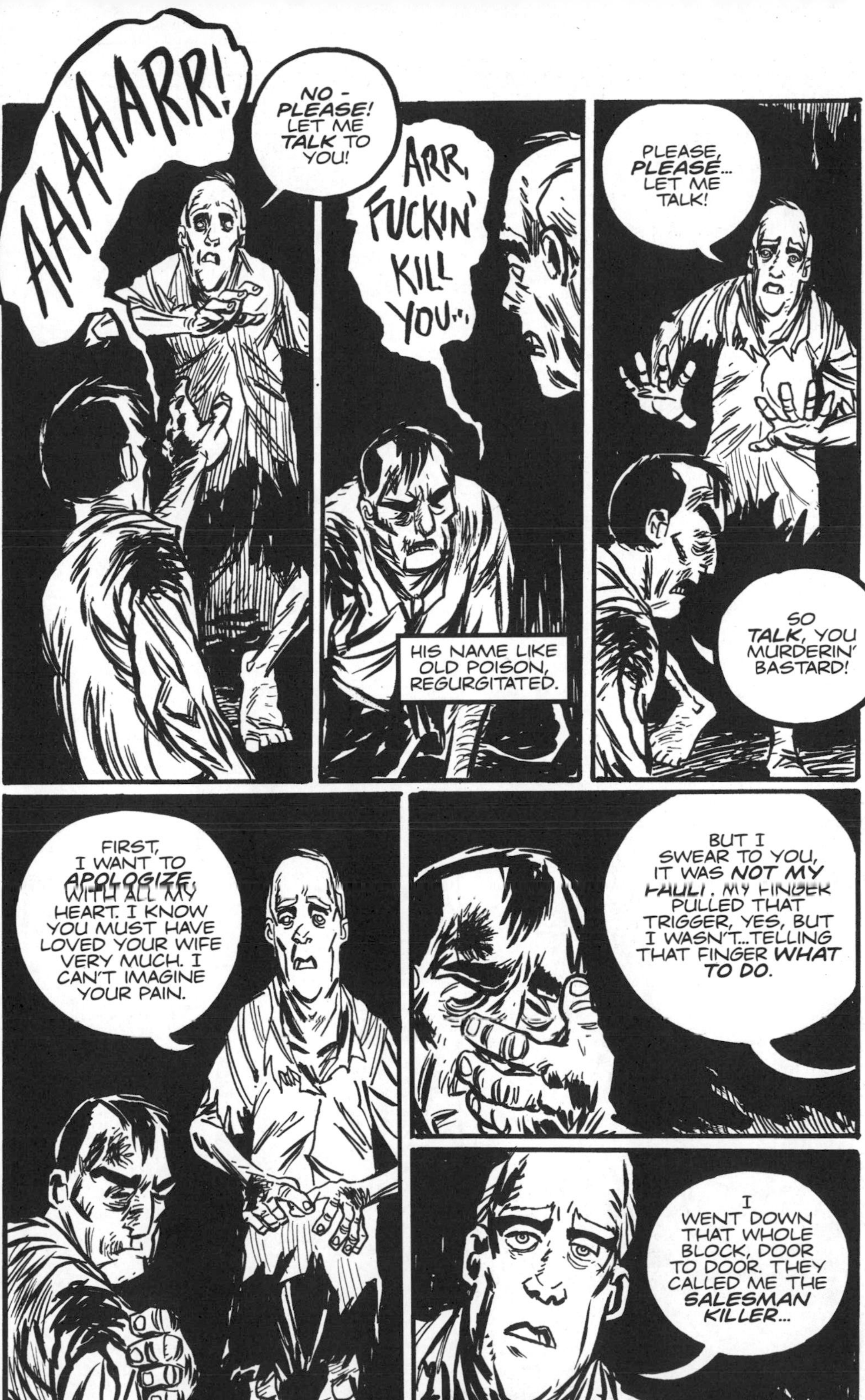
AAAAARR!
NO - PLEASE! LET ME TALK TO YOU!
ARR, FUCKIN' KILL YOU...
HIS NAME LIKE OLD POISON, REGURGITATED.
PLEASE, PLEASE... LET ME TALK!
SO TALK, YOU MURDERIN' BASTARD!
FIRST, I WANT TO APOLOGIZE, WITH ALL MY HEART. I KNOW YOU MUST HAVE LOVED YOUR WIFE VERY MUCH. I CAN'T IMAGINE YOUR PAIN.
BUT I SWEAR TO YOU, IT WAS NOT MY FAULT. MY FINGER PULLED THAT TRIGGER, YES, BUT I WASN'T...TELLING THAT FINGER WHAT TO DO.
I WENT DOWN THAT WHOLE BLOCK, DOOR TO DOOR. THEY CALLED ME THE SALESMAN KILLER...

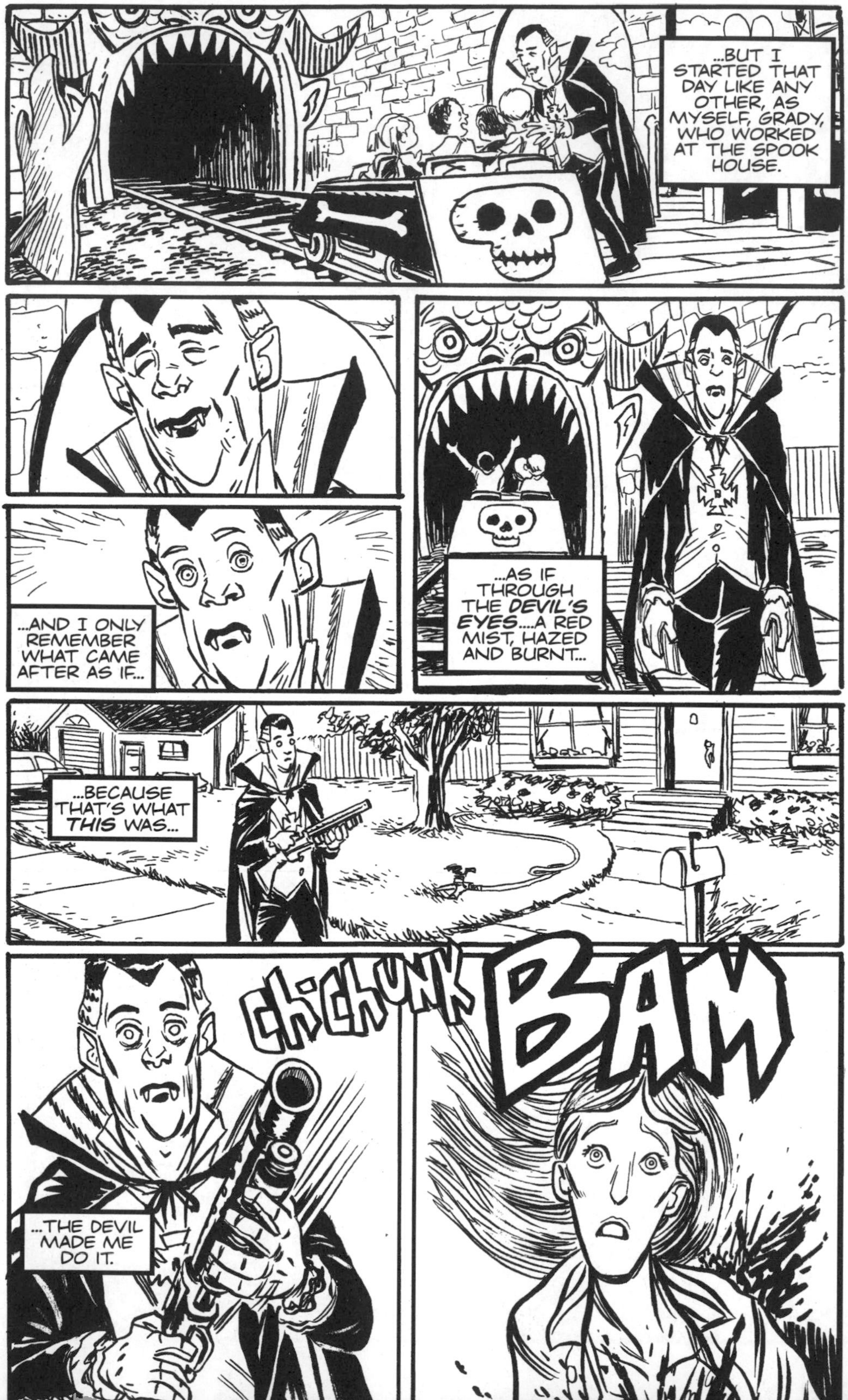
...BUT I STARTED THAT DAY LIKE ANY OTHER, AS MYSELF, GRADY, WHO WORKED AT THE SPOOK HOUSE.
...AND I ONLY REMEMBER WHAT CAME AFTER AS IF...
...AS IF THROUGH THE DEVIL'S EYES....A RED MIST, HAZED AND BURNT...
...BECAUSE THAT'S WHAT THIS WAS...
...THE DEVIL MADE ME DO IT.
CHi-CHUNK
BAM

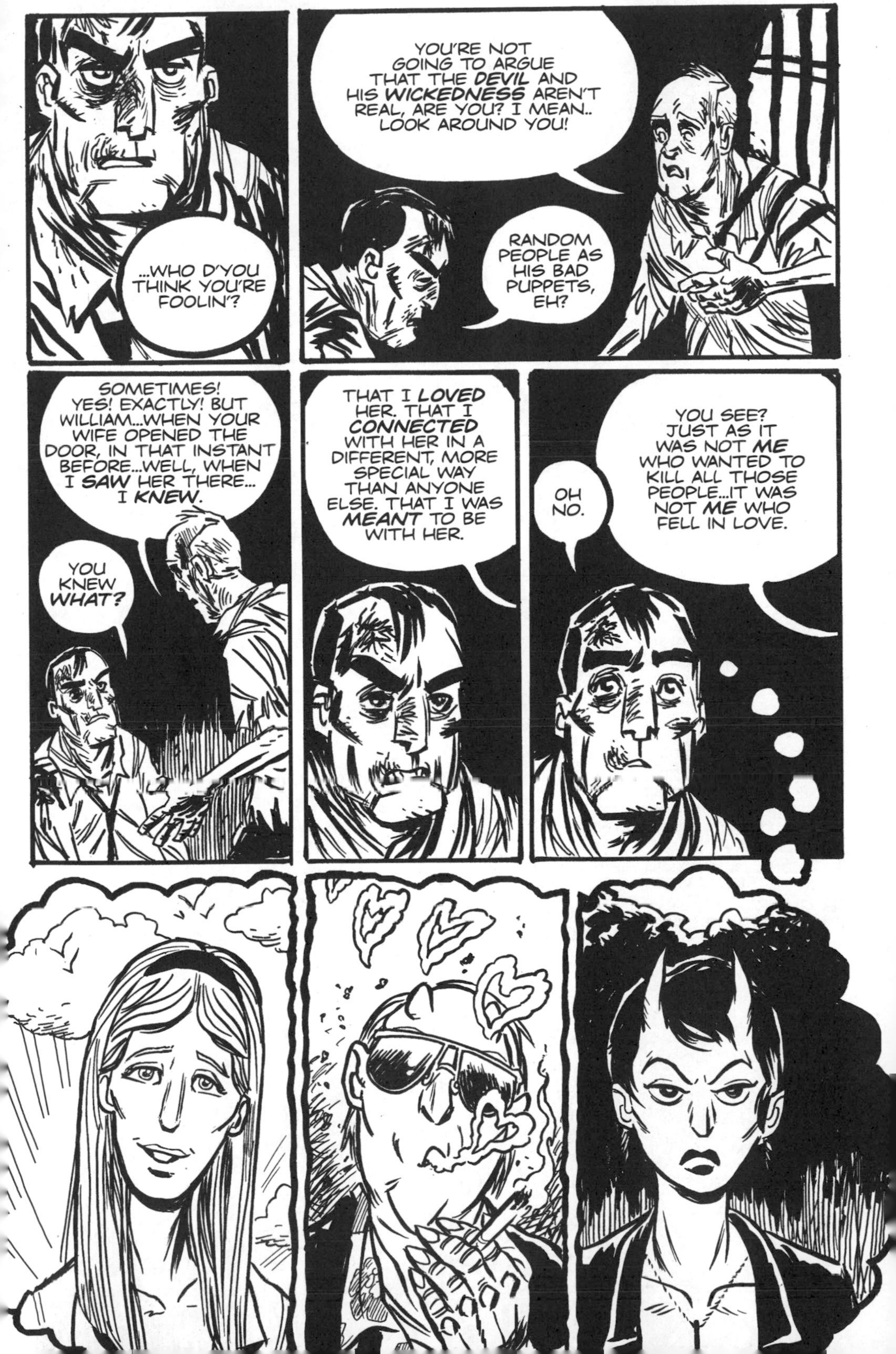
...WHO D'YOU THINK YOU'RE FOOLIN'?
YOU'RE NOT GOING TO ARGUE THAT THE DEVIL AND HIS WICKEDNESS AREN'T REAL, ARE YOU? I MEAN.. LOOK AROUND YOU!
RANDOM PEOPLE AS HIS BAD PUPPETS, EH?
SOMETIMES! YES! EXACTLY! BUT WILLIAM...WHEN YOUR WIFE OPENED THE DOOR, IN THAT INSTANT BEFORE...WELL, WHEN I SAW HER THERE... I KNEW.
YOU KNEW WHAT?
THAT I LOVED HER. THAT I CONNECTED WITH HER IN A DIFFERENT, MORE SPECIAL WAY THAN ANYONE ELSE. THAT I WAS MEANT TO BE WITH HER.
OH NO.
YOU SEE? JUST AS IT WAS NOT ME WHO WANTED TO KILL ALL THOSE PEOPLE...IT WAS NOT ME WHO FELL IN LOVE.

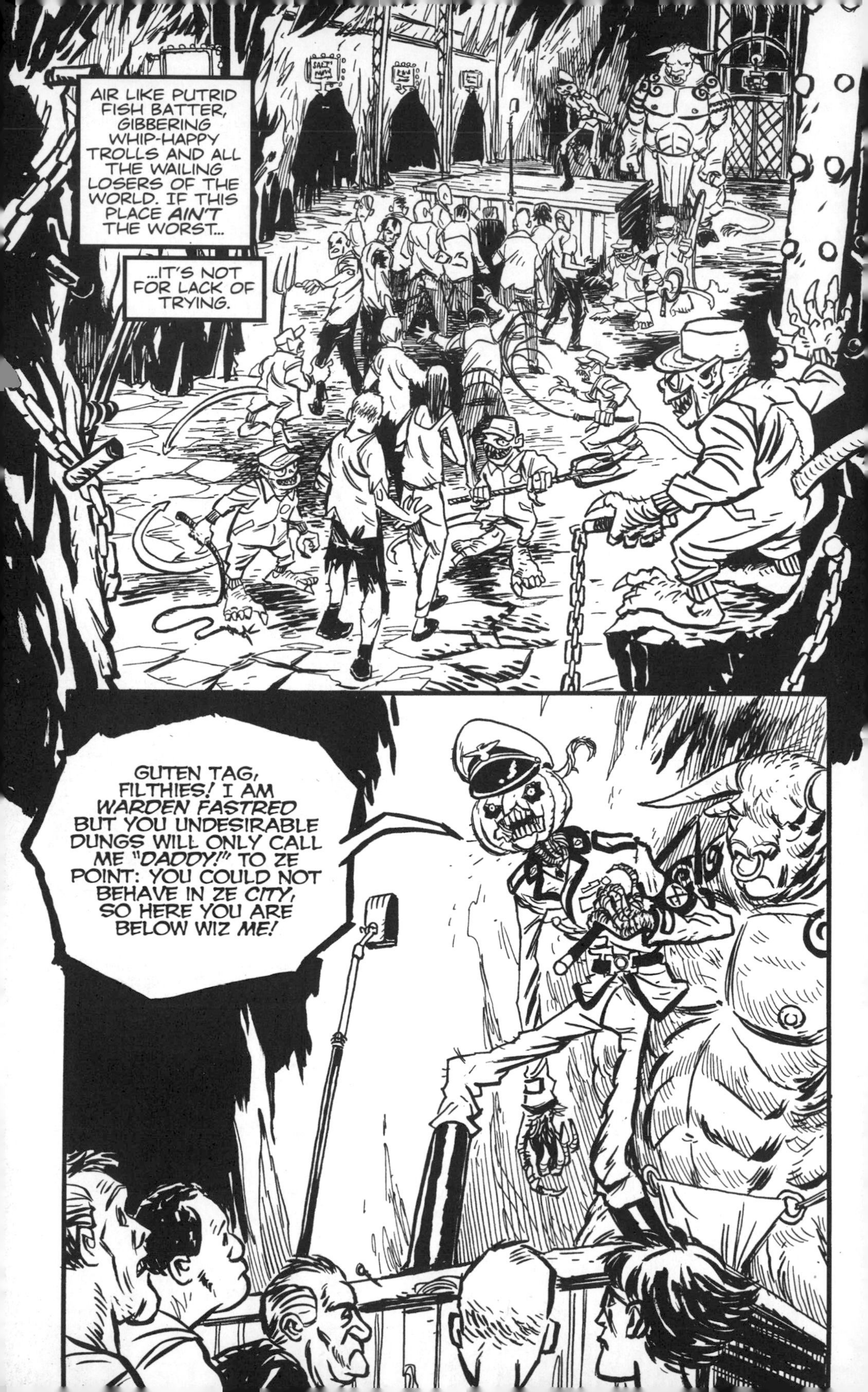
AIR LIKE PUTRID FISH BATTER, GIBBERING WHIP-HAPPY TROLLS AND ALL THE WAILING LOSERS OF THE WORLD. IF THIS PLACE AIN'T THE WORST...
...IT'S NOT FOR LACK OF TRYING.
GUTEN TAG, FILTHIES! I AM WARDEN FASTRED BUT YOU UNDESIRABLE DUNGS WILL ONLY CALL ME "DADDY!" TO ZE POINT: YOU COULD NOT BEHAVE IN ZE CITY, SO HERE YOU ARE BELOW WIZ ME!

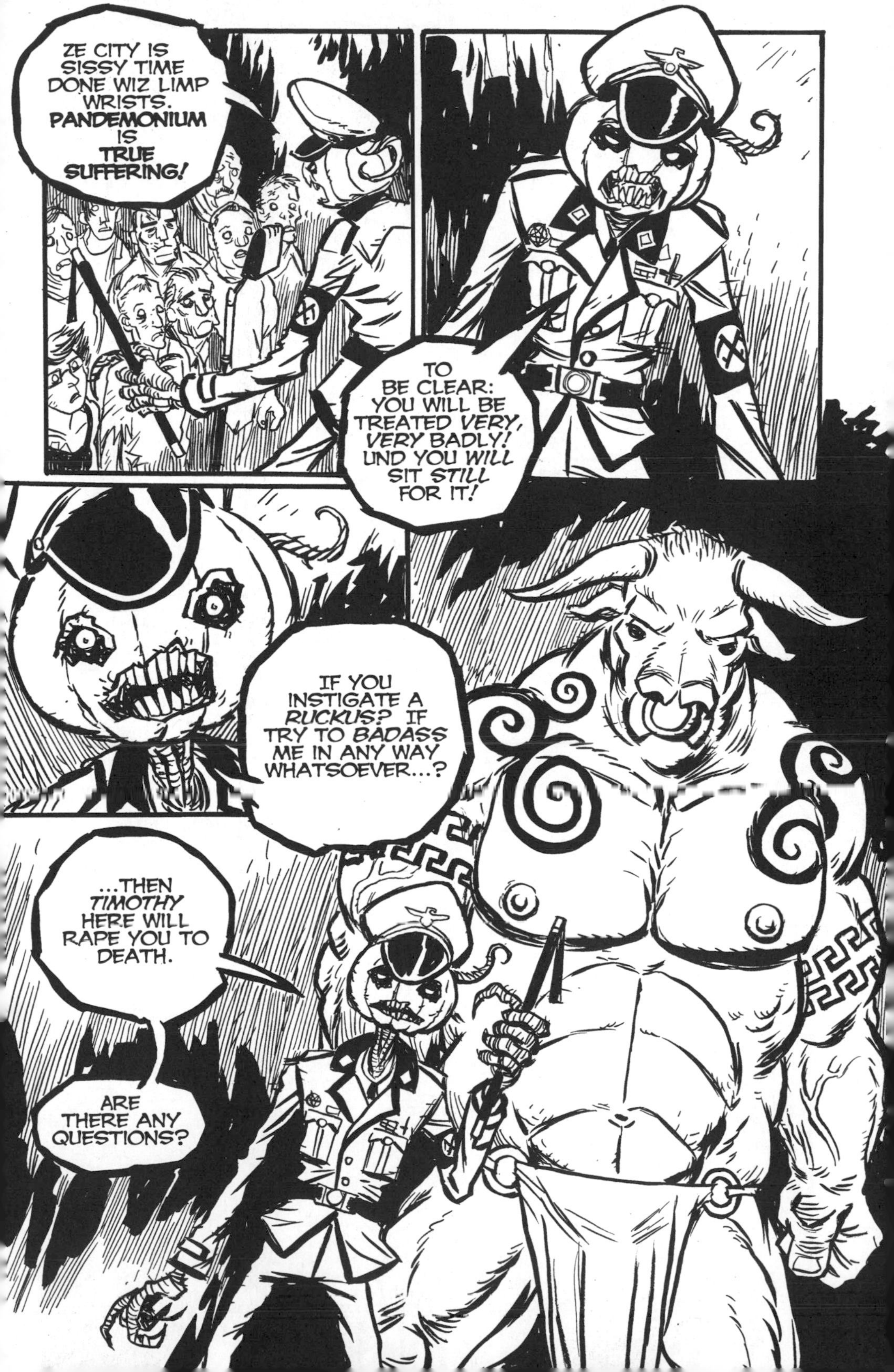
ZE CITY IS SISSY TIME DONE WIZ LIMP WRISTS. PANDEMONIUM IS TRUE SUFFERING!
TO BE CLEAR: YOU WILL BE TREATED VERY, VERY BADLY! UND YOU WILL SIT STILL FOR IT!
IF YOU INSTIGATE A RUCKUS? IF TRY TO BADASS ME IN ANY WAY WHATSOEVER...?
...THEN TIMOTHY HERE WILL RAPE YOU TO DEATH.
ARE THERE ANY QUESTIONS?

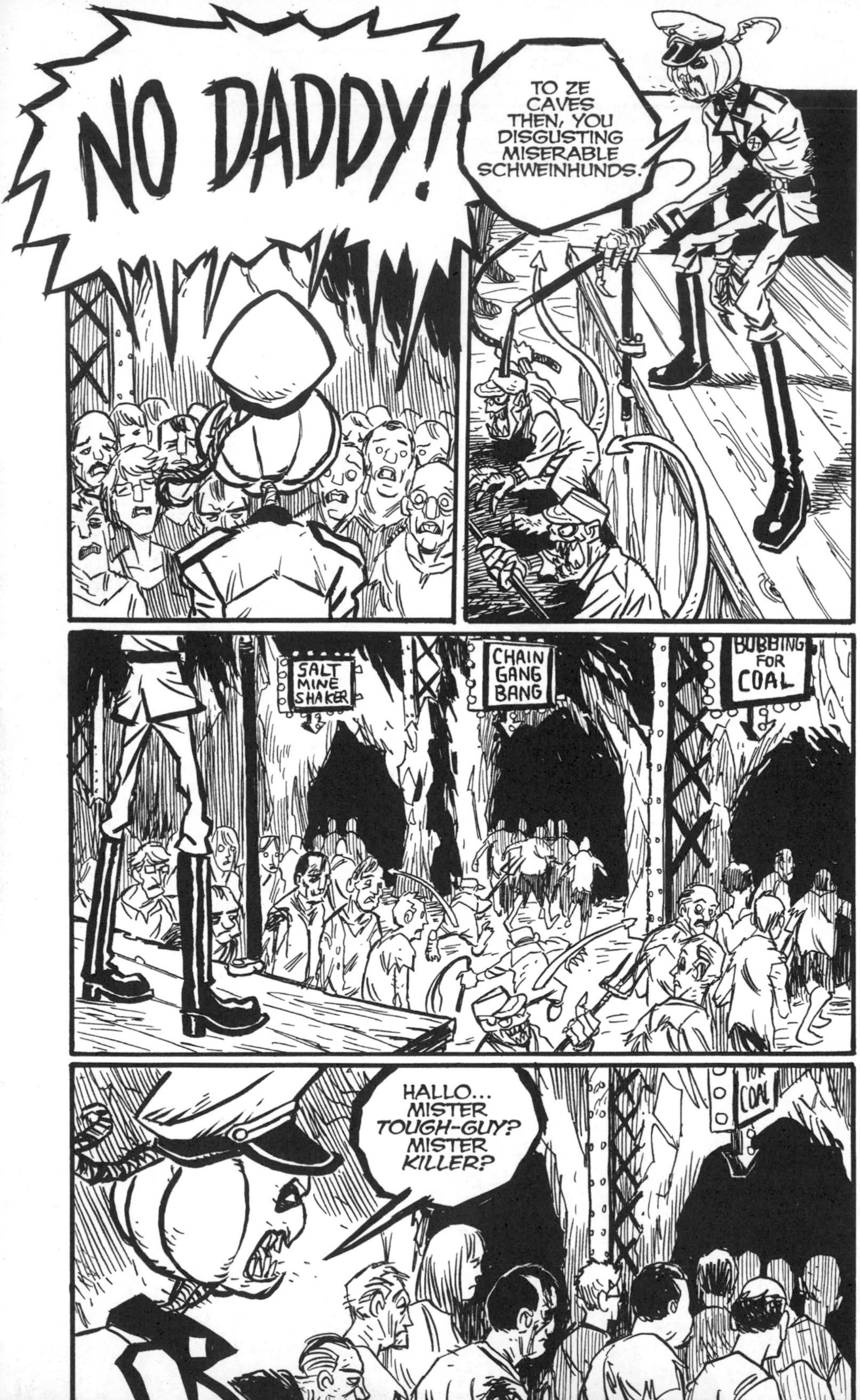
NO DADDY!
TO ZE CAVES THEN, YOU DISGUSTING MISERABLE SCHWEINHUNDS.
SALT MINE SHAKER
CHAIN GANG BANG
BOBBING FOR COAL
HALLO... MISTER TOUGH-GUY? MISTER KILLER?

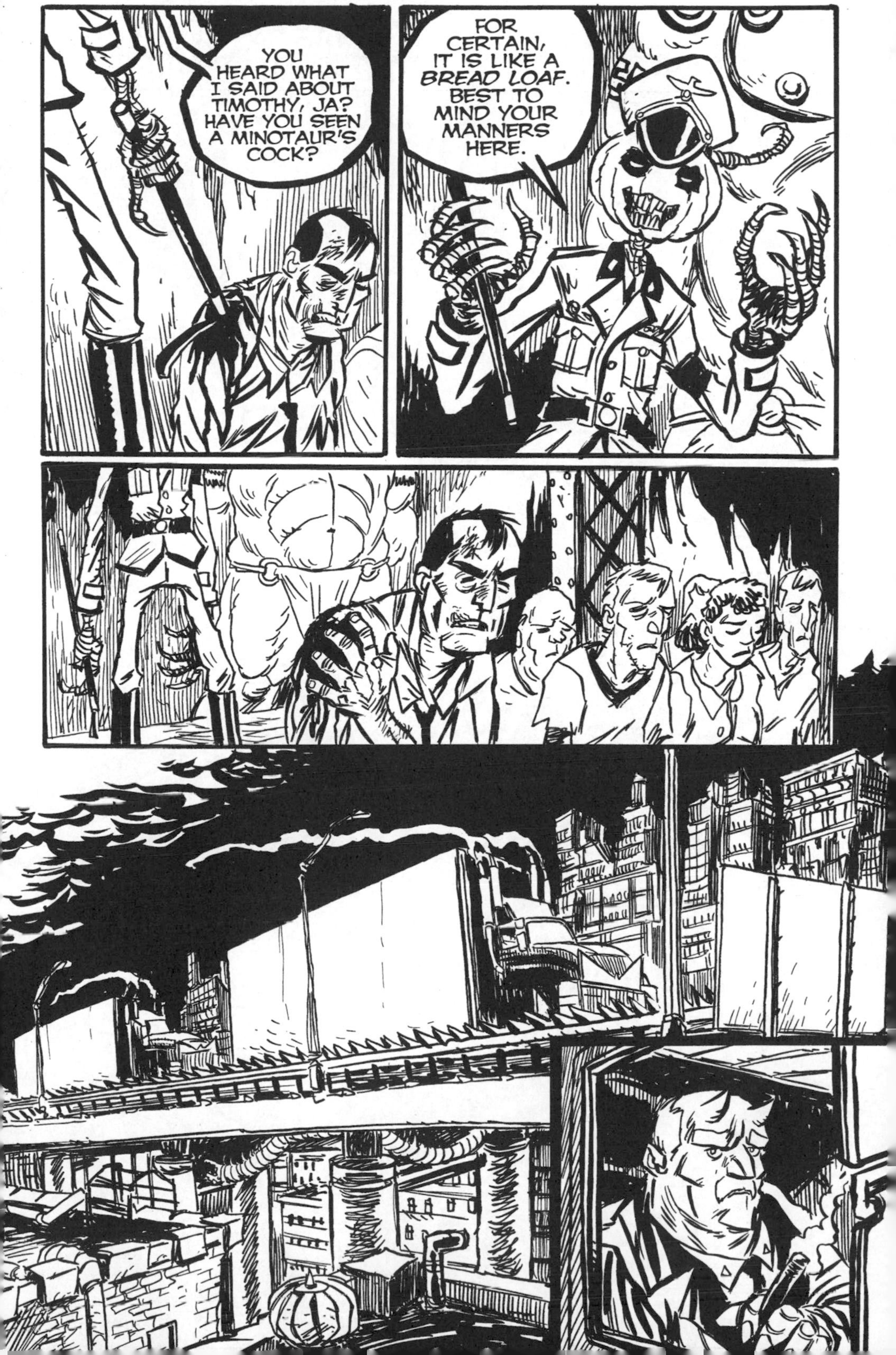
YOU HEARD WHAT I SAID ABOUT TIMOTHY, JA? HAVE YOU SEEN A MINOTAUR'S COCK?
FOR CERTAIN, IT IS LIKE A *BREAD LOAF*. BEST TO MIND YOUR MANNERS HERE.

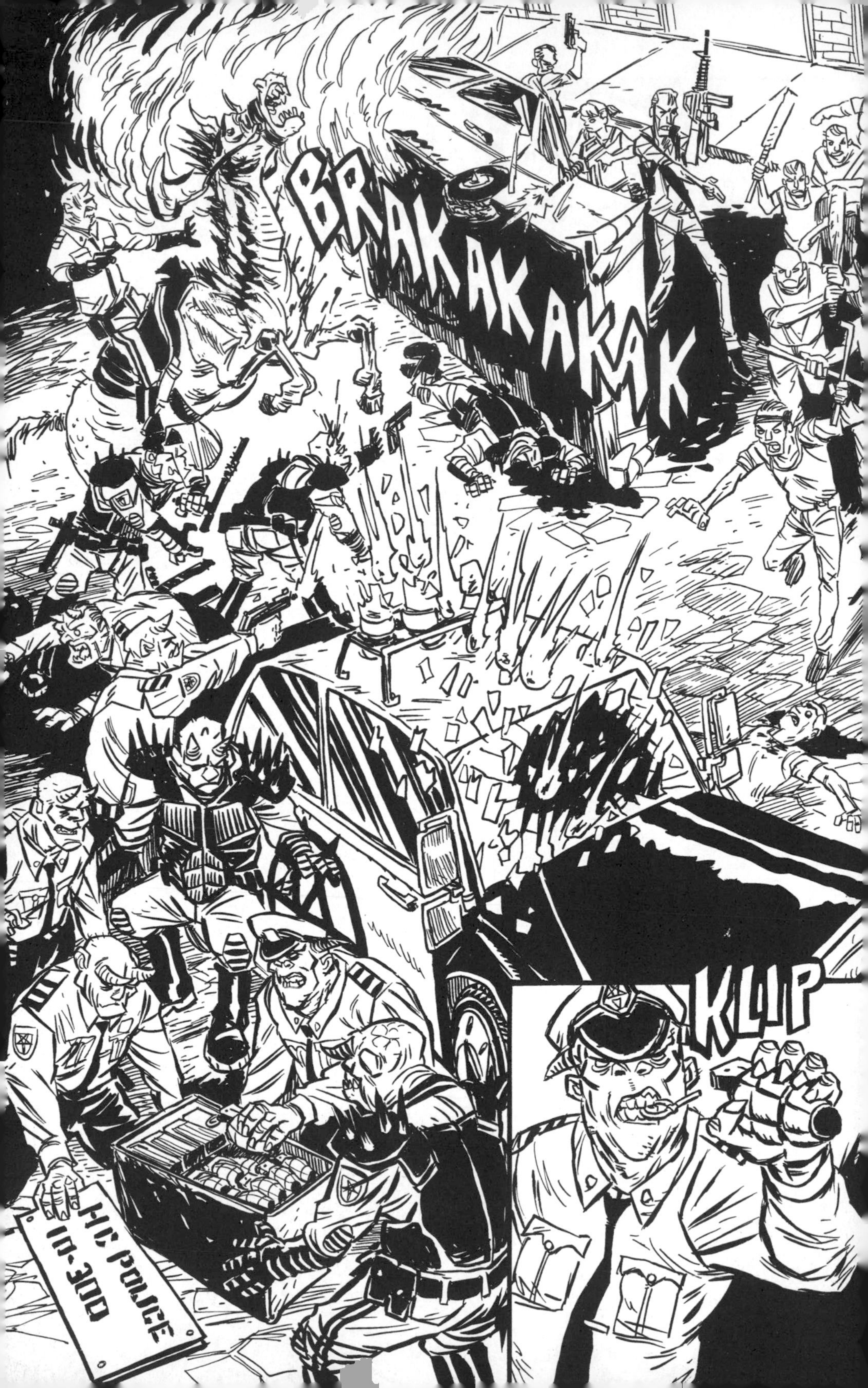
BRAKAKAKAK
HC POLICE
ID-3000
KLIP

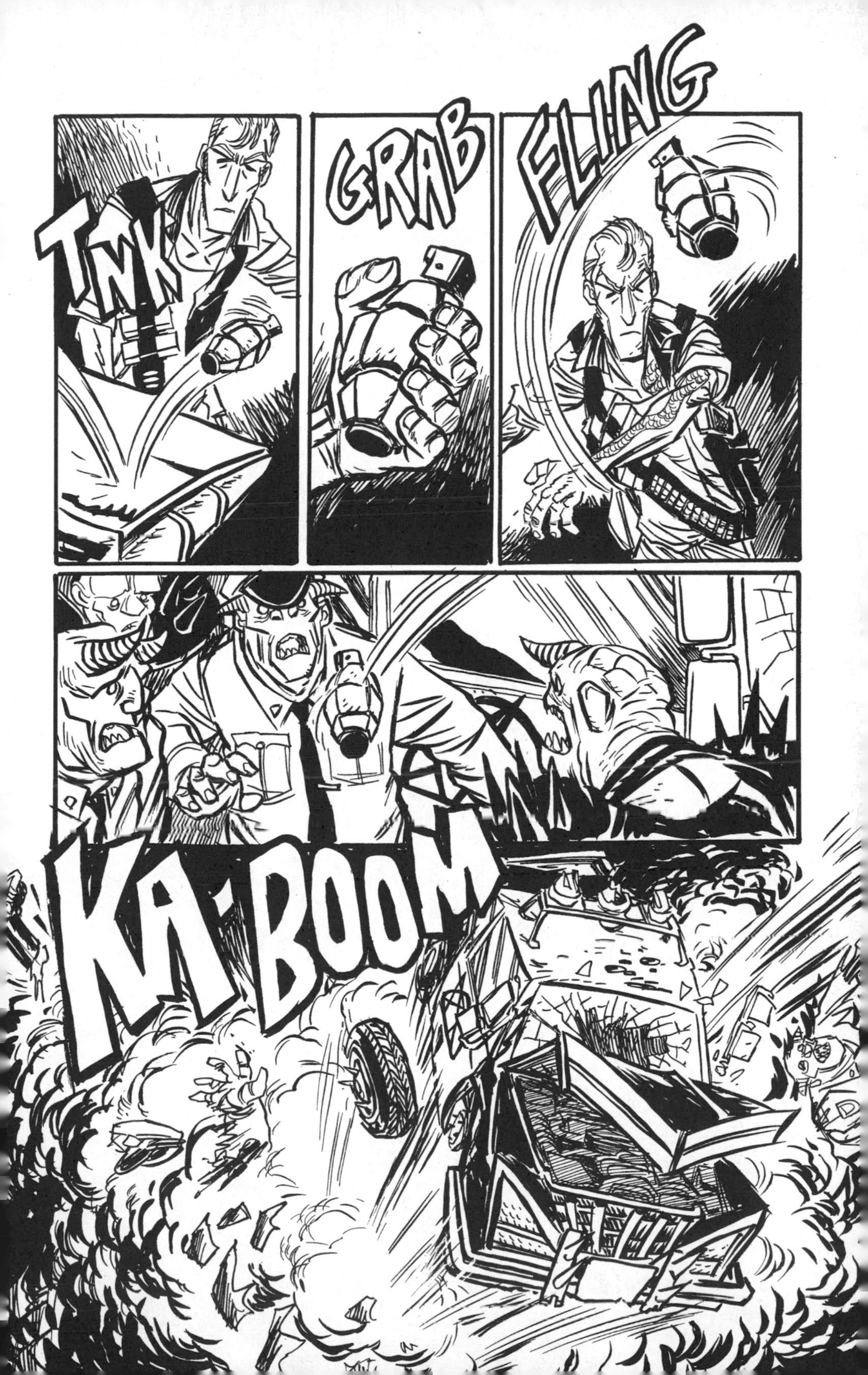
TNK
GRAB
FLING
KA-BOOM

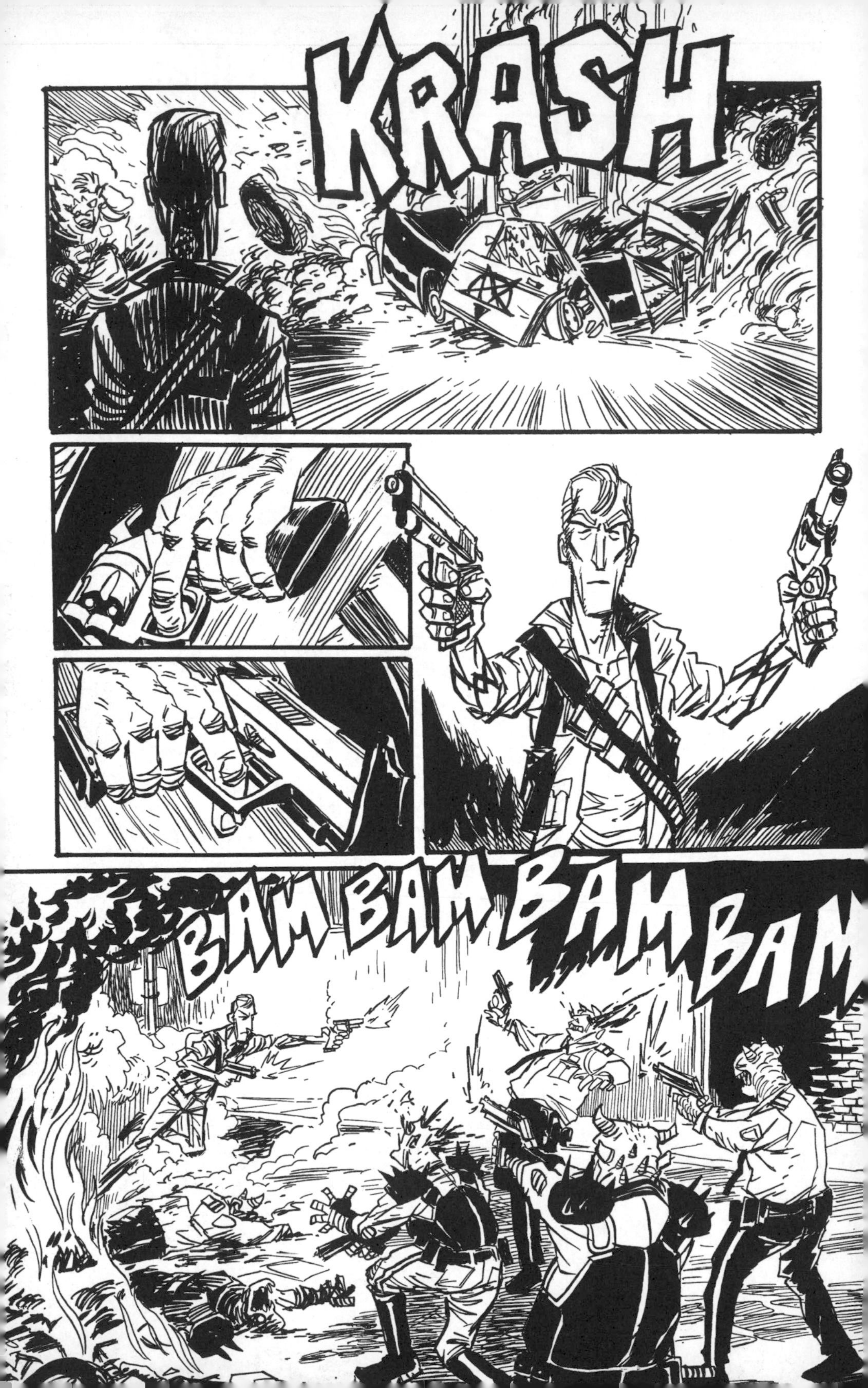
KRASH
BAM BAM BAM BAM

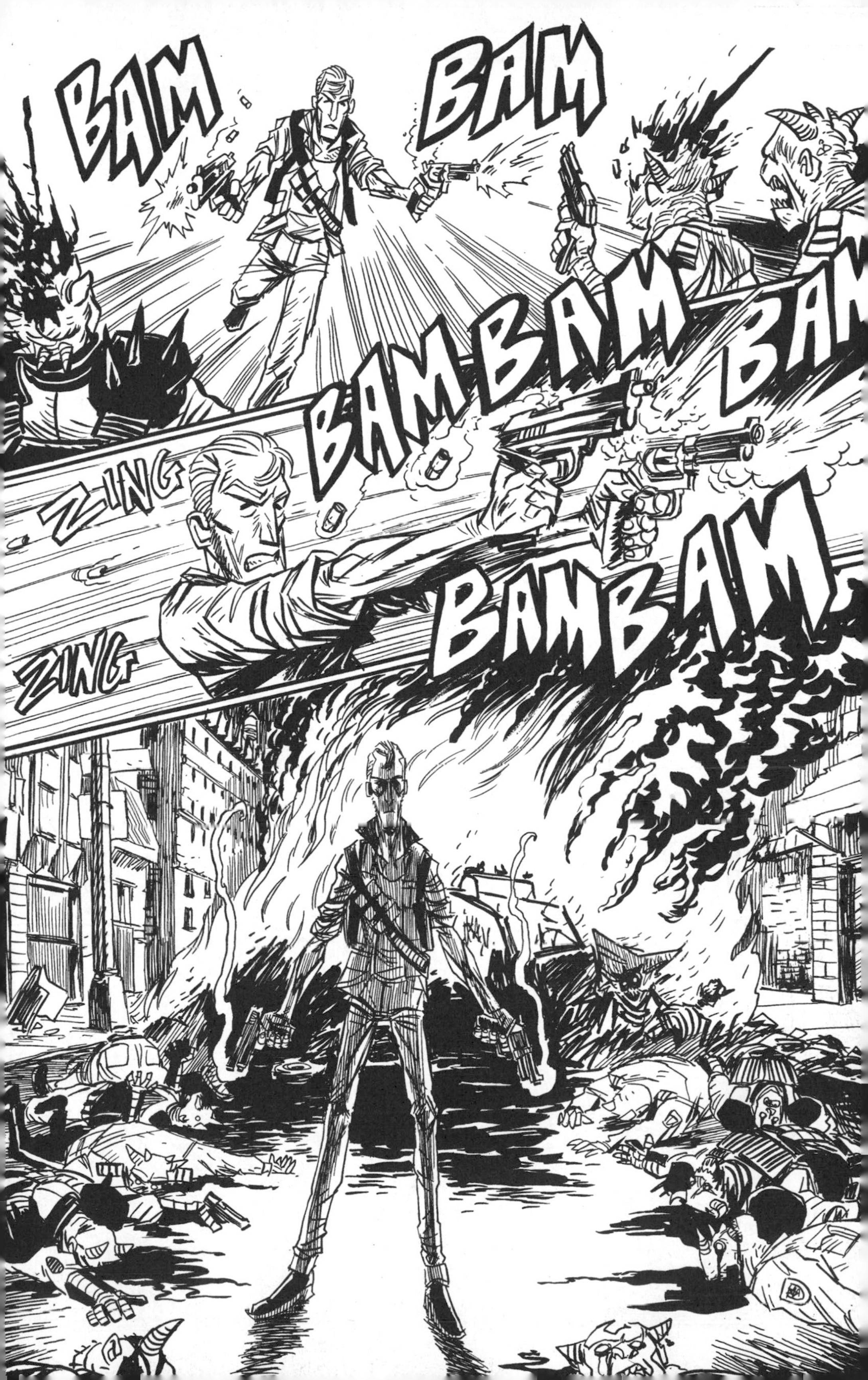
BAM
BAM
BAM BAM
BAM
ZING
ZING
BAM BAM

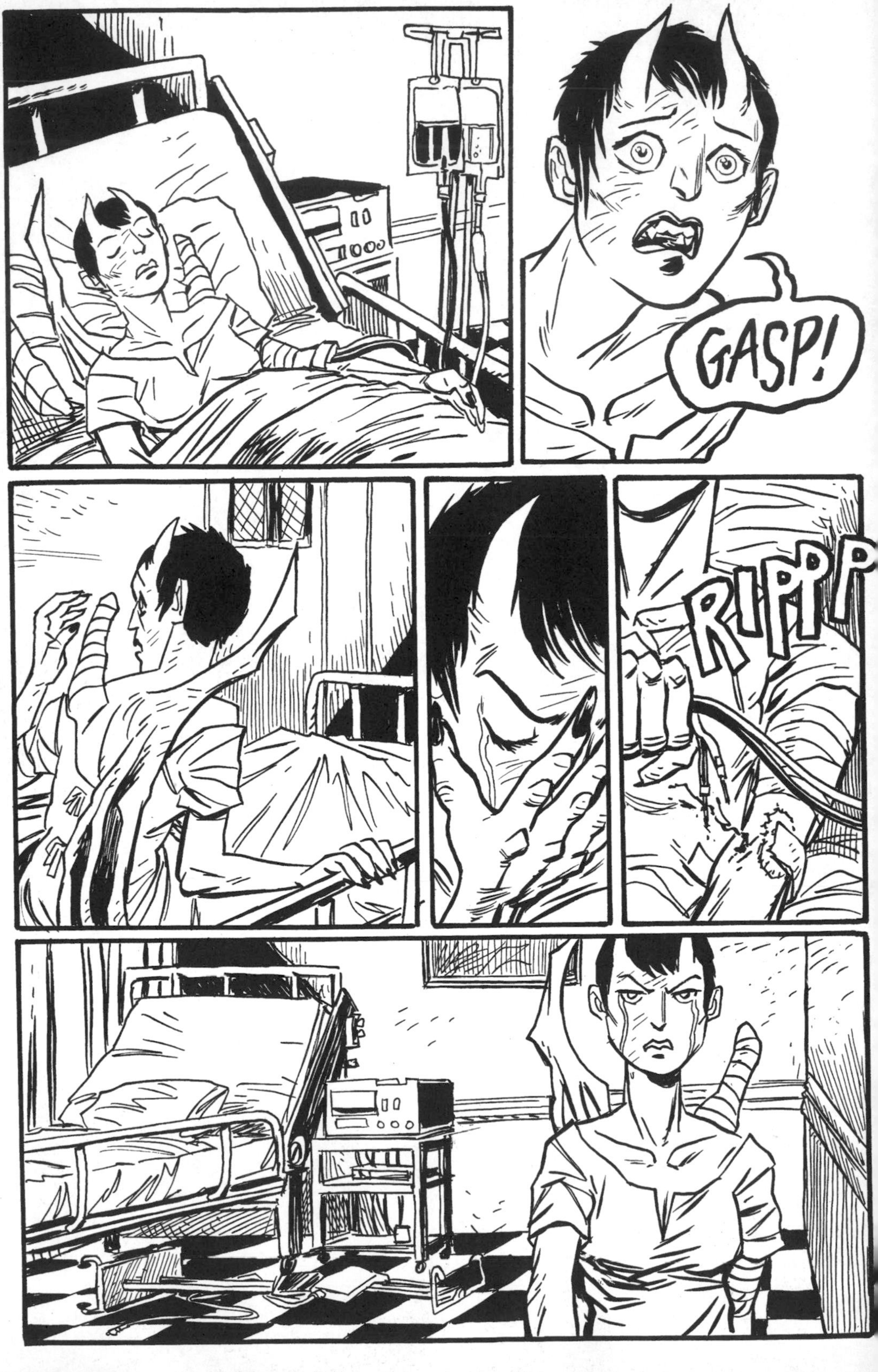
GASP!
RIPPP

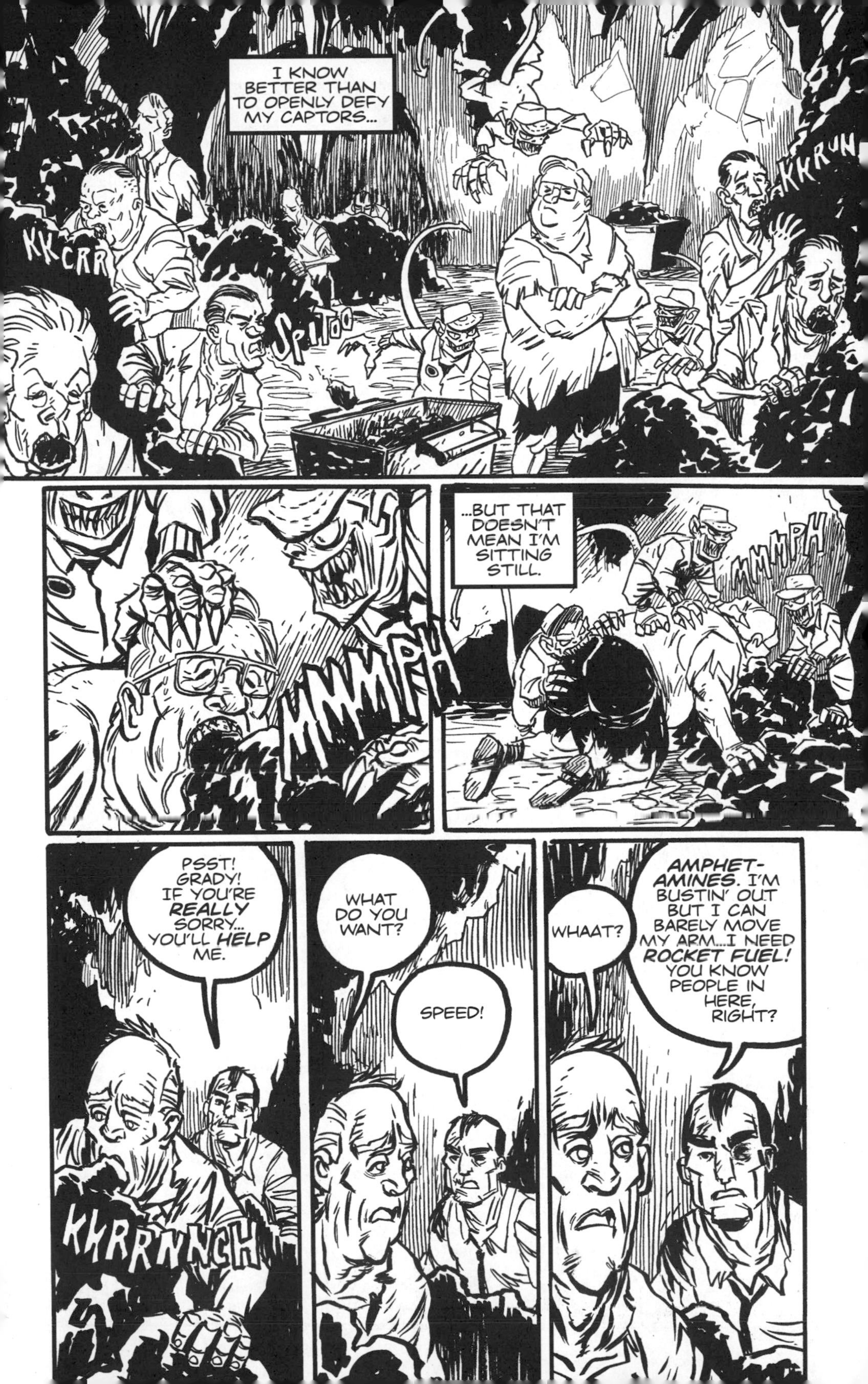
I KNOW BETTER THAN TO OPENLY DEFY MY CAPTORS...
KKCRR
SPITOO
KKRUN
...BUT THAT DOESN'T MEAN I'M SITTING STILL.
MMMPH
MMMPH
PSST! GRADY! IF YOU'RE REALLY SORRY... YOU'LL HELP ME.
KHRRNNCH
WHAT DO YOU WANT?
SPEED!
WHAAT?
AMPHET-AMINES. I'M BUSTIN' OUT BUT I CAN BARELY MOVE MY ARM...I NEED ROCKET FUEL! YOU KNOW PEOPLE IN HERE, RIGHT?

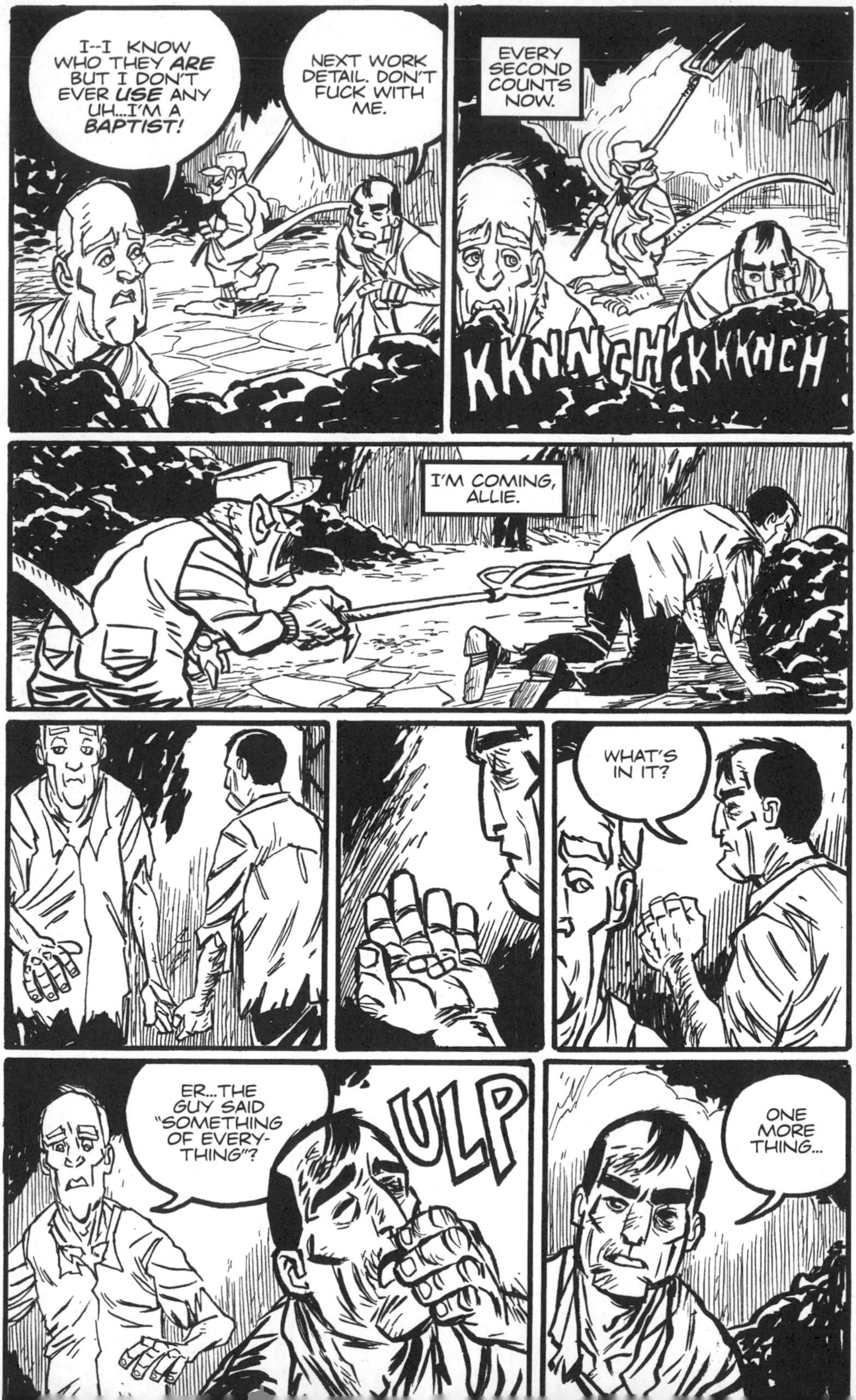
I--I KNOW WHO THEY ARE BUT I DON'T EVER USE ANY UH...I'M A BAPTIST!
NEXT WORK DETAIL. DON'T FUCK WITH ME.
EVERY SECOND COUNTS NOW.
KKNNCH KKNNCH
I'M COMING, ALLIE.
WHAT'S IN IT?
ER...THE GUY SAID "SOMETHING OF EVERY-THING"?
ULP
ONE MORE THING...

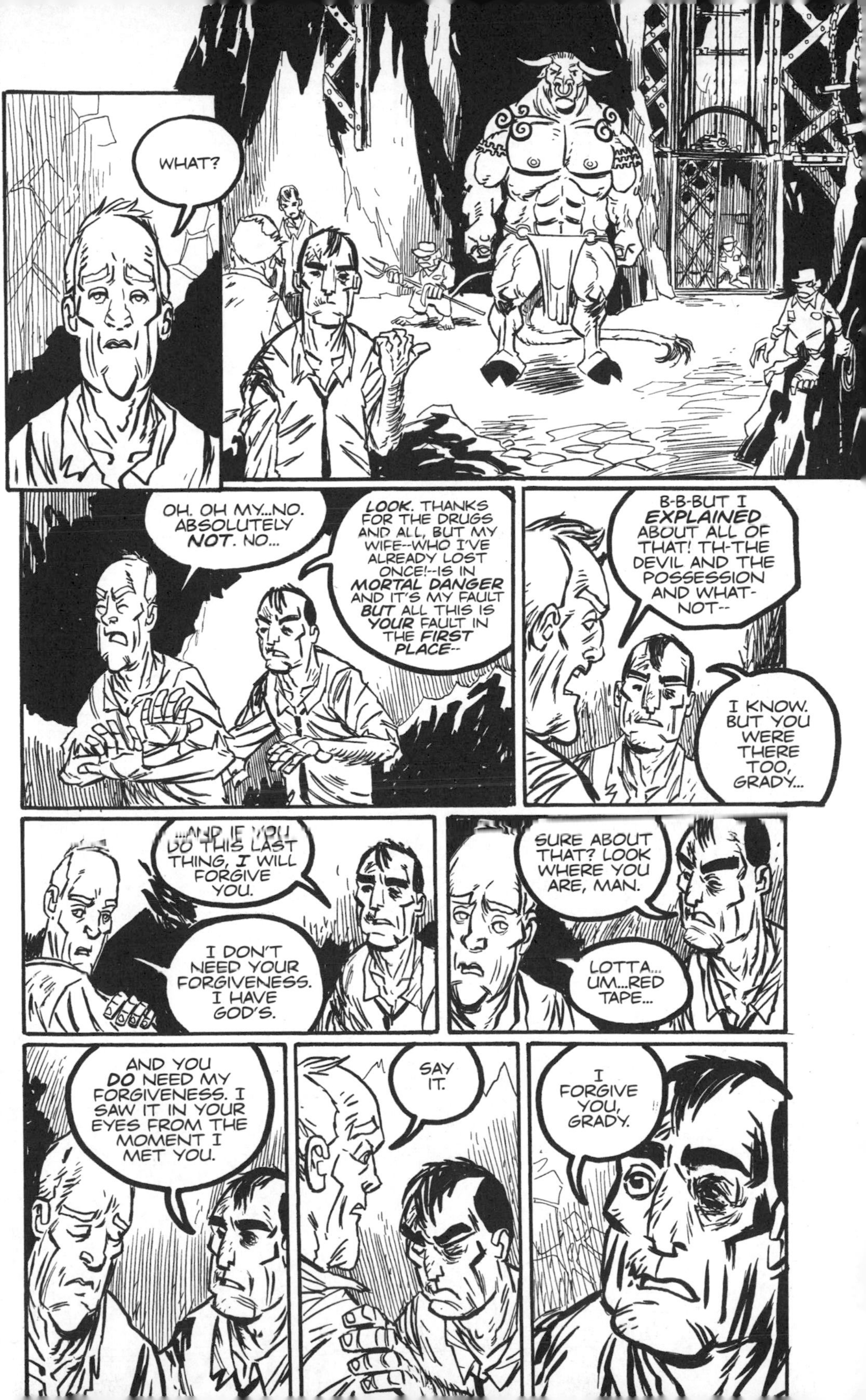
WHAT?
OH. OH MY...NO. ABSOLUTELY NOT. NO...
LOOK. THANKS FOR THE DRUGS AND ALL, BUT MY WIFE--WHO I'VE ALREADY LOST ONCE!--IS IN MORTAL DANGER AND IT'S MY FAULT BUT ALL THIS IS YOUR FAULT IN THE FIRST PLACE--
B-B-BUT I EXPLAINED ABOUT ALL OF THAT! TH-THE DEVIL AND THE POSSESSION AND WHAT-NOT--
I KNOW. BUT YOU WERE THERE TOO, GRADY...
...AND IF YOU DO THIS LAST THING, I WILL FORGIVE YOU.
I DON'T NEED YOUR FORGIVENESS. I HAVE GOD'S.
SURE ABOUT THAT? LOOK WHERE YOU ARE, MAN.
LOTTA... UM...RED TAPE...
AND YOU DO NEED MY FORGIVENESS. I SAW IT IN YOUR EYES FROM THE MOMENT I MET YOU.
SAY IT.
I FORGIVE YOU, GRADY.

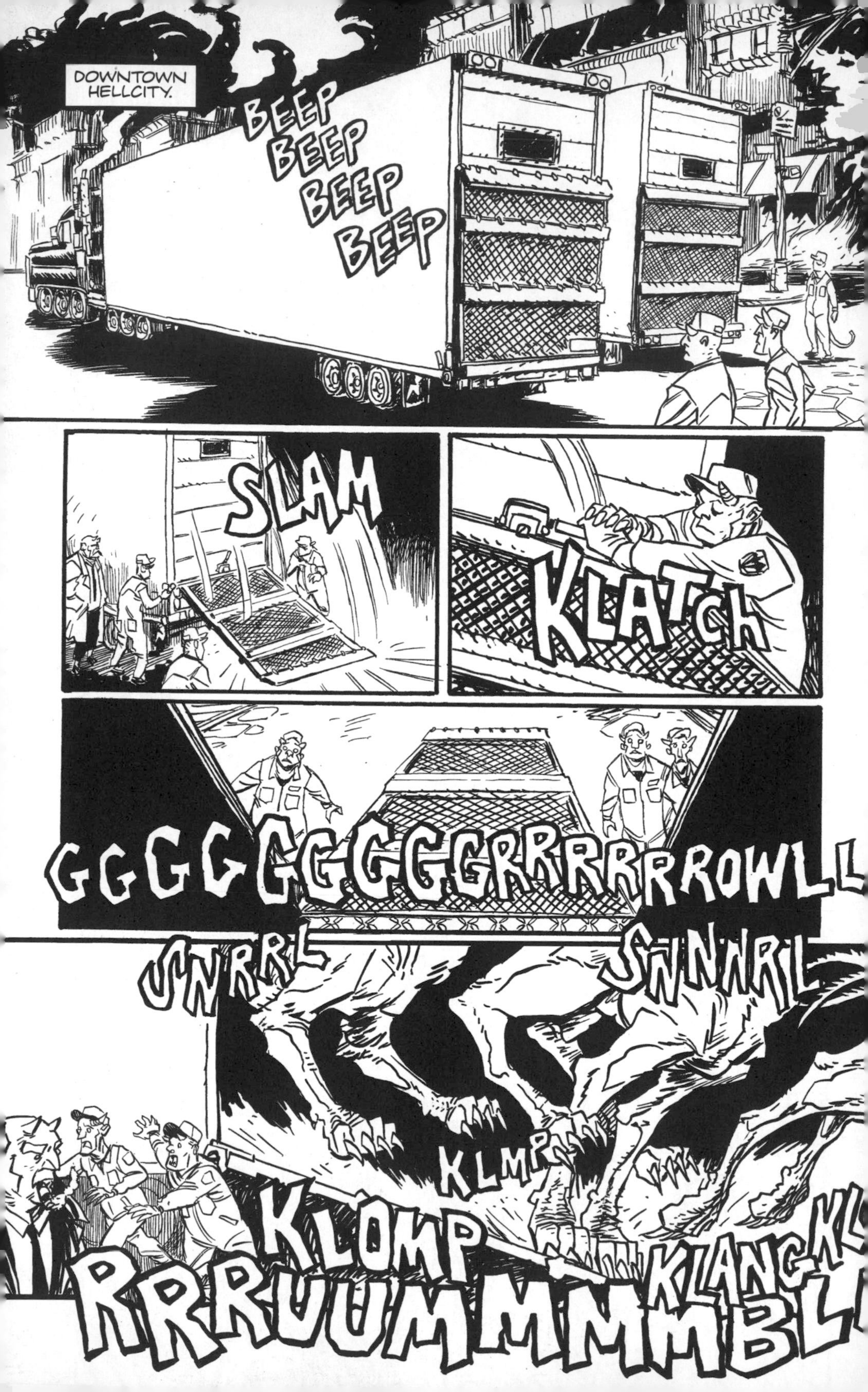
DOWNTOWN HELLCITY.
BEEP BEEP BEEP BEEP
SLAM
KLATCH
GGGGGGGGRRRRRRROWLL
SNRRL
SNNNRL
KLMP
KLOMP
KLANGKL
RRRUUMMMMBL

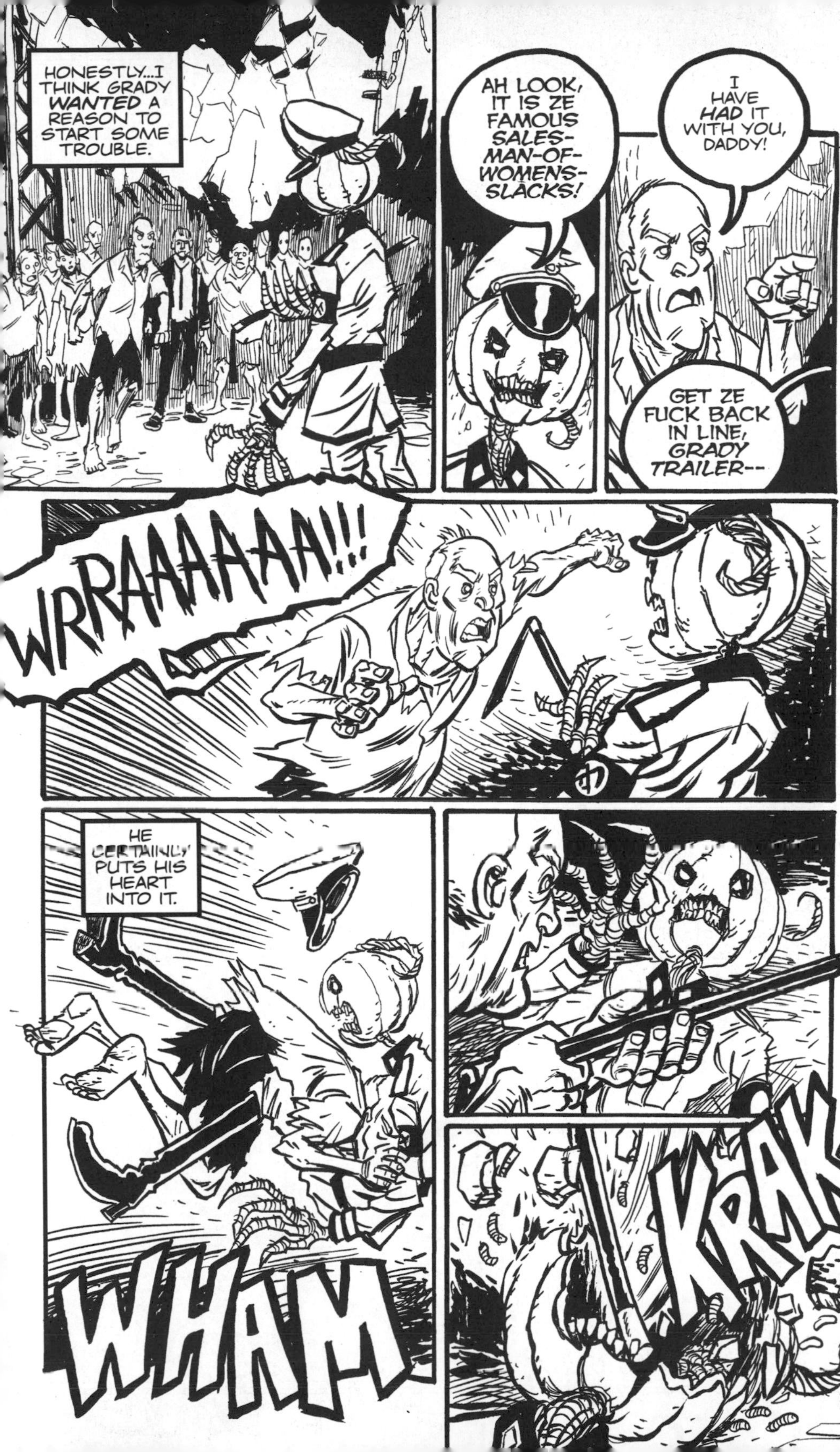
HONESTLY...I THINK GRADY WANTED A REASON TO START SOME TROUBLE.
AH LOOK, IT IS ZE FAMOUS SALES-MAN-OF-WOMENS-SLACKS!
I HAVE HAD IT WITH YOU, DADDY!
GET ZE FUCK BACK IN LINE, GRADY TRAILER--
WRRAAAAAAA!!!
HE CERTAINLY PUTS HIS HEART INTO IT.
WHAM
KRAK

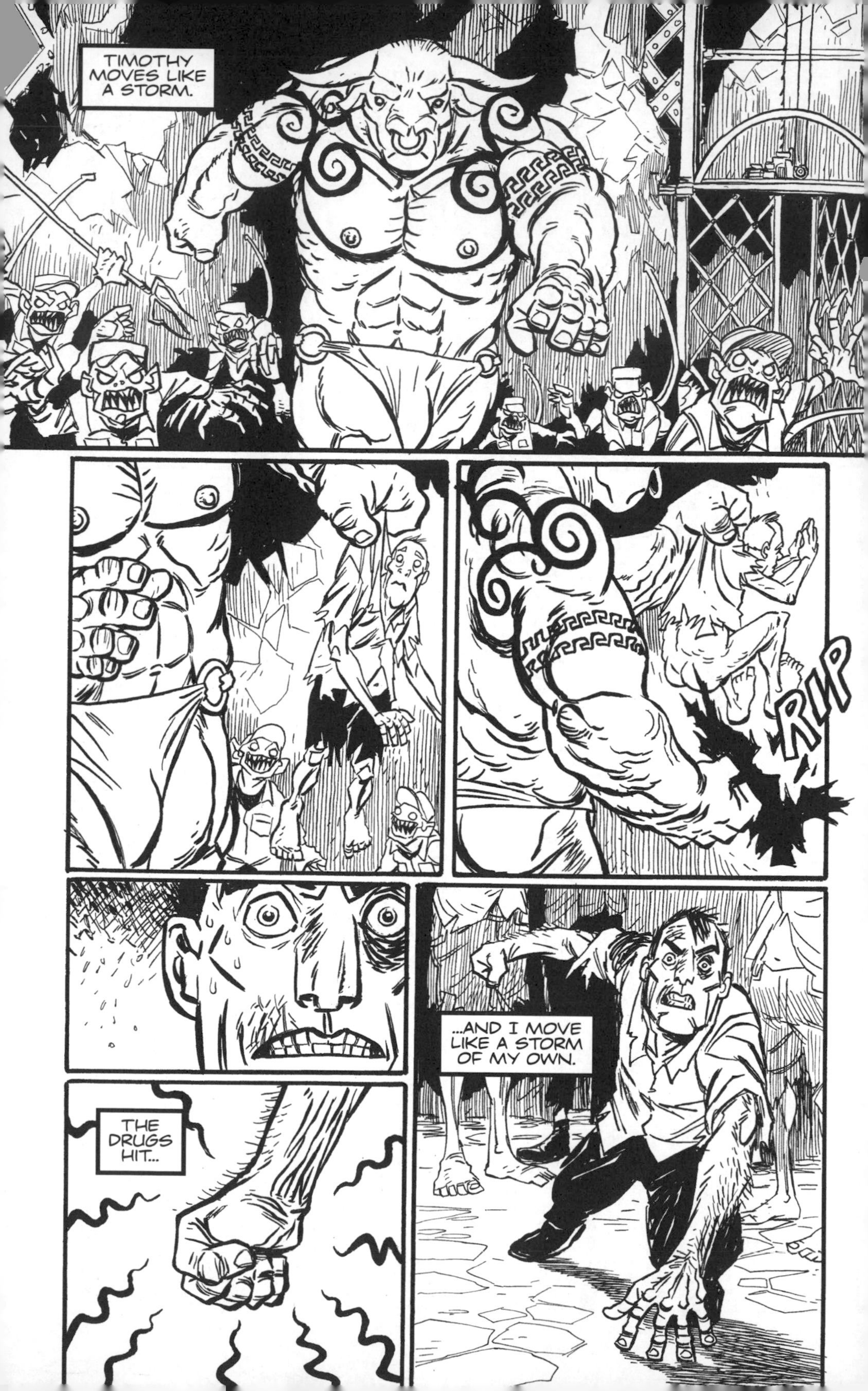
TIMOTHY MOVES LIKE A STORM.
RIP
THE DRUGS HIT...
...AND I MOVE LIKE A STORM OF MY OWN.

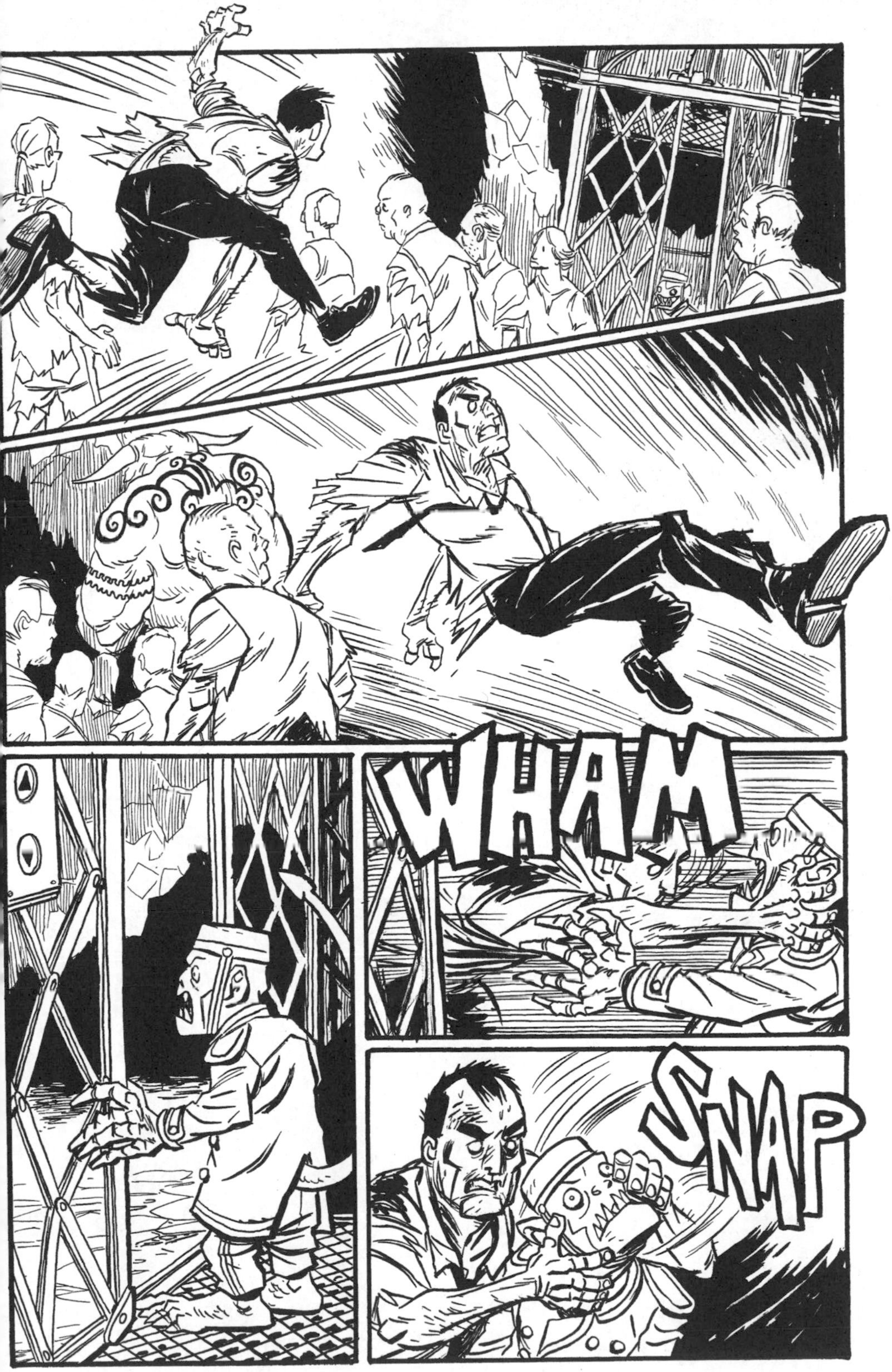
WHAM
SNAP

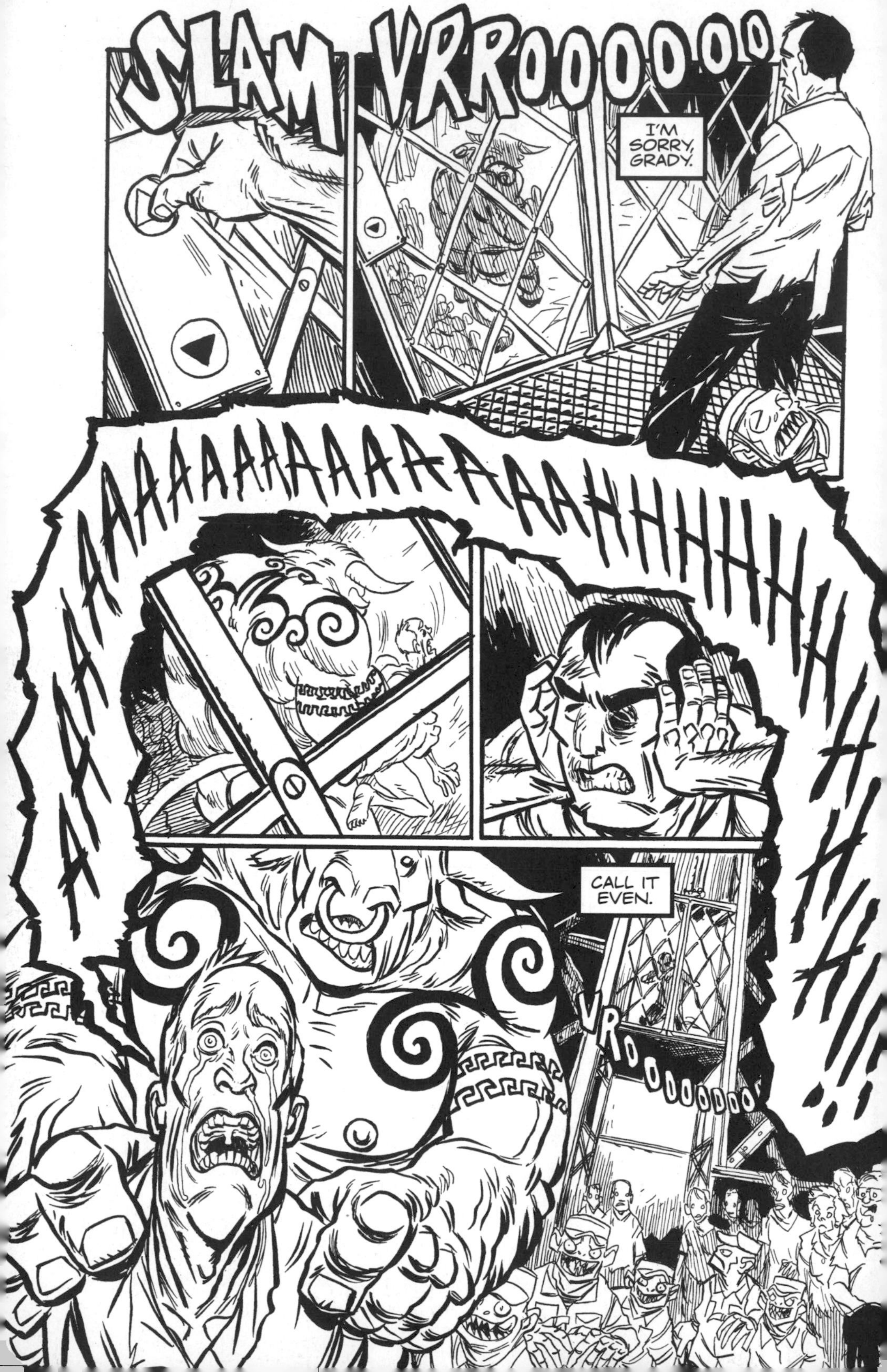
SLAM
VRROOOOOOO
I'M SORRY, GRADY.
AAAAAAAAAAAAAAAAAAAHHHHHHHHHHH!!!
CALL IT EVEN.
VROOOOOOOOO

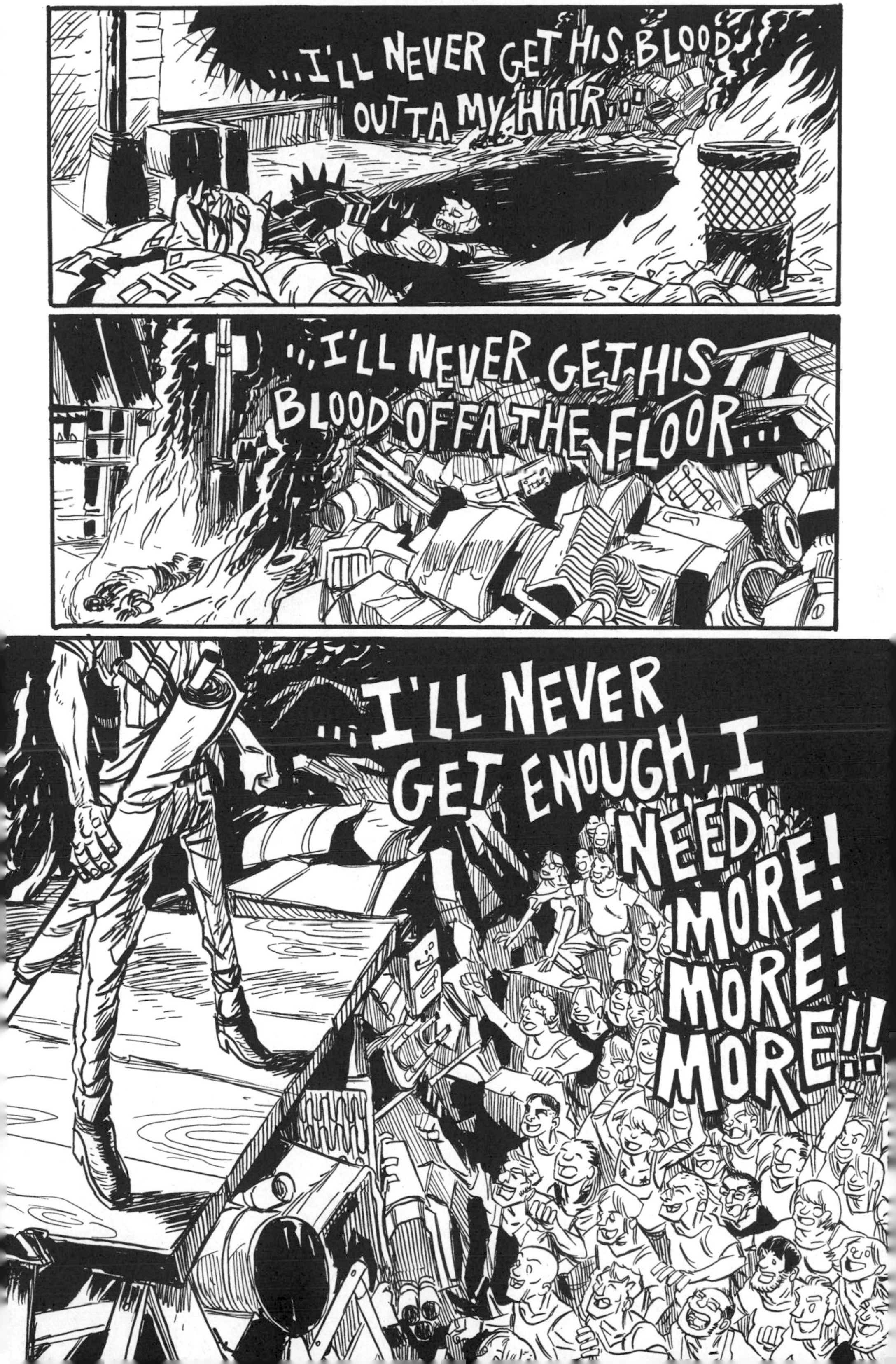
...I'LL NEVER GET HIS BLOOD OUTTA MY HAIR...
...I'LL NEVER GET HIS BLOOD OFFA THE FLOOR...
...I'LL NEVER GET ENOUGH, I NEED MORE! MORE! MORE!!

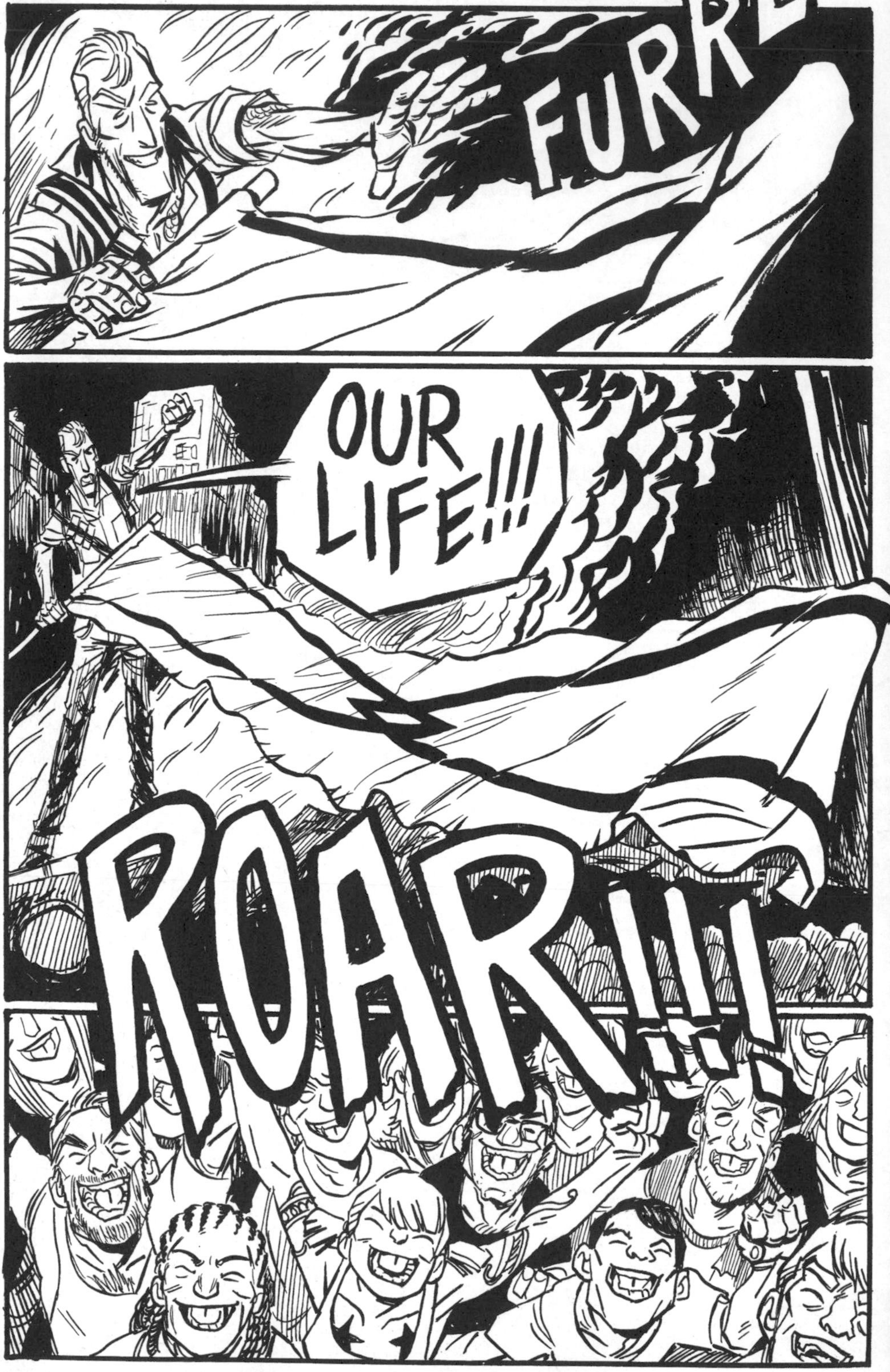
FURRL
OUR LIFE!!!
ROAR!!!!

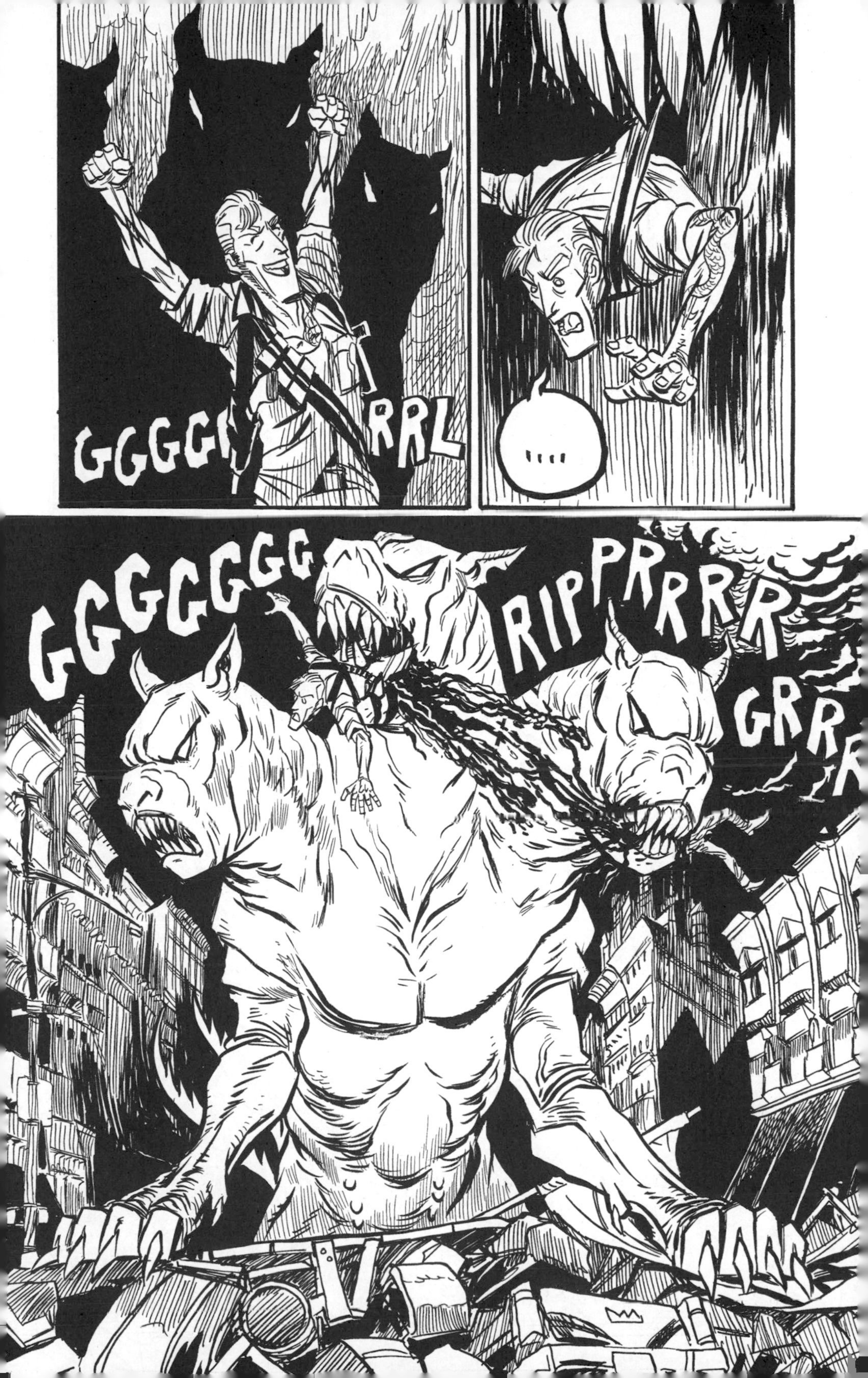
GGGGG RRRL
....
GGGGGGG RIPPRRRRR
GRRR

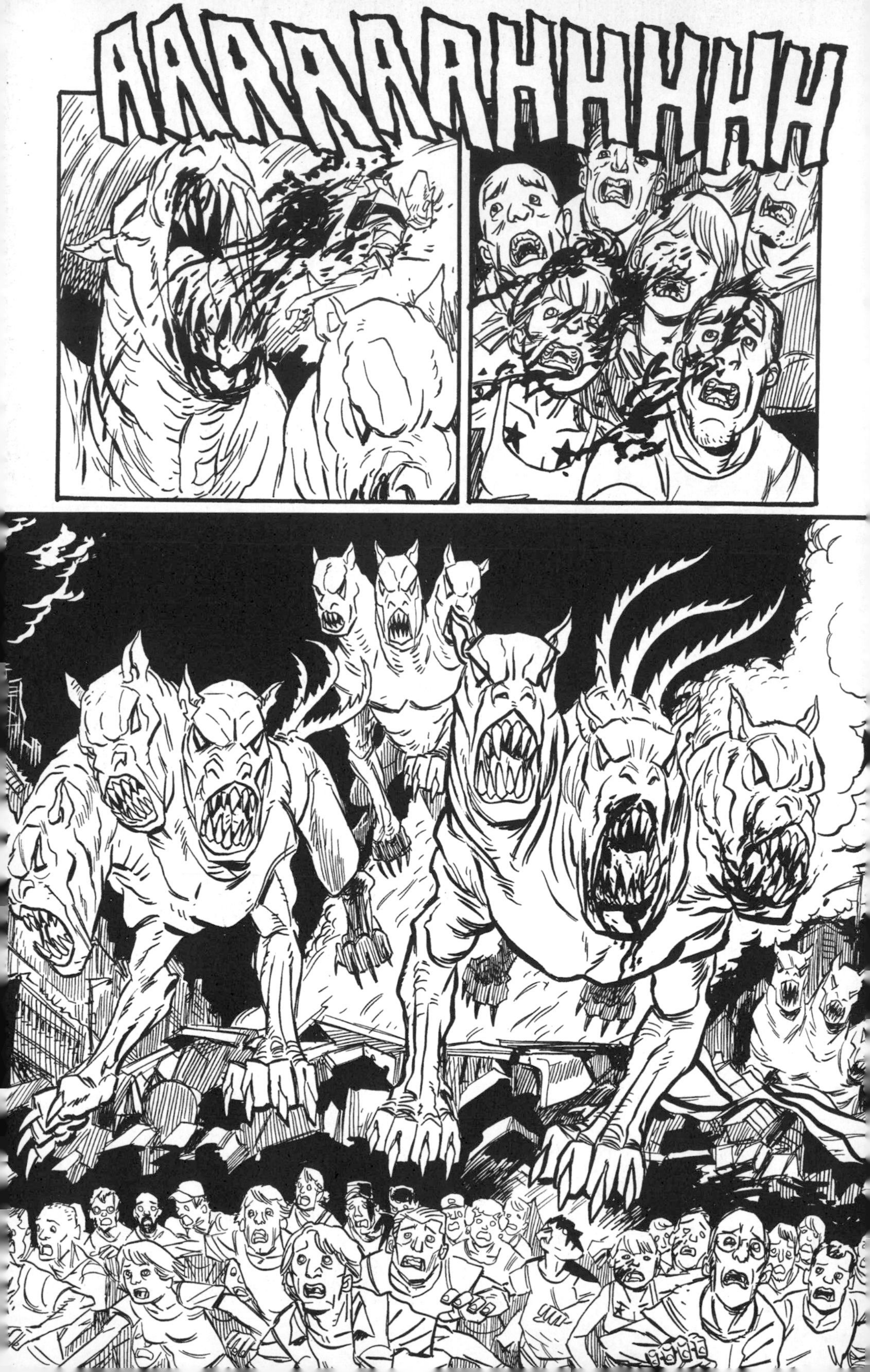
AARRRAHHHHH

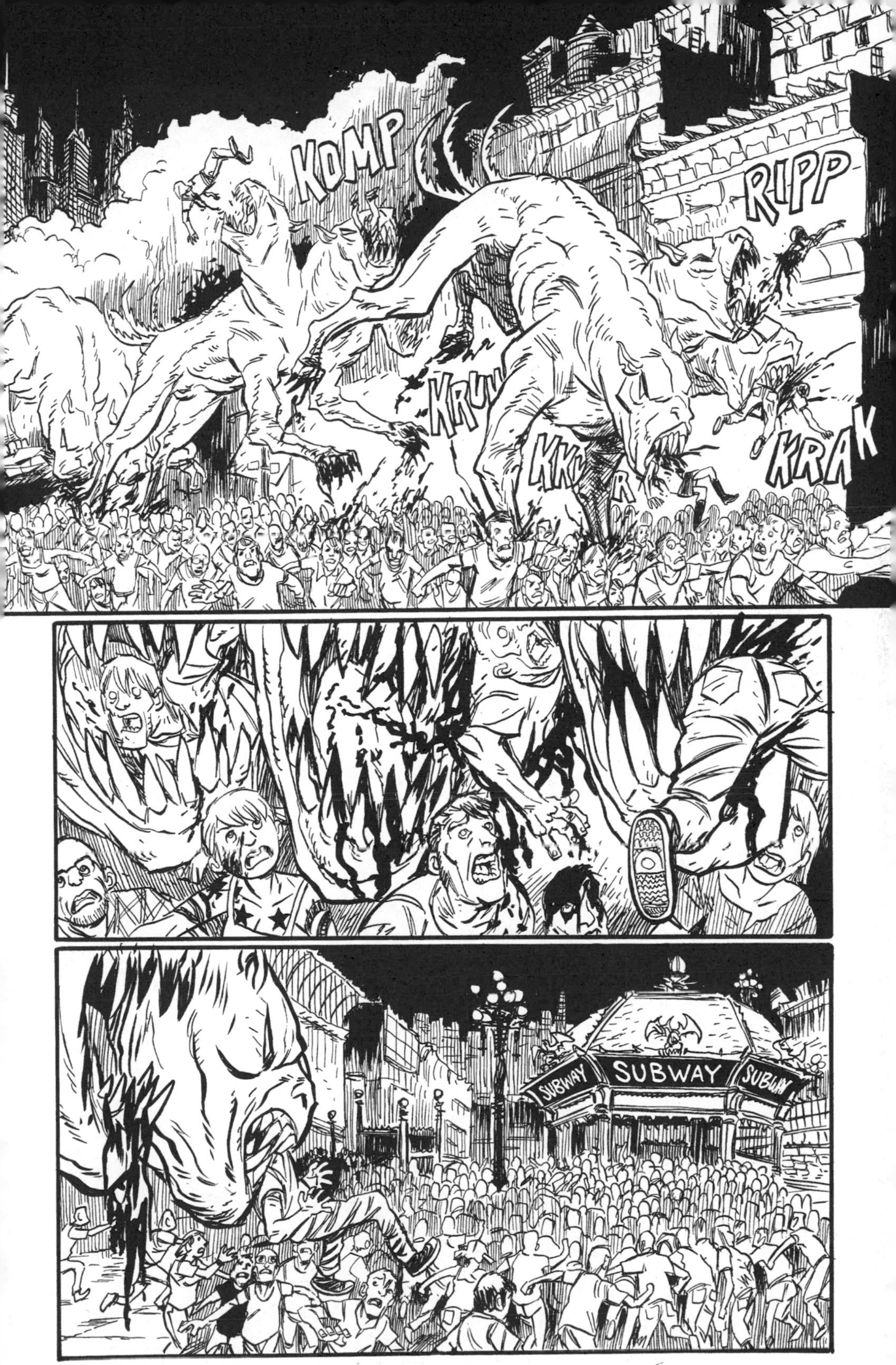
KOMP
RIPP
KRAK
SUBWAY
SUBWAY

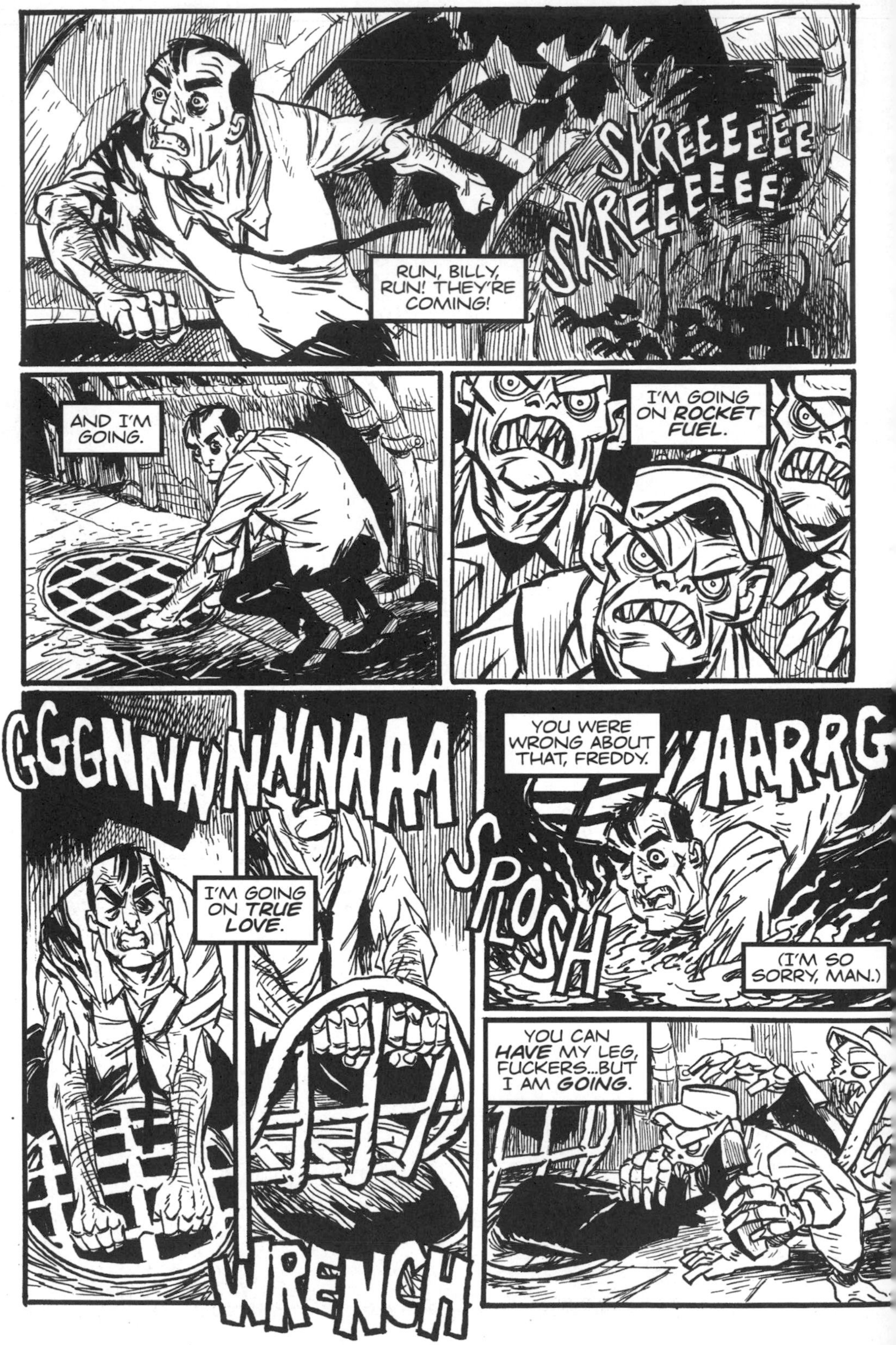
SKREEEEEE
SKREEEEEE
RUN, BILLY, RUN! THEY'RE COMING!
AND I'M GOING.
I'M GOING ON ROCKET FUEL.
GGGNNNNNNAAA
I'M GOING ON TRUE LOVE.
WRENCH
YOU WERE WRONG ABOUT THAT, FREDDY.
YAARRG
SPLOSH
(I'M SO SORRY, MAN.)
YOU CAN HAVE MY LEG, FUCKERS...BUT I AM GOING.

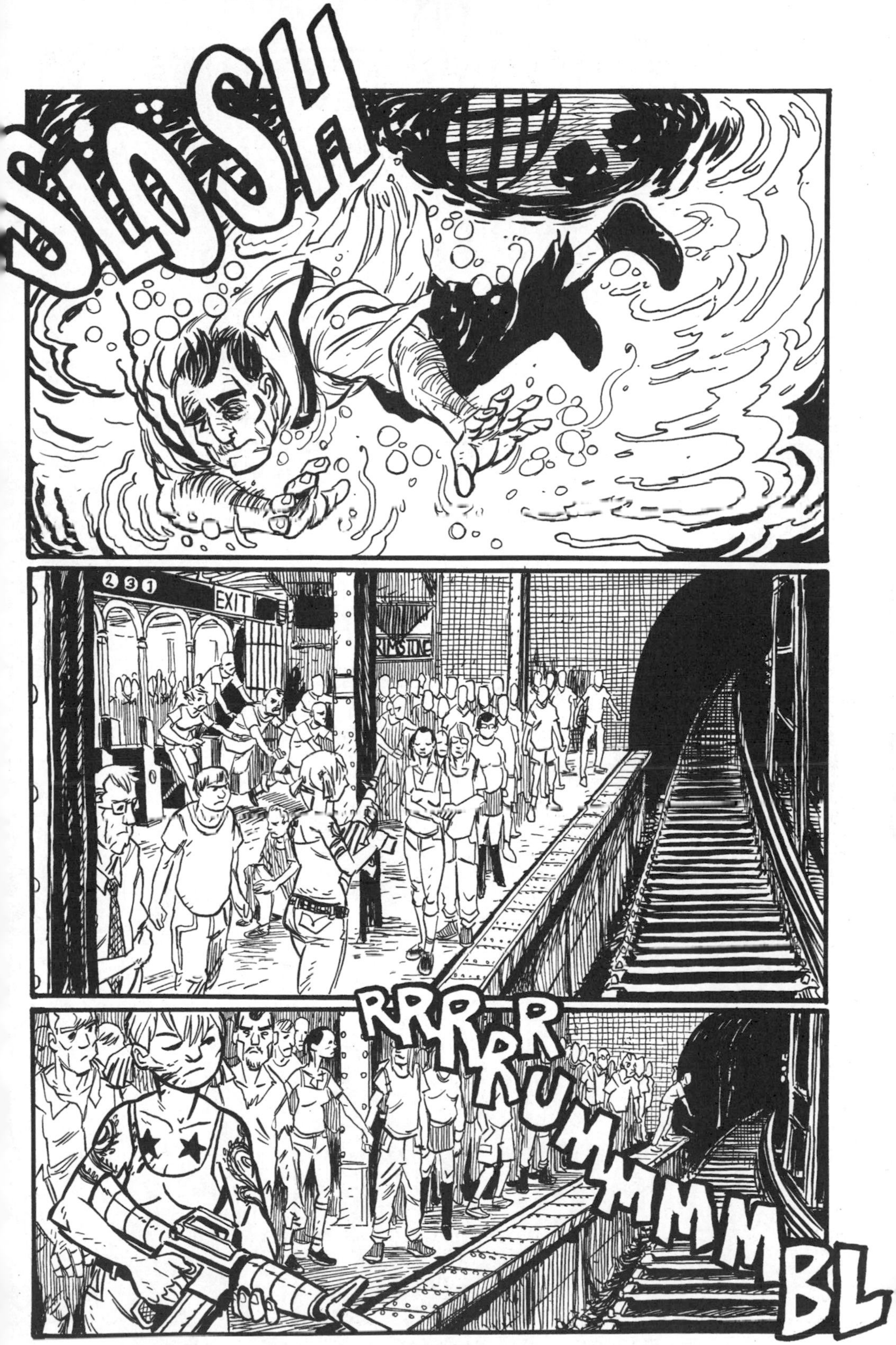

SLOSH
2 3 1
EXIT
RRRRRUMMMMMMBL

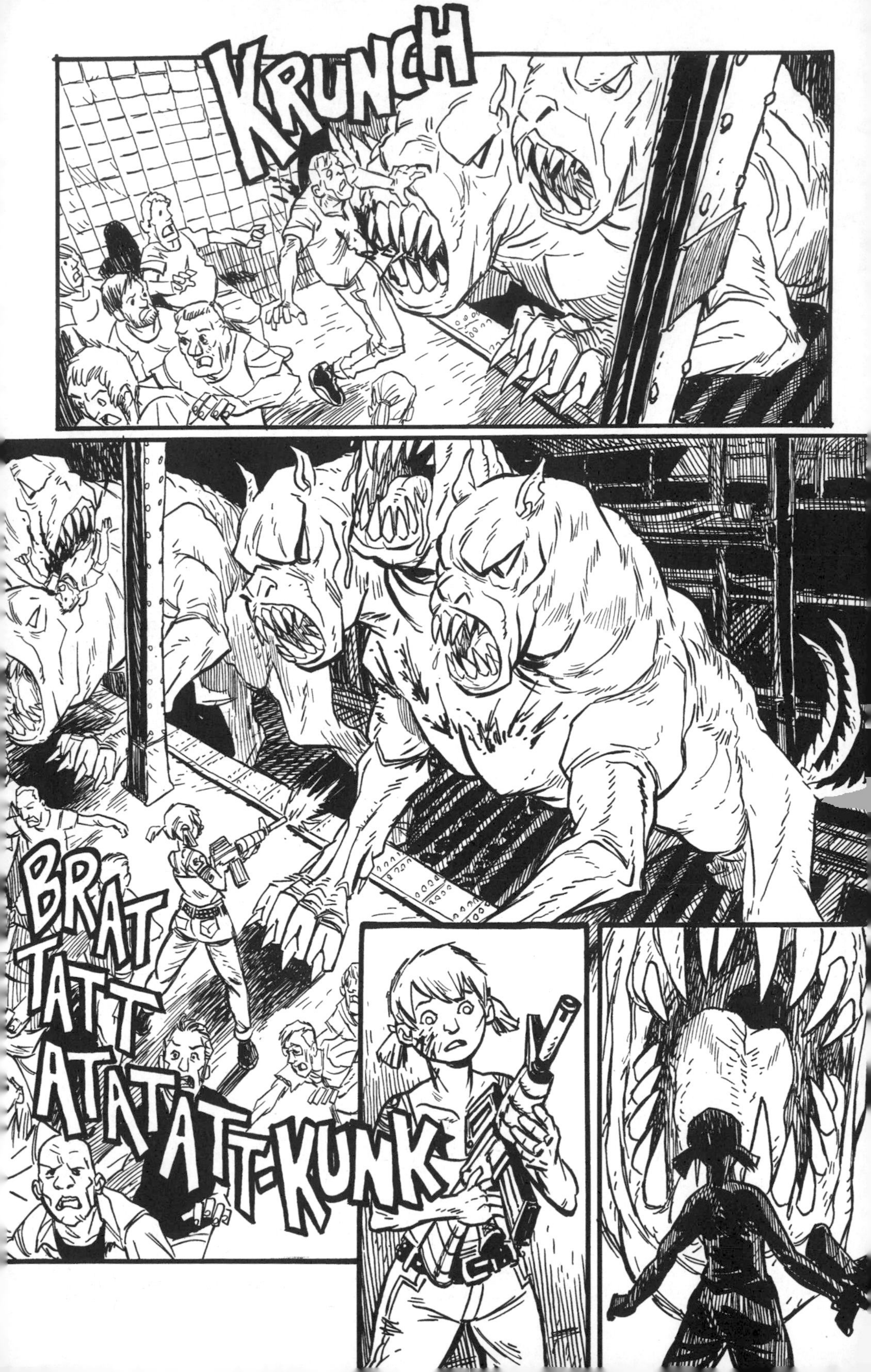
KRUNCH
BRAT TATT ATATATT-KUNK

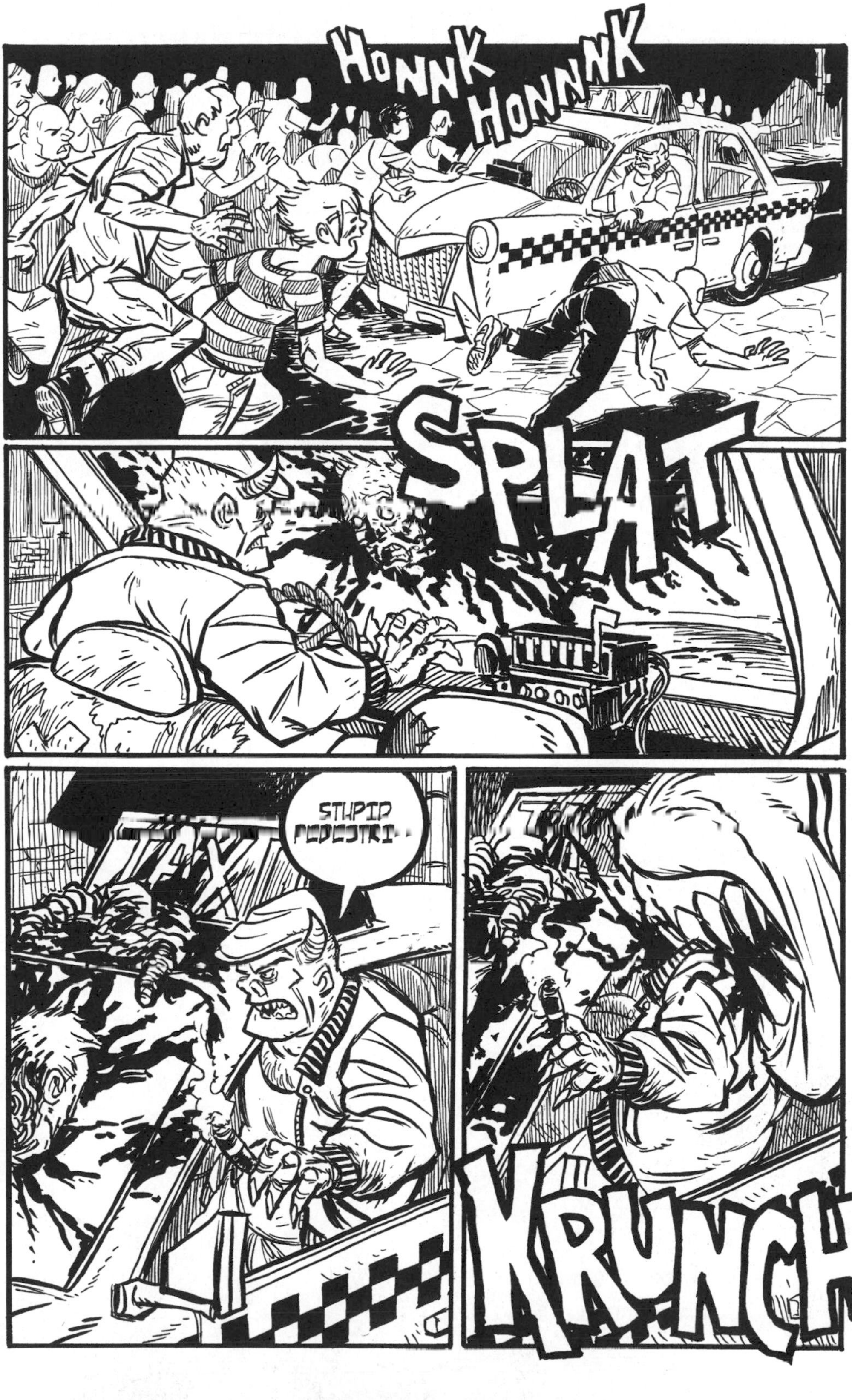
HONNK
HONNNK
TAXI
SPLAT
STUPID PEDESTRI...
KRUNCH

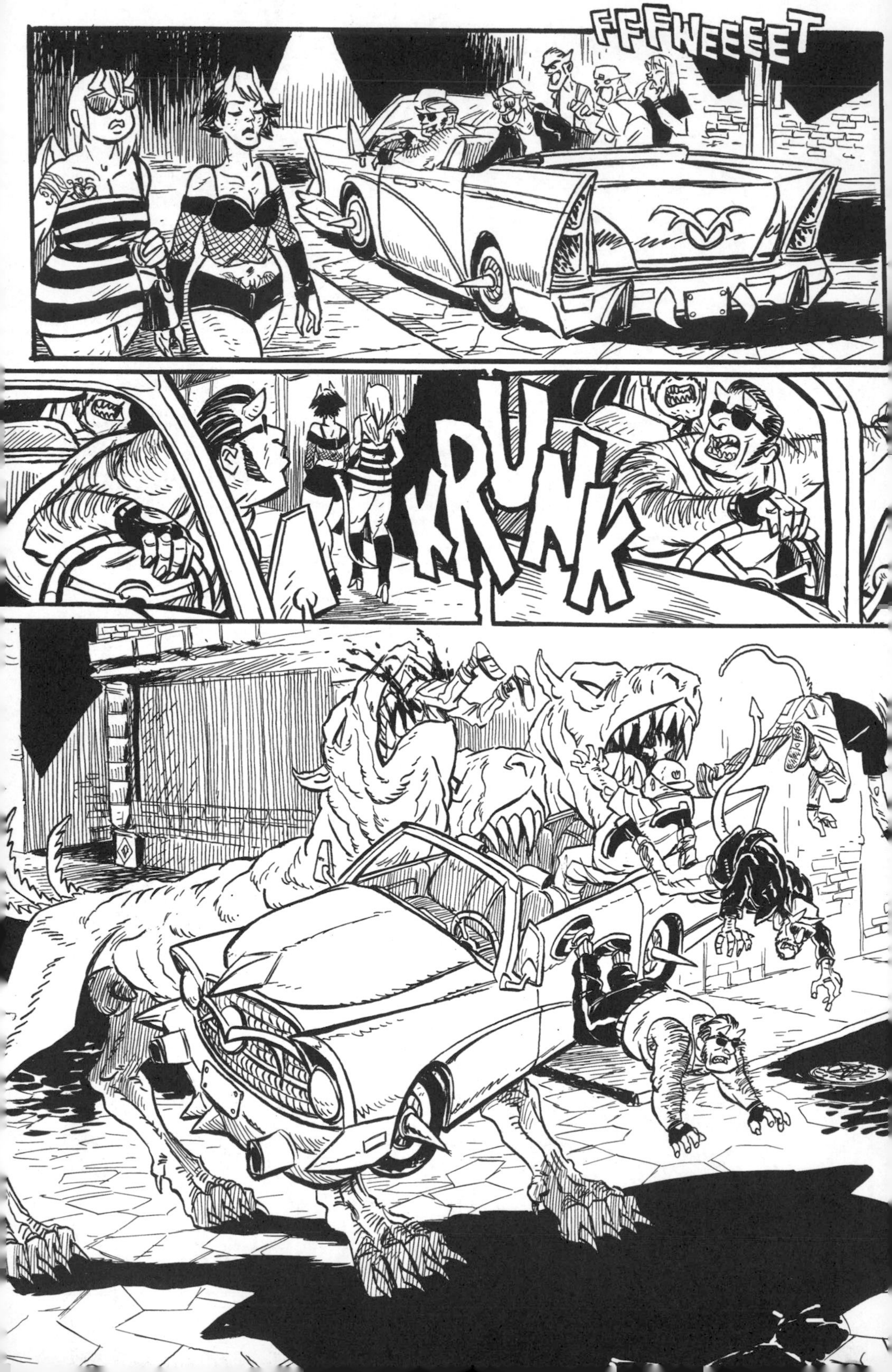
FFFWEEEET
KRUNK

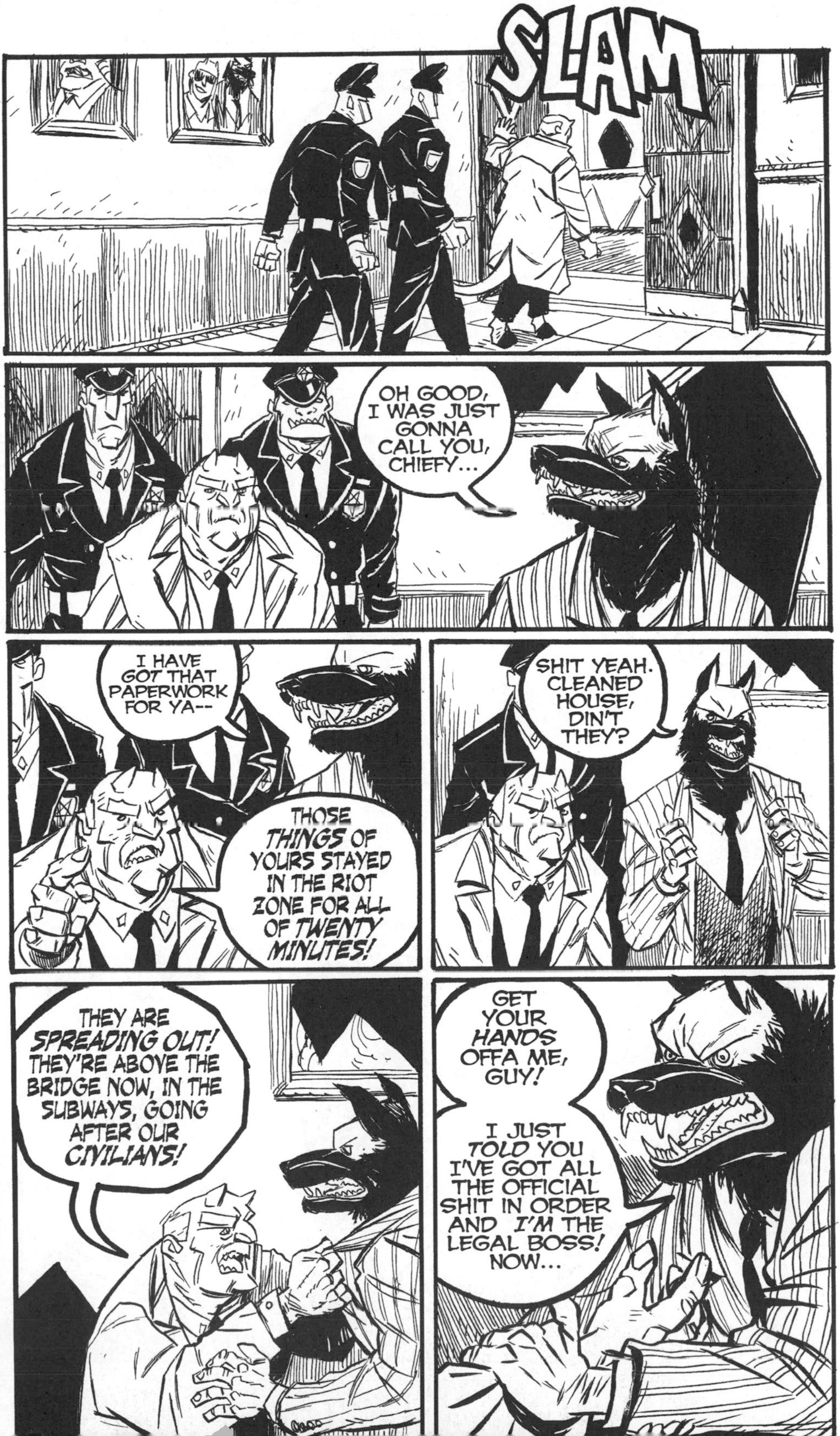
SLAM
OH GOOD, I WAS JUST GONNA CALL YOU, CHIEFY...
I HAVE GOT THAT PAPERWORK FOR YA--
THOSE THINGS OF YOURS STAYED IN THE RIOT ZONE FOR ALL OF TWENTY MINUTES!
SHIT YEAH. CLEANED HOUSE, DIN'T THEY?
THEY ARE SPREADING OUT! THEY'RE ABOVE THE BRIDGE NOW, IN THE SUBWAYS, GOING AFTER OUR CIVILIANS!
GET YOUR HANDS OFFA ME, GUY!
I JUST TOLD YOU I'VE GOT ALL THE OFFICIAL SHIT IN ORDER AND I'M THE LEGAL BOSS! NOW...

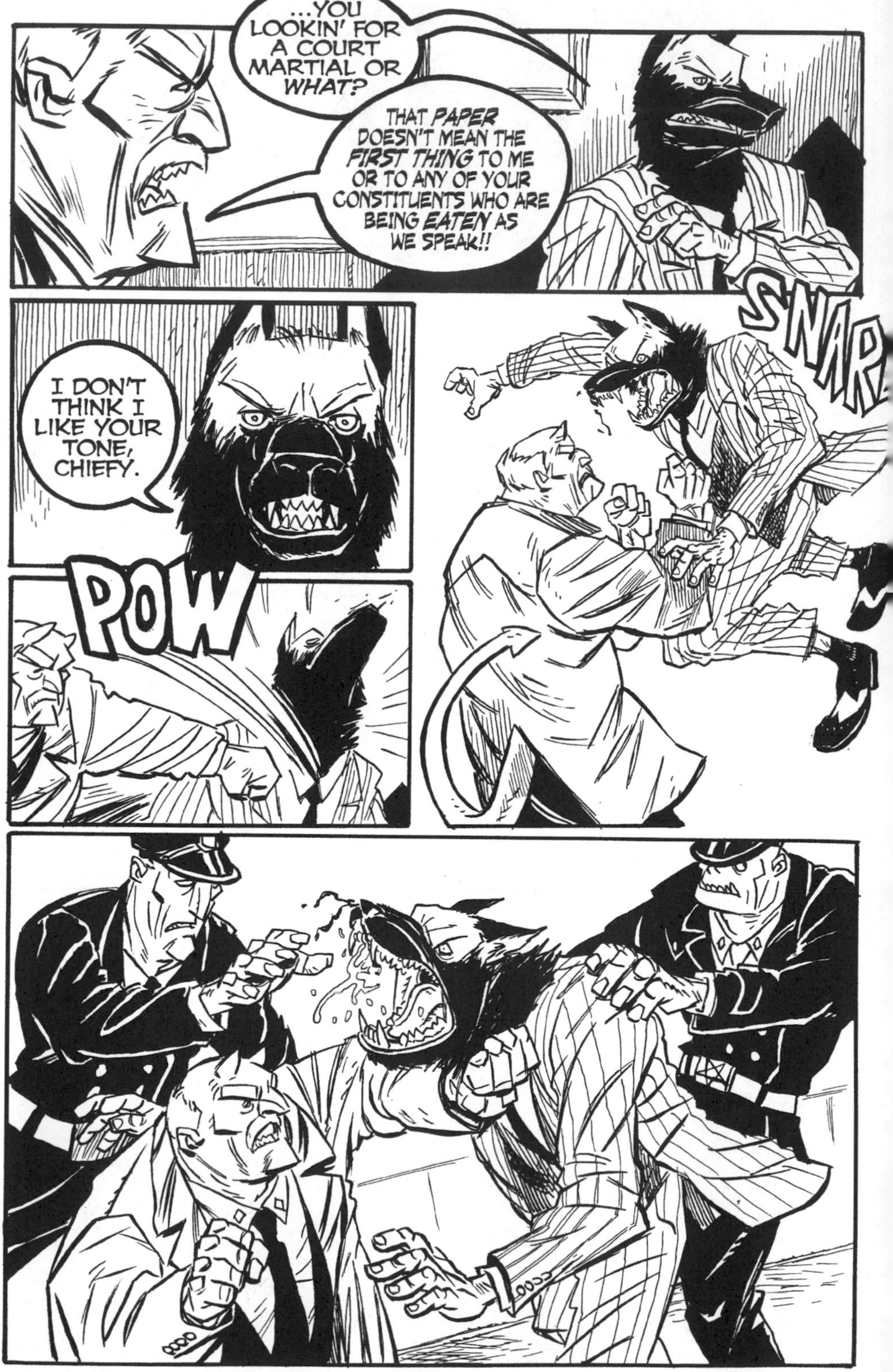
...YOU LOOKIN' FOR A COURT MARTIAL OR WHAT?
THAT PAPER DOESN'T MEAN THE FIRST THING TO ME OR TO ANY OF YOUR CONSTITUENTS WHO ARE BEING EATEN AS WE SPEAK!!
I DON'T THINK I LIKE YOUR TONE, CHIEFY.
POW
SNAR

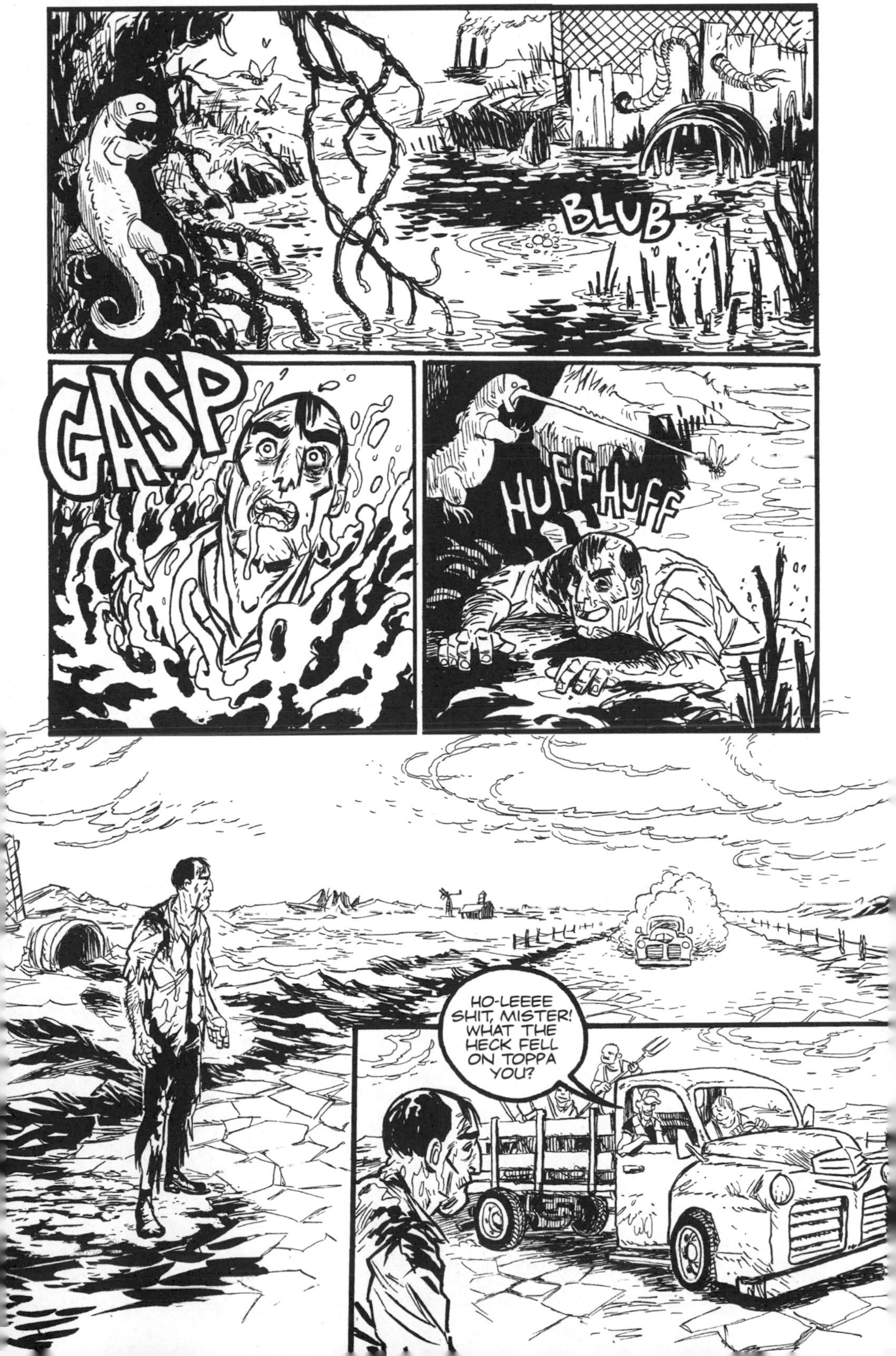
BLUB
GASP
HUFF HUFF
HO-LEEEE SHIT, MISTER! WHAT THE HECK FELL ON TOPPA YOU?

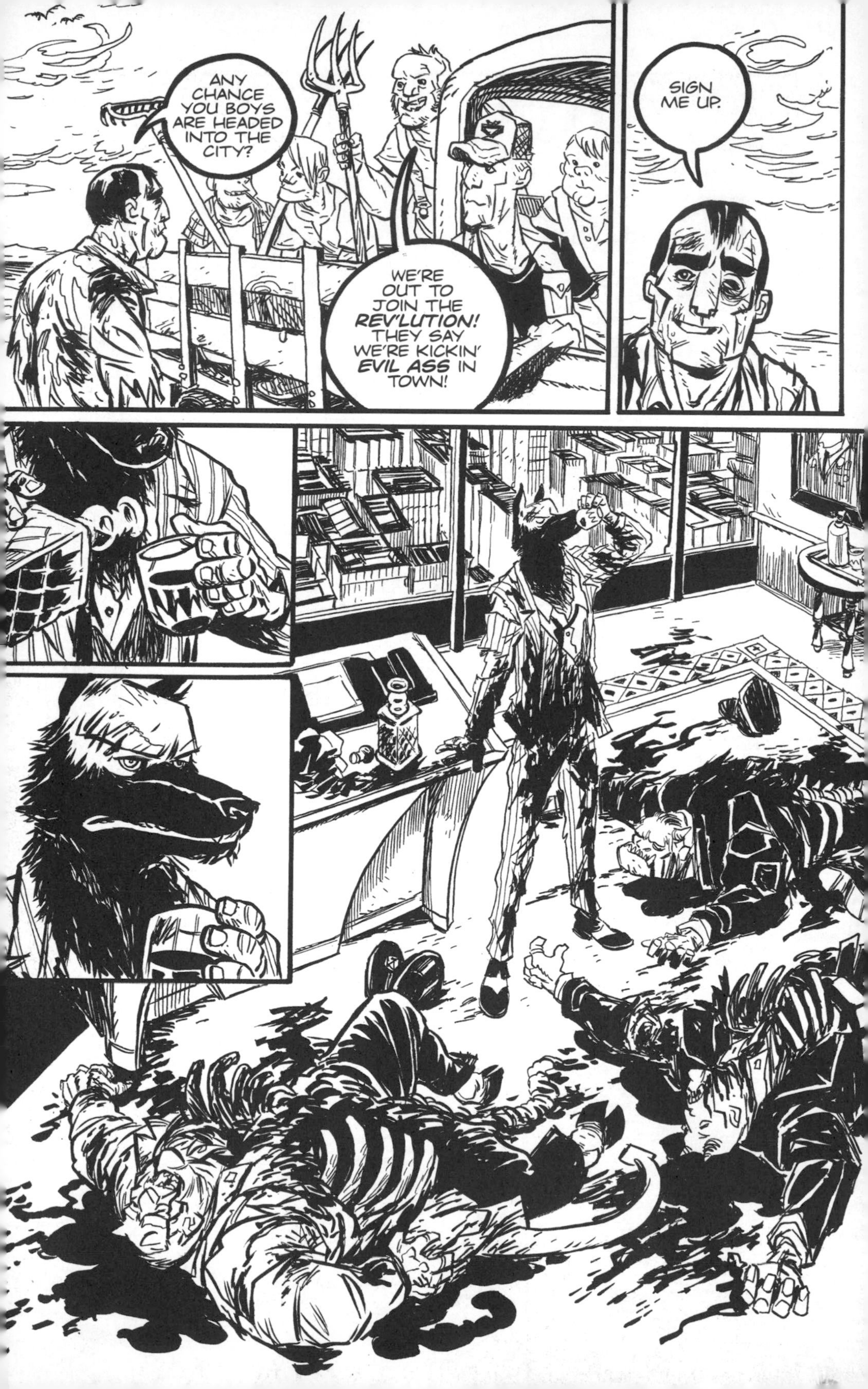

ANY CHANCE YOU BOYS ARE HEADED INTO THE CITY?
WE'RE OUT TO JOIN THE REV'LUTION! THEY SAY WE'RE KICKIN' EVIL ASS IN TOWN!
SIGN ME UP.

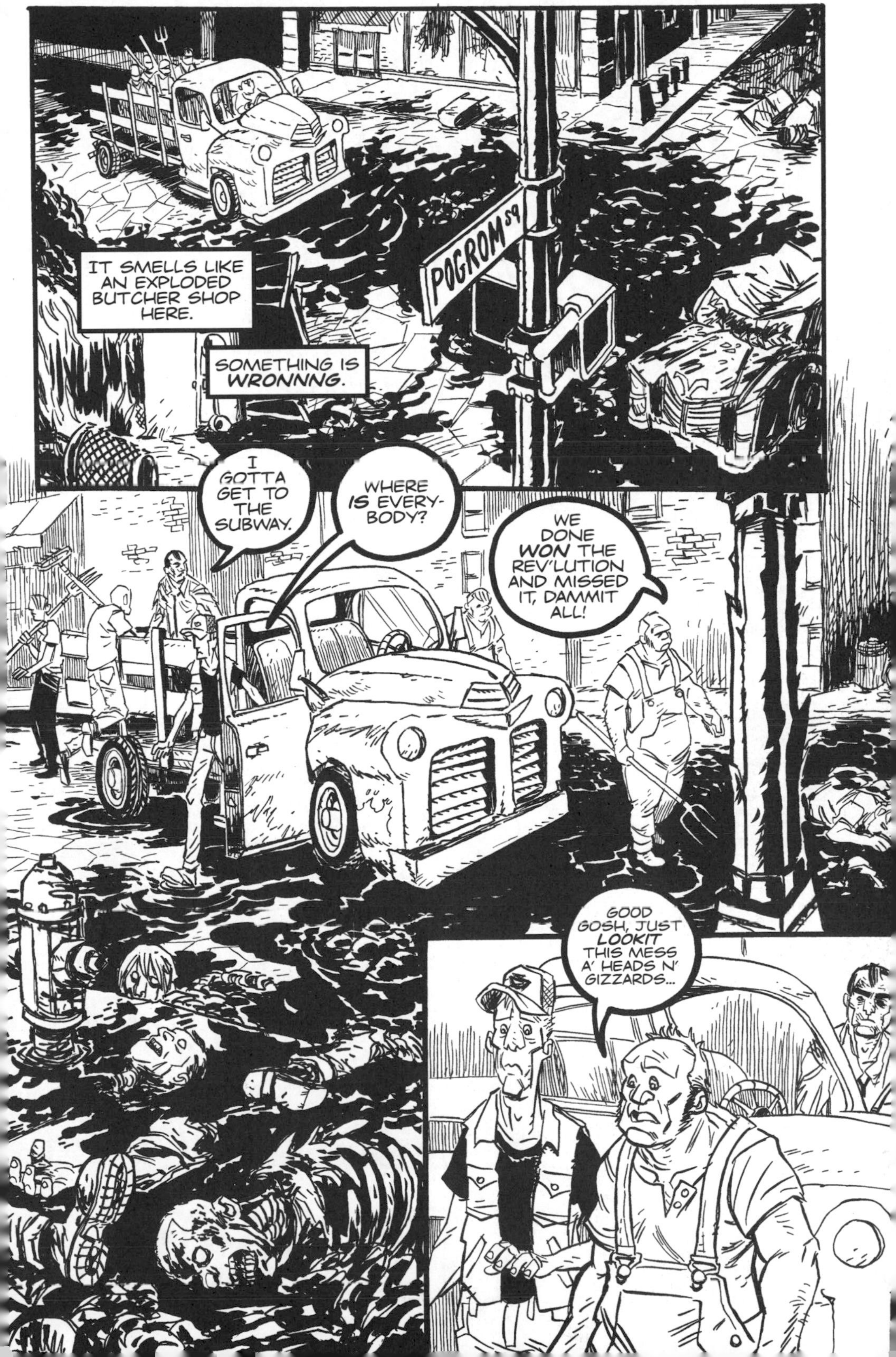

POGROM SQ
IT SMELLS LIKE AN EXPLODED BUTCHER SHOP HERE.
SOMETHING IS WRONNNG.
I GOTTA GET TO THE SUBWAY.
WHERE IS EVERY-BODY?
WE DONE WON THE REV'LUTION AND MISSED IT, DAMMIT ALL!
GOOD GOSH, JUST LOOKIT THIS MESS A' HEADS N' GIZZARDS...

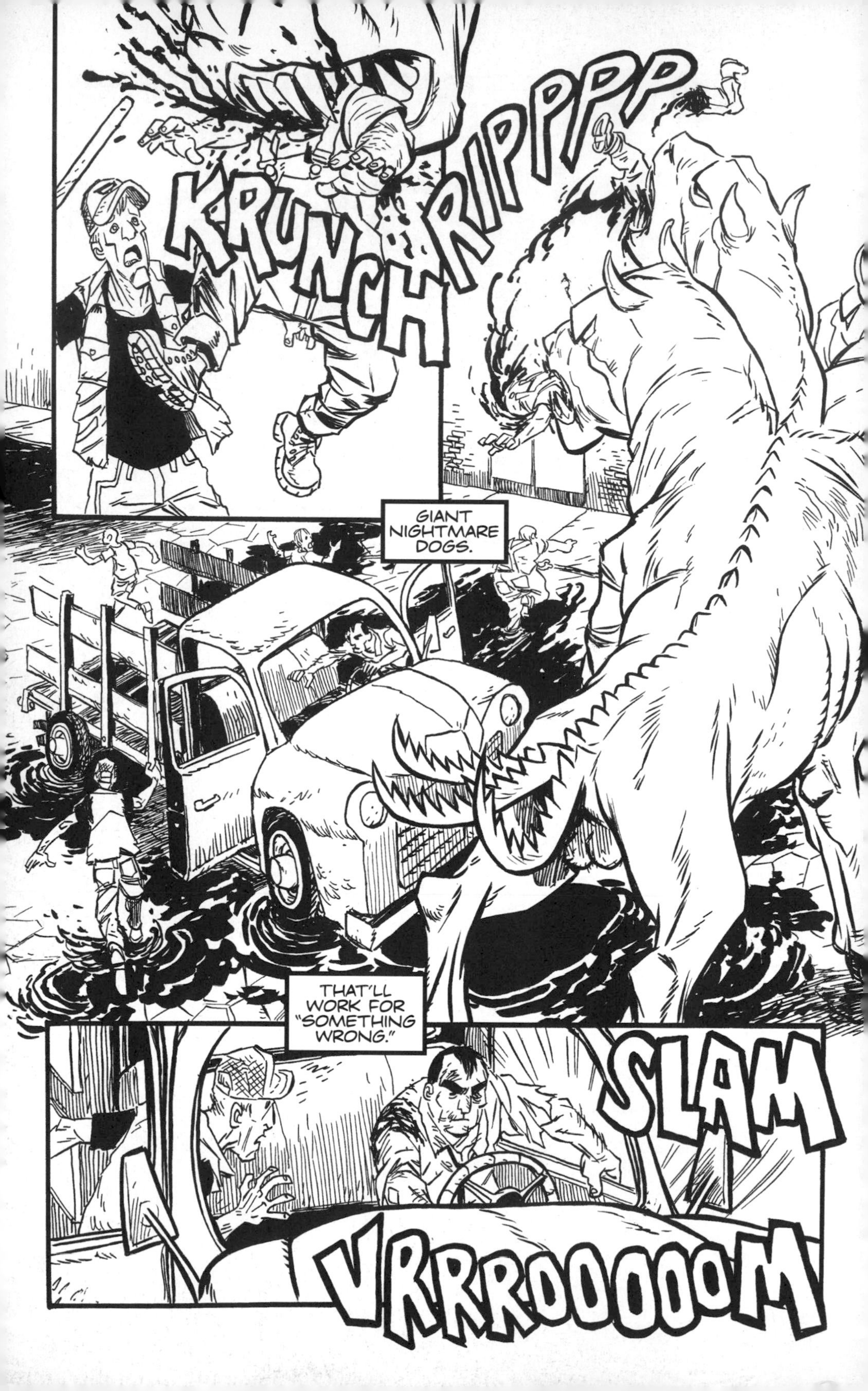
KRUNCH
RIPPPPP
GIANT NIGHTMARE DOGS.
THAT'LL WORK FOR "SOMETHING WRONG."
SLAM
VRRROOOOOM

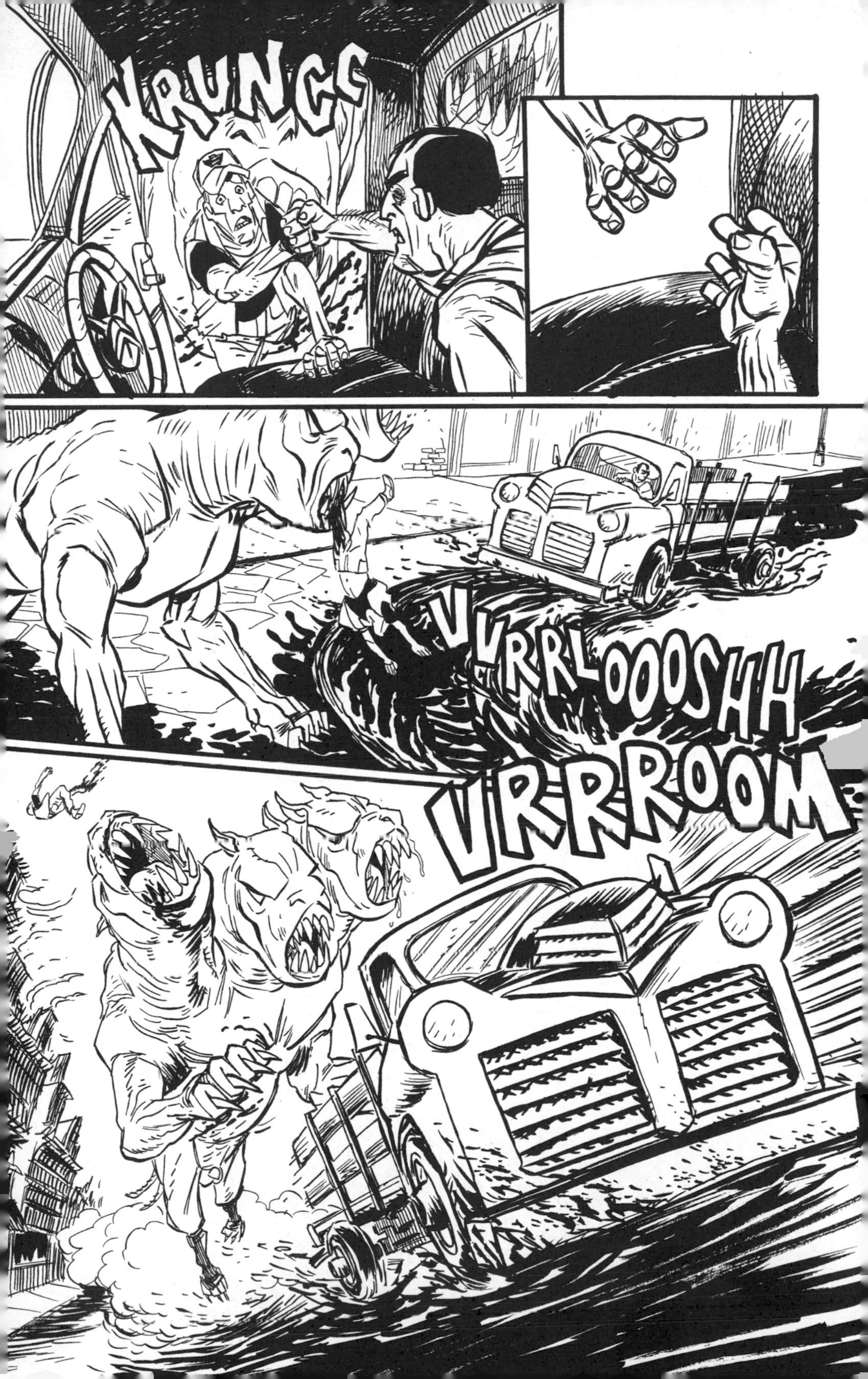
KRUNCC
VURRLOOOSHH
VRRROOM

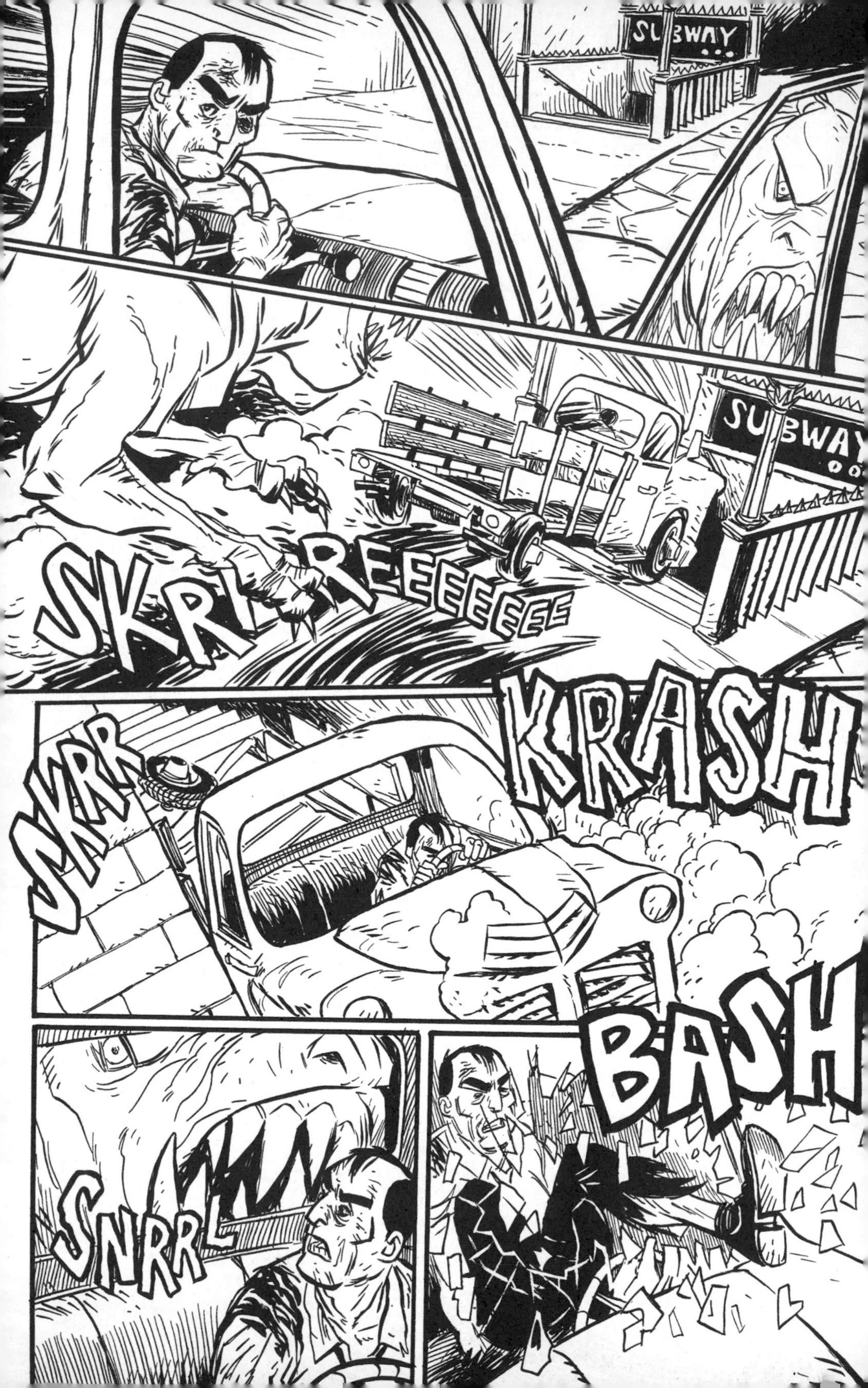
SUBWAY
SUBWAY
SKRI-REEEEEEEE
SKRR
KRASH
BASH
SNRRL

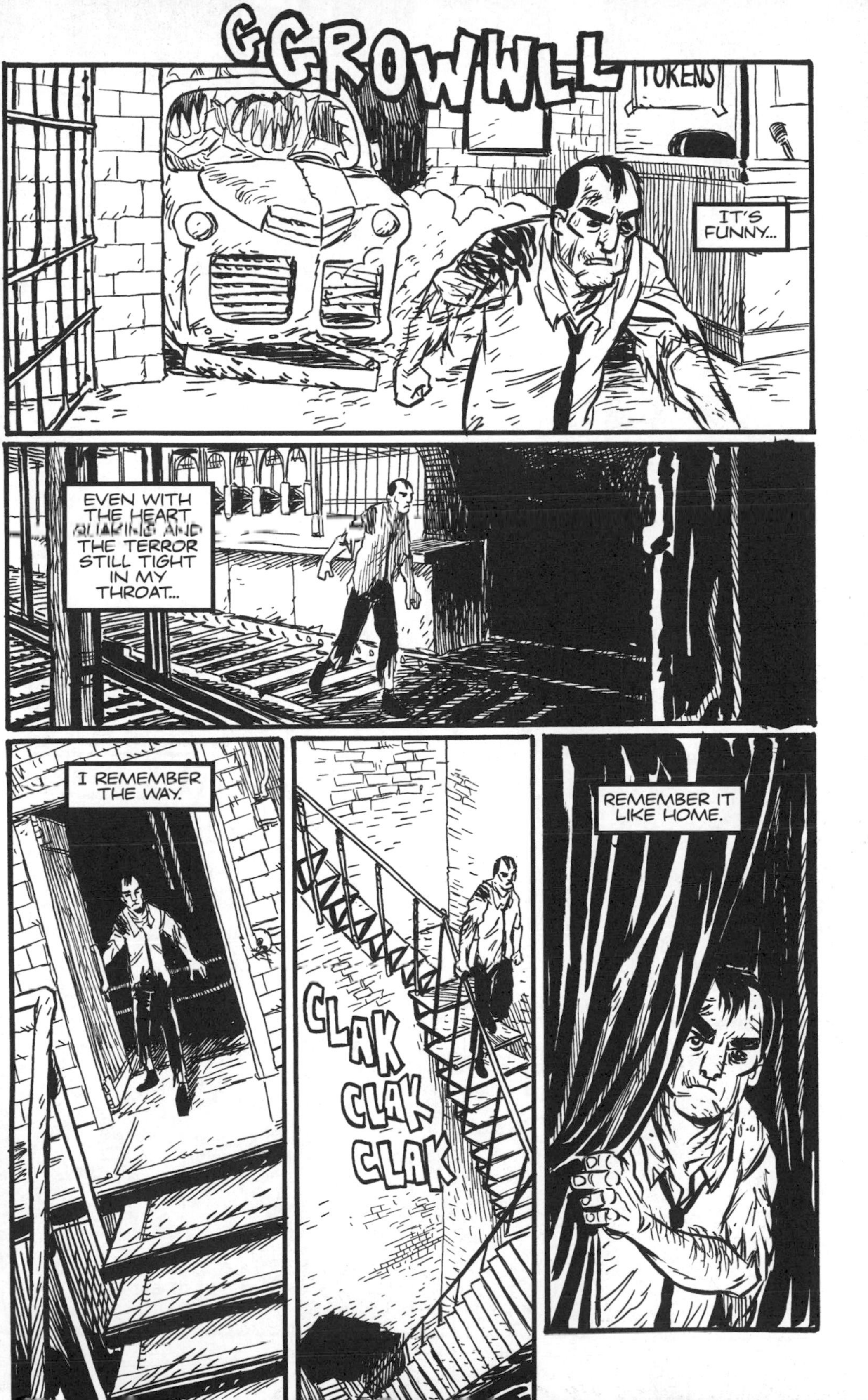
GGROWWLL
TOKENS
IT'S FUNNY...
EVEN WITH THE HEART QUAKING AND THE TERROR STILL TIGHT IN MY THROAT...
I REMEMBER THE WAY.
CLAK CLAK CLAK
REMEMBER IT LIKE HOME.

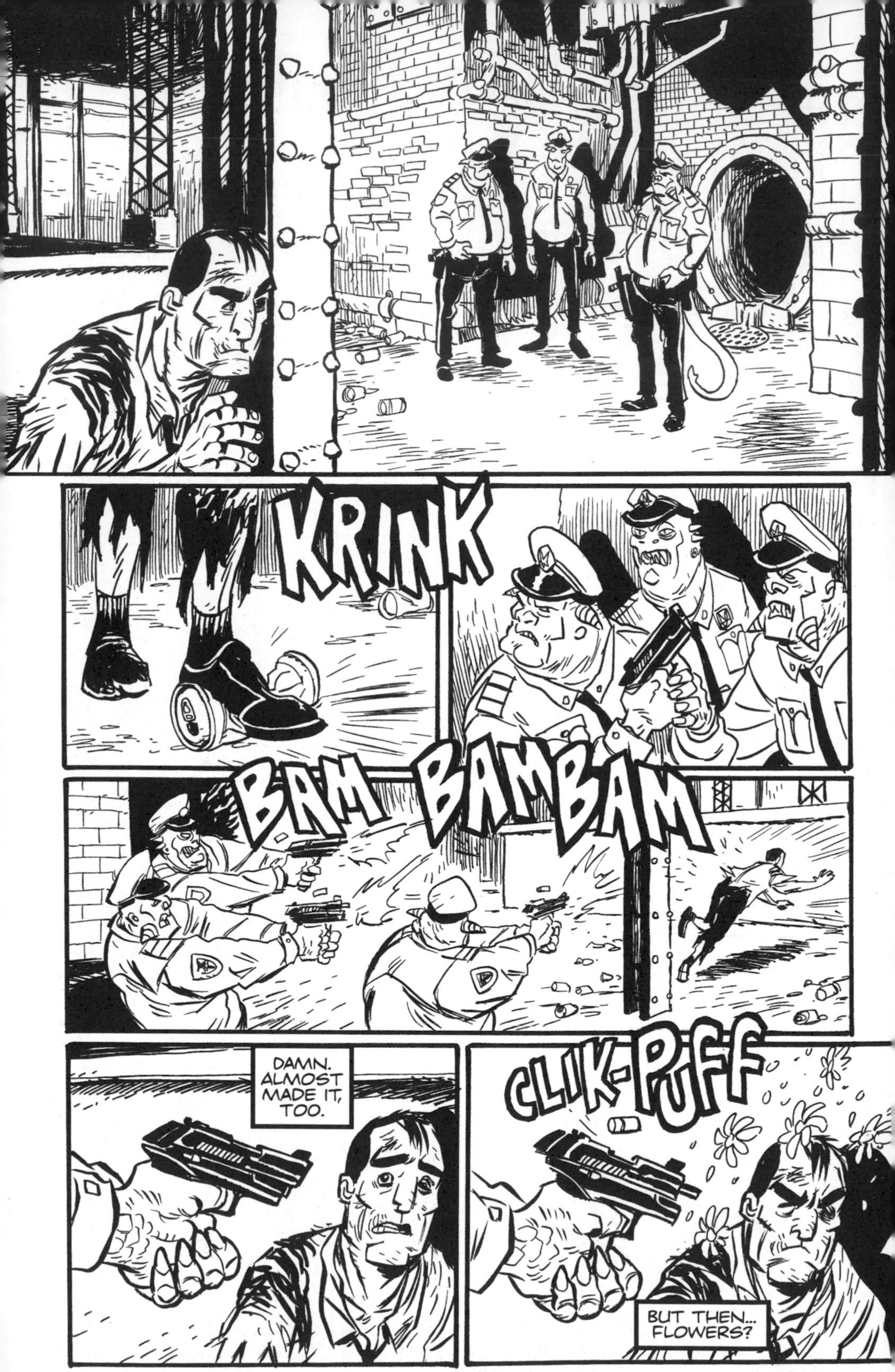
KRINK
BAM BAM BAM
DAMN. ALMOST MADE IT, TOO.
CLIK-PUFF
BUT THEN... FLOWERS?

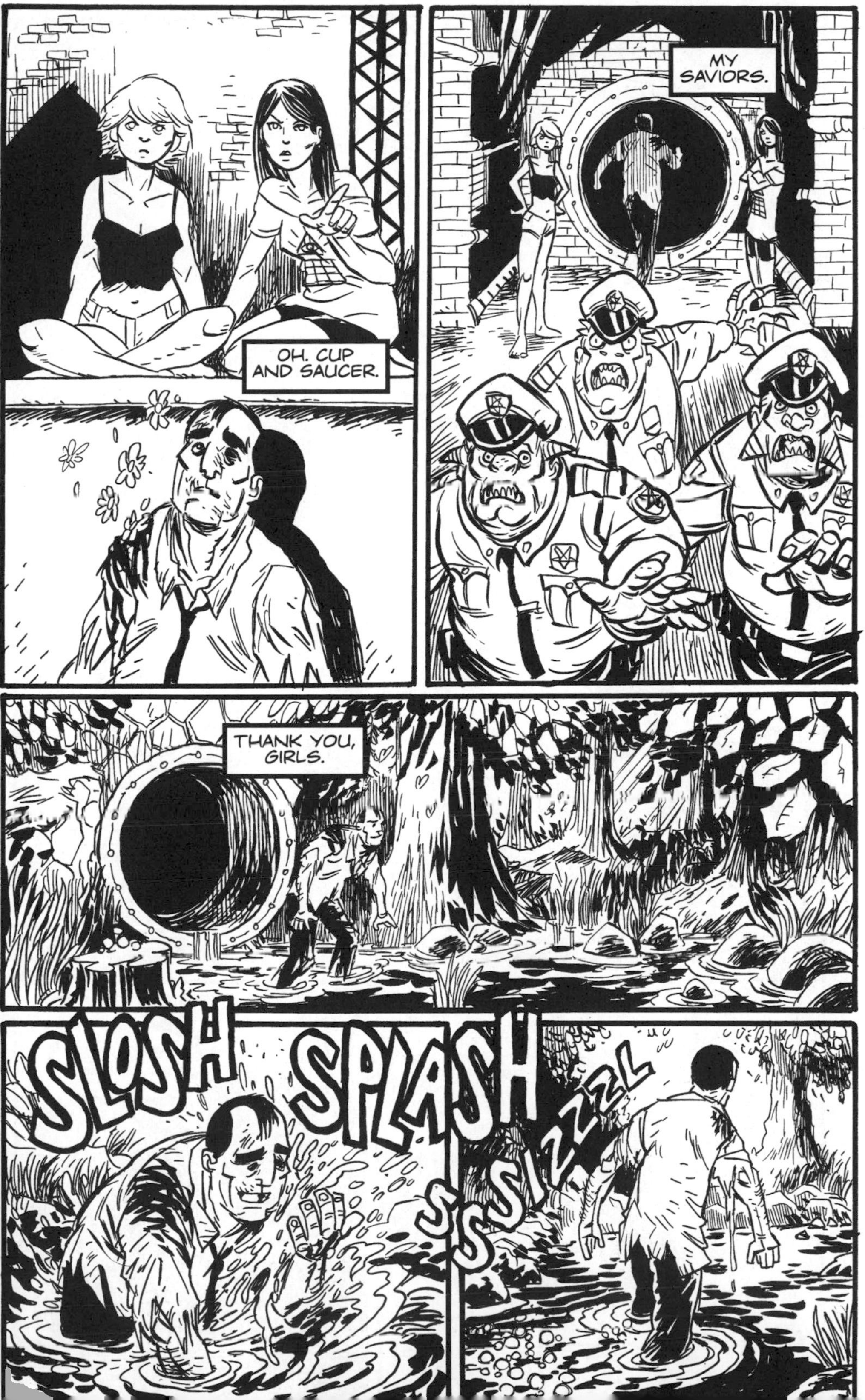
OH. CUP AND SAUCER.
MY SAVIORS.
THANK YOU, GIRLS.
SLOSH
SPLASH
SSSIZZZL

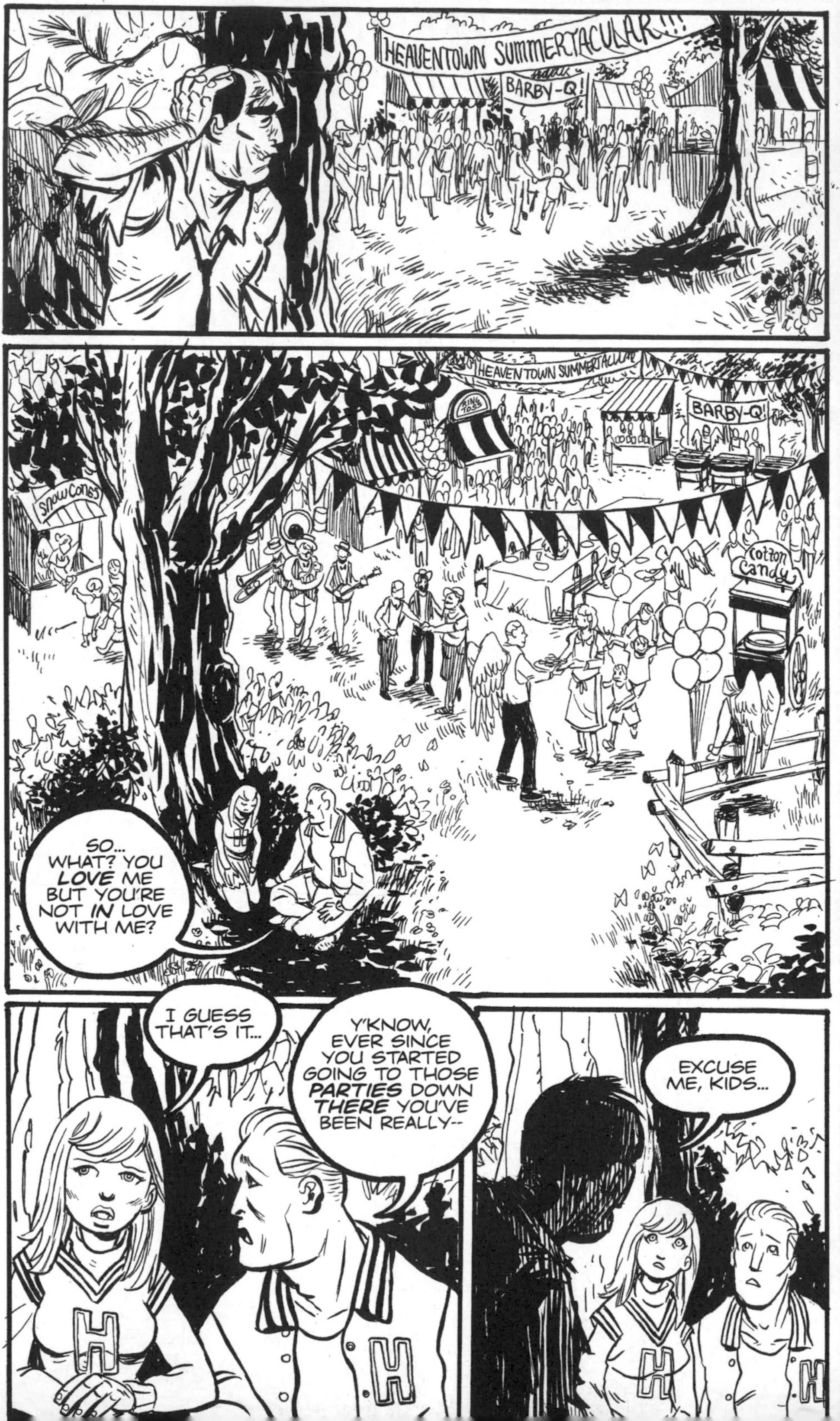
HEAVENTOWN SUMMERTACULAR!!!
BARBY-Q!
HEAVENTOWN SUMMERTACULAR
RING TOSS
BARBY-Q
SNOW CONES
COTTON CANDY
SO... WHAT? YOU LOVE ME BUT YOU'RE NOT IN LOVE WITH ME?
I GUESS THAT'S IT...
Y'KNOW, EVER SINCE YOU STARTED GOING TO THOSE PARTIES DOWN THERE YOU'VE BEEN REALLY--
EXCUSE ME, KIDS...

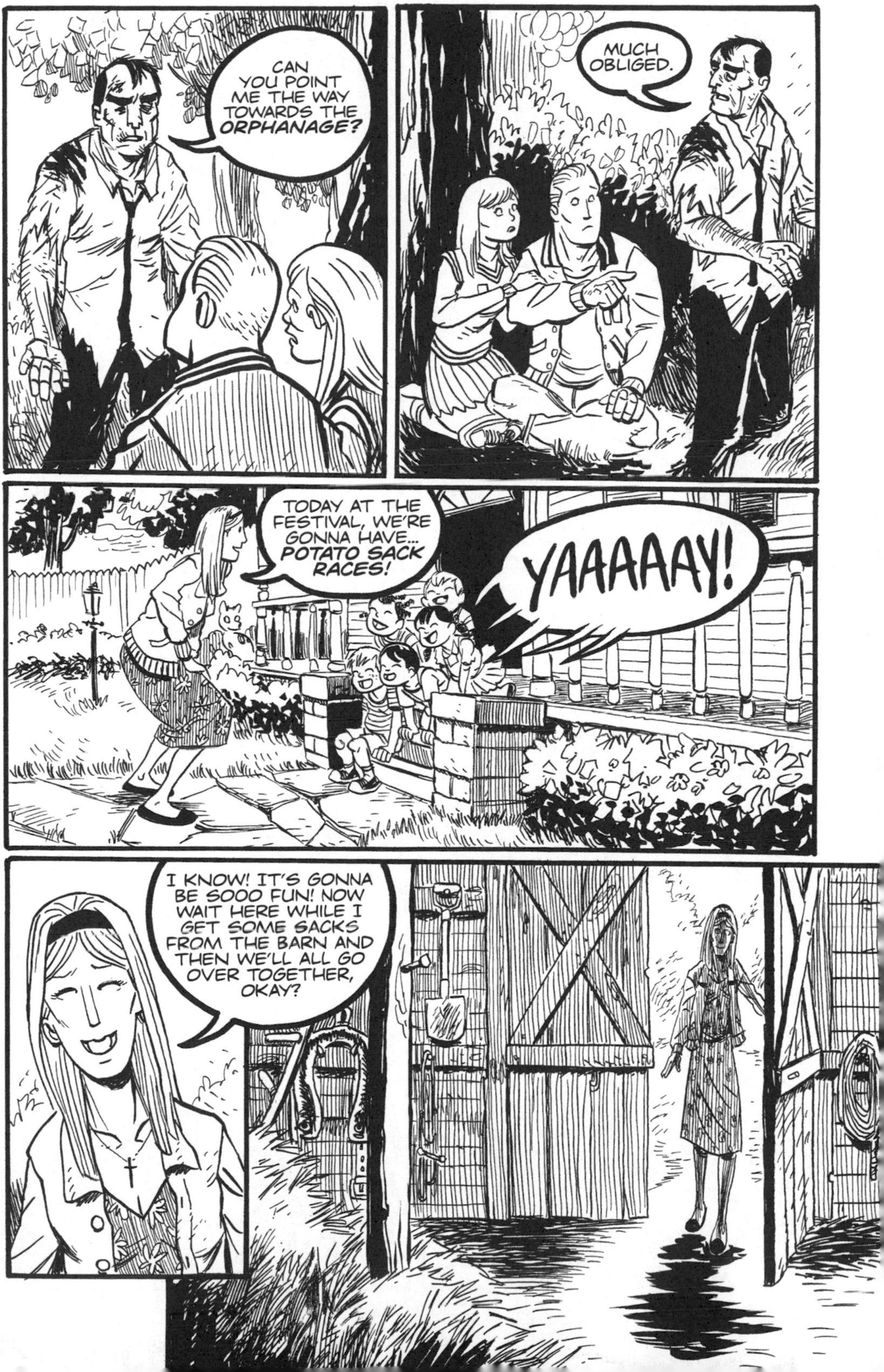
CAN YOU POINT ME THE WAY TOWARDS THE ORPHANAGE?
MUCH OBLIGED.
TODAY AT THE FESTIVAL, WE'RE GONNA HAVE... POTATO SACK RACES!
YAAAAAY!
I KNOW! IT'S GONNA BE SOOO FUN! NOW WAIT HERE WHILE I GET SOME SACKS FROM THE BARN AND THEN WE'LL ALL GO OVER TOGETHER, OKAY?

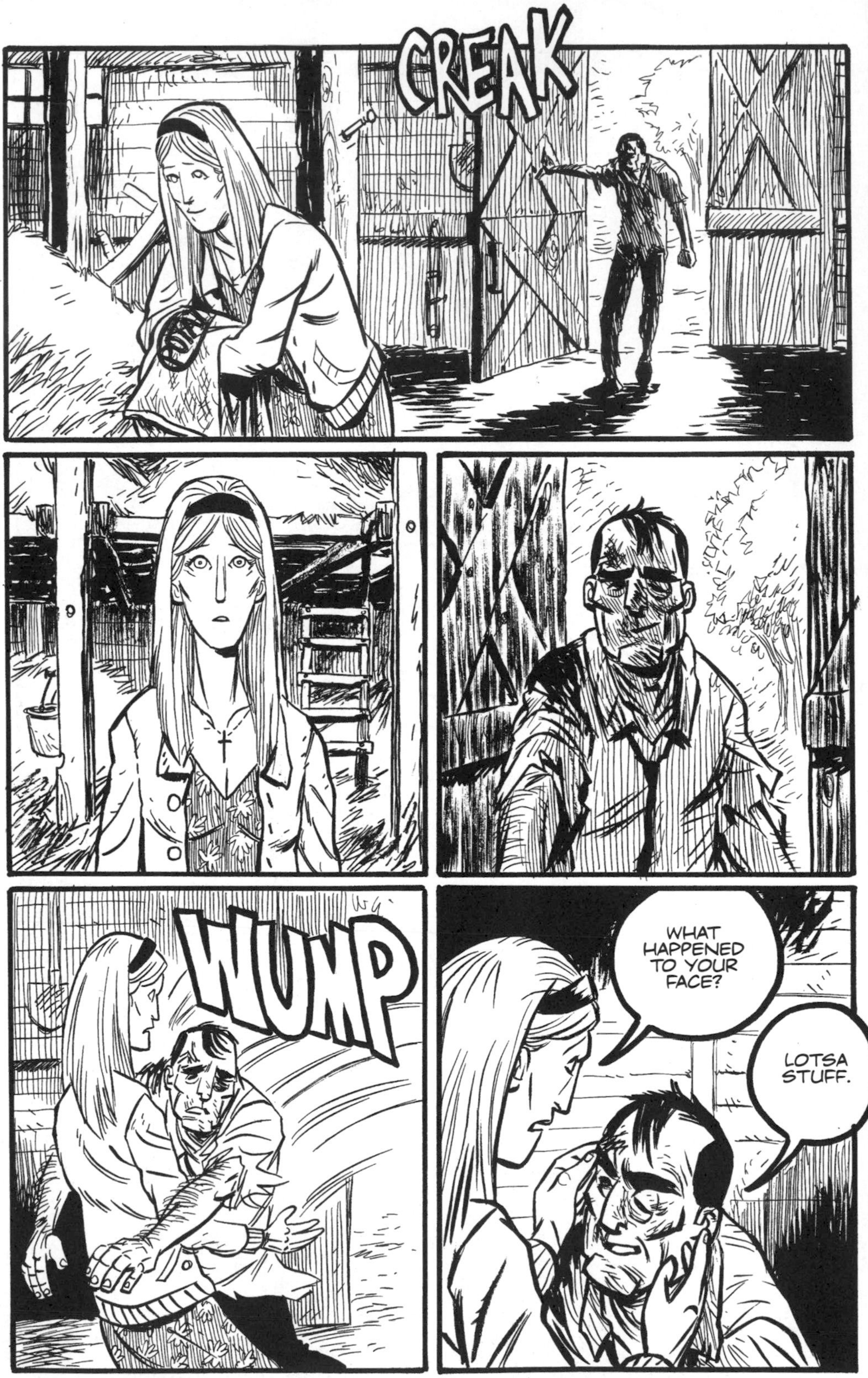
CREAK
WUMP
WHAT HAPPENED TO YOUR FACE?
LOTSA STUFF.

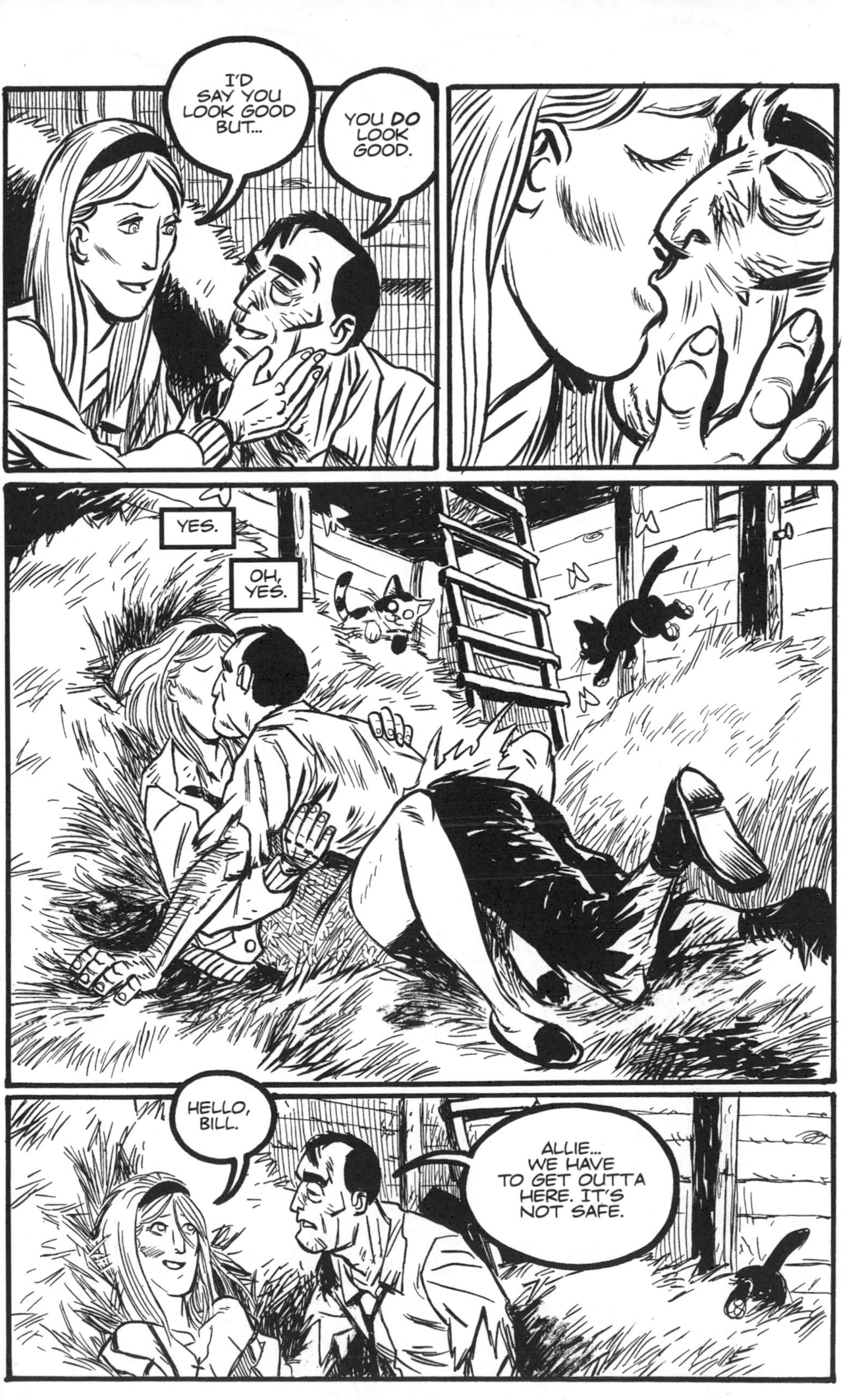
I'D SAY YOU LOOK GOOD BUT...
YOU DO LOOK GOOD.
YES.
OH, YES.
HELLO, BILL.
ALLIE... WE HAVE TO GET OUTTA HERE. IT'S NOT SAFE.

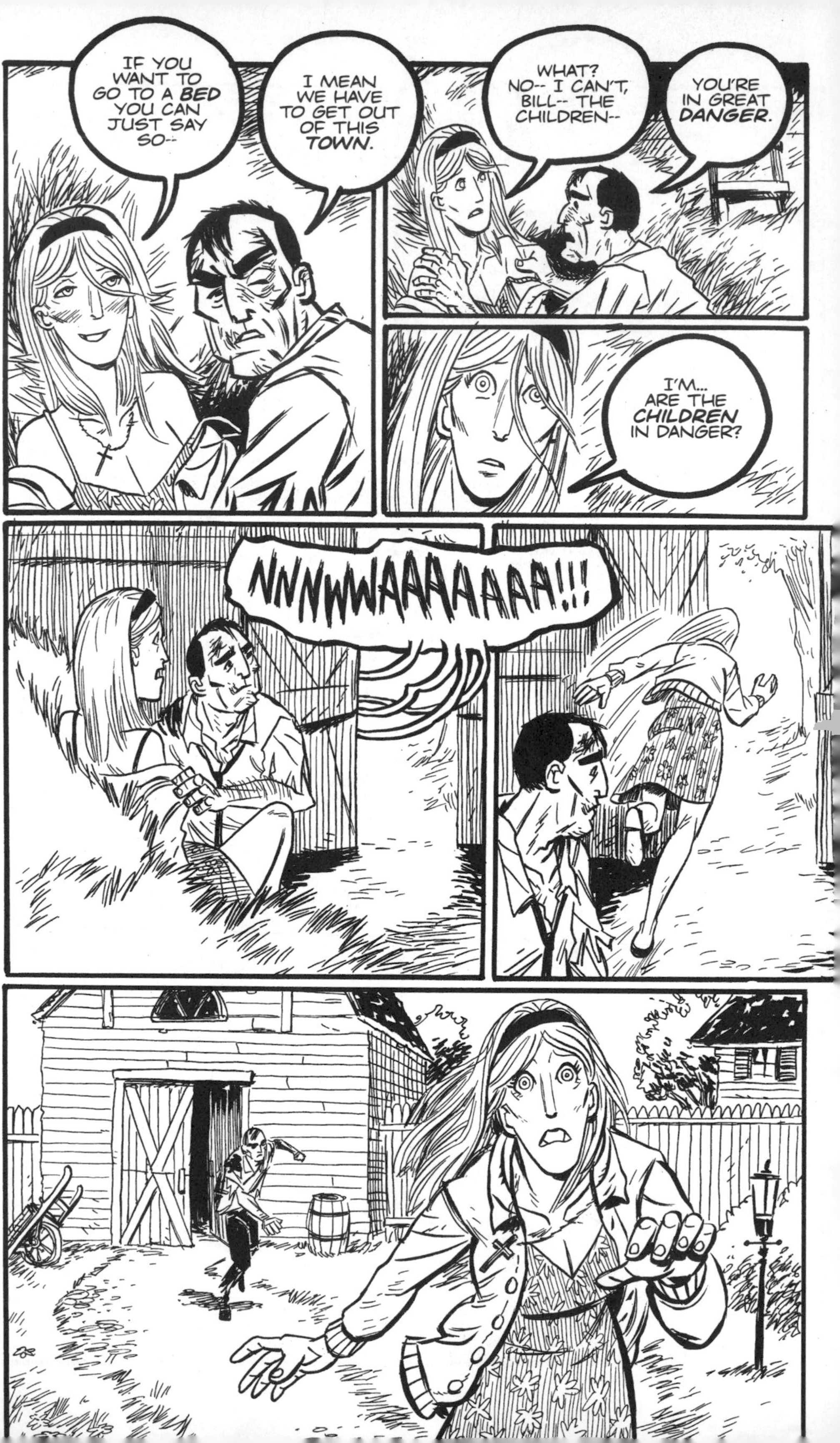
IF YOU WANT TO GO TO A BED YOU CAN JUST SAY SO--
I MEAN WE HAVE TO GET OUT OF THIS TOWN.
WHAT? NO-- I CAN'T, BILL-- THE CHILDREN--
YOU'RE IN GREAT DANGER.
I'M... ARE THE CHILDREN IN DANGER?
NNNWWAAAAAAAA!!!

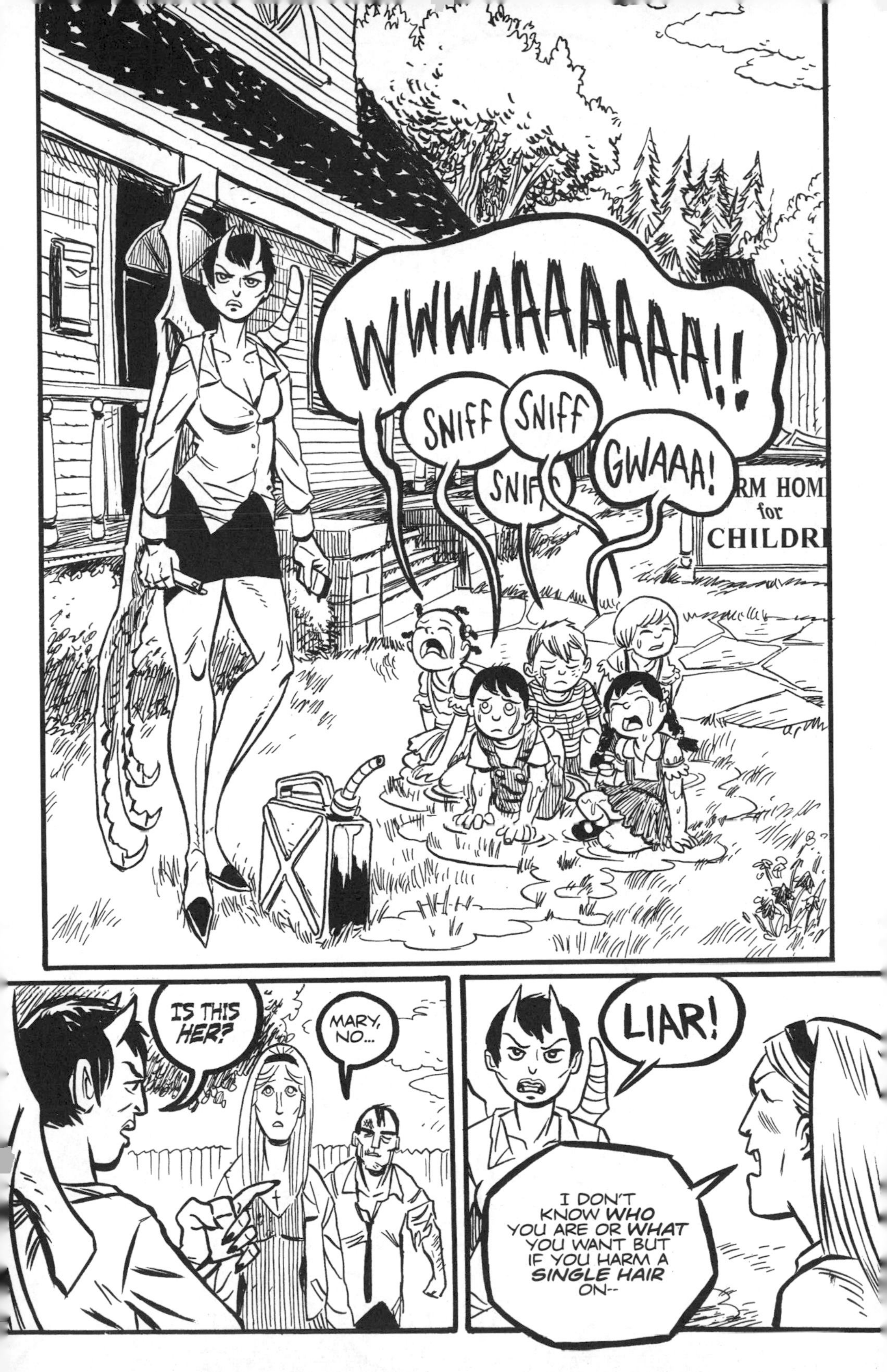
WWWARAAAAAA!!
SNIFF
SNIFF
SNIFF
GWAAA!
...RM HOM...
for
CHILDR...
IS THIS HER?
MARY, NO...
LIAR!
I DON'T KNOW WHO YOU ARE OR WHAT YOU WANT BUT IF YOU HARM A SINGLE HAIR ON--

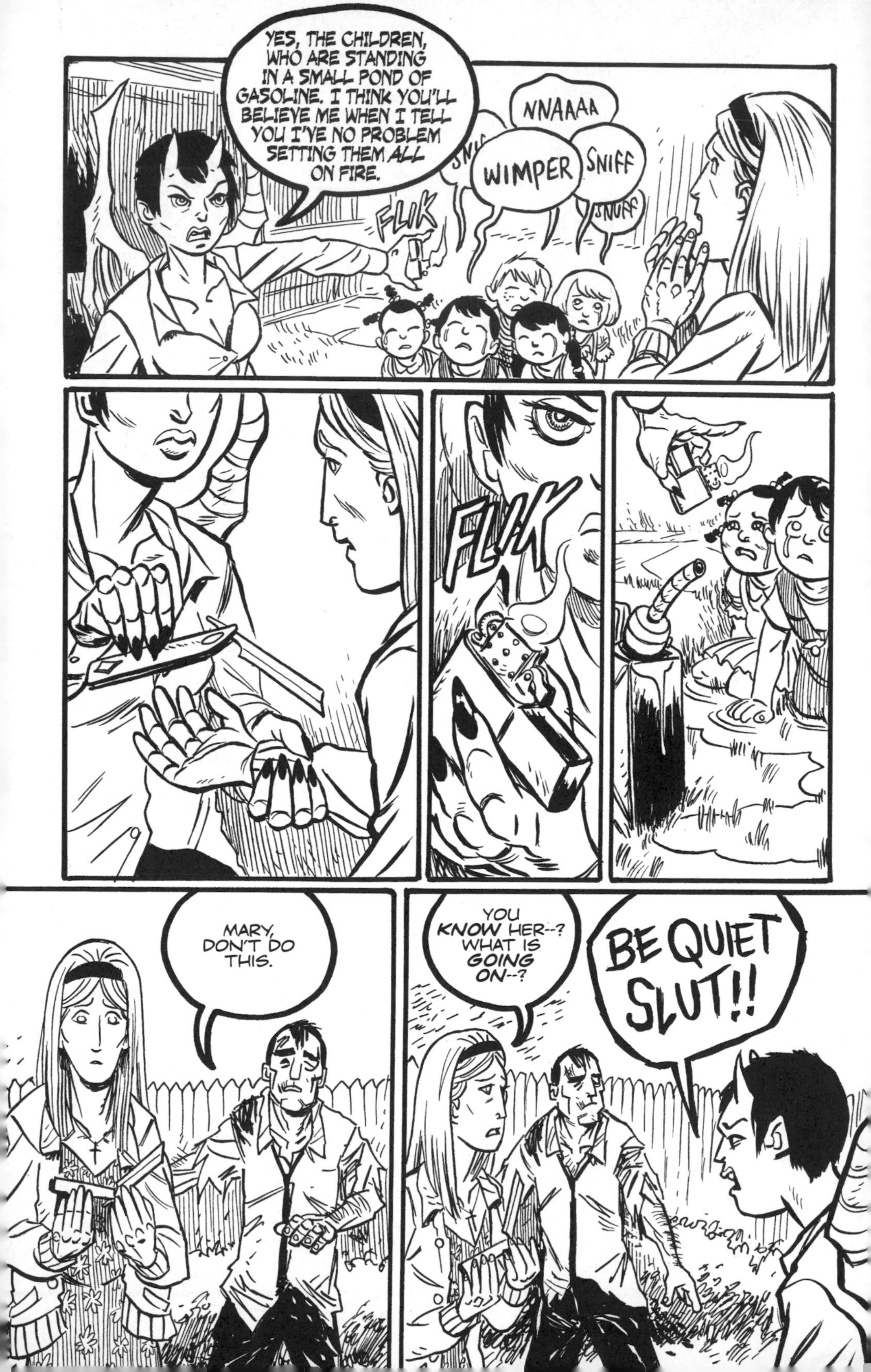
YES, THE CHILDREN, WHO ARE STANDING IN A SMALL POND OF GASOLINE. I THINK YOU'LL BELIEVE ME WHEN I TELL YOU I'VE NO PROBLEM SETTING THEM ALL ON FIRE.
NNAAAA
WIMPER
SNIFF
SNUFF
FLIK
FLIK
MARY, DON'T DO THIS.
YOU KNOW HER--? WHAT IS GOING ON--?
BE QUIET SLUT!!

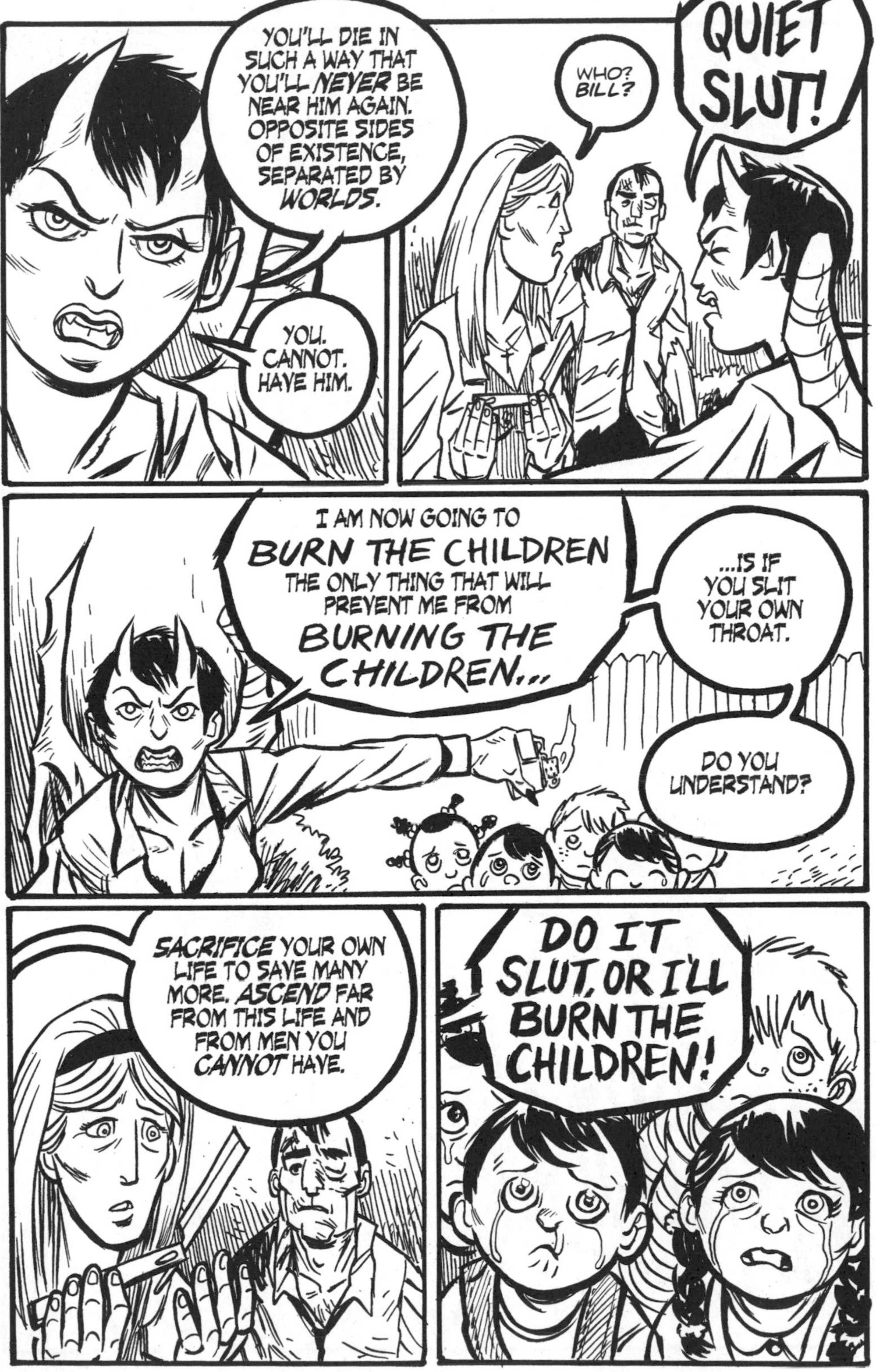
YOU'LL DIE IN SUCH A WAY THAT YOU'LL NEVER BE NEAR HIM AGAIN. OPPOSITE SIDES OF EXISTENCE, SEPARATED BY WORLDS.
YOU. CANNOT. HAVE HIM.
WHO? BILL?
QUIET SLUT!
I AM NOW GOING TO BURN THE CHILDREN THE ONLY THING THAT WILL PREVENT ME FROM BURNING THE CHILDREN...
...IS IF YOU SLIT YOUR OWN THROAT.
DO YOU UNDERSTAND?
SACRIFICE YOUR OWN LIFE TO SAVE MANY MORE. ASCEND FAR FROM THIS LIFE AND FROM MEN YOU CANNOT HAVE.
DO IT SLUT, OR I'LL BURN THE CHILDREN!

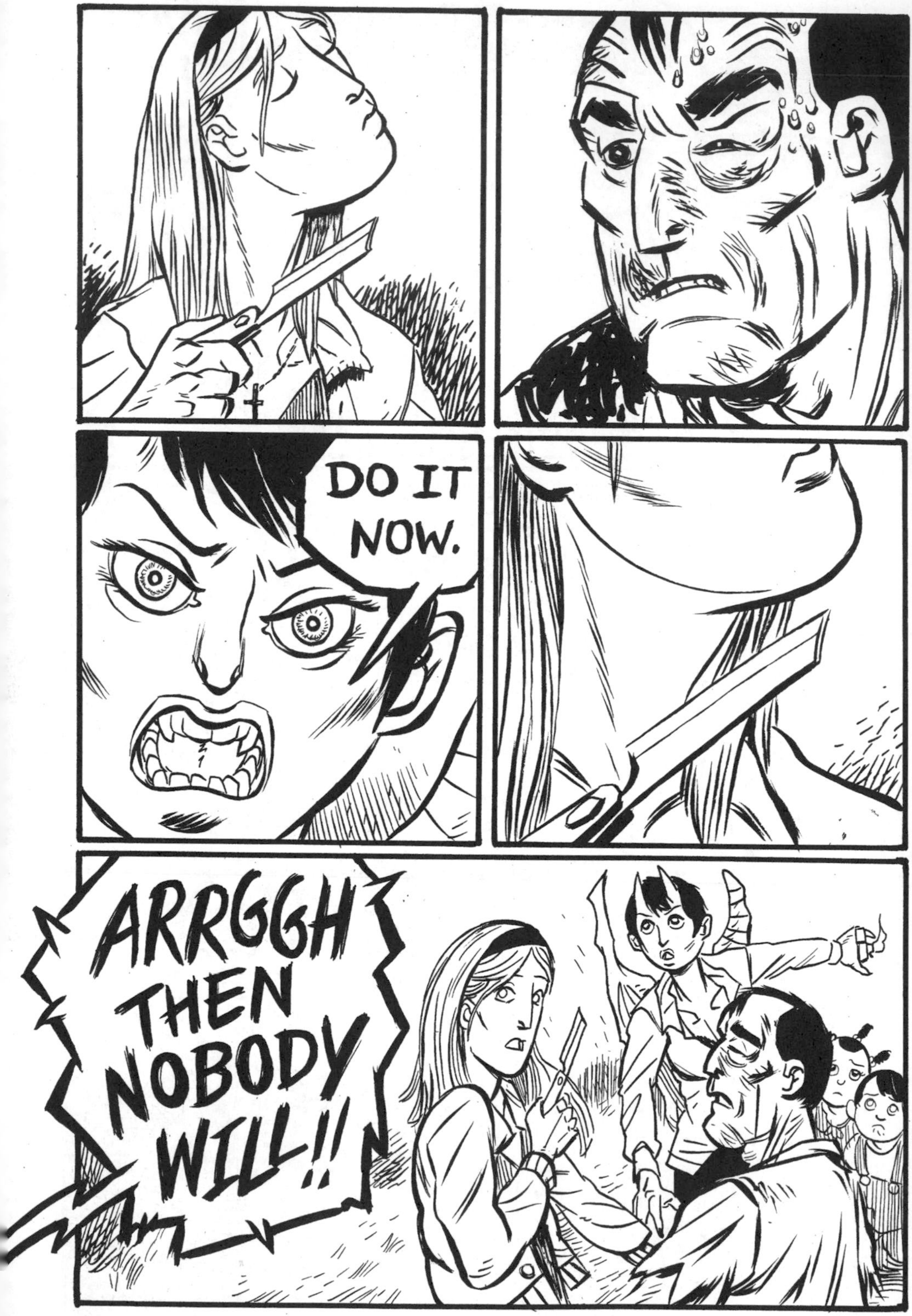
DO IT NOW.
ARRGGH THEN NOBODY WILL!!

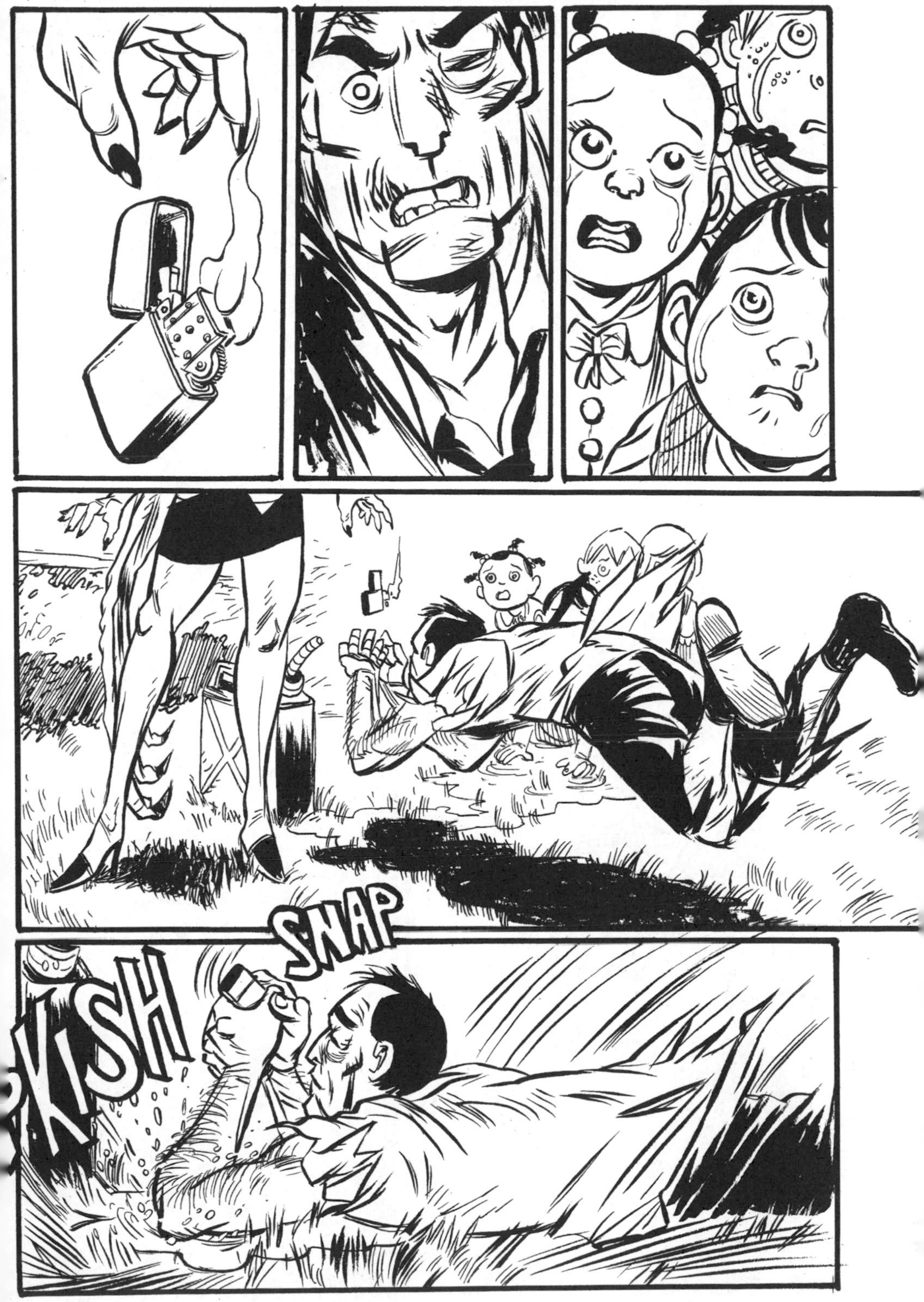
SNAP
KISH

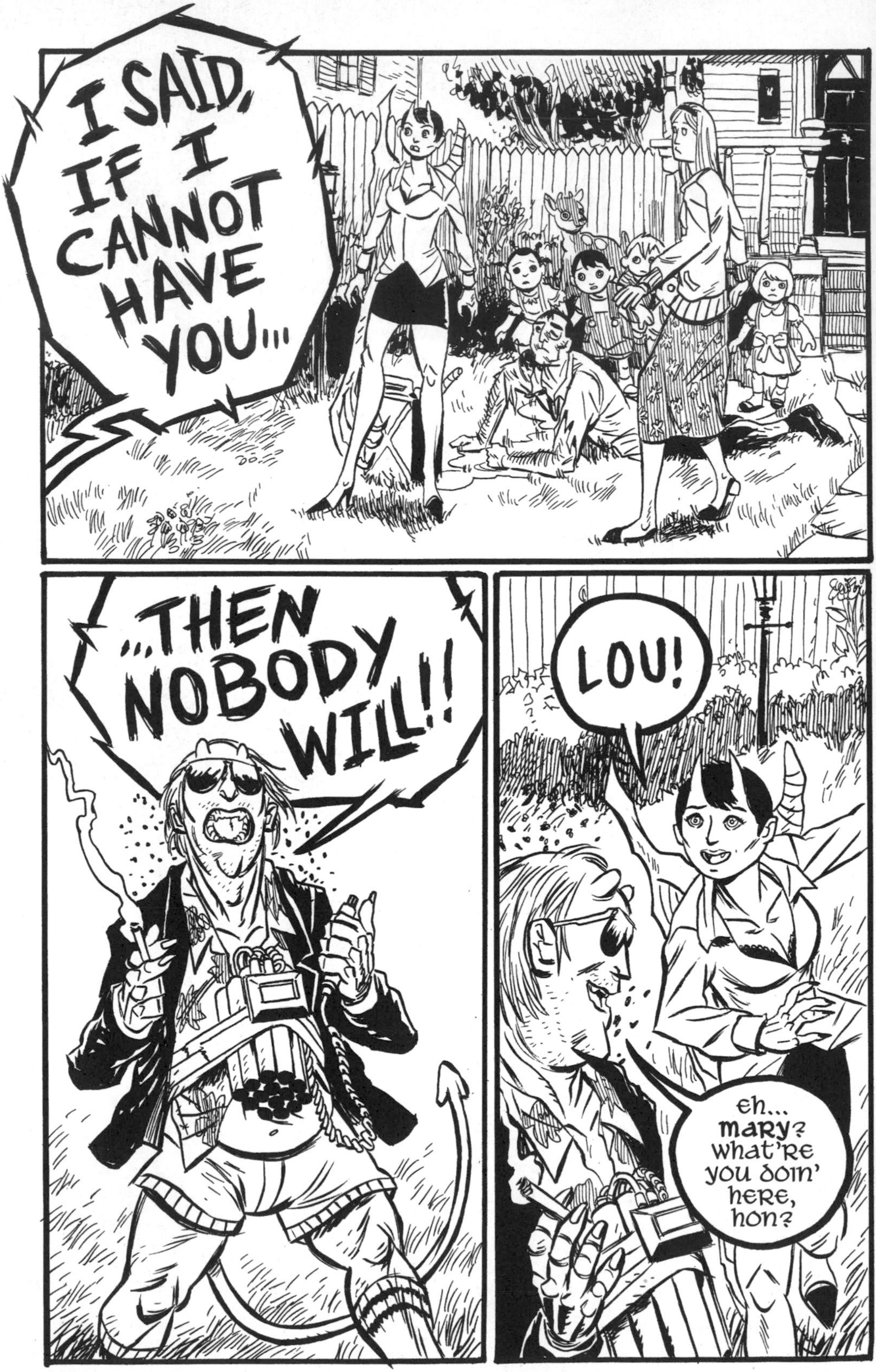
I SAID, IF I CANNOT HAVE YOU...
...THEN NOBODY WILL!!
LOU!
eh... mary? what're you doin' here, hon?

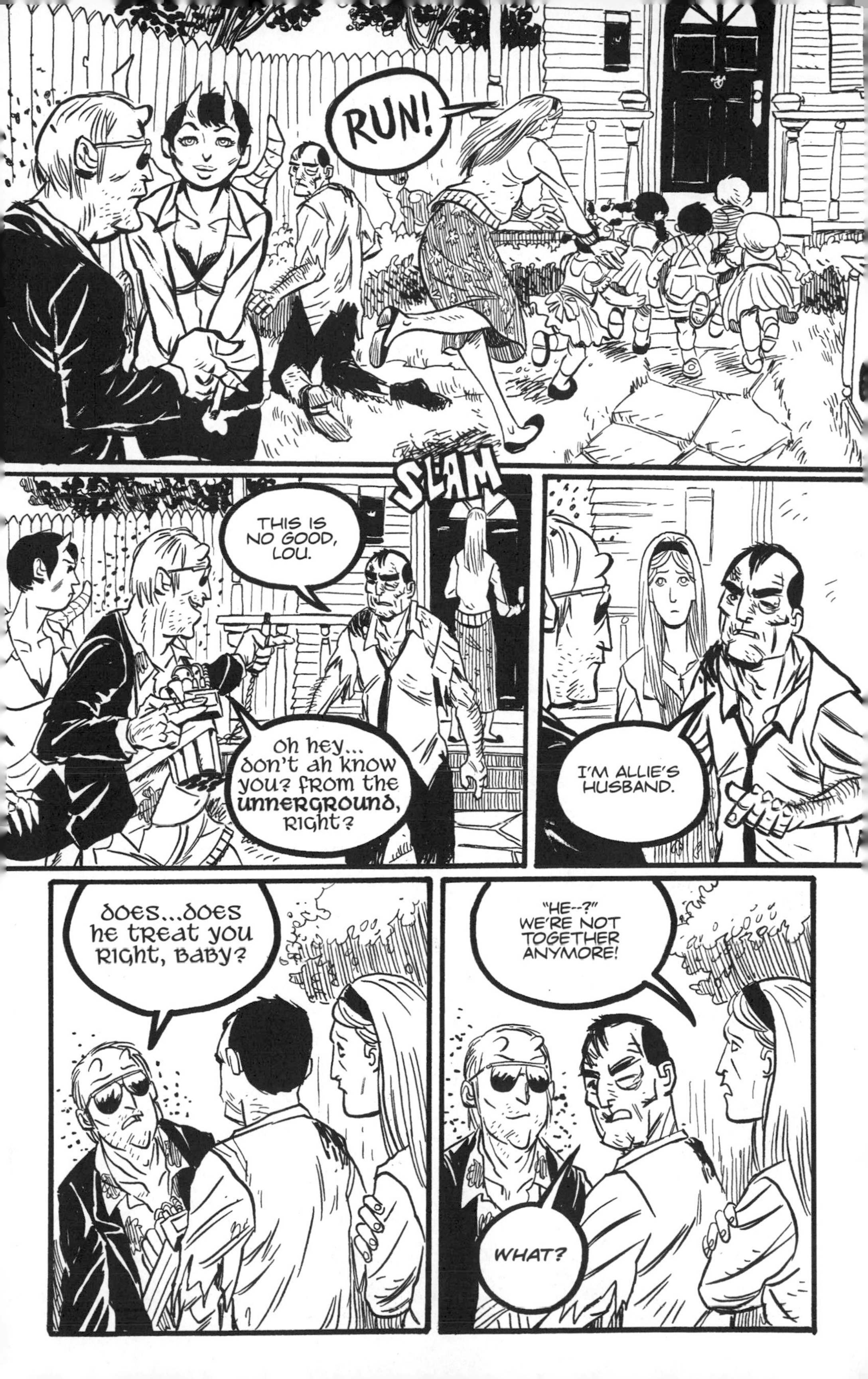
RUN!
SLAM
THIS IS NO GOOD, LOU.
oh hey... don't ah know you? from the unnerground, right?
I'M ALLIE'S HUSBAND.
does...does he treat you right, baby?
"HE--?" WE'RE NOT TOGETHER ANYMORE!
WHAT?

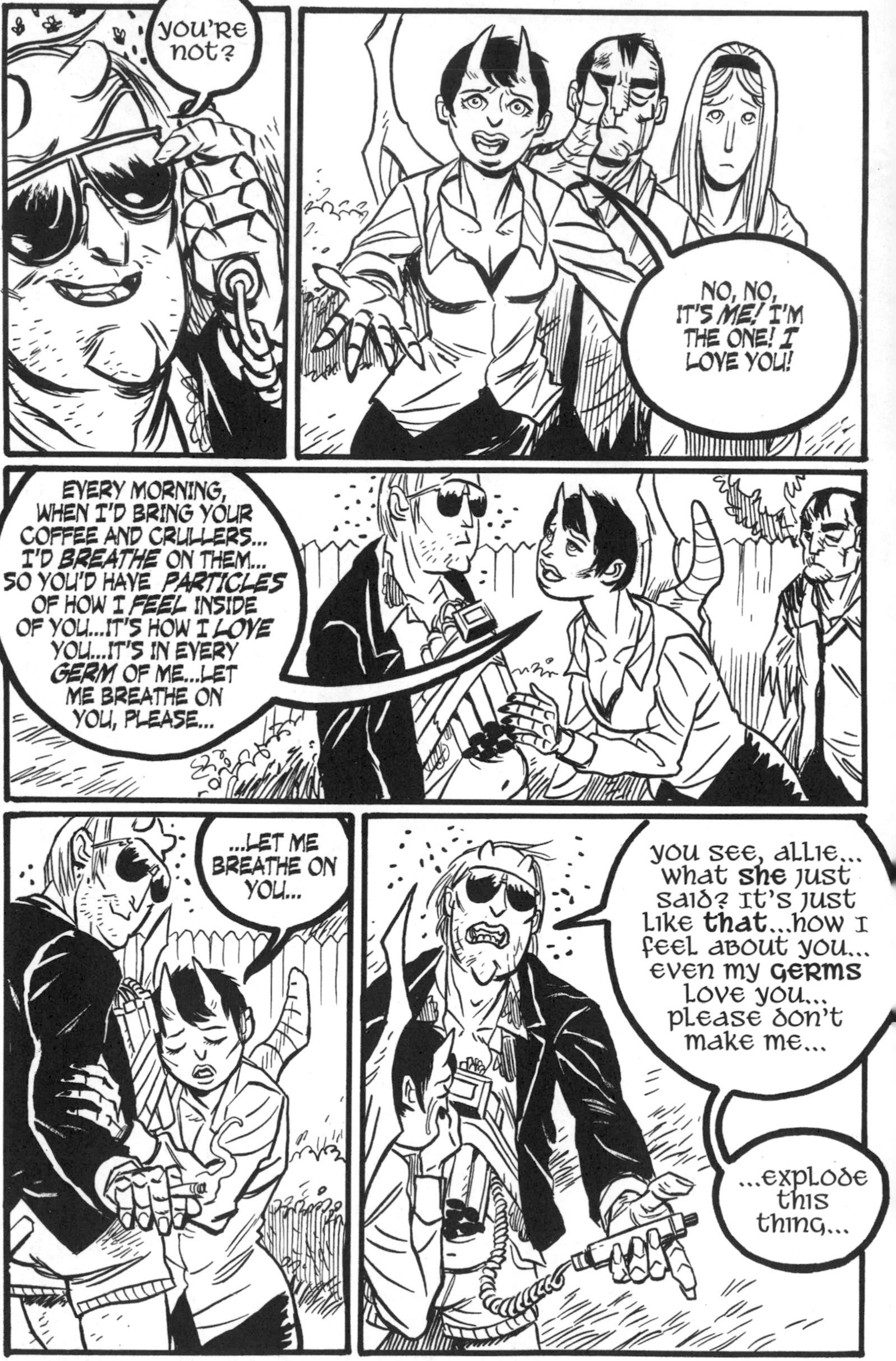
you're not?
NO, NO, IT'S ME! I'M THE ONE! I LOVE YOU!
EVERY MORNING, WHEN I'D BRING YOUR COFFEE AND CRULLERS... I'D BREATHE ON THEM... SO YOU'D HAVE PARTICLES OF HOW I FEEL INSIDE OF YOU...IT'S HOW I LOVE YOU...IT'S IN EVERY GERM OF ME...LET ME BREATHE ON YOU, PLEASE...
...LET ME BREATHE ON YOU...
you see, allie... what she just said? It's just like that...how I feel about you... even my germs love you... please don't make me...
...explode this thing...

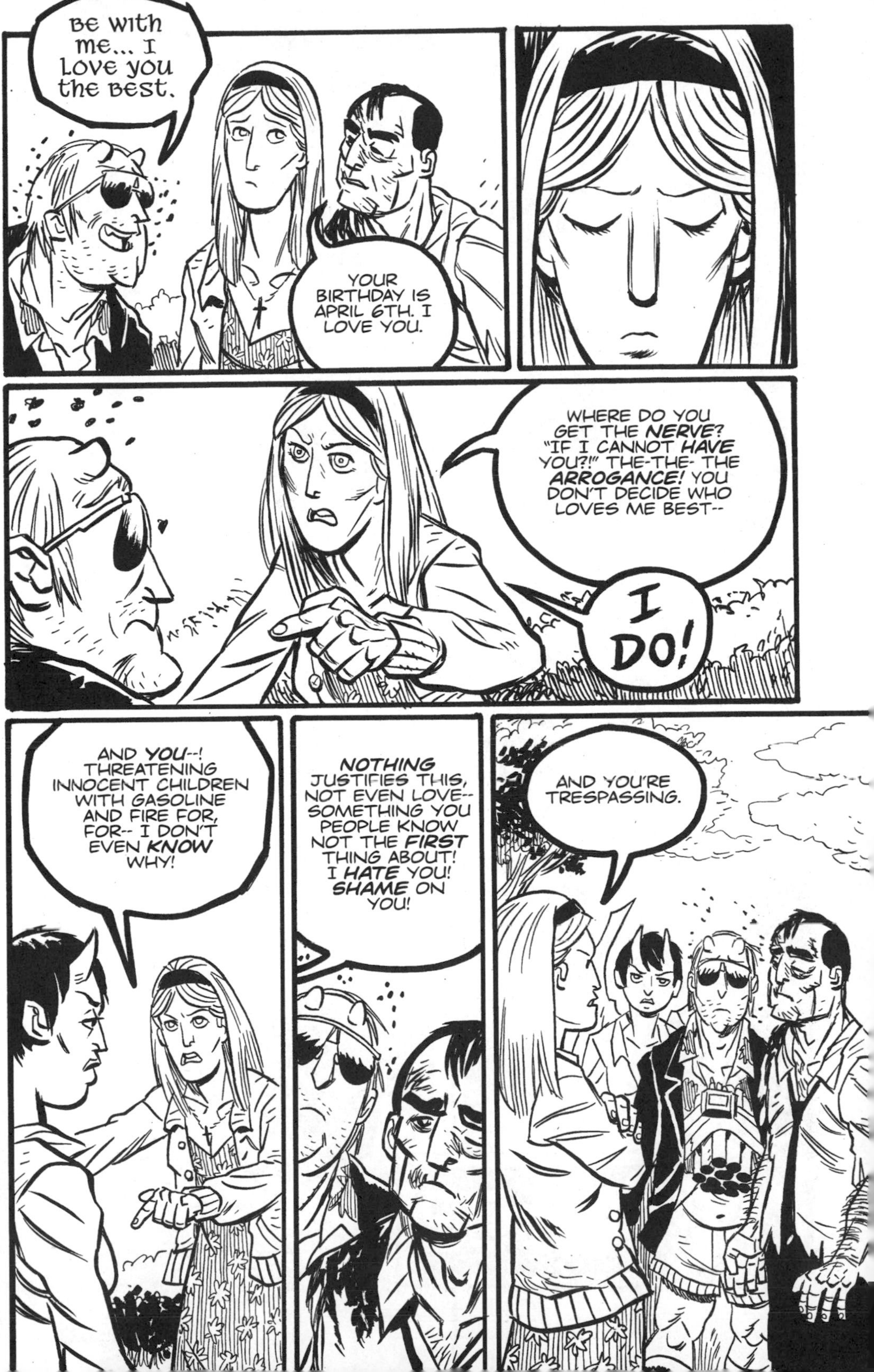
BE WITH ME... I LOVE YOU THE BEST.
YOUR BIRTHDAY IS APRIL 6TH. I LOVE YOU.
WHERE DO YOU GET THE NERVE? "IF I CANNOT HAVE YOU?!" THE-THE- THE ARROGANCE! YOU DON'T DECIDE WHO LOVES ME BEST--
I DO!
AND YOU--! THREATENING INNOCENT CHILDREN WITH GASOLINE AND FIRE FOR, FOR-- I DON'T EVEN KNOW WHY!
NOTHING JUSTIFIES THIS, NOT EVEN LOVE-- SOMETHING YOU PEOPLE KNOW NOT THE FIRST THING ABOUT! I HATE YOU! SHAME ON YOU!
AND YOU'RE TRESPASSING.

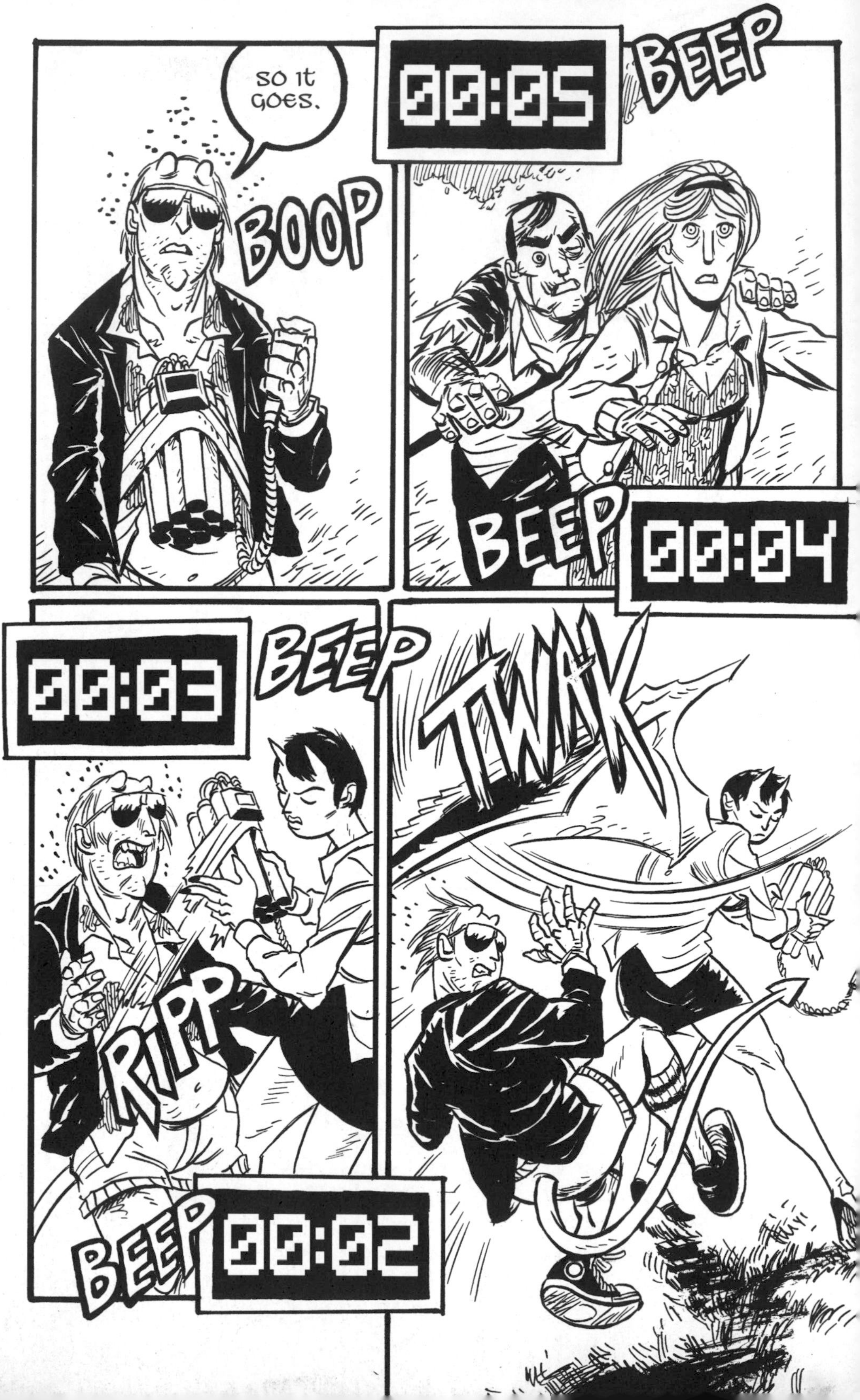
SO IT GOES.
BOOP
00:05
BEEP
BEEP
00:04
00:03
BEEP
RIPP
BEEP
00:02
TWAK

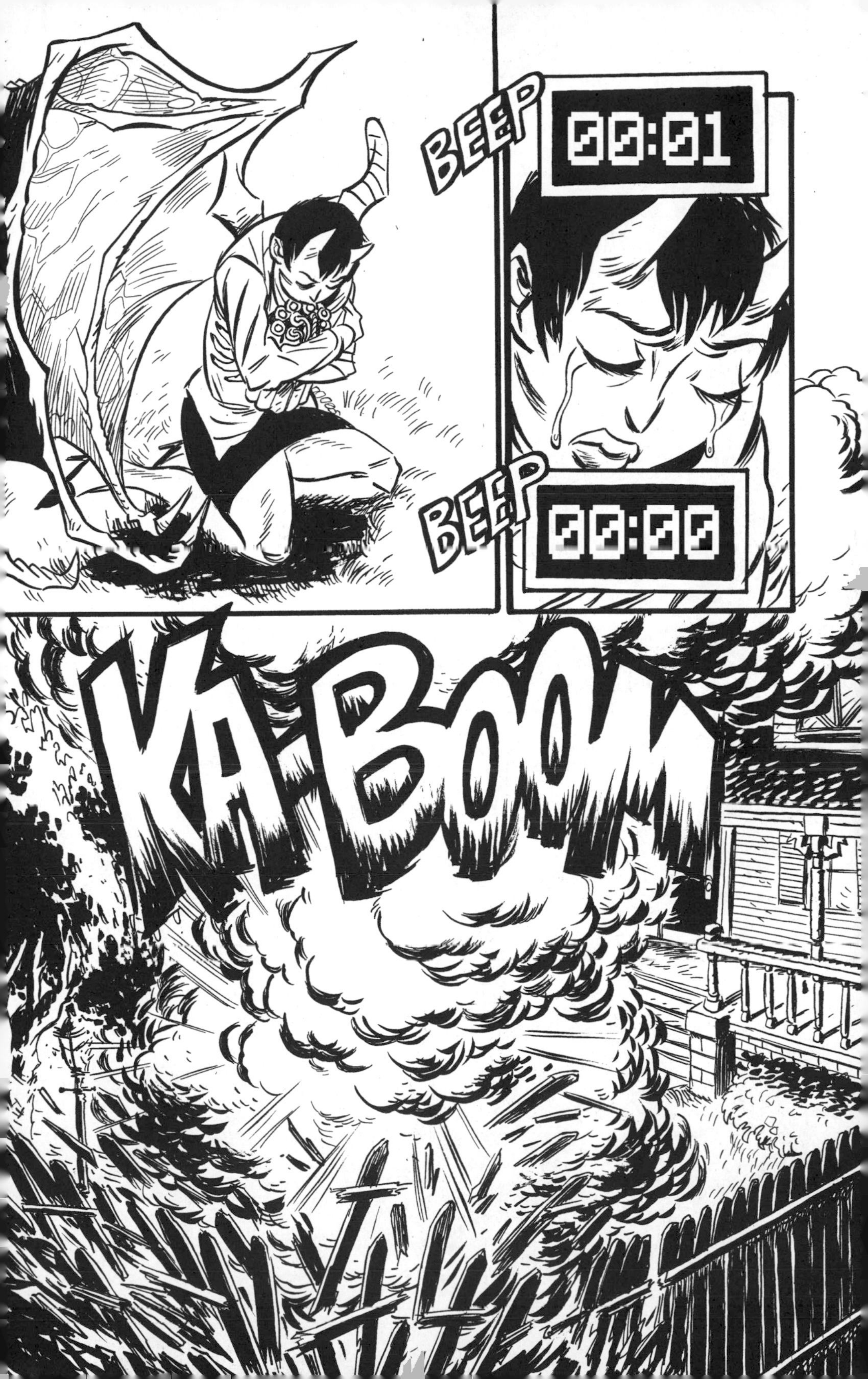

BEEP
00:01
BEEP
00:00
KA-BOOM

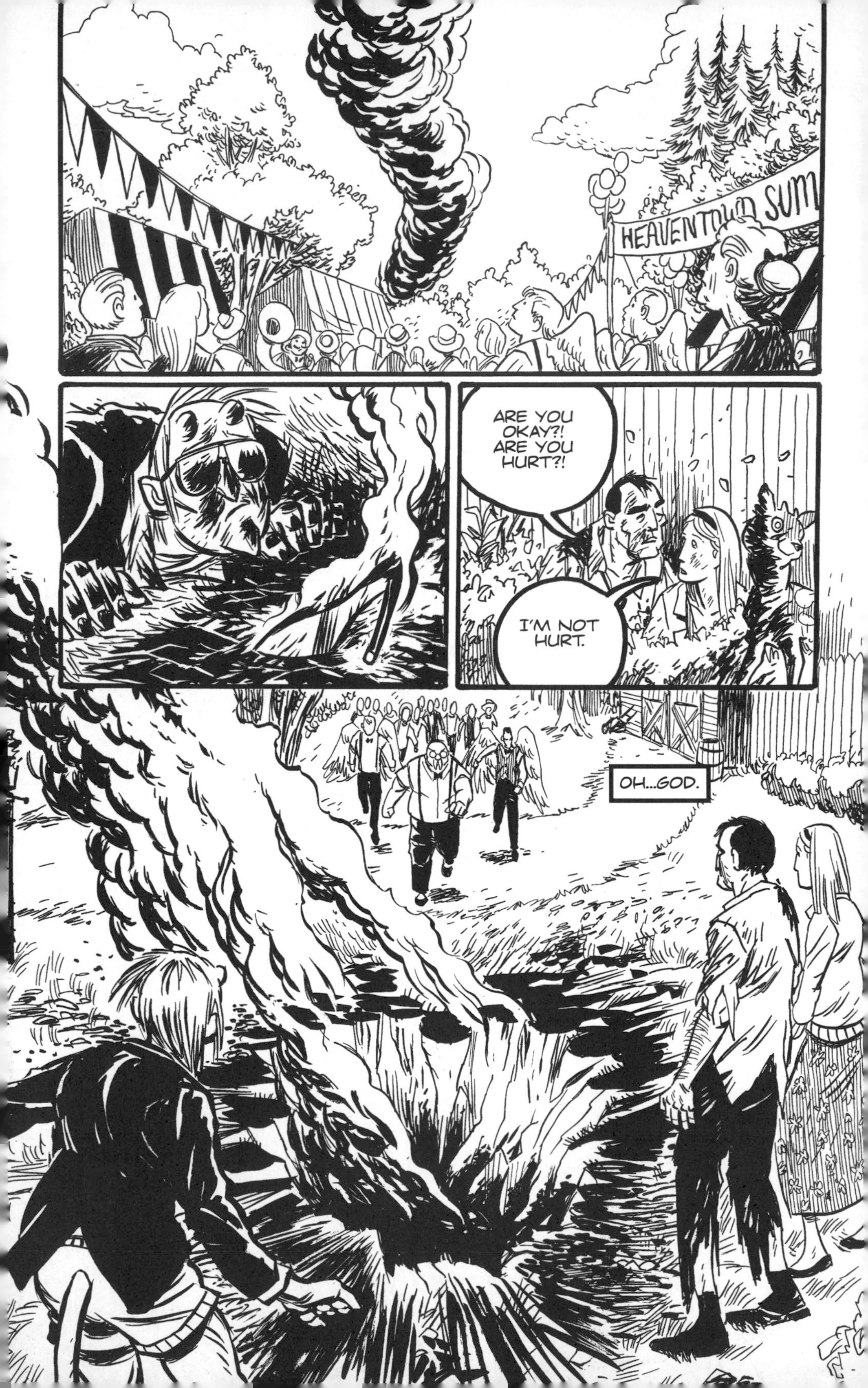
HEAVENTOWN SUM
ARE YOU OKAY?! ARE YOU HURT?!
I'M NOT HURT.
OH...GOD.

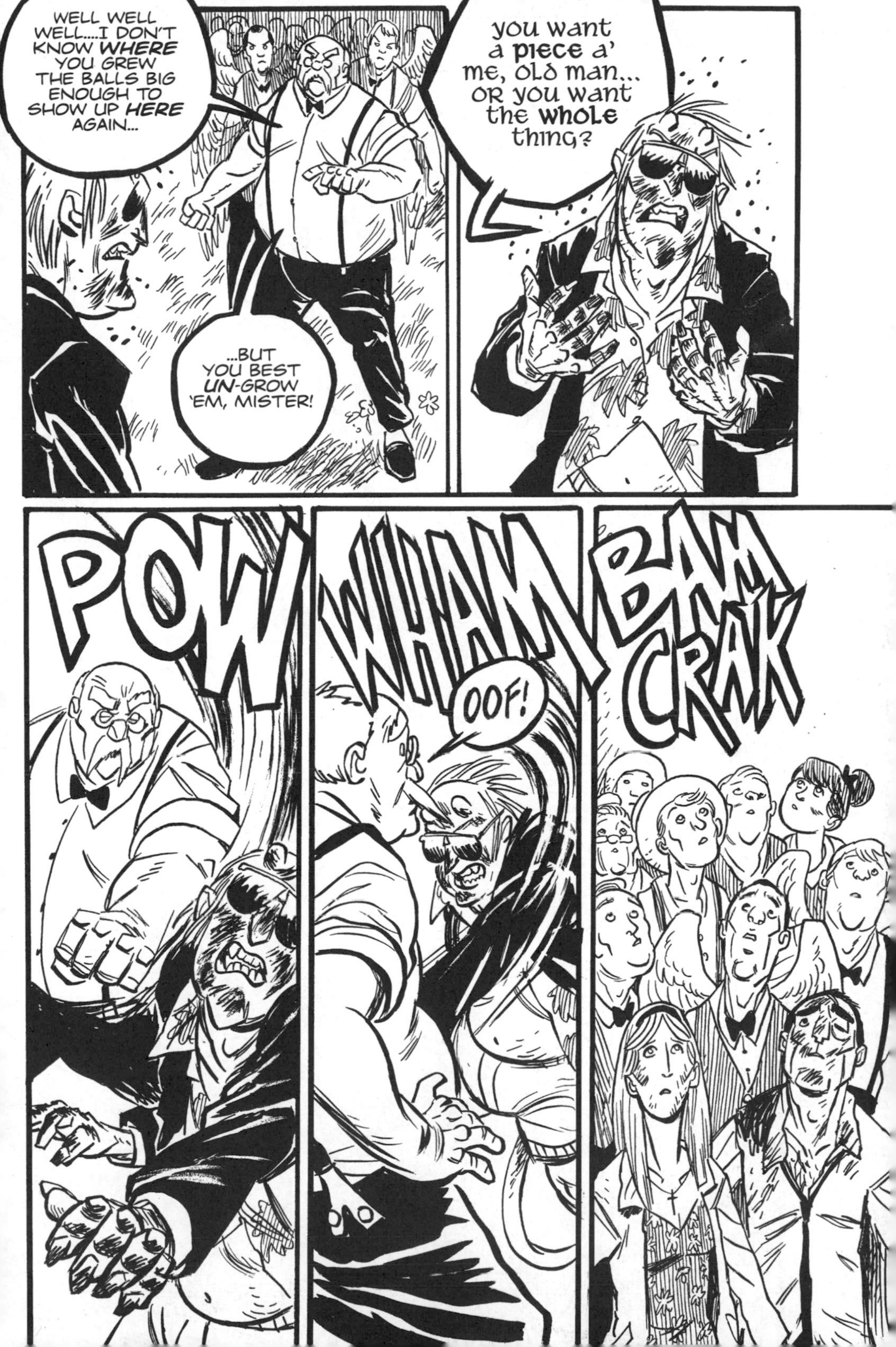
WELL WELL WELL....I DON'T KNOW WHERE YOU GREW THE BALLS BIG ENOUGH TO SHOW UP HERE AGAIN...
...BUT YOU BEST UN-GROW 'EM, MISTER!
you want a piece a' me, old man... or you want the whole thing?
POW
WHAM
OOF!
BAM
CRAK

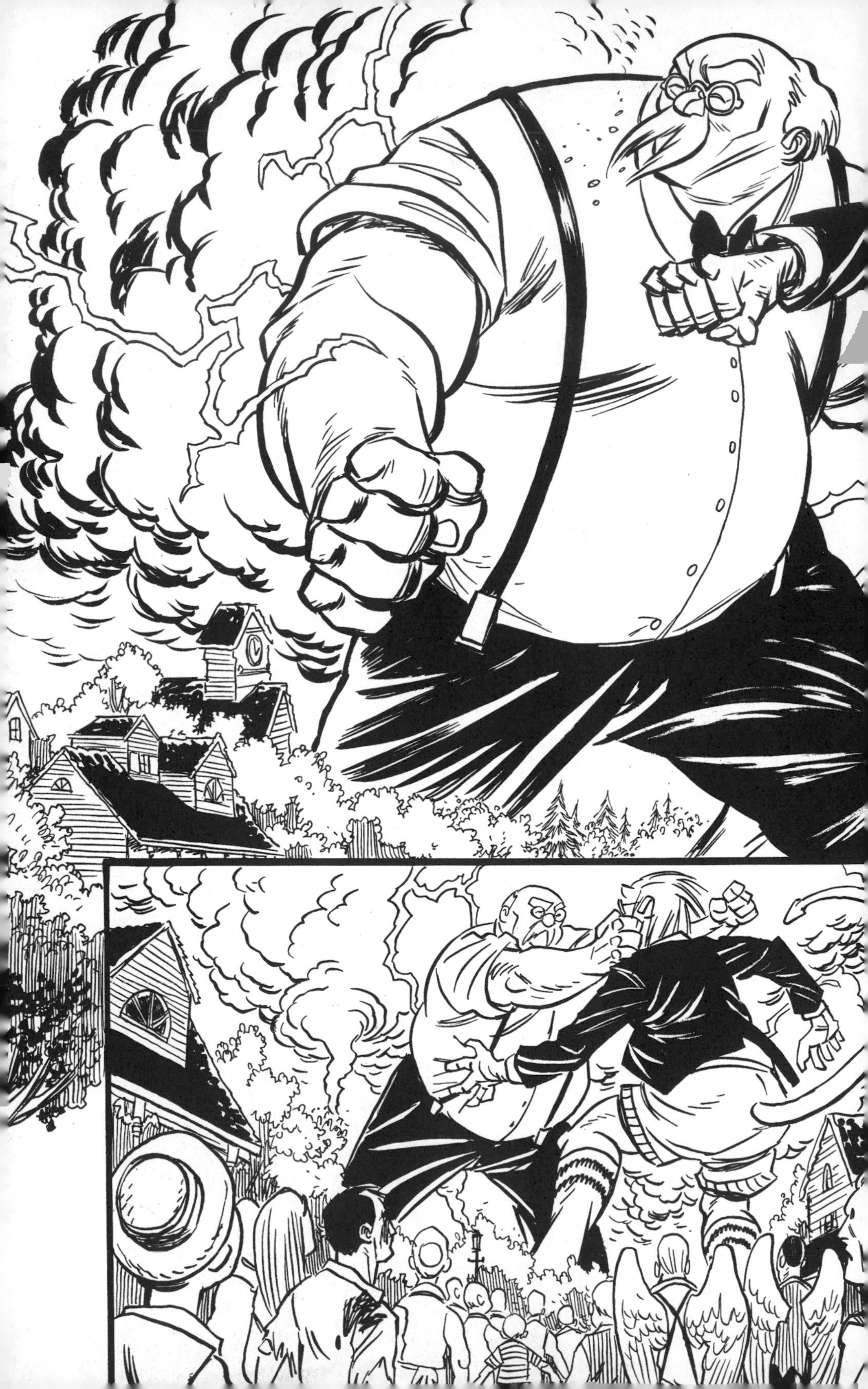

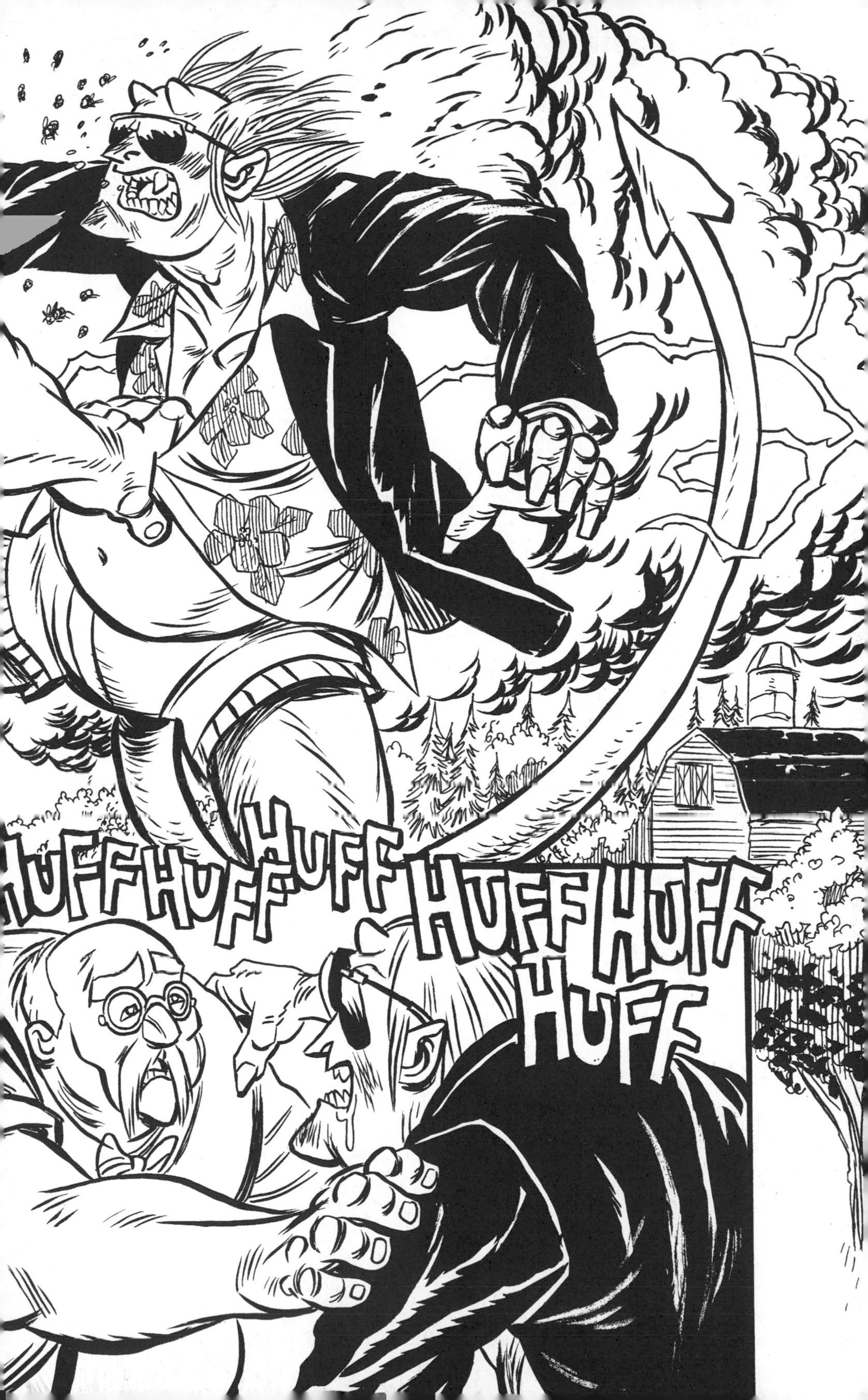
HUFF HUFF HUFF HUFF HUFF HUFF HUFF

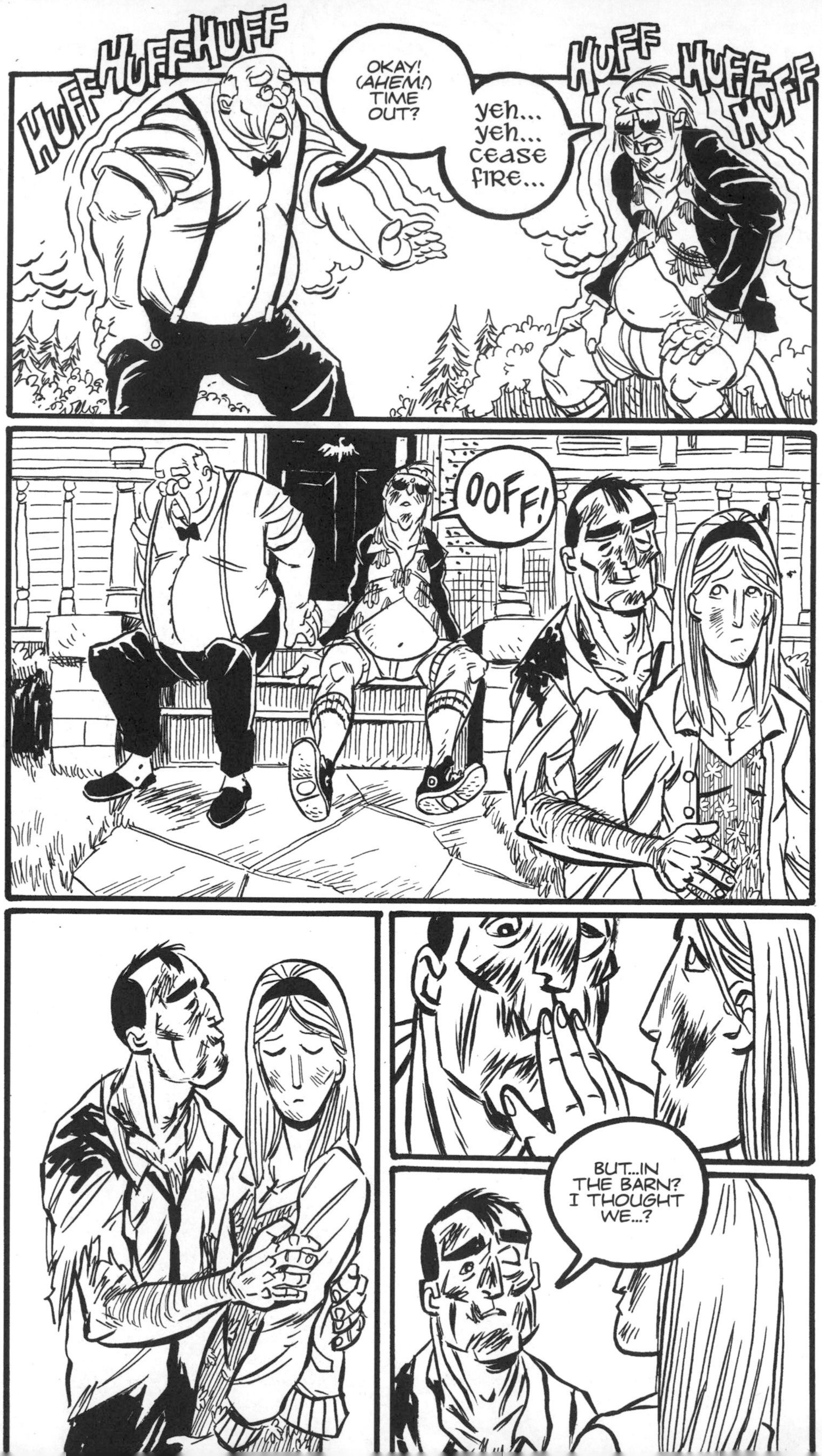
HUFF HUFF HUFF
OKAY! (AHEM!) TIME OUT?
yeh... yeh... cease fire...
HUFF HUFF HUFF HUFF
OOFF!
BUT...IN THE BARN? I THOUGHT WE...?

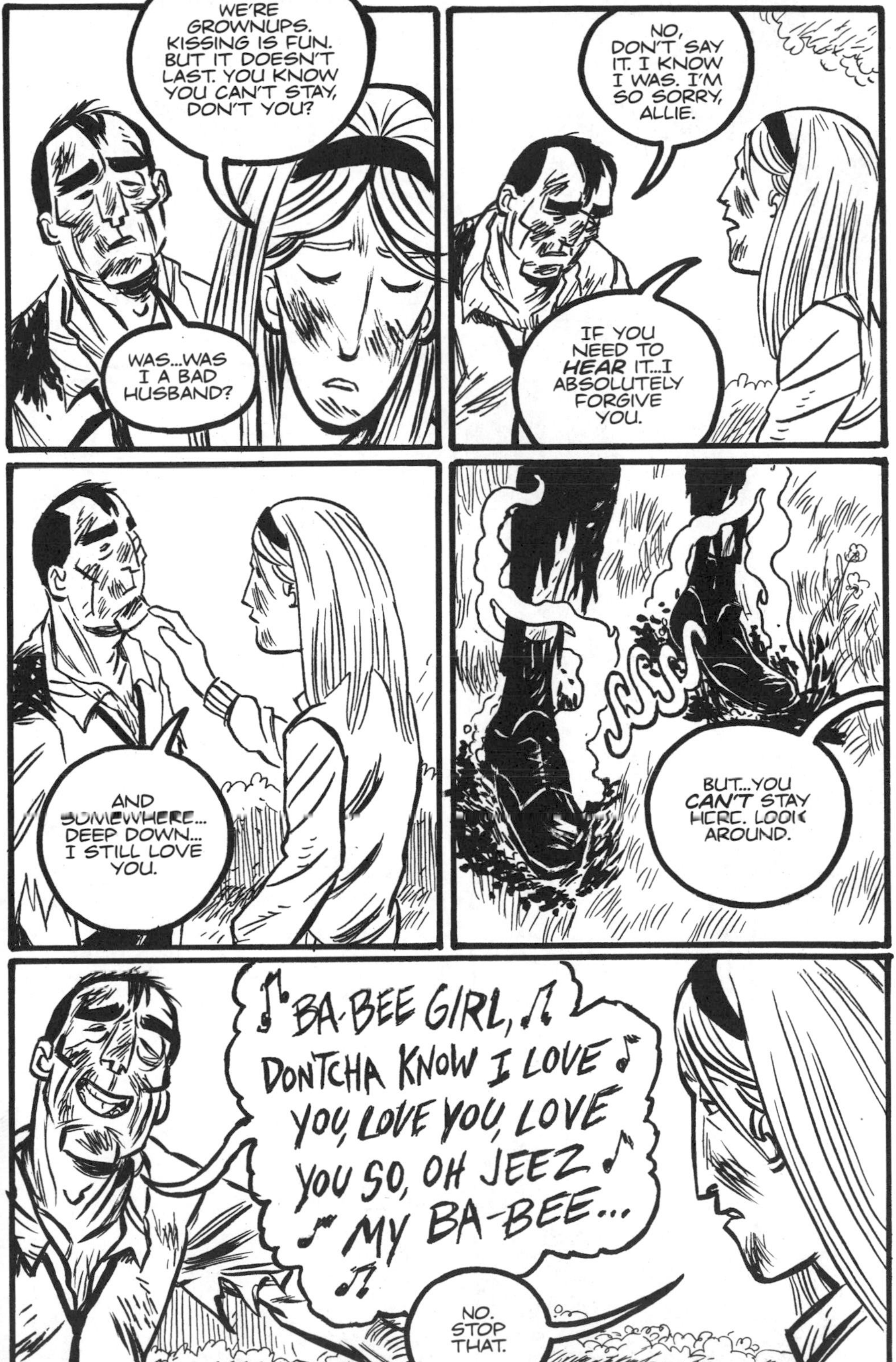
WE'RE GROWNUPS. KISSING IS FUN. BUT IT DOESN'T LAST. YOU KNOW YOU CAN'T STAY, DON'T YOU?
WAS...WAS I A BAD HUSBAND?
NO, DON'T SAY IT. I KNOW I WAS. I'M SO SORRY, ALLIE.
IF YOU NEED TO HEAR IT...I ABSOLUTELY FORGIVE YOU.
AND SOMEWHERE... DEEP DOWN... I STILL LOVE YOU.
BUT...YOU CAN'T STAY HERE. LOOK AROUND.
BA-BEE GIRL, DONTCHA KNOW I LOVE YOU, LOVE YOU, LOVE YOU SO, OH JEEZ MY BA-BEE...
NO. STOP THAT.

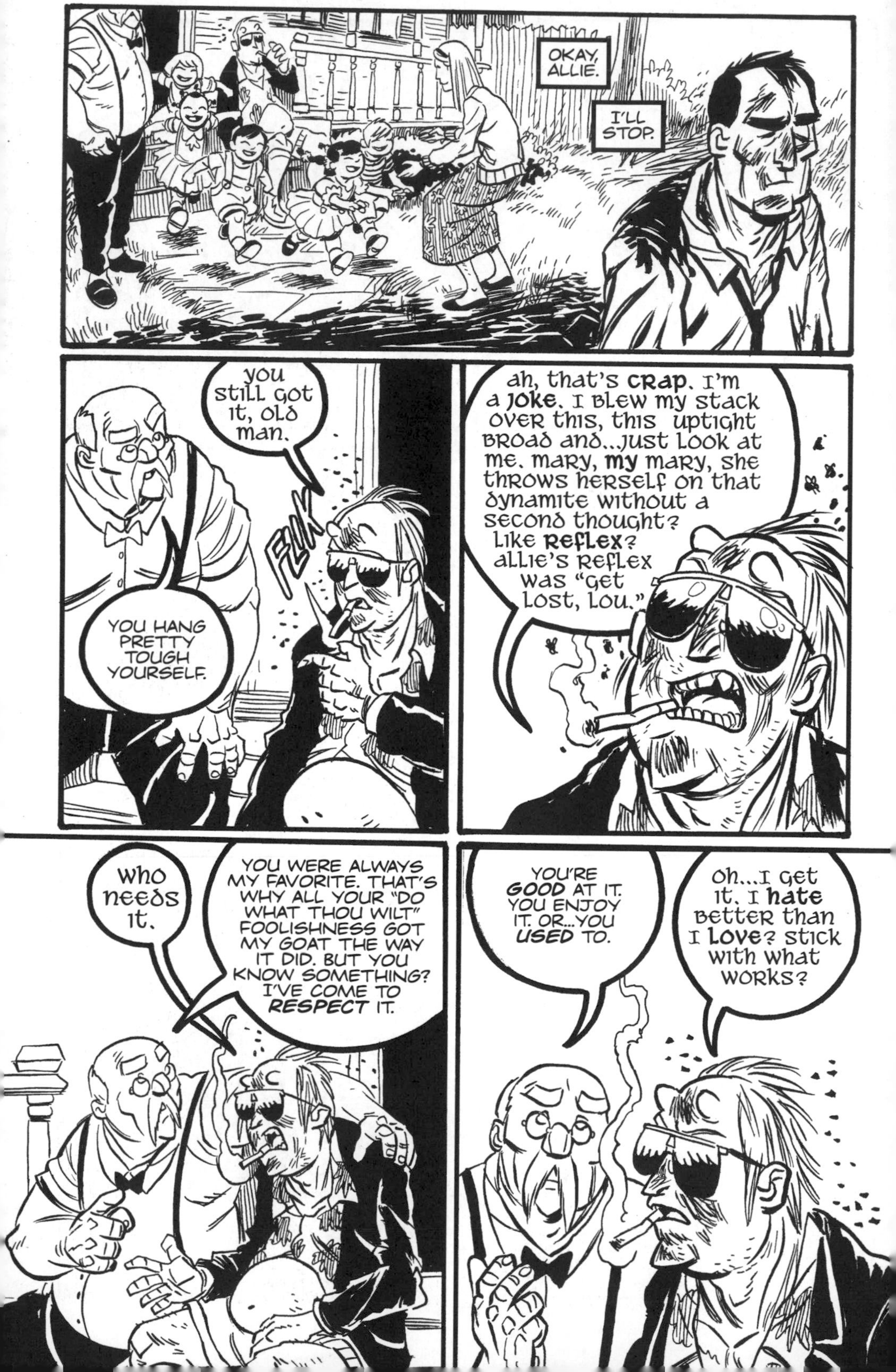
OKAY, ALLIE.
I'LL STOP.
you still got it, old man.
FLIK
YOU HANG PRETTY TOUGH YOURSELF.
ah, that's CRAP. I'm a JOKE. I blew my stack over this, this uptight broad and...just look at me. mary, my mary, she throws herself on that dynamite without a second thought? like REFLEX? allie's reflex was "get lost, lou."
who needs it.
YOU WERE ALWAYS MY FAVORITE. THAT'S WHY ALL YOUR "DO WHAT THOU WILT" FOOLISHNESS GOT MY GOAT THE WAY IT DID. BUT YOU KNOW SOMETHING? I'VE COME TO RESPECT IT.
YOU'RE GOOD AT IT. YOU ENJOY IT. OR...YOU USED TO.
oh...I get it. I hate better than I love? stick with what works?

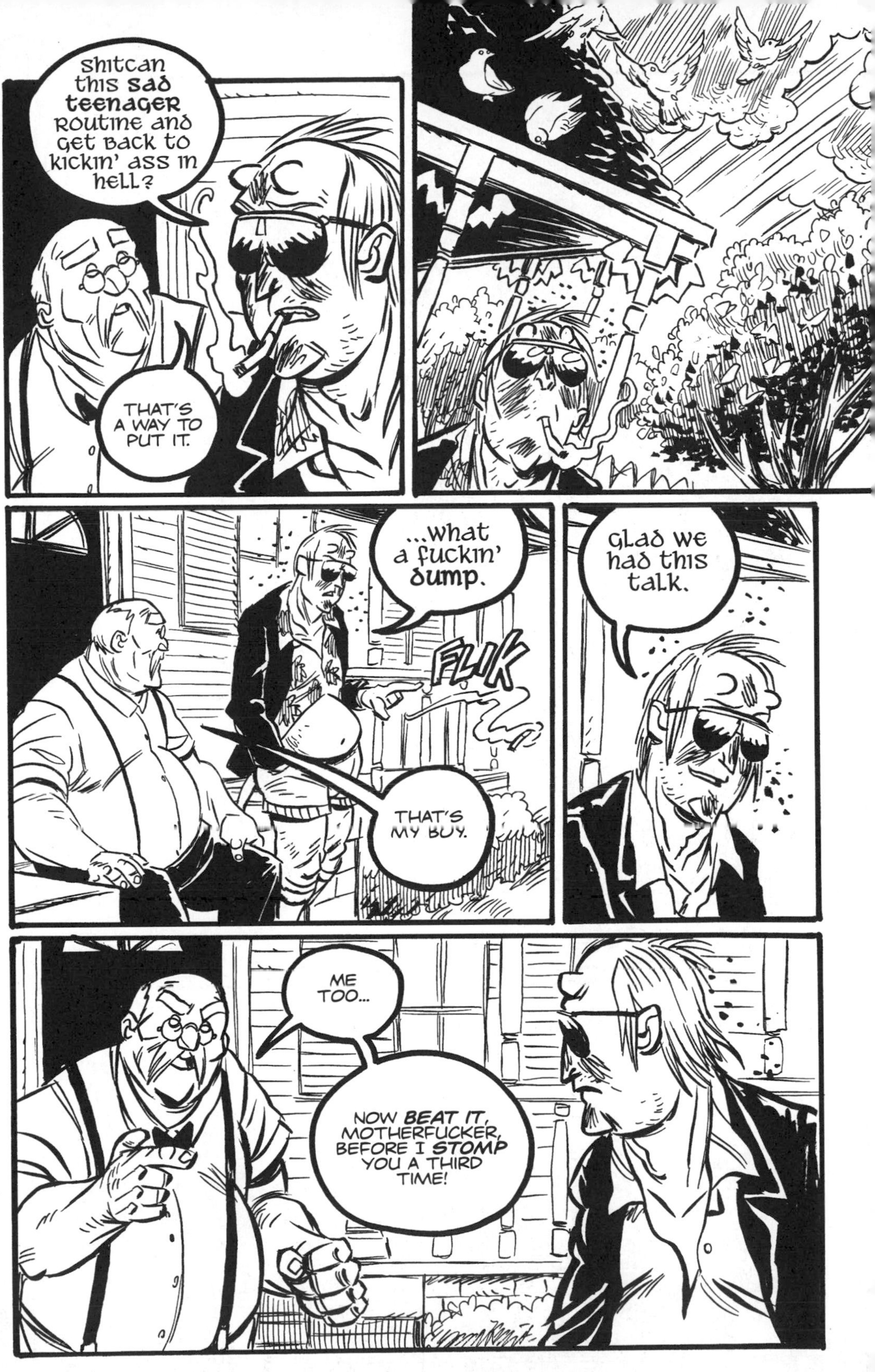
Shitcan this sad teenager routine and get back to kickin' ass in hell?
THAT'S A WAY TO PUT IT.
...what a fuckin' dump.
FLIK
THAT'S MY BOY.
Glad we had this talk.
ME TOO...
NOW BEAT IT, MOTHERFUCKER, BEFORE I STOMP YOU A THIRD TIME!

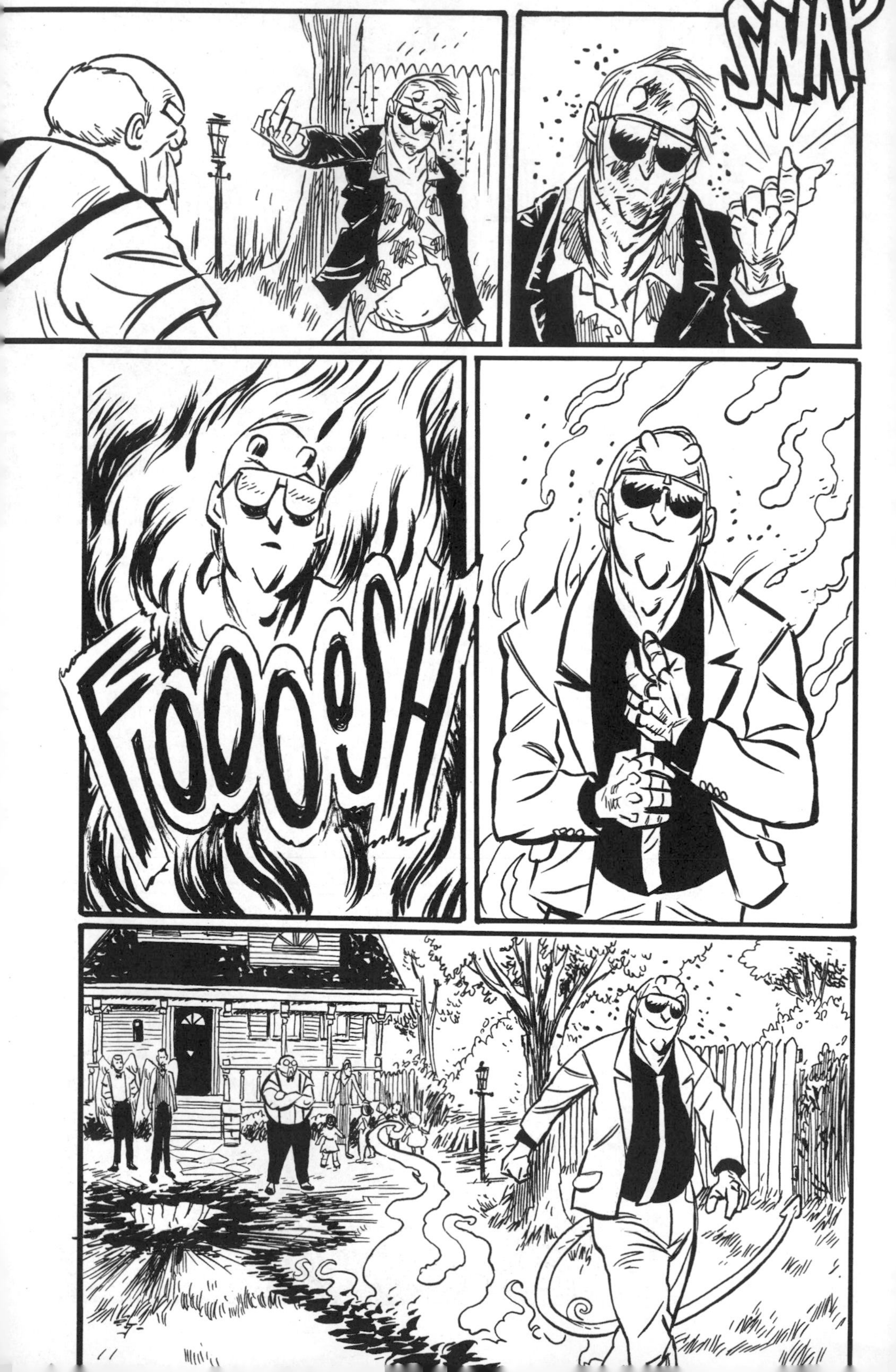
SNAP
FOOOOSH

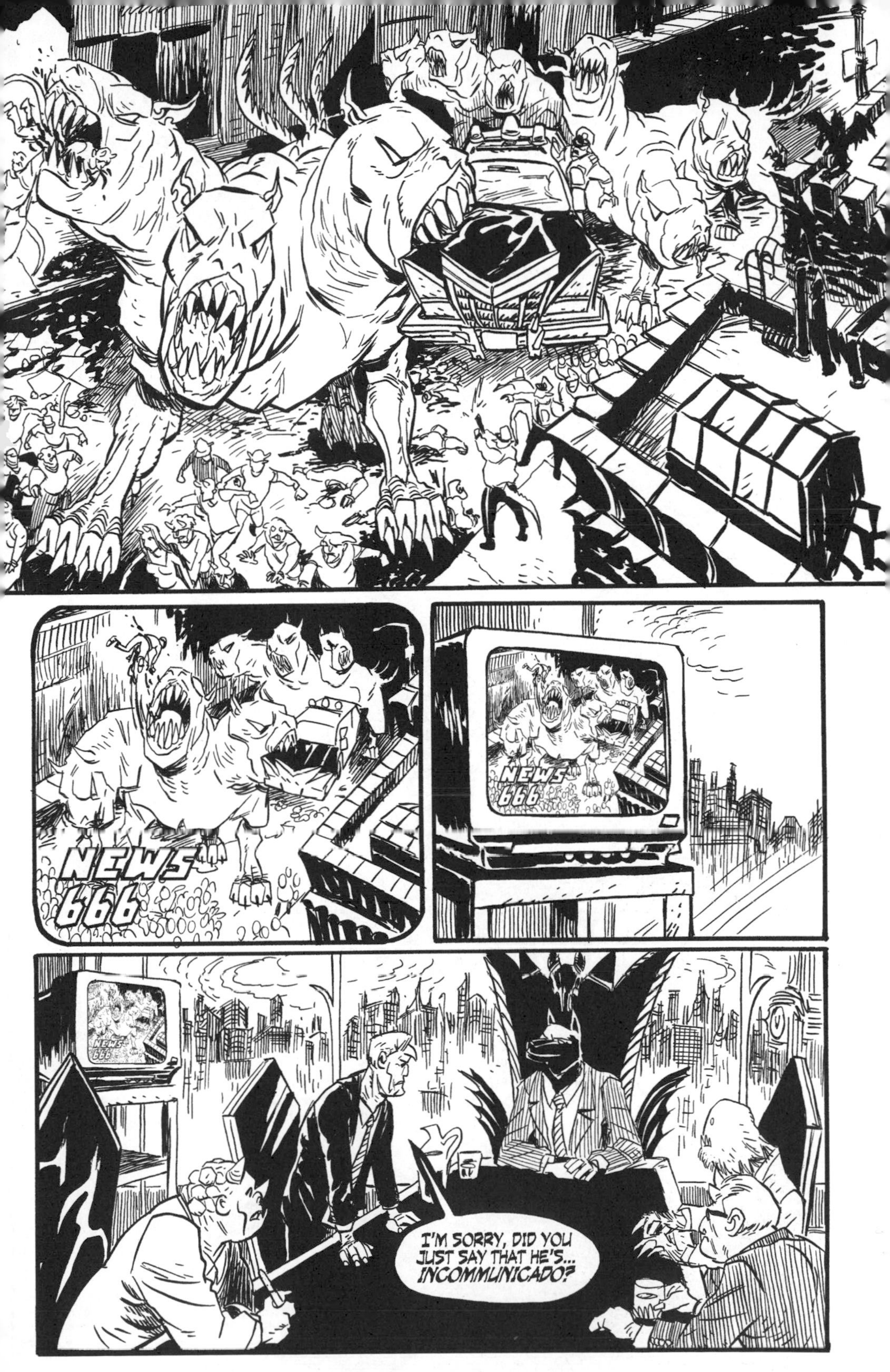
NEWS 666
NEWS 666
NEWS 666
I'M SORRY, DID YOU JUST SAY THAT HE'S... INCOMMUNICADO?

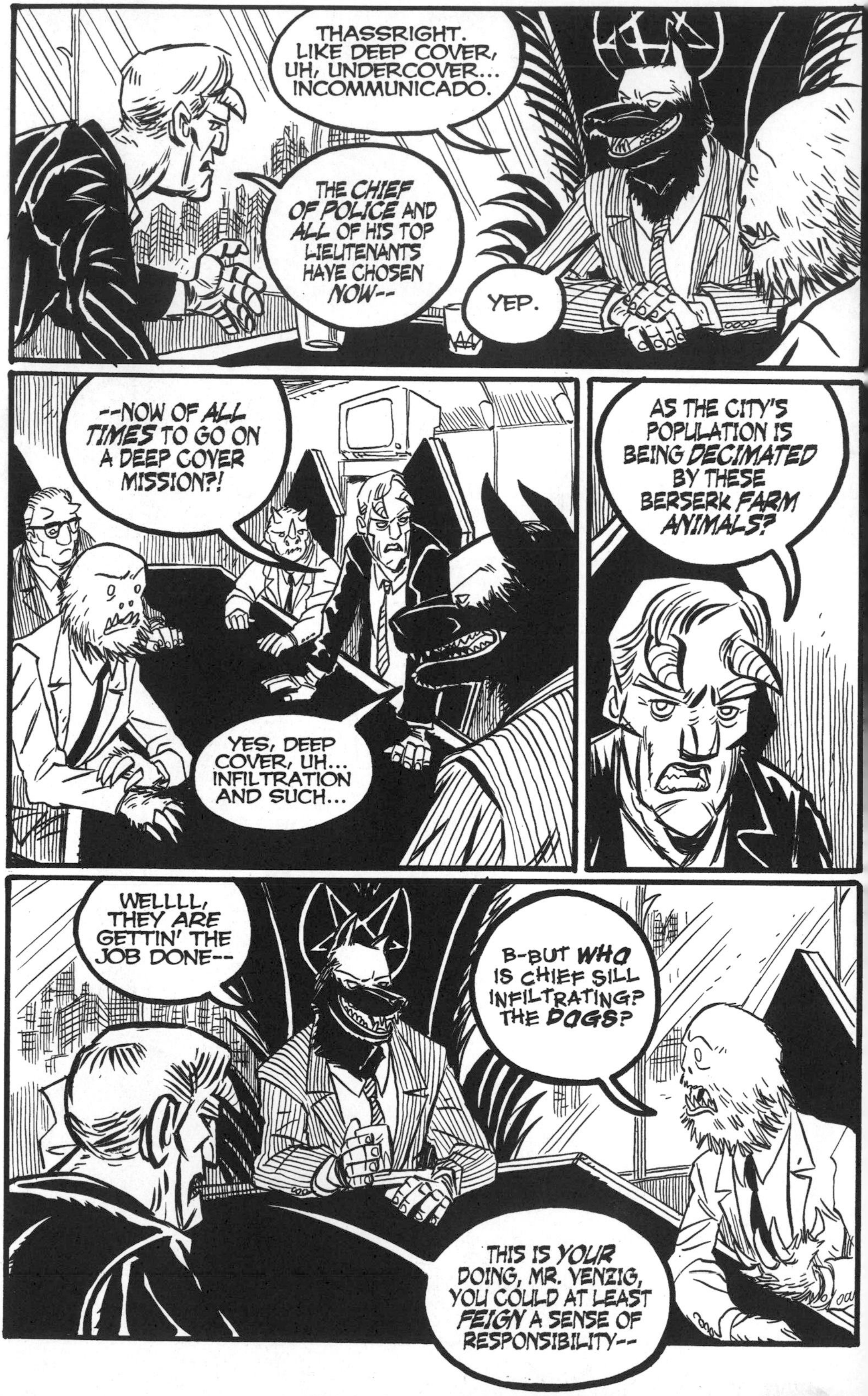
THASSRIGHT. LIKE DEEP COVER, UH, UNDERCOVER... INCOMMUNICADO.
THE CHIEF OF POLICE AND ALL OF HIS TOP LIEUTENANTS HAVE CHOSEN NOW--
YEP.
--NOW OF ALL TIMES TO GO ON A DEEP COVER MISSION?!
YES, DEEP COVER, UH... INFILTRATION AND SUCH...
AS THE CITY'S POPULATION IS BEING DECIMATED BY THESE BERSERK FARM ANIMALS?
WELLLL, THEY ARE GETTIN' THE JOB DONE--
B-BUT WHO IS CHIEF SILL INFILTRATING? THE DOGS?
THIS IS YOUR DOING, MR. VENZIG, YOU COULD AT LEAST FEIGN A SENSE OF RESPONSIBILITY--

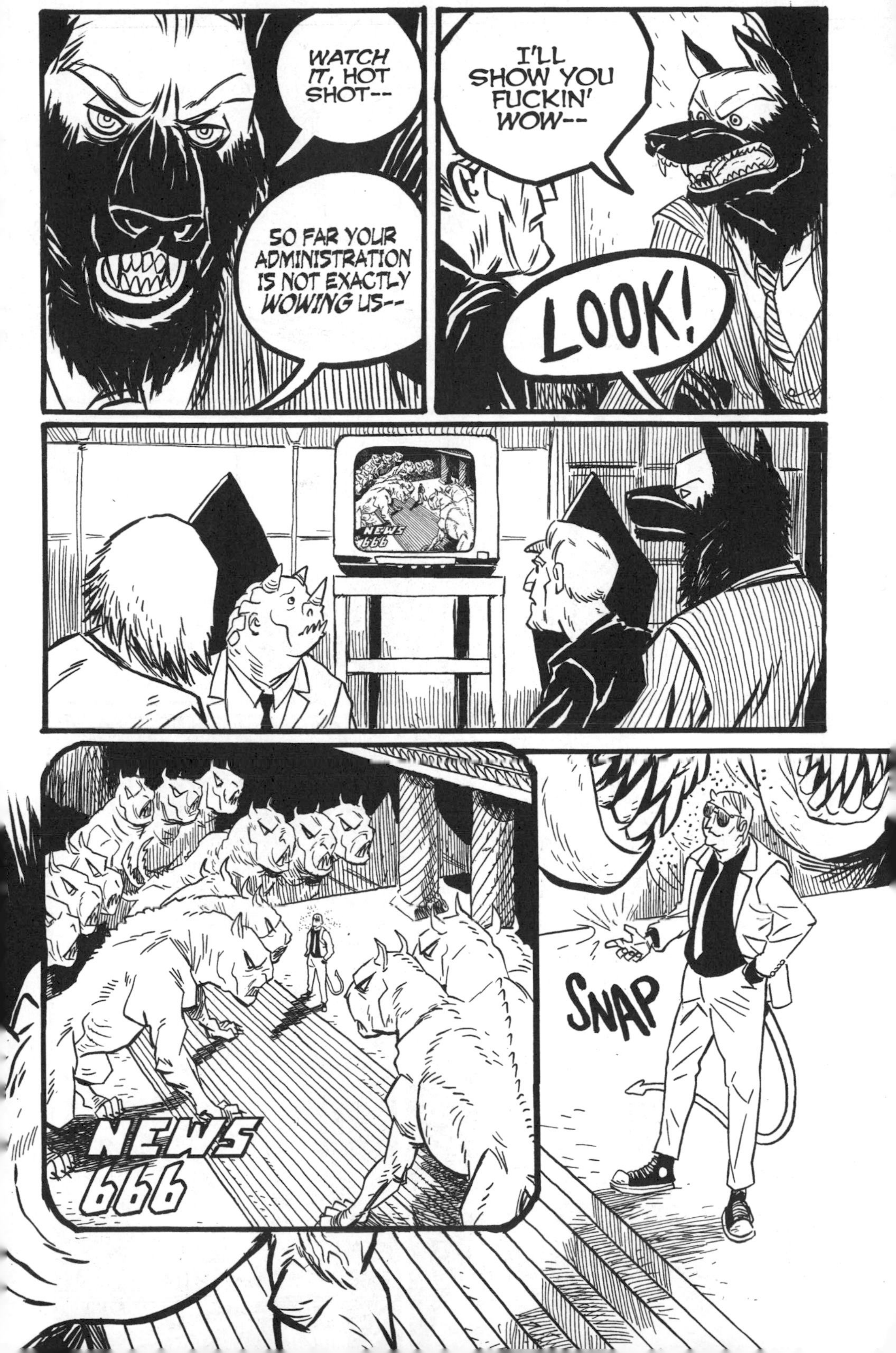

WATCH IT, HOT SHOT--
SO FAR YOUR ADMINISTRATION IS NOT EXACTLY WOWING US--
I'LL SHOW YOU FUCKIN' WOW--
LOOK!
NEWS 666
NEWS 666
SNAP

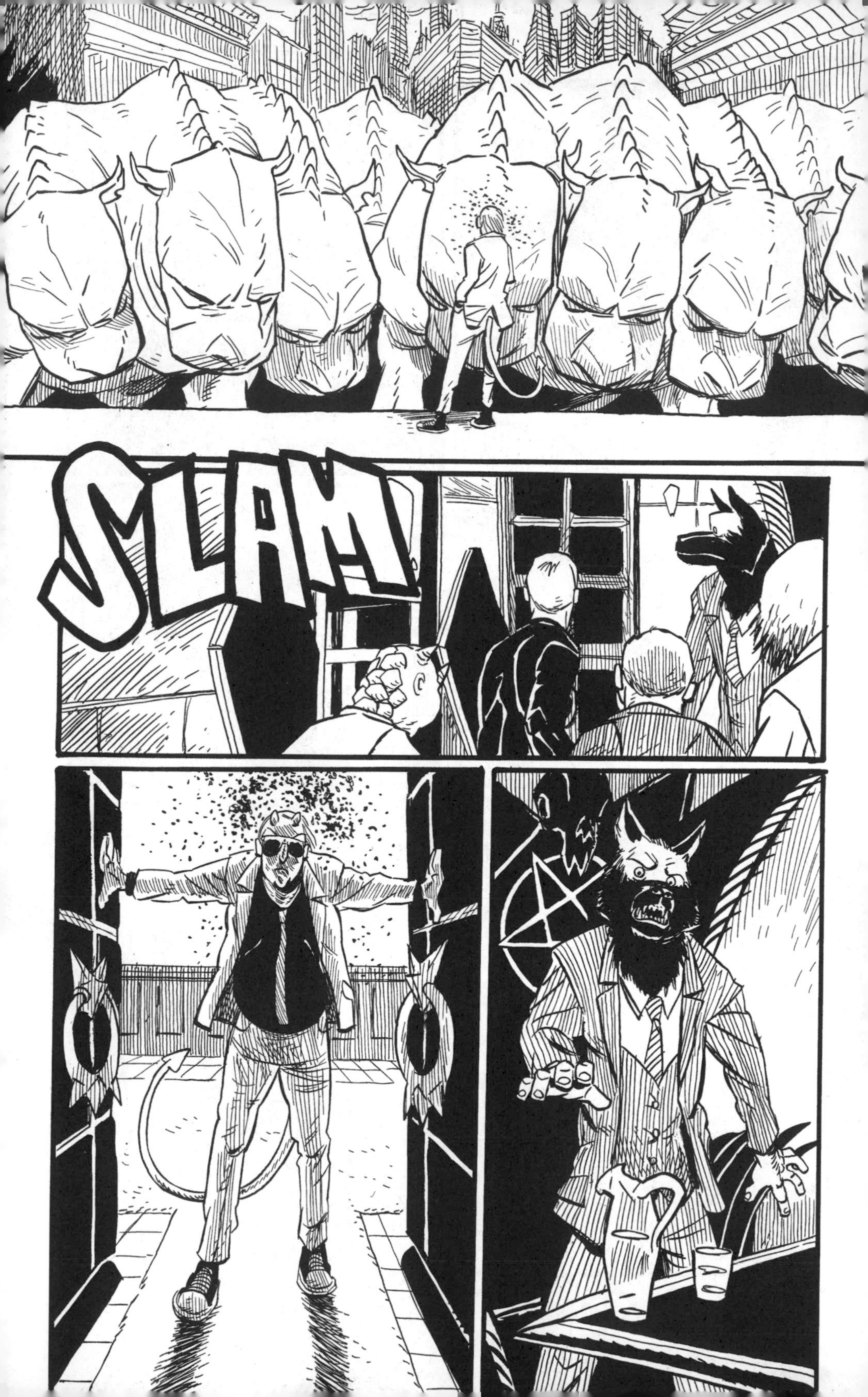
SLAM!

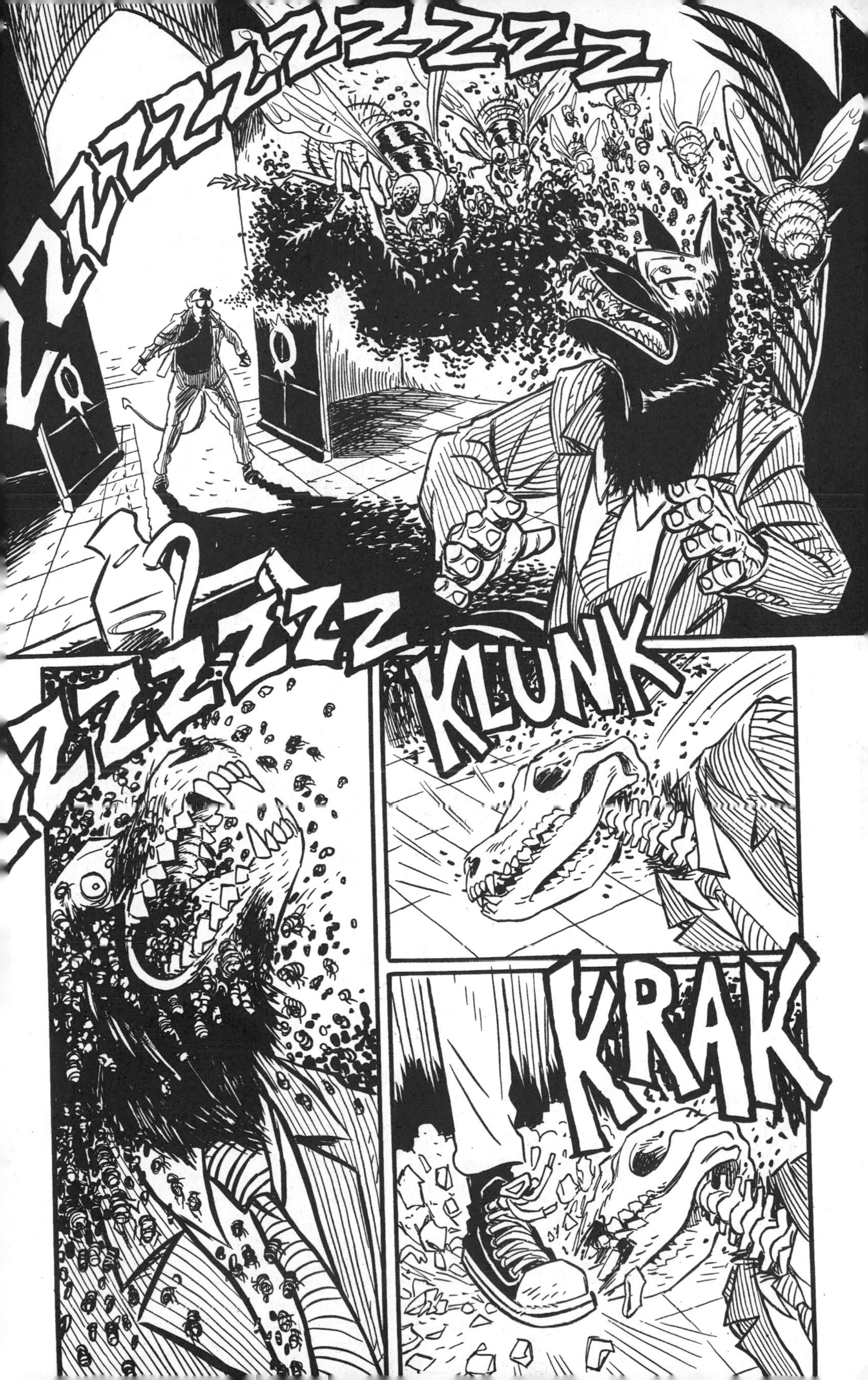
ZZZZZZZZZZZZZ
ZZZZZZZZ
KLUNK
KRAK

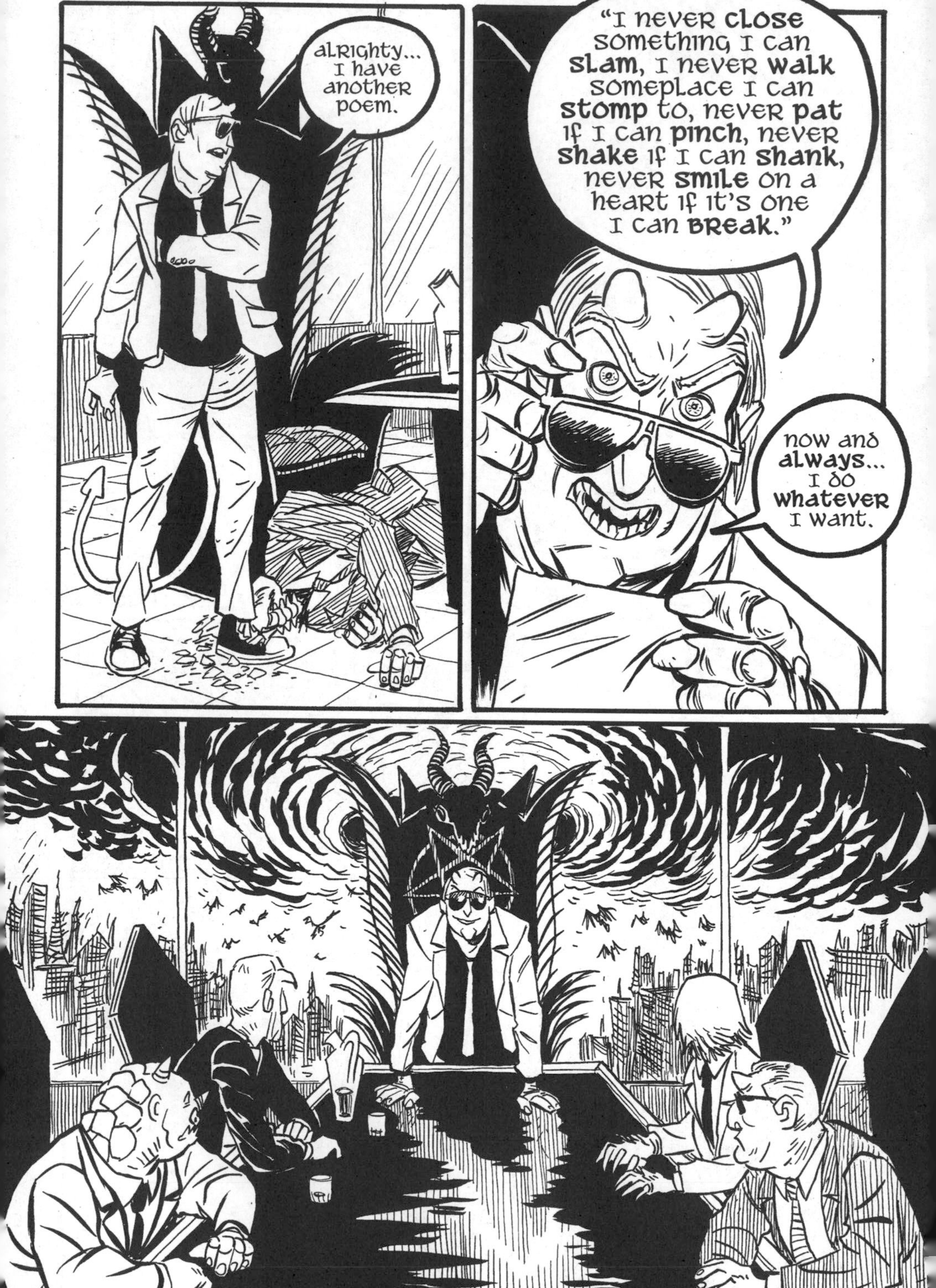
alrighty... I have another poem.
"I never close something I can slam, I never walk someplace I can stomp to, never pat if I can pinch, never shake if I can shank, never smile on a heart if it's one I can break."
now and always... I do whatever I want.

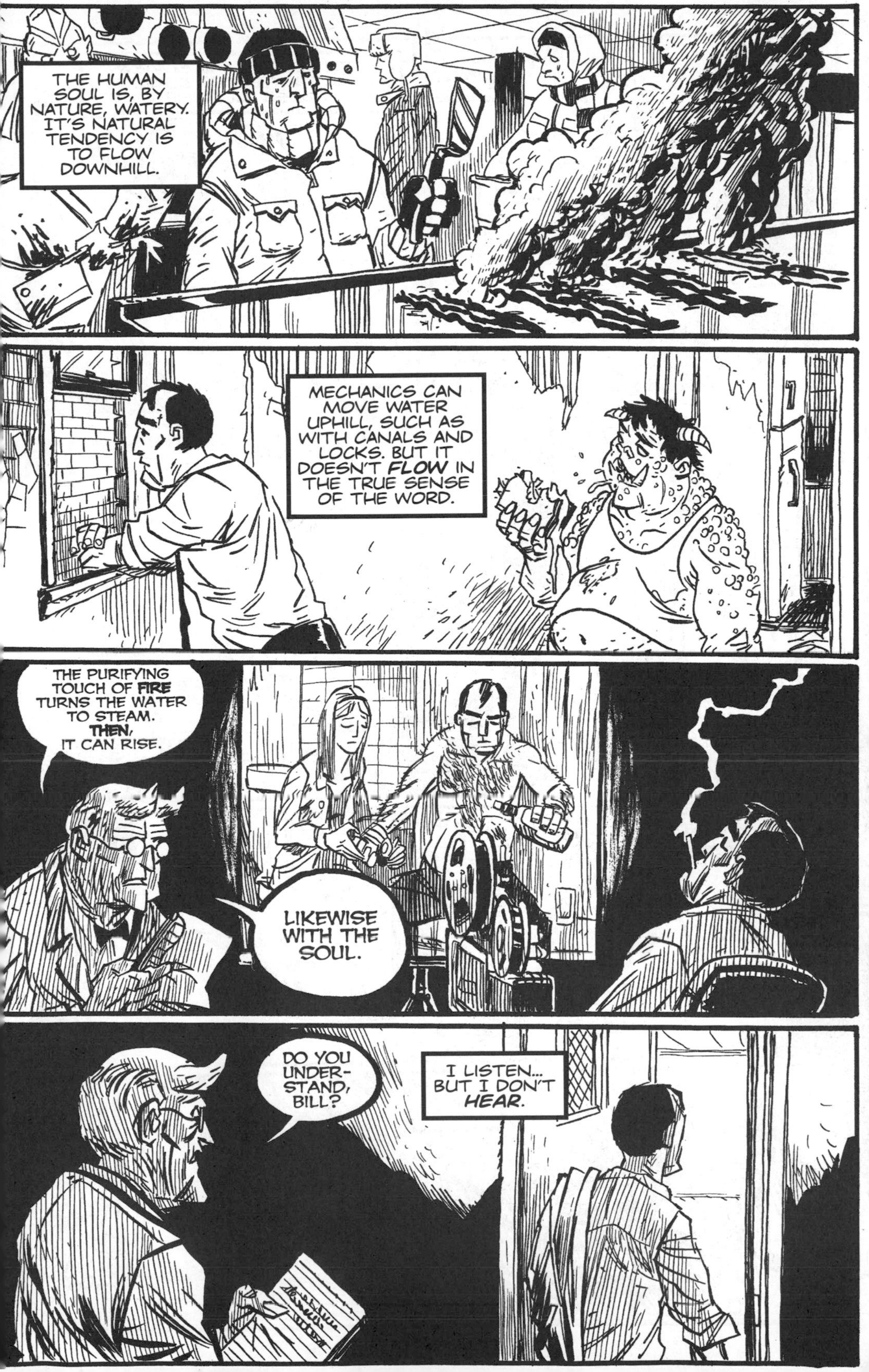
THE HUMAN SOUL IS, BY NATURE, WATERY. IT'S NATURAL TENDENCY IS TO FLOW DOWNHILL.
MECHANICS CAN MOVE WATER UPHILL, SUCH AS WITH CANALS AND LOCKS. BUT IT DOESN'T FLOW IN THE TRUE SENSE OF THE WORD.
THE PURIFYING TOUCH OF FIRE TURNS THE WATER TO STEAM. THEN, IT CAN RISE.
LIKEWISE WITH THE SOUL.
DO YOU UNDER-STAND, BILL?
I LISTEN... BUT I DON'T HEAR.

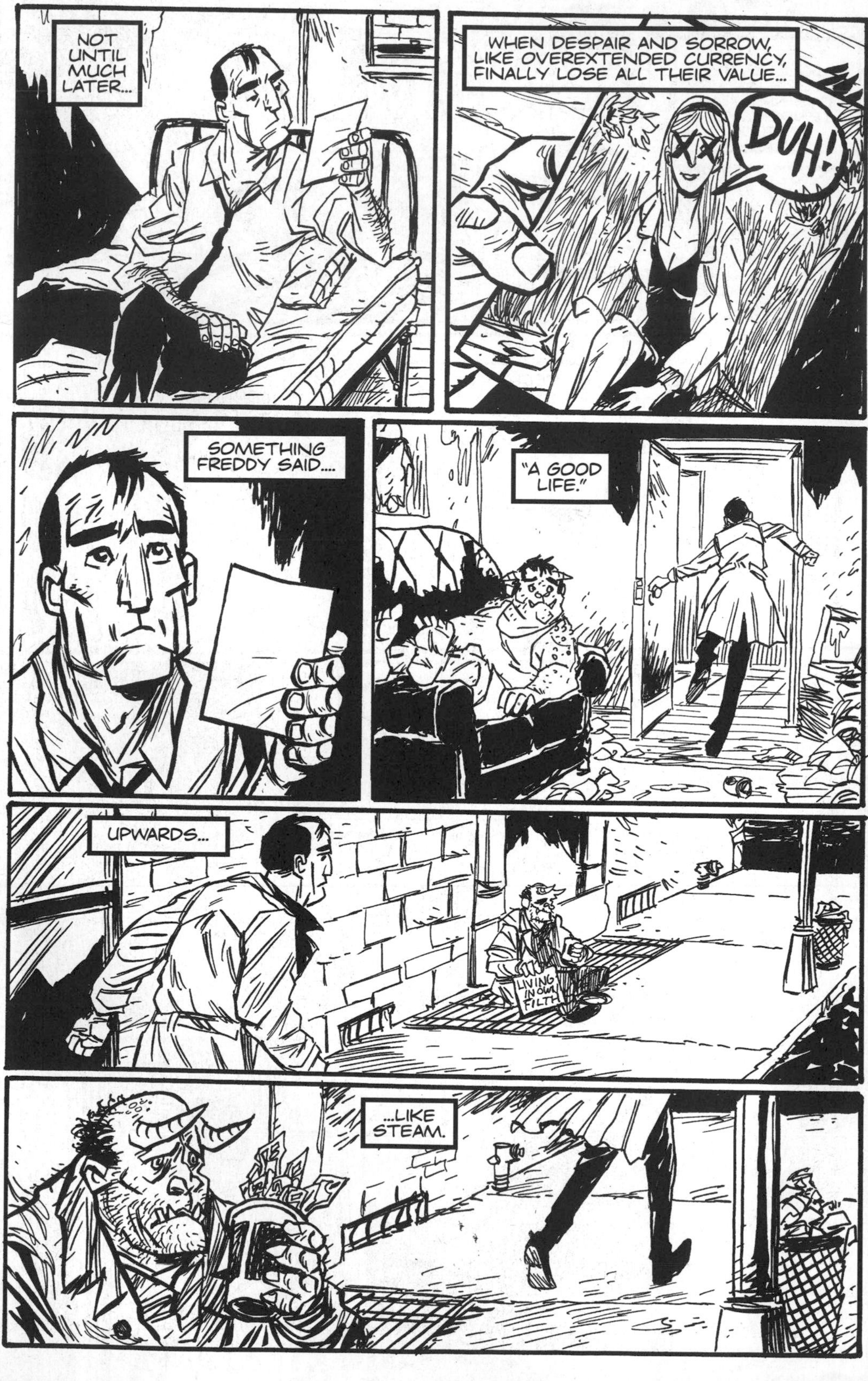
NOT UNTIL MUCH LATER...
WHEN DESPAIR AND SORROW, LIKE OVEREXTENDED CURRENCY, FINALLY LOSE ALL THEIR VALUE...
DUH!
SOMETHING FREDDY SAID....
"A GOOD LIFE."
UPWARDS...
LIVING IN OWN FILTH
...LIKE STEAM.

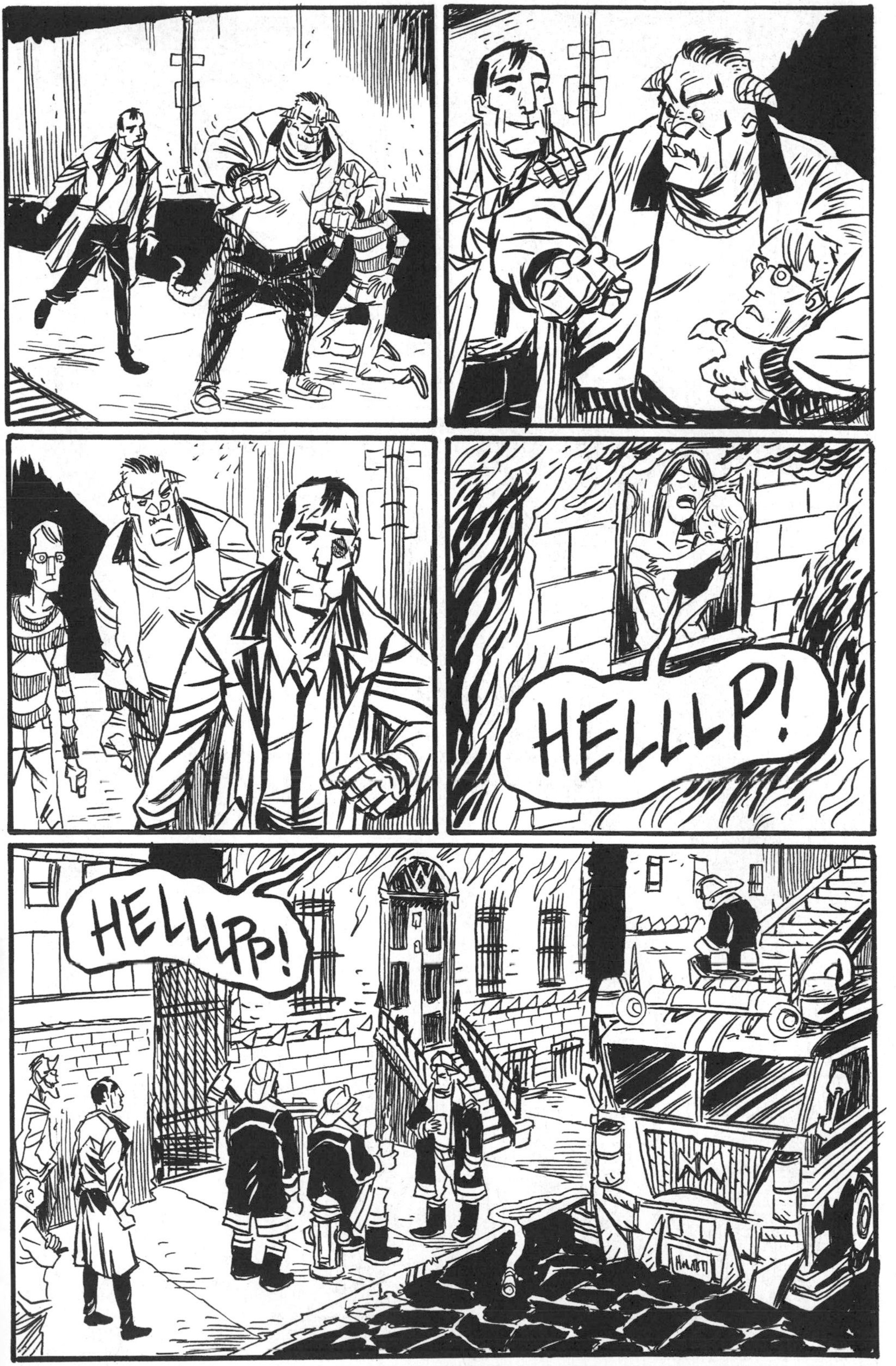
HELLLP!
HELLLPP!

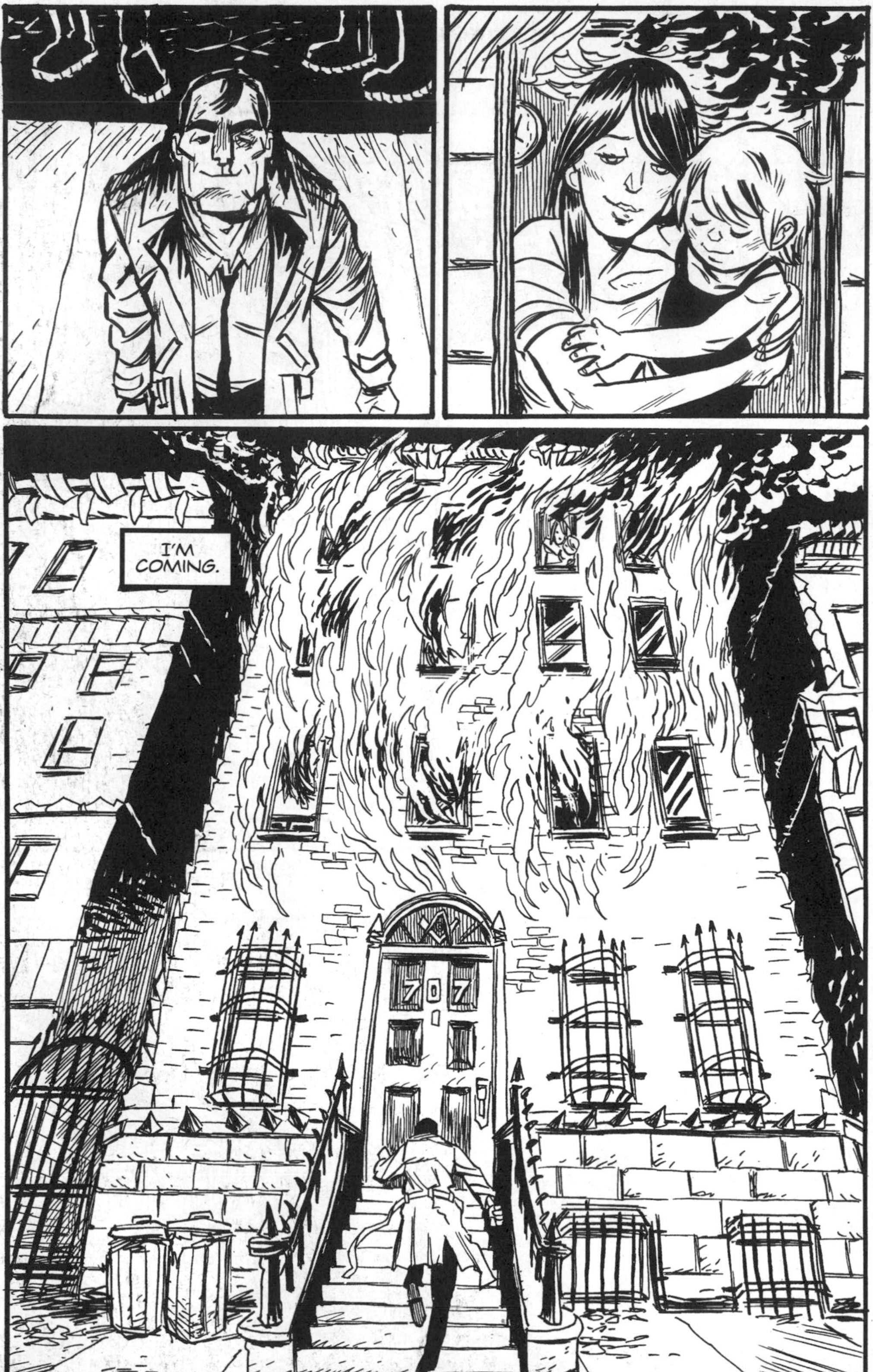
I'M COMING.
707